D1351735

This book is due for return on or before the last date shown below.

Hygiene
for
Management

A text for food safety courses

Ideal for use on LEVEL 4 • HABC • CIEH • • REHIS • RSPH • Courses

Richard A. Sprenger,
BSc(Hons), DMS, FCIEH, FREHIS, FSOFHT

Chairman Highfield.co.uk Limited

PUBLISHED BY
©HIGHFIELD.CO.UK LIMITED

Highfield House, Heavens Walk, Lakeside,
Doncaster, South Yorkshire, DN4 5HZ United Kingdom
Tel: +44 0845 2260350
Tel: +44 (0)1302 363277
Facsimile: +44 0845 2260360
E-mail: rsprenger@highfield.co.uk

Websites:
www.highfield.co.uk
www.foodsafetytrainers.co.uk

ISBN 978-1-909749-26-9

Highfield .co.uk limited

Improving Food Safety

TO JAYNE, JASON, CHRISTIAN, BECKY, BETHANY, EVIE, ISAAC, NATHANIEL, SEBASTIAN, NOAH, ZACHERY, ALEXANDER, ELIJAH AND ZAVIER

First published 1983

Reprinted 1985, 1988, 1989, 1991, 1993, 1995, 1998, 2002, 2003, 2004, 2005, 2007, 2008

15th Edition 2009 (reprinted February 2011)

16th Edition 2012

17th Edition 2014

©HIGHFIELD.CO.UK LIMITED

Printed by Charlesworth Press • Telephone: 01924 204839

MIX
Paper from responsible sources
FSC® C016379

Contents

Acknowledgments

During the compilation of this book, I have discussed the content with, and received information from, several food hygiene experts. I am grateful for their comments and assistance. I am indebted to Pat Sprenger for correcting errors and making the English more readily understandable. I record sincere thanks to the following people and organisations for their contributions and support: Adrian R. Eley (University of Sheffield), Adrian N. Meyer (Acheta), Dr. Chris Barry (Achor Partners), Terry A. Roberts, Andy Bowles, Dr. Slim Dinsdale, Barry S. Michaels, Euan MacAuslan, Roger Hart, Vic George, Dennis Farrar, Mark Kieran, Mark Du Val (LACORS), Graham Walker (REHIS), Steve Bagshaw and Peter Littleton (Holchem Laboratories Ltd.), Andy Barnard (Campbell Grocery Products), Richard North, Bob Hutson and Coleen Rudge.

I would also like to thank the following companies for providing photographs:

Company	Details
Acheta	Garden Cottage, Horsemoor, Chieveley, Newbury, Berkshire, RG12 8XD. Tel & Fax: +44 (0)1635 248084 www.acheta.co.uk
Anticimex	Thunes vei 2, N-0274 Oslo. Box 472 Skøyen, N-0212 Oslo. Tel: +47 22542880 www.anticimex.se
Biotrace Ltd	The Science Park, Bridgend, Mid Glamorgan, CF31 3NA. Tel: +44 (0)1656 641400 www.biotrace.com
Comark Ltd	Bury Mead Road, Hitchin, Hertfordshire, SG5 1RT Tel: 0844 (+44 844) 815 6599 Fax: 0844 (+44 844) 815 6598 www.comarkltd.com
Foster Refrigerator	Oldmedow Road, King's Lynn, Norfolk, PE30 4JU. Tel: 0843 216 8800 www.fosterrefrigerator.co.uk
Gemini Data Loggers (UK) Ltd	Scientific House, Terminus Road, Chichester, West Sussex, PO19 8UJ. Tel: 01243 813000 www.geminidataloggers.com
Holchem Laboratories Ltd	Premier House, 175 Grane Road, Haslingden, Rossendale, Lancashire, BB4 5ER. Tel: 01706 222288 www.holchem.co.uk
Johnson Diversey	Weston Favell Centre, Northampton, NN3 8PD. Tel: +44(0)1604 405311 www.johnsondiversey.com
Rentokil Initial plc	2 City Place, Beehive Ring Road, Gatwick Airport, West Sussex RH6 0HA www.rentokil-initial.co.uk
Vikan (UK) Ltd.	1 - 3 Avro Gate, Broadmoor Rd, South Marston Park, Swindon, Wiltshire SN3 4AG Tel: 01793 71 67 60 www.vikan.com

The importance of food safety

All organisations work towards achieving objectives. The primary objectives of commercial **food** businesses are to produce, distribute, store, handle, prepare and sell food at a profit. High standards of **hygiene** are imperative to prevent **food poisoning**, food **spoilage**, loss of productivity, **pest infestation** and prosecutions for contraventions of legislation. However, these standards must be achieved at a reasonable cost to ensure that the business remains profitable.

To ensure a profitable operation, managers must implement policies and systems relating to all their activities. One of the most important of these policies is maintaining cost-effective hygiene, by way of a food safety management system based on principles of **HACCP** (hazard analysis **critical control point**).

To implement an effective food safety management system, managers will require an understanding of all aspects of **food hygiene**, including basic **microbiology** and food science, together with the latest information on causes of **foodborne illness**, food **vehicles** and preventive measures.

Managers should be aware of the **hazards** and controls relating to their food business, especially in relation to temperature and microbiological, physical and chemical **contamination**. They should be able to identify points that are critical to food safety and implement effective control and monitoring procedures at these points. If monitoring reveals that a problem has occurred at a critical control point, a system must be in place to ensure timely and appropriate corrective action is taken.

High standards of **personal hygiene**, especially handwashing, are essential to reduce the risk of foodborne illness from **low-dose pathogens**, such as **viruses** and *E. coli* O157. Managers, supervisors and food handlers must be committed to food safety and trained commensurate with their work activities so they are competent to produce safe food. Effective supervision, including the motivation and coaching of staff, is the key to the continuous implementation of good hygiene practices. Managers must lead by example.

The correct storage and handling of food is essential to profitable operation. Food that is stored at incorrect temperatures may result in food poisoning or spoilage, and failure to carry out **stock rotation** will result in waste food and pest infestations. Supervision of food throughout processing is essential to avoid contamination, and suitable packaging, storage facilities and distribution vehicles must be provided.

To ensure hygienic and efficient operation, premises must be planned, designed and constructed in accordance with certain basic principles. The correct materials must be selected for surface finishes and equipment. **Cleaning**, **disinfection** and maintenance costs must be considered at the planning stage, as a modest increase in capital expenditure may considerably reduce the day-to-day operational costs.

Infestations of insects, rodents or birds are likely to result in food contamination, food wastage, prosecutions and even closure of food premises. Managers must be aware of the basic principles of pest control and the action to take in the event of an infestation.

Control and monitoring are essential functions of management, which ensure the production of safe food and **compliance** with legal requirements. Managers should provide a food safety policy and ensure the satisfactory implementation of HACCP. The skills to **inspect** the food operation and, where necessary, an understanding of microbiological sampling will be advantageous.

Managers must know the legal requirements placed on themselves and the business. A knowledge of relevant food safety acts and regulations, plus the role and powers of enforcement agencies and officers, should ensure the business complies with legislation and can prioritise its food safety activities to remain profitable.

MANAGEMENT RESPONSIBILITIES

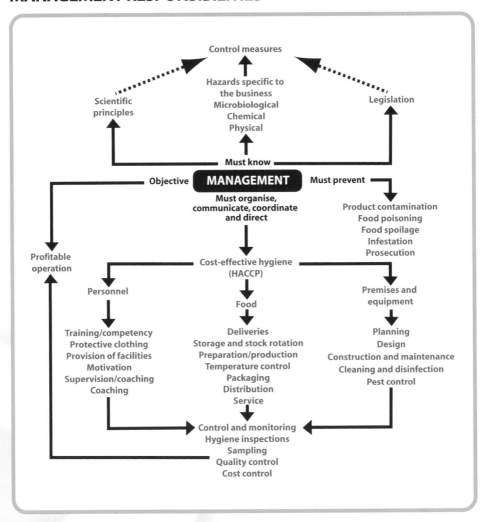

1 An introduction to food hygiene & food poisoning

Hygiene is the science of preserving health. A hygienic operation presents no risk of illness from the operations carried out therein. **Food hygiene** is much more than cleanliness, it involves all measures necessary to ensure the safety and **wholesomeness** of food during preparation, processing, manufacturing, packaging, storage, distribution, handling and offering for sale or supply to the consumer. This will involve:

♦ rejecting contaminated food or food from unreliable sources;
♦ decontaminating food, for example, by washing;
♦ protecting food from risk of **contamination** of any kind – this includes the effective **cleaning** and **disinfection** of food premises and equipment, requiring high standards of **personal hygiene** and training of staff;
♦ preventing any organisms multiplying to an extent that would expose consumers to **risk** or result in premature decomposition of food;
♦ destroying any harmful **bacteria** in the food by thorough cooking or processing; and
♦ discarding unfit or contaminated food.

The cost of food poisoning and poor food safety

Persons running a food business have legal, commercial and moral obligations to provide **safe food**. The costs resulting from **food poisoning** can be very high, as are those from poor hygiene. These costs, both financial and social, fall on employers and employees as well as those persons who are ill. Costs for employers include:

♦ the loss of working days and productivity from illness caused by employees eating contaminated food. Even minor infections increase costs for employers through absence of employees;
♦ the closure of food premises by local authority action;
♦ a loss of business and reputation either from bad publicity or from public reaction to poor standards, food poisoning **outbreaks** and even deaths;
♦ fines and costs of legal action taken because of contraventions of hygiene legislation or because of the sale of unfit or unsatisfactory food. In 2005, the owner of a curry restaurant in Bradford was jailed for 12 months, banned for life from working in a food company and required to pay over £34,000 in costs. This followed a salmonella food poisoning outbreak involving more than 340 people. In 2007, Cadbury were fined £1 million following an outbreak of *S.* Montevideo in chocolate bars. In the first few months of 2009, Tesco were fined over £120,000 with legal costs of around £100,000 for selling out-of-date food at 14 of its stores;
♦ civil action taken by food poisoning sufferers. In the USA, compensation for **foodborne illness** is a major business. In May 1998, Ochralla Inc. paid around $15 million to five children who were very ill after consuming apple juice contaminated with *E. coli* O157. In 2007, over 1,000 UK holiday makers staying at the Bahia Principe hotel in the Dominican Republic contracted salmonella, shigella, *E. coli* and giardia. In 2009, over 500 of these received a compensation package of £2.5 million;

♦ food losses due to premature **spoilage** or damage because of poor stock rotation, incorrect storage temperature or pest infestations;
♦ higher staff turnover, with attendant costs and inefficiencies from staff unwilling or unable to tolerate poor standards;
♦ food complaints and costs of internal investigation;
♦ loss of production; and
♦ decontamination, cleaning and replacement of equipment.

Food employees may suffer by:
♦ losing their jobs because of closure, loss of business or because they become long-term **carriers** of food poisoning organisms, especially salmonella; and
♦ losing overtime or bonuses.

Cost-effective hygiene

Cost-effective hygiene involves the identification of steps in the operation critical to food safety and the allocation of available resources to control and monitor **hazards** at these **critical points.** To achieve this objective, it is imperative to implement a food safety management system based on the principles of **HACCP** (hazard analysis and critical control point) that is reviewed periodically.

High-risk foods

High-risk foods are those foods that are most likely to be the vehicles of the food poisoning organisms consumed in food poisoning incidents. They are **ready-to-eat foods** that, under favourable conditions, support the multiplication of **pathogenic** bacteria and are intended for consumption without treatment that would destroy such organisms. They are usually high in protein, requiring strict temperature control and protection from contamination. High-risk foods include:
♦ all cooked meat and poultry;
♦ cooked meat products including gravy, meat pies, pâté, cook-chill meals and stock;

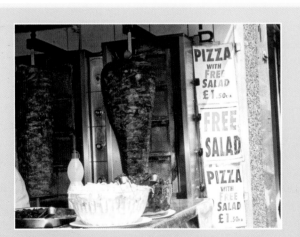

Examples of high-risk foods, including doner
kebabs, exposed to risk of contamination.

- milk, cream, artificial cream, custards and dairy produce, especially unpasteurised milk and products made from unpasteurised milk, ripened soft and moulded cheeses;
- cooked eggs and egg products, especially those made with raw eggs and not thoroughly cooked, for example, mayonnaise, mousse and home-made ice cream, but excluding pastry, bread and similar baked goods;
- shellfish and other seafoods, for example, raw oysters, mussels and cooked prawns;
- baby foods; and
- cooked rice (not high in protein).

Low-risk foods

These are usually ambient stable foods such as bread, biscuits, cereals, crisps and cakes, but not cream cakes. These foods are rarely implicated in food poisoning and include:

- **preserved** foods such as sterilised milk or canned food, whilst unopened;
- dried foods or food with little available moisture, such as flour, rice, bread, and biscuits. When adding liquid to powdered food, such as milk, the food becomes high-risk and must be stored under refrigeration;
- **acid** foods such as fruit, vinegar or products stored in vinegar (pH <4.5);
- fermented products such as salami or pepperoni; and
- foods with high sugar/salt/fat content such as jam or chocolate.

Ready-to-eat raw foods

Raw fruit and salad vegetables would normally be considered low-risk. However, an increasing number of outbreaks of foodborne illness are being associated with raw ready-to-eat foods. Between 2000 and 2012 there have been 29 reported outbreaks of food poisoning and recalls involving cantaloupe, mainly in the USA and South America (http://bites.ksu.edu/cantaloupe-related-outbreaks). The bacteria on the rind are transferred to the flesh when the melon is cut and will multiply if not refrigerated. Between 2000 and 2012, 31 outbreaks of food poisoning (*E. coli* and salmonella) have been reported in Europe,

Several outbreaks of food poisoning have involved ready-to-eat salads.

the USA, Canada and Australia involving bean, clover, alfalfa and onion sprouts (http://bites.ksu.edu/sprouts-associated-outbreaks). *E. coli* O157 has also been responsible for many outbreaks of illness involving apple juice, lettuce, tomatoes, spinach, strawberries and raspberries.

It is therefore recommended that all ready-to-eat food, which is intended for consumption without further treatment that would remove or destroy any foodborne pathogens, be treated as high-risk. Some ready-to-eat foods may be stored safely at ambient temperatures but they must always be protected from contamination, handled hygienically and never stored with raw food that may be a **source** of foodborne pathogens.

Bacteria

Bacteria are essential to life. They are minute organisms, often referred to as germs, which are found everywhere, including on and in man and food. Bacteria on the body are usually confined to a particular site and are known as **commensals** (part of the normal flora). For example, some species of staphylococcus are found on the skin and in the mouth and nose, other species are transient and may cause skin infections, such as boils. If harmful (pathogenic) species of staphylococcus, especially those which cause skin infections, are transferred to food they may cause illness. Most bacteria are harmless, some being necessary, for example, in yogurt and cheese manufacturing. However, two types of bacteria create major problems within the food industry:

♦ *spoilage bacteria* – responsible for the decomposition of food; and
♦ *pathogenic bacteria* – responsible for causing illness such as dysentery, typhoid and food poisoning.

Food poisoning

Food poisoning is an **acute** illness, usually of sudden onset, brought about by eating contaminated or poisonous food. The symptoms normally include one or more of the following; abdominal pain, diarrhoea, vomiting and nausea.

*Food poisoning may be caused by:
♦ bacteria or their **toxins**;
♦ marine toxins produced by dinoflagellates;
♦ chemicals including metals;
♦ plants or fish; and
♦ **mycotoxins** (moulds).

* As **viruses** do not multiply in foods and are **low-dose** organisms that primarily cause illness by routes other than food, they are included with foodborne diseases in Chapter 4.

Salmonella Enteritidis bacterium
©A.B. DOWSETT/SCIENCE PHOTO LIBRARY

Bacterial food poisoning

Bacterial food poisoning may be defined as "an acute disturbance of the gastrointestinal tract resulting in abdominal pain, with or without diarrhoea and vomiting, due to eating food contaminated by specific pathogenic bacteria or their toxins". The incubation period is normally short (between one and 36 hours). The number of bacteria required to cause illness in the healthy adult is usually large and multiplication of bacteria normally occurs within the food.

Patients usually recover in a few days but where body defences are low, illness may be prolonged and lead to complications. Botulism is usually much more serious, has different symptoms, often results in death, and survivors can take many months to recover. The use of anti-motility agents and **antibiotics** to treat ill people can sometimes be counterproductive. The carrier state can be prolonged. If gut movement is slowed down by using anti-motility agents, toxin from the bacteria stays in the intestines longer, so a greater amount can be absorbed into the bloodstream. The destruction of bacteria may also result in more toxin being released and absorbed into the bloodstream.

Carriers

Carriers are people who show no symptoms of illness but excrete food poisoning or foodborne pathogens that may contaminate food, for example, salmonellae or shigellae. Organisms may be excreted intermittently.

Convalescent carriers are people who have recovered from an illness but still harbour and excrete the organism. The convalescent state may be quite prolonged and salmonellae are sometimes excreted for several months.

Healthy carriers are people who have displayed no symptoms but harbour and excrete the causal organism. Healthy carriers may have become infected with pathogenic bacteria from contact with raw food with which they work, particularly poultry or meat.

Symptomless carriers can only be confirmed by bacteriological or, in some cases, serological screening, i.e. examination of faecal specimens or blood. However, routine screening of **food handlers** to detect carriers is not cost-effective. Intermittent excretors may be missed and a person may become a carrier the week after screening.

Medical questionnaires/interviews of new starters (important to identify persons with a history of gastrointestinal illness), induction training, effective communication and supervision of company rules, counselling, bacteriological testing of persons returning to work after illness involving diarrhoea or vomiting or illness whilst on holidays abroad and contacts of persons suffering from food poisoning are all useful to assist in the detection of carriers.

THE INCIDENCE OF FOOD POISONING

Because high standards of food hygiene should prevent the contamination and multiplication of food poisoning bacteria in food, trends of food poisoning statistics are often used as a measure of hygiene standards or as an indication of the success or failure of control systems or enforcement procedures. Unfortunately, one of the weakest areas of a surveillance system can be the reporting of food poisoning statistics and the failure of Health Authorities and laboratories to communicate essential up-to-date information to the food industry and enforcement officers. Those people who need to change practices quickly require rapid and reliable information, especially about food vehicles and causes of outbreaks. Publication of food poisoning statistics is often delayed and the way they are collected is frequently changed so comparison of trends may be of little value. Government departments and Health Authorities should improve their websites to allow rapid and easy access to information which will assist in the reduction of food poisoning.

National statistics on the reported number of confirmed food poisoning cases are unavailable. Furthermore, trends in reported food poisoning statistics can be seriously distorted by factors that may have nothing to do with hygiene standards, such as the inclusion of new "infectious intestinal pathogens", which may or may not be transmitted by food, for example, viruses. The number of ill persons seeking medical help and the number of faecal specimens submitted will also affect the statistics, for example, because of new legislation or increased publicity.

Notifications of food poisoning

Doctors attending a case of suspected food poisoning (any disease of an infectious or toxic nature caused, or thought to be caused, by the consumption of food or water) are legally required to notify the Proper Officer of the local authority. Each week the Proper Officer sends details of notified infections to the Health Protection Agency, Centre for Infections, which collates this data for England and Wales. This notification scheme facilitates the rapid identification and investigation of suspected cases of foodborne illness by authorised officers and enables implicated food premises to be identified as quickly as possible.

These notifications include cases that are bacteriologically unconfirmed and many cases of persons who are suffering from diarrhoea and/or vomiting that may not be foodborne. They could more accurately be described as "notified cases of **gastroenteritis**," and should not be used to indicate trends in food poisoning or hygiene standards.

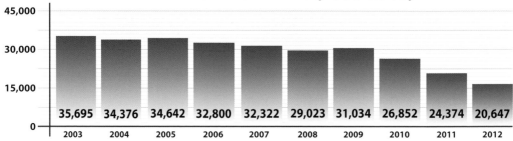

NOTIFICATIONS OF FOOD POISONING IN ENGLAND AND WALES (2003-2012)

	2003	2004	2005	2006	2007	2008	2009	2010	2011	2012
	35,695	34,376	34,642	32,800	32,322	29,023	31,034	26,852	24,374	20,647

These figures are much lower because "otherwise ascertained" statistics are no longer included. All statistics relating to England and Wales are provided courtesy of the Health Protection Agency Centre for Infections Gastrointestinal and Emerging Zoonotic Infections. www.hpa.org.uk

In the absence of information on the number of confirmed food poisoning cases, alternative statistics should be used by persons interested in trends of food poisoning. Arguably, the most representative statistics of actual trends of food poisoning are laboratory isolations relating to specific food poisoning organisms such as salmonella.

Salmonella statistics

A case of bacterial food poisoning is a person with symptoms, usually diarrhoea and/or vomiting, who has become ill as a result of eating contaminated food. This can only be confirmed if the person is part of a confirmed food poisoning outbreak or by isolating food poisoning organisms or toxin from faecal or vomitus specimens. Statistics relating to isolates and suspect cases should not be confused with confirmed cases.

The bar chart showing the annual totals of salmonellosis is based on laboratory isolations from faecal specimens. Although the vast majority of isolates will be cases of salmonella food poisoning, these statistics also include symptomless excreters, persons who may have non-foodborne salmonellosis and persons who acquired the illness abroad. Nevertheless, at the present time, these statistics are the most accurate representation of salmonella food poisoning trends over the last ten years.

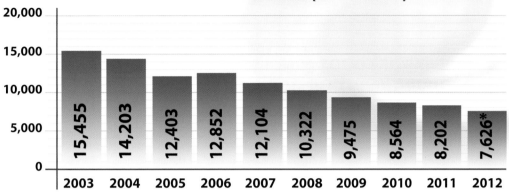

SALMONELLA ISOLATES FROM HUMANS IN ENGLAND AND WALES (2003-2012)

Excluding *S.* Typhi and *S.* Paratyphi.

*Provisional.

A survey in Yorkshire and Humberside between June and August 1986 showed that 27.4% of reported cases of salmonella food poisoning in that period originated abroad, although the national percentage is considered to be around 20%.

The Food Standards Agency (FSA)

The Food Standards Agency made a commitment to reduce the level of foodborne disease by 20% by the year 2006 (from a base of 2000). They did not use "notifications of food poisoning statistics", probably for the reasons outlined above. They have acknowledged that the most accurate statistics available are laboratory isolations of specific organisms.

Actual levels of foodborne illness

The number of cases of foodborne illness is significantly under-reported. However, claims that millions of people in the UK suffer from foodborne illness as a result of eating food from commercial catering premises are difficult to justify.

In order to determine and compare trends of the actual levels of food poisoning from commercial premises it is preferable to use confirmed outbreaks or adjusted statistics of laboratory isolations. The first thing is to select those organisms which are most likely to be foodborne, for example, salmonella, campylobacter, *E. coli* O157, norovirus, *Clostridium perfringens* and *Listeria monocytogenes*. It is essential to keep the statistics for each organism separately. The statistics then need to be adjusted to take account of illness acquired abroad. In the UK the FSA reduced the numbers by 20%. It is then necessary to determine the actual level of under-reporting for each organism. This is usually determined by the severity and length of time the symptoms last. The FSA "Studies of Infectious Intestinal Diseases" suggested that the actual number of salmonella cases was three times greater than reported and eight times greater for campylobacter.

The figures then need to be adjusted to take account of non-foodborne cases. Salmonella is usually considered to be 100% foodborne, although transmission from frogs, snakes, turtles and mice have been recorded, along with airborne transmission from contaminated aerosol. Campylobacter may be less than 70% foodborne and norovirus much lower. Finally some allowance could be made from illness resulting from bad practice in the home.

It would appear that the number of actual cases resulting from commercial premises, especially catering premises, could be a lower figure than the millions alleged in other books and the media. The Food Standards Agency claimed there were approximately 850,000 cases of foodborne illness in 2005 and since then figures have remained fairly stable apart from campylobacter.

OUTBREAKS OF FOODBORNE INFECTIOUS INTESTINAL DISEASE *(EXCLUDING PRIVATE RESIDENCES)* IN ENGLAND AND WALES (2003-2012)

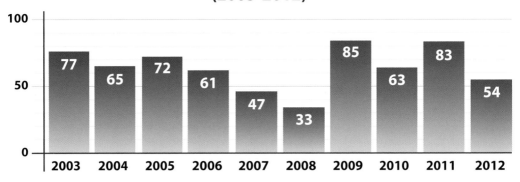

These figures are a further indication that food poisoning from commercial premises may be much lower than some organisations and the media suggest.

Management failures resulting in food poisoning (Dr Richard North)

♦ A failure to carry out a risk-assessment when there is a change of menu, ingredients or recipes, for example, increasing the pH of mayonnaise.

♦ Lack of contingency planning, for example, when the refrigerator breaks down.

♦ Communication - a failure of management or head office to provide the front-line staff with the correct information. Communication breakdown may also involve the government and government bodies, for example, the failure to give timely warning to pregnant women on the dangers of eating pâté and soft cheeses (listeria).

♦ Management disincentives, for example, bonus paid in relation to the amount of cleaning chemicals used.

♦ Commercially driven misuse or abuse of equipment or premises, for example, overloading refrigerators or catering for numbers beyond the capacity.

♦ A failure to recognise potentially hazardous procedures of the operation, for example, colour-coded equipment all being washed in the same sink with no disinfection.

♦ Failure to learn lessons or implement recommendations following an earlier outbreak.

♦ Failure to replace complex or time-consuming operations, for example, refrigerators positioned a considerable distance from workstations. This militates against small amounts of food being prepared, which results in temperature abuse.

♦ Unrealistic demands placed on junior management or untrained staff.

♦ The absence of routine planning and consistent procedures.

CAUSAL FACTORS RELATING TO 1479 OUTBREAKS OF FOOD POISONING IN ENGLAND AND WALES (1970-1982)*

	Causal factor	Total number of outbreaks in which factor recorded (%)**	
1	Preparation too far in advance	844	(57)
2	Storage at ambient temperature	566	(38)
3	Inadequate cooling	468	(30)
4	Inadequate reheating	391	(26)
5	Contaminated processed food	246	(17)
6	Undercooking	223	(15)
7	Contaminated canned food	104	(7)
8	Inadequate thawing	95	(6)
9	Cross-contamination	94	(6)
10	Raw food consumed	93	(6)
11	Improper warm holding	77	(5)
12	Infected food handlers	65	(4)
13	Use of leftovers	62	(4)
14	Extra large quantities prepared	48	(3)

*Roberts D. 6th Edition of Food Poisoning and Food Hygiene.
**In some outbreaks more than one factor was involved.

LABORATORY REPORTS OF FOODBORNE DISEASE IN ENGLAND AND WALES (2003-2012)

ORGANISM	2003	2004	2005	2006	2007	2008	2009	2010	2011	2012*
Campylobacter spp.	46,285	44,544	46,724	46,868	51,989	50,009	57,772	62,688	64,608	63,293
E. coli O157	675	699	950	1,001	828	950	1,034	793	1,182	-
Giardia lamblia	3,460	3,209	2,938	2,959	3,032	3,407	3,471	3,804	-	-
Hepatitis *A*	1,011	632	485	398	363	354	352	367	-	-
Listeria monocytogenes	233	211	189	185	227	182	214	159	147	-
Shigella spp.	996	1,176	1,332	1,087	1,487	1,393	1,484	1,747	-	-
Cryptosporidium	5,923	3,621	4,540	3,684	3,075	4,166	4,831	3,902	2,988	-
Norovirus	2,327	3,133	2,922	4,611	6,009	6,828	7,715	11,780	8,548	10,845
Typhoid	204	210	232	253	287	307	263	319	-	-
Paratyphoid	205	233	240	293	238	274	218	250	-	-
Yersinia enterocolitica	34	18	24	11	50	20	32	19	-	-

*Provisional.

STATUTORY NOTIFICATIONS OF FOOD POISONING AND LABORATORY ISOLATIONS OF SALMONELLA IN SCOTLAND 2003-2012

The reported cases of food poisoning in Scotland include laboratory isolations of campylobacter.

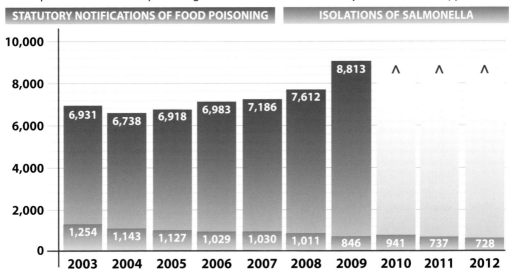

^ Changes relating to the Public Health etc. (Scotland) Act 2008 and the reporting of notifiable diseases was amended on the 1 January 2010. Food poisoning is now classed as a non-notifiable disease and therefore notification data is not available after 2009.

*Provisional.

LABORATORY REPORTS OF SPECIFIC FOODBORNE DISEASE IN SCOTLAND (2003-2012)

ORGANISM	2003	2004	2005	2006	2007	2008	2009	2010	2011	2012*
Campylobacter spp.	4,445	4,365	4,558	4,865	5,192	4,878	6,415	6,601	6,366	6,333
E. coli O157	148	209	172	243	243	241	237	212	253	234
Giardia lamblia	191	188	197	200	220	221	209	217	195	185
Listeria spp.	14	15	31	17	23	15	17	17	14	11
Shigella spp.	79	104	118	136	166	131	131	126	137	95
Cryptosporidium	805	465	709	612	510	656	698	584	443	710
Norovirus	1,441	1,321	1,552	2,324	2,043	2,170	2,200	3,109	1,668	2,920
Yersinia enterocolitica	47	51	28	23	19	18	13	4	4	10

*Provisional.
All statistics relating to Scotland courtesy of Health Protection Scotland.
www.hps.scot.nhs.uk

LABORATORY REPORTS OF SPECIFIC FOODBORNE DISEASE IN IRELAND (2004 - 2012)

ORGANISM	2004	2005	2006	2007	2008	2009	2010	2011	2012*
Bacillus cereus	1	0	0	0	0	1	0	0	0
Botulism	0	0	1	0	7	0	0	1	0
Clostridium perfringens (type A)	5	1	0	0	1	1	0	0	0
Cryptosporidiosis	435	568	369	608	415	445	294	428	556
Giardiasis	52	57	64	62	71	61	57	57	54
Hepatitis A *(acute)*	47	55	39	32	42	50	46	19	30
Listeriosis	11	12	7	21	13	10	10	7	11
Norovial *infection*	1,116	1,043	1,633	1,310	1,768	1,633	1,926	990	1,705
Paratyphoid	4	0	1	4	8	10	5	2	5
Shigellosis	56	36	53	43	75	70	60	42	29
Staphylococcal food poisoning	3	6	0	0	1	1	0	0	0
Trichinosis	0	0	0	2	0	0	0	0	0
Typhoid	5	5	9	9	5	9	8	14	9
Yersiniosis	6	3	1	7	3	3	3	6	2

All statistics relating to the Republic of Ireland are provided courtesy of
Health Protection Surveillance Centre. www.ndsc.ie/hpsc
*Provisional

NOTIFICATIONS OF SALMONELLA IN IRELAND 2003-2012

*Provisional

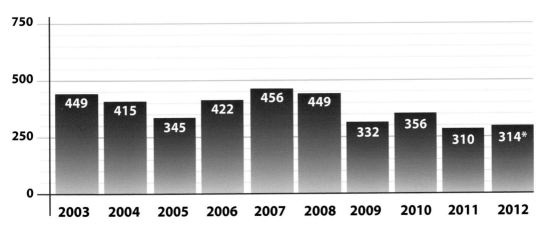

CASES OF VEROTOXIGENIC ESCHERICHIA COLI INFECTIONS IN IRELAND 2005-2012

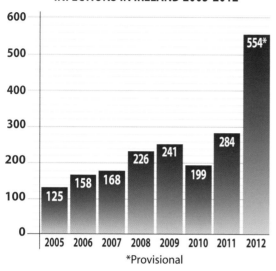

*Provisional

CASES OF CAMPYLOBACTER IN IRELAND 2005-2012

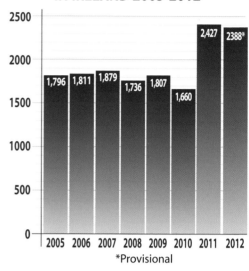

*Provisional

NOTIFICATIONS OF INFECTIOUS INTESTINAL DISEASES IN NORTHERN IRELAND 2002-2011

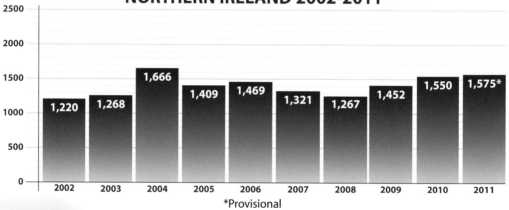

*Provisional

LABORATORY REPORTS OF FOODBORNE DISEASE IN NI (2003-2012)

ORGANISM	2003	2004	2005	2006	2007	2008	2009	2010	2011	2012*
Campylobacter spp.	743	841	891	937	885	848	977	1,040	1,175	1,211
E. coli O157	53	19	49	47	54	59	48	77	57	197
Giardia lamblia	19	18	18	15	14	9	38	16	35	50
Hepatitis *A*	3	5	7	2	0	17	36	4	0	4
Listeria spp.	3	4	3	6	5	11	4	2	3	7
Salmonella spp.	214	451	180	206	159	187	158	180	168	146
Shigella spp.	13	8	7	9	16	16	13	5	8	9
Cryptosporidium spp.	141	136	164	134	85	119	118	119	140	177
Norovirus	109	276	209	385	439	439	424	643	445	592

Courtesy of the Public Health Agency. www.publichealth.hscni.net

2 *Microbiology* edited by Adrian Eley

Bacteria are single-celled organisms found everywhere; in soil, air, water, on people, animals and food. Bacteria are measured in micrometres (µm) and 1µm = 1/1000mm. Staphylococci have a diameter of around 0.75µm and salmonellae are about 3µm in length. The naked eye can see to approximately 75µm and consequently bacteria are only visible in large numbers when they form colonies or occasionally as a slime on the surface of food. Bacteria may be examined at a magnification of 1000 times using a powerful microscope. (A housefly similarly magnified would be nine metres long.)

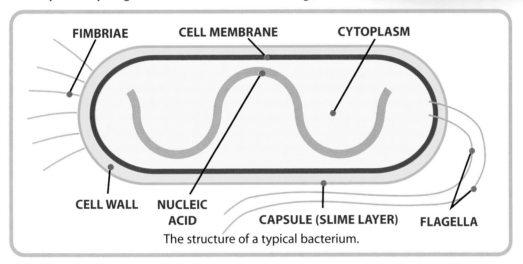

FIMBRIAE   CELL MEMBRANE   CYTOPLASM

CELL WALL   NUCLEIC ACID   CAPSULE (SLIME LAYER)   FLAGELLA

The structure of a typical bacterium.

Capsule	a gel-like secretion which surrounds many bacteria, protecting them against desiccation and harmful chemicals.
Cell wall	a rigid, permeable structure which surrounds the bacterium and gives the cell its shape and strength.
Cell membrane	a selectively permeable membrane which controls the passage of nutrients and waste products both into and out of the cell.
Cytoplasm	the major part of the cell and the medium within which the metabolic reactions occur.
Flagella	present in some bacteria for locomotion.
Fimbriae (or pili)	often involved in adherence.
Nucleic acid (such as DNA)	determines the genetic characteristics of the bacterium.

Appearance of bacteria

Bacteria vary considerably in shape:

♦ *Cocci* are spherical; some form chains, for example, streptococci. Others form clusters, for example, staphylococci.
♦ *Rods* are sausage-shaped, for example, salmonellae and *Escherichia coli.*
♦ *Spirochaetes* are spiral.
♦ *Vibrios* are comma-shaped.

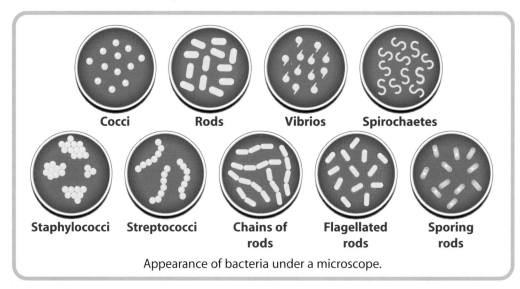

Appearance of bacteria under a microscope.

Spore formation

With minor exceptions only two bacterial genera, *Bacillus* and *Clostridium*, are able to form **spores** that are capable of surviving adverse conditions, such as lack of nutrients. Temperatures achieved in normal cooking may destroy the **vegetative bacteria** but any spores present will probably survive. Furthermore, these high temperatures trigger the spore into **germination** and as the food cools down, providing the environment is suitable, a new mature vegetative cell capable of reproduction is formed.

Spores may be resistant to desiccation, disinfectants and heat. Very high temperatures in excess of boiling (100°C) are often required, for long periods, to ensure their destruction. The time and temperature used in the canning of **low-acid foods** is based on the destruction of *Clostridium botulinum* spores (121°C for three minutes). The survival of spores is a hazard.

Toxin production

Certain bacteria release poisons known as **toxins**. Some toxins, such as those produced by *Cl. botulinum,* are often the cause of death of persons consuming food contaminated by this organism.

Exotoxins

These are highly toxic proteins usually produced during the multiplication, or **sporulation**, of some Gram-positive bacteria, for example, *Staphylococcus aureus* and *Bacillus cereus*. Quite often these toxins are produced in food and occasionally are heat-resistant so that, although cooking may destroy the bacteria, the toxin is unaffected and can still cause problems if the food is eaten. Toxins which are not destroyed are a hazard. Botulinum **exotoxin** is not heat-resistant. **Enterotoxins** are exotoxins that affect the gastrointestinal tract.

Endotoxins
These reside in the outer membrane and are released on the death of many Gram-negative bacteria. **Endotoxins** are commonly produced in the intestines of persons consuming food contaminated by such organisms as salmonella.

The identification of bacteria
As individual bacteria are so minute it is not practical to work with a single cell, so the first stage in identification is to obtain a pure **culture** containing millions of organisms. This involves spreading the bacterial mixture onto the surface of a solid culture medium in a petri-dish using a sterile wire loop. The usual medium is nutrient agar, which consists of beef extract, peptone water and agar to solidify the medium.

Pre-enrichment involves the use of a liquid medium, such as peptone water, to allow damaged cells to recover. Selective enrichment involves using a medium to suppress unwanted competitors and encourage the multiplication of the desired species to a detectable level. For example, the addition of crystal violet inhibits the growth of Gram-positive bacteria. MacConkey agar, which contains bile salts to inhibit the growth of non-intestinal bacteria, is used to grow some enteric bacteria such as salmonella. Selective atmospheres are used in a similar manner, for example, strict **anaerobes** such as *Clostridium perfringens* will not grow in air.

The inoculated medium is then incubated at a constant temperature for an appropriate length of time, for example, 24 hours. The temperature is often critical in promoting or precluding growth. Most of the common **food poisoning**/borne disease organisms prefer a temperature of 37°C whereas 42°C is used to isolate *Campylobacter* species. During incubation each bacterium can become a pure culture of millions of bacteria, which appear as small, discrete characteristic spots on the agar and are known as colonies.

The shape, size, colour and consistency of a colony can be of great value to identification. However, other methods will probably need to be used, including staining reactions, microscopical examination and biochemical reactions. In order to identify individual members of bacterial groups it may be necessary to use more complex tests such as **serotyping, phage typing** and plasmid typing.

The Gram stain
Bacteria can be divided into two major groups, the Gram-positive and Gram-negative types, depending on whether or not they retain a crystal violet/iodine dye complex after treatment with alcohol and safranin. Gram-positive bacteria retain the dye and are blue-purple whereas Gram-negative are pink. Staining is carried out after a suspension of the bacteria is applied to a microscope slide, using a sterile wire loop. The slide must be heated to fix the bacteria before the application of the stain.

Microscopical examination
Light microscopes are normally used to observe staining reactions, cell shape, the presence of spores and the motility of a particular bacterium.

Staphylococcus **(a)** showing Gram-positive cocci and
E. coli **(b)** showing Gram-negative bacilli.

Biochemical reactions

Bacteria that cannot be identified by **morphology** (shape and size) and cultural characteristics may be distinguished by their biochemical reactions. For example, some bacteria will ferment sugars to produce an acid, which changes the colour of a liquid medium, and gas which can be collected in a small inverted test tube immersed in the medium. Other biochemical properties of bacteria include the production of coagulase by *S. aureus*; the production of indole by *E. coli*; the ability to digest gelatin, egg and serum; to split fats; reduce dyes such as methylene blue; and produce ammonia and hydrogen sulphide.

Pulse field gel electrophoresis (PFGE)

PFGE is a technique used for characterising various strains of bacteria. It is widely used when investigating food poisoning outbreaks to determine if the bacteria detected in the food vehicle is the same strain as that which is isolated from the specimen of the ill person.

Serological typing

This test is used to distinguish different sub-types of the same species of bacteria. It involves observing the agglutination (clumping together) reaction between the **antigens** of the test bacteria and the **antibodies** produced in the blood serum (antisera) of human beings or animals infected with the same bacteria. Examples include *Salmonella* Enteritidis and *Salmonella* Typhi.

Phage typing

Phage typing enables even finer differentiation of sub-types. **Bacteriophages** are **viruses parasitic** on bacteria. Each virus is host specific and will only attack one particular type of bacteria. The bacteriophages are inoculated on to the bacteria culture. Susceptibility of the bacteria to the virus enables positive identification of the phage type. Phage typing is particularly useful for identifying salmonellae and staphylococci. Examples include *S.* Enteritidis PT4 and *S.* Enteritidis PT2.

Immunoassay

The use of specific monoclonal antibodies to detect bacterial antigens or toxins, for example, ELISA (enzyme-linked immunosorbent assay).

THE MULTIPLICATION OF BACTERIA

Bacteria reproduce vegetatively (non-sexually) by the process of **binary fission** (dividing into two). After cell division each daughter cell grows to maturity and itself divides. The time between each division, (known as the generation time) varies between species but, given the right conditions, is commonly around 20 minutes. However, under **optimum** conditions *Cl. perfringens* and *Vibrio parahaemolyticus* are both capable of division in ten minutes or less.

Given a generation time of ten minutes, 1,000 bacteria could become 1,000,000 in only one hour 40 minutes (1,000,000 bacteria per gram of food may cause food poisoning and 1,000 bacteria per gram of food is not an uncommon level of **contamination**). The multiplication of pathogens in food is a hazard.

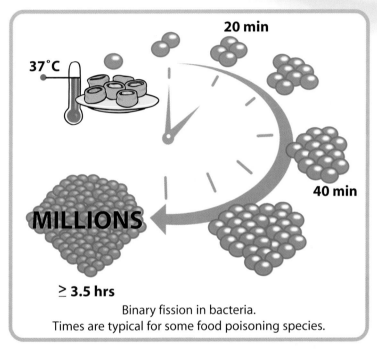

Binary fission in bacteria.
Times are typical for some food poisoning species.

Multiplication

When bacteria contaminate food and conditions are favourable, they begin to multiply. The increase in numbers does not occur at a uniform rate but passes through a succession of phases. These phases are described as follows:

1 to 2 the **lag phase** –	no multiplication as the bacteria "acclimatise".
2 to 3 the logarithmic phase –	rapid multiplication.
3 to 4 the stationary phase –	numbers of bacteria remain constant as the number produced is equal to the number dying.
4 to 5 the decline phase –	numbers decrease as numbers dying exceeds those produced.

The lag phase is short if there are large numbers of young bacteria in optimum growth conditions.

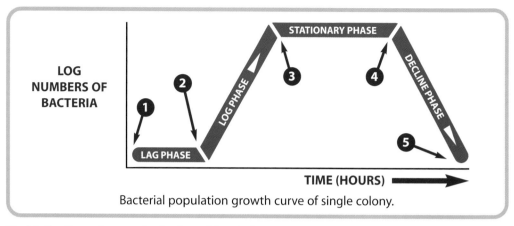

Bacterial population growth curve of single colony.

Multiplication of several colonies of bacteria

Although the population growth curve may follow the standard pattern in the laboratory, this is unlikely in food in practice. If the food is mixed or the colony disturbed in some way, a new supply of nutrients will be provided and levels of toxins reduced. It is extremely unlikely that a single colony or species would exist in isolation. Therefore, there will be many colonies at different stages of growth as they compete and as the substrate is changed by the preceding culture. The number of bacteria in food in favourable conditions will probably remain in a series of logarithmic phases interspersed by stationary and lag phases. The numbers of bacteria overall will therefore continue to increase until unfavourable growth conditions occur.

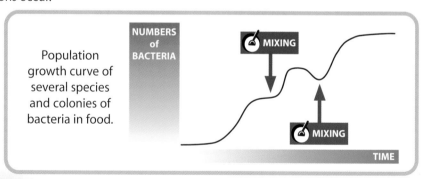

Population growth curve of several species and colonies of bacteria in food.

Factors influencing bacterial multiplication

Nutrients

Bacteria require carbon, hydrogen, oxygen and nitrogen with smaller amounts of sulphur and phosphorus, together with trace elements such as sodium, potassium, magnesium, iron and manganese. All nutrients must be in solution (dissolved in water) before they can enter the bacterium. The elements are converted into the constituents of cytoplasm by a process described as a **metabolic reaction**. Certain vitamins may be required to facilitate these reactions.

Most **pathogenic** and **spoilage bacteria** obtain the essential basic elements from sugar, amino acids, fats and minerals. The types of food favoured include high protein food such as milk, eggs, meat and fish. Foods with a high sugar or salt content are unsuitable for the growth of most bacteria and are therefore potentially safe. *S. aureus* and *Listeria spp.* are exceptions.

Hydrogen-ion concentration (pH)

The **pH** of a solution is measured on a scale of 1 to 14 (hydrogen-ion concentration). Acid foods have pH values below 7 and alkaline foods above 7; a pH value of 7 being neutral.

All bacteria have their own optimal, minimal and maximal pH for growth with most preferring a pH near neutrality. Most bacteria will not grow in food with a pH below 4·0 and at this pH it allows lower processing temperatures to be used in preservation techniques, such as canning, to render food safe and free of spoilage organisms. However, a large number of pathogens introduced into an acid food will not die off immediately and may still cause illness. S. Typhimurium has survived in fruit juices (pH 3.2 at 22°C) for up to five days. A food poisoning outbreak occurred in New Jersey, USA, following the consumption of apple juice (pH 3.6) contaminated with S. Typhimurium.

Generally, **moulds** and **yeasts** are less sensitive to the pH of food than bacteria.

Moisture

All life requires water, which is used to transport nutrients into the cell and take away waste products. Dry products are poor media for the multiplication of bacteria, for example, flour, biscuits and bread, and may be described as low-risk foods. However, some bacteria, especially spore formers, are able to survive **dehydration** and when dried egg or milk powder is reconstituted by the addition of liquid, the food once again becomes **high-risk**. Most other foods contain sufficient moisture to promote bacterial growth.

Water activity (a_w)

The amount of moisture in any food available to bacteria is normally considered in terms of water activity. The a_w of pure water is 1.00 (a saturated salt solution 0.75). Bacteria prefer an a_w around 0.99 and many will not grow below 0.95. However, S. aureus will grow at an a_w of 0.89 and some bacteria can exist below 0.75. Yeasts and moulds tolerate lower levels of a_w, some as low as 0.62. Fresh meat has an a_w of 0.95 to 1.00, bread 0.94 to 0.97, cured meat 0.87 to 0.95, jam 0.75 to 0.80, flour 0.67 to 0.87 and sugar 0.19.

Temperature

Bacteria have a maximum and minimum temperature for growth between which there is an optimum temperature when multiplication is the most rapid. The range of temperature for the fastest multiplication of most pathogens is 20°C to 50°C. Some pathogens grow between 0°C and 20°C but they multiply more slowly at the lower temperatures. The lowest recorded temperature for the growth of pathogenic bacteria is –2°C. Usually bacteria are separated into four groups:

	Optimum	Range	Importance
Psychrophiles	< 20°C	–8° to 25°C	Include bacteria which cause spoilage in refrigerators and cold stores.
Psychrotrophs	>20°C	–5° to 40°C	Include *Cl. botulinum* type E, *Listeria monocytogenes*, *Yersinia enterocolitica*, and *Aeromonas hydrophila*.
Mesophiles	20° to 45°C	10° to 56°C	Include most common pathogens that cause food poisoning.
Thermophiles	> 45°C	35° to 80°C	Important in canning – some are very heat-resistant and if not destroyed will cause spoilage if cans are stored at high temperatures.

Presence of oxygen

Some micro-organisms will only grow in the presence of oxygen and these are known as obligate **aerobes**. Others flourish in the absence of oxygen (obligate anaerobes). Micro-organisms that grow either with or without free oxygen are known as facultative. Some food poisoning bacteria are anaerobic, such as clostridia, others are facultative anaerobes, such as salmonellae and staphylococci. However, they usually prefer aerobic conditions. **Microaerophilic** bacteria grow in the presence of reduced quantities of free oxygen, for example, campylobacter.

Free oxygen is normally present in food, except those foods with a high liquid content that have been thoroughly boiled, roast joints and vacuum-packed foods.

Competition

When there are many different bacteria present, they will compete for the same food. Fortunately, most food poisoning bacteria are not as competitive as the normal flora found on food and, unless present in high numbers, will usually die. Modified atmospheres will favour anaerobes.

Viruses

Viruses are much smaller than bacteria. They vary from about one hundredth to a third of their size and can only be seen through an electron microscope. They consist of a single strand of nucleic acid surrounded by a protective protein coat. They multiply rapidly in living cells not in food. They survive well on inanimate surfaces and in the environment. Transmission through food depends on contamination of the food, for example, by food handlers or sewage. Filter feeding bivalves, such as oysters, harvested from sewage-polluted waters, are a major problem because of their ability to concentrate viruses from contaminated water. Viruses in food can be destroyed by the time and temperature combinations used to destroy bacteria, for example, in cooking or sterilisation. Viruses may be resistant to some chemical disinfectants and other bactericidal chemicals such as hand gels.

Incidents of gastroenteritis are being increasingly attributed to **viruses** such as norovirus and hepatitis A and undoubtedly contribute to a large number of notified cases of 'food poisoning'. However, rotaviruses, adenoviruses, astroviruses and calciviruses are predominantly faecal-oral, paediatric infections which are rarely incriminated in foodborne transmission. Outbreaks in hospitals, nursing homes and other 'closed' communities including cruises are common and are often considered to be person-to-person spread. However, airborne and environmental spread from vomit may be of greater importance. Inhalation of particles from desiccated vomit and faeces may be a significant transmission vehicle in 'closed settings'.

Outbreaks have been associated with contaminated ice and sewage-polluted water, although standard water treatment should prevent problems.

Moulds

Moulds are aerobic, or facultative anaerobes, multinucleate, chlorophyll-free **fungi** that produce thread-like filaments (hyphae) and form a branched network of mycelium. Moulds, which may be black, white or of various colours, will grow on most foods, whether moist or dry, acid or alkaline and high in salt or sugar concentrations. The optimum growth temperature is usually 20°C to 30°C, although they will grow well over a wide range of temperatures and may cause problems in refrigerators. Growth has been recorded as low as −10°C. High humidities and fluctuating temperatures accelerate mould growth.

Mould growth on food due to can punctures.

Mouldy food complaints may result in prosecutions.

Microscopic **mould spores** are inseparable from atmospheric dust and large numbers may be present in food premises. Moulds commonly affect bread and other bakery products, and although spores are usually destroyed in baking, subsequent contamination is difficult to avoid. Rapid cooling of bread and wrapping below 27°C will reduce mould problems. Also important is the removal of dampness and mould growth in factories and the thorough cleaning and disinfection of plant and equipment.

Food must always be stored in accordance with the manufacturer's instructions and never sold outside its **use-by** date. Mishandling of vacuum packs of cheese may result in punctures and consequential mould growth. As the mycelium grows over the food, hyphae penetrate the substance and consequently mould soon returns if scraped off the surface. Regular checking of stock is imperative to avoid customer complaints. The presence of mould on food is usually considered to render it unfit for human consumption. Cheeses produced with specific moulds are an exception.

Certain species of mould, for example, *Aspergillus flavus* and *Fusarium spp.*, are capable of producing poisonous metabolites, known as **mycotoxins**, which may affect animals and humans. Even toxins produced by some species of *Penicillium* have induced **carcinogenic** effects in animals including marked damage to the liver and kidneys and may, in large doses, constitute a hazard to man. Both aspergilli and penicillia are common in nuts and cereals, especially rice. Incidents of poisoning by mycotoxins in the UK over the last 50 years have been extremely rare: a few cases of ergotism were recorded in Manchester in 1927. However, constant vigilance is required by authorised officers employed at ports to prevent the import of mouldy food or animal feed. In 1984, several tons of peanuts intended for human consumption were found to be contaminated by small amounts of aspergilli and were condemned.

Mould **spores** will be present in the atmosphere, on surfaces, especially damp surfaces, and on mouldy food. Food should always be covered and mouldy food must be segregated. Furthermore, mould must not be allowed to grow on walls, ceilings and window frames. Mould growth often occurs if food is stored at the wrong temperature, at high humidity and in excess of the recommended **shelf life**. It may also affect cheese stored in vacuum packs that are pierced. Canned foods that are removed from cases opened with unguarded craft knives may become punctured, thus giving rise to mould growth inside the can.

Yeasts

Yeasts are microscopic unicellular fungi that reproduce by budding. They vary in size from around 5μm diameter to 100μm in length. Most yeasts grow best in the presence of oxygen, although fermentative types grow slowly anaerobically. The majority of yeasts prefer acid foods (pH 4 to 4.5) with a reasonable level of available moisture (a_w above 0.88). However, many yeasts will grow in high concentrations of sugar and salt with an a_w as low as 0.62. The optimum growth temperature for yeast is around 25°C to 30°C with a maximum of around 47°C. Some yeasts can grow at 0°C and below.

Yeasts are used in the manufacture of foods such as bread, beer, wine and vinegar. They are not usually considered to be responsible for food poisoning, although large numbers of yeast in unpasteurised, home-made fermented beer has resulted in mild illness.

Yeasts grow slowly in low-acid, moist food and are unable to compete with faster growing spoilage bacteria. However, they will outgrow bacteria in acidic or low water activity environments. Packaging, poor design of equipment and unsatisfactory cleaning procedures may result in contamination of foods such as fruit juice and dairy products. Processed fruit, dried fruit and jam products also provide the high-sugar and high-acid environment ideal for spoilage by yeast. Signs of spoilage are gas production and off-flavours. Meat and bakery products are less likely to be affected by yeasts other than some dried meats and low-water products such as marzipan and icings.

3 Food poisoning *edited by Adrian Eley*

Classically, **food poisoning** is commonly associated with symptoms such as diarrhoea and vomiting and may also include headache, stomach cramps and fever. **Bacteria** are responsible for most food poisoning **cases**, with **mycotoxins**, poisonous plants, chemicals or metals occasionally causing problems. Viral **gastroenteritis** is caused by **low-dose viruses**, which do not multiply in food, and is therefore dealt with in chapter 4 "Foodborne diseases".

Because food poisoning organisms are commonly found in **foods**, it is impossible to operate a food business without them being present in either small or large numbers. This is why good hygiene practices are so important to minimise **risk** of illness from consuming **contaminated** food.

BACTERIAL FOOD POISONING

There are at least eight types of bacteria known to be responsible for causing most food poisoning **outbreaks** in the United Kingdom:

Salmonella spp.
Clostridium perfringens
Staphylococcus aureus
Bacillus cereus and other *Bacillus spp.*

Clostridium botulinum
Vibrio parahaemolyticus
Escherichia coli
Yersinia enterocolitica

TYPES OF FOOD POISONING

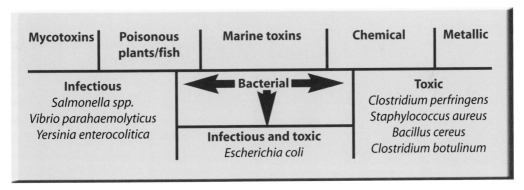

Salmonella

Salmonellae are Gram-negative, facultative **anaerobic** rods. There are approximately 2,500 **serotypes** of salmonella, the commonest being *S.* Enteritidis and *S.* Typhimurium.

Nomenclature of the salmonellae does not follow the conventional rules in that the classification systems usually refer to serotypes rather than to species. More recently, it has been proposed that all serotypes of salmonella be considered as members of a single species, *S.* Enterica. In this scheme, individual serotypes are referred to as, for example, *S.* Enterica subspecies *enterica* serotype Typhimurium. However, it is likely that for routine use *S.* Enterica serotype Typhimurium, *S.* serotype Typhimurium or *S.* Typhimurium will be acceptable.

CLASSIFICATION OF SALMONELLA

	Old classification	New classification
Family	Enterobacteriaceae	Enterobacteriaceae
Genus	Salmonella	Salmonella
Species/serotype	*enteritidis*	
Species		*enterica*
Subspecies		*enterica*
Serotype (Serovar)		Enteritidis
Type	*enteritidis* PT4	Enteritidis PT4

The growth range of these bacteria is from 7°C to 47°C with a generation time of ten hours at 10°C. Some salmonella can grow at a pH as low as 3.8. If present in sufficient numbers in consumed food (normally 100,000+ per gram), the digestion process may not destroy them. The bacteria multiply in the intestine and diarrhoea results after penetration of the intestinal wall. The **endotoxin** released on the death of the cell probably produces the fever associated with salmonellosis. Salmonellae are able to survive in soil for several months.

The primary **sources** of salmonella are the intestinal tracts of animals and birds. 90% of reptiles carry salmonella. Animals may become infected from the consumption of contaminated feed or contact with **carriers** or infected animals. Ill animals should always be isolated and animal feed treated to ensure it is free of salmonellae. Raw meat, especially poultry, is the main source of salmonellae in food premises. In 2009, the Food Standards Agency published the results of a survey of salmonella and campylobacter contamination of chilled and frozen chicken on retail sale in the UK. Findings showed an average salmonella contamination level of 6.6%, whereas campylobacter was present in 65.2% of chicken samples and 76.1% of whole chicken samples.

Although most outbreaks of salmonella involve high-risk foods such as cooked poultry and ready-to-eat products containing raw or lightly cooked egg and cheese, usually made with unpasteurised milk, several outbreaks have involved low-risk foods. In 1982, *S.* Napoli in imported Italian chocolate bars resulted in an unusual outbreak affecting 272 people. The chocolate was at least seven months old, the incubation period was up to ten days and the infective dose was commonly less than 100 organisms. The low moisture and high sugar content of chocolate increase the temperature resistance of the salmonellae and enable some organisms to survive the process. The low infective dose of salmonella in chocolate is thought to be due to the high fat content, which protects against the stomach acid. Chocolate was also responsible for outbreaks of salmonella in the USA (1973, *S.* Eastbourne), Finland (1987, *S.* Typhimurium), Canada (1985-6, *S.* Nima) and England (2007, *S.* Montevideo).

In 1984 (UK) aspic glaze contaminated with *S.* Enteritidis PT4 resulted in 766 cases and two deaths. In 1984 in Canada, *S.* Typhimurium in cheddar cheese (<10 organisms per gram) resulted in 2,700+ cases. An outbreak of *S.* Typhimurium at Stanley Royd Hospital, Wakefield in 1984 involved 455 cases and 19 deaths. In 1985, a UK outbreak involving dried baby milk contaminated with *S.* Ealing resulted in 60 cases and one death. The adverse publicity resulted in the closure of the factory responsible. In 1985, pasteurised milk with *S.* Typhimurium in the USA, resulted in 16,284 cases and seven deaths. The dairy was permanently closed. An egg sandwich shared by two women at Manchester Airport in 1988 resulted in compensation of £183,500 for food poisoning, irritable bowel syndrome, constipation and heartburn. In Germany in 1993, paprika crisps resulted in 1,000 cases of salmonella. In 1994 (USA), ice cream contaminated with *S.* Enteritidis resulted in 740 cases. In 2005, over 2,000 cases of *S.* Hadar in the USA resulted from consuming precooked vacuum-packed roast chicken. In 2006, the Brenalta brand

Salmonella bacterium dividing
©STEVE GSCHMEISSNER/SCIENCE PHOTO LIBRARY

of bottled water sold in Lanzarote and Gran Canaria was found to be contaminated with salmonella. In 2006/2007, 628 persons in the USA were affected by *S.* Tennessee following the consumption of peanut butter. *S.* Tennessee was recovered from unopened jars of ConAgra peanut butter. In the summer of 2008, 1,442 people in America reported being ill as a result of eating fresh hot chilli peppers such as jalapenos or tomatoes contaminated with *Salmonella* Saint-paul. The peppers originated from Mexico. In 2008/9 over 22500 people in the USA suffered from *Salmonella* Typhimurium and nine of them died following the consumption of contaminated peanut butter from the Peanut Corporation of America, Blakely Georgia. Over 1,000 products were recalled.

In 2010, 63 cases of *S.* Typhimurium DT8 occurred as a result of consuming duck eggs from UK farms. Between May and July 2010, 2000 cases of *S.* Enteriditis were reported in the USA as a result of eating contaminated eggs. 500 million eggs were recalled. In July 2011, a multistate outbreak of *S.* Agona in the USA resulted from eating contaminated Mexican Papaya.

Clostridium perfringens

These bacteria are Gram-positive, anaerobic rods, which form **spores** under adverse conditions such as exposure to free oxygen. The normal growth range is between 15°C and 52°C and there is no division at 10°C. *Cl. perfringens* can reproduce every ten minutes at its **optimum** growth temperature of 43°C to 47°C. Growth in meat was shown to be preceded by a **lag** of two to four hours at 35°C but no lag at 46°C*. Spores may survive boiling for several hours.

Illness is caused when large numbers of ingested organisms **sporulate** in the intestine and in so doing release an **exotoxin**, also described as an **enterotoxin**. The infective dose for adults is around 1,000,000 per gram of food.

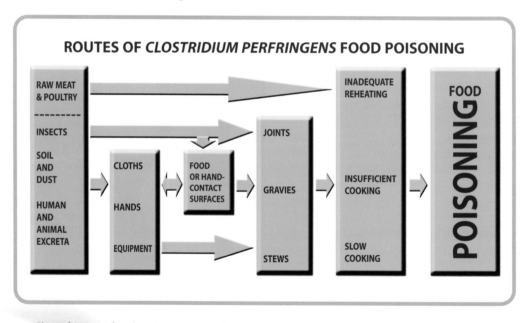

ROUTES OF *CLOSTRIDIUM PERFRINGENS* FOOD POISONING

Cl. perfringens food poisoning usually occurs as a result of food handling malpractices in large kitchens, especially institutional catering where large quantities of food are prepared hours before service. On cooking, oxygen is driven from the food creating anaerobic conditions ideal for the growth of the heat activated spores. Stews, gravies and large joints of meat allowed to cool slowly in warm kitchens are most commonly associated with outbreaks of *Cl. perfringens* food poisoning. Because *Cl. perfringens* is commonly found in the intestine of healthy individuals, sporadic cases are difficult to identify. Statistics therefore relate to numbers of cases involved in outbreaks and may be seriously underestimated.

Hall H. and Angelotti R. (1965). "Clostridium perfringens in meat and meat products."
Appl. Microbiol., 13:352-357.

Cl. perfringens has been shown to sporulate in meat products and produce enterotoxin in the food. Although not common, this explains why the incubation period for this type of food poisoning has been reduced to as little as two hours.

It is estimated that for every 343 cases of *Cl. perfringens* in the community only one is reported and that there are around 144,000 cases per year in the UK.

Cooking and simmering bulk fluids

Temperature distribution within bulk liquids during cooking is not uniform. Variations can be extreme and under certain conditions cool spots can form. Because of the nature of heat transference in liquids, stable convection currents are set up and liquid outside these currents may remain stationary at a low temperature.

Where a number of adverse factors combine, parts of a bulk liquid may be visibly boiling, whilst other areas of the liquid may be at a temperature that allows the multiplication of *Cl. perfringens*. The most dangerous combination is when a large volume of a viscous liquid, such as gravy or stock, is boiled and then simmered in an open pan on a solid type cooker, especially when the pan has no lid, the kitchen is cool and the pan contents are left unstirred. The initial boiling activates *Cl. perfringens* spores from which the **vegetative** bacteria grow. Furthermore, the boiling destroys other organisms, thereby reducing competition. Clostridia within the cool spot survive and multiply under virtually ideal conditions.*

Clostridium perfringens bacterium
©CNRI/SCIENCE PHOTO LIBRARY

COOL SPOTS

CENTRE HEATING

EDGE HEATING: SIMMERING

Circulation currents and the formation of cool spots.

*North R. A. E.: Unpublished information.

THE FORMATION AND PREVENTION OF COOL SPOTS

Problem	Remedy
Volume of liquid, especially greater than 25 litres	Cook in smaller volumes: use several small pans in preference to one large pan
Intensity of heat, especially low edge heating	Use heat source equal in diameter to pan base
Large tall pans	Use wide low pans
Failure to stir	Stir frequently, at least every ten minutes using a clean utensil
Cool draughts and absence of lids	Keep excessive cold air draughts away from cooking area. Keep lids on pans between stirring
It is preferable to use alternative equipment such as jacketed kettles or bratt pans.	

Clostridium botulinum

Clostridium botulinum is a Gram-positive, anaerobic, spore-forming, gas-producing rod. There are several types of *Cl. botulinum* that produce **neurotoxins** in food, which, if consumed, often cause fatalities. Types A, B, E and F are associated with food poisoning. Types A and B are commonly found in the soil and are usually associated with vegetables and meats. They produce objectionable smells when they grow in foods. **Psychrotrophic** type E is found in mud, streams, oceans and fish. The optimum growth temperature is 20°C to 30°C but toxin production is possible down to a temperature of 3°C. Spores of type E are much more sensitive to heat and are killed at around 85°C. Non-proteolytic strains producing types E and F toxins can produce lethal amounts of toxin with no detectable changes in the food, i.e. no smell. The toxin of all strains is **heat labile** (sensitive to heat) and is destroyed by boiling.

Unfortunately, the spores of proteolytic types A and B *Cl. botulinum* are very heat-resistant, for example, a temperature of 121°C for three minutes is used as a basis for ensuring their destruction in canned **low-acid foods**. Strict canning controls are essential. Toxin production does not occur below a pH of 4.5. If consumed by adults, spores are usually harmless as they are unable to grow and produce toxin in the human intestinal tract.

Outbreaks of botulism are most frequently associated with improperly processed or handled low-acid canned foods, fermented products, traditional and smoked fish products, vegetables in oil, and garlic in oil (neutral pH, long shelf life, grown in soil, ambient storage, anaerobic conditions). Vegetables should be rendered safe prior to placing them in oil, for example, by heat, acidification or high salt. If contaminated, fish products may

Botulinum toxin, computer model
©ALFRED PASIEKA/SCIENCE PHOTO LIBRARY

become toxic before they become unacceptable through spoilage. It is preferable, therefore, to store such products below 5°C to ensure their safety. Nitrates and nitrites are often added to cooked meats, bacon and ham to prevent the **germination** of spores in vacuum packs. Refrigerated processed foods, especially fish, anaerobically packaged with long **shelf lives** are of particular concern.

Although gas may be produced, which causes cans contaminated with *Cl. botulinum* to blow, this does not always occur and cannot be relied on as a method to detect suspect cans. In 1978, four elderly people in Birmingham developed botulism after eating a contaminated can of Alaskan salmon. Two of them died. In 1989, 26 cases of botulism type B occurred following the consumption of hazelnut yogurt and only one person died, primarily due to the administration of polyvalent botulinum antitoxin. Underprocessing of canned hazelnut purée, used in the yogurt production, was stated to be the cause as a change from sugar to saccharin increased the a_w, allowing germination of the spores.

In 1991 in Egypt, 91 people were ill and 18 died after eating salted fish that was spoilt before salting. In 1996, eight cases of botulism in Italy resulted from the consumption of contaminated acidified dairy cream (mascarpone cheese). In 1998, two people were ill and one died following the consumption of home-bottled mushrooms, brought back from Italy.

In 1999 in Morocco, 80 people were ill and 15 died following the consumption of a temperature-abused meat and chicken dish contaminated with *Cl. botulinum*. In 2006, six cases of botulinum in the USA and Canada were linked to pasteurised carrot juice that probably had not been stored under refrigeration. In 2011, two cases of botulism in Scotland resulted from eating Loyd Grossman Korma Sauce.

From 1980 to 2010, there have been 11 cases of infant botulism reported in the UK, where spores have apparently germinated in the infant gut and toxin has subsequently been produced. In the UK in 2001, a baby-food manufacturer recalled cans of powdered baby milk after a five-month-old girl contracted infant botulism. In 2009, three cases were linked to feeding honey contaminated with *Cl. botulinum* spores to babies under one year old.

Staphylococcus aureus
©SCIENCE SOURCE/SCIENCE PHOTO LIBRARY

Staphylococcus aureus

This organism is a Gram-positive, facultative anaerobe that is salt-tolerant and can, therefore, survive in some cured products. Approximately 40% of adults carry *S. aureus* in the nose and throat and 15% on their skin, especially the hands. Around half of these strains are **enterotoxigenic**.

If present in food, *S. aureus* will, under ideal conditions, produce an exotoxin, which may survive boiling for 30 minutes or more. The growth range for *S. aureus* is between 7°C and 48°C and the generation time at 10°C is 30 hours. However, it requires at least 100,000 organisms per gram and a temperature of at least 10°C to form toxin. (No toxin formation above 45°C).

The majority of outbreaks are caused by the direct contamination of cooked foodstuffs by

ROUTES OF STAPHYLOCOCCAL FOOD POISONING

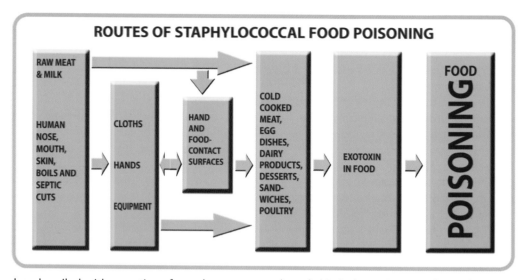

hands soiled with secretions from the nose, mouth and skin lesions. Frequently, ready-to-eat food has been handled while warm, and storage conditions have encouraged the organism to multiply and produce its toxin. *S. aureus* is commonly added to cooked meat during slicing or deboning at levels of around ten to 100 per gram. Such levels are harmless but storage at ambient temperatures for a few hours would allow significant levels of toxin to be produced. It is not very competitive unless the food has a significant salt content.

In 1965, an outbreak of *S. aureus* involving Cheddar cheese resulted in 42 cases. A typical outbreak in Texas, USA involved 1,364 children out of 5,824 attending 16 schools. They had eaten chicken salad that had been prepared the day before but had not been cooled correctly after boning. After transport on the day of the outbreak it was left at **ambient temperature**. Outbreaks have also involved fermented sausage. In 1985, 47 cases of *S. aureus* in the UK were caused by the consumption of imported Italian lasagne.

Bacillus cereus

Bacillus cereus is a facultative anaerobic, Gram-positive, spore-forming bacterium that grows predominantly **aerobically**. It is capable of causing two distinct forms of food poisoning. The more common type in this country is characterised by nausea and vomiting one to five hours after ingestion of contaminated food, including rice dishes, vegetables, cornflour, custards, soups, vanilla slices and raw vegetable sprouts. The spores survive normal cooking, and rapid growth and exotoxin production will occur if the food is

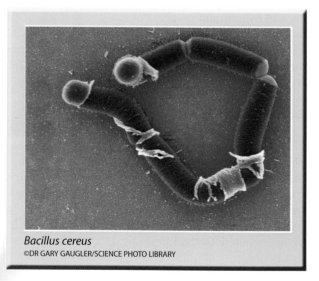

Bacillus cereus
©DR GARY GAUGLER/SCIENCE PHOTO LIBRARY

not cooled quickly and refrigerated. One of the exotoxins produced is very heat-resistant and can survive a temperature of 126°C for 90 minutes. Consequently, once the toxin is produced subsequent reheating is of little value. The second type of *B. cereus* food poisoning is rare in the UK and has an **onset** period of eight to 16 hours. Toxins are produced in the intestine and symptoms are usually diarrhoea and abdominal pain.

B. cereus grows between 4·4°C and 48°C with an optimum between 28°C and 35°C. It is distributed throughout the environment but is particularly common in soil, vegetation, cereals and spices. It also causes spoilage of cream – referred to as bitty cream.

B. cereus is often isolated in low numbers in many types of food. However, large numbers (100,000+ per gram) must be isolated to prove that a contaminated food has caused food poisoning. It is recommended that faecal specimens be sent to the laboratory under refrigeration to avoid other organisms multiplying.

Bacillus subtilis and Bacillus licheniformis

Bacillus subtilis and *Bacillus licheniformis* are spore-forming bacteria, which have occasionally been implicated in food poisoning incidents. The main symptoms are nausea and vomiting, usually within one hour of consuming contaminated food. Diarrhoea is less common but may occur after approximately 12 hours. In 1994, an outbreak of *B. subtilis* involved meat pasties seasoned with contaminated black pepper. The spores had survived the cooking process. Main vehicles include meat or vegetables and pastry products.

Vibrio parahaemolyticus

Vibrio parahaemolyticus is a Gram-negative, marine facultative anaerobe that grows between 8°C and 44°C, with an optimum of 35°C to 37°C. Given ideal conditions the generation time may be as short as five to seven minutes. Rapid growth may occur in seafoods or the human intestine.

Outbreaks of *V. parahaemolyticus* food poisoning in the UK are infrequent and usually caused by the consumption of imported seafood, such as cooked prawns and dressed crab from the Far East. However, it is occasionally isolated from the UK coastal waters, especially in the South. In 1998, 28 faecal **isolates** were reported to the Communicable Disease Surveillance Centre (CDSC). The organism is sensitive to heat and outbreaks are normally caused by contamination after cooking and multiplication due to unrefrigerated storage. *V. parahaemolyticus* is one of the commonest causes of food poisoning in Japan as it prefers the warmer coastal waters, and seafoods form a high percentage of the staple diet. In 2002, an outbreak of *V. parahaemolyticus* in Hong Kong involved 56 suspect cases. The suspect foods were escargots and squid which had been stored at ambient temperatures for too long.

Escherichia coli

Escherichia coli is a Gram-negative, facultative anaerobic rod that is a normal part of the intestinal flora of man and animals. It is usually used as an **indicator** of faecal contamination of food or water. However, certain strains are known to be pathogenic and some produce a toxin in the intestine that results in symptoms of abdominal pain and diarrhoea. One group of pathogenic *E. coli* is responsible for severe infantile diarrhoea and another group causes travellers' diarrhoea. A major outbreak in the USA was traced to the consumption of soft, fermented cheese. Growth of *E. coli* has been recorded as low as 4°C. *E. coli* O157 is a particularly serious foodborne pathogen and is dealt with in chapter 4.

Yersinia enterocolitica

Yersinia enterocolitica is a psychrotrophic, Gram-negative, facultative anaerobic rod that is quite widespread in nature, particularly in wild and domestic animals. Not all strains of *Y. enterocolitica* are pathogenic for humans. Faecal–oral transmission involving infected animals or persons or the consumption of contaminated food and water are the usual ways of spread and it is not heat-resistant. *Yersinia* has been incriminated in several major outbreaks of food poisoning in the USA and is commonly isolated as a cause of diarrhoea in Sweden, Norway and Germany. Foods involved are usually of animal origin. Outbreaks have involved raw pork and pork products, chocolate milk, reconstituted powdered milk, turkey and chow mein. In recent years, there has been a marked decline in the reporting of confirmed cases of *Y. enterocolitica* infection from laboratories in England and Wales.

Symptoms include diarrhoea, abdominal pain, fever, headache, pharyngitis, occasional vomiting, acute mesenteric lymphadenitis, pseudoappendicitis (especially in children) and arthritis. The incubation period is usually one to five days (occasionally longer) and bacteria may persist in the stools for several months. *Yersinia* has been isolated from raw milk, shellfish, raw and cooked meat, particularly pork, poultry, liquid egg, salami, dairy products, salads and vegetables. Of particular concern is the ability of *Y. enterocolitica* to grow on food during refrigerated storage, despite the normal microflora. This is in contrast to the majority of pathogens, which are usually not able to grow competitively at low temperatures. In April 2011, 21 cases of *Y. enterocolitica* in Norway were linked to eating bagged salad mix.

Other bacteria

Vibrio vulnificus is a rare cause of food poisoning but has a high death rate. In the USA it is responsible for around 47 cases and 18 deaths each year. The onset period is around 16 hours. Symptoms include fever, chills and nausea. It has been associated with the consumption of raw or recontaminated oysters, clams and crabs.

Very occasionally, *Enterococcus faecalis*, organisms belonging to the *Streptococcus viridans* group and *Aeromonas* species, have been implicated in food poisoning outbreaks. However, there is still controversy with the role of these and other bacteria as a cause of food poisoning and further studies are warranted.

THE PREVENTION OF BACTERIAL FOOD POISONING

Businesses must implement a food safety management system based on the principles of **HACCP** (hazard analysis critical control point). This will include a satisfactory environment, competent and properly trained personnel, suitable equipment and facilities to prevent contamination and adequate temperature control to ensure that food at all stages of production, storage, distribution and sale is as safe as reasonably practicable.

The food poisoning chain

The chain of events associated with an outbreak of food poisoning usually consists of:
♦ contamination of ready-to-eat food with food poisoning bacteria;
♦ multiplication of these bacteria; and
♦ consumption of the food.

In order to prevent illness, this chain must be broken and it is essential that care be taken to ensure that contamination of food is kept to an absolute minimum. This may be achieved by:

♦ separating raw and ready-to-eat food at all stages of preparation, storage and distribution. The same equipment or working surface must not be used to handle raw and high-risk foods, or ready-to-eat foods such as lettuce, unless **disinfected** between uses. The liquid from thawed, frozen meat and poultry must not come into contact with high-risk or ready-to-eat foods;

♦ maintaining the highest standards of **personal hygiene** at all times. Handwashing, particularly after using the toilet, is essential;

♦ the exclusion of ill persons and, where appropriate, carriers;

♦ high standards of **pest** exclusion and control (**integrated pest management**); and

♦ using the correct **cleaning** procedures. **Hand-contact** and **food-contact** surfaces must be kept clean and, where necessary, disinfected at appropriate frequencies. Care should be taken with wiping cloths, disposable paper cloths are preferable.

Failure to separate raw and cooked food during storage.

♦ **Bacteria already in food are prevented from multiplying by:**
   ♦ keeping food out of the **danger zone**. Food should be kept below 5°C, for example, in a refrigerator, or kept above 63°C, for example, in a bain marie;
   ♦ ensuring that refrigerators and cold stores are maintained at the correct temperature, usually below 5°C;
   ♦ ensuring that when food is removed from chilled storage for preparation, this work is carried out as quickly as practicable. High-risk food must not be left in the ambient temperatures of kitchens, serving areas or food rooms;
   ♦ cooling food as rapidly as possible, prior to refrigeration, or serve and consume immediately;
   ♦ precooling all salad ingredients, especially for sandwiches, overnight;
   ♦ not allowing dried foods to absorb moisture; and
   ♦ using suitable preservatives.

♦ **Those bacteria within food are destroyed by:**
   ♦ thorough cooking, usually to a **core temperature** of 75°C;
   ♦ heat processing such as **pasteurisation**, **sterilisation** or canning; and
   ♦ a suitable **preservation** technique, for example, **fermentation**.

A combination of a suitable temperature and sufficient time is always required to destroy bacteria. The time and the temperature required will depend on the particular organism. For example, spores of *Cl. perfringens* are much more heat-resistant than salmonellae. Furthermore, a time/temperature process only destroys a percentage of vegetative bacteria and the greater the numbers that are present the more likely it is that some will survive. Practical work carried out in Hull indicated that under certain circumstances large joints of ham had to be cooked to a centre temperature of 70°C for one hour to ensure the destruction of *Salmonella* Give.

- ◆ **The consumption of potentially contaminated food is avoided by:**
    - ◆ obtaining food from reputable suppliers;
    - ◆ washing all raw fruit and vegetables. **Blanching** at around 71°C for 15 seconds may be preferable for ready-to-eat products to be consumed raw;
    - ◆ never adding leftovers/old food to fresh food; and
    - ◆ avoiding consuming raw foods known to be a common source or vehicle of pathogens, for example, raw oysters, raw milk or raw egg dishes.

FOOD POISONING BACTERIA

SOURCE	FOOD VEHICLES	ONSET (HOURS)	SYMPTOMS & DURATION	ADDITIONAL SPECIFIC CONTROLS
Salmonella (Infection)				
Raw meat, milk, eggs, poultry, birds, carriers, pets, rodents, terrapins, sewage/water	Poultry, "raw egg products", meat, dairy products, cheese, mayonnaise, sauces and salad dressings, bean sprouts and coconut	6 to 72 usually 12 to 36

10 days in the case of low-dose outbreaks | Severe abdominal pain, diarrhoea, dehydration, nausea, vomiting and fever (1 to 7 days) | Sterilisation and strict control of animal foodstuff. Slaughterhouse hygiene. Safe sewage disposal and chlorination of water. Screening of carriers or suspects. Avoid products made with raw eggs and not fully cooked. Thorough thawing and cooking of frozen poultry. Avoid raw milk, use heat treated |
| ***Clostridium perfringens* (Toxin in intestine)** | | | | |
| Animal and human excreta, soil, dust, insects and raw meat | Meat, meat products, poultry, gravy, rolled joints and stews | 4 to 24 usually 8 to 12 | Acute abdominal pain and diarrhoea. Vomiting is rare (12 to 48 hours) | Eat immediately after cooking, store above 63°C or rapid cooling and refrigeration within 1.5 hours of reaching 63°C. Joints should not exceed a size of 2.25kg. Thorough reheating of foods |

The Health Protection Agency (preventing person-to-person spread following gastrointestinal infections:) guidelines for public health physicians and environmental health practitioners/officers (2004) were used as the main reference for onset times in this table.

SOURCE	FOOD VEHICLES	ONSET (HOURS)	SYMPTOMS & DURATION	ADDITIONAL SPECIFIC CONTROLS
Staphylococcus aureus (Toxin in food)				
Human nose, mouth, skin, boils and cuts. Raw milk from cows or goats with mastitis	Cooked meat, meat products, poultry, egg products, salads, cream products, milk and dairy products, and dried foods (toxins are heat stable)	1 to 7 usually 2 to 4	Abdominal cramps, nausea, vomiting, some diarrhoea, subnormal temperatures and collapse (6 to 24 hours)	Avoid handling food, use utensils. Good personal hygiene, especially regarding handwashing. Exclude handlers with respiratory infections involving coughing or sneezing. Cover cuts with waterproof dressings. Exclude persons with boils or septic cuts. Avoid the use of raw milk
Vibrio parahaemolyticus (Infection)				
Seafoods	Raw, improperly cooked or recontaminated shellfish and fish	2 to 96 usually 12 to 18	Diarrhoea, nausea, abdominal cramps, some vomiting, fever, **dehydration**, blood or mucus in stools (1 to 7 days)	Cook fish well. Take care to avoid cross-contamination between raw and cooked shellfish and fish. Avoid raw shellfish
Clostridium botulinum (Toxin in food)				
Soil and aquatic sediments, fish, meat and vegetables	Improperly canned low-acid or fermented foods. Smoked fish in vacuum packs. Vegetables in oil	2 hours, to 8 days usually 12 to 36 hours	Difficulties in swallowing, talking and breathing, weakness, double vision and vertigo. Fatalities common, recovery of survivors may take months	Strict control over processing low-acid canned foods. Discard blown cans or those with holes or defective seams. Strict control over smoking and handling of smoked fish. Store smoked fish in a freezer. Care in gutting and preparing raw fish. Strict attention to the shelf life of vacuum packed food
Bacillus cereus (i) (Toxin in food)				
Cereals, especially rice, herbs, spices, dried foods, milk and dairy products, meats, dust and soil	Rice products, starchy food such as pasta and potato, cornflour, vanilla slices, custards, soups and vegetables	1 to 6	Acute nausea, vomiting, abdominal pains and some diarrhoea (12 to 24 hours)	Thorough cooking and rapid cooling. Storing at correct temperatures. Avoid rewarming

SOURCE	FOOD VEHICLES	ONSET (HOURS)	SYMPTOMS & DURATION	ADDITIONAL SPECIFIC CONTROLS
Bacillus cereus (ii) (Toxin in intestine)				
Cereals, especially rice, herbs, spices, dried foods, milk and dairy products, meats, dust and soil	Rice products, starchy food such as pasta and potato, cornflour, vanilla slices, custards, soups and vegetables	6 to 24	Abdominal pain, fever, watery, diarrhoea and some vomiting (1 to 2 days)	Thorough cooking and rapid cooling. Storing at correct temperatures. Avoid rewarming
Escherichia coli (Infection and toxin)				
Human sewage, water and raw meat	Cooked foods especially buffets, water, milk, cheese, seafoods and salads	10 to 72 usually 12 to 24	Abdominal pain, fever, diarrhoea and vomiting (1 to 5 days)	High standards of hygiene. Thorough cooking. Avoid cross-contamination. Storage at correct temperature. Safe sewage disposal and chlorination of water used for drinking or food production
Yersinia enterocolitica (Infection)				
Milk and raw pork	Meat, raw milk, fish, shellfish, oysters, poultry, dairy products and salads	3 to 7 days	Severe abdominal pain, fever and diarrhoea, rarely nausea and vomiting (1 to 7 days). Complete recovery in most cases	Thorough cooking. Care with shelf life of foods stored under refrigeration (psychrotrophic)

CHEMICAL AND METALLIC POISONING

Some chemicals are extremely poisonous and if ingested may result in severe vomiting within a few minutes, and in some cases fatalities. Other chemicals may cause cancer or other serious **chronic disease**. In 2008, over €125 million of Irish products had to be destroyed due to pork and beef contamination with dioxins. The pork contained levels of up to 200 times the safety limit. The source of contamination was animal feed contaminated with industrial oil. In 2006, Seven Seas Ltd recalled batches of cod liver oil when levels of dioxins exceeded legal limits. In 2002, one of Britain's main suppliers of freshwater prawns withdrew several brands when tests demonstrated that 16 out of 84 samples contained nitrofurans, a potential cancer-causing drug.

Chemicals can enter foodstuffs by leakage, spillage, or other accidents during processing or preparation. Unacceptable levels of benzene migration from plastic packaging has been known to occur. However, acute chemical poisoning from food premises is rare and is usually caused by negligence, for example, storing weedkiller, pesticide or cleaning chemicals in unlabelled food containers. Following a survey in June 2008, the Food Standards Agency advised that rice drinks should not be used as an alternative to breast milk, infant formula or cow's milk for toddlers because of the unacceptable dietary exposure to inorganic arsenic. In December 2011, two one-year-olds were hospitalised with mouth and throat burns after their

Sippy cups were filled with pipe cleaning fluid from an unmarked jug at a Toby's Carvery in Sheffield, UK.

Chemical **additives** of food have to undergo rigorous tests before they are allowed and are usually harmless. However, some may cause problems if ingested in large amounts, for example, monosodium glutamate. The onset of symptoms usually occurs in less than one hour and may include burning sensations in the chest, neck and abdomen. The use of antibiotics in food production is usually prohibited because of the dangers of developing resistant bacteria, which could prove harmful to the populace. Nitrates and

Frozen prawns kept in detergent container.

nitrites are added to ham and bacon to inhibit the growth of *Cl. botulinum* and *Cl. perfringens* and to produce a desirable red colour. However, the maximum amounts allowable have been reduced because of the carcinogenic effect on animals. In 1997, three persons became ill after consuming sausages containing sodium nitrate and sodium nitrite at levels of 200 times that permitted for cured meats (not permitted in sausages). Symptoms included drowsiness, dizziness and a greying colour of the skin. In 2005, the Food Standards Agency initiated the UK's largest recall involving over 600 products contaminated with Sudan I, a red dye approved for use in polishes and solvents but not food. A large batch of chilli powder was adulterated and used to make Worcester sauce. The sauce was then used in the manufacture of hundreds of food products. Many countries were affected but most considered the risk of cancer to be so small that they did not issue a recall. The cost of the UK recall was millions of pounds.

In 2008, in China several children died and over 300,000 were ill after drinking milk adulterated with melamine, added to increase the nitrogen content. Melamine combined with cyanuric acid resulted in the formation of kidney stones. Two executives involved in the adulteration by the Sanla Dairy Company were sentenced to execution. The 66-year-old chairwoman was fined $4 million and sentenced to life imprisonment.

Residues of drugs, **pesticides** and fertilisers may be present in deliveries of raw materials. Pesticides sprayed onto fruit and vegetables just prior to harvesting may result in cumulative toxic effects and should be strictly controlled. Two outbreaks of chemical food poisoning in 1991 resulted from the contamination of watermelons (USA) and cucumbers (UK) with the pesticide aldicarb. Chemical poisoning may also occur because of waste, such as mercury compounds, polluting river water used for drinking or food production. Poisons may be taken up by fish, which may cause illness in humans if consumed. In 2002, the FSA issued a warning for pregnant women and children to stop eating shark, swordfish and marlin because of fears of high levels of mercury in the form of methylmercury. Symptoms include blurred vision and a prickling sensation of the skin. In 1984, a large outbreak of gastrointestinal illness in the north-west of England and North Wales was caused by drinking mains water contaminated by phenol. From May 1981 to December 1982, approximately 20,000 Spanish people became ill after using olive oil sold by street vendors, which allegedly contained industrial waste oil. At least 350 people died.

Several metals are toxic and if ingested in sufficient quantities, can give rise to food poisoning. The symptoms, mainly vomiting and abdominal pain, usually develop within an hour. Diarrhoea may also occur. Metals may be absorbed by growing crops or contaminate food during processing. Acid foods (pH <7) should not be cooked or stored in equipment containing any of the following metals.

Aluminium

Although concern has been expressed about aluminium being a factor in some cases of pre-senile dementia, contaminated food is unlikely to play a significant part.

Antimony

Antimony is used in the enamel coating of equipment. Under certain conditions antimony poisoning can occur. Vessels with chipped enamel should not be used. In 2006, research by Dr William Shotyk found traces of antimony in bottled water. Antimony is used in making polyethylene terephalate (PET) bottles, used by most mineral-water sellers. The longer the bottled water is stored, the greater the levels found. Up to 700 parts per trillion were found after three months, compared to official safety guidelines of six parts per billion.

Cadmium

Cadmium is used extensively for plating utensils and fittings for electric cookers and refrigeration apparatus. It is readily attacked by some acids including fruit and wines. Foods, such as meat, placed directly on refrigerator shelves containing cadmium may become poisonous. Earthenware from some countries may contain acid-extractable cadmium which may be hazardous if used with acid food.

Copper

Copper poisoning has been caused by a worn copper dispensing outlet on a soft-drink machine. Copper is also an initiator of rancidity development in fats and oils. Copper and bronze fittings must be avoided when processing foods such as milk.

Lead

Lead is a very poisonous metal and if ingested may cause acute poisoning. Consumption of food and drink is the main exposure route of people to lead, especially fruit, leafy vegetables, cereals (airborne lead from petrol and incinerators), kidneys, wine and shellfish (industrial effluent or geological sources). Lead is also released from containers made of ceramics and lead crystal. The glazing of earthenware vessels is compounded with lead oxide and the storage of acid products in such vessels should be avoided. Chronic poisoning from lead absorbed by soft water passing through lead pipes is not classed as food poisoning. The Lead in Food Regulations provide a maximum general limit for lead of 1ppm in most foods. Some imported cans may have lead seams and must be carefully examined.

Tin and iron

Most cans used for the storage of food are constructed of tin-plated iron sheet. Occasionally, due to prolonged storage, certain acid foods, such as pineapple, rhubarb, strawberries, citrus fruits and tomatoes, react with the tin-plate and hydrogen gas is produced. Iron and tin are absorbed by the food which may become unfit for human consumption. The Tin in Food Regulations, 1992 impose a statutory limit of 200ppm for the amount of tin permitted in food. Hundreds of students in Florida suffered from tin poisoning following the consumption of pineapple. The corrosion of the poorly lacquered imported cans from South Africa was responsible. In 2001, the EU Scientific Committee on Food concluded that levels of

150mg/kg in canned beverages or 250mg/kg of tin in other canned foods could cause illness in some people. In July 2002, cans of organic spaghetti were recalled by a major UK company because of high tin levels.

Zinc

Zinc is used in the galvanising of metals. Galvanised equipment should not be used in direct contact with food, particularly acid foods.

POISONOUS PLANTS AND FISH

Poisonous plants are rarely the cause of food poisoning in food premises. Plants responsible for causing acute poisoning include deadly nightshade, death cap (which may be mistaken for edible mushroom) and rhubarb leaves. In 1981, apricot kernels containing enzymatically produced hydrogen cyanide caused the poisoning of 24 children and four deaths in Israel. In 1983, several people in the UK became ill after drinking herbal tea contaminated with deadly nightshade. Natural toxicants in plants include: glycoalkaloids (sprouts and peel of potatoes, especially if green); furocoumarins (parsnips, celery and limes); phytoestrogens (soya-based products, cereals, peas, beans, cabbage, cucumbers, coffee and plums); and hydrazine derivatives (mushrooms). In March 2005, 27 children died and 100 became ill following the consumption of cassava (cyanide is present in the skin as linamarin) in the Philippines. In 2012, the chef and a food handler died and two other staff were ill after eating death cap mushrooms in a Chinese restaurant in Canberra, Australia. They mistook them for Chinese straw mushrooms.

The gonads, liver and intestines of some fish are highly toxic. For example, the puffer fish, which is considered a delicacy by the Japanese, has caused fatalities because of the failure to remove the toxic organs during preparation.

Several incidents of red whelk poisoning have been recorded in the UK since 1970. Symptoms include tingling of the fingers, disturbance of vision, paralysis, nausea, vomiting, diarrhoea and prostration. Recovery is usually within 24 hours. Intoxication is due to poisoning by tetramine, which is present in the salivary glands of these whelks.

Red kidney beans

Between 1976 and 1982 there were 26 reported incidents of food poisoning, affecting at least 118 persons, associated with the consumption of raw or undercooked red kidney beans (*Phaseolus vulgaris*).

The onset period is short, one to six hours, and recovery normally rapid. Symptoms may develop after eating only four raw beans and include nausea, vomiting and abdominal pain followed by diarrhoea. Recovery is usually around three hours but may be up to two days.

A naturally occurring haemagglutin, which can be destroyed by boiling for ten minutes, is responsible for the illness. The temperatures achieved by "slow cookers" are usually insufficient to destroy the haemagglutin.

In 1986, a number of people became ill after eating vegetable burgers containing haricot beans. The symptoms resembled those caused by red kidney beans and it is likely that undercooking resulted in a failure to destroy the high levels of haemagglutin in the raw beans. In 2006, 160 people who took part in a Japanese TV show promoting a weight-loss plan developed food poisoning. The diet included white kidney beans which contained lectin, which is toxic if the beans are not thoroughly cooked.

Scombrotoxic fish poisoning

Scombrotoxic fish poisoning is caused by toxins that accumulate in the body of some fish, mainly the Scombridae family, during storage, especially above 4°C. It is responsible for about 65% of the outbreaks of food poisoning associated with the consumption of fish in England and Wales. The onset period is between ten minutes and three hours. Symptoms last up to eight hours and include headache, nausea, vomiting, abdominal pain, a rash on the face and neck, a burning or peppery sensation in the mouth, sweating and diarrhoea. Scombrotoxic poisoning results from the conversion of histidine, an amino acid found in dark-fleshed fish, to histamine by the action of spoilage bacteria such as *Morganella spp.*, *Hafnia spp.* and *Klebsiella spp.* Histamine is normally found at levels in excess of 50ppm in fish responsible for illness and these levels may be reached before the fish appears spoiled. Problems arise in canning fish as, once formed, the toxin is very heat-resistant and will not be destroyed during processing. Refrigerated storage of fish should prevent toxin formation.

From 1992 to 2000, there were 78 outbreaks and 40 sporadic cases of scombrotoxic fish poisoning involving 341 people. No outbreaks were reported in 2001/2002. Incidents were confirmed by histamine analysis (levels greater than 5mg per 100g of flesh). Fish involved included raw and canned tuna, smoked, canned and soused mackerel, canned sardines, pilchards, herring, anchovies and salmon. Around 50 cases a year are investigated.

Ciguatera poisoning

Ciguatoxin enters the food chain through fish eating the toxic dinoflagellate, *Gambierdiscus toxicus,* which is associated with dead coral reefs and marine algae. Carnivorous fish accumulate toxins when consuming the smaller herbivorous fish. Species of fish involved include the moray eel, red bass, coral trout, Spanish mackerel, reef cod, grouper and surgeonfish. Fish affected look, smell and taste normal. The head, liver, gonads and roe are usually the most toxic parts of the fish. The toxin is unaffected by cooking, freezing or gastric juices.

The onset period is usually one to six hours and symptoms include malaise, headaches, disturbed vision, alternating feelings of hot and cold, respiratory paralysis, numbness or burning of the mouth, throat and tongue, weakness, numbness of the extremities, abdominal pain, vomiting and diarrhoea. Occasional deaths are recorded. In 1990, three people suffered ciguatera poisoning after eating a home-cooked red snapper imported from Oman. Ciguatera poisoning is the most common fish poisoning problem in the Pacific and Indian oceans and the Caribbean. As many as 50,000 cases are reported worldwide annually.

Paralytic shellfish poisoning (PSP) and diarrhetic shellfish poisoning (DSP)

PSP and DSP may result from the consumption of mussels and other bivalves that have fed on poisonous plankton (various species of dinoflagellates). The aquatic biotoxins causing PSP and DSP may withstand cooking. Symptoms for PSP include a tingling or numbness of the mouth almost immediately, which spreads to the neck, arms and legs within four to six hours. Death, when it does occur, is usually caused by respiratory paralysis within two to 12 hours. DSP symptoms include nausea, vomiting, abdominal pain, diarrhoea and chills with an onset time of 30 minutes to 12 hours.

In July 1997, an outbreak of DSP involving 30 cases resulted from the consumption of contaminated mussels served in two restaurants. Action is taken to prevent the consumption of bivalves if tests are positive for the presence of DSP toxin or if levels of PSP toxin exceed

80mg/100g shellfish flesh. In 2002, cockle fishing was banned on the Burry inlet in South Wales and a prohibition notice stopped the fishing of mussels, cockles, oysters and clams from Foulness to Canvey Island because of fears of DSP.

MYCOTOXINS

Mycotoxins are metabolites of some **moulds** that cause illness, and sometimes death, for example, aflatoxin and ochratoxin A. Symptoms vary depending on the particular mould. They are often carcinogenic but some may cause gastrointestinal disturbances, for example, *Aspergillus ustus*.

Aflatoxin M1 has been detected in milk and milk powder and there is increasing interest in the presence of patulin, a mutagenic mycotoxin produced by certain species of *Penicillium* and *Aspergillus* moulds, which infect apples and pears. Because of migration, cutting out the visible mould may not remove the risk. Patulin is not destroyed by pasteurisation. The FSA issued guidance on patulin, following concern over high levels in apple juice sold in the UK. Juice containing levels of patulin in excess of 50ppb should not be used. In 1992, 26% of samples of juices from pressed apples (cloudy juices) exceeded 50ppb. However, in 1996, only 2% of samples of juices from pressed apples exceeded this limit. In 2002, the FSA ordered the recall of James White apple juice because of unacceptable levels of patulin.

Aflatoxicosis

Aflatoxicosis is a **foodborne illness** caused by the consumption of aflatoxin produced by the common moulds, *Aspergillus flavus* and *Aspergillus parasiticus*. The illness may be either acute or chronic but the effects include liver cirrhosis and the induction of tumours. Foods usually implicated include cereals and nuts. Most illnesses caused by aflatoxins occur in underdeveloped countries where considerable amounts of mouldy cereals are consumed over prolonged periods. The Aflatoxins in Nuts, Nut Products, Dried Figs and Dried Fig Products Regulations, 1992 (SI. 3236) prohibit sales of the above products if levels of aflatoxin exceed 4μg/kg. In 1994, two samples of peanut butter and one sample of peanuts from a major retailer had a mean aflatoxin concentration of 20μg/kg for the peanut butter and 23μg/kg for the peanuts. Voluntary withdrawal was undertaken. A UK survey of herbs and spices in 1994 found 5% had levels of aflatoxin above 10μg/kg, but none above the action level of 50μg/kg.

Domestic cooking will not destroy aflatoxin. In 1997, the EC Commission banned the import of pistachio nuts from Iran because of high levels of aflatoxin B1. In 2001, a survey by Suffolk C.C. Trading Standards found that five out of 20 peanut butter samples contained unacceptably high levels of aflatoxin.

Mycotoxin producing mould (Courtesy of Anticimex).

THE INVESTIGATION OF FOOD POISONING OUTBREAKS

The definition of an outbreak is an incident in which two or more people, thought to have a common exposure, experience a similar illness or proven infection (at least one of them having been ill). A general outbreak is an outbreak affecting members of more than one private residence or residents of an institution. Some general outbreaks are, therefore, from private residences and they are not all from commercial food premises. They may also include waterborne outbreaks.

The effective investigation of food poisoning outbreaks, by all disciplines involved, is essential to limit the spread and to obtain accurate information for use in surveillance. This information can then be disseminated to food businesses and enforcement officers to assist in a risk-based approach to food production and control, making a major contribution to preventing foodborne illness. The sale of food that results in food poisoning is a criminal offence and may also result in successful claims for civil damages by sufferers.

The objectives of the investigation of an outbreak are to:

- contain the spread of the outbreak;
- identify the **outbreak location** (place where food vehicle was prepared or served);
- identify the food vehicle(s) involved (the food eaten which gave rise to illness);
- identify the **causative agent** (the organism, toxin or poison associated with the illness that is recovered from sufferers and/or food and/or the environment under investigation, for example, salmonella, scombrotoxin or mercury);
- trace cases and carriers, especially food handlers;
- trace the source of the causative agent (the vehicle that brought the causative agent into the outbreak location, for example, raw food or a food handler, and/or the origin of the causative agent, for example, a cow in the case of raw milk);
- determine **causal factors** (how the food vehicle became contaminated and what stage of food preparation allowed bacterial multiplication);
- recommend how food should be prepared in the future to prevent recurrence;
- provide data for use in surveillance; and
- provide evidence for legal action.

The isolation of the causative agent in food and/or from environmental swabs of surfaces and equipment provides the best evidence to confirm the food vehicle and the outbreak location in the event of a food poisoning outbreak. Consequently, the suspect outbreak location should be inspected, with food remains and environmental swabs taken, at the earliest possible opportunity. Causal factors may be grouped as:

- pre-process contamination (includes eating contaminated raw food);
- survival of pathogens (inadequate cooking/processing/reheating/thawing);
- post-process contamination;
- multiplication of pathogens (abuse of time/temperature, inadequate cooling);
- infected food handlers; and
- management failures.

The role of management

A manager will become involved in food poisoning investigations when:

- a food handler reports that he or she is suffering from diarrhoea and/or vomiting;
- persons purchasing food from, or eating at, the premises complain that they are ill.

The complainants may contact the local Environmental Health Department, who will inform the manager;

♦ persons attending a function begin to vomit whilst on the premises. If a manager is notified of a suspected case of food poisoning, he or she should immediately contact the Environmental Health Department (EHD) and then make enquiries to find out:

> ♦ whether any staff have been ill;
> ♦ which food or meals were implicated and how they were handled or prepared; and
> ♦ whether or not any other persons were affected.

It is essential to cooperate fully with the investigating officer and to provide required information as soon as possible. Immediately upon becoming aware of a foodborne outbreak associated with the premises, the person in charge should:

♦ stop serving any more food and stop any more food being eaten;

♦ telephone a doctor or ambulance if necessary (if people are ill on the premises);

♦ retain any remaining food, cans, cartons or other forms of food packaging that may be needed to trace suspect food consignments;

♦ telephone the EHD to arrange for an investigation by an Environmental Health Practitioner/Officer (an-out-of hours emergency number should be available);

♦ telephone the owner of the business;

♦ not clean up until bacteriological investigations have been carried out;

♦ prepare a relevant menu list and, as far as possible, details of food preparation (when purchased, storage temperature, method of cooking, cooling or reheating and monitoring records);

♦ if possible, make a complete list of persons consuming the suspect meal, including their addresses;

♦ prepare a complete list of all food handlers and other staff, especially those involved with the suspect meal. Absent staff should be included, the reason for the absence should be given;

♦ prepare a list of suppliers;

♦ remain available on the premises to give the necessary information to the investigating officer, for example, when the meal was served, the number of people known to be affected, etc; and

♦ when the investigation has been completed, thoroughly clean and disinfect the premises. Advice should be obtained from the Environmental Health Practitioner/Officer.

The HACCP system will need to be examined and any necessary amendments implemented.

The role of the authorised officers (environmental health practitioners/officers) in food poisoning investigations

The circumstances of an outbreak investigation may vary considerably. Notifications require different levels of response. However, all activities must be carefully coordinated and structured. Investigations should be undertaken in a way that protects public health without prejudicing future legal action (including formal cautions). There are six key stages:

♦ *Preliminaries*: reviewing notifications; formulating an initial hypothesis of the nature of the disease; determination of case definition, population at risk and general case search area; deciding on resources needed to investigate; defining responsibilities and reporting systems; setting up communication channels; briefing investigators; and issuing documents/forms etc. Officers should keep accurate and comprehensive personal daily logs of events.

♦ *Case finding*: searching for cases, carriers and contacts; recording detailed case histories of sufferers, food consumption details, symptoms, times of onset, personal and occupational details, obtaining specimens; assembling data to formulate a hypothesis as to outbreak location, meals/foods eaten, and approximate time of food preparation. Possible **food vehicles** should not be suggested. Telephone interviews can be useful and quick. Questionnaires, if used, should also be completed by persons attending the same function who were not ill. Appropriate detailed information must accompany all specimens and samples sent to the laboratory to maintain the integrity of evidence.

♦ *Site investigation:* secure assistance of managers, collect menus, details of food and suppliers; identification of all food production staff and their functions, staff records and sickness returns; locating production areas, food and waste stores and meal remains; seizing or detaining suspect food; postponing cleaning and **disinfection**;

terminating or modifying food production, if necessary, to prevent spread of disease; collecting food and other relevant samples and swabbing surfaces (in accordance with the Food Safety [Sampling and Qualifications] Regs, 1990); inspecting and recording site conditions; interviewing managers and staff (contemporaneous notes of the interviews should be made); arranging for collection of specimens from staff. Food handlers with symptoms must be excluded from food handling duties. Officers should not allow the sale of food from the premises to be resumed until they have, as far as is reasonably practicable, satisfied themselves that food can be produced safely with no identifiable risk to the consumer. Site investigations are the most important part of the investigation to ascertain the causal factors and require the special skills of an officer experienced in inspecting food premises and interviewing techniques.

♦ *Intermediate review:* assemble all available data; assess control measures needed; formulate a provisional hypothesis as to suspect food vehicle(s), causal factors and sources; review investigation progress and determine whether the outbreak is foodborne, as opposed to person-to-person spread, and whether a **due-diligence** defence is likely to succeed. If a prosecution is likely, all witness statements will need to be dealt with in accord with the Criminal Justice Act, 1967, as amended, and interviews of persons likely to face prosecution should be carried out under the Police and Criminal Evidence Act, 1984. Determine what further investigations are needed, prepare an interim report and, if appropriate, issue public warnings.

♦ *Source tracing:* sample ingredients used, to identify contamination levels; assess possibility of organisms surviving processing; analysis of food sample results, swabs and specimens; trace the distribution chain of suspect ingredients or other foods; investigate primary produce/animals or birds.

♦ *Consolidation:* collating and processing all data to test the hypothesis; carry out, as necessary, further detailed investigations of critical factors in the outbreak; discussion of a draft final report with investigators, agreeing final hypothesis and formulating remedial and control measures; publishing the final report.

The Food Law Code of Practice provides advice in relation to food **hazards** and foodborne illness. In the case of a serious localised incident or a wider problem, the relevant government department should be notified. Responsibility at local level remains with the Food Authority. Where a public health hazard has been identified and **risk assessment** indicates consumers could be exposed to the hazard, it is essential to provide information to assist in protecting public health. Consultation with the relevant food industry, government departments and the business affected should occur prior to the release of information to the media to avoid contradictory statements. However, delays should not be allowed to expose the public to risk.

Consultants in communicable disease control

The majority of consultants in communicable disease control (CCDC) are employed by district health authorities and work in public health. Most consultants are the nominated 'proper officer' of the local authority and possess delegated legal powers relating to communicable disease control. Consultants are specialists in public health medicine. Outbreak investigation is an important function of the consultant who may have the responsibility to coordinate the investigation. Once an infectious disease outbreak is declared, the local authority concerned will convene an outbreak control team (OCT). The consultant may assume lead responsibility for a multidisciplinary team which consists of a range of professionals, including environmental health officers/practitioners and medical practitioners, both within the authority and from other authorities that may be affected by the outbreak. Depending on the nature of the outbreak, other professionals may be included on the OCT such as veterinary specialists or representatives from the Food Standards Agency.

Some photographs used to illustrate this chapter were provided courtesy of
The Royal Borough of Kensington and Chelsea.

4 Foodborne diseases *edited by Adrian Eley*

A **foodborne disease** may be considered to differ from **food poisoning** in that:
♦ a relatively small number of organisms is capable of causing the illness; and
♦ the **food** acts purely as a **vehicle** and the multiplication of the organism within the food is not an important feature of the illness.

There are potentially a very large number of organisms that could **contaminate** food and lead to foodborne disease. In such a text as this it is not possible to give a complete review. Instead, important examples are given, some of which may lead to symptoms unrelated to **gastroenteritis**.

Typhoid and paratyphoid fever
Sometimes known as enteric fever, typhoid is caused by the **bacterium** *Salmonella* Typhi and paratyphoid by the bacterium *Salmonella* Paratyphi. Only a few *S.* Typhi are needed to cause illness, whereas 100,000 *S.* Paratyphi may be needed to cause illness. The **incubation period** is 3 days to 1 month (usually 8 to 14 days). Symptoms include sustained fever, severe headache, nausea, loss of appetite, slow pulse, spleen enlargement, rose spots on the trunk and constipation or sometimes diarrhoea. The fatality rate for typhoid is between 2% and 10% depending on use of **antibiotics**. Paratyphoid is generally much less severe and symptoms may be similar to salmonella food poisoning. The organism is excreted in the faeces and urine of patients and **carriers**. Up to 5% of persons affected become permanent carriers. Typhoid fever affects 17 million people worldwide each year with approximately 600,000 deaths. There are a few hundred cases of enteric fever in England and Wales each year, the majority of cases being acquired from **endemic** areas abroad. Enteric fever may be waterborne, due to contamination by urine or sewage, or foodborne, for example, shellfish taken from sewage-contaminated beds, vegetables fertilised by human manure and eaten raw, milk or cooked meat contaminated by polluted water or by carriers who are **food handlers**. Laboratory confirmation is by bacteriological examination of blood, faeces or urine. In 1993 an outbreak of *S.* Paratyphi B in France resulted from eating cheese made from raw goats' milk. In July 2001 an outbreak of typhoid fever occurred in the Newport area of Wales. The only link between the five cases (four children and one young adult) was the consumption of food from a local kebab restaurant. In 2012 the Health Protection Agency published the "Public Health Operational Guidelines for Typhoid and Paratyphoid" (http://www.hpa.org.uk/webc/HPAwebFile/HPAweb_C/1317132464189)

Prevention
♦ Ensure the safety of all water supplies. Water used for food preparation or drinking should be chlorinated.
♦ Ensure the satisfactory disposal of sewage.
♦ Ensure the heat treatment of milk and milk products, including ice cream.
♦ Prevent the sale of raw shellfish from sewage-polluted waters.
♦ Identify carriers and ensure that they are not employed within the food industry. Medical questionnaires should be used as an aid to recruitment.
♦ Maintain high standards of **personal hygiene** amongst food handlers, especially with regard to thorough handwashing after visiting the toilet.

- Ensure high standards of **hygiene** in food production and distribution.
- Double-wash ready-to-eat fruit and vegetables.

Dysentery
Bacillary dysentery

In the UK bacillary dysentery is usually caused by the Gram-negative bacterium *Shigella sonnei* and less frequently by *Shigella flexneri* and *Shigella boydii*. It is an **acute disease** of the intestine characterised by diarrhoea, fever, stomach cramps and often vomiting. Stools may contain blood, mucus and pus. Fatality is normally less than 1% and the severity of illness depends on the type of *Shigella* causing the infection. The incubation period is normally around one to three days, although it varies between twelve hours and seven days. Dysentery is almost always spread through faecal–oral transmission from an infected person or more rarely by the consumption of contaminated foods, including water or milk. In 1994 imported iceberg lettuce was implicated in several **outbreaks** of *Sh. sonnei*. In December 2001 Japan banned oysters from S. Korea after 159 people became ill with dysentery and the organism was isolated from the oysters. Outbreaks often involve children. Parents caring for ill children commonly become infected. Consequently some food businesses exclude food handlers with household contacts suffering from dysentery. Preventive measures are similar to those used for typhoid, with the emphasis on personal hygiene.

Amoebic dysentery

This form of dysentery is rare in the UK apart from persons becoming infected whilst visiting tropical and sub-tropical countries where it is endemic. There are approximately 100 reported cases annually in England and Wales. The **causative organism** is *Entamoeba histolytica*, a microscopic single-celled **protozoan**. Symptoms include abdominal pain and mild or severe diarrhoea alternating with constipation. The incubation period is usually 2 to 4 weeks.

Campylobacter enteritis

Campylobacter has been implicated as a cause of acute enteritis since 1977 and it is thought that up to 70% of cases may be foodborne. Even though the **epidemiology** of campylobacter infection remains poorly understood, it is the commonest cause of acute bacterial gastroenteritis in England and Wales and this must be due in part to its **low infective dose** (up to 500 organisms).

Campylobacters are Gram-negative spirally curved rods and most species are **microaerophilic**; oxygen at normal atmospheric pressure prevents growth and numbers decline. They multiply quickly between 37°C and 43°C but not below 28°C. At 48°C they are inactivated.

Campylobacter jejuni bacterium
©CAMR, BARRY DOWSETT/SCIENCE PHOTO LIBRARY

The causal species of human enteritis are *Campylobacter jejuni* (approximately 90%) and *Campylobacter coli* (approximately 10%). Symptoms vary in severity and include headache, fever, diarrhoea (often blood-stained), persistent colicky abdominal pain (may mimic acute appendicitis) and nausea (vomiting is rare). The incubation period is from one to ten days but usually between two and five days. The normal duration of illness is one to seven days. A second "dose" of symptoms may occur three weeks after the first.

Most reported cases are **sporadic** and peak in the late spring. Mortality is minimal and complications are rare. Campylobacters disappear from the stools within a few weeks of illness and long-term carriers have not been detected. Because of the low transmissibility and inability of campylobacter to multiply at room temperatures, infected food handlers should usually be allowed to resume normal duties when their stools are firm.

Animals and wild birds are the main reservoirs of infection and as campylobacters can survive in water for several weeks at low temperatures, untreated natural water is a potential source. Furthermore, water storage tanks could be contaminated by birds or small animals. Campylobacters are commonly found on raw poultry, in raw milk and sewage and on carcase meat and offal.

Transmission is thought to be from raw and undercooked poultry and meat, raw milk, bottled milk pecked by birds, especially magpies, contaminated water (private supplies) and infected dogs and cats. Person-to-person spread and secondary cases are rare. The hands can carry campylobacters for up to an hour. Freezing reduces the number of campylobacters but once frozen they can survive for several months. The organisms may be destroyed by heating food to 75°C and are sensitive to drying, chlorination and salt in excess of 2%.

Control measures include reducing the campylobacter in raw meat and the food chain, hygiene training of food handlers, especially on the dangers of cross-contamination and the importance of thorough cooking, and raising the hygiene awareness of consumers.

The luxury Tilney Hotel in Hampshire, UK was fined £36,500 with £4,039 costs after causing campylobacter food poisoning from undercooked chicken liver parfait to 13 diners in December 2010. In 2011, 13 (443 cases) of the 14 outbreaks of campylobacter reported from catering premises in the UK were linked to eating undercooked poultry liver parfait or pâté. One of the outbreaks in October involved 80 people who had eaten at the Lowry Hotel, Manchester.

Listeriosis

Although food is not the only means of transmission, and in the majority of cases a vehicle of infection is not identified, listeriosis may be considered as a foodborne disease and is caused by *Listeria monocytogenes*, a Gram-positive, **psychrotrophic** bacillus that is widely distributed in the environment (soil, water and drains). It is commonly found in effluents and sewage sludge and survives many weeks after spraying. In one outbreak involving coleslaw, the cabbage, stored for several months, had

Listeria monocytogenes bacteria
©EYE OF SCIENCE/SCIENCE PHOTO LIBRARY

been grown in a field fertilised by sheep manure. Human or animal carriers may excrete the bacteria, and many cases of cross-infection have been recorded. The incubation period is one day to three months. Symptoms include influenza-like illness, fever, diarrhoea, **septicaemia**, meningitis and abortion; **neonates**, pregnant women, **immunocompromised** persons and the elderly are most at **risk**. It causes little illness in healthy people and not all subtypes of *L. monocytogenes* have been proven to be pathogenic.

The organism, which is described as a low temperature pathogen, is salt tolerant and multiplies at a **pH** as low as 4.4 and between −1.5°C and 42°C, although growth at 3°C is very slow. It has the lowest temperature growth of any pathogenic bacteria. Under refrigeration, especially above 3°C, small numbers of listeria can soon dominate competing organisms and may also become more infective due to the production of a **toxin** (listeriolysin O). The trend to longer **shelf life** makes this of particular concern. Hypochlorite dips may be ineffective at removing the bacteria from contaminated vegetables.

Thermal death time is widely disputed: the bacteria may have a greater ability than normal to recover from heat damage. However, most reports state listeria is not especially heat-resistant, and is rapidly destroyed at 75°C.

In the mid-1980s, an outbreak in Los Angeles associated with soft cheese resulted in 148 cases and 48 deaths among Mexicans. In 1987, Switzerland banned the production of Vacherin Mont d'Or cheese following more than 60 deaths over a period of around four years. In 1989, the UK government issued a belated warning to risk-groups to avoid soft cheeses, reheated cook-chill meals and pâté. An outbreak in France in 1992, probably due to pork tongue in aspic, resulted in 279 cases, 63 deaths (including seven neonates) and 22 abortions. In 2003, 17 pregnant women in the North-East of England developed listeriosis. The suspected food vehicle was butter. The death rate for listeriosis is usually around 30% but mainly involves persons with other serious illness or with immune deficiencies. Surveys in the UK have shown that soft cheese and pâté now contain lower levels of listeria, which is also isolated in raw meat/poultry/fish/vegetables/milk, fried rice, salads, dairy products and retail processed-chilled food. Outbreaks have implicated turkey frankfurters, dried mushrooms, salami, hospital sandwiches and undercooked chicken.

An outbreak which started in September 2011 in Colorado, USA, resulted in 146 ill people and 30 deaths from eating cantaloupe melon contaminated with *L. monocytogenes*. The farm involved, Jensons, had been given a 96% grade (superior rating) by a third-party audit only two months before and renewed the arguments about the effectiveness of such audits and potential conflict of interest. In February 2012, 150,000 pounds of hard-boiled eggs in brine in the USA were recalled because of listeria contamination.

Streptococcus zooepidemicus

This bacterium may cause a serious flu-like illness together with septicaemia, meningitis and bacterial **endocarditis**. *Streptococcus zooepidemicus* is found in a variety of animals including horses and cows, when it may cause **mastitis**.

In 1984, 12 persons in West Yorkshire, ten over 70 years of age, were hospitalised after being infected with *S. zooepidemicus*. Eight of these subsequently died, including a day-old premature baby. All eleven adults drank raw milk. The organism was isolated from a bottle of milk and three cows from the supplier's herd. In 1994 two persons drinking raw milk were infected by *S. zooepidemicus* and one of them subsequently died.

Brucellosis (undulant fever)

A **systemic disease** caused by the Gram-negative bacteria *Brucella abortus* and *Brucella melitensis*. Symptoms include intermittent fever, extended depression, headache, weakness and generalised aching. The illness may last from a few days to several months. Fatality is less than 2%. The incubation period is usually five to 21 days. Transmission is normally by contact with an infected cow or by the consumption of raw milk or milk products. The brucellosis eradication scheme, which involved slaughtering all infected animals, and the heat treatment of milk have largely eliminated this disease. In 2001, six cases of *Brucella melitensis* were reported in England and Wales (probably contracted abroad).

Tuberculosis

A **chronic bacterial disease** caused by *Mycobacterium tuberculosis*, the human tubercle bacillus, and *Mycobacterium bovis* in cattle. The bovine type also affects man and can result in extra-**pulmonary** tuberculosis involving the bones, lymph nodes, kidneys, intestines and skin. The incubation period is four to six weeks but development of the later stages may take years. Airborne transmission and contact with infected sputum occur, although bovine tuberculosis is primarily spread by the consumption of raw milk or dairy products. Tuberculosis used to be a very common disease of bovines but is now rare, due to the slaughter of all infected animals. Heat treatment of milk was introduced primarily to combat this disease.

Vero cytotoxin-producing *Escherichia coli* O157:H7 (O157 VTEC)

Most *E. coli* that are found in the intestine are harmless. However, those capable of producing Vero cytotoxins often cause serious illness, which is sometimes fatal, particularly in young children and the elderly. Although there are many strains of VTEC, the main one associated with human disease in the UK is O157. The first documented outbreak of haemorrhagic colitis caused by *E. coli* O157 was in 1982, when it was linked to consuming hamburgers from a fast-food restaurant in the USA.

Symptoms vary from a watery diarrhoea, nausea and abdominal pain to bright red bloody diarrhoea (haemorrhagic colitis) and severe abdominal cramps, usually without fever. Up to 30% of patients develop haemolytic uraemic syndrome (HUS), although it is usually between 2% and 7%. This generally involves young children and *E. coli* O157 is the major cause of acute renal failure in children in the UK. Some adults develop HUS together with neurological complications. Fatality rates range from 1% to 5%, but in some outbreaks, for example, involving the elderly, these may be much higher. The onset period is one to eight days, usually three to four days. The duration of illness is approximately two weeks, unless complications, such as HUS, develop. *E. coli* O157 disappears from adult faeces within a few days and specimens should be examined within six days of the onset of symptoms. Young children may excrete *E. coli* O157 intermittently for three or more weeks.

Although *E. coli* O157 can multiply in food, it has a very low infective dose involving fewer than 100 bacteria. Infection results from eating contaminated foods, person-to-person spread and direct contact with animals, especially farm animals and their faeces. There have been many outbreaks from children "petting" farm animals. The main food vehicles are undercooked meat products, especially burgers and mince. Other foods implicated include raw milk, cheese made with unpasteurised milk, and apple juice. (*E. coli* O157 can grow at a pH of 4.4.) However, because of the low infective dose, cross-contamination of many **ready-to-eat foods** from raw meat is likely to result in illness. There have been several outbreaks associated with cooked

E. coli O157:H7 bacteria
©DR KARI LOUNATMAA/SCIENCE PHOTO LIBRARY

meat, especially from butchers. Bathing in contaminated water has occasionally caused infection.

The main reservoir of *E. coli* O157 is the stomach and intestines of cattle and, possibly, sheep. Manured vegetable and fruit crops may therefore be a **source** of the organism. Cattle excrete *E. coli* O157 intermittently and the infected animals show no signs of illness. The first isolation of *E. coli* O157 in food was in Sheffield in 1993, when it was discovered in raw milk, although it had been isolated on cattle carcases in Sheffield in 1992.

The bacterium survives freezing and is relatively tolerant to **acid** conditions. It survives and multiplies in some foods between 3°C and 46°C although numbers may decline below 3°C. It can double every four hours at 10°C. It is destroyed by normal, effective cooking processes. Most outbreaks occur in summer and secondary cases from person-to-person spread are common.

In 1996, several linked outbreaks of *E. coli* O157 in Central Scotland were traced back to a butcher's shop in Wishaw. The food vehicles involved included cold cooked meats and cooked steak/gravy. The outbreak(s) resulted in over 500 cases and 21 deaths, most victims being over 69 years old. As a result, the government set up an expert group, chaired by Professor Hugh Pennington, to examine the Wishaw outbreak(s) and recommend control measures.

In 1999 over 100 people in Cumbria developed *E. coli* O157 following the consumption of milk which did not meet the pasteurisation requirements.

The Pennington recommendations following the 2005 Outbreak of *E. coli* O157 in South Wales

1. Food businesses must ensure that their systems and procedures prevent the contamination of food with *E. coli* O157.
2. Food businesses must ensure HACCP is a core part of the way they run their business.
3. Additional resources should be made available to ensure that all food businesses in Wales understand and use an effective, documented, food safety management system which is embedded in working culture and practice.
4. The principles underpinning the Butchers' Licensing Scheme, should guide food hygiene measures in businesses processing raw meat and unwrapped ready-to-eat foods.
5. The Food Standards Agency (FSA) should generate new guidance where needs are identified.
6. The FSA should remove the confusion that exists among food business operators about what solution(s) should be used to prevent cross-contamination from surfaces and equipment.
7. Regulatory and enforcement bodies should keep the choice of "light touch" enforcement for food businesses under constant review.
8. The inspection of HACCP plans must be audit-based.
9. Training provision should be developed to ensure that all officers in Wales who check HACCP and their managers, have the necessary knowledge and skills.
10. Environmental Health Officers should obtain a copy of a business's HACCP plan at each inspection, which should be held on the business's inspection file.
11. A system of logging issues, concerns or potential problems, whether by "red flagging" specific documents or by file notes, should be standard practice.
12. Decisions about confidence in a business's management of food safety should be evidence-based.
13. All inspections must be unannounced unless, exceptionally, there are justifiable reasons for a pre-arranged visit.
14. Discussion with employees must be a standard part of food hygiene inspection visits.
15. The FSA should develop, as part of its Audit Scheme, a means of assessing how food hygiene inspections are undertaken by local authorities, including the assessment of HACCP.

In 2005, John Tudor and Sons of Bridgend, Wales were responsible for an *E. coli* O157 outbreak that affected 158 people and one death. The owner was given a one-year jail sentence and the company, which supplied cooked meat to schools, closed down.

In 2009 the report of the public enquiry, led by Professor Pennington, outlined the failures resulting in the outbreak and made 15 recommendations to prevent future outbreaks.

In 2006, in the USA and Canada, 204 cases of *E. coli* O157 resulted from the consumption of fresh spinach; three people died and 31 developed haemolytic uraemic syndrome. Between May and July 2011, *E. coli* O104 contaminated bean sprouts, mainly in Germany, resulted in around 4,000 cases, with 53 deaths and 22% HUS cases.

In 2011, 15 cases and one death occurred in Oregon, USA as a result of eating strawberries contaminated with *E. coli* O157 from wild deer droppings. In May 2011, 70 cases and four deaths occurred in central Japan after eating raw meat (yukhoe – similar to tartare) in a restaurant chain run by Foods Forus Co.

Norovirus

Noroviruses are the major cause of viral foodborne cases and outbreaks in the UK. Symptoms include vomiting, the predominant symptom and usually projectile, some diarrhoea, abdominal pain, fever, nausea and **dehydration**. Symptoms usually last around 12 to 60 hours and patients are infectious for a further two days. Recent studies have suggested symptoms may last up to two weeks. Virus particles can be shed for up to ten or more days. The incubation period is 10 to 50 hours, usually 24 to 48 hours, and is dose dependent. Specimens are required within 48 hours of the first symptoms. The infective dose is very low,

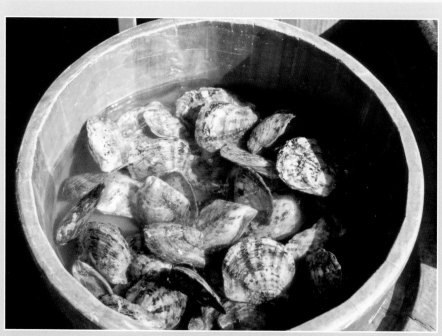

In 2011, an FSA report stated that 76% of oysters tested from 39 UK growing beds were contaminated with norovirus.

between 10 and 100 particles. Humans were thought to be the only reservoir for noroviruses but pigs and cattle are now suspected. Astroviruses are occasionally foodborne and have a four-day onset period.

The virus is present in vomit and the mode of transmission is person to person, through **fomites** or environmental contamination with around 10% being foodborne or waterborne. Outbreaks peak in the winter and are characterised by a high secondary attack rate. Re-infection is common. Outbreaks of norovirus can be suspected if stool specimens are negative for bacteria, average duration of the illness is 12 to 60 hours, vomiting is present in the majority of cases and the incubation period is 10 to 50 hours. The average attack rate is usually 45% or more. **Asymptomatic** infections are also common

Norovirus particles
©CENTRE FOR INFECTIONS/HEALTH PROTECTION AGENCY/ SCIENCE PHOTO LIBRARY

(up to 5%). Viruses thrive in cold conditions and are destroyed at temperatures above 60°C. A heat treatment of 90°C for 90 seconds is recommended for destruction in shellfish, but is disliked as it makes the shellfish rubbery. **Depuration** of shellfish is ineffective against viral contamination. Freezing does not destroy the virus and 15 outbreaks in Finland were traced to imported frozen raspberries. Illness has also been caused by eating shellfish pickled in brine and vinegar. They also survive high levels of chlorine.

Control measures include:

♦ the exclusion of **symptomatic** food handlers until 48 hours after they are symptom-free. This may be extended to 10 days if they cannot be relied on to wash their hands properly and/or handle high-risk food. (Disposable gloves may be considered);
♦ the use of reputable suppliers, especially for bivalves, salad vegetables and fruit;
♦ the washing or **blanching** of ready-to-eat raw fruits such as melons and berries;
♦ staff training, particularly in relation to handwashing;
♦ the implementation of HACCP;
♦ environmental decontamination of public areas. Steam cleaning of carpets, furniture and soft furnishings;
♦ ensuring that toilets always have adequate accessible supplies of liquid soap, disposable paper towels, nailbrushes and warm running water;
♦ the destruction of potentially contaminated foods;
♦ the separation of potential sources of noroviruses, such as bivalves, from ready-to-eat foods;
♦ ensuring that any contaminated food preparation surfaces, hand-contact surfaces and toilets are thoroughly cleaned and disinfected using 500ppm hypochlorite; and
♦ the detection and elimination of noroviruses from the food chain.

The first recorded outbreak of foodborne viral gastroenteritis was identified in an American school in the town of Norwalk, Ohio in 1968. The first time that similar virus particles were detected in both oysters and the faecal specimens of ill persons who had consumed the oysters was in Kingston-upon-Hull in 1980. Noroviruses are of major concern on cruise ships. Between February and March 2009 over 500 diners at the three Michelin starred Fat Duck restaurant, run by Heston Blumenthal, became ill with norovirus after consuming contaminated oysters. It was alleged that many symptomatic food handlers were allowed to continue working and that this significantly contributed to the number of cases.

Hepatitis

Hepatitis is caused by a virus and the two main types are hepatitis A and hepatitis B. Type A is the more common. Some statutory notifications of hepatitis A are foodborne and associated with shellfish. Hepatitis type B is transmitted sexually and by blood. It is often spread by the use of contaminated needles.

The onset of hepatitis A is abrupt and symptoms include fever, **malaise**, nausea, abdominal pain and later jaundice. The duration of the illness varies from one week to several months. Man is the reservoir for the virus and transmission is often by the faecal–oral route. Faeces, blood and urine may be infected and can contaminate food, especially water, shellfish and milk. The incubation period is from 15 to 50 days. The fatality rate is less than 1%. Preventive measures are similar to those used for typhoid. A temperature of 90°C for 90 seconds will inactivate hepatitis A virus.

In 1988, an outbreak in Shanghai, China involved over 300,000 cases and 11 deaths, due to infected clams. In 1994, 79 cases of hepatitis A resulted from the consumption of cinnamon buns in New York. The baker, who was positive for hepatitis, had applied cinnamon glaze to the buns. Handwashing was unsatisfactory. In 2004,

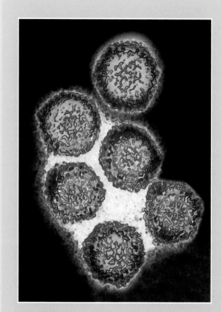

Hepatitis A
©JAMES CAVALLINI/SCIENCE PHOTO LIBRARY

351 cases of hepatitis A were traced back to a hotel in Hurghada (Egypt) following the consumption of fruit juices. In 2013 the Department of Environment, Food and Rural Affairs advised that 10% of UK raw pork sausages tested positive for hepatitis E. There were 657 reported cases of hepatitis E in 2012, an increase of 39% from 2011. Undercooking of pork products may be contributing to this increase.

Transmissible spongiform encephalopathy

Spongiform **encephalopathy** is thought to be caused by **prions** (proteinaceous infectious particles) and is responsible for scrapie in sheep, bovine spongiform encephalopathy (BSE) and Creutzfeldt-Jacob disease (CJD) including variant-CJD (vCJD) in humans.

vCJD is a rare and fatal neurodegenerative disease that is considered to be related in part to the consumption of BSE-contaminated food. Between 1970 and December 2001 there were 944 cases of CJD in the UK. 730 cases were classified as definite, the remainder being probable. Risk factors for the development of vCJD include age and host genotype.

Proposals agreed by the European Commission in February 2001 on restrictions to limit infected material entering the food chain were:

♦ the removal of the vertebral column from all cattle over 12 months and prohibiting mechanically recovered meat from bones of ruminants;

♦ requirements to pressure-cook rendered animal fats from ruminants for food and feed; and

♦ authorising certain hydrolysed proteins from fish and feathers.

Unfortunately, much remains unknown about BSE and vCJD. For example, assuming a causal relationship between vCJD and oral consumption of BSE-infected food, we do not know the infective dose and whether it is a single dose or cumulative. It is obvious that there is an urgent need to carry out research in a number of areas to answer basic but important questions. There is currently no treatment or cure for BSE or vCJD.

Information on CJD is available from www.cjd.ed.ac.uk

Vibrios vulnificus

Vibrios vulnificus is a bacterium that effects people consuming raw oysters or clams, harvested from warm coastal waters. It is not a result of pollution and has no effect on the oysters which look and taste normal. Immunocompromised people, for example, with liver disease, diabetes, transplants, AIDS or cancer are much more likely to be affected than healthy people. Symptoms include vomiting, diarrhoea and a blistering dermatitis. Severe symptoms and death occurs in up to 50% of people if the bacterium enters the bloodstream.

PARASITES AFFECTING FOOD AND/OR MAN

A **parasite** is a plant or animal that has the ability to live on another plant or animal known as the host. The parasite obtains its nourishment from the host. Parasites may pass through complicated life cycles that depend on intermediate hosts for the cystic stage of their life.

Giardiasis

Giardiasis is a type of gastroenteritis caused by the parasitic protozoan *Giardia duodenalis (Giardia lamblia or Giardia intestinalis),* which is a common inhabitant of the intestinal tract. The incubation period is 3 to 25 days and symptoms include watery diarrhoea, flatulence, abdominal pain and distension. Alternatively, there may be less acute diarrhoea with fatty stools (steatorrhoea), **lassitude** and weight loss. The infective dose is very low and may only require one viable cyst. The main sources are human cases and carriers and animals. Transmission

Coloured Scanning Electron Micrograph of *Giardia lamblia* in human intestine
©PROFESSORS P.M. MOTTA & F.M. MAGLIOCCA/SCIENCE PHOTO LIBRARY

is by the faecal–oral route. Cases involving food are rarely proven. Waterborne outbreaks occasionally occur and chlorination without filtration is ineffective. Most laboratory reports of giardiasis in England and Wales affect children, and many of these probably originated abroad.

Cryptosporidiosis

Cryptosporidiosis is a gastrointestinal infection caused by parasitic protozoa, *Cryptosporidium spp.* Symptoms include diarrhoea, vomiting, abdominal pain and **anorexia**. The incubation period is probably around ten days. The sources are cattle and other domestic and wild animals. The protozoa cling to the surface of the intestine and produce oocysts that pass out in the faeces. The oocysts (4 to 6mm in diameter) are unaffected by the chlorine levels in tap water. Transmission is by the faecal–oral route, although it is believed that close contact with infected animals is more significant than contaminated food. Most large outbreaks involve water, although other vehicles have included raw milk and unpasteurised apple juice.

Cyclosporiasis

Cyclosporiasis is a gastrointestinal infection caused by the parasitic protozoan *Cyclospora cayetanensis.* Symptoms include a prolonged relapsing watery diarrhoea with a duration of one to eight weeks; there may also be vomiting, abdominal pain, fever, flatulence, bloating, anorexia and weight loss. The incubation period is often seven to eleven days. Oocysts are excreted unsporulated in human faeces but need to **sporulate** to be infective. The main vehicles identified in outbreaks include untreated drinking water, soft fruit especially raspberries, lettuce, basil and vegetables. In 1996 and 1997 outbreaks of cyclosporiasis in the USA and Canada were linked to raspberries imported from Guatemala. Transmission is unknown although it is considered that the infective dose is low. Around 50 laboratory reports of *C. cayetanensis* are made in England and Wales each year and the biggest risk seems to be from imported food. However, current laboratory procedures in the UK might fail to identify the organism, and hence the true incidence could be underestimated.

Toxoplasma gondii

Toxoplasma gondii is a protozoan which may increase in significance as it is alleged that there are millions of people infected in the USA each year. Most infected people do not have symptoms but it can be serious for developing foetuses and people with compromised immune systems.

Infections mainly result from contact with the faeces of infected cats containing the oocysts and less frequently by the handling or consumption of undercooked pork, lamb, beef, or venison. Cooking to 75°C should destroy the parasite.

Taenia saginata

The adult tapeworm attaches itself to the intestine of man (adult host), eggs are passed out in faeces and if they reach grazing land may be eaten by cattle (intermediate host). The eggs hatch in the gut and the resultant cysts *(Cysticercus bovis)* migrate to the

Scolex (head) of a beef tapeworm, *Taenia saginata* Tapeworm head.
©ALFRED PASIEKA/SCIENCE PHOTO LIBRARY

muscle via the blood. If infected, undercooked meat is eaten, the cysts become adult tapeworms. In 2001, 97 cases were reported in England and Wales.

Trichina spiralis

Adult worms live in the gut of the host, for example, rats. Larvae are produced and are carried to the muscles, via the blood, and encyst. If infected meat is eaten the life cycle begins again. In 1996, 23 cases in France were linked to eating imported horse meat, which had probably been undercooked. In late 2001 an outbreak of trichinosis in the former Yugoslavia affected over 247 cases following the consumption of contaminated smoked sausages.

In 2005, 25 people from Kochkovsky in Russia developed trichinellosis following the consumption of undercooked badger meat. In 2006, 17 cases of trichinellosis in Eastern Germany occurred from the consumption of undercooked pork.

Colour Scanning Electron Micrograph of *Trichinella spiralis* roundworms
©EYE OF SCIENCE/SCIENCE PHOTO LIBRARY

Fasciola hepatica

The adult fluke lives in the bile duct of the host, for example, cattle. Eggs are passed out in faeces and hatch on wetland. If the cysts find a mud snail (intermediate host), further development occurs before they end up on vegetation waiting to be eaten by sheep or cattle. They infect persons who, for example, eat watercress grown in contaminated water. Cases are rare in the UK.

Fluke in sheep's liver, light micrograph
©STEVE GSCHMEISSNER/SCIENCE PHOTO LIBRARY

Echinococcus granulosus (hydatid cyst)

The adult host for this small tapeworm is usually the dog but also foxes. The worms attach themselves to the wall of the small intestine. Ova are passed out in faeces after around seven weeks and may be ingested by cattle, sheep, horses and pigs. The embryos are released and may end up in the liver, lungs, heart, kidneys or spleen. Man may become infected by eating food contaminated by ova. Infection is more likely from a dog licking the hands or face after licking its anus. Ten cases were reported in England and Wales in 2001.

In August 2006, at least 87 people at a Chinese restaurant in Beijing who had eaten raw or undercooked Amazonian snails affected with the parasitic eel worm developed meningitis.

5 Food contamination & control

Contamination of **food** is a major **hazard** and may be considered as the occurrence of any objectionable matter in or on the food. Thus, carcases may be contaminated with **faecal material**, **high-risk food** may be contaminated with **spoilage** or **food poisoning bacteria** and flour may be contaminated with rodent hairs. To prevent the consumption of unacceptable or unsafe food, contamination must be kept to a minimum.

There are four types of contamination/hazards:

♦ *Microbiological hazards caused by* **bacteria** *and* **toxins, moulds**, *viruses* **(micro-organisms)** *or* **parasites**. Usually occurs in food premises because of ignorance, inadequate space, poor design or because of **food handlers** taking short cuts. In the early stages it will not be detectable. Contamination of this sort is the most serious and may result in food spoilage, food poisoning or even death.

♦ *Physical hazards from foreign bodies including insects.* Physical contamination may render food unfit or unsafe but often involves pieces of paper, plastic, metal or string and is usually unpleasant or a nuisance.

♦ *Chemical hazards.* Examples include **pesticides**, mercury in fish and residues from **cleaning chemicals**.

♦ *Allergenic hazards.* Examples include peanuts, milk, eggs and cereals.

Food safety legislation requires that food shall not be exposed to **risk** of contamination. However, for an offence to have been committed it must usually be proved that there is a risk to the health of people consuming the food and regard must be had to the nature of the food, any further treatment, such as cooking, that the food may receive before sale and the manner in which it is packed.

In the USA the Food Service Sanitation Manual of the Food and Drug Administration states that: "At all times, including storage, preparation, display, service and distribution, food shall be protected from potential contamination, including dust, insects, rodents, dirty equipment, unnecessary handling, coughs and sneezes, flooding, drainage and overhead leakage or condensation".

MICROBIOLOGICAL HAZARDS AND CONTROL MEASURES

Sources of microbiological contamination

Bacterial contamination is the most significant as it results in large amounts of spoilt food and unacceptable numbers of food poisoning **cases**. Food poisoning bacteria may be brought into food premises by the following **sources:**

♦ food handlers/visitors;
♦ raw foods and water;
♦ insects, rodents, animals and birds; and
♦ from the environment, including soil and dust.

Food handlers/visitors

People commonly harbour food poisoning organisms in the nose, mouth, intestine and also on the skin. The hands are never free of bacteria and the soiled hands of food handlers are likely to harbour large numbers of moulds, yeasts and bacteria, some of which may be **pathogenic,** for example, *Staphylococcus aureus*. The presence of boils and septic cuts usually guarantees the presence of staphylococci and food handlers suffering with these conditions should be excluded from working in food premises, unless they present no risk.

Carelessness, ignorance of, or disregard for, hygienic food handling may result in contamination and possibly food poisoning. All food handlers must have high standards of **personal hygiene**, wear suitable **protective clothing** and, as far as possible, avoid handling food directly; tongs and other equipment should be used. The importance of thorough and regular handwashing cannot be overstressed.

Raw food

Foods such as raw meat, vegetables, milk, shellfish and eggs are all likely to be contaminated with large numbers of bacteria, which may include food poisoning bacteria. Even when produced under hygienic conditions raw foods must be considered potentially hazardous.

Raw meat and poultry

The contamination of meat starts on the farm and poultry meat is the most common food implicated in **outbreaks** of food poisoning, especially salmonellosis. Eggs from infected breeding stock may result in the introduction of chickens that are already excreting salmonellae. The younger the chicken the more susceptible it is to becoming infected and becoming an excreter. Other possible sources include man, dogs, cats, rodents, insects and wild birds. Overcrowded and badly constructed sheds, which cannot be cleaned and **disinfected**, encourage the spread of infection throughout flocks.

Animals that are ill should be segregated and infections treated as soon as possible. Stress, excitement, fatigue and overcrowding increase the likelihood of animals excreting salmonellae. Symptomless excreters remain a major problem. In the UK significant improvements in hygiene and **biosecurity**, and the vaccination of layers has resulted in a major reduction in poultry carcases contaminated with salmonellae (often below 10%). However, the majority of poultry is now contaminated with campylobacter.

Animals and birds should be transported to slaughterhouses in **clean** and disinfected vehicles. Slaughtering should be carried out in slaughterhouses that comply with the appropriate regulations. Animals should be kept as clean as possible before and after slaughtering. The flesh of healthy, live animals is virtually free of micro-organisms. However, on slaughtering, the walls of the intestine lose the ability to resist bacterial penetration. Consequently, evisceration must be carried out as quickly as possible.

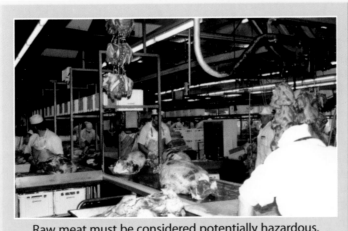

Raw meat must be considered potentially hazardous.

The hide is a possible source of food poisoning organisms, although most contamination of the carcase is likely when the stomach and intestines are removed. All dressing must take place clear of the floor. Areas and procedures that may result in contamination should be eliminated. Poor hygiene amongst slaughterhouse operatives, dirty equipment and unsatisfactory practices will undoubtedly contribute to the amount of contaminated raw meat or poultry leaving the slaughterhouse.

The skin of poultry is usually heavily contaminated with bacteria and S. Enteritidis has been isolated in the muscle. Bruises also harbour many bacteria, a large number of which may be staphylococci. Many birds in the slaughterhouse become contaminated by processes such as scalding, mechanical defeathering and evisceration. Scald tanks operating at 52°C are a much greater risk than those operated at 60°C, as fewer organisms will be destroyed at the lower temperature. Thorough spraying of poultry, with clean water, after evisceration is essential to reduce bacterial loads.

Physical inspection of animals, meat and offal will not detect food poisoning organisms. However, as one of the best ways of reducing levels of food poisoning is to minimise the number of pathogens on animals and raw food, we must ensure farms and slaughterhouses adopt the highest standards of hygiene. A study undertaken by the Food Safety Research Group of the University of Wales Institute, Cardiff in 2001 confirmed that the packaging of raw poultry was likely to be contaminated with salmonella and/or campylobacter. It was found that 3% of external and 34% of whole packaging was contaminated with campylobacter and 11% of whole packaging (non external) was contaminated with salmonella. The way that packaging is handled in the home means there is a significant risk of **cross-contamination** especially as many people do not wash their hands after handling packaging.

Fish and shellfish

Apart from *Vibrio parahaemolyticus* and *Clostridium botulinum*, which rarely cause problems in this country, most pathogenic bacteria are introduced into fish by poor handling. As fish spoil rapidly they should be gutted and stored under hygienic conditions on ice, in refrigerators or freezers, as soon as possible after removal from the water.

Shellfish are often contaminated with food poisoning organisms, especially bivalves such as cockles, oysters and mussels grown in sewage-polluted water. The amount of heat used to remove the meat from the shells is usually inadequate to destroy the pathogens and recontamination is always likely. A significant number of cases of viral food poisoning and hepatitis are attributed to the consumption of shellfish. Even shellfish that have been relaid in clean water and subjected to UV treatment may still contain viruses. Between 1981 and 1990, 42 outbreaks of illness, in the UK, were associated with eating crustacean species, mainly prawns, and 151 outbreaks associated with molluscs. Of these, confirmatory microbiological or **epidemiological** evidence was obtained in seven and 107 outbreaks respectively.

Eggs

Although the shell of eggs, especially if dirty, may be contaminated with salmonellae, it is considered that infected reproductive tissues are the main **route** of internal contamination, usually of the albumen. Other than in cracked eggs, numbers of salmonellae are likely to be low and the **bacteriostatic** properties of the albumen should prevent significant growth for at least 21 days if temperatures remain below 20°C.

A survey of salmonella in raw shell eggs used by caterers was carried out by the Food Standards Agency (FSA) between November 2005 and January 2007. Eggs were collected throughout the UK. 0.38% (0.31% *Salmonella* Enteritidis) of pooled samples of eggs were contaminated on the shell and one sample was found in the contents. Salmonella was detected in 2.6% and 0.4% of egg samples that were produced in Germany and the UK respectively. 55% of caterers did not store eggs under refrigeration and 20.7% of egg samples had expired best-before dates or had less than seven days before the expiry of the best-before date.

An FSA survey carried out between March and July 2006 found that 13.3% of imported Spanish eggs were contaminated with salmonella.

Most of the food poisoning outbreaks associated with hens' eggs have in fact involved dishes containing raw egg, for example, home-made mayonnaise or lightly cooked egg white, for example, meringue, and are more likely to have been caused by incorrect food handling and failures in temperature control, notwithstanding the source being contaminated eggs. The use of **pasteurised** egg is recommended for dishes that will not be cooked sufficiently to destroy salmonellae. However, in 2007, following two salmonella outbreaks in the UK and Jersey involving French pasteurised liquid egg, the FSA advised the product had been withdrawn.

Food handlers must always wash their hands after handling eggs and never take risks with egg products. Cross-contamination must be avoided.

Milk

Milk is an ideal medium for the growth of micro-organisms, which may be introduced from:

♦ the animal itself, especially if ill or very dirty;

♦ the person carrying out the milking; and

♦ unhygienic equipment or storage tanks.

In an effort to reduce the problems from milk, government schemes have been carried out to ensure that all herds are tuberculin tested (accredited) and free from brucellosis. Milk from cows or goats suffering from **mastitis** must not be used for human consumption as it may be infected with staphylococci and streptococci.

Raw or underprocessed milk, including goat's milk, has been implicated in several large food poisoning outbreaks involving *Salmonella spp.* and *Staphylococcus aureus,* in addition to several outbreaks of campylobacter enteritis, *Listeria monocytogenes* and *E. coli* O157. Since 1997 problems of spoilage have resulted because spores of *Bacillus sporothermodurans* have survived UHT processing.

Water supplies and drainage

Although not an ideal medium for the multiplication of bacteria, water can nevertheless transport certain pathogenic organisms considerable distances, for example, salmonellae, *Giardia intestinalis* and *Cryptosporidium spp.* Furthermore, bacterial spores may survive for several months in water. Pollution of water is usually caused by human sewage or faecal contamination from animals. The Aberdeen typhoid outbreak (1964) was associated with cans of Argentinian corned beef that had been cooled in sewage-polluted water.

Cold water supplies used for washing food or equipment require suitable treatment and must be of **potable** quality. Pipework must be properly installed and maintained. Potable and non-potable supplies must never be connected or confused. Regular bacteriological and chemical checks of water used in food production are essential.

Satisfactory drains must be installed to carry away waste water. Flooding, leakage, back-siphonage and blockages must, as far as practicable, be prevented. Food, including canned or packaged food, that has been in contact with sewage-polluted water must be regarded as unfit.

Vegetables and fruit

Vegetable crops, cereals and fruit must be grown on land that is free from toxic materials and must only be sprayed with **insecticide** and other such chemicals in accordance with manufacturer's instructions. Irrigation must not be carried out with sewage-polluted water, which may contain pathogens, tapeworm eggs or other **parasites**.

After harvesting, vegetables must be stored under conditions that do not expose them to risk of contamination, for example, from poisonous chemicals or rodents. Animals and birds must be kept away from storage areas.

Sorting and packing of fruit, and raw vegetables used in salads, may introduce pathogens from food handlers, especially via the hands. All such foods must be thoroughly washed before use. Particular care must be exercised to avoid contaminating vegetables to be eaten raw. An outbreak of salmonellosis in the USA involving coleslaw and onions was traced back to contamination of the vegetables prepared on the same work surface used for cutting up raw chickens. In 1997, raspberries imported into the USA resulted in a major outbreak due to the parasite cyclospora. Outbreaks of salmonella have involved cut melon, bean sprouts and tomatoes. Outbreaks of *E. coli* O157 have involved apple juice (unpasteurised), spinach and lettuce. Lettuce has also been implicated in the following outbreaks in the UK: in 2000, 361 cases of *S.* Typhimurium; in 2001, 19 cases of *S.* Newport; in 2004, 250 cases of *S.* Newport; and in 2005, 96 cases of *S.* Typhimurium (associated with imported Spanish lettuce irrigated with sewage-polluted water).

Animals and birds

Both domestic and wild animals are known to carry pathogens on their bodies and in their intestines. Large numbers of *Staphylococcus aureus* are commonly found on the skin and noses of cats and dogs. Salmonellae are often present in the intestines. Consequently, pets must always be kept out of food rooms. Persons handling animals should always change their clothing and wash their hands before touching food. Pet food may be contaminated and should be kept out of food rooms. Terrapins are occasionally implicated in food poisoning cases through contact with infected water. Wild birds have been responsible for an outbreak of salmonellosis in a hospital kitchen.

A mouse found in a milk bottle.

Salmonella has also been isolated from songbirds in the USA, and there have been outbreaks recorded with the handling of sick birds. Campylobacter carried by pets and *E. coli* O157 carried by farm animals are major contributors to cases of "foodborne disease" from these organisms.

Insects

Insects are capable of contaminating food by defecation, feeding, walking on or dying in the food. Insects of particular concern, with regard to bacterial contamination, are flies, cockroaches and pharaoh's ants.

An ant found in a prawn.

Rodents

Rodents, including both rats and mice, commonly excrete organisms such as salmonellae. Contamination of food may occur from gnawing, defecating, urinating or walking over food or food-contact surfaces.

Dust

There are always large numbers of bacteria and spores in dust and moisture droplets floating about in the air. **Open food** should always be removed or covered during cleaning. The ventilation of premises should always be from high-risk areas to low-risk areas unless each area is independently ventilated. All air drawn into food premises should be filtered and intakes of ventilation ducts must be positioned to avoid introducing contaminated air. The ventilation system should not produce turbulence within the premises. NLV outbreaks are often a result of airborne formites transmission.

Soil

Soil harbours a considerable number of pathogens such as *Clostridium perfringens and Bacillus cereus* and care must be taken when bringing raw vegetables such as potatoes, carrots and lettuce into food rooms.

VEHICLES AND ROUTES OF BACTERIAL CONTAMINATION

Sometimes bacteria pass directly from the source to high-risk food, but as bacteria are largely static and as the sources are not always in direct contact with food, the bacteria have to rely on other things to transfer them to food. These things are known as **vehicles** and the main ones are:

- ♦ hands;
- ♦ cloths and equipment; and
- ♦ hand-contact surfaces;
- ♦ food-contact surfaces.

Cross-contamination can be defined as 'the transfer of bacteria from contaminated foods (usually raw) to other foods.' This includes direct contact, drip and indirect contamination by, for example, hands, equipment or work surfaces. However, cross-contamination is also used to describe the transfer of, for example, food poisoning bacteria from a source to something else. This means that the transfer of bacteria from one food handler to another via a nailbrush could be considered as cross-contamination. The path along which bacteria are transferred from the source to **ready-to-eat** food is known as the route. Knowledge of sources, vehicles and routes is vital to food

Wiping cloths and cutting boards, especially in poor condition, are common vehicles for bacteria.

poisoning prevention, as different controls apply to each. It must be assumed that all sources are contaminated, i.e. every worker is a carrier and all raw meat, animals, insects and the surrounding environment are contaminated.

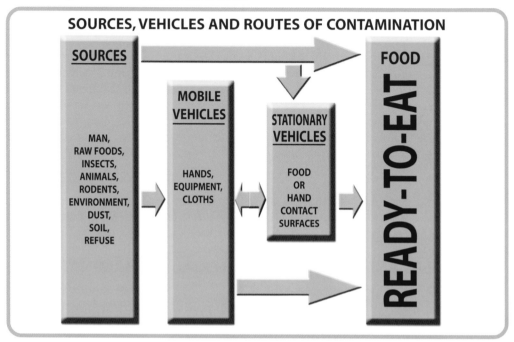

Prevention of contamination depends on either removing the sources, or putting barriers between them and the vehicles or between them and food. Thus human access to ready-to-eat food must be restricted, raw foods handled in separate areas, vermin excluded and work areas enclosed in suitably constructed and ventilated rooms. Similarly, vehicles must, where possible, be excluded. Handling should be minimised, wiping cloths used sparingly, disposable are preferred, hand-contact surfaces, such as tap handles, replaced with non-hand operable taps, and the number of surfaces with which the food comes into contact limited.

In the nature of food preparation, however, routes between sources and vehicles survive, giving rise to contaminated vehicles. Consequently, routes must be disrupted by cleaning and disinfection. For example, should a work surface come into contact with a contaminated source, raw meat for instance, the surface must be cleaned and disinfected before it is used for ready-to-eat meat.

The interrelation between sources, vehicles and food can be complex with many diverse routes being taken by the contaminants.

CHECK LIST FOR CONTAMINATION CONTROL

♦ Purchase food and raw materials from known, reliable and hygienic suppliers. Set specifications, obtain relevant hygiene records and, if practical, **inspect** suppliers' premises.

♦ Accept deliveries only if transported in clean, properly equipped vehicles, with clean drivers wearing satisfactory protective clothing. Refrigerated vehicles may be necessary.

♦ Inspect deliveries immediately on arrival. Reject or segregate any damaged, unfit or contaminated material. Where relevant, check temperature, codes and date markings and reject out-of-date food.

♦ After checking, remove deliveries immediately to appropriate storage, refrigerator or cold store.

♦ Keep any unfit food, chemicals and refuse away from stored food. Use only food containers for storing food.

Cooked and raw foods stored together.

♦ Keep high-risk foods and ready-to-eat foods apart from raw foods at all times, in separate areas with separate utensils and equipment. Colour coding is useful.

♦ Maintain scrupulous personal hygiene at all times and handle food as little as possible. Exclude potential carriers.

♦ Keep food covered or otherwise protected unless it is actually being processed or prepared, in which case bring food out only when needed. Do not leave food lying around.

♦ Keep premises, equipment and utensils clean and in good condition and repair. Report or remedy defects with the minimum of delay. Disinfect food-contact surfaces and hand-contact surfaces as often as necessary.

♦ Ensure that all empty containers are clean and disinfected prior to filling with food, for example, empty cans or milk bottles.

♦ Control cleaning materials, particularly wiping cloths. Keep cleaning materials away from food. Remove food and food containers before cleaning. Care must be taken to ensure that all cleaning residues, including water, are drained from food equipment and pipes.

♦ Remove waste food and refuse from food areas as soon as practicable. Store in appropriate conditions, away from food.

♦ Implement **integrated pest management**.

♦ Control visitors and maintenance workers in high-risk areas. Ensure hygiene disciplines apply to all personnel, including management.

♦ Inspect food areas and processes frequently, act on any defects or unhygienic practices. Train staff and monitor competence. Food handlers and other operatives must be aware of the bacteriological and physical contamination they may introduce.

♦ Ensure adequate thawing of foods, separate from other foods.

♦ Make suitable provisions for cooling food prior to refrigeration.

MICROBIOLOGICAL HAZARDS
- MULTIPLICATION AND SURVIVAL

In addition to contamination, microbiological hazards also include the multiplication and survival of micro-organisms, for example, due to undercooking or ineffective disinfection.

Most pathogenic bacteria will not multiply below 3°C. Although *Listeria monocytogenes* is capable of slow multiplication as low as −1.5°C, it takes around 24 hours to double in numbers. It is estimated that around 1000 organisms per gram of food could make people ill. An initial contamination level of 100 *L. monocytogenes* per gram would become 800 in three days at 5°C. Food should be kept below 4.4°C and 3.3°C respectively to prevent the growth of *B. cereus* and *Cl. botulinum*. Salad vegetables should be precooled to less than 10°C to prevent the production of *S. aureus* toxin in salad sandwiches. Spores cannot germinate in food held above 55°C. The highest temperature at which pathogens may multiply is 52°C (*Cl. perfringens*).

Spoilage bacteria usually inhibit the production of toxin from *S. aureus*, *Cl. botulinum* or *B. cereus* in raw food, however, problems are likely in temperature-abused high-risk food.

pH can also be used to control the multiplication of pathogens, for example, a pH of 4.1 will control salmonella multiplication and a pH of 4.5 will prevent the growth of *Cl. botulinum*.

Slow cooling of food provides another opportunity for bacterial multiplication or spore germination. However, if food is cooled from 55°C to 7°C within 15 hours the maximum growth of *Cl. perfringens* or *B. cereus* following spore germination is 10^3.

Cooking food to a core temperature of 75°C will reduce levels of vegetative bacteria, such as salmonella, by log 10^5 to log 10^7. However, Hepatitis A virus may require 85°C for two minutes to reduce it to a safe level.

Double washing of raw fruit and vegetables may reduce 1000 organisms per gram to 10 organisms per gram. Blanching in hot water around 70°C may reduce levels of bacteria by 10^5.

PHYSICAL HAZARDS AND CONTROL MEASURES

Foreign bodies found in food may be brought into food premises with the raw materials or introduced during storage, preparation, service or display. It is essential that managers are aware of the types of foreign bodies commonly found in their particular sector of the food industry and that they take all reasonable precautions and exercise all **due diligence** to secure their removal or prevent their introduction. A record should be kept of all customer complaints and steps should be taken to identify the source of the contaminant.

Reported complaints involving foreign bodies (undesirable contaminants that are usually solid matter) are at an unacceptable high level and may pose a threat to consumer health and leave manufacturers and retailers vulnerable to prosecution and lost sales.

Examination of consumer complaints reveals a high incidence of problems associated with processed foods and in particular:

♦ milk and milk products;
♦ cakes and confectionery;
♦ fruit and vegetables (canned, bottled, dried and jams); and
♦ meat, poultry and fish products.

Contamination of food by **extraneous** matter will cause customer dissatisfaction and may result in bad publicity. If press and media coverage results, the impact on the business can be disastrous leading, in the worst possible case, to loss of product confidence and even company viability. It is therefore in the interests of the manufacturer to minimise the risk of foreign body contamination.

Foreign bodies, such as bone in chicken meat or stalks in vegetables, are **intrinsic** and should be minimised by care in harvesting and processing, although foreign body detection and removal systems, such as inspection belts, will also be necessary. The presence of **extrinsic** foreign bodies in food, such as glass or rodent droppings, is usually of greater concern as this indicates a breakdown in hygiene and will not be tolerated by the consumer. Contamination may occur at any step from storage through to service but is most likely during processing.

Extrinsic foreign bodies may be considered as those that:

♦   originate from the structure of the building, installations or equipment;
♦   originate from food handlers;
♦   originate from the activities of maintenance operatives;
♦   originate from packaging;
♦   originate from **pests** or unsatisfactory pest control;
♦   originate from cleaning activities; or
♦   are a result of post-process contamination including sabotage by disgruntled employees, blackmail attempts or from the kitchens or equipment of consumers.

Although in the minority, some foreign bodies may be considered as a serious health hazard, such as glass, stones, wire or rodent droppings, which may result in cut mouths, dental damage, choking or illness. However, all foreign bodies are, at the very least, a nuisance and manufacturers in particular must implement appropriate systems to prevent or remove such contamination.

EXAMPLES OF FOREIGN BODIES FOUND IN FOOD PRODUCTS

A can lid found in a meat fritter.   Half a mouse found in sausage meat.

Raw ingredients

The variable nature of raw material quality is one of the main sources of problems in food processing. Raw materials have traditionally been a major source of extraneous matter and food manufacturers use a range of cleaning, sorting and grading operations to separate out the offending material. In the manufacture of frozen peas, for example, stones, metal screws, cigarette ends, stalks, sticks, caterpillars and dirt often accompany the vined peas as they arrive at the factory.

Control measures should include specifications to detail maximum permissible levels of contaminants in incoming materials. By agreeing specifications with suppliers and monitoring and evaluating the supplier performance in meeting the specifications, the company has an effective tool in minimising the risk posed by extraneous matter. Standards of cleaning and sorting in the initial handling of raw materials by the supplier is an important control measure.

Before using raw materials, cleaning or washing and inspection may need to be carried out. For example, vegetables used in food factories must have stones and less-dense material removed. The vegetables should then be conveyed on an illuminated inspection belt of an appropriate colour. The speed of the belt and number of operatives involved in the detection and removal of foreign bodies will depend on the product and the original amount of contamination. Belts should be illuminated to at least 540 lux. Conveyor belts should be designed to eliminate crevices and to allow access to facilitate cleaning and repair. They must be kept clean and inspected frequently for signs of wear or damage. Plastic coated and woven belts should be repaired or replaced if frayed. Wooden sides and rubber strips should not be used and tracking control is recommended to prevent wear. Where practicable, conveyor systems after inspection (and metal detection if present) should be completely enclosed. Food conveyors should be above waist height, as should the tops of boxes, cans and bottles.

Liquids used in food production should be filtered and powders sieved. Filters, screens and sieves should be as fine as possible and must be cleaned and checked regularly. Worn equipment must be replaced. Wooden-framed sieves are unacceptable.

Packaging materials

Packaging may be a source of extraneous matter in the form of warehouse and transport dirt/dust, wood from the pallets, paper and polythene strips from over-wraps and a variety of insects and even rodents. Containers (cans, jars, bottles and plastic pots) may be used directly for filling with minimal cleaning, and any rogue material in the container (metal splinters, glass, dirt, insects, etc.) may end up in the final product.

Staples, cardboard, string, fibres, cloth, rubber, plastic and polythene

Food may be delivered in various containers including paper sacks, cardboard boxes and polythene bags. Particular care is necessary when emptying containers to avoid contamination of food. As far as practicable, all unpacking and packing should be carried out in areas separate from food preparation, if open food is exposed to risk of contamination.

String removed from hessian sacks and ties removed from bags should immediately be placed in suitable containers provided specifically for the purpose. As an extra precaution, coloured string may be specified to aid detection should it end up in the product. Paper sacks should be cut open, although care must be exercised to ensure pieces of paper do not finish up in the food. It is preferable for raw materials to be emptied into suitable lidded containers and not dispensed direct from paper sacks.

Particular care is needed to ensure that staples, which tend to fly considerable distances when boxes are prised open, do not contaminate food. Suppliers should be requested to use adhesive tape to fasten boxes, instead of staples. Many products are delivered in black polythene bags and small pieces of polythene often end up in the product.

Effective measures in terms of good manufacturing practice should be adopted in conjunction with HACCP to minimise the risk of contamination. An example would be the thorough examination of product and the removal of secondary packaging, before delivery to a high-risk area.

The building, installations and equipment
Wood splinters

As far as possible the use of wood should be eliminated from food production areas. Wooden containers used for transporting raw materials should be phased out. Pallets should not be double stacked over open food.

Bolts, nuts and other pieces of metal

As far as practicable nuts should be self-locking. Bolts, nuts and screws should be non-corroding and positioned to ensure that, should they fall off equipment, they do not drop into the food. In December 2001, 250,000 pounds of ham in the USA was recalled by IBP Inc. due to contamination by nails as a result

Metal washer baked in breadloaf.

of sabotage by a disgruntled employee. Also in 2001 the Food Standards Agency issued a food hazard warning after stainless steel wire was found in chocolate bars.

Flaking paint or rust

Ceiling structure, pipes or equipment, should be non-flaking and rust-free. This is especially important when such fixtures are positioned directly above open products. In some older factories this problem is very difficult to overcome and consequently additional protection is necessary, for example, enclosed systems for conveying food and empty containers such as cans. New factories should be designed so that fixtures, ducts and pipes are not suspended over working areas or food if the product is exposed to risk of contamination.

Grease and oil

Wherever necessary, food-grade grease and lubricants should be used. It is important that engineers use the minimum amount necessary to lubricate moving parts and that grease is not left on the machine. Careful control will ensure the absence of complaints relating to grease in food. It is preferable for motors not to be positioned above open food. When this occurs, suitable non-corroding, cleansable drip-trays should be fixed underneath to catch oil spillages.

Glass

The use of ordinary glass, porcelain and enamelware in food factories should be avoided. Perspex or wired glass windows should be used. Diffusers, or protective non-breakable sleeves, should be fitted to all fluorescent tubes. All beakers, funnels, etc. used by the quality control staff in production areas should be unbreakable. Glass containers, other than those used for the final product, drinking cups, glass mirrors and gauge covers must all be eliminated from food production areas. Scales coated in vitreous enamel should be replaced, preferably by stainless steel. Particular care is necessary with glass containers used for product as any line breakages may result in glass contaminating other products. Brushes used for sweeping up broken glass may be colour coded and should be discarded after use.

In the event of any glass breakage it is important to ensure that:
- ♦ the supervisor is notified;

♦ production and preparation ceases where contamination is likely;
♦ food containers should be checked for broken glass and cleaned;
♦ the glass is cleaned up using a vacuum cleaner and/or brush (discard the brush);
♦ all potentially contaminated product should be discarded; and
♦ the area should be fully cleaned and inspected before food preparation starts again.

In factories, all filling hoppers, elevators and belts conveying open food should be protected against overhead contamination. Guards must be easy to remove to facilitate cleaning. Hoppers, silos and tanks containing food must be checked and cleaned before use and protected from contamination with close-fitting lids or covers, which must always be used correctly.

Regular checks should be made of conveyor belts, rubber seals, gaskets, brushes, etc. as deterioration can result in small pieces of rubber or bristles ending up in the food.

In 2001, The Food Standards Agency issued a food hazard warning after glass particles were found in bottles of an orange cocktail drink. In 2002, a major sweet company recalled a batch of mint creams after finding particles of glass in them.

Notices

Notices used for warnings, advice or instructions should be properly fixed and permanent. Sheets of paper sellotaped to equipment or close to open food are unacceptable. Recipe instructions should be enclosed in sealed polythene bags. Drawing pins should never be used.

Notice boards should be kept out of areas where open food is handled and should be covered in perspex or similar sheeting. Velcrose notice boards may be acceptable.

Processing or reworking of product

The manufacturing process is a major source of extraneous material that may find its way into the product during processing as a result of the following:
♦ cross-contamination resulting from poor layout, unsatisfactory cleaning or inadequate removal of waste material from the processing area;
♦ inadequate consideration of hygienic design principles when purchasing and installing plant and equipment and subsequently poor maintenance;
♦ premises not suitable for hygienic food production or poor maintenance of the fabric of the building;
♦ problems with conveying packaging materials, filling and sealing; and
♦ delays/breakdowns in processing.

Maintenance operatives

Engineers must be trained/briefed to take extra care when working with food equipment to ensure that they do not leave loose nuts, swarf and pieces of wire in food rooms on completion of maintenance. Written instructions may be useful. Temporary repairs with string should be avoided. It is good practice for managers to check areas where engineers, builders or contractors have been working before food handling commences.

During production, areas that are being decorated, or where repair or maintenance work is being carried out, must be suitably segregated by screens, such as heavy duty polythene, to avoid exposing product to risk of contamination. Maintenance workers should not wear grossly soiled overalls and should not stand on or climb over machinery or open food if there is the slightest risk of introducing contamination. If necessary, all food and food containers should be removed or protected with clean polythene sheeting. The use of ladders over open food or hoppers can result in dirt falling off shoes or rungs and ending up in the final product. After the work has been completed all tools, screws, swarf, grease, etc. must be removed and the area cleaned and, if necessary, disinfected before use. Whenever possible, equipment should be removed from food areas for repair.

Cleaning activities
Care must be taken during cleaning and all staff involved should be trained to ensure they do not expose product to risk of contamination by using worn equipment, especially brushes that are likely to lose their bristles, or by using inappropriate methods such as high pressure spraying in the presence of open food. Particular care must be exercised when using paper towels or cloths to ensure small pieces of paper or cloth do not end up in the product.

Food handlers
Contaminants originating from personnel include earrings, hair, fingernails, buttons, combs and pen tops. Protective clothing, including head covering, must be of a suitable type and worn correctly. The personal hygiene of food handlers must be beyond reproach, and earrings and jewellery, other than plain wedding rings and sleeper earrings, should not be worn. Pencils, pens and pieces of chalk must not be used in situations that expose food to risk of contamination, for example, near filling hoppers and mixing vessels.

Sweet papers, cigarette ends and matches are common contaminants and staff should not eat sweets, chew gum or smoke in food rooms. Continuous coaching and reinforcement, such as posters, should be used together with strict supervision and enforcement of company rules.

Post-process contamination
Contamination of the product may occur during warehousing or distribution. Furthermore, malicious tampering of products in supermarkets continues to pose a threat to manufacturers and retailers. Finally, contamination of the product may occur in the consumer's home and this should always be considered when investigating a complaint.

Control measures for tampering
Tamper-evident packaging is now widely applied in the food industry as a result of sabotage and blackmail by unscrupulous individuals. Most notably, the case of Rodney Witchelo, who was convicted in December 1990 for 17 years after being found guilty on charges of a £3.75 million blackmail plot after contaminating food products and threatening to kill customers. The food industry acknowledges that tamper-proof packaging is difficult to achieve but tamper-evident packaging is now widely used and examples include:
- roll-on aluminium pilfer-proof enclosures;
- heat shrunk plastic sleeves;
- adhesive labels or strips on the side of the cap and jar;
- vacuum sealed containers with audible click feature; or
- a combination of the above.

Pests and pest control
Rodents, rodent hairs and droppings may be brought into food premises with the raw materials or introduced during the preparation or storage of food in **infested** premises. Food showing evidence of rodent contamination is unfit and should be rejected.

a) Rat in frozen sweetcorn. b) Snail in jam. c) Mouse in canned green beans.

Insects, **larvae** and eggs may also be present in raw materials, although some may find their way into food rooms via openings. Several insects multiply rapidly and infestations can soon spread throughout food premises. Infested food should be discarded and appropriate control measures introduced.

A reputable pest control contractor, experienced at working with food businesses, should be employed to lay rodent bait or traps and control pest infestations should they arise. Bad pest control is likely to result in food contamination. For example, UV fly killers positioned above open food, work surfaces or containers will probably result in dead insects in the food, as will the use of **insecticides** to destroy flying insects in the presence of open food.

Cleaners and other staff must be instructed not to touch bait boxes, unless authorised to do so, and never to put bait trays on shelves above open products whilst cleaning is being undertaken.

Customer contamination

Customers may contaminate food which is not adequately protected, especially when they serve themselves. Handling and sneezing over food is probable and inquisitive customers may break seals to examine the contents of jars and tubs. Furthermore, malicious tampering of products in supermarkets continues to pose a threat to manufacturers and retailers. Finally, contamination of the product may occur in the consumer's home and this should be considered when investigating a complaint.

The use of HACCP to control foreign body contamination in food processing

Conduct an analysis of all possible hazards associated with product.

♦ Prepare a flow diagram of the steps in the process, from harvesting through to filling of a closed container or to the purchase of the food by the customer.
♦ Identify and list the hazards and specify the control measures.
♦ Set critical limits, target levels and tolerances and establish a monitoring system to ensure effective control.
♦ Establish appropriate corrective action and satisfactory record keeping.

Having defined the starting and finishing point for HACCP, a team should be selected that, if possible, includes those with experience in production, Quality Assurance, engineering, purchasing of packaging and raw ingredients, hygiene and transport. Extraneous matter may result from poor control in any of these areas and a broad base of experience is vital if HACCP is to be effective. The first task of the team is to clearly define the products under consideration and then construct and verify a flow diagram. The team should consider which foreign body hazards exist and the risk and significance of contamination and then use this **risk assessment** to identify critical control points. The consequences of a particular hazard (serious health risk or nuisance value) will need to be considered when determining controls and critical control points. Account must also be taken of good manufacturing practices and any industry guides to good hygiene practice.

Control systems

When identifying control systems it will be necessary to consider:
♦ the training of staff. Training programmes should include a training needs analysis, induction training, competence training relating to their activity, reinforcement and refresher training. Records of training should be kept on personal files;
♦ the design, structure, layout and maintenance of food rooms and the implementation of a clearly defined policy relating to use of glass;
♦ the design, construction, lighting and maintenance of equipment and especially deterioration with age;
♦ personal hygiene and practices, including protective clothing (staff and visitors);
♦ cleaning and disinfection procedures;
♦ instruction and training of maintenance and pest control operatives; and
♦ instructions relating to deboxing and packaging.

Foreign body detection and removal in food manufacture

No system can guarantee to remove every contaminant and the effectiveness of a particular machine or system will depend on the type of foreign body, the initial level of contamination and the maintenance of the equipment. The performance of most machines will deteriorate with age and use, and constant testing is essential. There are many contaminant detection and removal systems available including:
♦ metal detection systems;
♦ X-ray systems;
♦ sieves and filtration;
♦ vision systems including monochromatic, colour and laser sorters;
♦ magnets;
♦ air or liquid separation systems; and
♦ the use of operatives, for example, as spotters, on bottle lines or illuminated inspection belts.

Metal detection

Metal detection systems should be provided on production lines after visual inspection of the food just before packaging or preferably just after packaging. Metal detection is also useful to screen raw ingredients to avoid damaging processing equipment. Systems must be installed in accordance with manufacturers' instructions and routine maintenance checks are important. Regular checks on performance must be carried out, as must checks on the efficiency of metal detectors and rejection systems. Appropriately sized rods or balls made from different metals should be used, for example, stainless steel, copper and aluminium (1mm to 3mm). Sensitivity is affected by the ratio of the aperture size to product size, the orientation of the metal contaminant, by salt, moisture, vibration, moving metal, the proximity of other detectors, the cleaning methods and by changes in temperature and humidity. The use of a metal detector will only assist a defence of due diligence if there is a controlled system for its operation. If a metal detector is found to be defective during routine testing, all product passing through since the earlier satisfactory check must be retested. All reject product must be examined to identify the reason for the rejection and to trace sources of contamination within the factory.

The latest detectors provide automated self-checking and adjustment, automated compensation for product effect, confirmation that reject product has been deposited in the reject bin and warn of low air pressure, which may prevent effective rejection.

Although products in aluminium foil can be checked for ferrous contamination, non-ferrous metals and non-magnetic stainless steels, commonly used for food equipment, will not be detected.

In 1995, on appeal from Crown Court, a company had its fine reduced to £7,000 with costs of £7,834 for selling chocolate confectionery containing a Stanley knife blade. Although many steps had been taken to avoid contamination, metal detection was not provided at the end of the processing line. The Lord Chief Justice stated that even though this was a first offence the seriousness warranted a large fine. Furthermore, the costs should stand because the company had elected for jury trial.

X-ray inspection systems

Several companies are now using X-ray inspection as a central feature of their contaminant management system. (A documented system that includes comprehensive detection and rejection equipment, that is regularly tested, with records being kept.)

Contaminant management system using X-ray inspection.
(Courtesy of Graseby GK Intertest Ltd.)

Detection levels of under 1mm can be achieved depending on product speed and presentation. Pipeline systems are claimed to inspect up to 1.5 tonnes per minute and still achieve a 2mm resolution. Product presented in a uniform way facilitates the most accurate detection of contaminants.

Current applications include the detection of bone in meat products, stone and glass in fruit and vegetables, and steel, plastics and natural rubber from processing machinery. Usually the greater the density of the contaminant the easier it is to detect. Contaminants can be identified in plastic, card or glass packaging and even in sealed cans. Because foreign bodies are precisely located and rejected there is a reduction in wastage of non-contaminated product, which may be rejected by metal detection.

X-ray systems can simultaneously be used to inspect the size and shape of product, which enables packages with missing product, or underfills, to be rejected.

Vision systems

Vision systems are primarily used for rejecting unsatisfactory raw materials containing stones, insects, stalks and leaves etc. Cameras are used to measure light reflected in monochromatic and colour sorters. A pre-set threshold on a black and white or colour range determines which products are rejected. When combined with UV or infrared, monochromatic and colour sorters are used to detect and reject by density.

Laser sorters are used for product within a narrow colour range. Photo-multipliers, which can detect minute differences in reflected light, are used for rejecting unsatisfactory products. Rejecting systems rely on compressed air guns which require regular maintenance to ensure effectiveness.

REMOVING DIRTY CANS AND BOTTLES

Single-use containers such as cans should be inverted and cleaned immediately before use. Canwashers are preferable but compressed air may also be used. If practicable, some form of inspection of empty containers, for example, using highly polished metal mirrors, should be employed.

Returnable bottles, which are washed and disinfected before refilling, pose much greater problems. Unacceptable dirty or cracked bottles should be removed prior to washing. Filling lines should be fitted with sniffer devices to reject bottles contaminated with pesticides or household chemicals. Removal of pathogens from bottle surfaces depends on optimising the use of detergents, disinfectants, temperature, pH and additives. The bottlewasher should be well-maintained and always operated in accordance with the manufacturer's instructions.

Spotters should be employed to remove dirty bottles, which pass through the bottle-washer. The number of spotters required will depend on the speed of the line and the number of unsatisfactory bottles leaving the bottlewasher. Lines operating at speeds greater than 300 per minute may require two or more spotters. Black and white backgrounds for empty bottles, and suitable mirrors positioned behind filled bottles assist in the detection of those that are unsatisfactory. Spotters should be changed at regular and frequent intervals, for example, every 30 minutes. Dirty bottle bases are almost impossible to detect by personnel, and side and base-scanners are essential. These devices consist of several beams of light, which travel through the glass and on to a photo-electric cell. If one of the beams

Cans awaiting inspection.

of light is broken, for example, by a piece of dirt, the bottle is rejected automatically. Quality control staff should carry out regular checks to establish the number of dirty bottles escaping detection and how the effectiveness of any of the above measures can be improved.

All reasonable precautions and all due diligence

A food company facing a prosecution as a result of selling a contaminated product will need to demonstrate that they have installed and used an effective, documented detection and rejection system, which is checked regularly, if they are to successfully use the **due-diligence** defence. It will be up to the courts to decide what is "reasonable" having regard to good trade practice, industry hygiene guides and the risk and consequences in relation to cost.

All complaints should be fully investigated. In order to identify the contaminant, and its origin, all relevant details must be recorded. If the complainant will not release the object a photograph may be beneficial.

The presence of the foreign object indicates a breakdown in procedures and control and monitoring systems will need auditing, preferably using the HACCP approach, and modifications made to prevent a recurrence. If the defence of due diligence is to succeed, accurate and complete records will be needed including:

♦ number and type of specific complaints and action taken to prevent recurrence;
♦ documentation relating to the HACCP system including good hygiene practices, identification of hazards and controls, monitoring, corrective action, recall procedures and reviews;
♦ details of staff training/competency;
♦ details of pest control; and
♦ cleaning schedules.

If practicable, records should be retained for up to three years depending on product shelf life. If a reasonable precaution has not been taken the defence is unlikely to be successful.

CHEMICAL HAZARDS AND CONTROL MEASURES

Sources of chemical hazards

a) Present in raw materials - Naturally occurring toxins in plants, fish or shellfish. Examples include red kidney beans, toadstools, daffodil bulbs, puffer fish and parts of crab. Toxic chemicals may also result from spoilage, for example, scombrotoxic fish poisoning, or as a result of fish or shellfish eating poisonous algae, for example, ciguatera poisoning, paralytic and diarrhetic shellfish poisoning. (All of these are dealt with in greater detail in the chapter on food poisoning).

Poisons introduced on the farm

Examples include pesticides, herbicides, fungicides and fertilisers, mainly affecting plants, vegetables and cereals, but may also affect animals and be present in meat or milk. Antibiotics or hormones used to treat animals may end up in the meat or milk. Animal feed additives or contaminated feed similarly may end up in meat or milk. Plants grown on land contaminated with, for example, heavy metals such as copper or lead may also cause illness. Furthermore, plants and animals may be affected by industrial chemicals or radionuclides, for example, dioxins from incinerators. Milk from cows grazing near incinerators has been unsafe to drink. Radioactive fallout from Chernobyl resulted in the contamination of both plants and animals.

Poisons introduced during transport

This usually occurs when food is delivered in lorries that have previously been used for the transport of poisonous chemicals.

b) Introduced during production or preparation - for example, the inappropriate use or storage of chemicals including cleaning chemicals and pesticides. The use of unsafe additives such as Sudan 1 or the excessive use of additives such as nitrates and nitrites.

The use of unsafe equipment or pipes, for example, copper pans used for cooking, copper dispensers for acid drinks or leadpipes used for soft water.

Fumes from diesel/petrol fork-lift trucks have resulted in contaminated food.

Control of chemical hazards

- Safe use and storage of chemicals on the farm.
- Vehicles used for transporting food should not be used for chemicals. Chemicals should not be transported with food if there is any risk of spillage, leakage or contamination of food.
- Chemicals should be delivered in suitably labelled containers which are fit for purpose.
- Food should only be purchased from reputable suppliers who, for example, guarantee food such as fish has not been obtained from polluted waters. They should also guarantee that food is grown, harvested and transported free from chemical pollution or adulteration.
- Chemicals should always be stored separately from food.
- Food should never be stored in old chemical containers.
- Chemicals should never be stored in old food containers or unlabelled containers, or containers which are not intended for the storage of the specific chemical.
- Chemicals must be diluted and used in accordance with the manufacturer's instructions. Use the right chemical for the job.
- Where required, rinsing following chemical cleaning must be undertaken.
- Only food-grade chemicals should be used if, for example, there is a risk of contaminating food.
- Food should be protected or stored away when cleaning or pest control is being carried out.
- Staff must be trained and effectively supervised to ensure they are using chemicals safely.
- Only food-grade packaging should be used for food to prevent migration of chemicals into food, especially food with a high fat content.
- If food additives are used, the staff involved must be fully trained and effectively supervised to ensure their safe use.
- If there is any risk of contamination of food from fumes, electric vehicles should be used in preference to diesel/petrol, for example, fork-lift trucks.
- Product sampling may be appropriate for large organisations.

In 1999 a major recall of Belgian products, including poultry, pork, beef, eggs, milk, dairy products and other products made using these ingredients, was instigated because of high levels of the carcinogen, dioxin. It is thought that contaminated animal fat used to make animal feedstuff was the source of the problem.

In 2005, Nestlé recalled over 2 million litres of baby milk in Italy, France, Portugal and Spain when traces of Isopropil Thio Xantone were detected. The potentially toxic chemical had leached from the packaging. The milk was packaged in Spain.

Cleaning chemicals

To avoid taint, some cleaning chemicals such as phenols and perfumed soap must not be used in food premises, especially by those handling dairy/fatty foods. All cleaning materials must be kept in properly labelled containers and stored in a manner that obviates any risk of contamination.

ALLERGENIC HAZARDS AND CONTROL MEASURES

The number of people suffering from food allergies is increasing. As well as the increase in prevalence, the proportion of complex, multiple allergy cases is increasing where cross-reaction between two or more allergens causes a problem to the individual. All sectors of the food industry have the same legal and moral obligation to provide safe food to allergy sufferers as they have when providing food for other customers. A true food allergy involves the body's immune system. The difference between food allergy and food intolerance must be clearly understood by the food producer as the consequences can be fatal if those suffering from true food allergies mistakenly consume incorrectly labelled food or food which has been contaminated with an allergen. In April 2011, a teenager in Merseyside with an allergy to nuts died after one bite of chicken purchased from a fish and chip shop, probably because of peanut oil being used. The term 'allergen' is given to the substance, usually a protein, which causes an allergic reaction in a susceptible individual. Food intolerances are usually less severe and do not always involve the immune system. Intolerances may be due to the lack of a particular enzyme, for example lactose intolerance, or as a response to an irritant.

Any allergic reaction, including the most extreme form, anaphylactic shock, occurs because the body's immune system reacts inappropriately in response to the presence of a substance that it wrongly perceives as a threat (the allergen). The result of the reaction causes a series of chemical responses which can cause varying symptoms in an individual, including:

- flushing of the skin;
- swelling of the throat and mouth;
- difficulty in swallowing or speaking due to constriction of the airways;
- abdominal pain, nausea and/or vomiting;
- sudden fall in blood pressure causing weakness and unconsciousness;
- skin rash, hives and urticaria (a severe skin reaction which can last for several weeks);
- severe asthma; and
- the most extreme reaction is anaphylactic shock and if this goes untreated, can cause death.

Food (allergens) labelling

The Food Labelling (Declaration of Allergens) (England) Regulations 2008 require that if any of the following 14 foods are used as an ingredient in pre-packed food, they need to be declared on the food label. This rule covers all European Union countries. The 14 foods are:

- Celery – including celeriac
- Cereals containing gluten – e.g. wheat, barley, rye and oats
- Crustaceans – e.g. prawns and lobster
- Eggs – e.g. mayonnaise, cakes, mousses, pasta, sauces and quiche
- Fish – e.g. anchovies used in salad dressings, sauces, relishes and on pizzas
- Lupin flour
- Milk – e.g. yogurt, cream, cheese, butter, milk powder
- Molluscs – e.g. mussels and squid
- Mustard
- Nuts – e.g. walnuts, hazelnuts, brazil nuts, cashew, pecan, pistachio, macadamia, Queensland nuts and almonds.
- Peanuts
- Sesame seeds
- Soybeans
- Sulphur dioxide and sulphites – (preservatives used in some foods and drinks) at levels above 10mg per kg or 10ml per litre.

Labels also need to give clear information about ingredients made from these listed foods, for example a glaze made from egg. Legislation also covers derivatives of the list of allergens.

With very few exceptions, manufacturers must list all ingredients on food labels of pre-packed food and drink products. The presence of allergenic ingredients, as good practice, may also be displayed separately alongside the list of ingredients as Allergen Advice.

All labelling information must be clearly and prominently displayed. The use of simple terms is preferred, for example, 'milk protein' rather than 'casein'. Where a manufacturer cannot guarantee that products are free from allergens, then it is appropriate to state that the product 'may contain (traces of) X', for example, peanuts, where the product may have been contaminated in the factory.

> **INGREDIENTS**
> **Wheat flour, Sugar, Fat, Syrup, Egg, Malt Extract, Ground Ginger, Raising Agents, Flavouring**

> **CONTAINS**
> **Wheat, Egg**
>
> **MAY CONTAIN**
> **Peanuts**

Caterers should clearly state when describing a menu item that it contains an allergenic ingredient, for example 'strawberry mousse with almond shortcake'. Great care must be taken to ensure that 'hidden' allergenic ingredients are also listed, such as nuts used in a cheesecake base. Caterers must be careful to amend menu descriptions when recipes change, and avoid using the term 'free from' unless careful checks have been made to ensure that this is true. It is good practice to inform customers that if they have a food allergy they can ask staff advice about what dishes contain. There must be specific allergen training for kitchen staff. Waiting staff must clearly communicate to the kitchen staff the dietary requirements of customers who have a food allergy.

Control of allergens

One of the most important controls when dealing with customers who are allergic to certain foods is good communication. The information supplied to caterers on food packaging and directly from manufacturers must be followed through to the point of consumption. For example, if a product has a 'may contain' statement then this information must be used when deciding whether a food is suitable for an allergen sufferer. Assumptions should never be made.

This need for clear understanding and communication will require a good level of competence by those taking food orders and handling and serving food. Managers and supervisors must ensure that all staff are aware of the importance of communicating the correct information to those preparing food and to customers.

The Food Standards Agency has issued guidance on how controls can best be put into place and it is imperative that every business has a system to demonstrate that suitable controls are in place. There are no safe limits for allergen proteins in food so the only effective control is absence.

In addition to using approved suppliers, allergen control should be effective from delivery of food to point of sale in the same way a Food Safety Management System operates. Consideration should be given to controls during the storage, preparation and service of foods.

If a customer asks whether a particular menu item is safe for them as they suffer from an allergy, then strict controls must be in place to prevent cross-contamination when preparing their food. This will require exacting standards when cleaning equipment, the use of separate utensils and cloths, effective handwashing before preparing the allergen-free foods and clear segregation of these foods from any foods containing allergens from storage to service.

Prevention of contamination

Food handlers should be trained in awareness of allergens and the effects of ingesting allergens by sensitive consumers. Training must include prevention methods to avoid cross-contamination by food handlers through, for example, adherence to the correct handwashing and correct cleaning procedures. The ideal approach to avoiding cross-contamination with allergens is to have separate production facilities. This may not always be an option, and procedures must be in place to separate allergen-containing products from those that are allergen-free. These procedures include:

♦ dedicating separate parts of the factory to allergen-free and products containing allergens. The layout of the factory should be such as to avoid cross-over of production lines;

♦ setting up physical barriers to prevent cross-contamination of high-risk products like milk in baby foods from production involving products containing allergenic ingredients;

♦ using dedicated equipment such as scoops, weighing scales, and separate lidded and labelled storage containers. Use of colour-coded equipment should be considered;

♦ organising production runs wherever possible so that allergen-free products are manufactured before products containing allergenic ingredients;

♦ implementing stricter cleaning procedures to remove the minute amounts of allergens that may not be removed by cleaning procedures that are adequate for general hygiene purposes. There must be effective cleaning procedures in place for both production and packing equipment to prevent recontamination of cleaned areas through, for example, top-down cleaning in areas where dry ingredients are handled; and

♦ where possible, establishing dedicated packaging lines to reduce the risk of incorrect labelling. Care must be taken to prevent packaging used for non-allergenic products being used for products containing allergens.

The role of supervision in prevention of contamination

Management must ensure that there is adequate supervision to prevent contamination of food. Food handlers should be supervised, on a daily basis, to ensure that they comply with personal hygiene rules. Supervisors should report to management any defects in premises and equipment that could cause contamination. Unsatisfactory deliveries should be reported to management. Attention should be paid when checking deliveries to ensure that all packaging is intact. Maintenance contractors and other visitors should be supervised so as to ensure that they follow the allergen policy rules and do not expose food to contamination. Supervisors should carry out daily checks to ensure that the rules on preventing contamination and cross-contamination are followed during food processing. A planned programme of audits should be implemented by the supervisor to identify non-compliances with allergen control procedures that could result in contamination. Audit reports should be provided for management. Reports of corrective actions taken should also be provided for management.

6 The storage & temperature control of food

The storage of foods is important to ensure adequate provision throughout the year and to overcome fluctuations in supply. Furthermore, bulk purchasing is normally cheaper and more convenient. However, it is preferable for fresh produce, particularly perishables, to be supplied daily. All suppliers should be approved and deliveries monitored as part of the **HACCP** system.

Correct storage of food is fundamental to the **hygienic** and profitable operation of any food business. Failure to ensure satisfactory conditions of temperature, humidity, **stock rotation** and the integrity of packaging can result in problems of unfit or **spoiled** food but will, at the very least, result in a considerable reduction in **shelf life**. Inadequate temperature control of **high-risk food** is the most common cause of **food poisoning**. The time and temperature of storage, thawing, preparation, processing, cooking and cooling is critical to food safety. Critical limits, target levels and tolerances should be established, controlled and monitored. Control systems will need to take into account:

♦ the nature of the food including a_w, **pH**, **preservatives**, and the initial level and types of **micro-organisms** present;

♦ the proposed shelf life unless intended for immediate consumption;

♦ the methods of packaging and processing;

♦ any further treatment the product is likely to receive, for example, cooking; and

♦ the intended consumers and the potential for abuse by the consumer.

Raw materials

Most raw food of animal origin, shellfish, vegetables and some fruits may be **contaminated** with **pathogenic** micro-organisms and should be considered as potentially **hazardous**. Inadequate cooking/processing or **cleaning** and **cross-contamination** of high-risk foods are common causes of food poisoning.

Food premises must have adequate and suitable storage facilities to keep all raw materials satisfactorily. The quality and bacteriological condition of raw materials has a significant influence on the finished product. Furthermore, unsatisfactory deliveries may introduce problems such as insects, rodents or **mould** into the storage area.

To demonstrate **due diligence** and to ensure that deliveries meet the agreed specification an effective, documented checking system must be implemented. The **inspection** required will depend on the type of product and the condition of other deliveries from the same source. Checks may include quantity, temperature, date code and quality. Damaged or discoloured packaging must be regarded with suspicion and the consignment thoroughly examined by trained staff, preferably before unloading from the delivery vehicle. Leaking cartons, rusty cans and old stock should all be rejected. A documented system detailing reason for rejection should be maintained.

Perishable food must be checked quickly and removed to cold stores, freezers or refrigerators without delay. Unloading of vehicles should take place, as far as practicable, in covered bays screened from adverse weather. Raw food and high-risk, or **ready-to-eat food** should be completely segregated to avoid **risk** of contamination. Non-food items and strong-smelling foods, which may cause taint problems, should normally be delivered separately. Once unloaded, batches of food should be clearly marked to ensure they are used in strict rotation and to identify the date of delivery in the event of subsequent complaints, for example, mould growth.

Raw meat and poultry

Raw meat joints should be stored between –1°C and +1°C, with a relative humidity of approximately 90%. Humidities above 95% encourage unacceptable microbial growth and humidities below 85% result in excessive evaporation and subsequent weight loss. Air speeds of around 0.3 metres per second minimise drying of meat but are only intended to remove heat coming through the insulated wall, or introduced when opening the door. Higher air velocity is required for cooling meat. Only cooled meat should be placed in the refrigerator/cold store. Meat should not touch the wall surface.

Given the correct temperature and humidity the shelf life of meat depends on the initial bacterial loading. For example, meat with a **total viable count** of less than 100 organisms per gram will have a shelf life of at least double that of meat with a count of approximately 1,000,000 organisms per gram. This fact clearly illustrates the need for the hygienic handling of meat in the slaughterhouse. The avoidance of contamination and multiplication during distribution is also important to maintain low counts of micro-organisms. Joints of beef packed in a temperature-controlled atmosphere and stored at –1°C to +1°C should keep for up to a week. Beef usually has a longer shelf life than pork, lamb, poultry and fish. Processed raw meats, offals and such products as sausages have the shortest life.

The unsatisfactory storage of meat.

Eggs

As soon as possible after lay, eggs should be stored in a **clean**, dry place, at a constant temperature below 20°C (ideally between 10°C and 15°C). Temperature fluctuations result in condensation and must be avoided. Eggs should not be stored near heat sources such as fridge motors or in direct sunlight. Eggs must be sold to the final consumer within 21 days of lay. The maximum permissible 'best before date' is 28 days from lay. This means, for example, eggs sold 21 days after lay have to be used by the consumer within seven days. Stock rotation is essential and cracked or dirty eggs should not be sold. After delivery to consumers and caterers, eggs should be stored below 8°C under refrigeration. Large numbers of salmonellae have been isolated from contaminated eggs stored for 21 days above 20°C.

Meat pies, pasties and sausage rolls

These products must be obtained from a reliable source and should preferably be stored under refrigeration. Temperatures of around 7°C, with good air movement, are recommended so that the pastry remains crisp. As these foods are cooked to temperatures as high as 90°C very few **bacteria** survive and, consequently, they remain bacteriologically safe at this higher than normal temperature of refrigeration. However, stock rotation is important and such products should be sold on the day of production or the following day. Pies or pasties to which something has been added after baking, such as jelly, should be stored at or below 5°C. Fluctuations in temperature result in condensation and mould growth.

As these products may be consumed without further cooking they must never be stored with raw meat or vegetables. Strong smelling foods such as cheese may introduce taint or mould problems. Price tickets must not be stuck into pies or any other food. If pies are to be sold hot from retail outlets they must be cooked thoroughly and if stored, maintained above 63°C. Alternatively, pies may be microwaved as required. They must never be rewarmed.

Fruit and vegetables

The quality and shelf life of fresh fruit and vegetables depend on the way in which they are harvested, handled, transported and stored. Deterioration may be physical, physiological, chemical or pathological. Storage conditions should reduce the rates of **respiration** and transpiration (loss of water by evaporation) to ensure the maximum shelf life. Although each fruit and vegetable has its own optimal storage conditions, a general guide is to keep them refrigerated (0°C to 2°C) at a relative humidity of 90%. However, tropical fruits such as pineapples and bananas should be stored around 10°C to 13°C to avoid "chill injury". Rapid turnover and practical difficulties such as lack of separate refrigerators usually results in catering premises storing fruit and vegetables in cool rooms without undue problems.

Care must be taken to avoid warm moist conditions and condensation, which will encourage bacterial **spoilage** and mould growth. Low humidities and excessive ventilation result in **dehydration** and must also be avoided. Fruit should be examined regularly and mouldy items removed to avoid rapid mould spread. Transit wrappings may need to be removed to avoid condensation.

Ice cream

During production and at **ambient temperatures**, ice cream is an ideal food for bacterial growth and must be handled with care. Ice cream should be kept in a clean freezer, preferably by itself, and open ice cream must never be stored with raw products. It should always be kept frozen and if defrosted must be discarded. One tub of a particular variety should be used completely before opening a fresh one and nothing should be placed on top of an open tub. Lids should normally be kept on. The texture of ice cream is more temperature sensitive than other frozen foods and it may be held at −12°C for one week before use.

Clean scoops should be used for serving ice cream and these should be rinsed in clean, running water after each use and wiped dry using disposable paper. After service the scoop must be cleaned, **disinfected**, allowed to dry and stored in a protected place.

Milk and cream

Milk used to be a major source of disease and even now raw or inadequately heat-treated milk continues to cause problems. Milk and cream should be stored under refrigeration (below 5°C) and should be placed in the refrigerator or cold store as soon as received. Imitation cream should also be stored under refrigeration. Raw milk will be labelled untreated and should not be used by any food business. Crates of milk should not be stored below raw meat.

Between 1992 and 1996 there were 20 general outbreaks (600 cases) of food poisoning associated with dairy products. Two outbreaks (32 cases) implicated home-made ice cream and two outbreaks (eight cases) implicated cheese.

Flour and cereals

Flour and cereals should preferably be stored in mobile stainless steel containers. Lids must be tight-fitting. Large stocks of flour kept in original sacks must be stored clear of the ground and free from damp. Condensation may result in mould growth on wet flour and must be prevented. Regular cleaning of containers used for flour storage must not be overlooked. Frequent **inspections**, at least weekly, should be carried out for rodents or insects. Permanent bait points, laid by trained operatives, are recommended.

Canned foods

The risk from canned foods is very small compared with the number produced and the excellent safety record of cans filled in this country will be maintained if:

♦ blown cans are not used;
♦ badly-dented, seam-damaged, holed or rusty cans are not used; and
♦ stock rotation of cans is carried out. Stocks should be marked with the date of delivery to ensure older cans are used first.

Canned goods should be examined regularly and blown or leaking cans must be rejected. Cans from the same batch should not be used until clearance has been received from the manufacturer or the local environmental health department.

The shelf life of canned foods

High-**acid** cans of fruit, such as prunes, rhubarb, tomatoes and strawberries, may blow if kept longer than recommended by the manufacturer. The **acid** nature of these foods enables them to attack the tin and iron of the can, especially at the seams, and hydrogen gas is released causing the can to blow. An unacceptable amount of tin and iron may be present in the food and even if the can is not blown, high levels of these metals, with or without a metallic taint, will render the food unfit for human consumption. Fortunately, new canning techniques and lacquers for these products has reduced this problem and increased their shelf life. However, some imported canned fruit could still be affected.

Some large cans of meat, especially ham, may only have been **pasteurised** and therefore need to be stored under refrigeration. If this is the case, the can should be clearly labelled.

Once the can is opened the contents should be placed in a suitable plastic or stainless steel container, if the food is not for immediate use. If the food is discoloured or has an unusual smell or texture, it must be rejected. The inside of the can should be inspected and if there is any rust or discolouration, the food must not be used.

Wrapping and packaging

Packaging of food is important not only to assist marketing but also to:

♦ prevent chemical, physical and bacteriological contamination;
♦ retain quality and nutritional values;
♦ prolong shelf life; and
♦ provide a water vapour and gas barrier.

Packaging materials must be economic, non-toxic and easy to remove. Chemicals from packaging materials must not leach into the food or expose the food to risk of contamination when opened or removed. Materials must be capable of withstanding the storage conditions to which they could be exposed, for example, freezing. The integrity of seams is particularly important and seams must withstand the pressures, handling and distribution systems that they are likely to experience.

The use of laminates and plastics is increasing whilst the more traditional materials such as wood are declining in popularity. Laminates may consist of several materials including duplex board, polyethylene and aluminium. Plastics include polyethylenes, polypropylene, polystyrene and polyvinyl chloride (PVC). Greaseproof paper or aluminium foil can also be used.

Packaging and wrapping materials must be stored in clean areas where they are not exposed to risk of contamination. Wrapping of food must be carried out under hygienic conditions by staff who observe the same high standards as employees involved in food preparation. Suitable handwashing facilities should be available close to wrapping and packaging areas.

Cling film

Cling film is useful for preventing the dehydration of food and protecting it against contamination (special breathing films are available for raw meats). Under certain conditions, however, it can speed up spoilage and mould growth by trapping moisture against the surface. It is important therefore that:

♦ raw meat or wet food is unwrapped when removed from the refrigerator; and
♦ food wrapped in cling film is not left in bright light or sunlight.

In 1995, the Department of the Environment, Food and Rural Affairs advised that, because of the risk of chemical migration, cling films should not be used where they could melt into food (such as in conventional or microwave ovens), or for wrapping foods with a high fat content (such as cheese, meats with a layer of fat, fried meats, pastry products and cakes with butter icing or chocolate coatings) unless the manufacturer's advice indicated their suitability for this purpose.

Vacuum packing

Vacuum packing is widely used for an increasing number of foods, particularly fresh meat, bacon, poultry, cooked meat and cheese. The use of a vacuum pack for fresh meat was pioneered by the Cryovac Division of W. R. Grace Limited in the USA in the 1950s. (Cryovac is a registered trade mark of W. R. Grace & Co.)

Materials such as nylon/polyethylene laminate, which are used in vacuum packing, prevent the entry of oxygen and moisture thus reducing spoilage of food by bacteria, moulds and rancidity. Furthermore, the food is protected against contamination, excessive drip and weight loss due to dehydration. The storage life of food is prolonged considerably, often being doubled or more. Immediately after opening the vacuum pack the contents should be removed. The slightly darker colour of meat and the acid odour will disappear shortly after being removed.

Vacuum packing will not improve the quality of a poor product and strict observance of **hygiene** and temperature control throughout the operation is essential. After the air is removed, closure may be affected by heat sealing or the application of a metal clip.

Vacuum packs may allow the growth of **anaerobic** food poisoning organisms and if not stored under refrigeration there is a possibility of consuming unspoiled but unsafe products. Cooked meat that is contaminated with food poisoning organisms just prior to vacuum packing is particularly hazardous. The absence of competition from other organisms will, if temperatures permit, enable the rapid growth of these pathogens.

Vacuum packing of fish, especially smoked salmon and trout, is a worrying development as conditions are ideal for the multiplication of *Cl. botulinum* which is commonly isolated from the intestines of these fish. Storage of these products should always be below 3°C.

Care must be taken to avoid puncturing packs, for example, with sharp bones or rough handling. Defective seams commonly result in the loss of pack integrity. However, air-tight vacuum packaging may blow because of the presence of fermentative lactobacilli. Semi-permeable films favour the growth of **aerobic** bacteria, which produce slime and off-flavours. It is advisable to purchase branded vacuum packs from reputable suppliers to avoid receiving low-grade meat of dubious origin. Unmarked packs without "**use-by**" dates should always be regarded with suspicion.

Modified atmosphere packing (MAP)

Modified atmosphere packing is being used increasingly for products such as raw meat and fish, to reduce spoilage rates and maintain a more attractive colour. Gases used include carbon dioxide, nitrogen and oxygen, which must each be at the correct concentration depending on the product. A mixture of gases is injected at sealing. Storage under refrigeration remains essential to retain product quality, safety and shelf life.

Damaged stock

All damaged stock should be segregated and thoroughly examined before use. If there is any doubt regarding the fitness of food it should be discarded, or the local environmental health department may be asked for advice. The practice of some supermarkets of selling damaged packets of food or dented cans is not recommended. In the event of a justified complaint of unfit food the company is unlikely to be able to avail itself of the "due-diligence" defence.

The greenhouse effect

Food, especially high-risk food, should not be stored in windows or in glass display cabinets that are exposed to direct sunlight. The heat within the cabinet will build up in the same way that it does in a greenhouse, with the result that ideal temperatures for bacterial multiplication are provided. The greenhouse effect may even occur in chill cabinets without proper chilled air circulation, and fluorescent tubes may exaggerate the problem.

Storage systems and equipment

Safe food storage and stock rotation are facilitated by the use of systems and associated equipment.

 ♦ *Mobile racks* – wheel-mounted stainless steel shelving on adjustable supports allow free standing storage, shelf spacing to be set for specific stores and easy inspection.
 ♦ *Slotted trays* – available in high-density coloured plastics, frequently used by bakeries for bread deliveries. They enable stacks to be set up to store a variety of different items. They can be dismantled and stacked in space-saving nests when not in use.

♦ *Bins* – bulk dry-foods may be stored in mobile plastic or stainless steel bins and wheeled from the store to the point of use.
♦ *Mobile silos* – as above but larger, with a gravity fed hopper discharge allowing substances such as flour to be stored in safety and transported to the site of use.
♦ *Pallets* – large quantities of bulk goods can be stored on pallets and moved around with fork-lift trucks or hand-operated pallet trucks.

Stock rotation

Satisfactory rotation of stock, to ensure that older food is used first, is essential to avoid spoilage. Stock rotation applies to all types of food. Daily checks should be made on short-life perishable food stored in refrigerators whereas weekly examination of other foods may suffice. Stock that is undisturbed for long periods will encourage **pest** infestations. Good stock rotation has the added advantage of assisting in the maintenance of the correct levels of stock. Remember the rule: **"First in, first out."**

Management of stock rotation systems

Food businesses must have in place documented procedures to ensure that raw materials and food products are used in the correct order and within the stated shelf life. There must be a procedure for accepting deliveries that include checks on 'use by' and 'best before' date labelling. The acceptance procedure must be clearly written so that nominated employees understand what to do regarding, for example, expired 'use by dates' or lack of product traceability and ingredient labelling information. Supervision and instruction will be required to ensure that employees understand and implement the acceptance procedure, and accurately complete delivery and stock rotation records. There must be written and communicated procedures in place to ensure that all food products and raw materials are used within date and that stock rotation procedures, like dot colour codes, are adhered to, and that these items are stored hygienically. Management audits and daily visual checks are required to identify failures in delivery and storage procedures. It is necessary to take corrective action in the event of rejected deliveries and audits that identify failures in stock rotation. For example, a retraining programme may be required in stock rotation procedures. Non-compliances should be recorded following regular supervisory checks on stored products, together with information about completed corrective actions. A management review may be required on the effective operation of delivery and stock rotation procedures.

Codes

Stock rotation has been much easier since the advent of open-date coding but some products do not require a "use-by" date and, in these cases, retailers should adopt their own code to identify the date of delivery. A colour code system is one of the easiest to use; a blue line for Monday, a red line for Tuesday, etc. The practice of selling old stock cheaply is not recommended and it is an offence to sell foods bearing an expired "use-by" date or to change this date (see the food labelling regulations, chapter 15).

Dry-food stores

Rooms used for the storage of fruit and vegetables, dried, canned and bottled foods should be dry (relative humidity of 60 to 65%), cool, well-lit, well-ventilated and large enough to facilitate the tidy packing and rotation of stock. They must be kept clean and spillages should be cleared away promptly. Internal walls should be free of cavities. External walls should be north-facing. Wall surfaces should be smooth and impervious. Joints and cracks harbour dust, prevent efficient cleaning and encourage pest infestations. Floors should be impervious, jointless and capable of being kept clean. Sufficient strength is required to support loads and any vehicles used in the store. The method of cleaning must be considered when selecting finishes. Where practicable, wall/floor joints should be **coved**. Ceilings should be easily cleaned and not encourage condensation, if this is likely to be a problem. Ledges collect dust and should be avoided. Wooden pallets should be replaced, for example, by reinforced plastic pallets, as they allow a build-up of dirt and dust, which provides ideal conditions for mites and insects.

Stores should be rodent- and bird-proof; doors should be provided with metal kick-plates, and airbricks, if present, fitted with wire gauze. Holes around pipes passing through walls should be effectively sealed. As far as possible food should be kept in rodent-proof containers. All goods should be stored clear of the wall and floor to allow cleaning and pest control. Stores should be close to the areas in which it is intended to use the food and also be readily accessible to delivery men, who should not have to pass through food preparation areas.

Natural ventilation will assist in keeping the temperature of the room low, but in the summer, mechanical ventilation and circulation will probably be necessary. The absence of windows will prevent solar heat gain. Temperatures of around 10°C to 15°C should be maintained for the best storage conditions and stores should not be situated next to a source of heat, for example, adjacent to the boiler room.

Shelves should have a non-absorbent, cleansable finish. Tubular mobile racking made of non-corroding metal is recommended. Cupboards should be avoided. Non-food items, including cleaning equipment and chemicals, and strong smelling foods, should not be stored in dry-food stores. Packs of food should be handled carefully to avoid damage. Part-used packs should be adequately resealed to prevent contamination. Alternatively food may be transferred to clean containers with pest-proof lids.

The storage of perishable foods

High-risk perishable foods may be contaminated by pathogenic organisms, which can multiply to dangerous levels without altering the appearance or taste of the food concerned. For this reason all premises should have adequate cooling and cold storage facilities to keep perishable food that is not intended for immediate consumption.

REFRIGERATORS

Refrigeration must be considered as a means of delaying and not preventing food spoilage by bacteria and moulds. Furthermore, although the common food poisoning organisms are incapable of multiplication or **toxin** production below 5°C, there is concern regarding certain **psychrotrophic** pathogens capable of growth below 5°C, including *Yersinia enterocolitica* (1°C), *Listeria monocytogenes* (–1.5°C), *Aeromonas hydrophila* (1°C) and *Clostridium botulinum* type E (3°C). Fortunately, growth and toxin production at temperatures just above 0°C takes several days or weeks and should not usually cause problems during short-term refrigerated storage. The consequences for prolonged refrigerated storage of food, even in vacuum packs, are of more significance. The nearer the refrigerator operates to 1°C the safer it will be.

Siting

Refrigerators should be readily accessible and should not be positioned near any heat source. Ideally they should be in well-ventilated areas away from the direct rays of the sun.

Multi-deck cabinets may be affected by draughts from doorways, high room temperatures and ventilation and heating grills fitted in ceilings, which may result in a significant increase in temperatures. High humidities will eventually result in problems of condensation and sweating. The siting of the unit should allow the cleaning of the surrounding area as well as the cooling coils.

Construction and design

Refrigerators should be constructed to facilitate easy cleaning. Large motors are best positioned outside as they generate heat and collect dust. (This also ensures a good circulation of air.) The inner skin and shelves should be impervious, non-corrosive and easy to clean. The number, position and size of shelving are critical in ensuring the effective distribution of cold air to all parts of multi-deck units. Lighting inside cabinets can raise temperatures and, if used, should be of the cold cathode type. Floors should preferably be jointless, laid to a suitable fall and coved for ease of cleaning. Door seals should be checked regularly as they can become perished and difficult to clean. Large chill stores should be fitted with self-closing doors and protected by air-locks, air-curtains or plastic screens. Storage capacity must be adequate to cope with peak demands. Damage to the external or internal cladding of units, which enables moisture to penetrate the insulation, will reduce the effectiveness of the refrigerator by creating a "warm bridge". Domestic refrigerators are not designed or suitable for most commercial operations.

Defrosting and cleaning

Each unit must have an adequate number of defrost cycles to prevent ice build-up on the **evaporator** coil. This would reduce air flow across, and the surface area of, the coil and result in decreased efficiency and increased temperatures and costs. Assisted defrost systems prevent ice build-up and product warming.

Both exterior, especially door handles, and interiors should be cleaned regularly and internal surfaces of fans disinfected. Base plates and baffle plates should be removed to check for debris such as price tickets and packaging, which can obstruct air flow and block drains in multi-deck units. Drip trays, if present, should be emptied and cleaned.

Cooked and raw food stored on same shelf.
Unsatisfactory shelving.

Door seals on refrigerators
must be kept clean.

Dust on evaporator coils and air ducts must be removed to maintain performance.

After cleaning and disinfection, units should be completely dried and allowed to attain the correct operating temperature, usually 1°C to 4°C, before being reloaded. Stock should be kept in back-up chill stores during cleaning operations.

Food that experiences a significant increase in temperature, above 10°C, due to breakdown or power cut should be destroyed. Regular cleaning and maintenance will improve efficiency and reduce breakdowns.

Operating temperature

To prevent the growth of most pathogens and reduce spoilage, the majority of high-risk foods, including cans of pasteurised ham, should be stored below 5°C. The optimum temperature for multi-use refrigerators is therefore between 1°C and 4°C. Higher temperatures allow greater bacterial activity and also prolong the time taken to reduce the temperature of food placed in the refrigerator, i.e. prolonging the time the food remains in the **danger zone**.

From a food safety perspective the operating temperature of the refrigerator over a 24 hour cycle is much more important than a spot temperature taken once or twice a day. Constant use of the refrigerator, opening the door and stocking with warm food is likely to result in temperatures in excess of 8°C for a short time. However, provided the refrigerator operates throughout the night/early morning below 5°C, pathogenic growth is very unlikely to be a problem. In fact, as spoilage organisms grow faster at lower temperatures, the food is likely to spoil before it becomes unsafe.

The storage of some foods just below freezing results in the formation of large ice crystals and consequential loss of food quality and texture. Fan assisted cooling is recommended, as the circulated cold air maintains uniform temperatures and quickly establishes correct temperatures after the door has been opened.

Cook-chill foods with a maximum shelf life of five days must be kept between 0°C and 3°C to ensure safety and reduce the risk from *Listeria monocytogenes*. It is recommended that raw meat, poultry, fish and raw meat products such as sausages should be stored at −1°C to 1°C to maximise shelf life. Furthermore, regulations originating from EC legislation specify that carcases and cut meat in slaughterhouses and cutting premises should not exceed 7°C, offal 3°C and poultry meat 4°C.

Air velocity

Many refrigerators have a low air velocity, around 0.3 metres per second, to avoid drying the food. However, if reasonable cooling rates are to be achieved a minimum air velocity of around 1.7 metres per second is recommended. This level of air velocity is only likely to be found in blast chillers.

Hot food

Hot food should be cooled rapidly and not placed directly into a refrigerator as this will raise the temperature of food already stored, as well as increasing the ice build-up on the cooling unit. Condensation may also occur on some foods, resulting in an unacceptable drip on to food stored below. However, depending on the amount of food and the capacity of the refrigerator, it may be preferable to place a small amount of food, which has cooled to around 60°C, into a large capacity unit instead of leaving it in a warm place overnight. During the day a fan can be used to cool food prior to storage in the refrigerator.

Contamination

It is essential that precautions are taken to avoid contamination. Raw food must always be kept separate from ready-to-eat food. Ideally two refrigerators should be used, one for raw meat and the storage of food prior to cooking and the other refrigerator to store ready-to-eat food. Each refrigerator should be clearly labelled to indicate its intended use. If only one refrigerator is available, high-risk food must be stored on shelves above raw food. Shelves previously used for raw foods must not be used for ready-to-eat foods without disinfection. Again it is preferable to label shelves according to their intended use. All foods should be adequately covered to prevent drying out, cross-contamination and the absorption of odour.

Unsatisfactory storage in a walk-in refrigerator. Raw meat and cooked meat on the same shelf. Shelving and support corroded and filthy.

Unfit steak and cooked steak stored with raw meat.

Packing and rotation of food

Refrigerators should not be overloaded and they need packing in a manner that allows good air circulation. Food should not be placed directly in front of the cooling unit as this reduces efficiency. Non-perishables should not be stored in a refrigerator as this takes up valuable space. Good stock rotation is essential to avoid the spoilage of foods so daily checks should be made to remove out-of-date stock.

Staff responsibilities

Staff should be given clear instructions on how to use the refrigerator and ensure that the door is opened as little, and for as short a time, as possible. Acid foods should not be stored in opened cans within the refrigerator because of the acid attack on the internal surface of the can. The temperature of the refrigerator should be checked regularly throughout the day and recorded at least twice a day. Spillages should be cleared up immediately.

The shelf life of perishable food under refrigeration

The storage life varies considerably depending on the operating temperature of the refrigerator and the specific perishable food. For example, at 1°C most vegetables will keep for at least two weeks, butter for two months and fresh beef up to a week. A reduction in the initial numbers of bacteria on food can, provided it is stored correctly, increase its shelf life significantly.

Chilled display cabinets

Display cabinets should comply with BS 3053. Cabinets should be loaded correctly so that cold air inlets are not obstructed and load lines are not exceeded. Only chilled products should be loaded.

Radiant heat can have a significant effect on food stored in chilled cabinets, particularly on the upper shelves. Air temperatures may vary from 1.5°C at the back to 6.5°C at the front, and the temperature of such product as cartons of yogurt stored at the front of such units may vary from between 7°C and 11°C. Cabinets should be sited away from heating units, high-intensity lights and out of direct sunlight.

Monitoring temperatures

Cabinet thermometers rarely reflect product temperature accurately. Refrigerator temperatures should be checked using an accurate digital tip sensitive thermistor or an electronic thermocouple. Bare wire thermocouples provide a quick response and can also be used for testing between packs. **Probe** diameters should be 15mm or less and have a grounded junction at the probe point. Indicating or recording thermometers are essential and premises with a large number of units will need automatic monitoring equipment and alarms to warn of unacceptable temperatures. Bimetallic coil thermometers are inaccurate and often difficult to use.

Thermometers will need calibrating, as often as recommended by the manufacturer and always when involved with court proceedings and/or due-diligence defences. Calibration can be undertaken in slush ice and boiling water, or by electronic calibration devices. From a food safety perspective accuracy for measuring cooking temperatures is more important than refrigeration temperatures. For example a 1.5°C error can double the time necessary to destroy salmonella and make food safe. The salmonella kill takes 52 seconds at 65.5°C and 104 seconds at 64°C. (Dr P. Snyder Jr.)

The Food Law Code of Practice suggests a three stage approach to determining compliance with statutory food temperatures:

♦ an examination of daily records of air temperature monitoring at the premises;
♦ if records are unsatisfactory then non-destructive testing, between packs, should be carried out; and
♦ if concern remains then probing of the food should be undertaken.

The correlation between air and product temperature can be obtained by pre-chilling a probe thermometer (leave it in a refrigerator for five minutes), taking the product temperature, after at least 24 hours storage, then checking the unit's air temperature.

Each section in a long, refrigerated cabinet should be checked for defective fans and it should be noted that multi-deck cabinets vary by up to 2°C with the cold air being at the top. Variations of 2°C can also occur due to the **compressor** cutting in and out. Temperatures may be raised slightly during defrost and this can be checked as any highly polished surfaces are usually misted up. **"Air on" temperatures** are the most reliable indicator of performance as this is the warmer air at the return air vent. (**"Air off"** refers to the cold air leaving the evaporator coil where it enters the cabinet.)

Temperature monitoring should be recorded at least twice a day, preferably first thing in the morning, and at the end of the day. Accurate records of in-house checks should be retained and available for enforcement officers. They will be very useful to establish a **due-diligence** defence in the event of complaint.

Transportation of fresh lettuce that has to be kept within a set temperature band. The loggers are being used to ensure that this happens and have had their alarms set in order to highlight any discrepancies outside these limits. In the first picture you are also able to see the information being downloaded in situ using a palm unit. (Courtesy of Gemini Data Loggers (UK) Ltd.)

Infrared thermometers

Infrared thermometers, which work by measuring the amount of radiant energy, are assuming increasing importance for monitoring food temperatures. Products can be scanned very rapidly and any identified problems can be checked immediately with a digital thermometer. Additional advantages include the fact that it is non-destructive testing and there is no risk of cross-contamination. It is particularly useful for scanning retail cabinets, frozen food, deliveries and despatch as large consignments can be checked for hot spots.

Although simple to use, staff require training to ensure accuracy of measurement. The object to be measured needs to fill the field of view, or the reading will be an average of the object and its surroundings. Infrared is unsuitable for measuring temperatures of foods packaged in reflective foil unless a matt black spot is painted on the surface. Furthermore, care must be taken because the emissivity of surfaces, for example, packaging and food varies. It is inappropriate to use for checking centre temperatures during cooking, thawing or cooling as only the surface temperature is measured. Infrared thermometers may also be sensitive to the surrounding air temperature, for example, they can be inaccurate up to 6°C for around 15 minutes in a refrigerator. After this time they should come to equalibrium with the case.

Temperature/data loggers

Data loggers and printers will provide a variety of useful information about refrigerated storage including current temperature, maximum, minimum and trends of temperature over a specified period. Should temperatures rise above a predetermined level they can also trigger an alarm. Loggers may be preferable to routine manual recording of temperatures.

The selection of effective refrigeration units

When purchasing refrigeration units for commercial use, it is important to consider a whole range of factors apart from the obvious one of capacity. Choice must not be based solely on price, and units built for domestic use are unlikely to have the life or qualities that could be expected from a refrigerator purpose-built for commercial organisations. When selecting a unit, regard must be had to the following:

◆ *Storage temperatures* – units must be capable of maintaining satisfactory storage temperatures in the high ambient temperatures of commercial kitchens. Some busy kitchens, with inadequate ventilation, have been recorded as high as 43°C. Some units may need to operate at 10°C, for example, if used for wine storage, or others at temperatures of –1°C to 1°C, for example, for the storage of fresh meat or fish. Fan assisted cooling is essential to circulate cold air throughout the storage compartment and maintain uniform temperatures. After opening and closing the door the correct temperature will be quickly re-established.

♦ *Construction* – door(s) and floor should be stainless steel to provide the greatest resistance to impact damage. Heat-reflecting aluminium sides and interior surfaces are often used to save energy. White painted finishes are prone to chipping, cracking and rusting. Plastic liners are easily damaged.

♦ *Automatic defrost* – ensures that the coil remains free of insulating ice and keeps down running cost. Staff do not have to remember to defrost the unit on a regular basis. Air temperatures of units should not rise above 10°C when defrosting.

♦ *Thermometers* – all units should be fitted with an indicating or recording thermometer positioned to show the temperature of the warmest part of the unit. Thermometers should be located externally and should be easily readable with the door(s) closed. It is also useful if there is a light that indicates when the unit is on automatic defrost.

♦ *Fittings* – a comprehensive choice of fittings is available including: adjustable, nylon-coated, wire shelves; gastronome pans; locks; meat rails and fish drawers.

♦ *Labour saving options* – an increasing number of modifications are being provided to save staff time and at the same time increase safety, for example:

  ♦ pass-through cabinets, which reduce staff fatigue and prevent congestion between the kitchen and the servery;

  ♦ roll-in cabinets, which enable fully-loaded trolleys to be wheeled directly into storage so reducing handling;

  ♦ heavy-duty drawers, which are used to minimise stooping and reaching;

  ♦ door opening foot pedals, which leave hands free for carrying;

  ♦ glass doors, which enable stock checks without opening doors; and

  ♦ counter models, which can be sited under workbenches so reducing walking and minimising the time high-risk food is kept at ambient temperatures.

Cooking

Cooking is a form of **preservation** but is essentially used to make food more palatable and safe for immediate consumption. Temperatures achieved during cooking are usually sufficient to ensure an effective reduction, or the elimination, of **vegetative pathogens**, although some preformed **toxins** and **spores** may be unaffected. In some cases, cooking activates spores and a significant multiplication of **vegetative bacteria** may occur during subsequent cooling. Internal temperatures of 75°C should usually be achieved to ensure bacteriological safety, although heating food to a lower temperature for longer periods of time may be equally as effective. Faecal streptococci may survive these temperatures, especially in cooked ham.

The **core temperature** of cooked meat should be checked regularly with an accurate thermometer, which is always disinfected before use. The external surface of, for example, a joint may give the appearance of being thoroughly cooked but closer examination often reveals unacceptable centre temperatures. Rare beef will always have received a terminal centre cooking temperature of less than 62°C (at 62°C/63°C the myoglobin changes from red to brown/grey due to the **denaturing** of the albumen, which loses its transparency) and this may cause problems if pathogenic contamination is introduced to the centre of rolled joints during boning.

Particular care must be exercised when using the probe thermometer to ensure you are measuring the lowest temperature of food achieved through cooking. Food cooked in microwave ovens is notorious for cold spots. Food in microwave ovens should be fully enclosed in a suitable container and periodically stirred or rotated to ensure even heat distribution. After cooking food should be left for two minutes to achieve even temperature distribution.

Dr Brad Berry, USA advised that variations of up to 19°C were measured in cross sections of beefburgers cooked to 71°C. Burgers cooked from frozen had the greatest variations and were pink after cooking whereas thawed patties were brown. Slow cooking at low grill temperatures is usually safer.

Some products such as cakes and pork pies may be cooked satisfactorily but are exposed to risk because of the subsequent addition of contaminated cream or gelatin. Storage of these products must always be under refrigeration.

An Evolution logging food thermometer and a flexible type T thermocouple probe being used to check the temperature of cooked food as it emerges from a travelling oven. (Courtesy of Comark Ltd.)

Safe cooking temperatures in the USA are based on a log 7 reduction of salmonella, for example 1.6 seconds at 75°C, 12.5 seconds at 70°C or 95 seconds at 65°C. The United States Department of Agriculture and the US Food and Drug Administration recommend the following minimum temperatures:

Minced beef, lamb and pork	**71°C**
Minced chicken and turkey	**74°C**
Beef and lamb roasts and steaks (rare)	**63°C**
Beef and lamb roasts, pork and steaks (medium)	**71°C**
Whole poultry	**82°C**

60°C for 13 minutes also gives a log 7 reduction of salmonella. However, salmonella can triple in resistance to kill if it is held for some time around 43°C. This would mean that a temperature of 60°C for 39 minutes would be required to give the same salmonella kill. Potential increase in resistance of organisms after cooking may also be a reason for ensuring reheating temperatures of cooked food should be higher.

The colour of meat should not be relied on as a definite indicator that safe cooking temperatures have been achieved. Beefburgers can turn brown after cooking to 57°C or may still be pink after cooking to 74°C (Dr P. Snyder Jr.).

Generally speaking the safest cooking methods include roasting for long periods, casseroles or cooking thin slices under a hot grill or in a frying pan. If stir frying it is important to cut any meat into small cubes.

Infrared thermometer showing incorrect temperature.

Slow cooking

Cooking of foods at lower temperatures for prolonged periods can be dangerous if the food is between 20°C and 50°C for between ten and 15 hours. This would allow production of heat resistant toxins by *S. aureus* or *B. cereus*, which would not be destroyed by the final temperatures of cooking of around 65°C to 75°C.

Cooling of hot food

Rapid cooling of cooked foods to be chilled or frozen is extremely important. Bacteria may survive cooking as spores or even in the vegetative state and there is always a risk of contamination after cooking. By whatever **route** bacteria enter the food it is essential that their multiplication during cooling is minimised. It is recommended that food is cooled below 10°C in less than 1.5 hours and blast chillers are available that can achieve this specification, but only for relatively thin portions of food. Furthermore, cooling units must be cleaned regularly to avoid problems with mould growth.

Cooling methods vary depending on the type of food being cooled. They include:

♦ use of shallow containers, 2.5cm maximum recommended depth of food;
♦ using smaller or thinner portions;
♦ blast chillers;
♦ ice baths, increase cooling cooling rate by three to five times. Little difference in rates between metal and plastic;
♦ stirring food;
♦ using fans, food should be loosely covered and supported, for example, on racks, as about 75% of heat is extracted from the bottom of the pan;
♦ adding ice as an ingredient;
♦ cold water sprayers, for example, manufactured joints;
♦ cold running water, for example, rice, potatoes and pasta; and
♦ large walk-in refrigerators when there is no risk of a temperature rise of any other food in the unit. This should only be used as a last resort but is preferable to, for example, leaving food out in a warm room overnight.

During cooling, food should be loosely covered or protected from contamination to facilitate heat transfer from the food surface. If the joint is sliced or hot liquids drained off into shallow containers to assist cooling, extreme caution is necessary to avoid the risk of introducing pathogenic bacteria such as salmonella. Recently cooked food is an ideal medium for the growth of pathogens because there are few competing organisms.

Unfortunately, it is very difficult to cool large quantities of thick sauces and even relatively small joints of meat (or poultry) within the recommended times. A study undertaken by the AFRC Institute of Food Research, Langford, Bristol found that:

Rolled Joints	wt (kg)	Approximate Cooling time (min) 70°C to 10°C (50°C to 10°C)		
		Convection	Immersion	Pressure vacuum
Beef silverside	2.7	291(237)	186(153)	39(36)
Beef forequarter	2.7	304(261)	216(185)	24(21)
Boneless turkey	5.9–6.5	396(325)	335(275)	16(13)

Convection cooling was in air at 0°C and 1.2ms[1].
Immersion cooling was in water at 0°C.

A study by Dr Peter Snyder Jr. demonstrated that it took 6.5 hours for Alfredo cream sauce 2.5cm deep in a 30cm x 50cm stainless steel dish to cool from 60°C to just above 5°C in a refrigerator operating at 5°C with an air flow of around 0.25 metres per second. Sauce that was 5cm deep would take up to 14 hours. The same amount of sauce in a 10cm diameter jar would have taken ten hours to cool to 5°C.

As can be seen from these studies most catering/retail premises will not be able to achieve anywhere near the recommended cooling rate of below 10°C in 1.5 hours unless they have a very expensive blast chiller and use small joints.

The danger of slow cooling is the **germination** of spores activated during cooking and the multiplication and/or toxin production of the vegetative bacteria. *Clostridium perfringens* is the pathogen of most concern. However, a study by Juneja *et al.* demonstrated that only 1 log multiplication of *Clostridium perfringens* occurred when a cooked hamburger was cooled continually from 55°C to 7°C over 15 hours.

Forced cooling does not need to start immediately food is removed from the oven. The highest temperature from the multiplication of known pathogenic bacteria is 52°C (*Clostridium perfringens*). Food can be cooled for around 1.5 hours using, for example, a fan and then placed in a large capacity refrigerator operating at around 5°C.

Blast chillers

To avoid the formation of large ice crystals and consequential loss of quality, it is important that chilled foods do not freeze during the chilling process. Usually, chilled air at 2°C to −7°C is circulated around the product but some blast chillers use the vapour from liquid nitrogen and solid carbon dioxide.

Chillers are intended for the rapid removal of heat and not for the storage of food that is already chilled. Consequently, they operate at air velocities well in excess of those used in refrigerators, for example, 5ms[1].

Distribution of high-risk food

Vehicles used for the distribution of high-risk food must always be insulated and preferably refrigerated, even for short journeys. Insulation of the roof and floor is just as important as the insulation of the walls. Properly located thermometers should be fitted to all vehicles. The maximum temperature will be recorded by a sensor fitted in the returned air system and the minimum temperature can be measured near the outlet of the evaporators.

Refrigerated vehicles are designed to maintain temperatures of chilled or frozen food and must not be loaded with warm food. Vehicles should be precooled prior to loading. The refrigeration unit should be switched off whilst the doors are open to avoid icing-up of the cooling units. During loading or unloading breaks, the doors must be closed and the unit switched on. Loading must be carried out quickly to avoid unacceptable temperature rises.

Vehicles must be maintained in a clean and tidy condition. Raw food should never be transported with high-risk food unless they are completely segregated to avoid any risk of contamination. Stacking of vehicles should facilitate sufficient air circulation around the food.

Deliveries of high-risk foods should be in refrigerated vehicles.

Deliveries of high-risk food

The temperature of food should be checked on arrival. Food requiring refrigerated storage should be rejected if above 8°C and frozen food rejected if above −12°C. Deliveries must be placed in refrigerated storage as quickly as possible to avoid temperatures exceeding the rejection temperatures. The Quick-frozen Foodstuffs Regulations 1990 require quick frozen food to be delivered below −15°C.

THE STORAGE OF FROZEN FOOD

At temperatures of around −40°C, most frozen food should keep for several years without noticeable deterioration. However, most domestic and retail freezers operate at −18°C and at this temperature a gradual loss of flavour and a toughening of texture occurs. Above −10°C spoilage organisms, especially **osmophilic** yeasts, moulds and **halophilic** bacteria, commence growth and together with biochemical reactions cause spoilage problems including souring, putrefaction and rancidity. As the lowest recorded temperature for the growth of a pathogen, *L. monocytogenes,* is −1.5°C, food stored below this temperature should not become a health problem.

Spores and significant numbers of pathogenic bacteria are usually able to withstand freezing and prolonged frozen storage. After a suitable lag phase, survivors will commence multiplication on thawing. Strict precautions must therefore be taken in the manufacture of frozen foods to ensure the absence of pathogens. The storage life of frozen food depends on the initial number of micro-organisms, the final storage temperature and the temperatures, and times, of distribution and manufacture. Short periods at a temperature of approximately −15°C will have little effect on quality or shelf life.

The manufacturing temperature of frozen food is usually −23°C or below. Commercial cold stores are usually operated at an air temperature of between −25°C and −30°C.

The quality of frozen food will be affected if:
♦ food is frozen too slowly or not to a low enough temperature;
♦ there is a breakdown in the cold store, which results in a significant temperature rise.

Cold stores should always be fitted with temperature recording charts so that fluctuations in temperature, and times, are accurately recorded;
♦ distribution vehicles are incapable of maintaining temperatures of −18°C. Problems may occur if there are many small delivery points necessitating the opening of doors a large number of times;

Freezers must be defrosted regularly to avoid ice building up.

Condensation and mould in an ice-making machine.

Ice build-up in a machine room freezer.

Poor stacking and stock control.

A well organised cold store.

♦ there are excessive delays in loading or unloading that result in frozen food being left at ambient temperatures for considerable periods of time; and
♦ storage facilities at retail or catering outlets are inadequate.

All frozen food should be coded to enable the recall of suspect batches that have escaped manufacturing controls.

The storage of frozen food at retail premises

All cabinets used for the storage and display of frozen foods should comply with BS 3053: 1983. To ensure that customers receive the highest quality of frozen food, managers must:
♦ only use reputable suppliers;
♦ reject frozen food deliveries above −12°C, or −15°C for quick frozen foods, or which show signs of thawing or having been refrozen, for example, packs of peas that have welded solid;

♦ not allow frozen food to remain at ambient temperatures for longer than 15 minutes. Food will, of necessity, be at ambient temperatures during unloading of deliveries and stocking display units from back-up stores;

♦ not use display freezers for freezing fresh food, as they are only capable of maintaining the temperature of food that is already frozen;

♦ ensure that display units are not filled above the **load-line**;

♦ carry out regular inspections of freezers and check temperatures at least daily but preferably more frequently. Electronic probe thermometers should be used to ensure the accuracy of the indicating thermometers, which should be fitted to all units in an easily readable position;

♦ ensure that back-up stores are fitted with strip-curtains or air blowers and the doors are opened as little as possible to avoid unacceptable fluctuations of temperature. Ice build-up on the walls or floor of units must not be allowed;

♦ implement effective systems of stock control and stock rotation. It is advisable to code food on delivery to assist rotation; and

♦ ensure that food is not mishandled. Damage to packaging may result in loss of product, contamination and **freezer burn**. For similar reasons packaging, designed to protect frozen food, must not be removed. Stable air temperatures are important as warm air will result in a fall in vapour pressure and the **sublimation** of water vapour from the food to restore the balance. Dehydration of the product (freezer burn) results in a pale discoloured food surface, rather like balsa wood, that cannot be restored.

Storage times

All food should be used within the time recommended by the manufacturer. However, a general guide for food kept at −18°C is:

	Months
Vegetables, fruit, most meat	up to 12
Pork, sausages, offal, fatty fish, butter and soft cheeses	up to 6

Salad vegetables, non-homogenised milk, single cream, eggs and bananas should not be frozen. Cream can be whipped and stabilised to overcome the separation in desserts.

The star marking system is used to indicate the temperature and storage times of food in a frozen storage compartment.

✲	not above −6°C (one week)
✲✲	not above −12°C (one month)
✲✲✲	not above −18°C (three months)
✳✲✲✲	−18°C to −25°C (three months or longer and is capable of freezing fresh food)

The star marking system for frozen food compartments.

Freezing and refreezing

Freezing of food will not improve its quality. The slow freezing of food in domestic freezers results in the formation of large ice crystals, which rupture cells, leading to a slight deterioration in quality, due to changes in the composition of proteins in the presence of enzymes. This deterioration is much more noticeable if food is thawed and refrozen, apart from the obvious dangers if the thawed food is maintained above 8°C for a considerable time. Large ice crystals are particularly noticeable in ice cream that has been refrozen. However, food that has been frozen, thawed and thoroughly cooked may be refrozen quite safely, although flavour and texture will be altered and nutritional value lowered.

Effect of fluctuating temperatures

Clear plastic packaging of food may act as a greenhouse and the radiant heat from fluorescent tubes and air conditioning may increase the temperature of frozen food significantly. Fluctuations from –3°C to –18°C have been observed with the lower temperatures only being achieved during the night when heat sources have been switched off.

The presence of ice in packets of frozen food usually indicates fluctuating temperatures have allowed water to evaporate from the product and subsequently freeze. Individually quick frozen products, such as peas, weld together in a solid mass if exposed to fluctuating temperatures.

Freezer breakdown

If the freezer breaks down or food becomes thawed, for example, due to a power failure, the food may occasionally be treated as fresh. In certain circumstances the food may be cooked and refrozen. If the food has a solid core of ice it may be safe to refreeze without cooking. If in doubt advice should be obtained from the local environmental health department.

In the event of breakdown, the lid of the freezer should be left closed and the unit covered in newspapers and blankets until repaired. Food may remain frozen for at least two days in a well-stocked, well-insulated freezer.

Multichannel data logger monitoring product temperatures inside a freezer. The logger has been mounted on the freezer door, with the probe inside, attached to a food item. The logger can be removed at required intervals for downloading on to a computer.
(Courtesy of Comark Ltd.)

Thawing of frozen food

Most food taken from the freezer can be cooked immediately but poultry, joints of meat and other large items must be completely thawed before cooking. The manufacturer's instructions should always be followed. If food is not completely thawed, ice is likely to be present at the centre and the heat from subsequent cooking will be used to melt the ice and not to raise the internal temperature above that required to destroy pathogens.

However, thawing of food poses several problems and inadequate thawing of poultry frequently results in undercooking and subsequent food poisoning. Thawing at room temperatures (21°C to 25°C) for around 12 hours results in a small multiplication of spoilage bacteria on the surface of food. Thawing in a small refrigerator can be extremely hazardous. A 20lb turkey will take several days to thaw and the surfaces of the refrigerator, and ready-to-eat food, may become contaminated with thawed liquid containing pathogenic bacteria. Furthermore, the temperature at which the refrigerator is operating has a significant effect on thawing times. Work carried out by Mr T.C. Grey at the Bristol AFRC Institute of Food Research showed that a 1.1kg broiler took around eight hours at 20°C, 11 hours at 15°C, 13 hours at 10°C, 40 hours at 5°C and 70 hours at 1°C for the temperature to go above 0°C in the deep thigh. Birds left in polythene bags took longer especially at the colder temperatures. It is therefore essential for advice regarding thawing times under refrigeration to state actual temperatures. Thawing of frozen poultry is best carried out at 10°C to 15°C in an area entirely separate from other foods, in a thawing cabinet, or at room temperature (preferably at less than 21°C).

In 1968 a study by Klose, *et al.* concluded that it is satisfactory to thaw turkeys at room temperatures at or below 21°C. It takes a 10kg turkey 15 hours or less to get to 0°C while the surface temperature rises to 12°C or less. During this time spoilage organisms may multiply by four times but no detectable multiplication of salmonella occurs. In 1999, Jiménez, *et al.*, confirmed that chickens weighing over 3kg thawed to an internal temperature of 5°C within the breast in ten hours at room temperature. There was no increase in inoculated *Salmonella* Hadar or spoilage organisms during this time.

THAWING AND COOKING TIMES OF FROZEN POULTRY

Oven ready weight kg (lbs)	Approx. thawing time at room temp (21°C) (hours)	Cooking time at 180C/350F Gas 4* (in foil) (hours)
2.25 (5)	15	2.5
4.5 (10)	18	3.5
6.75 (15)	24	4.75
9.0 (20)	30	5.75

*These are minimum times. The bird is cooked when the juices run clear, and should be checked with a disinfected probe thermometer.

Food thaws slowly because of the low thermal diffusivity of food at 0°C. As soon as the surface thaws it acts as an insulating layer and this reduces the rate of heat flow into the product. Thawing in refrigerators is even slower because of the small temperature difference between the refrigerator operating at 1°C to 4°C and frozen food. Consequently, it takes a considerable time to provide the latent heat of thawing, i.e. the heat necessary to change ice to water.

Hot water and a wire pad wrongly used for the rapid defrosting of prawns.

Several techniques have been suggested for thawing food and some of these have been used commercially. Electrical methods of thawing, namely dielectric, microwave and resistive, are not affected by the low thermal diffusivity of food but, unfortunately, may give rise to an effect known as runaway heating: thawing does not occur evenly throughout the frozen food and areas that thaw absorb energy preferentially to areas that remain frozen. This results in some parts of the food cooking before the whole mass of food is thawed.

Rules for thawing and cooking frozen poultry
♦ Segregate from high-risk food.
♦ Thaw completely in a cool room at less than 15°C, in a thawing cabinet, or at room temperature (less than 25°C). Cold running water and refrigerators may be used but cross-contamination is likely. Furthermore, thawing may not be complete in the refrigerator, which is the major hazard. Poultry will be ready for cooking when the body is pliable, the legs are flexible and the body cavity is free from ice crystals.
♦ Remove giblets (handle with care because of risk of cross-contamination).
♦ Do not wash the birds as you will contaminate the sink, taps, dishcloth and adjacent work surfaces, possibly with campylobacter, salmonella, *E. coli* O157 or *Clostridium perfringens*.
♦ Once thawed cook immediately, or keep in the refrigerator and cook within 24 hours.
♦ Cook thoroughly and cook the stuffing separately.
♦ All utensils and surfaces used for the preparation of raw meat and poultry should be thoroughly cleaned and disinfected before being used for high-risk food. It is preferable to use separate work surfaces.
♦ Eat immediately after cooking or, if the bird is to be carved cold, cool it quickly and store in the refrigerator. As with all meats **refrigerated storage is essential within 1.5 hours.**
♦ Avoid handling the cooked bird unnecessarily.

In the USA it is suggested that frozen poultry can be safely cooked without thawing - cooking times are increased by around 50%.

COOK-CHILL

Cook-chill is the name given to a catering system in which food is thoroughly cooked and then chilled rapidly in a blast chiller to a temperature of 3°C or below within 1.5 hours. The food is stored between 0°C and 3°C until required for reheating. In mass catering, some form of cooking and chilling is often essential. There is no other way of bringing together all the components of a meal simultaneously without a disproportionately large labour force and an excessive cooking equipment provision. As such the chilling of cooked food is not a completely new concept. The rudiments are practised by virtually every large catering establishment. Sometimes, the regime is as basic as "chilling" the food to ambient in a cool part of the kitchen, but in most operations there tends to be an initial prechilling at ambient followed by retention in a cold store or refrigerated cabinet. Such uncontrolled practices have significantly contributed to a number of food poisoning cases in the UK.

The formalisation of cook-chill as a specific form of catering has, in this context, done nothing more than introduce specialist equipment for chilling and reheating, enabling that which was already practised to be undertaken safely and more efficiently. Large-scale schemes are, however, more than just cook-chill. To meet the costs of re-equipping with expensive equipment, a number of operations have centralised production in a single kitchen, known as a central production unit (CPU). The most cost-effective results are achieved using large-scale equipment such as bratt pans, tilting kettles, large steamers, computer controlled fast fryers and convection ovens. A major distribution system is then organised to get the food to the former producing kitchens, now known as end kitchens, where it is reheated.

The storage of cook-chill meals.

There are usually eight stages in a cook-chill system:
- bulk storage;
- preparation;
- cooking;
- portioning, packaging and labelling;
- blast chilling;
- storage at or below 3°C;
- distribution at or below 3°C; and
- reheating (regeneration) and serving.

With the introduction of cook-chill schemes there have been, coincidentally, and necessarily in respect of centralisation, developments in production aimed at systemising and standardising the catering process. The fundamental nature of these operations is that they have more in common with food processing than catering. However, there are significant differences. Batch size tends to be smaller than would be handled in food processing and the menu is considerably more varied. A key difference, however, is that the CPU can rarely, if ever, cook all the food used in a scheme. Anything up to 60% of total consumption may simply pass through after being portioned and packed. The CPU, therefore, as well as being a manufacturing plant is also a distribution centre, often handling a high proportion of precooked foods. These high-risk foods must be integrated into the mainstream production line. Composite foods such as salads and sandwiches may also require integration. In effect, the CPU is two separate operations under one roof, combining to form a single operation at the end. This mixing of functions has a far-reaching effect on the layout. The simple "dirty in one end – clean out the other" flow, favoured in operations as diverse as food factories and sterile supply units, cannot usually be achieved. A far more sophisticated flow and layout is required.

The responsibility of the designer is even greater than for conventional kitchens. The operations heavily influence the design requirements, but the design controls the operation

REFRIGERATION FOR COOK-CHILL

to an even greater degree. The designer should seek to impose a specific regime and set methods of working to ensure a systemised operation. The aims are to ensure that the operation works in the most efficient and safe way and to prevent it working in any other way.

The following benefits are claimed for the cook-chill system:

♦ cost-effectiveness – savings are possible because:
  ♦ of centralisation and better utilisation of equipment;
  ♦ centralised purchasing and accurate portion control results in less wastage;
  ♦ careful design and planning can reduce energy consumption;
  ♦ less floor space is required;
  ♦ fewer staff are required in both the CPU and satellite kitchens; and
  ♦ a reduction in overtime. Careful planning results in a steady workload instead of troughs and peaks throughout the day;
♦ better staff conditions and less work in unsociable hours. Staff turnover is usually reduced;
♦ flexibility – orders for meals can be accepted at much shorter notice; and
♦ improved quality and palatability compared with meals kept hot, above 63°C, for long periods. Complaints of dried-up and overcooked food should not occur. Meals are also more consistent.

The safety of cook-chill

Because of the emphasis on strict temperature control throughout the system and the provision of recording thermometers on all units, a properly controlled cook-chill system is safer than most conventional systems of mass catering. Furthermore, as staff are not working under immense pressure for short periods of time, there is less rushing about and mistakes are less likely. However, the reduction in risk tends to be offset, at least on a statistical basis, by the larger scale of production. Where more meals are produced, a unit has to be safer than a smaller operation, just to maintain the same statistical risk of food poisoning. There is also the essential matter of extended shelf life: foods to be consumed some days after cooking have obviously to be at a higher standard than food produced for immediate consumption. The general approximation that cooking kills germs, which governs conventional catering, does not apply. The cooking process is seen as a reducing factor only. Where initial bacterial loading of the raw product is too high, the cook-chill process cannot produce food at an acceptable standard, no matter how well it operates or how hygienic it is. Raw produce standard assumes a much greater importance.

Spores of *B. cereus* and *C. botulinum*, will not be destroyed during cooking. As some strains of *B. cereus* can grow below 8°C and some strains of *C. botulinum* can produce toxin under refrigeration, strict attention to cooling, storage temperatures and shelf life is essential. The potential of the low temperature pathogens such as *Yersinia enterocolitica* and *Listeria monocytogenes* to cause problems must not be overlooked, notwithstanding that it appears that multiplication and toxin production over a five day period is insignificant at temperatures below 3°C. Furthermore, most low temperature pathogens should be destroyed during the reheating process.

In order to ensure the safety of cook-chill the following rules should be observed:

♦ all raw materials should be of good microbiological quality. Purchasing contracts should include product specifications and suppliers should be monitored to ensure compliance. Raw products should be stored at appropriate temperature and humidities, which are monitored;

♦ cross-contamination must be avoided; the preparation of raw materials must be in areas physically separated from cooking and post-cooking areas. Personnel handling raw foods should be confined to the raw material area. Separately identifiable equipment should be used for raw products;

♦ controlled thawing equipment is required if frozen raw materials are used;

♦ the highest standards of hygiene, especially **personal hygiene**, must be observed throughout all stages of preparation, cooking, storage and reheating. Staff will require additional training;

♦ immediately prior to cooking, excess prepared food must be held below 10°C;

♦ to ensure the destruction of *Listeria monocytogenes,* food should be cooked to a temperature above 70°C for not less than two minutes, at the slowest heating point (checks should be made with a probe thermometer). Recording thermometers should also be used;

♦ food should be portioned and chilled to below 3°C within two hours of cooking. Chillers must be capable of reducing the temperature of a 50mm layer of food from 70°C to 3°C in not more than 90 minutes when fully loaded. Automatic controls are required including an accurate ($\pm$0.5°C) indicating thermometer and temperature recorder. Product depth during chilling should not exceed 50mm and may need to be reduced to achieve chilling specification. Joints of meat should not exceed 2kg and 100mm in thickness. Uniform shapes of joint should be used. Handling of food should be minimised and the use of disposable gloves does not remove the need for frequent handwashing;

◆ reusable lidded containers, capable of being cleaned and disinfected, or disposable containers may be used for cooked food portions. (Use of lids during chilling reduces dehydration but slows down chilling.) Containers should be date marked to ensure strict stock rotation. The label can also indicate type of food and reheating time (with or without the lid);

◆ the refrigerated store, fitted with indicating and recording thermometers and alarms, should maintain food between 0°C and 3°C and should only be used for cook-chill products. The maximum life of cooked products is five days, including the days of cooking and consumption;

◆ should the temperature of the food exceed 10°C during storage or distribution and before reheating, it should be destroyed. If the temperature exceeds 5°C the food should be eaten within 12 hours;

◆ insulated containers, chilled before use, may be used for short distribution runs but refrigerated vehicles are preferred and are essential for long journeys, especially during warmer months;

◆ food should be reheated as soon as possible after removing from chill and never longer than 30 minutes. The centre temperature of food should reach at least 70°C and be maintained for at least two minutes. Service of food should commence as soon as possible and within 15 minutes of reheating. Temperatures must not be allowed to fall below 63°C. Unconsumed, reheated food must be destroyed;

◆ reheating is preferable using infrared units, forced air and steamer convection ovens (traditional ovens may cause dehydration);

◆ foods intended to be eaten cold should be consumed as soon as possible and within 30 minutes of removal from chill; and

◆ to avoid health hazards documented HACCP should be implemented. Action plans should be formulated to deal with deviations at critical control points.

Management

Cook-chill demands considerable management and supervisory skills. Menu planning must take account of the keeping quality of different types of food. Foods with a high unsaturated fat content may oxidise more quickly and may not be suitable for the full five day storage. Work scheduling so that chilling times are rigidly observed, taking into account the differing rates of chilling of food for different types and densities, is also challenging for managers. Equipment failure and abnormal temperature readings can lead to difficult decisions and high losses. Increased complexity of equipment demands increased expertise from both managers and maintenance staff.

CRITICAL CONTROL POINT CHECKS FOR A COOK-CHILL SYSTEM

RAW MATERIALS TQ	PREPARATION C	PORTIONING C	STORAGE TCR	REHEATING T
STORAGE TCR	COOKING TCR	COOLING TCR	DISTRIBUTION TC	SERVING C

C= TIME, T=TEMPERATURE, R= RECORDING THERMOMETER, Q=QUALITY,

Microbiological guidelines to be used for setting up the system (Chilled and Frozen Guidelines on Cook-Chill and Cook-Freeze Catering Systems: DH 1989)
Total aerobic colony count (48 hours at 37°C) < 100,000 per gram.
Salmonella and *Listeria monocytogenes* not detected in 25g.
Staphylococcus aureus (coagulase+ve) and *Clostridium perfringens* < 100 per gram.
Escherichia coli < 10 per gram.
(100g samples to be taken immediately prior to reheating.)

SOUS VIDE COOK-CHILL

Sous vide cook-chill, also known as cuisine sous vide, is an interrupted catering system in which raw or par-cooked food is sealed in a vacuumised plastic pouch or container, heat treated by controlled cooking, rapidly chilled and then reheated for service after a period of chilled storage. The advantages include:
♦   extended shelf life;
♦   enhanced sensory quality; and
♦   improved nutritional quality.
Disadvantages include:
♦   significant capital and operating costs;
♦   limited number of products are suitable for this operation; and
♦   poorly designed systems and badly controlled systems may result in serious consequences, such as the growth of *Clostridium botulinum or B. cereus* in the product.

The sous-vide process
Ingredient purchasing, delivery and *storage*
All raw materials should be of the highest quality and stored at correct temperatures and humidities for the minimum time.

Preparing and portioning
High standards of hygiene must be maintained at all times. Prepared food must be held, or if pre-heated, chilled to below 10°C prior to vacuum packaging. Single portion pouches are

preferred but if multi-portion pouches are used product thickness should not exceed 50mm, to ensure acceptable heat transfer. Adequately sized pouches are essential. It should be possible to pinch 12.5mm of plastic together on all four sides of the product and the opening of the pouch should be folded back to prevent soiling during filling.

Vacuum packaging
After the removal of air and heat sealing of the pouch, it should mould tightly to the contours of the food. All pouches should be checked and any with defects such as air or product movement should be repackaged.

*Prime cooking/***pasteurisation**
Controlled heating may be undertaken using atmospheric steamers, combination ovens (set on "steaming" mode) or water baths. Food should be heated as soon as possible after preparation and always within two hours. Pouches of differing thickness should be processed separately and pouches must not be stacked on top of each other.
One of the following time/temperature treatments should be used:

Core temperature (°C)	Minimum holding time (minutes)
80	26
85	11
90	4.5
95	2

Chilling
Chilling may be achieved by blast, immersion or cryogenic chillers and should commence immediately after pasteurisation and always within 30 minutes. Food must be chilled to at least 3°C within two hours of cooking.

Chilled storage and distribution
Products must be labelled with their name, date of production (or batch number), **use-by date** and reheat instructions. In the UK the maximum shelf life is usually considered to be eight days including days of production and consumption. Storage and distribution must be between 0°C and 3°C. If the food temperature rises to between 5°C and 10°C the food must be consumed within 12 hours, if it exceeds 10°C the food should be destroyed.

Reheating and service
Prior to reheating (regeneration), any defective pouches should be destroyed. Reheating should take place immediately after removing from chilled storage and always within 30 minutes and never more than 15 minutes prior to service. A minimum centre temperature of 75°C should be achieved and the temperature of the food must not fall below 63°C before being served. Unconsumed reheated products must be destroyed.

THE SAFETY OF CHILLED FOODS

In 1992 The Advisory Committee on the Microbiological Safety of Food recommended that in addition to maintaining the temperature of prepared, chilled foods with a shelf life of more than ten days below 10°C, at least one of the following controlling factors should be used, to prevent the growth and toxin production of psychrotrophic *Cl. botulinum*:

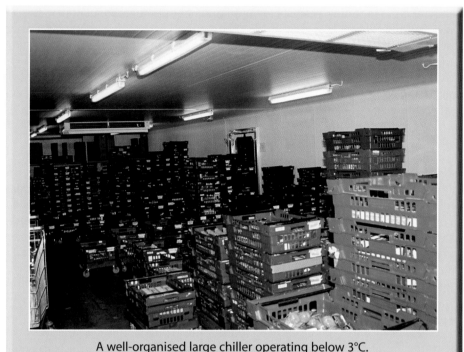

A well-organised large chiller operating below 3°C.
(Courtesy of Marks & Spencer.)

- a heat treatment of 90°C for ten minutes or equivalent lethality;
- a pH of 5 or less throughout the food;
- a minimum salt level of 3.5% in the aqueous phase throughout the food;
- an a_w of 0.97 or less throughout the food; or
- a combination of heat and preservative factors, which can be shown consistently to prevent growth and toxin production of psychrotrophic *Cl. botulinum*.

The Advisory Committee also recommended that a code of practice for the manufacture of vacuum and modified atmosphere packaged chilled foods should be drawn up containing detailed guidance on:

- raw material specification;
- awareness and use of HACCP;
- process establishment and validation (including thermal process);
- packaging requirements;
- temperature control through production, distribution and retail;
- factory auditing and quality management systems;
- the requirements to establish a safe shelf life;
- the control factors necessary to prevent the growth of bacteria and toxin production;
- the application of **challenge testing**;
- equipment specifications, particularly with regard to heating and refrigeration; and
- training.

COOK-FREEZE

Traditional catering involves considerable fluctuations in workload with a peak of around two hours, based on the time of meals. Cook-freeze is a system of catering devised to ensure a planned daily workload that utilises division of labour techniques and reduces wastage. The system takes advantage of economies of scale and operates on the same principle as a factory production line. Requirements can be forecast months in advance but fluctuations in demand can be dealt with as they occur. Furthermore, skilled staff are fully utilised throughout the day and a greater proportion of unskilled staff can be employed, for example, in serving kitchens.

The first four stages of cook-freeze are the same as cook-chill, namely: bulk storage; preparation; cooking and portioning; packaging and labelling. The fifth stage is blast-freezing. Precooked, lidded packs are loaded on to trolleys, which are wheeled into tunnel-type blast-freezers that reduce the temperature to –20°C in less than 90 minutes. Rapid freezing is essential to avoid the formation of large ice crystals, which result in poor texture and loss of nutritional value on regeneration. The frozen containers are kept at –20°C and may be stored for up to 12 months.

The exact number of meals required can be removed from storage on demand and regenerated to a temperature of at least 75°C in serving kitchens using, for example, forced-air convection ovens.

Cook-freeze systems may be installed as purpose-built, self-contained production units, which ensure a positive flow line, or, alternatively, existing equipment can be used with the addition of portioning, wrapping, blast-freezing and low-temperature storage. Cook-freeze is most suitable for operations requiring at least 1,000 meals per day, although some units have proved viable serving 200 meals per day.

Hot storage of food

Temperatures used for keeping food hot prior to service must be high enough to prevent bacterial multiplication, especially pathogenic bacteria. However, appliances such as hot cupboards and bains-marie are designed for storing hot food that has been thoroughly cooked; they must not be used for warming up cold food. Storage temperatures must not be relied on to destroy pathogens.

Hot food storage.
(Courtesy of Marks & Spencer.)

Hot food storage.
(Courtesy of Marks & Spencer.)

Very few bacteria are able to multiply above 55°C, including those that commonly cause problems of food poisoning. Consequently, the law requires all food businesses to keep hot food at or above 63°C.

It is important to remember that temperatures of cooking may cause the germination of *Clostridium perfringens* spores and the vegetative bacteria will commence rapid multiplication at approximately 50°C. Consequently, a slight reduction in storage temperatures can have disastrous consequences.

VENDING MACHINES

The use of automatic vending machines continues to increase. The complexity and types of machine and range of food dispensed are considerable. The hygiene of vending machines is controlled by Chapter 111 of the Regulation EC No 852/2004. Vending machines must be sited, designed, constructed and maintained to ensure the safety and wholesomeness of all dispensed food. Machines must be kept in good condition to avoid the risk of contaminating food. They must be durable and capable of being kept clean and, where necessary, disinfected, both internally and externally. Pests must be denied access. **Food-contact surfaces** should be smooth, impervious, non-toxic, corrosion resistant and be able to withstand the repeated cleaning to which they will be subjected.

Drinks vending machines must be connected to a supply of water of acceptable quality. Storage of water in machines must not result in an unacceptable deterioration of quality and carbon filters should be changed regularly. Plumbing of drinks vending machines must comply with any relevant local water byelaws. Hot drink vendors must be designed to prevent steam from affecting dry ingredients.

Machines must not be sited in direct sunlight or adjacent to sources of heat, for example, boilers, which could affect the temperature of food. Lights and other heat-generating mechanisms within machines must be fitted so that the temperature of food is not significantly affected. Location of machines should facilitate the thorough cleaning of adjacent wall and floor surfaces. External or internal sites that expose food to risk of contamination, including dust, condensation or odour, should not be used for vending machines. The name and address of the machine operator should be clearly visible on the machines. Adequate litter containers, which are emptied as frequently as necessary, should be provided next to machines.

Vending machines are increasing in popularity. (Courtesy of Marks & Spencer.)

Stock rotation of food is essential. All items should be given a use-by date, or a suitable code, to ensure that unsatisfactory food is removed. It is extremely desirable for vending machines dispensing high-risk foods, which are stored under refrigeration or above 63°C, to be fitted with chart recording thermometers, to ensure that food that has been subjected to unacceptable temperatures, for example, during a power cut, is not sold. At the very least, an indicating thermometer, visible externally, should be provided.

Vending machines must not be used for heating up cold food or for cooling down high-risk food from ambient temperatures. Hot food placed in vending machines must be thoroughly cooked and placed in the unit above 63°C.

A supply of hot and cold potable water must be available for cleaning machines vending **open food**. Regular and thorough cleaning and, if necessary, disinfection of vending machines is essential to ensure food safety and quality. Machines should display precise cleaning instructions on the inside of the front service door, and operators must always follow these instructions. The date and time of each cleaning should be noted in the machine.

Appropriate facilities must be available to maintain adequate personal hygiene for personnel involved in loading open food or cleaning food-contact parts.

Adequate arrangements and/or facilities must be available for the hygienic storage and disposal of hazardous and/or inedible substances and waste.

Some photographs used to illustrate this chapter were provided courtesy of
The Royal Borough of Kensington and Chelsea.

7 Food spoilage & preservation

FOOD SPOILAGE

Immediately vegetables and fruit are harvested or animals slaughtered, they usually commence to decompose due to the release of **autolytic** (self-splitting) **enzymes** from dying cells. The enzymes break down the largest **food** molecules and **spoilage** is then accelerated by bacterial exoenzymes, which degrade the complex molecules into their constituent molecules, which are then absorbed by the **bacteria**. Spoilage usually starts with **aerobic** and facultative bacteria and then obligate **anaerobes** take over as oxygen levels are reduced. **Moulds** and **yeasts** are responsible for some spoilage, especially when conditions do not favour bacteria. The rate of decomposition depends on the condition of the food, the **pH, a**$_w$, temperature, oxygen tension, the presence of inhibitory substances and the type and number of spoilage organisms present. As off-flavours and odours develop and a breakdown in texture occurs, the food will eventually become unfit for consumption.

Spoilage may also be caused by insects or vermin, **parasites**, chemical **contamination**, physical damage, such as **freezer burn**, and oxidation. Perishable **foods** such as meat, poultry, fish, dairy products, fruit and vegetables, unless preserved in some way, are the most susceptible to microbial spoilage and must be handled carefully. Some foods such as sugar, flour and dried fruit are often described as stable or non-perishable and are unlikely to be affected by spoilage unless they are handled badly, for example, by storing under damp conditions.

As spoilage bacteria multiply more rapidly than moulds and use up the available surface oxygen, meat at **ambient temperatures** or stored in refrigerators of high humidity will usually be spoiled by aerobic bacteria, such as *Pseudomonas,* growing on the surface. Off-odours and slime will be produced. However, in low humidities the surface of meat may be too dry for rapid bacterial growth and consequently moulds such as *Cladosporium herbarum* (Blackspot) and *Thamnidium elegans* (Whiskers) will develop. The presence of mould usually results in food having a musty odour and flavour and, although usually considered to be harmless, increasing concern is being expressed because of the possible presence of **mycotoxins**. The **acidity** of fruit ensures that most primary spoilage is caused by moulds and yeasts, which are able to multiply at a lower pH than bacteria. Although several species of bacteria do cause spoilage of vegetables, moulds are much more commonly involved, for example, those belonging to the genera *Botrytis, Rhizopus* and *Penicillium*.

Vegetables stored in vinegar, such as beetroot, may be attacked by yeasts, which gain access to jars after processing, for example, if the lid on the jar is defective, damaged in transit or removed and replaced by inquisitive customers. The beetroot turns a rusty-brown colour and a pinky-white precipitate may be observed on the base of the jar, which is attributable to **fermentation** by the yeast. Yeast spoilage of food can often be detected by the alcoholic taste and smell and the presence of bubbles in liquid.

Moulds are responsible for most of the spoilage of baked products, especially bread and pies. As mould **spores** are destroyed by normal cooking temperatures, post-process contamination from airborne spores and contact with contaminated surfaces must be prevented. Particular care must be taken to remove debris and waste food that would support mould growth. Cleansable surfaces and effective ventilation to stop condensation are also important to prevent growth. Products should be cooled quickly and not wrapped whilst warm as the resultant condensation will encourage rapid mould growth, especially if the food is stored at ambient temperatures. Moulds commonly involved include *Rhizopus* and *Mucor spp.* (white growth with black spots), *Penicillium spp.* (green) and *Monilia sitophilia* (red/pink).

Staleness of bread usually develops with prolonged holding due to physical changes in the carbohydrates. Refrigeration increases the rate of staling, however, staling does not occur during frozen storage at −18°C.

Rope

Rope in bread is caused by *Bacillus subtilis* and **spores** of this bacterium may be present in flour. They are able to withstand baking temperatures, and slow cooling and warm, humid storage ensure rapid **germination** and multiplication. Affected bread develops a fruity, sickly smell and a soft, sticky texture. Internally the loaf discolours, becoming yellow or brown. Rope is prevented by the use of proprionates. Other products such as cakes and doughnuts may occasionally be affected by rope.

Rope in bread.
(Courtesy of C & C Food R A.)

Rancidity

Fat in dairy products may be broken down into free fatty **acids** by **micro-organisms** or by naturally occurring enzymes, lipases, with the production of off-odours and flavours. This process is described as hydrolytic rancidity. Heating may destroy lipase-producing bacteria but not any lipase already formed and rancidity may still occur.

Oxidative rancidity may also occur in dairy products, often due to the presence of copper or iron contamination. Off-odours and flavours are due to the formation and decomposition of peroxides. The prolonged cold storage of fatty fish, bacon and pork results in rancidity unless vacuum packed.

COMMON FOOD SPOILAGE BACTERIA

FOOD	SPOILAGE BACTERIA Commonly isolated	TYPICAL SIGNS OF SPOILAGE
Fresh meat and poultry	*Clostridium, Flavobacterium, Pseudomonas* spp., *Micrococcus, Achromobacter, Acinetobacter* and *Psychrobacter immobilis, Brochothrix thermosphacta*, psychrotrophic Enterbacteriaceae, and occasionally cold-tolerant clostridia	Slime, greenish discolouration, white spots (bacterial **colonies**), souring, putrefaction, off-odours and flavours
Processed meats	*Achromobacter, Micrococcus, Pseudomonas, Clostridium Lactobacillus, Streptococcus**	Souring, gas production, discolouration, surface slime
Bacon**	*Streptococcus*, Micrococcus, Lactobacillus*	Slime formation, white spots, discolouration, off-odours. Souring of vacuum packs (which may blow)

Fish	Acinetobacter, Pseudomonas spp., Shewanella spp. (marine fish), Acinetobacter/Moraxella, Aeromonas spp. or other members of the Vibrionaceae if fish held above 5°C, Photobacterium phosphoreum when packed in modified atmospheres	Off-odours, discolouration
Vegetables ***	Pseudomonas, Corynebacteria Erwinia, Leuconostoc Bacillus, Clostridium	Soft rot, foul odour, discolouration, black spots
Raw milk	Streptococcus, Micrococcus Lactobacillus, Bacillus, Pseudomonas	Tainting, off-flavours and odours, souring (above 15°C), rancidity
Pasteurised milk	B. cereus, Streptococcus,**** Lactobacillus****	Bitty cream (sweet curdling), off-odours and flavours

Streptococcus faecalis is quite salt tolerant.
**Packs of bacon with faulty seams are vulnerable to mould spoilage.
***Frozen green vegetables, which defrost, become yellowish and khaki, odours and slime develop. The organism commonly responsible is *Leuconostoc mesenteroides*.
****Thermoduric strains, which survive **pasteurisation**, e.g. *Streptococcus faecalis*.

Spoilage of poultry

The spoilage rate is dependent on the storage temperature and the number and type of spoilage organisms present. Spoilage is evident at around 10^8 organisms per cm^2.

The smell of spoilt chicken is due to the production of hydrogen sulphide by spoilage bacteria. The hydrogen sulphide diffuses into the muscle tissue and combines with the haem pigments of blood and muscle in the presence of air to form the green pigment sulphaemoglobin just under the skin.

SPOILAGE RATE OF POULTRY*

Temperature	100 organisms/cm^2	10,000 organisms/cm^2
0°C	11.5 days	7.6 days
5°C	6.2 days	4.1 days
10°C	3.9 days	2.6 days
15°C	1.8 days	1.2 days

*Mead G. C. (personal communication).

Soft drinks and fruit juices

Spoilage of soft drinks and fruit juices is caused by bacteria, Gluconobacter (Acetomonas) and *Alicylobacillus acidoterrestris*, yeasts, *Zygosaccharomyces bacilli* (often resistant to preservatives) and heat-tolerant **fungi**, *Byssochlamys fulva, B. nivea, Neosartorya fischeri* and Talaromyces species.

Alicyclobacillus acidoterrestris is an aerobic bacterium that grows between 45°C and 70°C. Its optimum pH is 2.5 to 4.5. Reported **D values** (decimal reduction time) range from 60.8 to 94.5 minutes at 85°C, 10 to 20.6 minutes at 90°C and 2.5 to 8.7 minutes at 95°C. Spoilage from *Alicyclobacillus acidoterestris* is easily detected due to a distinct **antiseptic** off-odour attributed to guaiacol, a **metabolic** by-product of the bacterium off-flavour due to, 2, 6-dibromophenol. Spoilage can be prevented by the addition of lysozyme.

FOOD PRESERVATION

Preservation is the treatment of food to prevent or delay spoilage and inhibit growth of pathogenic organisms, which would render the food unfit. Preservation may involve:

♦ the use of low temperatures or high temperatures;
♦ the use of **dehydration**, i.e. moisture control;
♦ the use of chemicals;
♦ controlled atmospheres and the restriction of oxygen; and
♦ physical methods including smoking and irradiation.

FOOD PRESERVATION BY THE USE OF LOW TEMPERATURES

This form of preservation is based on the fact that all metabolic reactions of micro-organisms are enzyme catalysed. The speed of enzyme reaction depends on temperature and the colder it is, the slower the reaction. Temperatures used may be:

♦ above freezing (refrigerator);
♦ at freezing (commercially used with chilled beef); or
♦ below freezing (freezer).

Temperatures above freezing

Refrigerators are used both commercially and domestically and should usually operate at between 1°C and 4°C. They are suitable for the storage of most perishable foods over a relatively short period of time. Most common pathogenic organisms cease multiplication below 5°C, although increasing concern is being expressed about *Yersinia enterocolitica, Aeromonas hydrophila* and *Listeria monocytogenes,* all of which are capable of growth under refrigeration. **Psychrophilic** spoilage bacteria that cause problems include those belonging to the genera *Pseudomonas, Acinetobacter, Flavobacterium* and *Alcaligenes.* Mould genera capable of growth at low temperatures include *Penicillium, Mucor, Cladosporium* and *Botrytis.*

Temperatures below freezing

As well as the inhibition of enzyme reactions, freezing also relies on reducing available moisture to ensure effective preservation. The a_w of water at 0°C is 1.0 whereas at −15°C the a_w of ice is approximately 0.85. The freezing of food destroys some bacteria, including pathogens, and a gradual reduction of survivors occurs during storage. Generally, the lower the storage temperature of frozen food the greater is the survival rate of micro-organisms. Spores and toxins are practically unaffected by freezing or frozen storage. The greatest number of bacteria are killed between −2°C and −5°C; unfortunately, many enzymes are extremely active at around −2°C and food stored at this temperature would soon deteriorate.

Some parasites can be destroyed by freezing, for example, trichina cysts in pork stored at −18°C for 21 days, *Cysticercus bovis* in beef carcases stored at −10°C for 14 days and the fish nematode anisakis, which is destroyed at −20°C in 24 hours.

Moulds and yeasts are more likely to grow on frozen food than bacteria as they are better able to withstand lower a_w and temperatures. In practice very few organisms grow below −8°C. Even at temperatures of around 0°C it takes the most rapidly growing **psychrophiles** a day to achieve a tenfold increase in numbers.

On thawing, after a short lag time, a rapid growth of those bacteria that survive freezing will soon compensate for those destroyed, especially if food is allowed to reach temperatures of 20°C to 30°C.

Before vegetables are frozen they must be blanched. **Blanching** is carried out by immersion in hot water for a short period, approximately one minute. Its function is to destroy enzymes, such as peroxidases, which produce off-odours and flavours, reduce bacterial load, fix colour, remove trapped air and induce wilting in some vegetables to aid packing. Overblanching will result in excessive loss of vitamin C by leaching and must be avoided. Care must be taken when operatives handle frozen food to avoid contamination, especially by staphylococci.

As the temperature is reduced, pure water will commence freezing at 0°C. (The freezing point is depressed by the presence of solutes such as salts and sugars.) However, the rate of cooling slows due to the loss of the latent heat of fusion prior to ice formation. As most of the water is converted to ice, the rate of cooling once again increases. Quick freezing involves passing through this zone of maximum crystallisation of ice as quickly as possible. The faster the process the smaller the ice crystals, the better the food quality and the smaller the amount of liquid (drip) produced on thawing.

The actual rate of freezing depends on:

♦ the shape and weight of the product;
♦ the initial and final temperature;
♦ the surface heat transfer coefficient and thermal conductivity;
♦ the amount of heat to be removed (enthalpy);
♦ the temperature of the refrigerant; and
♦ the type of packaging.

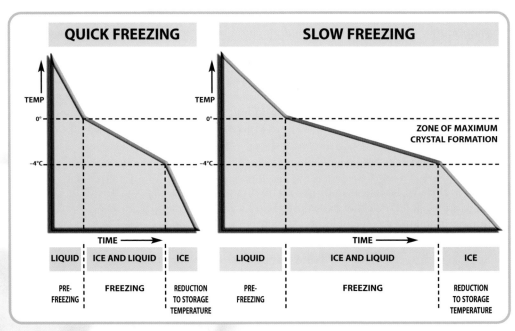

Rates of freezing: the latent heat zone and zone of maximum crystal formation overlap and, if food is frozen slowly, considerable damage and loss of quality occurs.

Most foods will keep for prolonged periods in a freezer, although a recommended **shelf life** is given because of loss of texture, flavour, tenderness, colour and overall nutritional quality. Foods must be properly wrapped to avoid loss of moisture from the surface, i.e. freezer burn. The oxidation of food is slower at −18°C and this also assists in preservation. However, vacuum packing is essential to extend the shelf life of frozen food susceptible to oxidative rancidity, for example, bacon, and the shelf life of kippers can be extended from three to nine months. Very sophisticated laminate packaging is used for some **ready-to-eat** meals and boil-in-the-bag products. Films of low-density polyethylene, polyesters, aluminium foils and polypropylene are all used to improve packaging characteristics. Some products such as fish fillets are given a thin coat of ice to avoid dehydration during storage.

Freezing systems

Fluidised-bed freezing
Particulate vegetables such as peas are moved along a tunnel on a perforated tray, through a blast of very cold air. They are normally borne along by a cushion of freezing air forced up from below. This ensures that each item is individually quick frozen, so ensuring that the product does not weld together. The process takes about three to eight minutes.

Air-blast freezing
Air-blast freezers are the commonest method of freezing and include: static tunnels where trolleys of boxed product such as beef and cakes are pushed through; solid continuous belt freezers, which are used for fish fillets, patties and pizzas; and spiral belt freezers, which are relatively small and allow the refrigerated air to pass through the open link belt. They are used for pizzas, fish fillets, meals and cakes. Air circulates around the food at temperatures of −30°C to −40°C and as with all freezing systems, the freezing time depends on the dimensions of the food. The process usually takes two to three hours.

Plate freezing
This method is used for food packed in flat cartons, for example, fish blocks and meals. The cartons are placed between narrow metal shelves in which a very cold refrigerant circulates, so ensuring freezing. Revolving plate freezers are used, for example, for boil-in-the-bag products. Plate freezing usually takes two to three hours.

Cryogenic freezing
The food is sprayed with, or dipped into, a refrigerant such as liquid nitrogen. It is a very quick technique and, although capital costs are relatively low, high refrigerant costs restrict its use to high-cost, small products such as raspberries and prawns. Studies have shown that after a few months of frozen storage there is no significant difference between liquid nitrogen frozen and air-blast frozen foods.

Pellofreeze system
The "pellofreeze" system is an interesting development in freezing technology, which involves freezing liquids and semi-solids in pellet form. Spinach, cream, orange juice, egg and soup have all been frozen commercially by this method.

FOOD PRESERVATION BY THE USE OF HIGH TEMPERATURES

Heat energy is used to destroy both spoilage and pathogenic organisms and so preserves food. However, heat-resistant bacteria, some toxins and spores may survive heat treatment. The number of organisms that survive heating is related to the initial numbers and strain of organism, the time and temperature used, the pH and the presence of protective substances such as proteins and fats. For example, the thermal death point of *E. coli* in cream is 73°C and in skimmed milk 65°C. The destruction of micro-organisms depends on their D value, which is the time required at a specific temperature to destroy 90% of the organisms present. Therefore if the D value of an organism is one minute at 75°C and there are 10^6 organisms present then after one minute there will be 10^5, after two minutes 10^4, three minutes 10^3, etc. The D value of *salmonella spp., S. aureus, L. monocytogenes* and *E. coli* is less than ten seconds at 72°C. Therefore, heating food at 72°C for one minute will result in reducing one million of any of these bacteria to one. Any equivalent heat energy will produce the same effect. However, the D value of spores of *Clostridium perfringens* and *Bacillus cereus* may be up to 20 minutes at 100°C and spores will not be destroyed at 72°C. Examples of equivalent cooking time/temperatures for the destruction of bacteria include: 60°C for 45 minutes, 65°C for ten minutes, 70°C for two minutes, 75°C for 30 seconds, and 80°C for six seconds.

This log reduction of bacteria by heating clearly demonstrates the need to minimise the number of pathogenic bacteria in raw food.

Care must always be taken to avoid the recontamination of food after processing, or the multiplication of bacteria not destroyed during heating will occur. This involves the use of suitable packaging, for example, bottles or cans, or storage under conditions that inhibit bacterial growth, usually refrigeration.

Pasteurisation

Pasteurisation normally involves heating food at a relatively low temperature for a short time. For example, milk may be heated at 72°C for 15 seconds. The time and temperature combination chosen depends on the particular type of food and must be sufficient to destroy **vegetative** pathogens and a considerable proportion of spoilage organisms. Toxins and spores generally survive pasteurisation and, to avoid the growth of heat-resistant organisms and **vegetative bacteria** that may be present because of spore germination during heating, refrigerated storage is often essential.

Organisms preferring to multiply at temperatures above 45°C are known as **thermophiles** and those capable of withstanding heat treatment, but not necessarily multiplying at the higher temperatures, are known as **thermoduric**.

The main advantage of pasteurisation is that food is rendered safe with the minimum effect on flavour and nutritional value. Foods that are pasteurised include milk, ice cream, eggs and liquid egg, wines, canned fruit and large cans of ham.

Guidelines to the types of food products stabilised by pasteurisation treatments and recommendations for the design of pasteurisation processes are provided in "Food Pasteurisation Treatments: Technical Manual No. 27. Campden and Chorleywood Research Association, 1992".

Sterilisation

Sterilisation involves the destruction of all micro-organisms and as this is sometimes difficult to achieve, heat treatment adequate to destroy all viable organisms may be utilised.

In this case food may be considered **commercially sterile**. This means that any organisms remaining after treatment will be of no significance under normal methods of storage. **Low-acid** canned food is given such a treatment. Temperatures required for sterilisation normally exceed 100°C and are usually achieved by means of steam under pressure.

There are several factors affecting the heat-resistance of organisms.

♦ *Humidity* – the lower the moisture the more resistant the organism, i.e. dry heat is not as lethal as steam at the same temperature.

♦ *Fat, sugar and proteins* – the presence of these substances usually increases heat resistance.

♦ *pH* – neutral pH is preferred, acid and **alkaline** conditions increase heat sensitivity. For this reason acid foods such as fruit require a much lower temperature to render them commercially sterile.

♦ *Chemicals* – the presence of certain chemicals such as nitrites may decrease heat resistance.

♦ A_w – the heat-resistance of salmonellae and other bacteria increases significantly by reducing the a_w.

The main advantage of sterilisation is the prolonged shelf life. The main objections are a lowering of nutritional value, including loss of vitamins, and a marked difference in texture and flavour.

Ultra heat treatment (UHT)

The ultra heat treatment of milk is a result of research carried out to find a product with an extended shelf life without the organoleptic changes caused by sterilisation. Milk is heated to a temperature of not <135°C for one second before filling **aseptically** into sterile containers. This reduces the amount of caramelisation and also enhances keeping quality. UHT milk will usually keep for several months without refrigeration.

Ohmic heating

Ohmic heating involves heating food by passing a high-voltage electric current through a liquid and solid type food such as chilli con carne. The **commercially sterile food** is then cooled and packed under aseptic conditions to provide a product that has a prolonged shelf life at ambient temperatures. Products must be capable of being pumped and can have a solids content of up to 60% with particulates having a diameter of about 25mm.

DEHYDRATION AS A MEANS OF PRESERVATION

This method of preservation relies on the fact that all micro-organisms require moisture to facilitate their metabolic reactions. Dehydration reduces the amount of available water, and dried foods normally contain less than 25% moisture with an a_w of less than 0.6. Most bacteria require an a_w of at least 0.95 and very few micro-organisms can exist at levels around 0.6. However, some bacteria form spores that will germinate on the reconstitution of the dried product, for example, *Bacillus cereus*. Gram-negative rods are the most sensitive bacteria to drying and Gram-positive cocci are usually the most resistant, with some able to grow down to an a_w of 0.85. Yeasts and moulds usually grow at lower levels of a_w than do bacteria. Organisms growing under dry conditions are usually referred to as **xerophilic** (dry loving).

The role of dehydration in food preservation became more important in the food industry with the development of packet convenience foods. Mould and enzyme spoilage is also prevented and, provided that food is stored in suitable air-tight packs, it will keep for a considerable period of time.

Sun drying was the earliest method of dehydration and is still practised in hot climates, for example, for drying currants, raisins and figs. Artificial drying is quicker and normally more effective than natural means. Unfortunately, food undergoes irreversible changes to the tissue structure during drying, which affects both texture and flavour.

Methods of drying may be divided into those using hot air, for example, tunnel drying, fluidised-bed drying, roller drying and spray drying, and those using warm air such as accelerated freeze drying. Hot air **denatures** protein; foods are more difficult to reconstitute and it induces greater changes in flavour. However, the choice often depends on the type of foodstuff and the degree of dehydration required. Blanching of vegetables must be carried out before drying to obviate enzyme activity during storage.

In spray drying a solution, paste or slurry is dispersed as small droplets into a stream of hot air. The small droplets result in a rapid loss of moisture and a large proportion of the colour, flavour and nutritive value of the food is maintained. However, because the evaporative cooling effect keeps the temperature of the droplets low, a pasteurisation process is usually required prior to spray drying.

In roller drying, a paste of the food is made and fed on to a heated drum from which the moisture is driven off and the dried cake is scraped from the drum. Generally, the quality of the product is not as good as the spray dried product.

For fruits and vegetables a tunnel drier is used. This consists of a tunnel 10 to 15 metres long in which trays of product are passed along. Hot air is blown across the trays and a continuous process leads to a gradual loss of moisture.

Total removal of moisture may not be necessary. Water that does remain forms a strong solution of salts and soluble proteins. This water remaining is not available to micro-organisms and thus the food has a low a_w.

Accelerated freeze drying

Food is frozen quickly and then subjected to a mild heat treatment under vacuum. The ice in the food changes directly to water vapour, which is then removed, a process known as **sublimation**. The cells of the food are substantially less affected than by other methods of drying and the product reconstitutes with very little change.

The advantages and disadvantages of dehydration

The advantages of dehydration over other methods of preservation include:

♦ the food is lighter and takes up less space; this results in cheaper transport and storage;

♦ costly insulated or refrigerated distribution vehicles and storage facilities are not required; and

♦ the relatively long shelf life of the food.

The disadvantages include:

♦ considerable care is necessary in packaging to eliminate oxygen; if the packaging is damaged or permeable then spoilage will occur and oxidative rancidity may be a problem in foods containing fats;

♦ non-enzymic browning may occur in foods;
♦ there may be a significant alteration in flavour and a lowering of nutritional value, especially vitamin C;
♦ spore-forming bacteria survive and on reconstitution will germinate;
♦ many foods do not **rehydrate** very well and may become tough; and
♦ **rehydration** damages cell walls, which increases the rate of decomposition.

To minimise chemical changes, particularly browning, in dried foods it is important to:
♦ keep the moisture content as low as possible;
♦ minimise the level of reducing sugars;
♦ use clean blanching water with low levels of leached soluble solids; and
♦ use sulphur dioxide as a preservative.

All dried food should be stored at low levels of relative humidity and kept dry in order to prevent spoilage, especially mould growth.

CHEMICAL METHODS OF PRESERVATION

A wide range of chemical **additives** is available for food preservation and may be used to prevent microbial spoilage, chemical deterioration and mould growth. The use of additives is strictly controlled by legislation and maximum permitted levels are usually specified. Ministers are advised by the Food Standards Committee and the Food Additives and Contaminants Committee and are empowered, under the Food Safety Act, 1990, to make regulations and orders to control their use. However, a preference for milder flavours, and in some instances increasing public resistance, has resulted in a reduction in the amount of some preservatives such as nitrite used in food manufacture. Although this is desirable, extreme caution must be exercised if preservatives are being used not only to increase shelf life but also to prevent pathogen multiplication. As the amount of preservative is reduced, satisfactory handling and refrigerated storage are becoming even more important. Initially, therefore, the safety of an altered or new recipe containing reduced preservative must be microbiological **challenge tested**. (The "new" product is inoculated with appropriate pathogens and then subjected to various temperatures to ascertain the effect on, for example, previous recommendations for cooking and storage.)

Any chemical used in food processing must be used in the best interests of the consumer and not as a device to deceive the consumer or to hide faulty processing and handling techniques. All food additives used must be shown to be safe for the consumer. In the UK a positive list principle is applied, that is, only those compounds specifically listed can be used for food and, in most cases, the maximum amount of material allowed in specific types of food is also specified.

Salt

Salt has been used as a preservative since ancient times. In part, preservation is due to osmosis. When salt is added to food, water passes out of the cells by diffusion to create an equilibrium concentration. This moisture becomes unavailable for micro-organisms. When added to 100g of water, 1.7g of sodium chloride will depress the a_w by 0.01, 3.4g by 0.02, 5.1g by 0.03, etc. The effectiveness depends on the concentration and this is related to many factors including water content, contamination levels, pH, temperature, protein content and the presence of other inhibitory substances. The salt tolerance of micro-organisms is usually decreased by lowering the temperature or the pH. Moulds are less exacting in their water requirements than bacteria and consequently, for effective preservation the available moisture must be less than will permit mould development. Salt may be rubbed into the meat, used as a brine solution, injected into the muscular tissue as a concentrated solution or added directly, for example, in the manufacture of sausages.

Organisms that can grow in high concentrations of salt are known as **halophiles** (salt loving). Those that can withstand high levels but do not grow are termed **haloduric**. Staphylococci will grow in relatively high salt concentrations and are often associated with food poisoning from semi-preserved salted meats.

In preservation the use of salt, with the addition of other chemicals such as sodium nitrate, is termed curing whilst its use for flavour or colouring is termed brining.

The salt used for food preservation must be pure and free from contaminants and extraneous matter, for example, sea salt can often contain a range of mineral substances in addition to sodium chloride.

Nitrates and nitrites

Sodium nitrate ($NaNO_3$) and sodium nitrite ($NaNO_2$) are used in curing meat to stabilise red pigmentation and reduce spoilage. They are also essential for use in such products as pasteurised ham to stop the production of botulinum toxin by preventing the germination of spores. Traditionally, salt and nitrate solutions were injected into the meat, which was then immersed in the brine solution to enable salt tolerant bacteria to convert nitrate to nitrite. However, the current trend is to use nitrites direct as they are much more effective than nitrates. Unfortunately, nitrites react with amines to form nitrosamines, many of which are said to be **carcinogenic**. For this reason the levels allowed are strictly controlled. Both nitrates and nitrites gradually disappear during storage and heating.

The effectiveness of curing salts depends on various factors, including the pH of the meat, the number and types of micro-organisms present and the curing temperature.

Sugar

Sucrose acts in a similar manner to salt but concentrations need to be about six times higher. Moulds and yeasts are less susceptible than bacteria and can withstand up to 60% of sucrose. Organisms that are able to grow in high concentrations of sugar are designated **osmophiles** (loving high osmotic pressures) and those that withstand high levels without multiplying are **osmoduric**. The substitution of sucrose by artificial sweetening agents must be carefully evaluated because of the implications for reduced product stability and increased potential for growth of pathogens.

This method of preservation is commonly used for jam and other preserves, candied fruit and condensed milk. Certain types of cake have increased shelf life due to the effect of sugar.

Benzoic acid/sodium benzoate

This chemical occurs naturally in some foods, for example, cranberries. It is used to inhibit the growth of moulds and yeasts in high-acid foods such as fruit juice, pickles and dressings, but is not generally effective in neutral foods. It acts by inhibiting the cellular uptake of amino acids. Excess benzoate can cause an unpleasant burning taste.

Sulphur dioxide/sulphite

Sulphur dioxide may be used in gaseous or liquid form or as a salt. It is an antioxidant and also inhibits growth of bacteria and moulds. It is utilised in the dehydration of some foods to prevent enzymatic browning. Sulphur dioxide is used in wine, beers, fruit juice and comminuted meat products including sausages, where it is allowed up to 450µg/g. Apart from reducing the growth of spoilage organisms, sulphur dioxide also limits the growth of salmonellae.

Sorbic acid/potassium sorbate

Like benzoate, sorbate is only effective in acid food. It is particularly effective against moulds and yeasts and it is also reported to inhibit the growth of salmonellae, faecal streptococci and staphylococci but not clostridia. It may be used in hard cheese, as lactic acid bacteria are unaffected. It is also used in bread, jam, syrups and cakes.

Fermentation

Fermentation involves the **anaerobic** oxidation of carbohydrates by micro-organisms and the production of acid which lowers the pH and preserves the food. For example, starter cultures of lactic acid bacteria ferment glucose in milk to produce lactic acid and yogurt. Yeasts ferment carbohydrates to produce ethanol (beers and wines) and moulds are involved in the production of blue cheeses and soy sauce. Fermented foods also include butter, sauerkraut, bread, olives, salami and pepperoni. Sodium chloride may be added to inhibit the growth of competing spoilage organisms. Sugar may be added, especially to meat, to increase the amount of lactic acid produced.

The production of vinegar (acetic acid) involves the fermentation of sugar into alcohol by yeast and the fermentation of the alcohol into acetic acid by vinegar bacteria.

The pH limit for bacterial growth is around 4.5 for *Cl. perfringens, Cl. botulinum* and *Staphylococcus aureus*; 4.2 for most *Bacillus spp., Salmonella spp.* and *E. coli,* and below 4.0 for *Lactobacillus.* Some salmonella can grow as low as 3.8. However, many yeasts and moulds will grow below a pH of 3.0.

Acidification or pickling

This process involves lowering the pH of food by using an organic acid, for example, citric acid or acetic acid, i.e. vinegar. It is essential that the acidification process is controlled so that the pH of each part of the product is below 4.5. Acetic acid is used in the production of mayonnaise and salad dressings. Sufficient time must be allowed for any pathogens, such as salmonella, to die off after the acid has been added.

Sodium and calcium propionate

Propionates are active in **low-acid foods** and very useful to prohibit mould growth. They are used in bread, cakes, cheese, grain and jellies.

Antibiotics

These chemicals have a preservative role in addition to their normal function. Their use is strictly controlled by regulations to avoid the build-up of resistance by pathogenic organisms. An example of an **antibiotic** is nisin, sometimes used in cheese and canned foods. Nisin is heat-resistant but is destroyed in the stomach by trypsin and should not cause problems of pathogen drug resistance.

PHYSICAL METHODS OF PRESERVATION

Controlled atmospheres

Modified atmosphere packaging

One of the simplest food processing/preservation methods using a physical method is to change the atmosphere around the food. This is termed **modified atmosphere packaging** (MAP). The air around a product is modified to contain a different proportion of the gases normally present, for example, lower levels of oxygen and higher levels of nitrogen and carbon dioxide, and will slow down the growth of many spoilage organisms thus giving an extended shelf life to the product. MAP should also be combined with correct chilled temperature control in order to further guarantee the control of microbial proliferation. Concentrations of 10% carbon dioxide may be used to keep chilled beef free from spoilage for up to 70 days. Comprehensive guidelines for the good manufacturing and handling of modified atmosphere packed food products have been produced.*

The restriction of oxygen

The development of oxidative rancidity and the growth of strict aerobes such as moulds can be prevented by vacuum packing. However, removal of oxygen allows the growth of anaerobes such as *Clostridium perfringens,* and sufficient oxygen normally remains in so-called vacuum packs of meat to facilitate the growth of some aerobes.

Regular sampling shows that vacuum packs of ham are generally no better bacteriologically, and may even be worse, than ham sliced off the bone. Vacuum packs of cooked meat must be stored under refrigeration to achieve a reasonable shelf life. A vacuum pack of cooked ham with an initial count of 10^2 organisms per gram will have a count of 10^6 after 39 days if stored at 2°C; 20 days at 5°C; and seven days at 15°C.

Smoking

Smoking is used primarily with meat and fish, after brining or pickling, by suspending the food over smouldering hardwoods, such as oak and ash, which should be free from chemical preservatives. The principle purpose nowadays is to enhance the flavour. The smoking process also has some dehydrating effect and, when properly controlled, there may be some preserving action due to the presence of bactericidal chemicals such as phenols, alcohols and aldehydes, which are absorbed by the food. Most non-sporing bacteria will be destroyed but moulds and *Cl. botulinum* type E may survive, especially if there is a low salt concentration. Smoked products should, therefore, always be stored under refrigeration, preferably below 3°C to prevent toxin formation if *Cl. botulinum* is present. Poor control of the process may allow incubation and hence an increase in numbers of spoilage organisms.

Another way of adding a smoke flavour to the food is to use a liquid, produced by trapping smoke in water and spraying this on to the food. The preserving effect of this process is limited and no dehydration of the food takes place.

Food irradiation

There has been a considerable debate regarding the use of irradiation as a method of food preservation. It involves subjecting the food to a dose of ionising radiation, for example, gamma rays emitted from an isotope such as cobalt 60. (X-rays with energies up to 5MeV (million electron volts) or accelerated electrons with energies up to 10MeV could also be

*Source: Technical Manual No. 34, 1992. Campden and Chorleywood Research Association.

used.) Several countries irradiate food, and from the scientific studies carried out it seems to present an effective and safe method of extending the shelf life of food. It destroys parasites, insects including eggs, bacteria, moulds and yeasts thus reducing the risk of food spoilage and foodborne illness. However, microbial spores and toxins remain unaffected at the levels used. Foods most commonly irradiated include chicken, fish, onions, potatoes, spices and strawberries. The irradiation of burgers started in the USA in 2002.

One particular advantage of food irradiation as a food preservation method is that it introduces virtually no temperature rise in the treated product and is often referred to as a "cold pasteurisation process". Fish, fruits and vegetables remain "fresh" and unchanged. Irradiation of packaged food is possible and may be particularly important in areas where hygiene is difficult to maintain or control. Frozen food can be treated without thawing but higher doses are required. However, irradiation must never be considered as a substitute for good hygiene practices. Irradiated foods must be handled and stored with the same hygiene considerations as non-irradiated foods.

The dose of irradiation used (which is measured in Grays (Gy) or kiloGray (kGy) is a measure of absorbed energy by the food. One Gy is equivalent to one joule per kilogram. (1Gy=100 rads.) It should be noted that doses of around 5Gy can be lethal to man. Irradiation may be used as part of a continuous process or for controlled batches.

Spores are least sensitive to radiation, then viruses, Gram-positive bacteria and moulds with Gram-negative bacteria being the most sensitive. Type E botulinum spores have survived the irradiation of fish and produced toxin more rapidly than those in non-irradiated fish.

Food irradiation as a method of preservation has the same limitations as many other food preservation technologies. Vitamins may be destroyed and enzymes are not deactivated. Other disadvantages include the encouragement of oxidative rancidity in fatty foods, the possible production of free radicals in food, which stimulate a range of chemical reactions, and the softening of some fruit.

The dose of irradiation received varies throughout the product depending on thickness, orientation and packaging. It is important to ensure that the minimum dose necessary to achieve the end result is delivered to all parts of the food but that the maximum average dose of 10kGy is not exceeded in order to limit the adverse effects.

DOSE RANGES NEEDED FOR EFFECTIVE TREATMENT

	kGy
Inhibition of sprouting in onions and potatoes	0.03-0.1
Sterilisation of insects and parasites	0.03-0.2
Killing insects and parasites	0.05-5.0
Reduction by 10^6 of vegetative bacteria	1-10
Complete sterilisation of food	20-40
(would result in unacceptable off-odours and flavours together with a cooked texture)	

The following matters need to be considered when determining the acceptability of the food irradiation process.

Production of toxic agents
Irradiation of food will result in some chemical reactions in the food but it is alleged that no toxigenic compounds have been demonstrated in treated foods. In 2002 the Centre for

Food Safety and the Public Citizen urged the USA Food and Drugs Authority to halt the approval of irradiated food until it could be proved that a new class of chemical, cyclobutanones, formed during irradiation were harmless.

Microbiological interactions

A high dose of irradiation sufficient to achieve commercial sterility should cause no health problems, however, at lower dose levels when some micro-organisms survive, problems may arise. An increase in radiation-resistant organisms will occur but normally only on repeated exposure to irradiation.

A second problem in the use of sub-lethal treatments is that they might result in shifts in microbial flora and the possibility of spoilage being unrecognised through odour before toxins reach dangerous levels. In practice this does not seem to occur and irradiated foods appear to follow the normal spoilage pattern.

Possible carcinogenicity

There is no proof that food that has been irradiated shows any carcinogenic activity.

Induced radioactivity

Only at very high doses could the food become radioactive. At the levels used for food processing there is no danger of the food developing radioactivity.

Nutritional quality

The changes produced in the nutrient content of food will depend on many factors including the type of food, the radiation dose and the processing temperature. Generally, vitamins A and E are the most susceptible to irradiation damage. Although the shelf life of food is prolonged, some bacteria survive and irradiated food must be stored at correct temperatures. Irradiation cannot replace refrigeration.

THE MAIN USES OF IRRADIATION

♦ To destroy a percentage of spoilage and pathogenic bacteria on food.
♦ To control mould growth particularly on soft fruits such as strawberries.
♦ To disinfest fruit and grain (limited to a depth of around 8cm).
♦ To inhibit the sprouting of potatoes, onions or garlic.
♦ To inactivate parasites such as *Trichina spiralis*.
♦ To delay the ripening of fruit such as bananas.

The main disadvantages claimed by opponents of irradiation include:
♦ inadequate information exists to assess the long-term effects of consuming irradiated food;
♦ some reduction in the nutritional value of food, particularly vitamin loss;
♦ the production of undesirable flavour changes in some foods, for example, eggs and some dairy products. Some foods are softened to a mulch;
♦ food of poor bacteriological quality and shelf life may be irradiated to disguise this fact;
♦ hygiene standards will be reduced as some manufacturers will rely on irradiation to produce an acceptable final product;

- ◆ spoilage bacteria are more easily destroyed than pathogens and reducing competition may allow more prolific growth of pathogens in certain circumstances; and
- ◆ more dangerous mutants of pathogens may be formed.

The Food Labelling (Amendment) (Irradiated Food) Regulations, 1990 require food that has been irradiated to be so labelled.

The Food Irradiation (England) Regulations, 2009 set out the requirements for producing, importing and selling irradiated food in the UK. Parallel legislation exists in Wales, Northern Ireland and Scotland. The Regulations include details of the seven categories of food that may be irradiated before importation to and sale in the UK. The licensing of food irradiation facilities and Regulation 5 sets out the restrictions applying to imports.
http://www.food.gov.uk/business-industry/imports/importers/irradiated

In the UK, Isotron PLC has a licence that allows the irradiation of a seasoning blend to a maximum overall average dose of 10kGy. However, surveys undertaken by the Scottish Universities Research and Reactor Centre at East Kilbride and Suffolk Trading Standards have discovered several irradiated foods on sale, for example, seven out of 18 samples of prawns.

Further information on the irradiation of food is available in the WHO Technical Report Series no. 890 (1999) High-dose Irradiation: Wholesomeness of food irradiated with doses above 10kGy. (WHO, Geneva).

The symbol indicating food has been irradiated.

In total, 9263.4 tonnes of food products were irradiated in European Union countries in 2010, mainly in three member state countries: Belgium (63%), the Netherlands (17%) and France (11%). The three types of foods irradiated the most were frog legs (48%), poultry (23%) and dried herbs and spices (16%).

Since 2002 in the USA hamburgers have been irradiated to reduce the risk of *E.coli* O157.

One angström unit = 1/10,000,000mm

Part of the electromagnetic spectrum of interest to the food industry.

8 Personal hygiene

High standards of **personal hygiene** are essential to reduce the **risk** of **foodborne illness** and a prerequisite to the implementation of **HACCP**. The risks associated with **food handlers** contaminating **high-risk foods** with **low-dose organisms** such as *E. coli* O157, norovirus, hepatitis C, *S.* Typhi, *Shigella spp.* and campylobacter should not be underestimated. Personal **hygiene** of staff is a management responsibility and must be dealt with proactively. It must not be assumed that good personal hygiene is common sense that will be implemented automatically by all staff.

Documented procedures and rules for staff hygiene should be part of the **food** safety policy and brought to the attention of new employees during induction training. Staff must then be trained, motivated, supervised and monitored to ensure the continuous implementation of good hygiene practices.

The law, and the industry guides to good hygiene practice, require every person working in **food handling** areas to maintain high standards of cleanliness and wear suitable, clean and, where appropriate, **protective clothing**. Personal cleanliness may be considered to include good hygiene practices necessary to prevent the **contamination** of food. This interpretation prohibits smoking, spitting and the wearing of excessive jewellery, and requires any cuts to be covered with waterproof dressings.

Food handlers should be in good health, have good eyesight and be able to read, especially if they are responsible for checking thermometers, instructions on labels, date coding and the condition of food. Furthermore, clean staff wearing clean protective clothing and exhibiting good practices will promote customer confidence and increased business.

All visitors to food premises, including managers from head office, enforcement officers and maintenance operatives, should observe the same hygiene rules as staff, and wear appropriate protective clothing. Major customers undertaking inspections will expect strict adherence to company rules.

Implementation of a personal hygiene policy

Management should formulate a personal hygiene policy setting out its objectives with a list of the main areas covered. The policy should include reference to appropriate personal hygiene facilities, the food handlers' legal responsibilities and personal hygiene rules including handwashing, protective clothing, jewellery and hygiene rules for visitors. When formulating the Personal Hygiene Policy, management should have regard for the guidelines in "Food Handlers - Fitness to Work" (Department of Health), and should implement the personal hygiene policy through clearly communicated procedures that include:

- ♦ providing all food handlers with written rules on personal hygiene;
- ♦ explaining to food handlers and visitors what the rules are for good personal hygiene;
- ♦ implementing a training programme, and appropriate supervision procedures in safe food handling;
- ♦ instructing visitors, including contractors, in personal hygiene rules to be observed and ensuring that visitors are adequately supervised;
- ♦ explaining to food handlers their legal obligation to report infectious or potentially infectious conditions to management;

- excluding infectious or potentially infectious food handlers from working with food; and
- ensuring that there is a planned monitoring programme regarding the effective implementation of personal hygiene rules, together with appropriate corrective actions, such as retraining, in the event of non-compliances with the rules, and checks on the adequacy of the hygiene facilities such as handwash provision.

STAFF SELECTION

The foundations of high standards of hygiene are built by the employment of the right calibre of staff and the provision of satisfactory training. The first stage in successful recruitment is the formulation of job specifications and descriptions that clearly define the level of responsibility and skill required. A reasonable salary commensurate with these requirements must then be offered. The following points should be considered when interviewing and appointing staff.

Personal appearance and attitude

Food handlers must have:
- a clean, neat and tidy appearance;
- an absence of skin infections;
- good dental hygiene;
- clean hands with short fingernails and no evidence of nail biting;
- an absence of excessive personal jewellery or make up;
- clean shoes, suitable for the work area; and
- a belief in the need for hygiene.

Persons who cannot take the trouble to present a good appearance at interviews will not respond to hygiene disciplines imposed in the food environment. They should show enthusiasm and have a suitable attitude relevant to the position for which they are applying. Hygiene awareness and a recognised qualification, especially for supervisors, is also advantageous.

Medical screening

It is advisable to ascertain some details of an applicant's medical history, particularly relating to foodborne illnesses, **food poisoning** or persistent diarrhoea. Applicants should have to complete a medical questionnaire (see Appendix II) and in large companies may be interviewed by a doctor or nurse. When necessary, persons should be asked to submit a faecal or blood specimen, although this is not normally recommended for routine screening of all applicants. Chest X-rays may also be required.

POST APPOINTMENT

The role of management

Before any staff are allowed to commence work they should be advised, in writing, of their personal obligations in respect of hygiene. They should be informed of the training they will be expected to undertake, including attendance on courses. It should be made clear that a breach of hygiene rules could result in disciplinary action. It is particularly important to stress that they have a legal obligation to notify their supervisor if they are suffering from any condition that exposes food to risk. Food handlers should be aware that if they are suspected of having, or have been in, close contact with a person who has had food poisoning, they would be expected to cooperate by providing faecal specimens. Interference with the personal freedom of the individual is likely to arouse resistance and possibly resentment, unless staff appreciate the reasons for particular restrictions.

After attending hygiene training, food handlers must be encouraged to implement what they have been taught. Effective instruction, supervision and competency-based testing will be essential to maintain high standards of hygiene. Continuous coaching is important to keep staff up to date and to reinforce the need for high standards.

Management must lead by example and provide a hygienic working environment together with adequate resources to facilitate the achievement of high standards, for example, suitable and sufficient protective clothing, constant replenishment of liquid soap, paper towels and **cleaning** materials with adequate cleaning time. A wash-hand basin at the entrance of food rooms, together with close supervision, is the best way of ensuring staff always wash their hands before handling food.

HAND HYGIENE

The role of the hands in transferring **pathogens** to high-risk food, especially from **carriers**, is probably underestimated in the UK. In the USA, infected food handlers are much more commonly implicated in outbreaks of foodborne illness, especially from campylobacter (45%), viral **gastroenteritis**, hepatitis, shigella (94%) and *Staphylococcus aureus* (71%). It is considered that up to 25% of foodborne illness in the USA may be due to improper handwashing. Barry Michaels of Georgia Pacific Corporation reported that his review of 260 outbreaks of foodborne illness attributed 40% to food handlers exhibiting symptoms of infectious intestinal disease or who were **asymptomatic**.

Furthermore, research undertaken in care homes demonstrated that when a programme of vigorous handwashing was implemented there was a 33% reduction in common colds and a 50% reduction in **cases** of diarrhoea. The US Centre for Disease Control and Prevention advise that "handwashing" is the single most important means of preventing the spread of infection. However, there is so much confusion and misinformation regarding handwashing, that even if it is undertaken, it may not be very effective.

Skin magnification by around 3400 showing staphlococci, streptococci and bacilli, for example, *E. coli* or possibly salmonella.

The skin

To understand handwashing we need to understand the physiology of the skin. The skin consists of three layers, the epidermis, the dermis and the subcutaneous tissue. The epidermis is made up of millions of microscopic cells known as skin scales and contains many cracks and crevices that provide harbourage for resident and transient **micro-organisms**. A layer of dead skin cells is lost around every two days, although injuries and practices such as scrubbing with a hard nailbrush will result in a much more rapid loss of skin layers and eventually bleeding. A water repellent film produced by the sebaceous glands protects the outer layer of the skin. Removal of this layer by excessive handwashing or use of alcohol **disinfectants** is likely to cause irritation, dryness and roughness and increase the risk of dermatitis. All of these conditions deter people from washing their hands.

Resident micro-organisms such as *Staphylococcus epidermis, Staphylococcus saprophyticus, Enterobacter spp.* and **yeasts** are found throughout the epidermal layers and are impossible to remove, even with the most rigorous scrubbing. The presence of resident micro-organisms is important in preventing pathogens from colonising the skin. We, therefore, would not want to **sterilise** the skin, even if it was possible. The only pathogen included as a resident micro-organism on healthy skin is *Staphylococcus aureus*, although it is only likely to be present in relatively low numbers. *Staphylococcus aureus* usually needs to grow in food to around 10^6 organisms per gram to cause illness by producing sufficient amounts of **toxin**.

Transient micro-organisms, including **bacteria**, viruses, **moulds**, **parasites** and yeasts, are those organisms that "hitch a temporary ride" on and in the epidermis. They do not usually live in the skin and the types present depend on our environment and what we touch. This means that food handlers touching contaminated poultry and raw meat are likely to have salmonella, campylobacter, *Staphylococcus aureus* and *E. coli* on their hands. High numbers of transient pathogens on the hands, fingertips and nails are also likely from faecal contamination after using the toilet, changing nappies or cleaning up after pets or ill people. High levels of *Staphylococcus aureus* are likely after touching infected cuts or boils or changing a dressing. Food handlers are also much more likely to have *Listeria spp.* on their hands than, for example, office workers. Transient micro-organisms may survive on the skin from a few minutes to several hours; so, effective, regular handwashing is essential.

Handwashing strategies

Probably the most important thing is to ensure food handlers wash their hands as often as necessary. This involves explaining the hazards and demonstrating the correct procedure, which should be documented in the food safety policy. Staff will require supervision and need to be motivated to follow the procedure every time they wash their hands. Managers should lead by example.

Strategies to secure **compliance** will need to be developed. Handwashing should be monitored and may even be documented and verified, for example, by using hand swabs, **agar** plates or a fluorescent dye and ultraviolet light. Posters and signage will aid reinforcement. Disciplinary action may be necessary against employees who fail to wash their hands.

The learning process to change behaviour goes through the following stages:
♦ unconscious incompetence;
♦ conscious incompetence;
♦ conscious competence; and
♦ unconscious competence.

(Abraham Maslow)

Requirements for handwashing

Handwashing is best carried out at a designated hand-wash station and will require:

- an accessible wash-hand basin or trough, preferably with non-hand operable taps;
- a supply of clean, warm (35°C to 45°C) running water (4 to 8 litres per minute);
- suitable soap, preferably liquid, non-irritating in a replaceable cartridge;
- paper towels, preferably using an infrared dispenser; and
- a foot-operated or open-topped bin for used towels, which is emptied as often as necessary.

Misused hand basin in kitchen.
(Courtesy of Runnymede Borough Council.)

Effective handwashing

The objective of most food handlers when washing their hands should be to reduce the number of transient pathogens to a safe level. The method used will therefore depend on the number of pathogens likely to be present and this will usually depend on the last activity of the food handler. Activities likely to result in large numbers of pathogens should be followed by a double wash.

These activities include:

- entering the food room at the start of the day or after taking a break;
- using the toilet when there is a risk of faecal contamination, especially on the fingertips (toilet paper is porous and tends to slip). It should also be remembered that several cultures do not use toilet paper;
- cleaning up or contact with vomit or faecal material, for example, a guide or guard dog, a nappy, pest droppings or an ill person;
- changing, putting on a dressing or touching an infective cut, wound or boil; and
- after handling raw poultry, meat or vegetables before handling **ready-to-eat food**.

The double wash procedure

Effective handwashing relies on friction and dilution to remove transient pathogens to a safe level. The first stage of the double wash requires the use of a clean, soft-bristled nailbrush. Running warm water is required to wet the hands and the nailbrush. The temperature of the water is not critical, although a temperature of around 35°C to 45°C is recommended, as no one likes washing hands in cold water (<20°C) or hot water (>49°C).

Around 3 to 5ml of a good quality, unperfumed liquid soap should be applied to the nailbrush. **Bactericidal** soaps are not necessary, as in the majority of food handling situations, **aseptic** conditions are not achievable or required. However, because some bacteria, such as

Pseudomonas spp., may contaminate and multiply in liquid soap, only cartridge replacement containers should be used.

Brushing under running water should produce a good lather and will remove contaminants from the fingertips and under the fingernails. Continue brushing until the lather disappears; this should result in a reduction of bacteria on the fingertips of around 1000 to one. (Dr P. Snyder, Jr.) The nailbrush should then be stored bristles up. In practice, **cross-contamination** from one food handler to another via the nailbrush is unlikely. However, nailbrushes should be changed at least daily. Cleaning and **disinfection** of nailbrushes may be achieved in a dishwasher, or by the use of chemical disinfectants followed by drying.

Highfield Poster,
How to wash your hands.

The single wash procedure

The second stage of the double wash is also used as a single wash on all other occasions when washing the hands. Around 3 to 5ml of liquid soap is added to wet hands. A good lather should be produced by vigorously rubbing the hands and fingertips together. The area inbetween the fingers, around the thumbs, the forearms and wrists should be thoroughly lathered for around 20 seconds. This time may be longer if the hands are heavily soiled, for example, with blood.

The hands should be rinsed thoroughly in warm running water (around 4 to 8 litres per minute) until all lather, dirt and contaminants are removed. The rinsing process is critical as it provides dilution and friction. A further reduction of bacteria by around 100 to one will result. The hands and arms should be completely dried, preferably using paper towels. Drying is an integral part of effective handwashing as the friction removes more transient bacteria, around 100 to one. The paper towel should, if necessary, be used to turn off the tap. It should then be placed in a foot-operated, or open, waste container. The container or lid must not be touched with clean hands.

A single wash procedure should normally be used in the following situations:

♦ after combing or touching the hair, nose, mouth or ears;
♦ after eating, smoking, coughing or blowing the nose;
♦ after handling external packaging or flowers;
♦ after handling waste food or refuse;
♦ after cleaning, or handling dirty cloths, crockery etc;
♦ after shaking hands;
♦ after handling money;
♦ after touching shoes, the floor or other dirty surfaces;
♦ before putting on and taking off gloves; and
♦ as often as necessary throughout the day to remove soil and prevent product contamination.

Warm air dryers

Warm air dryers are not recommended for food handlers, as they often take too long to completely dry the hands. This results in food handlers walking away, shaking wet hands or drying their hands on their protective clothing. Dryers are unlikely to reduce the levels of bacteria remaining on the hands and some dryers may even increase the number of bacteria after washing. Residual moisture on the hands after "drying" plays a significant part in the transfer of bacteria and viruses. If roller towels are used they must not result in contamination of the hands. Only clean sections of the towel should be used and clean and dirty parts of the towel must be segregated. Care must be taken to ensure the towel is changed before it runs out.

A non-hand contact paper towel dispenser and a knee operated handwashing station.
(Courtesy of Holchem Laboratories.)

Surfaces that have been found to be contaminated with coliforms and *E. coli* include the washhand basin, the tap and the paper towel dispenser. Occasionally the door handle may be contaminated. Disinfection of these surfaces is therefore necessary during cleaning. Non-hand operable taps and paper towel dispensers are recommended.

Common reasons for failure in handwashing:
♦ failure to train and motivate food handlers to wash their hands;
♦ failure to provide adequate facilities, soap or drying materials;
♦ poor accessibility of wash-hand basins;
♦ inadequate supervision, reinforcement or management commitment;
♦ poor quality soap, which does not remove fat from hands or is affected by hard water salts and fails to lather;
♦ lack of notices/posters regarding handwashing;
♦ lack of an effective system for handwashing;
♦ inadequate time allowed;
♦ extremely high handwashing frequency disrupting the skin barrier properties resulting in skin cracking and sores, especially in winter;
♦ high staff turnover;
♦ an unpleasant experience, including use of scalding or cold water, or the use of a poor quality soap with no emollient, which dries up the skin and increases the risk of dermatitis. Some bactericidal soaps also increase the risk of dermatitis;

- failure to remove all soap residue from the hands during rinsing, resulting in skin irritation;
- overuse of a stiff nailbrush resulting in damaged skin and/or inflammation; and
- long or false fingernails.

AREAS COMMONLY MISSED DURING HANDWASHING

BACK   **FRONT**

Most frequently missed   Less frequently missed   Not missed

Hand contact during high-risk food service should be minimised and several procedures are used including tongs, utensils, plastic bags and gloves. However, cross-contamination can still occur if good practices are not observed.

The use of gloves for handling high-risk food

The use of disposable vinyl, latex and non-latex gloves has not been proved to be a safer method of handling food compared to food handlers who use effective handwashing techniques. Opponents of gloves claim they give a false sense of security, become contaminated if hands are not washed prior to putting them on and can result in cross-contamination from raw to high-risk food in the same way as hands. Furthermore, a significant number of gloves have defects and pinholes, which enable bacteria from the hands to pass through the gloves. Latex gloves may produce an **allergic** reaction in some people. The hand environment created by wearing gloves provides ideal conditions for the growth of pathogens such as *Staphylococcus aureus*. Punctures in the gloves during use may result in contamination of the high-risk food with large numbers of pathogens.

Proponents of gloves claim that, provided hands are washed before putting on the gloves and they are disposed of frequently, they minimise the risk of contamination of high-risk food, especially if effective handwashing is not being achieved. It is also claimed that food handlers with gloves are more aware that they are handling high-risk food and are less likely to scratch their head, pick their nose or carry out other bad hygiene practices. Hands should also be washed when gloves are removed as significant multiplication of pathogens may have occurred. The use of suitable gloves is recommended, for example, when handling high-risk foods for vulnerable groups or when effective handwashing is not possible.

If gloves are used a glove policy should be provided. Food handlers should be trained on how and when to put on gloves and how they should be used to prevent cross-contamination. Clear instructions regarding the changing and disposal of damaged and contaminated gloves should be given. Effective monitoring and supervision of glove use, including checking for dermatitis, is essential.

Hand disinfection

The use of bactericidal soap or disinfectants such as alcohol and chlorhexidine solutions rarely produces significant improvements in the removal of transient pathogens compared to the double wash technique. Furthermore, they tend to be less pleasant to use, dry and irritate the skin and increase the risk of dermatitis. However, formulations are improving all the time and the use of hand disinfectants, with emollients to prevent drying of the skin, may be appropriate if handwashing by the double wash method cannot be undertaken and/or aseptic food production is required. It is always preferable to wash hands prior to using a hand disinfectant although some users claim excellent results from some alcohol base gels on hands that are not visibly soiled.

Skin lotions

Skin lotions are not usually recommended, as some support bacterial growth, and result in product contamination. However, in certain situations such as very frequent handwashing, an antimicrobial-containing skin lotion may assist in maintaining skin health and minimising drying and/or cracking.

For more information on effective handwashing check www.hi-tm.com and www.gphealthsmart.com

Cuts, boils, septic spots and skin infections

Employees with boils and septic cuts should be excluded from ready-to-eat food handling areas, as such lesions contain *Staphylococcus aureus*. Uninfected wounds should be completely protected by a conspicuously coloured waterproof dressing. Cuts on hands may need the extra protection of waterproof fingerstalls. Waterproof dressings are necessary to prevent blood and bacteria from the cut contaminating the food and also to prevent bacteria from food, especially raw meat or fish, making the cut septic. Furthermore, waterproof dressings

Brightly coloured plasters should be used to cover cuts.

do not collect grease and dirt. It is preferable that green- or blue-coloured detectable plasters be used, to improve their visibility in food should they become detached. Metal strips incorporated in dressings assist detection where metal detectors are in use. Loss of dressings must be reported immediately. Perforated plasters are not recommended. Staff who report for work wearing unacceptable dressings must have them changed before they enter a food room or commence food handling duties.

The hair

Hair is constantly falling out and, along with dandruff, can result in contamination of food. As the scalp often contains pathogenic organisms such as *Staphylococcus aureus,* steps must be taken to prevent contamination from this source. The hair should be shampooed regularly and completely enclosed by suitable head covering. Hairnets (blue) worn under turbans, helmets and hats are recommended in very high-risk food handling areas, especially manufacturing. Combing of hair and adjustment of head covering should only take place in cloakrooms and should not be carried out whilst wearing protective clothing, as hairs may end up on the shoulders and then in the product. Hairgrips and clips must not be worn. After having a haircut staff should wash their hair before handling food or working in food rooms.

The nose, mouth and ears

Up to 40% of adults carry *Staphylococcus aureus* in the nose and 15% on their hands. Coughs and sneezes can carry droplet infection for a considerable distance and persons with bad colds should not handle open food. The hands should be washed after blowing the nose and soiled handkerchiefs should not be used; single-use paper handkerchiefs are preferable. The mouth may harbour staphylococci and food handlers should not eat sweets whilst working. Spitting is aesthetically unacceptable, can result in food contamination from staphylococci or streptococci and would result in enforcement action. Staff with discharges from the ears or eyes must not handle food.

Smoking

Not only is smoking illegal it also exposes food to risk of physical and microbiological contamination.

This is not only because ash or cigarette ends may find their way into open food but also because:

- it encourages coughing;
- there is a risk of contaminating food from fingers touching the lips while smoking and then touching food without effective handwashing; and
- cigarette ends, contaminated with saliva, are placed on work benches.

Legible notices should be clearly displayed, emphasising the requirement not to smoke.

Protective clothing

The proprietor must ensure that food handlers, visitors and maintenance personnel wear clean, washable (withstand up to 85°C), light-coloured, durable protective clothing, without external pockets. Protective garments should be appropriate for the work being carried out, should completely cover ordinary clothing and should not be removed whilst food handling. Jumper and shirt sleeves must not protrude and if short-sleeved overalls are worn, only clean forearms must be visible. Press studs are preferred to buttons as they are less likely to become detached. Clean overalls must be available as needed and stored away from contaminants. New products and practices may require a reappraisal of protective clothing provided.

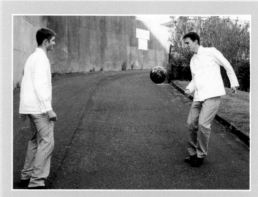

Don't play games in protective clothing during breaks.

Staff must be aware that protective clothing is worn primarily to protect the food from risk of contamination and not to keep their own clothes clean. Dust, pet hairs and woollen fibres are just a few of the contaminants carried on ordinary clothing. Protective clothing must not be worn outside food premises or for travelling to and from work.

When selecting protective clothing the manager must consider:

♦ the duties of the wearer and which parts of the body should be covered;
♦ how the garments are fastened;
♦ the colour and type of material;
♦ the smartness and fit (to improve customer image and generate pride in the wearer); and
♦ whether to purchase or use a laundry rental service.

Outdoor clothing and personal effects must not be brought into food rooms, unless stored in suitable lockers. Lockers should be adequately ventilated to keep them dry, eliminate odours and prevent mould growth. Cloakrooms which are well-ventilated and cleaned regularly are preferred.

Aprons, if worn, should be suitable for the particular operation and capable of being thoroughly cleansed. Disposable aprons may be obtained and should be disposed of after each use. The use of coloured aprons, to aid detection if damaged, is recommended. When used in factories, aprons are normally impervious. Aprons that are torn or have badly worn surfaces, which render them incapable of being cleaned, should be discarded. Facilities should be provided for cleaning aprons at various times during production and at the end of each working day. Cleansable hooks should also be provided for hanging up clean aprons.

Boots may be provided for wearing in wet areas. They should be anti-slip, unlined and easy to clean. Suitable facilities should be provided for cleaning boots, and storing cleaned boots.

Heavy duty rubber gloves may be worn for various jobs, for example, on inspection belts in factories or for cleaning operations. Gloves should be maintained in a clean condition and torn gloves should be discarded. If in contact with food, gloves should be of a different colour so that any detached pieces can be easily detected. After use, gloves should be thoroughly cleaned and dried. Only plain, unperfumed talc should be provided for use with gloves. The inside of all gloves provides a warm, moist environment ideal for the multiplication of bacteria, and gloves should not be left on **food-contact surfaces** during, for example, breaks.

Jewellery and perfume

Food handlers should not wear earrings, watches, jewelled rings or brooches, which harbour dirt and bacteria. Furthermore, stones and small pieces of metal may end up in the food and result in a customer complaint. Food handlers should not wear strong-smelling perfume or aftershave as they may taint foods, especially food with a high fat content.

Practices

Bad habits are not easily broken and if they are exhibited by a food handler, and present a risk of contaminating food, careful and conscientious control is required. Common bad practices include:

- wetting fingers to open bags or to pick up sheets of wrapping paper;
- picking the nose;
- scratching the head or spots;
- tasting food with an unwashed spoon;
- coughing and sneezing on to hands and handling food without first washing;
- using a food sink for handwashing;
- using a wash-hand basin to rinse utensils;
- handling the inner parts of crockery or glasses; and
- chewing gum, eating food or sweets in food rooms other than dining areas.

The supervisor's role in maintaining high standards of personal hygiene

Food business operators must put in place effective supervisory management to ensure high standards of personal hygiene of all food handlers. Supervisors must lead by personal example, especially in relation to handwashing and wearing protective clothing. Supervisors must ensure that the appropriate facilities are provided and that soap, paper towels, clean protective clothing and a supply of waterproof plasters are always available. They will assist in the implementation and the communication of the food business's personal hygiene policy and procedures through, for example, training sessions (one-to-one and group) and staff meetings. Supervisors should provide clear instruction and training of staff, including arranging induction and refresher training. Training and instruction should emphasise matters such as the correct handwashing procedure, avoidance of bad personal habits and individual responsibility to adhere to protective clothing and jewellery policies and sickness reporting procedures. Posters and notices may be provided to remind food handlers of their personal hygiene responsibilities.

Supervisors should check that food handlers understand personal hygiene rules. For example, the supervisor may ask an employee to demonstrate the correct handwash procedure. Monitoring includes spot visual checks throughout the day to confirm that correct handwashing procedures are being practised, and that clean protective clothing is being correctly worn. Supervisors may also carry out random swab tests of hands and record the results. If, for example, hand swabbing results or visual spot checks indicate failures in personal hygiene, then the supervisor must report findings to management and take corrective actions. Supervisors should periodically check that sickness-reporting rules are being followed, and that health questionnaires and other due diligence records are being kept and fully completed. Retraining of food handlers may be required if swab results indicate poor handwashing standards. Supervisors may need to report to management defects in personal hygiene facilities, for example, inadequate provision of soap and paper towels. Supervisors should discipline, as a last resort, food handlers who deliberately or consistently flout hygiene rules.

Exclusion of food handlers

Management should be aware that even with the strictest application of health standards, a healthy, symptom-free employee may be excreting pathogenic bacteria or viruses. Furthermore, laboratory tests cannot be relied on to detect small numbers of pathogens even though they are being excreted. Consequently, it must be emphasised that high standards of hygiene are essential to prevent the contamination of food, rather than a laboratory report indicating the absence of pathogens from a faecal specimen.

Any food handler suffering from, or being a carrier of a disease likely to be transmitted through food or afflicted, for example, with infected wounds, skin infections, sores or diarrhoea, must report to management immediately.

No person so affected is permitted to handle food or enter any food handling area if they are likely to contaminate food, i.e. they should be excluded. This includes managers, maintenance contractors and inspectors.

In 2009 the Food Standards Agency published an updated version of "Food Handlers: Fitness to Work – Regulatory Guidance and Best Practice Advice for Food Business Operators" to reduce the spread of infection to other people through food.

(www.food.gov.uk/multimedia/pdfs/publication/fitnesstoworkguide09v2.pdf)

The Guide provides advice on best practice and meeting the requirements of Annex II, Chapter VIII of Regulation (EC) 852/2004 on the hygiene of foodstuffs. However, it is not legally binding and only the courts have the power to interpret the law.

Managers should discourage any unnecessary visitors to food handling areas and minimise direct contact with the food and food-contact surfaces to reduce the risk of contaminating food. Persons with diarrhoea or vomiting, or with skin infections etc. should be excluded, usually for 48 hours after symptoms stop and once any treatment has ceased. Good hygiene, especially handwashing is essential. However, some more serious diseases require prolonged periods of exclusion including the provision of negative faecal specimens.

Because absenteeism is undesirable managers must ensure staff are well motivated to report ailments that they believe may result in salary reduction or even a loss of their job.

All reports of illness must be noted on staff records. New staff and staff returning from holidays abroad, particularly from countries with warm climates and suspect sanitation, should complete a short medical questionnaire (Appendix II). Any positive answers will require further medical investigation and may result in exclusion.

New staff should also be given verbal and written instruction of their legal responsibilities regarding the notification of foodborne diseases and skin infections that may give rise to contaminating food.

Correct handwashing and drying, especially after using the toilet, and minimising the handling of food remain the best way of preventing food contamination as many food handlers may be unaware they are excreting foodborne pathogens.

THE EXCLUSION OF FOOD HANDLERS WITH SPECIFIC INFECTIONS WHO COULD EXPOSE FOOD TO RISK OF CONTAMINATION

(Food Handlers: Fitness to Work 2009)

Organism/disease	Criteria for clearance to return to work when symptom-free
Bacillus spp. *Campylobacter spp.* *Clostridium perfringens* *Cryptosporidium and Giardia lamblia* Norovirus *Salmonella spp.* (excluding typhoid and paratyphoid) *Shigella sonnei* *Staphylococcus aureus* *Vibrio (except vibrio cholerae O1 and O139)* *Worms except threadworm and Taenia solium* *Yersinia spp.*	48 hours after first normal stool, or when other symptoms stop, providing good hygiene is practised
Typhoid and paratyphoid (enteric fever)	*Six consecutive negative stool specimens, one week apart starting three weeks after the completion of **antibiotic** treatment (Usual advice from Health Protection Agency)
Verocytotoxin-producing *Escherichia coli* (e.g. *E. coli* O157) *Shigella dysenteriae, flexneri and boydii*	In addition to the 48-hour exclusion, medical clearance usually requires two consecutive negative faecal specimens taken at intervals of at least 48 hours
Hepatitis A	Seven days after onset of jaundice and/or other symptoms
Entamoeba hystolytica	In addition to the 48-hour exclusion. One negative faecal specimen taken at least one week after the end of treatment
Threadworm	Until treated
Taenia solium	Two negative faecal specimens at one and two weeks post treatment
Vibrio cholerae O1 and O139	In addition to the normal 48-hour exclusion, medical clearance usually requires two consecutive negative faecal specimens taken at intervals of at least 24 hours

Where any of the above advice contradicts advice from the Health Protection Agencies then their advice takes precedence. On some occasions, food handlers suspected of being infected or carriers may be given duties that don't involve handling open, ready-to-eat foods. Managers must be confident that they observe good personal hygiene practices. Food handlers who have close family contacts with infected persons, especially suffering from enteric fever, *E. coli* O157, norovirus or shigella should be excluded from direct contact with open ready-to-eat foods until medical clearance has been obtained.

*The advice regarding typhoid carriers is of concern as there is an 8% risk that after six consecutive negative specimens the next specimen will be positive.

9 Training & education of food handlers

Training is intended to modify or develop knowledge, skills and attitude through learning experience and to achieve effective performance in an activity or range of activities. Although ignorance may be a factor, most **food poisoning** incidents are caused by a failure of managers and **food handlers** to implement good **hygiene** practice. Consequently, **food** becomes **contaminated**, **pathogenic** bacteria are provided with the opportunity to multiply or they survive inadequate cooking or processing.

Training of managers, supervisors and all people who can influence the safety of food is essential to reduce the unacceptable high levels of food poisoning. However, the emphasis on classroom-based, foundation courses and certification in isolation has not been particularly successful in reducing levels of food poisoning. The main reason for this is the belief that ignorance is the main reason for food poisoning. Furthermore, it is assumed that if food handlers are aware of their legal obligations and they are provided with knowledge and understanding on the prevention of food poisoning, this will automatically result in the implementation of good hygiene practices. As Foster and Kaferstein stated in 1985 "human beings are not empty vessels into which correct information can be poured, thereby eliminating undesirable actions".

This hypothesis can be tested by considering the number of people who break the speed limit when driving. They all know what the speed limit is but it is often ignored. Prior to breaking the speed limit, most people will undertake a **risk assessment**. They will consider:

♦ the importance of getting to their destination on time;
♦ the consequences of speeding, including the road conditions and the risk to themselves and others;
♦ whether or not they believe the legal speed limit on the particular stretch of the road is reasonable or necessary;
♦ the likelihood of detection; and
♦ the deterrent, i.e. the punishment if caught.

In the same way, food handlers can be provided with the knowledge of the importance of handwashing after using the toilet but many of them continue to ignore this simple, but essential, good hygiene practice. Reasons for this can include:

♦ a belief that it is not important and that it is unlikely to result in food poisoning;
♦ it is unlikely that their failure to wash their hands will be discovered;
♦ they will not be punished for not washing their hands;
♦ there are no handwashing facilities, no hot water, no soap or no towels;
♦ management don't appear to care whether or not staff wash their hands; or
♦ they have insufficient time to wash their hands.

The importance of training

Having recognised that the objective of food safety training is to provide competent food handlers who continuously produce **safe food**, management must be convinced of the importance and benefits of training to provide the necessary resources.

Training should be considered as an investment in the future and evidence is available to show that companies providing high levels of training usually have better growth and profits. Training is necessary to:

♦ enable staff to fulfill their potential by understanding their responsibilities and improving their skills;

♦ promote confidence, increase job satisfaction, improve performance/morale and develop team spirit; and

♦ reduce the amount of supervision required.

The benefits of hygiene training

Hygiene training of staff should stress the importance of hygiene to the commercial viability of the organisation and how a food poisoning incident or serious food complaint is likely to affect them. Such training should contribute significantly to the profitability of a food business by:

♦ assisting in the production of safe food;

♦ safeguarding the quality of the product and reducing food wastage;

♦ reducing complaints;

♦ generating a pride in appearance and practices, increasing job satisfaction and probably reducing staff turnover;

♦ contributing to increased productivity;

♦ ensuring that all the correct procedures, including cleaning, are followed;

♦ complying with any legal provisions or the requirements of industry guides or codes of practice;

♦ promoting a good company image, which should result in increased business; and

♦ improving the supervisory skills of managers.

The food industry will benefit by having available a pool of trained food handlers. Furthermore, if good food hygiene practices are also implemented at home, the level of food poisoning should reduce even more.

Effective food safety training

Effective food safety training involves two stages, firstly the provision of knowledge in a way that develops understanding and a positive attitude, for example, the importance of handwashing and the knowledge of when to wash the hands. The second stage involves the implementation of the knowledge by washing the hands properly when required. Practice, motivation and effective supervision, especially coaching, should result in the objective being achieved, i.e. the competency of the food handler and implementation of good practice at all times.

> **KNOWLEDGE + PRACTICE = TRAINING**

> **UNDERSTANDING (LEARNING) ➡ ATTITUDE ➡ BEHAVIOUR ➡ COMPETENCY**

To change behaviour, learning must be interesting, challenging, realistic, credible, relevant to the job and take account of existing knowledge.

LEARNING METHODS

Hygiene education revolves around some simple but important principles:

- ◆ if all **I** do is *hear* – **I** will *forget;*
- ◆ if **I** *hear* and *see* – **I** will *remember;*
- ◆ if **I** *hear, see* and *do* – **I** will understand.

Understanding helps *remembering* which leads to *learning.*

The first step in training is to motivate the employees to learn. They must appreciate that they could be a vital link in a chain of events leading to food poisoning and that suitable training will give them the knowledge to provide safe food.

The second stage in training involves explanation and demonstration to provide knowledge and skill respectively.

The third stage involves the trainee practising the task and the fourth stage should be to test that the task can be performed satisfactorily and that competency has been achieved.

Successful intervention (training)

There are many reasons why staff who have attended food safety courses fail to implement good hygiene practices, including:

- ◆ ignorance;
- ◆ poor working conditions;
- ◆ low pay;
- ◆ lack of job prospects;
- ◆ high turnover of staff;
- ◆ staff shortages; and
- ◆ lack of facilities, procedures and effective supervision.

To be successful, intervention must convince a person that:

- ◆ the problem can affect him/her;
- ◆ the outcome could be serious; and
- ◆ the proposed preventive measure is effective, practical and will benefit him/her.

Selling food safety solely on the basis of preventing a possible food poisoning outbreak is likely to be as successful as getting someone to stop smoking because of the long-term health effects to himself/herself or others. In other words some staff may respond, others won't. There are approximately 370,000 catering businesses and around 100 reported food poisoning outbreaks per year. Therefore, the chance of getting an identified outbreak in a catering premises is around one in 3,700. It is essential therefore to motivate food handlers to implement the knowledge gained, by using several factors in addition to "preventing food poisoning".

The motivation of food handlers to apply knowledge

The owners of the business must have a genuine commitment to achieving and maintaining high standards of food safety. Consequently they will:

- ◆ provide good working conditions and facilities for securing high standards of hygiene and **personal hygiene;**

♦ ensure managers and supervisors are committed and trained to provide the necessary coaching, instruction, motivating and training of staff;
♦ develop a culture of high standards, which ensures all staff believe that the right way is the hygienic way;
♦ provide the necessary resources and organisation including finance, suitable food safety expertise and sufficient time (adequate staff levels); and
♦ communicate their views to staff to engender a positive attitude towards safety. Staff must know what is expected of them.

Staff may be motivated to implement high standards because they believe:
♦ it results in improved professionalism;
♦ it is a legal requirement;
♦ customers demand them;
♦ they will not cause food poisoning;
♦ it will assist their promotion (or other incentives);
♦ failure to do so may result in disciplinary action (deterrent); and
♦ their colleagues will object if they don't (peer pressure).

Management responsibility

Although staff cannot avoid their individual responsibility, especially when supervisors are absent, it is important to remember that most food poisoning results from management failure. In particular managers should:
♦ communicate the company policy on hygiene to staff and demonstrate full management support for the policy;
♦ lead by example. Managers must wear the appropriate protective clothing, wash their hands on entering a food room and always follow correct procedures;
♦ ensure staff are competent to provide safe food;
♦ remove any barriers to good hygiene practice;
♦ ensure staff have sufficient time to undertake good hygiene practices;
♦ take appropriate action against staff who exhibit unhygienic practices; and
♦ appreciate the potential effect of bad hygiene on the profitability of the business.

Management knowledge and skills

Managers of **food businesses** must themselves be trained to a level appropriate to their position and should:
♦ be able to prepare and implement a satisfactory food safety policy;
♦ know the requirements of legislation relating to their operation;
♦ have sufficient food hygiene knowledge to enable them to analyse **hazards**, determine **risks**, implement effective control and monitoring procedures at all points in the food business operation that are critical to food safety and, when necessary, take appropriate corrective action and implement product recall; and
♦ have the skill to select, motivate, train and supervise staff who have the necessary attributes to become competent food handlers.

The legal requirement for training

Section 16(1) and para 5(3) of Schedule 1 of the Food Safety Act, 1990 empower Ministers to make regulations requiring the hygiene training of persons engaged in food businesses. Section 23 of the Act empowers food authorities to provide food hygiene training courses for such persons. Chapter XII of Regulation EC No 852/2004 states, "Food business operators shall ensure:

(1) that food handlers are supervised **and** instructed **and/or** trained in food hygiene matters commensurate with their work activity"; and

(2) that those responsible for the development and maintenance of the HACCP system or for the operation of relevant guides have received adequate training in the application of the HACCP principles.

The level of training, instruction or supervision of food handlers is a responsibility placed on the food business to determine, having regard to the nature of the business and the role played by food handlers within it, and should be assessed as part of the HACCP system. Authorised officers should take into account any relevant UK or EC industry guides to good hygiene practice when assessing training requirements, but it is recommended that persons preparing high-risk **open food** require the level of training equivalent to that contained in the level 2 accredited food safety courses.

It has also been suggested that food businesses may not successfully utilise the defence of **due diligence**, unless staff are properly trained and adequate records of training are kept.

Unfortunately the UK legislation, the codes of practice and the industry guides do not define "training" and fail to stress the need for the competency of food handlers.

Although the majority of food handlers engaged in high-risk food handling will benefit from attending an accredited course, it must be emphasised that obtaining an examination certificate relates to knowledge not competency. Consequently, a food handler who has a certificate but fails to implement the knowledge will not comply with the law.

It should also be made clear that food handlers involved solely with the handling and preparation of raw food, or staff handling only packaged high-risk food, will benefit from attending much shorter courses designed specifically for their needs. Two/three hours relevant on-site training will probably be more beneficial, and certainly more cost-effective than attending a classroom-based accredited course.

An alternative approach to training

The Food Safety Authority of Ireland are to be commended for their enlightened approach to food safety training. The FSA (Ireland) state in their "Guides to Food Safety Training" that food safety training is the key to food safety. It does not have to be certified. Training is only effective when training standards are being demonstrated in the food operation – effective training must be continuous.

Standards are expressed in terms of food safety skills, i.e. what the employee must be able to demonstrate in the area of food safety commensurate with their activity. For example:

Food safety skills	What the employee must do to demonstrate this skill	Employers, supporting activities
Monitor and record the temperature of foods.	Use a temperature probe correctly.	Provide appropriate, calibrated and maintained temperature probes.
	Know when to probe food products.	Provide appropriate rules for using and cleaning probes.
	Know the temperature limits (company/legal).	Provide relevant time/temperature recording sheets.
	Record the temperature.	Reinforce the need for time/temperature control using coaching, notices etc.
	Take corrective action and/or advise the supervisor if temperature outside specification.	Provide effective supervision.

A checklist may be designed to assess the knowledge and skills of food handlers during **auditing** or enforcement inspections. For example, food handlers should:

♦ know and adhere to their legal responsibilities regarding food safety;
♦ know the hazards and implement controls associated with their activities including **cross-contamination** and prevention of contamination;
♦ know high-risk and **low-risk foods**;
♦ avoid unnecessary handling of food/**food-contact surfaces**;
♦ avoid unhygienic practices that expose food to risk; and
♦ observe high standards of personal hygiene.

(If applicable):

♦ use a probe thermometer correctly;
♦ demonstrate effective checking of deliveries;
♦ demonstrate effective monitoring of controls; and
♦ know what appropriate corrective action to take if something goes wrong.

PLANNING AND IMPLEMENTING A TRAINING PROGRAMME

A structured approach to training will enable organisations to obtain the maximum benefits. Managers should consider future skill requirements, identify training objectives and set targets to achieve by specific dates. An appropriate budget allocation will be required. The first step is to determine whether sufficient expertise is available to plan and implement a training programme in-house. Many organisations will probably benefit from the use of experienced hygiene training consultants. Successful training programmes will usually involve the following stages.

Management of the training programme

One person should be responsible for the programme and continually monitor its progress and effectiveness. Management support will be essential and regular reports should be made to directors or the proprietor. A food safety policy statement should be signed by the chairman or proprietor to demonstrate his/her support for, and the commitment of the company to, training and high standards of hygiene. He/she must ensure, as far as practicable, that appropriate managers are appointed and systems established to ensure this policy is implemented.

Training needs analysis

The range of tasks and the risk to food safety of each task will need to be established, together with the existing level of skill and knowledge of all operatives, including managers, supervisors, cleaners and maintenance staff. (The definition of a food handler suggested by the Catering Industry Guide is "any person in a food business who handles food whether open or packaged [food includes drink and ice]".) The academic ability (the ability to assimilate knowledge, study, sit examinations and read and write) and competency of each person will need to be determined from personal records interviews, and observations. This will need to be carried out sensitively in the case of staff with literacy problems to avoid possible ridicule.

Assessment must also be made of the hygiene awareness, skill and behaviour of new employees, who should not be allowed to work in high-risk situations without appropriate induction training and close supervision. A recognised hygiene qualification is an indication of hygiene awareness but not a guarantee of competency.

Establishing a training committee

A training programme will probably be more successful if the views of the workforce are taken into account and it is not considered to be imposed.

In large organisations it may be beneficial to establish a training committee with representatives from appropriate departments and/or disciplines. Members may include the hygiene training/personnel manager, the production/catering/retail manager, an engineer, a supervisor and a first tier worker. All groups of staff should be given the opportunity to contribute, for example, by questionnaire or through discussion.

The committee will be responsible for considering the information collected and comparing the actual standards of hygiene with the required standards to determine the training needs. Objectives should be determined and targets set for the development and implementation of various parts of the programme. As far as practicable, the committee should ensure that the training undertaken is of benefit to individuals and the company as a whole.

The content of training programmes

The content of the programme will depend on the shortfall in standards/levels of skill, the time to be allocated and the finance available. These factors will also influence how, when, where and by whom the training will be undertaken. Competence assessment of operatives must be built into the programme at the beginning to ensure it is effective and provides value for money. The following questions will have to be answered:

Is the training to be provided in-house or are external consultants to be used?

To be effective, hygiene training must be continuous, accurate and up to date. It should include:
- ◆ pretraining assessment;
- ◆ induction training;

- on-the-job training (reinforcement, instruction and supervision);
- attendance of an appropriate food hygiene session/course (courses must meet the specific needs of the food business and be practical);
- continuous refresher training; and
- evaluation of training.

Trainers must have the ability to educate and motivate, and the necessary skill and knowledge to effect a change in behaviour of those persons being trained. In large organisations, managers with training skills who have attended an appropriate intermediate or advanced hygiene course may be able to provide level 2 hygiene training specifically designed for the company. Alternatively, an external trainer could provide a modified course to suit the requirements of the particular food business. One major advantage of in-house training is that it can be linked with

Food Safety Level 2
Highfield.co.uk ltd e-learning.

training for hazard analysis and the monitoring of critical control points. The supervisor should be responsible for on-the-job coaching, effective supervision and for continuous refresher training. In the event of a food handler failing to carry out an important food safety procedure, the supervisor should remedy the problem immediately. On-site computer-based programmes (e-learning) are ideal as retraining can be provided immediately when it is required. The need for, or value of, recertification of food handlers every three years has not been established in terms of the benefit to food safety. However, provision must be made to update training when, for example, new legislation or new food safety systems, such as **HACCP**, are introduced.

Who will be trained and to what level?
The industry guides to good hygiene practice identify the appropriate level of training for food handlers. All staff should understand the essentials of food hygiene as part of their induction training, prior to starting work for the first time. Most food handlers will then require hygiene awareness instruction, within four weeks, which may include:

- an overview of the company's food safety policy, confirmation of the company's commitment to hygiene and the consequences of a breakdown in hygiene;
- the potential of bacteria to cause illness;
- personal health and hygiene, including the legal responsibilities of food handlers and the need to report illness to their supervisor;
- preventing contamination, including foreign body contamination;
- cleaning and disinfection procedures, materials, methods and storage;
- food storage (protection and temperature control);
- recognition of **pests** and signs of pests; and
- waste disposal.

The actual content of, and requirement for, training will depend on the type of food being handled and the risk to food safety posed by the tasks undertaken, together with the level of supervision. Organisations with a high turnover of staff will require more emphasis on instruction and supervision, although training should still be provided. It is recommended that high-risk food handlers attend an accredited level 2 food safety course or an equivalent in-house course. Alternatively e-learning, distance learning or on the job training may be utilised to provide the relevant level of knowledge. In order to comply with the law this knowledge must be implemented by staff who follow good hygiene practice and demonstrate competency to produce safe food.

Supervisors and managers will benefit from attending either a level 3 (around 20 hours) or level 4 (around 40 hours) food safety course. If they are responsible for the HACCP system they will also require training in the application of HACCP principles. HACCP training may be incorporated within the level 3 or level 4 course.

What provision has been made for pretraining assessment and induction training?

Pretraining assessment of new employees can considerably reduce the amount of time spent on training. Courses that include a significant amount of information already known to food handlers are often counter-productive and demotivating. Pretraining assessment is just as important for new employees with a food safety qualification as for those who have attended in-house training with their previous employers, or those who have received no training. It is essential that all new starters are properly supervised/instructed and receive essential induction training prior to carrying out any **food handling** duties. All companies should provide new employees with a basic induction book, which states the company food safety policy and details the hygiene rules that they will be expected to follow. Operatives should complete a short test to confirm they have read and understood the content of the book. The booklet could be used as a basis for short induction training sessions, which will be necessary to emphasise the dangers of bad hygiene, what is expected of him/her and the consequences for the employee failing to adhere to essential hygiene rules. On-the-job training is critical in developing the correct attitude of new food handlers. Staff must be shown the most hygienic way of performing their job as bad habits, once cultivated, are difficult to break. As well as explaining how to carry out a task, staff must be told the reason for carrying it out in a particular way.

What training and examination techniques will be used?

Most food handlers involved with the preparation of high-risk food attend a formal course of lectures provided by an internal or external trainer. However, certified courses presented in a classroom style with written examinations may be inappropriate for some operatives and other methods of training designed to improve hygiene standards may be necessary. It is estimated that around 25% of people in the UK have literacy problems. National vocational qualifications (NVQs) and other competence-based routes to attaining national food hygiene qualifications should also be considered. Open learning programmes with workbooks may be of use in certain circumstances.

Computer-based training (e-learning)

A considerable increase in food safety training using computers has taken place in the last few years. Computer-based training, especially for induction, level 2, level 3 and refresher training, has several advantages compared to classroom-based courses.

Advantages of high quality computer-based training

♦ *Consistent* – the same high quality interactive information is available 24 hours a day;

♦ *Flexible and accessible* – training is provided at a convenient time for a realistic period of time, training missed through illness or unexpected busy periods is easily rescheduled;

♦ *Convenient* – all training can be carried out on site;

♦ *Value* – very cost-effective, no travel, no subsistence, reduced training time because pretesting ensures you only provide necessary training;

♦ *Complete solution* – some packages incorporate induction, level 2 and level 3 and facilitate continuous refresher training;

♦ *Monitoring* – an accurate overview of training progress will be available;

♦ *Records* – comprehensive information of the performance of each food handler can be printed out and may be used to support a due-diligence defence;

♦ *Understandable* – can be used successfully by people with reading difficulties or those whose second language is English, or those with learning difficulties including dyslexia; and

♦ *Certificated* – on successful completion of the programme a recognised certificate of training may be provided. Furthermore, it may be possible for food handlers to sit an accredited examination if this is required.

However, computer-based training should not be used to cut training budgets or make trainers redundant. As stated earlier the major reason for food poisoning and food complaints is the failure to implement good hygiene practice. Trainers should be involved with the development and auditing of systems that ensure the implementation of good hygiene practice at all levels. This will also involve additional training of supervisors and managers to ensure effective and continuous training, through coaching and reinforcement, of all food handlers.

Examinations and testing

Given the considerable number of food handlers with literacy problems, or whose second language is English, the use and type of examination should be considered carefully, especially at level 2. Examinations which include out-of-date, confusing or irrelevant questions may cause more harm than good. It is also essential, at level 2, that food handlers should be advised which questions they get wrong. At no time should the examination or qualification at level 2 ever assume more importance than the training. Examinations should be practically based and relevant to the job of the food handler to avoid trainers stating "in practice this is the correct procedure, but the correct answer in the examination is different", or "you won't need this information for your job but you may need it for the examination".

It should be remembered that the information provided at level 2 is essential for ensuring food safety, it is not to test the academic ability of food handlers. There is no need to provide unusual, complicated or obscure questions.

Testing by the use of projects and assignments relevant to the specific food business is receiving increased support in preference to the theoretical examination of level 3 and level 4 courses.

Have arrangements been made to continually assess the competency of the trained food handlers?

Increased knowledge, obtained by food handlers attending hygiene courses, may soon disappear. Prior to sending staff on courses a record should be made of their understanding and implementation of good hygiene practices. A further assessment should be made on completion of the course to ensure it provided value for money. In addition, competence assessment should be incorporated within the day-to-day role of supervisors to ensure hygiene practices are observed and to provide continuous refresher training. Interactive hygiene software will also be useful to provide immediate refresher training.

Accurate records of task assessment, standards achieved, courses attended and progress through training of each employee should be maintained. Staff appraisals can be linked to staff development to determine future training needs.

It is unfortunate that some organisations and auditors put more emphasis on paper records and certification than they do on the competency of food handlers at foundation level.

Competency assessment cards should be used to:

♦ ensure staff implement good hygiene practice;

♦ ensure supervisors accept responsibility for the competency of staff;

♦ demonstrate compliance with the legal requirement "that food handlers are supervised and instructed and/or trained in food hygiene matters commensurate with their work activity"; and

♦ assist in a due-diligence defence as they will form an essential part of the training records.

Highfield.co.uk ltd competency assessment cards.

Training sessions and methods

When planning training it is important to consider the background of the food handlers including their age, previous experience, ability, language difficulties and interests. Objectives for training must be established and, more importantly, achieved. Finally, the training method and content must be decided and visual aids selected. Food handlers must be encouraged to participate, especially if in groups, and this may be accomplished by asking questions beginning with the words, how, why, what, when, who, where and which. E-learning programmes must be interactive if they are to be successful.

There are many different ways of providing knowledge and training, however, they should all have regard to the key phases of information processing, namely: attention; comprehension; retention; and recall. Training can be provided to a single food handler, a group of food handlers, in each case on or off the job.

TRAINING METHODS

Individual	Group	On-the-job
Distance learning	Classroom/lectures	Practical instruction
Revision	Meetings/discussions	Coaching (supervision)
Research	Workshops/case studies	Experience/practice
E-learning (computer-based)	Seminars	Management

In large companies hygiene committees, similar to safety committees, could be established to discuss ways in which hygiene can be improved and customer complaints reduced.

Whichever method is adopted, it should be designed to ensure that the food handler retains as many important facts as possible. The length of training sessions depends to a large extent on the complexity of the material being presented, relative to the ability of the food handlers to concentrate and comprehend. However, for the majority of food handlers, sessions should be held frequently and kept short and simple.

It is often advantageous to invite visiting lecturers, such as environmental health practitioners/officers, to reinforce hygiene training, as they usually present a slightly different approach, which may stimulate renewed interest, even if it is only to highlight the legal obligations placed upon food handlers. The use of guest lecturers also demonstrates the importance the company places on hygiene training.

Communication skills

To get the message across, the hygiene trainer must take account of factors that interfere with effective communication and these may be considered as factors affecting either the trainer or the trainee.

Factors affecting the trainer

- *Voice* – should not be monotonous, too quiet or too loud.
- *Appearance* – should be smart and suitably dressed.
- *Habits* – should not be distracting, for example, rattling loose change, walking up and down, frequent repetition of words or phrases such as "ok", frequent touching of the hair or face.
- *Eye contact* – should be maintained with as many of the group as is possible. Each trainee should feel that he/she is being addressed.
- *Enthusiasm* – should be conveyed to the trainees, who must be given the impression that the trainer believes in the importance of what is being said. Questions should be encouraged.
- *Knowledge of the subject* – should be thorough as reasoned arguments are more likely to succeed than dogma.
- *Presentation* – must be at the appropriate level. Trainers must not talk down to people or over their heads. Sessions must be well-planned as disjointed, unrehearsed sessions are not effective.
- *Vocabulary* – must be appropriate. Long difficult speeches, words and jargon will not be appreciated.

Factors affecting the trainee
- ♦ *Motivation* – are the trainees aware of the importance of the subject and how it affects them either directly or indirectly?
- ♦ *Comprehension* – if trainees do not understand what is said they will soon lose interest.
- ♦ *Time of day* – large lunches, too much drink or training sessions after a hard day's work may result in student indifference.
- ♦ *Length of session* – as for as practicable training sessions at induction and foundation level should be kept to about an hour.
- ♦ *Design of training room/area* – can everyone see and hear the trainer/visual aids?
- ♦ *Visual aids* – professional, legible, informative, interesting and, sometimes, amusing.

The location and timing of training courses

Provided adequate training facilities are available, it is preferable for training courses to be organised on the food premises. Although six-hour level 2 courses can be completed in a day, improved results should be obtained by organising sessions of 30 minutes or an hour over several days or weeks. A frequent compromise is three x two hour or two x three hour sessions. Level 4 courses will usually be organised at training centres, hotels or colleges where appropriate facilities are available to allow use of videos and other hygiene aids as well as any necessary demonstrations.

Training should be undertaken at a time that is convenient to the business operation but also acceptable to the food handlers.

Visual aids equipment

DVDs, PowerPoint™ presentations, card games, desktop presenters, interactive games, photographs, posters and exhibits such as pests and food complaints are useful to break up training sessions and maintain interest. They are also useful for highlighting actual situations that would be difficult to recreate in a training room. Care must be taken to ensure the information presented does not become dated. Presentations should be carefully prepared and used to emphasise, clarify or supplement talks. Interesting or amusing coloured illustrations that maintain attention are preferable to black and white text, and essential at foundation level. Presentations on screens should be clear and legible to everyone in the audience and not be crammed with too much information. It is better to use two or more PowerPoint™ slides rather than cramming information. Graphs and illustrations are preferable to tables, and a good contrast between text and background is essential. The number of words should be limited to a maximum of around 40 with adequate spaces between lines. Presentations should be rehearsed to ensure familiarisation with sequences.

Multimedia projectors

The main advantage of the projectors are that they enable trainers to maintain eye contact with trainees and lectures must not be presented to the screen. PowerPoint™ presentations are much more flexible than the transparencies they replaced. They are also very easy to amend and customise.

Trainers should be familiar with equipment and should be able to carry out minor repairs such as changing bulbs or fuses. Focusing and volume control should be attended to before trainees assemble.

Piloting of the programme

Prior to the introduction of the programme, it should be piloted to a cross-section of employees. Close supervision and monitoring is essential to obtain accurate feedback from those trained to enable the programme to be evaluated. Competence assessments following training should be compared with assessments prior to training.

Implementation of the training programme

Provided the evaluation of the pilot exercise is satisfactory and any necessary corrective action is approved, the programme may be introduced to all parts of the organisation. Consultation with the local environmental health department during the planning and implementation of the training programme may be beneficial to confirm you are satisfying any legal requirement.

The programme must be flexible and monitored and evaluated continually to ensure the objectives are being achieved and, if necessary, modifications can be made.

Evaluation of the programme

Evaluation of the whole programme and each training session/course is essential. Evaluation of staff, supervisors and managers should be undertaken to determine:

- ◆ whether objectives have been achieved;
- ◆ if knowledge and awareness are greater;
- ◆ if attitude has changed;
- ◆ if behaviour has changed (improved skills, practices and standards);
- ◆ if staff are competent to provide safe food; and
- ◆ further training needs.

Various techniques of evaluation have been used following training and attendance at courses, including:

- ◆ pre- and post-training inspections;
- ◆ pre- and post-training interviews to assess knowledge gained;
- ◆ pre- and post-training testing, including practical assessment of competence and written assignments;
- ◆ the use of pre- and post-training questionnaires;
- ◆ bacteriological swabs taken of **hand and food-contact surfaces**;
- ◆ bacteriological food sampling (especially for the presence of **indicators**);
- ◆ trends in the number of hazards identified during audits; and
- ◆ trends in food complaints.

Evaluating specific courses

If possible, a control group of food handlers who have not attended the course should be compared to ensure that improvements in hygiene resulted from attendance on the course and not, for example, from improved supervision or on-the-job training. Managers who have attended advanced hygiene courses could be asked to report on hygiene improvements or achievements implemented three and six months after completing the course.

Highfield.co.uk ltd Poster
Handwashing When?

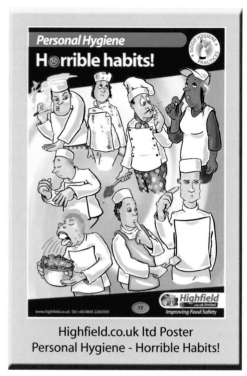

Highfield.co.uk ltd Poster
Personal Hygiene - Horrible Habits!

Reinforcement of training and staff motivation to ensure that hygiene standards are maintained

Effective supervision, reinforcement, coaching enforcement and continuous refresher training will be essential to ensure behavioural changes are maintained after attending training sessions. Incentives should be used to encourage high standards. In some countries deterrents have been used to maintain standards, for example, frequent hand swabbing, closed circuit television and fines.

Posters and notices may be used to encourage good practices and to reinforce the legal obligation of the individual. Posters may shock, amuse or instruct and should be prominently positioned and changed as often as necessary to maintain attention. Hygiene displays may be useful and free literature may be available from the local environmental health department.

Small groups of staff participating in hygiene sessions, for example, discussing case studies, can stimulate significant interest. External speakers may be brought in to chair such discussions.

Recognition may be given to employees who obtain hygiene qualifications and especially those who operate hygienically. This may take the form of increased remuneration or an award.

Many companies use some form of appraisal to determine whether or not supervisors and managers justify receiving larger increases in salary. Hygiene should be included as one of the categories on which this decision is made. Once managers realise that poor hygiene affects their salary, improved standards should be assured.

10 The design & construction of food premises

A considerable amount of thought must always be given to the design, construction and location of food premises, to ensure a cost-effective and **hygienic** operation. Newly built premises should comply fully with the requirements of the appropriate hygiene and safety legislation and the elimination of potential **hazards** and **risks** should be a key objective. Plans should be discussed with enforcement officers as it is much easier and cheaper to provide satisfactory finishes and facilities such as sanitary accommodation during construction, than it is to be told to provide alternative finishes or additional sanitary accommodation when the building is completed.

The use of satisfactory building materials and a well-planned layout are essential to achieve high standards of hygiene. The size of the premises must facilitate efficient operation and the site must be large enough to accommodate possible future expansion.

Selection of a suitable site

Choosing a suitable site for new food premises is of paramount importance. During the selection procedure, consideration must be given to the provision and availability of services, i.e. electricity and gas, water supply and effluent disposal and the accessibility for delivery and waste disposal. The site should not be liable to flooding or unacceptable **contamination** from chemicals, dust, odour or **pests**.

Close proximity of residential properties may cause problems for some premises, especially factories. Most **food businesses** generate noise, to a greater or lesser extent, and complaints from nearby properties can be expected, especially if noise is generated before 8.00 a.m. or after 6.00 p.m. Shift working, unloading or loading vehicles, extractor fans and refrigerated vehicles parked overnight are just a few examples of commonly occurring complaints. When the site has been selected, and outline planning permission obtained, time and effort must be devoted to the design of the premises.

General principles of design

Achieving a satisfactory design, which provides a linear workflow and so eliminates **cross-contamination**, facilitates effective **cleaning** and can be operated profitably, is far from simple. Full consultation between all involved parties, including architects, environmental health practitioners/officers and users is recommended. It should always be borne in mind that an increase in capital expenditure may well result in both increased life of the premises and a reduction in operating and cleaning costs. When designing food premises the following principles should be considered:

♦ the risk of contamination should be minimised under the proposed working conditions; clean and dirty processes must be separated. Where possible the work areas in large-scale manufacture should be segregated into precook and post-cook, and staff should not be allowed to move from one area to the other. If practicable, a separate area should be provided for de-boxing and unwrapping raw materials, especially when there is a risk of contaminating food with staples, paper, cardboard and string. Accumulations of refuse should not be permitted;

- workflow should be linear and progress in a uniform direction from raw material to finished product. Food should not be kept at ambient temperatures for longer than is absolutely necessary. Distances travelled by raw materials, utensils, food containers, waste food, packaging materials and staff should be minimised;
- facilities for **personal hygiene** and disinfection of small items of equipment should relate to working areas and process risks;
- where appropriate, suitable facilities must be provided for temperature, humidity and other controls;
- the premises should be designed to avoid accumulation of dirt in inaccessible places and the risk of contamination from condensation and must be capable of being thoroughly cleaned and, if necessary, **disinfected** at the end of production;
- insects, rodents and birds must be denied access and harbourage;
- yard surfaces and roads within the boundary of the premises must have a suitable impervious surface with adequate drainage, and provision made for refuse storage. Refuse should not have to be taken through food rooms when collected. Facilities for cleaning yards must be provided, for example, a stand-pipe; and
- suitable provision must be made for staff welfare, including cloakroom and, if necessary, canteen and first aid facilities.

THE CONSTRUCTION OF FOOD PREMISES

If the design of a food premises establishes the method of operation, the construction and structure determine how easily it can be cleaned. It is essential that the correct materials are chosen for all ceiling, wall and floor finishes and even more important that they are properly fixed or applied. Insufficient attention to fixing generally results in a potentially satisfactory material becoming totally unsuitable and advice should be sought from specialists. Materials should be non-toxic, suitably durable and easy to maintain. Before a material is selected, the

Unsatisfactory food premises, staff toilets and washing facilities.

supplier should be requested to provide details of similar premises using the particular product and existing applications should be visited. Whichever surface is chosen, it should be kept in good repair and be capable of withstanding the frequent cleaning to which it will be subjected.

Ceilings

Ceilings may be either solid or suspended. The latter are advantageous as horizontal pipework and services are concealed. Access for inspection, pest control and maintenance must be built in. Structural walkways are often necessary and should always be provided in large premises. Suspended ceilings are normally made of metal lattice incorporating cleansable panels. Aluminium backed and faced fibreboard has proved successful in many food factories. Flush-fitting ventilation grilles should normally be provided.

Solid ceilings give less scope for a hygienic finish, as pipework and ventilation trunking normally protrude. They should be well insulated to avoid condensation and **mould** growth. Generally, ceilings should be smooth, fire-resistant, light-coloured, **coved** at wall joints and easy to clean. Plasterboard with taped joints, skimmed with plaster and finished with a washable emulsion is common in smaller premises, although in factory areas with little steam, corrugated sheeting treated with suitable anti-fungal paint has proved satisfactory. Special attention must be paid to ceiling finishes above heat and/or steam-producing appliances such as ovens, sinks and retorts.

Ceiling height will vary depending on the type of operations being carried out but should only be high enough to provide satisfactory working conditions and allow the installation of equipment. Maintenance and cleaning is much easier if the ceiling is around 3.5m from the floor.

Walls

Smooth, impervious, non-flaking, light-coloured wall surfaces are required. Whichever finish is chosen it must be capable of being thoroughly cleaned and, if necessary, disinfected by the methods employed in the premises. Internal solid walls are preferable to those with cavities, which may harbour pests. Crevices and ledges that cause cleaning problems should be eliminated. False panelling must not be used.

Regard must be had to the operations carried out adjacent to

Broken and missing wall tiles present cleaning problems and risk of physical hazard.

the wall, as the surface may need to be resistant to spillages, chemicals, grease, heat and impact. Wall surfaces in use include resin-bonded fibreglass, ceramic-faced blocks, epoxy resin, glazed tiles with water-resistant grouting and rubberised paint on hard plaster or sealed brickwork, which is used in some food factories. Some paints incorporate a **fungicidal** additive but absorbent emulsion paint should not be used on walls.

Galvanised steel, aluminium and stainless steel are used, although they may warp and strain their fixings. In addition, these metals are prone to corrosion and attack by some cleaning chemicals. Plastic sheeting is becoming more popular, although standards and suitability vary considerably. Some sheets can be heat formed to fit corners and angles. Fire resistance of materials must always be considered. Stainless steel splash backs are recommended behind sinks and working surfaces that may be exposed to impact damage.

Wall or floor stops are needed to prevent doors damaging wall surfaces, and wall corners should be protected by non-corrosive metal or PVC angles. Stainless steel angles bedded in mastic with countersunk screw fixings are recommended. Protection of wall surfaces from trolleys may be required. Crash rails or specially designed **coving** have proved successful.

Pipework and ducting should be bracketed at least 150mm from walls to facilitate cleaning. All lagging to pipes must be smooth and impervious. Pipes passing through external walls must be effectively sealed to prevent the ingress of pests.

Precautions for painting within food premises

♦ Select the correct paint. The paint chosen should:
  - ♦ adhere firmly so that flaking is minimised;
  - ♦ be of low toxicity; the minimum standard should be in compliance with BS 4310: 1968 for low-lead paints;
  - ♦ be cleansable; the higher the gloss the better the washability. If vigorous cleaning is used, for example, using hoses, specialist paints will be required;
  - ♦ dry rapidly. It may be possible to use a rapid-drying, emulsion-based primer and undercoat system followed by an eggshell. This would allow a two-coat system to be applied within a working day and so minimise production losses.
♦ Cease production during redecoration. This requires careful planning. It may be possible to decorate out of normal production times, for example, at weekends.
♦ Ensure tainting of food does not occur. Solvent vapour may spread to other sections not being decorated and is especially likely to contaminate food rich in fat or oil, such as butter.
♦ All fixed equipment must be well covered.
♦ All paint must be kept in properly marked containers that are not made of glass.
♦ Ensure the contractor is aware of hygiene and safety rules.
♦ On completion of painting ensure that the area is clean, free from odour and painting materials before processing starts.

Further information may be obtained on specialist paints for the food industry, and precautions to be taken, by contacting paint manufacturing firms.

Doors, windows, stairs and platforms

Windows in factories are often omitted as they take up valuable wall space, and if used for ventilation purposes will allow the entry of insects and dust. If windows are provided they should be fixed on north-facing walls to reduce glare and solar heat gain. Where this is unavoidable solar film will assist in counteracting heat gain. Cleansable, well-fitting fly-screens must, where necessary, be fitted to opening windows. Windows should be constructed to facilitate cleaning. If present, internal window sills should be sloped to prevent their use as shelves. The design of frames, of both windows and doors, should avoid acute angles. Right-angled joints between frames and walls should be beaded or filled to form continuous surfaces. Architraves should be avoided and reveals tile-surfaced rather than wood carcased. Woodwork should be well-seasoned, properly knotted, stopped, primed and given three coats of polyurethane paint.

Doors should have smooth, non-absorbent surfaces capable of being thoroughly cleaned. They should be tight-fitting and self-closing. Door handles and finger-plates should be capable of disinfection. Swing doors with kick-plates are preferable to

A filthy window in a canteen.

handles. Many food factories use polypropylene or toughened rubber doors as they require little maintenance and are easy to keep clean. Clear plastic strips are also used. External doorways should, where necessary, be proofed against the entry of insects, and metal kick-plates should be provided to prevent gnawing by rodents.

Doorways must be large enough to allow for the movement of mobile equipment and possible replacement of fixed equipment. Swing doors that open both ways should be fitted with sight panels. Stairs, ladders and platforms must be capable of being thoroughly cleaned and should not expose food to risk of contamination.

Floors

When selecting a floor covering, the following criteria should be considered:
♦   the volume and nature of traffic, for example, fork-lifts;
♦   whether the area is wet or dry;
♦   how the area will be cleaned, particularly if steam is used;
♦   what chemical resistance will be necessary;

Area of floor beneath kitchen sink, main unit.

Dirt and flour build up on the floor and oven sides.

♦ whether production will need to be curtailed to effect repairs to the floor; and

♦ the type of sub-floor.

Failure to clean under equipment.

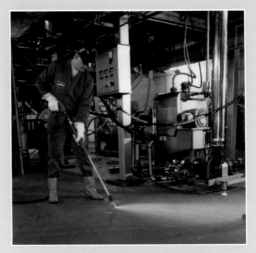

Ucrete flooring withstanding contamination from hot oil and potato starch, as well as heavy traffic and cleaning at high temperatures. (Courtesy of MBT Ucrete.)

To assess the cost-effectiveness of a finish, regard must be had to initial cost, durability, performance and safety. In food premises, floors should be durable, non-absorbent, anti-slip, without crevices and capable of being effectively cleaned. Where appropriate they must be resistant to **acids**, grease and salts and should slope sufficiently for liquids to drain to trapped gullies; a slope of one in 60 is the minimum recommended. The angle between walls and floors should be coved. Regard must be had to the possible odour taint of food during installation or repair. The base of H section vertical girders should be filled with concrete to avoid difficulties in cleaning.

Several types of floor covering may be used. For example, epoxy resin, granolithic (concrete incorporating granite chippings), welded anti-slip, vinyl sheet and slip-resistant ceramic or quarry tiles. Wooden floors are unacceptable. Whichever type of floor covering is chosen, it must be laid in accordance with the manufacturer's recommendations. Special attention must be paid to the jointing of quarry tiles and the sub-floor must be very smooth if anti-slip, vinyl sheeting is laid. If concrete is used, it must be steel-float finished and sealed with, for example, an epoxy sealant, to ensure that it is dust free and impervious.

Services

These include gas, electricity, water supplies, drainage, lighting and ventilation. Proper provision of services is essential to the hygienic and effective functioning of all food businesses.

Gas supplies

Specific hygiene implications are covered by more general safety and equipment fixing requirements. Supply pipes should always be mounted clear of the floor and never so close to other pipes as to restrict access for cleaning. Flexible connections, to facilitate removal of equipment for cleaning purposes, are recommended.

Electrical supplies

Adequate numbers of power points should be available for all electrical equipment, without the use of adaptors or the need for lengthy flexes. Provision should be made for maintenance, repair and cleaning operations. Cut-out switches for power circuits should be accessible and separate from lighting and ventilation supplies, so that cleaning can take place in safety. Separate cut-out switches should be provided for refrigeration equipment.

Controls should be fixed clear of equipment to avoid becoming dirty or wet during cleaning. Removable electrical components are advantageous. Electrical wiring should be protected by waterproof conduits. All switches should be flush-fitting and waterproof (especially in production areas).

Water supplies

All cold water supplies for use with food, for cleaning equipment or surfaces or for personal hygiene must be **potable** and should be mains supplied and not fed via an intermediate tank, unless chlorinated. The distribution system must not provide opportunities for contamination or the multiplication of **micro-organisms**. Water supplies should be subject to control and monitoring procedures determined by **hazard analysis** and, if necessary, include periodic microbiological and chemical sampling.

Hot water should have a target water discharge temperature of 60ºC. In hard-water areas, hot water supplies should be softened, otherwise scale build-up will cause cleaning and operational problems and add significantly to detergent usage. Water softeners and filters must be maintained in a good condition so that they do not contaminate the water.

Ice used in food, drinks or buffet displays must be made from potable water. Ice machines must not be exposed to risk of contamination and must be regularly cleaned and disinfected. Utensils must not present a foreign body hazard; glassware should not be used to "shovel ice". Ice for drinks should not be handled with bare hands.

Non-potable water used for steam generation or fire control must be conveyed in identifiable systems, which have no connection with, nor any possible reflux into, the potable water system. An external water supply for washing refuse areas and loading bays should always be available.

Drainage

Premises should have an efficient, smooth-bore drainage system, which must be kept clean and in good order and repair. Drains and sewers should be adequate to remove peak loads quickly without flooding. Sufficient drains should be installed to facilitate effective cleaning of rooms by pressure jet cleaners or other means.

Shallow, glazed, half-round floor channels within food rooms are best left uncovered, provided that they are not a safety hazard. If covers are necessary, these should be non-corrosive, continuous, of suitable strength and easily removed for cleaning. In certain circumstances trapped gullies are preferable.

To avoid fat solidifying and causing blockages, drainage systems must be well designed and constructed, with the minimum number of bends, and have an efficient self-cleaning velocity. Cleaning and flushing, at least six monthly, is essential. **Grease traps**, if fitted, should be large enough to allow adequate time for fat to separate. They should be emptied as frequently as necessary and, as the contents may be foul-smelling and obnoxious, traps should be positioned outside food rooms.

Inspection chambers should be placed outside food rooms but if interior location is unavoidable they must be airtight. Manhole covers should be double sealed, bedded in silicon grease and screwed down with brass screws. All drainage systems must be provided with sufficient access points to allow rodding in the event of blockages. Petrol interceptors may be required for yard drains.

Items of machinery such as potato peelers and dishwashers, connected directly into the drainage system, should be trapped to avoid waste pipes acting as vents for sewers. Waste pipes to fittings should be plastic with screw or push-fit connections to enable easy dismantling in case of blockage.

Drains should be constructed to inhibit the harbourage and movement of vermin. Defective drains may result in effluent, foul odours and rodents entering food rooms. They must be repaired as quickly as possible. All external rainwater fall-pipes should be fitted with balloon guards to prevent rodent access. Circumference guards should be fitted around all vertical pipes fastened to walls, to prevent rodents climbing up them. Waste pipes exposed to constant high temperatures should be constructed of Alkathene. The direction of flow should be from clean areas to dirty areas. Toilets should feed into the system after food rooms.

Ventilation

Suitable and sufficient ventilation must be provided to produce a satisfactory, safe working environment and to reduce humidities and temperatures that would assist the rapid multiplication of **bacteria**. Condensation encourages mould growth and drips onto food. Ambient temperatures should be below 25°C. The ventilation system, which should always flow from a clean to a dirty area, must prevent excessive heat, condensation, dust and steam, and remove odours and contaminated air. Good ventilation will assist in reducing grease and staining of ceilings, so reducing the need for frequent decoration.

When planning a ventilation system, expert advice should be sought to ensure that food rooms have the recommended number of air changes, for example, in kitchens, the minimum ventilation rate should not be less than 17.5 litres per second per square metre of floor area and not less than 30 air changes per hour. Inlets must be suitably filtered to prevent dust, dirt and insects being brought into the food room. The input capacity should be approximately 85% of the extract capacity. Natural ventilation through screened windows normally needs supplementing by mechanical ventilation to ensure effective air circulation.

Ducting should be as short as possible with man-sized access points at 3 metre intervals to facilitate cleaning and removal of dirt, grease and pests. Fan motors should be located outside

Filthy extraction canopies in kitchens.

the kitchen otherwise the noise produced may result in staff switching them off. Fans should be of a low-noise type but silencing may result in cleaning difficulty and fire risk.

Steam-producing equipment such as cookers, boilers and blanchers should be provided with adequately sized canopies constructed of anodised aluminium or other suitable material. Canopies should overhang by around 250mm. Filters, if fitted, should be cleaned frequently to eliminate fire hazards and maintain efficiency. Drainage gutters at the base of canopies should be provided to collect condensate.

Much of the equipment used in food rooms, especially for heat processing and cooking, emits radiant heat, which is not directly affected by air flow. Provision of lower heat-emitting equipment such as pressure vessels and microwave ovens, and upgrading insulation on ovens should be considered to reduce heat production.

Workroom temperature where food is handled

Generally, food hygiene law regulates food temperatures, and health and safety law regulates air temperature. Health and safety requirements can usually be met by:

♦ maintaining a "reasonable" temperature of 16°C (13°C if work involves serious physical effort); or if this is not practical

♦ providing a warm work station; or if this is not practical

♦ providing suitable protective clothing, suitable heated rest facilities and minimising the time in uncomfortable temperatures.

Hygiene of ventilation and water systems

Clean air and safe water are vital for a pleasant working environment and hygienic food production, and failure to carry out routine maintenance and cleaning of ductwork, pipes and cooling towers can result in increased risk of infection.

Water in cooling towers for industrial processes and air conditioning systems is often contaminated with legionella bacteria. This organism develops in neglected water and air

Sampling a header tank for harmful bacteria.
(Courtesy of Rentokil Initial PLC.)

conditioning systems and is spread by **aerosols**, for example, from showers and cooling towers. Poorly maintained water systems result in a build-up of slime and dirt, which support many bacteria and **algae** and can result in product contamination.

Those organisations without the necessary equipment or in-house experience should consider employing a reputable contractor to carry out regular surveys and maintenance. Filters, header tanks, cooling tower sumps, packing and drift eliminators, overflows and plant rooms should be cleaned and, where necessary, disinfected. Such servicing enables water treatment programmes to operate efficiently, reduces the risk of infection and prolongs the life of pipes.

Lighting

Suitable and sufficient lighting must be provided throughout food premises, including storerooms, passageways and stairways, so that employees can identify hazards and carry out tasks correctly. High standards of lighting will produce an environment conducive to clean and safe working without eye strain. Other advantages include the enhanced appearance of food in service and retail areas together with the fact that insects and rodents generally shun well-lit areas.

Artificial lighting is often preferred to natural lighting because of problems of solar heat gain, glare, shadows, and insects entering open windows. Fluorescent tubes, fitted with diffusers to prevent glare and product contamination in the event of breakage, are recommended. Suspended ceilings can incorporate flush light fittings, which are also satisfactory, but in certain premises, particularly bakehouses, panel lights incorporated into the ceiling may buckle due to excessive heat.

Standards of lighting may be identified in the industry guides. The Catering Guide suggests 150 lux in storerooms and 500 lux in preparation areas. As a general guide, in areas where decoration is bright and ceiling heights do not exceed 3 metres, 20 watts from a fluorescent fitting per square metre of floor space will give 400 lux.

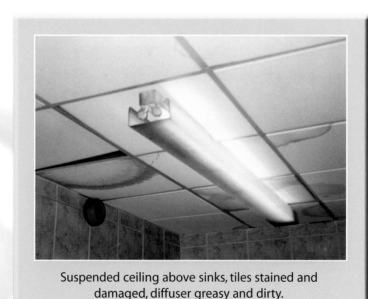

Suspended ceiling above sinks, tiles stained and damaged, diffuser greasy and dirty.

Untidy, dirty pot wash and food preparation area.

Wash-up area, sink not sealed to adjacent wall surfaces.

Handwashing facilities

Adequate facilities for handwashing and drying should be provided wherever the process demands. In particular, a suitable number of basins or troughs should be sited at the entrance of food rooms to ensure all persons entering wash their hands. Washbasins must be easily accessible and should not be obstructed. They must be kept clean and maintained in good condition. Non-hand operated spray taps providing warm water at 35°C to 45°C are essential to minimise the risk of cross-contamination. Washing facilities provided in food rooms should be additional to those used in conjunction with sanitary accommodation. All basins and troughs, preferably made of stainless steel, should be connected to drains by properly trapped waste pipes.

Cleaning and disinfection facilities

Where appropriate, adequate facilities for the cleaning and disinfection of utensils, crockery, cutlery, glasses and equipment should be provided. These facilities should be constructed of corrosion-resistant materials, normally stainless steel, capable of being easily cleaned. Twin sinks are preferable to facilitate washing and disinfecting/rinsing. Sinks should be provided with adequate supplies of hot and cold water. Mixer taps are acceptable. Taps should be wall-mounted with no direct connection to the sinks. It is good practice to provide facilities for draining and air drying equipment close to the area where it is washed. Waste pipes should be plastic push-fit ware. Sinks should be freestanding so that they can be removed easily after unscrewing the lower trap joint freeing the waste pipe. "**Sterilising**" sinks and units should be capable of operating at 82°C, as should the rinse cycle of dishwashing and tray-cleaning machines. It is recommended that if any of the above are positioned against the wall, a suitable stainless steel upstand of 300mm, or a splashback, be provided. If glasswashers are used they should clean and disinfect. Hoses and other equipment for cleaning and disinfecting fixed equipment may be required.

Separate sinks must be provided for food preparation and equipment washing if the volume demands it. In small operations the same sink may be used if there is no risk to food safety. Exclusive food sinks may be provided with cold water only. It is good practice to have signs above sinks indicating their use.

Sanitary conveniences and washing facilities

All new premises should be provided with adequate staff sanitary accommodation in accordance with the Workplace (Health, Safety and Welfare) Regulations, 1992 and the approved Code of Practice and Guidance L24. Suitable and sufficient sanitary conveniences must be provided at readily accessible places, in adequately ventilated and lit rooms that are kept clean and tidy. Rooms containing sanitary conveniences must not communicate directly with a room where food is processed, prepared or eaten. Internal wall and floor surfaces should permit wet cleaning.

Non-hand operated flushing devices are recommended. Doors to intervening spaces and sanitary accommodation should be self-closing and clearly illustrate the sex of the user. It is good practice to display a conspicuous notice requesting users of the toilet to wash their hands before leaving. Suitable and sufficient washing facilities must be provided at readily accessible places. In particular, facilities must be provided in the immediate vicinity of every sanitary convenience and supplied with clean hot and cold or warm water, liquid soap, nailbrushes and appropriate drying facilities.

Highfield.co.uk ltd self-adhesive hygiene notices.

Misused and dirty handwashing trough.

Cloakrooms

Adequate accommodation for outdoor clothing and footwear, not worn by the staff during normal working hours, must be available. Such articles must not be stored in a food room unless in suitable cupboards or lockers provided only for this purpose. Adequate facilities for drying wet clothing should also be provided. Cloakrooms must be kept clean and tidy and food scraps should not be allowed to accumulate under benches and behind lockers as this may result in cockroach or rodent infestations.

STAFF SANITARY CONVENIENCES AND WASH STATIONS

Males or females at work			Alternative, males only		
Males/Females	W.C.s	Washstations	Males	W.C.s	Urinals
1 – 5	1	1	1 – 15	1	1
			16 – 30	2	1
6 – 25	2	2	31 – 45	2	2
26 – 50	3	3	46 – 60	3	2
51 – 75	4	4	61 – 75	3	3
			76 – 90	4	3
76 – 100	5	5	91 – 100	4	4

Public sanitary accommodation

Section 20 of The Local Government (Miscellaneous Provisions) Act, 1976 enables a local authority to require the provision of sanitary appliances at places of entertainment and places selling food or drink to the public for consumption on the premises. The number of sanitary appliances is not stipulated, although hot water can be required. It is good practice for public toilets not to be used by food handlers.

PUBLIC SANITARY ACCOMMODATION RECOMMENDED FOR RESTAURANTS, PUBLIC HOUSES AND CANTEENS

	Males	Females
W.C.s	1 per 100	1 per 50
Urinals	1 per 25	
Washbasins	1 per W.C. + 1 per 5 urinals	1 per 2 W.C.s
Washbasins to be provided with hot and cold water supplies.		
Provision should also be made for at least one cleaner's sink.		

Sanitary disposal

Wherever women are employed or catered for, the law requires that suitable and hygienic provision is made for the disposal of sanitary dressings. Customer welfare should also be considered when selecting a disposal method.

Problems may arise from soiled dressings if the disposal of sanitary towels and tampons is inefficient or inadequate, and there is also a risk of blocked drains if attempts are made to flush such items down the toilet. Pedal bins are inevitably unhygienic and present cleaners with the unpleasant task of emptying and cleaning them. Mechanical macerators and incinerators may produce unpleasant smells and may not completely destroy used sanitary dressings – especially where dressings contain synthetic cellulose rather than natural fibres.

An alternative method of disposal is a regular contract service using specially designed containers placed within W.C. cubicles to afford privacy and which are regularly collected and replaced by fresh, sterilised ones. The contractor is responsible for the safe disposal of the contents away from the customer's premises.

Some containers use a **bactericide** that works as a vapour as well as a liquid to ensure adequate protection and elimination of unpleasant smells. The bactericide should be capable of keeping the contents sterile for periods well in excess of the normal frequency of exchange.

Contractors should be asked to undertake a survey to establish the optimum number of sanitary towel dispensers, rate of replenishment and the number, and siting, of disposal units required. Some contractors may also provide other hygiene services or amenities such as air fresheners, coin-operated dispensers of sanitary dressings and a disposal service for such things as hypodermic needles.

The storage and disposal of waste

Waste disposal systems must be planned, along with other services, when food premises are designed. Refuse must not be allowed to accumulate in food rooms and should not be left overnight. Waste generated within the premises may be stored in polythene bags which are removed when full and at the end of each working day. Stands for such bags, must be maintained in a clean condition. Employees must be educated to "clean as they go", to replace lids and wash their hands after receptacles are used. Sacks should not be overfilled and should be tied to prevent problems from insects. Refuse collectors should not have to enter food rooms or dining areas.

Waste food should be kept separate from paper and cardboard packaging. In some instances, waste may be stored under refrigeration pending collection, for example, bones in butchers' shops. It is preferable for all waste food to be removed from food premises at least daily and general refuse to be removed at least twice a week.

Suitable facilities must be provided for the storage of waste externally, prior to removal from the establishment. The number and type of receptacles used will depend on the type and quantity of waste, the frequency of collection and the access available for the refuse vehicle. Wheelie bins are commonly used, although skips and compactors are more appropriate for large food factories. All receptacles should be durable, impervious, capable of being cleaned and provided with suitable tight-fitting lids or covers to prevent insects, birds and rodents gaining access.

The refuse area must have a well-drained, impervious surface, which is capable of being kept clean. Standpipes, hoses and, possibly, high-pressure sprayers should be provided for cleaning purposes. The receptacles, and the refuse area, should be thoroughly cleaned after each emptying. Covered areas to protect refuse from the sun and rain are recommended. Satisfactory provision should be made for the disposal of liquid food waste, such as oil. It should not be flushed down the drain.

Accumulations of rubbish in room adjacent to wash-up area.

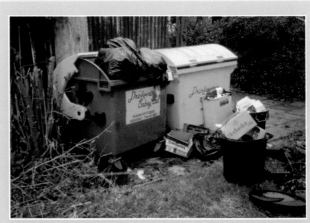

Unsatisfactory refuse storage.

Refuse areas should not be too far from food rooms to discourage their use but they should not be too close to encourage flies to enter the food rooms. They should not be sited next to the main food delivery entrance. Receptacles used for the storage or collection of food must not be used for refuse.

Refuse compaction

Charges for refuse collection are continually rising and, since levies are usually based on volume of waste produced, often a price per bin, it is advantageous to use a refuse compaction system. Compactors vary from units similar to a large dustbin to refuse-sack compactors and skip rams. A well-run compaction system improves hygiene, as flies and other pests are less likely to be attracted. Cleaning of refuse areas is also easier as spillages are considerably reduced. Capital costs for purchasing compactors should be compared against collection charges, cleaning and pest control. However, before ordering a compactor the local authority cleansing department should be consulted, as special arrangements may have to be made for emptying.

Perimeter areas

A concrete path, at least 675mm wide, abutting the external walls should be provided around all food buildings. This removes cover for rodents and enables early signs of pests to be discovered, for example, rodent droppings. Paths should be kept clean, free of vegetation and inspected regularly. A smooth band of rendering, around 450mm, at the base of external walls will discourage rodents from climbing.

Whenever possible, a perimeter fence should be constructed around food premises to deter unauthorised entry. Areas within perimeter fences must be kept clean and tidy.

Unsatisfactory drainage.

Cluttered rear yard offering harbourage for pests.

Rubbish, old equipment and weeds must not be allowed to accumulate or provide harbourage for insects or rodents.

Kitchen design

Kitchen design to operate cost effectively, meet the needs of users and satisfy essential safety requirements and enforcement officers, demands considerable expertise. The layout of a well-designed commercial kitchen has three main characteristics:

- ♦ clearly identified and separated workflows;
- ♦ defined accommodation, and services specific to the purposes allocated; and
- ♦ economy of space provision (commensurate with good hygiene practice).

The unit will also be so arranged that it can be easily managed. The layout will afford management personnel easy access to the areas under their control and good visibility in the areas that have to be supervised. Space will be allocated for the management function and for equipment such as telephones and computers.

Workflows

Four separate workflows need to be considered from delivery to service: product; personnel; containers, utensils and equipment; and refuse. Cleaning of premises, equipment, utensils, crockery and cutlery will also need to be considered.

Product flows should be subdivided into **high-risk** and ready-to-eat foods, and contaminated (raw food) sections. Clear segregation should be maintained between the two. As far as practicable, workflows should be unidirectional, without backtracking or crossover.

Accommodation and services

Accommodation should be sized according to operational need. Essentially, the working areas, stores, the equipment and its relative spacing should all be determined and laid out to suit the operation.

Areas should be allocated according to environmental compatibility; hot functions with hot, dirty with dirty, wet with wet, dry with dry, defined overall by segregation between high-risk and contaminated food handling.

Adequate working space and good staff changing facilities are important to create good working conditions. The siting of electricity, gas, water and drainage must be considered at an early stage. Sufficient connections must be provided for mobile equipment. Specially designed heavy-duty connections will be required.

Size

There should be a minimum of circulation and dead space, commensurate with the efficient functioning of the unit. Size should be neither too small nor too large; there are penalties in the over-provision of space as much as there are problems with too small a provision. The use of standard-size equipment will be beneficial on space requirements.

The size of the kitchen can only be determined when its exact purpose and function have been defined. A unit designed for a fast food operation will not work effectively for à la carte service. When a catering operation is planned, the kitchen should be designed first and the rest designed around it. Haute cuisine, for example, will require ample storage space for fresh vegetables, a larder and pastry area. Fast food will require none of these but will need ample space for freezer storage. Other items to take into consideration include:

- the state of raw materials, for example, ready prepared or not;
- the extent of the menu, for example, à la carte or set menus;
- the length of meal times and the number of sittings;
- the scope of the operation. Does the business support multiple outlets such as banquets, or does it operate as a wholesaler;
- is the kitchen used purely for residential or non-residential;
- the type of equipment used, for example, cook-chill, microwave oven etc.;
- the use of modular equipment;
- the type and amount of dishwashing and cleaning. Are disposable plates and utensils to be used;
- if ready prepared food, such as bread and pastries are to be used; or produced in the kitchen; and
- if such functions such as dish-wash and vegetable preparation are to be included in the kitchen area or ancillary rooms.

Siting of equipment

Great care is needed to ensure that the operation works as a single system, with equipment required for specific functions grouped and accessible, to avoid excessive walking and the temptation to take short cuts. For instance, refrigeration should be close to the working areas it serves, otherwise excessive amounts of food may be brought out to save the trips to and from the unit. Mis-en-place refrigeration is recommended. Washbasins should be strategically located to ensure that operatives entering clean areas wash their hands. Personnel should also be encouraged to wash their hands when leaving the dirty area. Depending on the size of operations, additional washbasins should be provided close to work stations. Minimising the distance that staff need to walk to undertake their duties improves safety (the easy way becomes the safe way) and reduces costs, as it saves time.

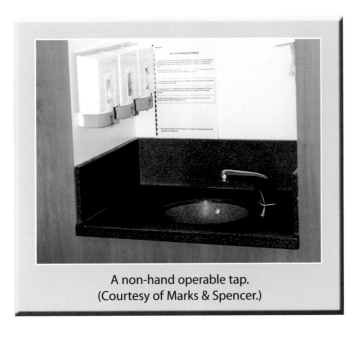

A non-hand operable tap.
(Courtesy of Marks & Spencer.)

LARGE KITCHEN PLAN

Moveable and temporary food premises

The following are examples of moveable or temporary food premises: marquees, market stalls, mobile sales vehicles, premises used occasionally for catering purposes such as church or village halls, premises used primarily as private dwellings, and vending machines. Although the requirements of food hygiene legislation apply to these venues, The Guides to Good Hygiene Practice (Catering and Retail) recommend that the following good hygiene practices be observed:

♦ tents or marquees should be made of washable materials, and work surfaces are maintained in good repair;

♦ where it is not possible to provide separate food or utensil washing sinks, then sinks must be cleaned, and preferably disinfected, between different activities. If practicable, an automatic dishwasher is recommended for domestic premises;

♦ an adequate supply of hot and cold potable water must be provided. Where mains water is not practicable, then enclosed water tanks may be used, emptied and refilled daily and periodically disinfected;

♦ special care should be taken to dispose of refuse hygienically, double-bagging kitchen refuse from mobile or temporary premises. If food preparation creates large amounts of waste, then arrangements should be made for collection on a more frequent basis than for domestic premises;

♦ food preparation should be minimised where space is limited in temporary or mobile premises by selecting menus requiring simple steps in preparation and cooking, or using a permanent base kitchen for more elaborate preparation;

♦ in domestic premises handwashing facilities may be situated in the bathroom. Wherever practicable, a separate hand washbasin should be provided in the kitchen, preferably with a 'Handwash Only' sign. Material for handwashing and drying must be provided, with antibacterial soap and paper towels as good practice;

♦ particular care must be taken to ensure that domestic refrigerators maintain a good practice maximum temperature of 5°C, and that raw foods are strictly segregated from high-risk foods. The use of a thermometer probe is recommended to monitor temperatures of refrigerated foods. It may be practicable to use, for short periods only, insulated boxes for chilled foods;

♦ vending machines should be sited in well-ventilated areas to avoid the build-up of condensation; and

♦ it is recommended that vending machines have a dedicated cleaning schedule, with strict adherence to the manufacturer's safe and hygienic operating instructions.

*The photographs used to show unsatisfactory premises in this chapter were provided by Kingston-upon-Hull City Council, Environmental Health (Food Team) and Runnymede Borough Council.

11 The design of equipment

Hygienic design of equipment is necessary to comply with legislative requirements, avoid product **contamination** and facilitate cost-effective **cleaning** and, if necessary, **disinfection** (downtime for cleaning will be minimised). Good design necessitates the consideration of the complete process, the environment and methods of cleaning and maintenance and not just the equipment in isolation.

Poorly designed equipment, which cannot be dismantled, may be uncleanable, incapable of being chemically disinfected and may result in product contamination by **pathogenic bacteria**, which will be disastrous in the case of **high-risk food**. Even if equipment can be dismantled, unhygienic design may make cleaning and disinfection prohibitively expensive. The ultimate test of whether or not a machine is hygienic is the standard of the product.

The legal requirements

Hygiene legislation requires all articles, fittings and equipment, with which food comes into contact, to be kept clean and be so constructed, of such materials and maintained in such condition and repair as to minimise **risk** of contamination and enable thorough cleaning and, where necessary, disinfection. Furthermore, equipment must be installed in a way that allows the surrounding area to be cleaned. Proprietors of businesses governed by specific regulations will need to comply with similar requirements and all businesses should be aware of the advice contained within any relevant UK or EC industry guides.

Failure to keep equipment clean and in good condition
is likely to result in prosecution.

Dirty can opener.

Dirty food production equipment.

A filthy microwave oven.

Unsatisfactory raw meat
preparation area.

The cleanliness of, and risk of contamination from, equipment will need to be considered as part of the identification of steps in the activities of the businesses that are critical to ensuring food safety.

In June 1989 the Council Directive relating to machinery (89/392/EEC) as amended by Directive 91/368/EEC, was published. Although mainly concerned with safety, an important section deals with the hygienic design of agri-foodstuffs machinery.

In the UK the requirements of the Directive are enforced using the Supply of Machinery (Safety) Regulations, 1992 (as amended in 1994). The responsibility for **compliance** rests primarily with the manufacturers and suppliers (including importers), although the user must ensure that the machine is properly installed and maintained and used for the purpose for which it is intended. The Directive requires that new machinery used for preparing and processing foodstuffs carries a CE marking and must be designed and constructed to avoid health risks and in particular:

♦ contact materials of foodstuffs must satisfy the conditions set down in the relevant directives. Machinery must be designed and constructed to facilitate cleaning;

Equipment must be kept clean and well maintained.

♦ all surfaces and joints must be smooth, without ridges or crevices that could harbour organic materials;
♦ projections, edges and recesses should be minimal. Continuous welding is preferable. Screws and rivets should not be used unless technically unavoidable;
♦ contact surfaces must be easily cleaned and disinfected. The design of internal surfaces, angles, etc. must allow thorough cleaning;
♦ cleaning residues must drain from equipment surfaces, pipework, etc., there must be no retention in voids;
♦ the design should prevent organic accumulations or insect **infestation** in uncleanable areas, for example, by the use of castors or alternatively, sealed bases; and
♦ lubricants must not come into contact with product.

In addition, equipment manufacturers must provide information on recommended products and methods of cleaning, disinfecting and rinsing. This requirement is particularly relevant as, no matter how well designed, equipment will lose the potential to be hygienic if clear instructions for installation, operating, cleaning and maintenance are not provided. The simpler the instructions the better, as workers often attempt to short cut complicated and time-consuming systems, sometimes with disastrous consequences.

The European Committee for Standardisation (CEN)
The European Committee for Standardisation has been charged with the task of preparing

new European standards and harmonising documents and promoting the implementation of international standards in relation to machinery safety and hygiene.

A series of technical committees has been established. CEN/TC 153 is concerned with food processing machinery, safety and hygiene specifications. Another working group is considering the principles of hygiene design that apply to all equipment. In addition, there are nine groups working on standards for specific machines: bakery; meat; catering; slicers; edible oils; pasta; bulk milk coolers; cereals; and dairy.

Construction materials

Materials in contact with food must be non-toxic, non-tainting and constituents from their surfaces must not migrate into the food or be absorbed by the food in quantities that could endanger health. Materials must have adequate strength over a wide temperature range, a reasonable life, be corrosion and abrasion resistant and be easily cleaned/disinfected.

The Machinery Regulations state that materials in contact with foodstuffs must satisfy conditions set down in the relevant EU legislation. Regulation (EC) No 852/2004 on the hygiene of foodstuffs requires surfaces of food-contact equipment to be smooth, washable, corrosion resistant non-toxic and easy to clean and disinfect. Equipment must be constructed, be of such materials and be kept in good condition so as to minimise any risk of contamination. Equipment must be installed to allow adequate cleaning of the equipment and the surrounding area.

The most widely used material is food grade stainless steel, either type 304 containing 18% chromium and 8% nickel or the more corrosion resistant, and expensive, type 316 with a 10% nickel content and 2% molybdenum. Handles of knives, brushes and other equipment should all be made from cleansable materials such as stainless steel or high-density polypropylene.

Aluminium is attacked by sodium hydroxide, which forms the basis of some **detergents**, and sodium hypochlorite. Even hard anodising fails to protect against severe pitting corrosion. Copper and alloys of copper hasten oxidation if in contact with oil or fat. Several metals, for example, copper, zinc and cadmium, are unsuitable as they are absorbed by **acid** food and may cause illness.

Some plastics may be suitable, but must be approved for food use. A useful indication can be obtained if materials comply with safety standards of the US Food and Drug Administration or the German Bundsgesundheitsamt. In the case of uncertainty, advice should be sought from the manufacturers, particularly with regard to high temperatures achieved during cleaning and disinfection.

Surface finish

Hygiene legislation requires surfaces to be in a sound condition and easy to clean and, where necessary, disinfect. This requires the use of smooth, washable, non-toxic materials unless food business operators can satisfy the competent authority that other materials used are appropriate.

Surfaces should be continuous, non-porous, non-flaking and free from cracks, crevices and pits. Surfaces will need to retain a satisfactory finish throughout their life including anticipated abuse and normal wear and tear. Instruments are available for measuring surface texture and a profile graph can be made of the shape, height and spacing of surface irregularities. The American National Standard for Food, Drug and Beverage Equipment suggests a value of no greater than the equivalent of 0.8mμRa for surface roughness of food-contact surfaces.

Examples of good and bad welded joints.

Grind &
Polish Flush

Unhygienic dismountable joints.

Unpolished cold rolled sheet from steel mills is well below this. (Roughness average Ra is the arithmetic average value of the department of the profile above and below the mean line throughout the specified sampling length.)

A rough surface provides a better mechanical "key" for soil. Furthermore, soiling is more apparent on bright surfaces, which is why it is cost-effective to electropolish stainless steel. (Care is needed with siting to avoid problems with sunlight reflecting.)

Joints

Joints should be made by welding or continuous bonding to reduce projections, edges and recesses to a minimum. Butt welding is preferred to lap joints provided the welds are ground and polished to the same standard as the rest of the surface, unless it can be demonstrated that the untreated weld is cleanable. Solders used in the construction of **food-contact surfaces** must also be non-toxic and should not contain cadmium or antimony. Silver soldering may be used to seal joints but must not contain cadmium.

Dismountable joints, for example, those relying on bolts, may contain product residue and high bacterial counts when disassembled. If such joints are not cleaned daily they should be sealed against the ingress of product and **micro-organisms** by means of a gasket. (Controlled compression of gaskets is essential.) Metal to metal joints, even if leak tight, may still permit the ingress and egress of micro-organisms. Flanged joints must present a smooth, continuous internal surface and be sealed with an appropriate gasket. (Some gaskets are made of materials such as rubber, which harden and crack over time.)

Hygienic and unhygienic fasteners.

Fasteners

Exposed screw threads, nuts, bolts and rivets should be absent from food-contact surfaces, although if removed daily for cleaning purposes are less likely to cause a problem. Annular recesses and screwdriver slots retain product residues. Nuts and bolts, etc. should be located on the non-product side where this can be achieved.

The hygienic design of equipment also includes avoiding physical contamination of the product. The accidental ingress of foreign matter such as bolts, nuts, washers and gasket materials must be prevented.

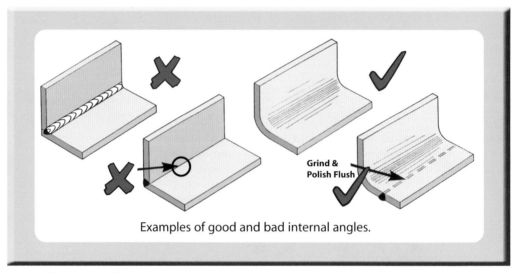

Examples of good and bad internal angles.

Internal angles and corners

The Machinery Regulations require inside surfaces to have curves of sufficient radius to allow thorough cleaning. When components are bolted or screwed together, sharp corners are usually unavoidable and metal that is bent or machined is preferred. Routine dismantling and cleaning is the only way to deal with unsatisfactory internal angles.

Dead spaces

Dead spaces allow product retention, bacterial growth and product contamination. They must be avoided in the design of equipment and not introduced during installation or as a result of modifications. The Machinery Regulations require the design and construction of equipment to prevent organic matter accumulating in, or liquids or insects entering, areas that cannot be cleaned. In effect, this means that gaskets of material approved for food use or contact must be used, or the design must enable regular dismantling for the space to be cleaned and disinfected.

Bearings

Bearings should, wherever practicable, be mounted outside product areas to avoid contamination by lubricants. Where this is not possible edible lubricants, or if liquid the product itself (as in the case of foot bearings), should be used.

Equipment exterior

The external surfaces of equipment must avoid ledges and dust traps, for example, round stretchers are preferred to rectangular. It is important to avoid recessed corners, sharp edges, unfilled seams, uneven surfaces and hollows and projecting bolt heads, threads, screws or rivets that cannot be cleaned. Inaccessible spaces, pockets and crevices where product may accumulate must be absent.

Examples of good and bad controls.

Instrumentation

Instrumentation must be constructed from appropriate materials and any transmitting fluids should be approved for food contact. Hygienic installation of instruments is essential. Controls such as push buttons must also be of hygienic design so they can be maintained in a clean condition and be capable of being cleaned by whatever system is in use. Dials that are fitted to machines must have adequate clearance to allow cleaning.

Fixing and siting of equipment

Equipment must be sited so that there is sufficient space to facilitate access to all external and internal surfaces and, where required, to allow for rapid dismantling and reassembly. Stationary equipment should be at least 500mm from walls and have a clearance of at least 250mm between the floor and underside of the equipment, to allow thorough cleaning of wall and floor surfaces. Alternatively, machines should be fixed firmly to the floor and sealed. Narrow areas or angled contact with the floor should be avoided. Machinery may be mounted on coved, raised platforms of concrete to facilitate cleaning. Where necessary, additional space may need to be provided. The bases and lower parts of machines, including motors and gears, may be difficult to clean and consequently collect dust and spillages, which make ideal breeding sites for insects. Skirting or cover plates tend to trap dust.

Where practicable, and with due regard for safety, equipment can be mobile to facilitate its removal for cleaning. This is particularly important if sited close to walls. Tubular metal storage racks, refrigerators and ovens should be castor-mounted with brakes on all wheels. Tables and benches should not be fitted with castors as even when braked, slight movement can still occur, posing a **hazard** to knife users.

When pipework is installed, future cleaning must be considered and sufficient space left between the pipes and floors or walls to allow easy access for cleaning. Alternatively, pipes may be built into the walls. Lagging of pipes must have an impervious cleansable finish. Pipework and equipment directly above open food must not expose food to risk of contamination from condensation, rust or flaking paintwork.

Conveyors can be designed to enable automatic cleaning. Manufacturers must be pressured to ensure that if dismantling is necessary it is as simple as possible.

Guards, required under health and safety legislation, should be capable of being cleaned and, where necessary, removed quickly and easily, even if special tools are required. Sheet-metal and wired-perspex guards are preferable to painted mesh.

Gas and electrical connections

The presence of electrical equipment such as motors and switches poses problems for cleaners, as even routine cleaning may expose users to some danger of electrocution. Such equipment must always be waterproof and/or capable of removal without tools, prior to cleaning the main equipment. If practicable, electrics should be sited outside food rooms, to reduce cleaning problems. It also enables servicing and maintenance to be carried out by electricians who do not need to enter food rooms.

Gas and electricity supply pipes to ovens should be flexible and capable of being disconnected. In the case of gas, the coupling to the mains must incorporate a self-sealing valve and a shut-off cock immediately upstream of the fitting. The flexible tube must conform to gas suppliers requirements and the appliance must be secured to a fixed point by a strong, detachable wire or chain, shorter in length than the tube, to avoid accidental stretching. Trailing wires and cables must be avoided.

Drainage of vessels.

Drainage of pipelines.

Drainage

All pipelines, vessels and equipment should be self-draining, not only to enable liquid deriving from foodstuffs to be discharged but also for cleaning and rinsing fluids. It is particularly important that pipelines and vessels cleaned by CIP systems are designed to facilitate complete drainage. Valves need to be accessible for cleaning.

Preparation surfaces

Preparation surfaces should be jointless, durable, impervious, the correct height and provide a firm base on which to work. If materials other than stainless steel are used, for example, food grade plastic, care should be taken to seal the edges and gaps, which may harbour food scraps. They must be able to withstand repeated cleaning and disinfection without premature deterioration, pitting or corrosion. Flanged-lip designs for tables and shelves, which harbour food residues and are difficult to clean, should be avoided. Abutting surfaces that can be separated for cleaning may be used.

Chopping boards

A variety of non-absorbent, plastic chopping boards is now being produced, for example, good quality polypropylene. However, some plastics are unsatisfactory and hardwood boards in good condition can be more hygienic. Soft wood and open jointed boards are unacceptable. When selecting a chopping board regard should be had to its:
- water absorbency;
- resistance to stains, cleaning chemicals, heat and food **acids**;
- toxicity and odour;
- durability; and
- cleanability.

Microwave ovens have been used to successfully disinfect wooden chopping boards but not plastic boards. Temperatures of 95°C can be achieved in 4 minutes in 800W ovens. Longer times may result in smoking. Increased moisture (wet boards) enhances killing efficiency of micro-organisms in wood. Furthermore, a good plastic board should not split or warp when passed through a dishwasher, which is one of the best ways of disinfecting it.

The use of boards containing the bactericide triclosan is increasing. Triclosan is used in toothpaste, mouthwash and deodorants and should remain active for the life of the

An unacceptable chopping board.

board. Concerns over the use of **bactericides** in chopping boards, equipment and wall finishes have been expressed because of the risk of developing resistance in pathogenic micro-organisms. As yet no ideal replacement has been found for hard wood chopping blocks used by butchers. However, these should be maintained in good condition and used solely for chopping or sawing raw meat.

Contamination

To avoid **cross-contamination**, it is important that the same equipment is not used for handling raw and **high-risk products** without being disinfected. To prevent the inadvertent use of equipment for high-risk and raw food it is recommended that, where possible, different colours and/or shapes are used. Colour coding may be extended from knives and chopping boards to include washing facilities, trolleys, **protective clothing**, cloths and packaging material. A common colour-coding system involves using: red (raw meat), green (salad), blue (fish), yellow (high-risk), white (dairy) and brown (raw vegetables).

Deterioration

Equipment deteriorates with age and eventually becomes incapable of being thoroughly cleaned. Routine maintenance is essential. Chipped, broken and badly pitted equipment allows the harbourage of dirt and bacteria and should be replaced. String or tape must not be used to repair defective equipment, including knife handles. Equipment that is no longer used should be removed from food premises.

The cleaning of equipment

All operating instructions and procedures must be clearly communicated to equipment users and cleaners. The equipment should be capable of being cleaned and, if necessary, disinfected safely, thoroughly and rapidly without the need for skilled fitters and specialised tools. If dismantling is necessary this must be achieved relatively easily, as should reassembly.

Sharp edges are a serious hazard for cleaners. A reluctance to clean equipment because of poor design will result in a lowering of hygienic standards. Hinges should be capable of being taken apart for cleaning. Angle iron is difficult to clean and tubular construction is preferred, open ends to tubular legs must be sealed.

Storage of clean equipment

Having spent a considerable amount of time cleaning and disinfecting equipment and utensils, it makes sense to ensure that subsequent storage does not result in contamination. The USA Food and Drug Administration Food Service Sanitation Manual states that clean equipment and utensils should be stored at least 450mm above the floor in a clean, dry location, in a way that protects them from contamination by splash, dust and other means.

MAINTENANCE OF PREMISES AND EQUIPMENT

Managing maintenance

Equipment must be maintained in efficient working order and good repair. This involves routine inspection and preventive maintenance as recommended by the manufacturer and determined by experience. Regular effective cleaning and waste removal will assist in extending the life of equipment. Maintenance must be carried out by competent persons who have received adequate information and training. Pressure systems must be inspected by engineering inspection companies.

Build up of flour dust and debris, leading to failure to keep equipment clean and in good condition is likely to result in prosecution.

Procedures should be in place for supervision of external contractors to ensure that they work safely and do not expose food to contamination. External contractors must complete a visitor's medical questionnaire. The manager or supervisor should check that contractors' working areas are screened off from food production. Contractors should ensure that they do not leave equipment or materials like wiring and metal waste that could result in physical contamination of food. The work areas should be carefully checked before food production can be resumed.

Cleaning

The supervisor should ensure that the premises and equipment cleaning schedules are fully implemented, and that external cleaning contractors' work standards are monitored. It is important that equipment be adequately cleaned to ensure that it works efficiently and does not develop unnecessary wear.

Routine monitoring

There should be procedures in place to ensure that daily supervisory checks are carried out to identify obvious defects in premises and equipment, for example:

◆ damaged flyscreens or leaking pipes and taps;
◆ damaged cables and defective electric plugs; and
◆ missing light covers.

There will need to be specific training so that supervisors and food handlers know what to look for, what needs checking, and how to report faults.

Planned maintenance

When organising a maintenance programme, management should identify the equipment or areas of the premises to be maintained, the actual work needed, the frequency of maintenance, the competencies of people to do it and the necessary supervisory arrangements. Suppliers of food processing equipment must provide the food business operator with accurate information on recommended products and methods of cleaning, disinfecting and rinsing - as well as operation and maintenance. Only competent and properly trained contractors should be allowed to carry out work in food premises, for example, for electrical or gas appliance maintenance. Management should monitor the correct implementation of planned maintenance, and take corrective action if any maintenance has not been carried out. Checks should be made that repairs, following a breakdown in equipment, are carried out by competent personnel using the correct components.

As far as is practicable, work schedules for planned maintenance should include periods when food production is not being carried out. For example, planned maintenance is best carried out during the annual 'shutdown', or at night and at weekends.

Inspections and tests

There is a legal requirement for some food processing equipment like steam ovens to be periodically tested. Specialist engineering inspection companies are usually employed to carry out tests on such equipment.

Electrical food processing equipment in factories and catering outlets should receive frequent inspections. Heavily used portable appliances such as food mixers should be formally inspected every month and given a combined inspection and test every six months. Management will monitor that periodic planned testing, such as portable appliance testing (electrical items), is carried out, that records are completed for each test and checks are made to ensure that follow-up maintenance is completed.

*The photographs used to show unsatisfactory equipment in this chapter were provided by Kingston-upon-Hull City Council, Environmental Health (Food Team), Runnymede Borough Council and the illustrations by Campden & Chorleywood Food Research Association.

12 Cleaning & disinfection

edited by Peter Bird & Steve Bagshaw

Even in the most highly automated **food business**, operating under the most controlled conditions, soiling of both surfaces and equipment is unavoidable. The type and extent of soiling will vary considerably but, whatever the operation, it is essential that such residues are not allowed to accumulate to levels that expose **food** to the **risk** of **contamination**. Removal of these residues is the process of **cleaning**.

The objective of the clean varies depending on the standard required. A physical clean may be used to prevent physical contamination of the product. However, operations involving **high-risk foods** require a **microbiological** clean, which involves cleaning to remove soiling plus **disinfection** to destroy **micro-organisms**. A clean surface has no soiling or objectional odour, is not greasy to touch and will not discolour a white paper tissue wiped over it.

The law and cleaning

Food safety legislation requires food premises and equipment to be kept clean. The standards of cleanliness and frequency of cleaning required will vary depending on the type of operation and the type of food being prepared. This means that, for example, the standard of cleanliness in a **cook-chill** kitchen will be higher than a room used solely for peeling potatoes. **Food-contact surfaces** in high-risk areas will require periodic disinfection, whereas thorough cleaning of areas used for **low-risk food** preparation may suffice.

The frequency of cleaning and the removal of waste and other refuse must ensure that there are no accumulations in food rooms, except so far as is unavoidable for the proper functioning of business. Adequate facilities must be provided for cleaning and disinfecting work tools and equipment and, where necessary, adequate provision for any washing of food.

All food must be protected from contamination that would render it unfit for human consumption, injurious to health or unreasonable to consume. This means that food must not be exposed to risk from cleaning. Several prosecutions have resulted from the contamination of food with cleaning chemicals, or with bits of metal, plastic or wood from cleaning equipment.

The benefits of cleaning

Cleaning is an essential and integral part of a profitable food business. In addition to satisfying legal requirements, cleanliness will:

♦ disrupt routes of contamination, e.g. cleaning and disinfecting tables used for raw and high-risk foods;

♦ ensure a pleasant, safe and attractive working environment, which will encourage effective working and reduce the risk of accidents to both staff and customers;

♦ promote a favourable image to the customer and assist in marketing the business;

♦ remove matter conducive to the growth of micro-organisms, so facilitating effective disinfection and reducing the risk of **food poisoning, spoilage** and wastage;

♦ remove materials that would provide food or harbourage for **pests** and prevent early discovery of **infestations**;

♦ reduce the risk of foreign matter contamination and thereby obviate customer complaints; and

♦ prevent damage to, or a reduction in, the efficiency of equipment and services, thereby reducing maintenance costs.

HACCP and cleaning

Cleaning must be carried out at every stage in the production of food, from the delivery bay to the service point, and is often included in **HACCP** plans. However, in most food businesses it is preferable for effective cleaning and disinfection to be considered as an essential prerequisite to the introduction of HACCP.

Hazards and problems from cleaning

Although cleaning is intended to eliminate **hazards** or reduce them to a safe level, negligent or ineffective cleaning can result in many serious hazards and other problems.

Hazards from cleaning

Microbiological contamination may result from:
♦ cleaning from raw to high-risk areas;
♦ using contaminated cleaning equipment, especially brushes and cloths;
♦ using the wrong chemicals or the right chemicals at the incorrect dilution;
♦ dust created during sweeping and dry cleaning; and
♦ aerosols created by pressure spraying, floor scrubbing and boot washing.

Microbiological multiplication may occur when:
♦ cleaning and disinfection are not carried out properly or at the correct frequency; and
♦ there is a failure to remove food debris thoroughly and frequently.

Microbiological survival may occur when:
♦ surfaces are not adequately cleaned prior to disinfection; and
♦ the type, concentration or **contact time** of a **disinfectant** is inadequate.

Chemical contamination may result from:
♦ using the wrong chemicals, which produce **tainting**, for example, phenolic **disinfectants**;
♦ using chemicals at the wrong concentration, for example, hypochlorite for disinfecting lettuce;
♦ a failure to rinse properly, for example, clean-in-place systems;
♦ storing chemicals in food containers or bottles; and
♦ storing chemicals with food.

Physical contamination may result from:
♦ using inappropriate, worn and defective cleaning equipment;
♦ using inappropriate cleaning substances, for example, abrasives;
♦ using defective **protective clothing**, especially torn rubber gloves; and
♦ a failure to remove food debris, waste and packaging material.

Problems from cleaning

In addition to food safety hazards, negligent cleaning results in many other problems:

♦ financial consequences arising from using the wrong chemicals, the wrong dilution, the wrong temperature and inadequate contact time. This not only applies to direct costs relating to product, equipment and premises, but also the cost of effluent treatment;

♦ a poor quality product, which may lead to a reduction in **shelf life**, customer complaints, loss of reputation, court proceedings, food poisoning, redress from suppliers and loss of sales;

♦ wastage of food and production re-runs;

♦ corrosion and premature replacement of equipment;

♦ production breakdowns, for example, following the incorrect use of caustic soda, which has removed grease from bearings;

♦ unacceptable deterioration of floor surfaces and drainage systems;

♦ fire hazards, for example, because of build up of grease in ventilation ducting from extract hoods; and

♦ accidents due to slipping on wet floors, mixing chemicals or not using appropriate protective clothing.

CLEANING TERMS

Technical terms commonly used in cleaning science include:

Abrasives

Abrasives include hard abrasives such as pumice and fine sand, which may be compounded with soaps to form pastes, and mild abrasives such as lime and chalk, which are used in cream cleaners. These are not generally approved of because of the risk of foreign body contamination.

Amphoteric surfactants

The active ions of amphoterics can be either positively or negatively charged, depending on the **pH** (**acidity** or **alkalinity**) of the solution. Some amphoteric surfactants are very mild in nature and are used in shampoos; others have excellent biocidal properties and are used as disinfectants. They have low human toxicity but high unit cost.

Anionic surfactants

Anionic surfactants separate in solution to form ions. The active ion is negatively charged. They are the most commonly used surfactants and are often mixed with non-ionic surfactants to form basic commercial **detergents** such as washing-up liquid. They are generally **biodegradable**, non-toxic and have good wetting properties.

Biodegradability

Biodegradability refers to the property of a surfactant, which allows it to be broken up by **bacteria** in sewage works, so reducing pollution and toxic hazard to fish. All modern surfactants tend to be biodegradable, although some form intermediate toxic compounds and have been banned in some countries.

Cationic surfactants

Cationic surfactants ionise in solution, the active ion being positively charged. Mixed with non-ionics, they are very commonly used as disinfectants or **sanitisers**. They are high foaming and have relatively poor wetting characteristics.

Compatibility

Detergents with different ionic charges should not be mixed as they are not compatible and become inactivated. Even mixing similar types of detergent may impair performance, as blends are carefully balanced to **optimise synergistic** effects.

Emulsion

An **emulsion** is a suspension of one liquid in another. Detergents have the ability to surround microdroplets of oil or fat and hold them in suspension as an "oil-in-water" emulsion that can be easily rinsed away.

Foaming activity

Foam is not an essential part of a detergent and can interfere with mechanical cleaning. In manual cleaning, however, foam increases the surface area of a solution, increasing the speed of activity and enabling more dirt to be suspended. Too much foam can cause rinsing difficulties.

Non-ionic surfactants

Non-ionic surfactants do not ionise in solution and therefore do not carry a charge. They are compatible with anionic, cationic and amphoteric surfactants, commonly being used as components of blends to improve overall cleaning performance. They can also be mixed with **acids** to form acid cleaners. They are generally biodegradable, non-toxic, have good wetting properties and may be high or low foaming.

Saponification

Saponification is the process of making soap, usually by boiling vegetable and mineral fats and oils with an alkaline material such as caustic soda. This also occurs in cleaning when alkalis react with fatty or oily **organic** soils. The soap thus formed assists in the further cleaning action. Soap is anionic in character and forms a scum in hard water when it reacts with the calcium and magnesium ions.

Scouring powder

Scouring powders are cleaning powders combining abrasive and often minute amounts of bleaching agent. They will seriously damage enamel or stainless steel surfaces and should not be used for cleaning these materials.

Sequestrants

Sequestrants are chemicals that counteract the effect of **water hardness** salts, preventing the formation of scum, which would interfere with the cleaning action of chemicals.

Solvents

Solvents are chemicals that have the effect of dissolving specific types of soil. Solvents, such as glycol ether, are often used in small amounts as a part of a detergent formulation to improve its performance for dealing with oils and fats.

Synergism

Synergism is an enhanced performance achieved by the mixture of two or more chemicals, the sum of the activity being greater than the total effect of the components acting separately. This effect occurs with ionic and non-ionic detergent blends and can also be important in disinfectant formulations.

MANAGEMENT FUNCTIONS OF CLEANING

Cleaning is essentially a management function but the physical process of removing dirt is only the final stage. The prime responsibility is to ensure that premises and their contents are capable of being effectively cleaned. Not only does this make economic sense but it is also a legal requirement.

Securing the commitment

Paying lip service to standards is not enough. Everyone involved in a food business must be personally committed to ensuring that satisfactory standards are achieved. Requisite standards must be clearly defined, effectively communicated and reinforced by management. Staff must be motivated, instructed, supervised and controlled.

Providing the means

Sufficient numbers of adequately trained cleaning staff, properly supervised and supplied with appropriate materials and equipment, must be employed. Adequate supplies of hot water are essential. To avoid confusion, the number of different cleaning chemicals used should be minimised.

Reducing unnecessary labour

Careful planning, assembly of materials and adopting the most suitable method will save considerable time and effort. Systematic wiping or spraying will avoid duplication of coverage and the risk of areas being missed. If "clean as you go" is in operation, cleaning will be easier as residues will not have hardened. Organising work in teams is often highly efficient.

The use of in-house and contract cleaning

External contractors may provide food businesses with services that they cannot undertake effectively themselves. These services include specialist cleaning of extractor systems and drains, waste collection and disposal. Large catering, manufacturing and retail businesses often contract out their cleaning requirements. Using an outside contractor for cleaning has a number of advantages. Specialised expertise and trained cleaning staff are provided by the contractor to achieve a standard of cleaning that in-house staff may not be able to attain. An external cleaning service removes the burden of cleaning from in-house staff, enabling them to concentrate on their key responsibilities such as retail service, cooking, and food production. The food business's premises and equipment will be protected from damage or theft by a reputable cleaning service's comprehensive insurance. An effective cleaning contract can reduce the food business's operating costs. There are cost savings because the contractor provides specialised cleaning equipment and appropriate cleaning chemicals. The food business's production or service activities will not be disrupted if the cleaning contractor provides out-of-hours service, for example, overnight. An effective cleaning contract reduces the risk of foodborne illness and provides a visual standard of cleanliness that creates a favourable impression to customers. A well-run and fully documented cleaning contract contributes to a due-diligence defence.

There are potential drawbacks to using an external contractor. The management of a food business have full control over in-house cleaning. Management understands the cleaning requirements of the business, and has the incentive to operate an effective cleaning schedule using well-trained employees. The external contractor may not have the same level of commitment to achieving and maintaining high standards of cleaning. There may be significant litigation costs in terminating an unsatisfactory cleaning contract, as well as costs arising from enforcement action taken because cleaning standards do not meet standards required under food safety legislation. A customer audit of the food business may identify an inadequate cleaning contract, or one that is poorly supervised by management. This could result in the loss of the customer. Sufficient management expertise and experience may not be available in-house to fully evaluate proposals for services and their costs. A badly drawn-up contract may fail to adequately cover key cleaning tasks and/or allocation of responsibilities on the part of management and the contractor. Management cannot leave the contractor unsupervised. Close supervision of the contractor is essential if cleaning standards are to be maintained. External contractors may be selected on cost grounds. The cheapest contractor might cut corners using unsuitable or ineffective cleaning chemicals, or poorly trained staff. Insufficient time may be allocated to key cleaning tasks. Contract staff shortages may result in poor cleaning standards or interruptions in waste collection, for example. Poor cleaning standards could result in a foodborne illness incident.

Cleaning schedules

Cleaning schedules are a communication link between management and staff and are necessary to ensure that equipment and premises are effectively cleaned and, if necessary, disinfected as frequently and as economically as possible. When planning a cleaning schedule, the following items should be considered:

- ◆ the size, type and temperature of area to be cleaned, the structure of the building and the wall, floor and ceiling finishes;
- ◆ the type of equipment and the material from which it is made. The manufacturer's recommendations should always be followed;
- ◆ whether or not the equipment can be dismantled;
- ◆ the type of soiling and the water hardness;
- ◆ the presence of electrics;
- ◆ the available water pressure and drainage system;
- ◆ the time constraints, manpower and training needs;
- ◆ if cleaning is necessary during food preparation, or if food should be removed;
- ◆ whether or not disinfection is required;
- ◆ the risk of spreading contamination, for example, the role of pressure hoses in disseminating *Listeria monocytogenes;*
- ◆ the requirements of the Health and Safety at Work etc. Act, 1974, and all relevant health and safety legislation;
- ◆ the controls available to monitor the effectiveness of cleaning; and
- ◆ the overall cost, including labour, equipment, chemicals, water and heat. In large premises the cost of effluent treatment must also be considered.

The cleaning schedule itself must be clearly and concisely written, without ambiguity, to ensure that instructions to staff are easy to follow and result in the objective of the schedule being achieved.

Cleaning failure.

Written schedules should specify:

- what is to be cleaned;
- the chemicals, materials and equipment to be used;
- the dilution and contact time of the chemical;
- how it is to be cleaned (method);
- when it is to be cleaned (frequency);
- the time necessary to clean it;
- who is to clean it;
- the protective clothing to be worn;
- the safety precautions to be taken; and
- who is responsible for monitoring and recording that it has been cleaned.

Control and monitoring of cleaning

A system for identifying problems must be established. Faults may be caused by poor management, administrative deficiencies, unsatisfactory staff, inadequate training or unreasonable expectations of individual performance.

Standards should be routinely monitored through **inspections**, which are carried out by management personnel not directly involved in cleaning operations. All findings should be recorded and utilised to rectify faults and improve the effectiveness of cleaning.

ADMINISTRATION

To implement management policy, certain administrative functions must be carried out. These include:

Selecting a chemical supplier

Price is obviously important, but cheap chemicals can result in expensive cleaning. Suppliers should have a knowledge of the type of operation, a satisfactory range of products, a knowledge of all appropriate health and safety legislation, the expertise to undertake a comprehensive audit to determine cleaning needs, the time to spend demonstrating how to use the product to best effect and easy to understand literature that does not mislead. They must be reliable, have the ability to respond to emergencies and, preferably, be quality assured.

Stock control

Provisions similar to those applicable to food stocks should apply, with proper **stock rotation**, delivery checking and inventory control. Comprehensive records should be kept of all transactions, while minimum and maximum stock levels should also be established. Authorisation to order should be restricted to named personnel.

Distribution

Transfer of materials from the store to the point of use should be properly organised to ensure that the correct materials, in the correct quantities, reach the correct people at the correct time. Over-supply or storage of bulk stocks in working areas, should be avoided.

Financial control

Records of expenditure on each item, identifiable with the area of use, should be kept. Expenditure norms should be established and any deviations investigated, as this is often the first indication to management that procedures are amiss. Underspending is as significant as overspending.

TECHNOLOGY OF CLEANING

Management and administration apart, the remainder of the cleaning function is the application of technology. In this sense, cleaning is defined as "the systematic application of energy to a surface or substance, with the intention of removing dirt". Central to the definition is the concept of energy.

Energy in cleaning

ENERGY IS AVAILABLE FOR CLEANING IN THREE DISTINCT FORMS

kinetic energy:	physical – manual labour;
	mechanical – machines;
	turbulence – liquids (clean-in-place);
thermal energy:	hot water; and
chemical energy:	detergents.

Normally, a combination of two or more energy forms is used. Manual labour is the most expensive and chemical energy the most economic, although adequate contact time is also important. The correct energy balance is essential for cost-effective cleaning.

Cleaning costs

CLEANING COSTS MAY BE APPORTIONED AS FOLLOWS

labour	70%	chemicals	6%
equipment	12%	heating	4%
water/effluent	6%	corrosion	2%

The above figures should only be considered as a rough guide, for example, if only buckets and mops are used, equipment costs will be lower and labour costs increased. If the wrong chemicals are used, corrosion costs may be significantly greater than 2%. Water and effluent costs have increased significantly over the last ten years and water use should be minimised.

Chemical cleaning

The usual cleaning medium is water, which dissolves certain residues and forms a solution that can be rinsed away. Water, however, is not efficient in dissolving many of the soils that occur in the food industry. To improve the efficiency of water as a cleaning chemical and to counteract the effect of the impurities in water (hardness salts), other chemicals, for example, detergents, are added.

Detergents

Detergents are chemicals, or mixtures of chemicals, made of soap or synthetic substitutes, with or without additives, which are used to remove grease or other soiling. They are available as powders, liquids, foams or gels.

Detergents can exhibit two types of action depending on their make-up and the soil they are acting upon. These are: chemical actions where a constituent of the detergent reacts chemically with the soil, for example, the reaction of mineral scale and acid detergents; and physical actions where a constituent of the detergent helps to penetrate, remove and disperse the soil from a surface, for example, the removal and **emulsification** of fats from a surface using a neutral detergent.

Manual detergents used in the food industry should be non-toxic, non-tainting, non-irritant, non-corrosive, free-rinsing, soluble in water and not form scum in hard water.

Surfactancy

This is the property of a detergent that enables it to increase the "wetting power" of water by reducing the surface tension. This increases the contact between the soil and the detergent solution, which is able to penetrate the minute irregularities of the dirt more effectively.

Dispersion

This is the ability of a detergent to break up large accumulations of matter into smaller particles.

Suspension

When dirt is broken up into particles, they become coated with a thin film of detergent which keeps the particles apart and buoyant, i.e. in suspension, allowing them to be rinsed away. This characteristic is commonly referred to as the emulsifying action of detergents.

| Oil globule in solution of detergent | Detergent molecules surrounding oil globule | Oil globule surrounded by hydrophilic parts of detergent molecules |

* hydrophilic part

detergent molecule

* lipophilic part

oil molecule

Emulsifying action (diagrammatic).
* hydrophilic means water loving and lipophilic means fat loving.

Classification of detergents

For convenience, detergents tend to be classified by their acidity or alkalinity.

Alkaline detergents

The most commonly used alkaline detergent is caustic soda (sodium hydroxide). It is corrosive to skin, aluminium and zinc, has poor wetting properties, but is effective for fat and protein solubilisation and is relatively cheap. Sequestering agents (chelates), such as the amino carboxylic acids, EDTA and NTA, are added to prevent scale formation in hard water. **Inorganic** phosphates are effective sequestrants used in the UK, mainly in powder products, but are banned in some European countries because of the eutrophication of rivers.

Acid detergents

These are mainly used to remove mineral, protein and vegetable deposits and commonly contain phosphoric acid, which is one of the least corrosive acids. It must never be allowed to come into contact with chlorinated compounds because of the consequential release of toxic chlorine gas.

Neutral detergents

These are generally blends of surfactants used for manual dishwashing and manual cleaning. They are by their nature relatively safe to use, but gloves should still be worn to avoid defatting of the skin and to reduce the risk of dermatitis.

Detergent action

The reduction of surface tension enables detergent solutions to penetrate dirt and grease and lift them from the surface to form a suspension.

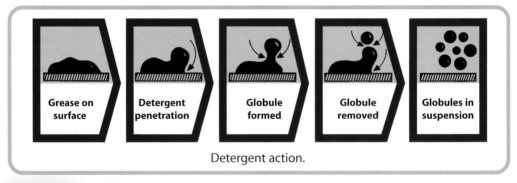

| Grease on surface | Detergent penetration | Globule formed | Globule removed | Globules in suspension |

Detergent action.

Types of soil

In very general terms there are two types of soil: organic and inorganic.

Organic soils

These are derived from living matter and include animal fat, vegetable oils, starch, sugars and proteins from milk, egg, meat or blood. Normally they may be removed by using neutral or alkaline detergents. However, if heated, dried or allowed to remain for a prolonged period, then alkalis must be used to remove them.

Grease or oil will, if heated, form a tenacious, dark, sticky deposit known as polymerised grease. This may be removed by a mild **alkali** such as sodium carbonate (washing soda) or sodium metasilicate. Further heating of polymerised grease results in the formation of carbon, which must be removed by the more aggressive, caustic alkalis such as sodium hydroxide or potassium hydroxide (caustic potash).

Another type of organic soil is tannin, which is derived from tea, coffee or wine. It is normally removed by an oxidising agent such as sodium hypochlorite (bleach) or sodium perborate. However, if the tannin is present with water hardness salts it may be better to use an acid detergent.

Inorganic soils
These include water hardness salts (scale), oxidised metals (rust), uric acid salts (urinal stains), beerstone and calcium salts deposited from milk (milkstone). Inorganic soils are normally removed by acids such as hydrochloric and phosphoric, although these should not be used on aluminium due to potential corrosion problems.

Soils are very rarely made up of one component, for example, a hard scale in a meat processing area may be a complex of a mineral scale and protein.

DISINFECTION

Disinfection is defined by British Standard 5283 as "the destruction of micro-organisms, but not usually bacterial **spores**; it may not kill all micro-organisms but reduces them to a level which is neither harmful to health nor the quality of perishable foods". Disinfection may be achieved by using heat, chemicals, irradiation or UV radiation. UV is usually effective for atmospheres and clear water but not for surfaces. The term **sterilisation** relates to the destruction of all micro-organisms and spores and is normally unnecessary and impracticable to achieve within the food industry.

Disinfection is commonly used to describe one of the last stages of the clean, where any remaining micro-organisms are reduced to an acceptable level. However, it must be remembered that the most important stages in the overall regime are cleaning and rinsing. The disinfection stage on its own, or following poor cleaning, will give poor microbiological results.

Heat disinfection
The application of heat is the most reliable and effective means of destroying micro-organisms, although it may not be the most practicable, especially for surfaces. It is used in machines, such as dishwashing machines, with a water temperature of 88°C and a contact time varying from one to 15 seconds. It is also used in "sterilising units" where articles may be fully immersed for a period of 30 seconds at 82°C.

Steam disinfection
Lances producing steam jets may be used in large food factories to disinfect machinery or surfaces that are difficult to reach. Steam-cleaned equipment is self-drying, although disadvantages may include:
♦ an adverse effect on some materials, for example, some plastics and certain wall and ceiling finishes, such as paint, may be stripped off;
♦ the removal of grease and lubricants from machinery;
♦ a safety hazard if steam lances are used by untrained personnel; and
♦ the formation of condensate on other equipment, especially overhead pipes and metal girders, leading to corrosion and potential product contamination.

Chemical disinfection

Disinfectants suitable for use in the food industry are limited to those that, when used correctly, will not have a deleterious effect on food, equipment or personnel. Types of chemical disinfectants available include:

Chlorine release agents

The commonest chemical **bactericides** are hypochlorites, which are salts of hypochlorous acid (HOCl). The most useful is sodium hypochlorite, which disinfects by oxidation of protein, an essential part of the structure of bacteria, **viruses, yeasts** and **fungi**.

They are normally supplied in solutions containing 6 to 14% available chlorine and should be diluted to between 100 and 2,000ppm of available chlorine, depending on the particular situation. A freshly made-up solution of hypochlorite containing 100ppm of available chlorine will satisfactorily disinfect a completely **clean surface**, provided a contact time of approximately three minutes is allowed. However, depending on the amount and type of soil, pH, contact time, temperature and organisms or spores present, a concentration of up to 2,000ppm of available chlorine may be necessary to ensure disinfection. In the event of doubt, the manufacturer's advice should be obtained. For general use, to minimise corrosion, it is recommended that hypochlorites are used below 40°C at a maximum of 200ppm with a contact time of up to 20 minutes. Upon completion of disinfection, they should be rinsed off with clean, cold water. They must never be used in conjunction with acid cleaners due to the production of chlorine gas. Hypochlorites may react with phenols, present in some resins used in glass fibre vessels, to form chlorophenols, which result in taint problems.

Hypochlorites are relatively cheap and are active against most micro-organisms. They are unaffected by hard water. However, they have a pungent odour, are corrosive to man and many metals and are readily inactivated by organic soil. They have no wetting power and therefore a surfactant may be added. Liquid hypochlorite should be stored in a cool, dark place. The use of chlorinated powders containing, for example, sodium dichloro-isocyanurate, eliminates most of the above disadvantages.

Provided they are used on clean surfaces, allowed adequate contact time, residues are rinsed off and suitable safety precautions are taken during handling, the advantages of using hypochlorites far outweigh their disadvantages.

Disinfectant soak.
(Courtesy of Holchem
Laboratories Ltd.)

Quaternary ammonium compounds (QACs or **quats**)

Cationic in characteristic, QACs are safe, non-corrosive, stable, and taint-free bactericides with some inherent detergent properties and little odour. In isolation, they have a narrow range of activity and are not as effective as hypochlorites against Gram-negative bacteria, viruses and fungi. They may be inactivated by hard water, organic material and some plastics. Effectiveness can be significantly improved by the incorporation of a sequestrant as part of a well-built formulation with non-ionic detergent and alkali ingredients. QAC-based disinfectants are the most widely used surface disinfectants in the food processing industry. Because of their inherent substantive properties, which can make it difficult to completely remove them by normal rinsing, they are not used in brewing as any residual QAC effects beer head retention.

Amphoteric disinfectants

Amphoterics exhibit bactericidal properties. They are of low toxicity, relatively non-corrosive, tasteless and odourless. They are good disinfectants but are expensive. They are high foaming and are unsuitable for use with machines and high-velocity sprays.

Biguanides

These are cationic bactericides, similar in function to QACs but with better all-round performance. They have no wetting properties and are therefore compounded with non-ionic detergents. They are sometimes used in the licensed trade for glass washing and are non-foaming. They are unsuitable for use in highly alkaline conditions and should not be used after caustics.

Iodophors

Iodophors are expensive but effective bactericides consisting of iodine and non-ionic surfactant in an acid medium. They have both detergent and disinfecting properties and their acid characteristics make them suitable for the dairy industry, breweries and soft drink manufacturers. Advantages include the ability to kill a wide range of organisms, effectiveness at low temperatures (iodine may sublime above 40°C), tolerance of soiling and hard water and brief contact time. Iodophors are stable, of low toxicity and virtually odourless if properly used, although they may combine with food to cause taint. Furthermore, if used negligently they may be corrosive.

Iodophors stain soiling matter such as milkstone and so indicate poor physical cleanliness. Plastics may be stained but metals are not. In use, the yellow-brown colour of the iodophor is absorbed by organic matter and the colour disappears, a useful indicator of potency. They should not be used on aluminium or copper.

Peroxy compounds

These fairly specialised products are increasingly used for terminal disinfection in dairies and breweries (per-acetic acid, replacing hydrogen peroxide) and as peroxy compounds within a detergent blend for agricultural and other applications.

Per-acetic acid destroys micro-organisms by an oxidative action and remains effective at temperatures as low as 0°C. Once diluted, it has a limited life and is only suitable on glass or stainless steel surfaces.

Alcohols

Where there is a requirement for light cleaning and disinfection in an essentially "dry" area, for example, delicatessen point of sale or packing belts on a production line, the use of an alcohol-based spray/wipe product is particularly useful. This is typically a blend of alcohol, QAC, and possibly mild detergent additives, formulated to provide good disinfection in lightly soiled conditions and without the use of water. The product flashes dry after application thus removing the need for an undesirable wipe-dry operation. Care must be exercised because of the flammability of alcohols.

Ethanol and iso-propanol are two of the alcohols commonly used for surface and hand disinfection.

Aldehydes

Formaldehyde and glutaraldehyde have a wide spectrum of activity but are not used because of their high toxicity and irritancy characteristics.

Ozone

Ozone consists of three oxygen molecules electrically bound together. It is unstable and once generated will only last for around 20 minutes in distilled water at 20°C. It can be used to destroy bacteria, moulds, viruses, yeasts and parasites in water or on the surface of fruits and vegetables, grains, seeds, nuts, shellfish, fish and meat. A few seconds contact time is usually sufficient to destroy pathogens. Ozone may also be used to destroy micro-organisms on packaging, food-contact surfaces and room surfaces.

Ozone extends the shelf life of food and leaves no chemical by-products. Although the use of ozone was considered to be dangerous, its advantages have resulted in a considerable investment in its safe application. The use of ozone is likely to increase over the foreseeable future.

Choosing a disinfectant

The choice of disinfectant depends on many factors including:
- amount of soiling;
- type of cleaning equipment;
- water hardness;
- contact time available;
- stability;
- type of micro-organisms that need to be destroyed;
- type, imperviousness and smoothness of surface to be disinfected;
- possibility of taint;
- temperature of application;
- toxicity of the disinfectant and the effect on personnel;
- ionic nature of the detergent used before disinfection; and
- the way the disinfectant is to be used/method of application.

Most suppliers of disinfectants to the food industry will have tested their products for effectiveness against a range of micro-organisms. Users should satisfy themselves that the product is suitable for the use intended.

Where to disinfect

Disinfection is not a universal process applicable to all surfaces. It should only be used on those surfaces where the presence of micro-organisms, at the levels found, will have an adverse effect on the safety or quality of the food handled. If disinfection is considered necessary, it should normally be restricted to:
- food-contact surfaces;
- **hand-contact surfaces;**

- cleaning materials and equipment;
- the surface of fruit and vegetables to be consumed raw; and
- hand disinfection (only when essential).

Disinfection of food and hand-contact surfaces

As micro-organisms are rarely mobile and need to be physically carried on to food, the disinfection of non-food contact surfaces, such as floors and walls, is rarely necessary. Surfaces not directly coming into contact with food, but frequently touched by **food handlers**, need disinfection to avoid the build-up of micro-organisms on hands.

Hand disinfection

Hand disinfection is only necessary in critical situations, for example, when the handling of high-risk food is unavoidable or to protect food handlers, such as fish filleters, from developing septic cuts. In the majority of **food handling** situations, washing the hands properly with liquid soap, rinsing in running water and thorough drying is quite satisfactory. If hand disinfection is considered necessary, it should be carried out after normal handwashing. Hand disinfectants should be fast-acting, rapid-drying and contain ingredients to protect the skin. Alcohol-based handrubs are becoming more popular.

Disinfection of cleaning equipment and materials

Cleaning equipment is often an important vehicle of contamination. It should be cleaned and disinfected frequently and always before storage. Normal machine laundering at 65°C or above, in the case of cloths and towels, will achieve this.

Disinfecting fruit and vegetables

An increasing number of food poisoning and **foodborne disease outbreaks** are being attributed to the consumption of contaminated fruit and vegetables, such as cut melons, lettuce

Incorrect storage of mop.
(Courtesy of Vikan (UK) Ltd.)

and tomatoes. Contamination can occur because of the use of animal fertiliser, sewage - polluted irrigation water or post-harvest washing with polluted water. Infected food handlers may occasionally be implicated, especially in the case of **low-dose pathogens**, such as *Shigella spp, Salmonella* Typhi, or Norwalk-like viruses and hepatitis A.

Blanching in hot water at around 70°C for 15 seconds is probably the most effective way of destroying organisms, although hypochlorites (50ppm free chlorine at pH of 6.00 to 7.5 for around two minutes) ozone or acetic acid and peroxide (around 75ppm) will also reduce levels of transient pathogens. Vegetables should be washed prior to disinfection to remove dirt which would inactivate the chemicals. Agitation during washing provides the friction to remove bacteria from the food surface. Each wash will reduce the numbers of bacteria by about ten to one. Some experts suggest that a double wash may avoid the need for disinfection.

Disinfecting cucumbers and tomatoes. (Courtesy of Drywite Ltd.)

It is recommended that the water used for washing vegetables and fruit should be around 10°C higher than the food being washed to avoid contaminated water containing bacteria being sucked into the food.

Airspace disinfection

Micro-organisms can be carried in the air and transferred to food or food-contact surfaces. This is only an issue where high-risk food is prepared. Disinfection of the air space can be carried out using a gas, such as ozone, or by aerosol misting using a liquid disinfectant. Airspace disinfection only takes place when no exposed food or personnel are in an area. It does not replace the need for surface disinfection.

Disinfection frequency

In most operations, contamination by micro-organisms takes time to build up to a significant level unless extraneous contamination is introduced by poor operational practice. Therefore, under normal circumstances, disinfection can correspond with cleaning intervals dictated by visual soiling or with work cycles. However, intermediate cleaning and disinfection may be needed to counter the effects of inherent bad practice, such as the use of the same surface or equipment for cooked and raw meats.

Resistance

Some bacteria, under certain circumstances, develop resistance to disinfectants at concentrations that would normally be lethal. This problem can be avoided by:

◆ ensuring that a fresh solution of disinfectant is used, at the correct concentration;
◆ ensuring that the components of a system are compatible with the disinfectants used;

Disinfecting fog. (Courtesy of Holchem Laboratories Ltd.)

- using disinfectants of adequate performance against the bacteria requiring control;
- using only disinfected equipment and/or disposable or freshly laundered cloths; and
- applying disinfectants to clean surfaces.

Only in extreme cases, where the above conditions have not been observed, is it necessary to change the type of disinfectant used.

Inactivation

This phenomenon occurs when a disinfectant mixes, or comes into contact, with a substance that interferes, partially or completely, with its ability to kill micro-organisms. Such substances are called inactivators, the primary one being dirt, which affects all disinfectants to a greater or lesser extent. Hard water will inactivate uncompounded QACs, and plastics, cork, cellulose and certain organic materials will inactivate cationic disinfectants in free solution.

Control procedures

It is unfortunate that there is no visible difference between a physically clean but bacteriologically contaminated surface and one that has been effectively disinfected. Furthermore, even minor deviations from manufacturers' instructions may render the disinfection process ineffective.

If necessary, the effectiveness of disinfection should be monitored by **bacteriological** swabbing of surfaces and also examination of the food product. It is important to establish trends over a period of time and not to react to isolated unsatisfactory results.

Rapid cleanliness testing

Systems are now available for use by non-technical staff to ascertain whether or not physically clean surfaces are microbiologically satisfactory. Tests measure the amount of adenosine triphosphate (ATP), a chemical found in food debris, bacteria, **moulds**, yeasts and all living cells, remaining on the surface. When the ATP comes into contact with luciferin luciferase, the chemical that causes the firefly to glow, light is produced proportional to the amount of ATP present. Measurement of the light can be undertaken in seconds and provides an accurate standard of cleanliness. Another test involves using Vericleen strips.

CLEANING METHODS

The first step in effective cleaning is to determine the most appropriate method. Factors to consider include:

♦ accessibility, are surfaces accessible, for example, work surfaces, or conveyor belts? Is dismantling required or are the surfaces enclosed, for example, pipes and tanks?
♦ what standards are required to ensure **safe food** production, quality and shelf life;
♦ the type and mixture of soils;
♦ the type and level of microbial contamination and the required level of reduction;
♦ the risks to food, people or equipment;
♦ the resources available, labour, time, equipment and finance; and
♦ the impact on the effluent disposal system.

Manual clean.
(Courtesy of Vikan (UK) Ltd.)

Manual clean

Hand cleaning utilises the physical energy from an operative (elbow grease) coupled with application of a neutral or mildly alkaline detergent or detergent/disinfectant or sanitiser to a clean surface. A cloth, scouring pad or brush and detergent from a bucket or sprayer provides a very effective and flexible cleaning method. However, hygiene and foreign body contamination issues exist with all cleaning tools.

Dry clean

Dry cleaning methods include wiping, scraping, brushing and vacuuming of dry debris and are commonly used for dry ingredient areas, for example, in bakeries. The absence of water reduces the opportunity for microbial growth but, unfortunately, may not result in effective soil removal. Disposable cloths dampened with either a water- or alcohol-based detergent/disinfectant are often used to enhance soil removal where excessive water can be a problem, for example:

♦ on electrical or electronic equipment; and
♦ during product change clean on lightly soiled surfaces in high care environments, for example, in sandwich production.

Hand sprayers containing sanitisers are commonly used with disposable cloths in fast food outlets and cafeterias to wipe tables between customers.

Dishwashing

Unfortunately, many catering premises only use a single sink for dishwashing. Wherever possible this should be supplemented by a dishwasher. Where a single sink is used it is essential to use water as hot as possible, just below 60°C, and to replace the water frequently as it becomes cool or greasy. Suitable gloves will be required at these temperatures. Air drying may not occur and disposable paper towels should be used in these circumstances.

Although the use of a single sink is not as effective or hygienic as either the double sink or the dishwasher, provided the crockery and cutlery are clean, free from grease and dry, then there will be minimal risk of causing illness to customers.

Detergents must be compatible with the local water supply and correct amounts, in accordance with manufacturers' instructions, must be used. Measuring equipment must be cleaned frequently.

Soak clean

Soak cleaning is used for small items to extend contact time with the detergent. It is beneficial on heavy or tenuously soiled items. Highly carbonised trays, for example, pizza trays can be successfully cleaned in this manner. Detergents are often highly alkaline and may need to be formulated to be suitable for use with aluminium. Ultrasonic energy can be used to enhance soil removal.

Foam or gel cleaning

A foam or gel is simply a vehicle to increase contact time between soil and detergent. A wide variety of foam and gel products are available, which when applied to a soiled surface, will remain in contact for typically 10 minutes to 1 hour. This contact time enhances the chemical actions between soil and detergent, making it easier to remove the soil.

However, the loosened or reacted soil still requires some physical energy to remove it. This can be provided by a cleaner and a brush and/or by energy from a washdown system. In a large number of cases, some manual energy is necessary while the foam detergent is in contact with the soil because the physical energy from the washdown system is insufficient on its own.

Foams are applied by a variety of application systems, for example, Jetstream Foamer. They all have the benefit of keeping the cleaning operative away from direct contact with the foam, and also enable large areas to be quickly covered.

Foam or gel cleaning can improve performance. (Courtesy of Holchem Laboratories Ltd. and Perkins Chilled Foods Ltd., Barnsley.)

Foam detergents include neutral, alkaline, caustic, chlorinated alkaline and acidic products.

♦ Alkaline products are the most commonly used foam formulations because of their good all-round performance on fats and proteins.
♦ The higher alkalinity the better the performance against carbonised and polymerised soils, such as those found in cooking and frying operations.
♦ Products safe for use on aluminium and other "soft metals" would typically be the neutral and alkaline products; but data sheets must be checked for compatibility.
♦ The chlorinated caustic products are highly effective at removing protein soils and staining. The chlorine donor in the formulation is primarily there to aid removal of proteins and not as a biocide.
♦ Acidic products are effective on mineral scale and also on proteins.

Automated washing machines

Trays, racks, bins and utensils can be automatically washed using purpose-built washing machines. The machines maximise energy through the washdown jets, high temperature and aggressive detergents, for example, highly alkaline, to enable quick cleaning. Typically a tray passing through a tunnel traywasher will be in the detergent zone for around ten to twenty seconds.

Highly alkaline or caustic-based detergents are used for washing plastic or stainless steel parts. These products are available in different formulations to suit site water hardness. A caustic detergent sequestered to deal with water hardness will keep the traywasher relatively free of mineral scale, although the rinse sections of the washer often need periodic descaling with an acid detergent.

Aluminium or tinned utensils are cleaned using either neutral or aluminium-safe alkaline products.

Disinfectants are typically low foam, quaternary ammonium compounds or amphoterics. An exception to this is in poultry processing, where live bird crate disinfection uses Department of Environment, Food, and Regions approved products, which are often per-acetic acid based.

Washdown systems

An increasing number of food premises are being designed to facilitate cleaning by the use of water hoses. Satisfactory fall and drainage of floors are essential and wall/floor finishes and equipment, must be resistant to water ingress and damage. Care must be taken to protect electrical components against the ingress of water.

A washdown system is used to provide energy for soil removal, to rinse away soil and detergent residues and may be used as a means of applying the detergent or disinfectant.

Pressures range from 20 to 196 bar (300 to 2,800 psi), although extreme care must be exercised at the higher pressures. Increasingly, lower pressures of around 20 bar are being used for many applications, particularly when combined with foam or gel detergents. The correct machine or system must be selected for a particular job. Inadequate pressure may result in poor cleaning, whereas excessive pressure will increase the risk of damage to surfaces and equipment. This may cause unnecessary splashing and misting which leads to potential **cross-contamination**. A volume of water of at least 9 litres per minute is required to wash away dislodged soils.

Nozzle design, pressure and flow rate are all important in achieving soil removal in each cleaning situation, without causing cross-contamination by overspray or aerosols. Various nozzle designs are available giving a spreading angle of between 15° and 40°.

Washdown systems may be fixed installations or mobile. The fixed systems are generally fed with hot water in the range of 55 to 65°C. Mobile systems may be electric, diesel or petrol driven. The large electric washers require a three-phase supply. Safety must be considered in relation to mobile electric units, which should be protected by an approved earth-leakage circuit breaker. All electrical installations should satisfy the requirements of the Electrical Engineers Regulations and should be checked regularly. Fumes from petrol- and diesel-driven washers may make them unsuitable for use in food premises unless fixed outside food rooms.

Clean-in-place (CIP) equipment

Cleaning-in-place has replaced hand cleaning in dairies, breweries and potable liquid installations. Some food processing plants, including cook-chill systems, are now using CIP systems. It involves circulating non-foaming detergents and disinfectants through process equipment in the assembled state. The combined effects of solution turbulence, chemical energy and heat remove soil debris and micro-organisms from pipework and ancillary plant, without time-consuming dismantling and manual cleaning. Efficiency of cleaning depends on the type of soil, temperature, concentration of detergent, velocity, turbulence and the design of the CIP system.

HIGH TURBULENCE

LOW TURBULENCE

SUPERIOR DIRECTION OF FLOW

INFERIOR DIRECTION OF FLOW

TRAPPED AIR (INADEQUATE CLEANING)

HEIGHT EXCEEDS THREE TIMES PIPE DIAMETER

Direction of flow and height of tees affects effects cleaning performance.

The use of heat changes the physical state of the soil, for example, melts fat. It also accelerates chemical reaction. As a rough guide, an increase of 10°C may be considered to double the speed of chemical reaction. The most cost-effective results are usually obtained by using detergents at the highest temperature possible, taking into account equipment, venting, stressing and detergent manufacturers' recommendations. Allowances must also be made for the expansion of pipe lengths during CIP when hot solutions are used. It may not be possible to use hot solutions for cleaning refrigerated systems or tanks because of the risk of damaging heat-sensitive thermometers and thermostats. For light soiling, a concentration of detergent between 0.1 and 1.0% causticity is preferred. Acid products are more effective on some soils. Disinfection normally involves QACs or amphoterics, terminal disinfectants or per-acetic acid.

Careful design of CIP systems is essential to avoid unsatisfactory results. Inaccessible crevices and pockets, which can become foci for bacterial multiplication, must be eliminated. Valves and other components must be installed in the correct orientation and configuration to avoid uncleanable dead legs and tees that retain air or debris. The maximum length of dead legs and height of tees should be three times the pipe diameter to ensure satisfactory cleaning. Direction of flow into a pocket is superior to flow away from the same pocket.

All sections of the pipe-line, including valves and fittings, must be filled with solution without leaving any pockets of air. A fluid velocity of around 1.5m per second is satisfactory for most applications, although 2m per second may be required to remove stubborn soil with low-temperature solutions. Suitable fall must be built in to horizontal pipes as all parts of the system must drain completely.

Tanks, exceptionally large diameter pipes and large containers may be thoroughly cleaned using spray balls or rotating jet devices, as this avoids the unnecessary and uneconomical filling of vessels with solution. It also obviates the need for men to climb into vessels to carry out manual scrubbing.

Mains services required by CIP units may include: electricity, which may be single- or three-phase; a suitable clean, softened water supply; a clean, filtered, oil-free air supply; a saturated, filtered steam supply; and a suitable splash-proof drain or gully, resistant to temperatures of up to 90°C, capable of transporting CIP acids and alkalis and removing effluent. All systems include cleaning solutions, reservoirs, pumps, feeds and control equipment, which may vary from simple timers and manually operated switches and clocks to complex, fully integrated computer operations.

A typical basic CIP sequence consists of five stages:
- ♦ pre-rinse with cold water to remove gross soil;
- ♦ detergent circulation to remove residual adhering debris and scale;
- ♦ intermediate rinse with cold water to remove all traces of detergent;
- ♦ disinfectant circulation to destroy remaining micro-organisms; and
- ♦ final rinse with cold water to remove all traces of disinfectant.

The time allowed for each operation can be determined for each particular plant or circuit being cleaned.

EFFECTIVE CLEANING

Having selected the appropriate cleaning method, the effectiveness of the whole cleaning operation depends on:
- ♦ choosing the correct chemical;
- ♦ applying it at the **optimum** temperature and concentration;
- ♦ allowing it time to function; and
- ♦ using it with the correct equipment.

The correct mix of the above will reduce the work required.

Choosing cleaning chemicals
Cleaning product choice (the detergent or disinfectant) cannot be considered in isolation

from the cleaning method or from the dispense and application method. A detergent or disinfectant is purely a tool in the overall cleaning procedure that assists in achieving the required end result; namely a clean facility that is safe for food production. For example, a neutral detergent applied with a bucket and brush can achieve an equally good cleaning result on a stainless steel tabletop as one cleaned using an alkaline foam detergent rinsed off with a medium pressure washdown system.

The primary choice of a chemical depends on the soil. However, other factors must be considered including: compatibility of surface being cleaned with detergent, for example, highly alkaline detergents may cause corrosion on soft metals; method of application; personal safety issues; suitability for use with water supply; time available; and compatibility with other chemicals used.

SELECTION MAY BE AIDED BY THE FOLLOWING CHECKLIST

- ◆ soil
- ◆ situation
- ◆ surface
- ◆ safety

The optimum temperature

Temperature can be critical to chemical performance, generally the higher the better. However, heat may **denature** the chemical or fix proteins such as egg, in which case warm or cold applications must be used initially.

Dosing aids and applicators

This classification applies to devices used to deliver or control chemicals. They may be manually operated or automatic. Dispensers may be of the plunger or proportioning or metering type. Applicators include aerosol, trigger spray, pump-up sprayer, backpack sprayer, air or electrically driven sprayer and foam or gel applicators.

Swan-neck or mushroom dispensers

These are spring-loaded, push-operated pumps, screwed vertically into concentrate containers.

Venturi proportioners

These draw detergent by water suction from a container. Consistency can be a problem with low or varying water pressure.

Proportioning pumps

These simple water driven-pumps are more expensive than venturi proportioners but give greater consistency of dilution.

Hand sprayers

Sprayers may be trigger-pump or pressure-operated and vary in size from 500ml to 25 litres. They can be adjusted to deliver an atomised mist or a fine, long-reaching jet.

Time to function

Chemicals must be given sufficient time to act. This period is normally referred to as the contact time. Vertical surfaces may not allow sufficient contact time due to run-off. Alternative cleaning methods, such as repeated applications, or the use of foams, gels, highly viscous liquids, or even soaking, can be used to extend contact times. Attempts to remove dirt before the chemical reaction is complete results in a considerable amount of extra work.

Equipment

A growing range of specialist equipment is available for cleaning operations and the correct choice will ensure that the most cost-effective cleaning is carried out. Cleaning equipment must be cleaned and disinfected prior to storage.

Selecting the right equipment

The quality of cleaning equipment varies considerably and is usually price related. Effectiveness and durability depend on the choice of materials used in manufacture, the design and quality of construction and the suitability for a particular task.

Manual cleaning aids

Consistent, high standards of cleanliness will only be achieved if the cleaning tools have been specifically manufactured for the stringent demands of the food industry. Correct choice is essential if operatives are to avoid recontamination of a cleaned surface with dirt or bacteria. The quality and

Cleaning equipment must be stored satisfactorily. (Courtesy of Vikan (UK) Ltd.)

cleanliness of tools that touch surfaces in direct contact with food is particularly important.

Design

The design must ensure that tools can be effectively cleaned and there are no hiding places for residues or bacteria to accumulate. If handles are hollow they must be properly sealed. The use of ergonomics in design minimises operator fatigue, improves safety and consistently results in higher standards. Correct length and diameter of handles reduce the risk of muscle tension and provide the most comfortable grip. Handles should reach the chin of the user, when measured from the floor.

Materials

Modern materials such as high-density polypropylene, polyester and rilsan are resistant to acid and alkaline cleaning agents and will withstand repeated heat sterilisation up to 130°C.

Colour coding

The use of colour coding for cleaning equipment, for example, handles of brushes, bristles and cloths used in high-risk situations, with different colours being used in potentially contaminated raw food areas, assists in reducing the risk of cross-contamination. It also reinforces hygiene training relating to the need to separate raw and high-risk food.

Colour-coded brushes and shovels can reduce the risk of cross-contamination.
(Courtesy of Vikan (UK) Ltd.)

Cloths

Cloths vary from the durable, high-strength textile to the semi-disposable, non-woven with high absorbency and relatively low mechanical strength. Disposable paper is commonly used in preference to cloths.

Brushes

Brushes constructed from modern materials such as high-density polypropylene for stocks with bristles of polyester or rilsan give improved performance and resistance to wear. They are capable of withstanding boiling water and the normal cleaning chemicals used throughout the food industry. Wood and natural bristles must be avoided and worn out brushes must be replaced. As brushes become worn they become less effective, they discolour and bristles are more likely to drop out. Blue coloured bristles are often preferred as they are more easily detected if they become loose. Nylon filaments are porous and quickly lose their stiffness in wet conditions, and inferior materials may even distort in hot water.

Care is necessary to ensure damage to surfaces does not occur because the bristles are harder than the surface being cleaned.

Mops

The common or socket mop should not be used in the food environment. The twist mop and the Kentucky mop, with its detachable head that can be washed and boiled, are much more appropriate. Mops must be thoroughly cleaned after use and then left to dry. The storage of mops in buckets, with or without disinfectants, should not take place as this may allow the multiplication of, or the development of resistant, bacteria.

Buckets

Buckets may be high-density nylon or polypropylene with steel handles. Domestic-grade buckets should be avoided. Buckets should not be placed on the floor and then on to food contact surfaces.

Unsatisfactory cleaning equipment. (Courtesy of Vikan (UK) Ltd.)

Sinks and tanks

Sinks are the basis of any manual utensil and small equipment cleaning and are essentially fixed vessels for the containment of a cleaning solution. Sizes may vary from 20 to 450 litres. Construction material should be food grade stainless steel.

Tanks are similar to sinks but are used for soaking. They tend to be under-exploited. A stainless steel tank containing an aggressive cleaning solution can be used to soak a variety of equipment, removing encrusted carbon with a minimal labour input.

Mechanical aids

These include floor scrubbers, rotating washers, power washers, air lines, steam cleaners, vacuum pick-ups, dishwashing and tray-cleaning machinery. Judicious use of mechanical equipment can significantly reduce labour requirements, but considerable care should be taken in selection to ensure that it is suitable for the use intended.

Vacuum cleaners

Suitable industrial vacuum cleaners, which suck up dirt and dust in a stream of air and then filter the air to trap the dirt, should be used to clean such areas as dry stores and carpeted public rooms. The suction must be powerful enough to ensure efficient operation and some models may be used to remove liquid spillages. Extension pipes are available to clean ceilings. The use of suction vacuum cleaners is preferable to sweeping as dust clouds are avoided.

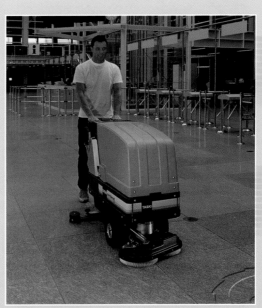

A single disc scrubbing machine and a suction vacuum cleaner.
(Courtesy of JohnsonDiversey.)

CLEANING PROCEDURES

Whatever the location, industry, soiling type or circumstances, cleaning and disinfection comprises six basic stages:

- ◆ pre-clean: sweeping, wiping or scraping off loose debris, pre-rinsing and/or pre-soaking;
- ◆ main clean: applying detergent and loosening of the main body of dirt;
- ◆ intermediate rinse: removal of loosened dirt and detergent residues;
- ◆ disinfection: destruction of remaining micro-organisms;
- ◆ final rinse: removal of disinfectant residues (if required); and
- ◆ drying: removal of final rinse water and storing to prevent contamination.

| Pre-rinsing prior to dishwashing. (Courtesy of Marks & Spencer) | Pre-clean (Courtesy of Vikan (UK) Ltd.) |

In light-soil conditions, the pre-clean may be combined with the main clean. Disinfection can be omitted on non-critical surfaces. Drying can either be natural, as in air drying, or physical, using disposable paper towels, hot air or a clean dry cloth.

Disinfection can take place in combination with the main clean using specific chemicals known as sanitisers, although this is not as effective.

Preliminary and post-cleaning actions

In the case of dangerous or electrical equipment, preliminary safety procedures and final safety checks will be required. Several types of equipment will need partial or complete dismantling to ensure effective cleaning.

Double-sink washing

This procedure is recommended for washing-up in catering premises, public houses and retail outlets selling high-risk foods, when suitable dishwashing machines are not available. It also applies to food-processing, packing and distribution plants where small items are hand washed. Thermal disinfection is usually more effective if double sinks are used. However, the evaporation of water often results in poor visibility and condensation, leading to mould growth on ceilings and walls. Furthermore, hot water at 82°C may pose an unacceptable health and safety risk. Because of these problems, a suitable chemical disinfectant such as a QAC, an amphoteric-based disinfectant or hypochlorite in a tablet form may be used. However, the rinse water should still be hot enough to allow air drying. The requisite temperature will depend on the particular piece of equipment/utensil and the material from which it is made, the temperature of the item prior to immersion and the time the item is left in the second sink. Melamine plates were found to air dry rapidly after immersion for 30 seconds at 65°C.

The full, six-stage procedure should always be followed:

- remove any heavy or loose soil by scraping and rinsing in cold water;
- place articles in the first sink in detergent solution at 53°C to 55°C, scrub with a suitable brush and/or wipe with a clean cloth to loosen dirt residues. Higher temperatures bake on proteins and are too hot for the hands;
- re-immerse in the first sink to wash off loosened dirt;
- place articles in the second sink to rinse off chemical residues;
- leave for sufficient time at a high enough temperature to ensure rapid air drying. Dilution (large volumes of water in sinks) also aids disinfection. Baskets for disinfecting purposes should be maintained in good condition and inspected regularly. They should be loaded so that all surfaces of crockery and equipment are fully exposed to the rinse water. Hollow items such as cups should be placed on their side; and
- remove articles, allow to drain and evaporate dry on a clean, disinfected surface.

The order of washing-up should be planned so that glasses and lightly soiled articles are cleaned first. For safety reasons, glasses should be washed one at a time. Some articles may need pre-soaking and treatment with abrasive pads. The temperature of the wash water should be so high as to be uncomfortable, necessitating the wearing of rubber gloves, but should never exceed 60°C to avoid fixing proteins. A rinse aid may be added to the rinse water to promote smear-free drying. Disposable paper towelling placed on the draining surface helps absorb water and reduces noise. Clean pans, cups etc. should be inverted and protected from contamination during storage. Gloves must be washed and dried after use, as must the sinks, drainers and any other surfaces involved in the process.

Dishcloths should be semi-disposable, discarded daily or, if woven fabric, should be withdrawn daily and laundered; normal laundry procedures are sufficient to secure disinfection. Cloths should never be left wet or soaked in disinfectant overnight as this can result in a build-up of resistant bacteria. Bleaching, if desirable, may take place prior to laundering but should not be considered as a substitute. High-density polypropylene brushes are preferable to cloths as they withstand autoclaving temperatures and can be cleaned and disinfected frequently.

Mechanical dishwashing

Mechanical dishwashing is preferable to, and often more economical than, manual washing, provided the machine is used according to the manufacturer's instructions. Machines, in addition to cleaning, are also a highly efficient means of disinfecting small items of equipment. They should be used for articles such as the removable parts of slicing machines, polypropylene chopping boards, nailbrushes and other items that come into contact with high-risk foods, provided that no damage to the item will result. The sequence is as follows:

- remove excess food into suitable waste bins; if necessary pre-soak or spray, unless the machine is fitted with a pre-wash cycle;
- pack articles in a neat, orderly fashion so that items do not overlap (racks may be used);
- articles pass through the wash cycle of hot detergent solution (49°C to 60°C);
- articles are rinsed at 82°C to 88°C, with the injection of rinse aid;
- the dishwashing cycles are complete and disinfected articles may be accessed; and
- allow cleaned items to drain and evaporate dry before storage (inverted).

To ensure that the best results are obtained, it is important that machines are serviced regularly, operated in accordance with manufacturers' instructions and that:

- utensils are washed as soon as possible after becoming soiled;
- the correct detergent for the level of water hardness is used. It is often more economic and efficient to install a water softener;
- the detergent dosing equipment is working properly and detergent rinse levels are properly adjusted;

Mechanical dishwashers.
(Courtesy of JohnsonDiversey.)

- sprayer arm jets are clear from obstruction and strainers are in place. Both should be cleaned daily; and
- track speed, where appropriate, is properly adjusted to give the contact time required for the detergents used.

As a rule-of-thumb guide to the efficiency of a machine, if items coming out are too hot to handle and dry rapidly to a clean, smear-free finish, then the machine is operating correctly.

Cleaning a work surface

The procedure for work surfaces will vary according to the finish and the types of cleaning chemicals used. For stainless steel and similar surfaces the routine is as follows:

- remove loose debris with a clean, loosely folded cloth (pre-clean);
- wash with hot detergent solution and a clean cloth or brush (main clean);
- rinse with hot water and a clean cloth (intermediate rinse);
- apply a suitable disinfectant and allow sufficient contact time;
- rinse off with fresh water and a disposable paper towel (final rinse); and
- allow to evaporate dry (drying).

Cleaning a slicing machine

Pre-clean

- Switch off power socket and remove the plug.
- Set the slice thickness control to zero.
- Dismantle the machine and pass removed parts through the dishwashing machine.

Where the machine is of a type that has a removable blade, a blade guard must be fitted before the blade is removed. Cleaning may then commence, with the proviso that no person may clean a slicer or other dangerous machine unless they have reached their eighteenth birthday and have been properly trained.

Filthy slicing machine.

If a dishwashing machine is unavailable, the blade may be cleaned and disinfected in situ or adjacent to the slicer. Alternatively the two-sink method may be used.

Post-clean
♦ Reassemble the machine.
♦ Redisinfect parts handled.
♦ Check the guards are properly fitted, reconnect the power and switch on the machine. Test run to check safe working. This procedure is vital because accidents have been caused by guards that were improperly fitted after cleaning. If any adjustments have to be made, the machine should be switched off and disconnected and the test run repeated.
♦ Switch off the machine, disconnect the plug and cover with a freshly laundered tea towel or other suitable covering.
♦ Supervisor to check.

Cleaning a soft ice cream machine
♦ Remove all ice cream from the machine.
♦ Rinse thoroughly with cold water.
♦ Switch off, disconnect the plug and dismantle the machine.
♦ Wash the parts and machine interior with a suitable detergent, reassemble the machine.
♦ Clean the outside of the machine and reconnect.
♦ Fill the machine with a suitable disinfectant solution, circulate for two minutes and drain. Leave the machine empty.
♦ Prior to use the next day, fill with fresh clean water, circulate and drain before filling with ice cream mix.

Beverage vending machines

These machines may present difficult cleaning problems. The complexity of some of the working parts, the time allocated for cleaning and the tenacious nature of the soil deposits has often resulted in machines being imperfectly cleaned, as well as accelerated surface damage from the use of abrasives.

While the prevalent and most troublesome soiling is often identified as tannin, it has been shown that the stubborn nature of the soil is caused by an intermediate layer of water hardness scale, bonding to machine parts. The scale and tannin deposits can be removed by soaking in a suitably formulated acid detergent for a few minutes. Specific tannin removers merely remove the tannin without affecting the scale.

Problems have also been identified with feed tubes. Conventional procedures do not remove all soil and when a brush is pushed down a tube and pulled out from the same end, an amount of the soil is redeposited. Brushes have therefore been adapted by crimping the end loops so that a whole brush can be passed through a tube in one direction. Complete soil recovery and disinfection are effected by inserting a small piece of disinfectant-soaked cloth in the crimped end-loop, which is pulled through in much the same way that a rifle barrel is cleaned.

Cleaning procedure

♦ Remove all contact parts from the machine, dismantle where necessary and soak in acid detergent solution. (The waste bucket, after emptying and cleaning, can be used.).

♦ Remove ingredient containers, clean auger discharges with a nylon scraper, refill as necessary, wipe down the exteriors and set aside.

♦ Wipe down the interior of the machine and dry thoroughly with a disposable paper towel.

♦ Remove soaked parts, wipe, brush and "pull through" as appropriate, disinfect and dry. Reassemble and replace.

♦ Replace ingredient containers.

♦ Empty, clean, disinfect and dry the waste bucket to prevent fungal growth. Replace bucket.

♦ Flush all lines with clean, hot water from the machine system, test-vend all drinks, close the cabinet and wipe down the exterior. Provided that high-risk beverages such as soups are closely monitored, the above procedure may be carried out every three days.

THE HEALTH AND SAFETY OF CLEANING

The main Act applying to the safety of cleaning is the Health and Safety at Work etc. Act, 1974. This Act requires employers to ensure the health and safety of all persons on site, including employees, visitors, members of the public and sub-contractors.

There are a large number of regulations made under this Act. The most common are known as the European Six Pack Regulations; namely:

1. Management of Health & Safety at Work Regulations, 1999

These Regulations cover a broad range of duties applicable to most work environments. They are general in nature and may overlap with specific regulations, for example, The Control of Substances Hazardous to Health Regulations. They include **risk assessment**, which is one of the main principles in Health & Safety. Risk assessment involves a careful examination of the workplace to identify hazards (anything that has the potential to cause harm), exposure (the likely contact with the hazard) and risk (the likelihood and seriousness of someone being harmed).

Stages in risk assessment
- Look for the hazards that may result in significant harm, for example, physical hazards from chemicals, slipping on wet floors, moving parts of machinery, work at height (steps), pressure systems (steam, water or air), electricity (contact with water), manual handling, noise, poor lighting and low or high temperatures.
- Consider who might be harmed and how.
- Evaluate the risks arising from the hazards. Establish the chance of exposure occurring, level, time and frequency of exposure. Conclude whether or not a significant risk exists.
- Is the risk adequately controlled? Control measures will involve providing information, training, instruction and setting up safe systems and procedures. Precautions must comply with legal requirements and reduce the risk as far as practicable.
  Preventive and protective measures may involve:
  - removing the risk completely;
  - using a lower risk option;
  - preventing access;
  - organising the work or area to reduce exposure;
  - issuing personal protective equipment; and
  - welfare and health surveillance.
- Assessments should be suitable and sufficient and recorded.
- Periodic reviews should be undertaken to establish any significant change.

2. Provision & Use of Work Equipment Regulations, 1998
These Regulations refer to the provision and use of all work equipment. The definition of work equipment is very broad, covering almost all equipment used at work.

3. Manual Handling Operations Regulations, 1992
Manual handling refers to lifting, putting down, pushing, pulling, carrying and moving by hand or bodily force. In addition to weight they deal with problems caused, for example, by sharp edges, slippery surfaces and extreme temperatures.

4. Workplace (Health & Safety & Welfare) Regulations, 1992
General requirements in the workplace including: working environment (lighting, temperature etc.); safety (access, falls, etc.); facilities (toilets, eating etc.); and housekeeping.

5. Personal Protective Equipment (PPE) at Work Regulations, 1992
These Regulations require the employer to provide suitable personal protective equipment for employees exposed to health and safety risks, when such risks cannot be adequately controlled by other means. PPE may include eye protection, respiratory protection, protective overalls and hand protection.

Employees must be fully trained in the use of such equipment, must be aware of the risks that the equipment will prevent or limit, must be aware of purpose and the manner in which the PPE is to be used and the maintenance required. Furthermore, employees must wear the PPE provided, take care of it and report any faults or damage.

6. Health & Safety (Display Screen Equipment) Regulations, 1992

These cover the health & safety requirements for work with display screen equipment. Additionally, the following regulations are applicable to the safety of cleaning.

The Control of Substances Hazardous to Health (COSHH) Regulations 2002 (as amended)

These Regulations are applicable to many cleaning chemicals. Hazardous chemicals should be identifiable by the presence of a warning label.

The COSHH Regulations require employers to assess the risks from substances that are hazardous to health. These substances are those classified as very toxic, toxic, harmful, corrosive, irritant or those with specified workplace exposure limits (WEL) or have biological or dust hazards. The risk must then be removed or reduced to acceptable levels.

Chemicals (Hazards Information and Packaging for Supply) Regulations, 2009 (CHIP 4)

The New European Regulation (EC) No 1272/2008 on Classification, Labelling and Packaging of Substances and Mixtures (CLP Regulation) will replace CHIP in June 2015 with a phased changeover up to that date, the main recognisable change to users of chemicals in the workplace will be new symbols to meet global requirements, the new symbols with their CHIP counterparts are shown below.

Under the requirements of REACH (Registration, Evaluation, Authorisation and restriction of Chemicals) suppliers provide a Safety Data Sheet with hazardous substances to enable the employer to assess the risks from those substances and put in place control measures to reduce that risk.

Guide for the storage, handling and dispensing of hazardous products
Receipt

All containers should be checked for damage, labelling and actual delivery against the delivery note.

Chemical stores

Lockable, clearly identified storage, which is separate from foodstuffs, should be made available for cleaning materials. Access to the store should be restricted. Stores should be dry, cool, well-lit, and well-ventilated and out of direct sunlight. There must be adequate space for safe and tidy storage, with sufficient racking to allow systematic placement of stocks. Information on storage and safety should be displayed.

Stores should be kept clean and spillages should be cleared away promptly. Stores should not freely drain and chemicals should not be allowed to enter the drainage system in quantities that could cause problems. Chemicals should be stored in original containers and used before the expiry date, which is usually written on the label or the container. Incompatible products must be kept apart, for example, acidic and chlorinated products.

Stores must be specially designed if bulk containers of potentially harmful chemicals are broken down, and a sink, water supply and adequate working surfaces should be provided. Care must be taken when making up cleaning solutions, and manufacturer's instructions must always be followed. For example, caustic soda flakes must always be added to water. If water is added to flakes, problems are likely because of heat and effervescence.

Hazardous chemicals
- Chemicals should never be transferred into unmarked containers.
- Lids must be firmly screwed on containers, especially when being carried/transported.
- There must always be adequate washing facilities for both routine and emergency situations. They should include eyewash facilities.
- There should be no contact with concentrated products.
- When transporting, decanting or dispensing concentrated products, appropriate personal protective equipment must be worn including overalls, gloves, and eye protection to the appropriate European norm.
- Protective clothing must be kept in good condition, dry and not contaminated with chemicals.

Dispense

Where available, automatic equipment is preferable for dispensing. Products must not be mixed because they may neutralise each other, form a very corrosive chemical, produce poisonous gases, or heat up rapidly causing boiling or an explosion.

First aid

The aims of first aid are to preserve life, to limit the effects of the condition and promote recovery. The first aid for cleaning chemicals generally involves the dilution of the product in or on the body.

- Eye and skin contact: dilute and remove the chemical by flooding with water. If necessary, arrange for the removal of the casualty to hospital. (Always take material safety data sheets.).

- Ingestion: maintain airways, breathing and circulation, obtain medical assistance and identify the substance swallowed. Do not induce vomiting.
- Inhalation: remove the casualty from the affected area, restore adequate breathing and obtain medical aid if necessary.

ENVIRONMENTAL CONSIDERATIONS

The cleaning process can have a significant impact on the environment and careful consideration must be given to minimise this impact. Waste food should be disposed of through dry waste handling and not rinsed to drains; thereby reducing the load on the effluent treatment system. Cleaning products can also have a negative impact on treatment systems if used excessively or at too high a concentration; always follow manufacturers' instructions.

Accidental spillage

In the event of chemical spillage, there is an immediate risk to site personnel and surfaces, and if chemicals mix in the drains there will be a subsequent risk to persons working in sewers.

Procedure in the event of spillage:
- wear appropriate personal protective equipment;
- contain the spillage to stop it reaching the drain;
- pump/decant the spillage into suitable containers for disposal/re-use, or absorb the spillage using sand or an absorbent material such as attapulgite; and
- if disposed of, use a registered waste disposal company.

Spillages entering the drain

The sewers may become dangerous for personnel working in them, while the effluent treatment plant may become damaged/overloaded so that the chemicals end up in a river. The Water Authority/Environment Agency must be contacted for advice, and prosecution may follow. Make sure the emergency numbers for the Water Authority and the Environment Agency are readily available.

Storage
- Store chemicals safely, locked away.
- Never transfer chemicals into other containers.

Use

Note: If used incorrectly, chemicals can be dangerous.
- Follow manufacturers' instructions.
- The hazard of chemicals can vary; a washing-up liquid is relatively safe whereas an oven cleaner will cause burns and blindness if splashed in the eye.
- Do not mix chemicals.
- Always wear appropriate personal protective equipment.

COMMON CLEANING PRODUCTS

GENERIC *OTHER NAMES*	TYPICAL USE	CONSIDER
General purpose detergent (neutral or mildly alkaline) *Hard surface cleaner*	◆ Used at 1% in hand hot water to clean all surfaces. ◆ When used on food contact surfaces must be thoroughly rinsed off before applying a disinfectant.	◆ If in same room as food or on food-contact surfaces then product must be unperfumed and of low taint. ◆ Ensure that product will not damage sensitive materials such as aluminium.
Heavy duty cleaner (highly alkaline) *Degreaser*	◆ Used at 2% to 10% in hot water to clean burnt or very heavily soiled surfaces. ◆ May be recommended to be used neat. ◆ Cleaning burn-on from heated surfaces, such as hobs, ovens, grills and rotisseries. ◆ Boiling out brat pans and fryers. ◆ Must be thoroughly rinsed.	◆ Generally hazardous to personnel, causing burns. ◆ May attack aluminium. ◆ Personal protective equipment.
Oven cleaner (highly alkaline)	◆ Commonly used neat. ◆ Cleaning burn-on from heated surfaces, such as hobs, ovens, grills and rotisseries. ◆ Must be thoroughly rinsed.	◆ Generally hazardous to personnel, causing burns. ◆ May attack aluminium. ◆ Personal protective equipment.
Sanitiser (QAC based)	◆ Light duty, single stage cleaning and disinfecting of surfaces (typically 1 to 2%). ◆ Must be thoroughly rinsed.	◆ Single stage cleaning using a sanitiser is **not** as effective as cleaning with a detergent, rinsing and then disinfecting.
Disinfectant (QAC based)	◆ Disinfect at recommended strength (typically 1%). ◆ May be suitable to leave on food-contact surface without rinsing.	◆ All detergents used for cleaning prior to the application of a disinfectant must be thoroughly rinsed away.
Disinfectant (sodium hypochlorite based) *Bleach*	◆ Disinfect at recommended strength (typically 0.1%). ◆ Must be thoroughly rinsed.	◆ Contact with acid products will produce toxic chlorine gas. ◆ Will produce taint even at low levels on certain foods.

GENERIC *OTHER NAMES*	TYPICAL USE	CONSIDER
Disinfectant (Amphoteric)	◆ Disinfect at recommended strength (typically 1%).	◆ Not inactivated by detergents. ◆ Inactivated by soil. ◆ May be suitable to leave on food-contact surface without rinsing.
Acid descaler (phosphoric or hydrochloric acid based) *Limescale remover*	◆ Specific products for limescale removal. ◆ Often used neat in urinals or toilet bowls.	◆ Contact with chlorinated products will produce toxic chlorine gas. ◆ Should not be used on food contact surfaces.
Washing-up liquid (neutral) *Neutral detergent*	◆ Used at 1% in hand hot water to clean surfaces. ◆ Used at 0.5 % in utensil sink for utensil, crockery and cutlery cleaning.	◆ When used on food-contact surfaces, should be thoroughly rinsed and followed by application of a disinfectant and allowed to air dry.
Dishwash detergent	◆ May be in tablet, powder or liquid form. ◆ Follow manufacturers' instructions.	◆ Should only be used in automatic dishwasher. ◆ Contact with acid products may produce toxic chlorine gas.
Dishwash rinse aid	◆ Usually in liquid form. ◆ Follow manufacturers' instructions.	◆ Should only be used in automatic dishwasher.

Dilution

◆ A 1% solution of a chemical is made by adding 1 part chemical to 99 parts water.
◆ Never use food utensils (for example, cups, jugs) to measure out chemicals; always use specific chemical dosing or measuring equipment.

Some photographs used to illustrate this chapter were provided courtesy of
The Royal Borough of Kensington and Chelsea and Runnymede Borough Council.

13 Pest control *edited by Adrian Meyer*

Pests are the direct cause of most of the statutory closures of **food businesses**, they are a major factor in the thousands of **food** complaints reported to Environmental Health Departments each year and they feature prominently in many of the prosecutions taken under **food hygiene** regulations. Furthermore, pest attack is responsible for a significant proportion of the unfit food surrendered each year. If one also takes into account the amount spent on **pesticides**, the damage to buildings and fittings, the distress to customers and the spread of disease, it is obvious that pest control is an inseparable part of profitable and hygienic food production. Pests are a **source** of foodborne **pathogens** and pest control is usually considered as a prerequisite for **HACCP**.

It should be the responsibility of a senior person to ensure effective pest control. Persons involved in pest control should be fully trained, and it is essential to ensure that the treatment itself does not expose food to **risk** of **contamination**.

The common pests found in the food industry include:

♦ rodents: rats and mice;
♦ insects: flies, wasps, cockroaches, psocids, silverfish, stored product insects and ants;
♦ birds: mainly feral pigeons and sparrows; seagulls and starlings also cause problems in some areas; and
♦ mites.

Pest infestation often results in the closure of food businesses.

Effective pest control necessitates rapid detection and identification of the species causing concern, a knowledge of its life cycle and the most economical, rapid and safe way of eliminating it. Pests require food, shelter, warmth and security. Denial of these environmental factors will prevent their survival. Access may be denied by **inspection** of raw materials, design, maintenance and proofing, and food and harbourage may be removed by good housekeeping. This form of control may be termed **environmental control** and is the first line of defence against possible **infestations**.

Environmental controls may not be entirely successful and other steps must be taken to destroy any pests that gain access to food premises. Eradication methods may be considered under two main headings:

♦ physical;   ♦ chemical.

Usually, physical control methods are preferable as the pest is caught, either dead or alive, and consequently is not able to continue contaminating food. Examples of physical control include electronic fly killers and rodent traps. Unfortunately, physical control methods are rarely completely effective and pesticides have to be used.

When chemicals are used the pest is not killed immediately and may, therefore, drop or crawl into food if adequate precautions are not taken. Furthermore, the safety implications of using pesticides must not be overlooked.

Pest control programmes should therefore encompass an integrated approach to pest control, i.e. **integrated pest management** (IPM). IPM is the cost-effective implementation of prevention and eradication strategies based on the biology of pests, intended to ensure a pest free food operation. This should include the following elements:

 ♦   early detection and identification of the pest species;
 ♦   the application of environmental management – improvements in **hygiene**, exclusion and proofing;
 ♦   the application of chemical and physical control. Undertaken with due regard to safety and the environment, i.e. the least toxic treatments; and
 ♦   the development of an effective monitoring strategy that will monitor the progress of any control operations.

Reasons for pest control

To prevent the spread of disease

Rodents, insects and birds are all hazards and can spread diseases which affect man and other animals. Rodents, sparrows, flies and cockroaches are all capable of transmitting **food poisoning** organisms and a range of additional **viral**, **bacterial**, **protozoal** and **endoparasitic** diseases, either by direct contact with food from their contaminated bodies or legs, by faecal deposits, or in the case of rodents, by urine. Furthermore, disease may be spread by:

 ♦   consuming food contaminated by rodent urine or droppings;
 ♦   contact with rat urine, which may result in Weil's disease (leptospiral jaundice). In the food industry, fish filleters and slaughterhouse operatives are most at risk;
 ♦   eating undercooked pork affected by Trichina cysts, which may infect pigs that have eaten dead rats;
 ♦   ectoparasites that live on rats; and
 ♦   rat bites.

To prevent wastage of food

Considerable financial loss is incurred by pest infestations in food and packaging materials. The presence of insects either dead or alive, rodents, droppings or hair, bird feathers or droppings found in food results in loss of production, recall of contaminated foods and the destruction of large quantities of food. Bagged foodstuffs under long-term storage can collapse due to heavy rodent attack and the cost of rebagging and **cleaning** can be considerable. Furthermore, birds and insects, but particularly rodents, eat food in fields, warehouses, commercial and domestic premises.

To prevent damage

As a consequence of the specially constructed incisors that grow throughout their lives, rodents are able to gnaw continuously; woodwork, soft metal pipes and electric cables are common targets. The damage caused by rodents from fire, flooding due to burst pipes, and

Rat damage to stored maize and rat bites on the neck of a young girl. (Courtesy of Acheta)

subsidence caused by burrowing results in considerable financial loss each year. Furthermore, at least one death has been recorded as a result of rodents gnawing gas pipes.

To comply with the law

Food safety legislation requires that all food premises must have adequate procedures in place, to ensure that pests are controlled. Food must be so placed and/or protected, as to minimise any risk of contamination. Food premises must be maintained in good repair and condition and designed and constructed to prevent contamination by pests.

Food safety legislation makes it an offence to sell food that is unfit or contains foreign bodies. Food contaminated with pests, parts of pests or droppings, etc. can be dealt with under the legislation. Furthermore, food premises with serious infestations of rodents, insects, particularly cockroaches, or birds that are a danger to the health of customers, could be the subject of closure procedure under the Food Hygiene (England) (Scotland) (Wales) (NI) Regulations 2006. The loss of business resulting from the prosecution of a food premises for offences involving pests can be considerable and may even result in bankruptcy. In 2006, a large supermarket was fined £30,000 for selling a packet of crisps that had been nibbled by rodents. In 2002, an unlicensed butcher in Coventry was fined £40,000 for having dirty premises with a mouse and cockroach infestation.

The Prevention of Damage by Pests Act, 1949 requires the occupier of any land or buildings to notify the local authority of any rodent infestation (not applicable to agricultural land). The authority can insist that the occupier carries out any necessary treatment, including the removal of harbourage and repair of buildings. This Act also requires local authorities to take steps to ensure that their district is kept free from rats and mice.

Under the Health and Safety at Work, etc. Act, 1974 employers have a legal obligation to ensure, as far as reasonably practicable, the health, safety and welfare of employees. The presence of an infestation of certain pests could result in unsafe working conditions.

To avoid losing business, staff and profit

Most customers object to shopping in pest-infested premises or purchasing food contaminated by the droppings of pests or their bodies. The adverse publicity arising from prosecution may result in similar effect. Good staff are unlikely to work in badly infested premises.

The design, maintenance and proofing of buildings

Harbourage in food premises is not only provided in dark, undisturbed areas but also within the very structure of some buildings. For this reason, false ceilings must always have access points to enable inspection and treatment to be carried out. Boxing or ducting of pipes creates ideal conditions for harbourage and should normally be avoided. Where ducting is installed, it should be fitted with access plates at two metre intervals and should never finish in an open end. Surface panels and finishes that are not properly fixed and sealed to walls often provide ideal harbourage. Cavities within internal walls should also be avoided. All parts of the structure should be capable of being easily cleaned. High ledges, pits for elevators and ovens must be fully accessible. Elevators and conveyor intakes must have tight-fitting doors at the delivery end. Shutter boxes for roller doors must be checked to ensure they are not used as nesting sites for rodents or birds. The use of cupboards should be minimised and no gaps should exist around pipework passing into cupboards.

The design and installation of cables, electrical trunking and motors should eliminate harbourage. Motor housings for refrigerator compressors make ideal nesting sites for mice. All structural damage such as holes in walls, broken windows, loose tiles and damaged insulation should be repaired immediately to obviate the potential for insect harbourage. Silicon mastics are particularly useful for sealing small gaps.

All buildings should be adequately proofed; a small mouse can pass through 9mm wire mesh and so all access points greater than 6mm should be proofed. Rats can jump to a height of 90cm and so all possible points of entry below this height should be closed.

Doors should be close-fitting and provided with metal kick-plates. Bristle strip is often used as a method of proofing the bottom of doors and other openings. Such strips are not rodent proof and can be accessed by rodents. In the absence of more thorough exclusion, they do however, act as a potential barrier. Gaps where pipes and girders pass through walls should be adequately proofed.

Defective drains, both above and below ground, must be made good. Tight-fitting inspection chamber covers must always be provided and replaced immediately if they become broken. Chamber walls should be kept in good condition with the mortar joints intact, otherwise rats may break through the walls. Disused drains should be properly sealed, especially foul drain inlets from toilets, which should be filled in using concrete mixed with broken glass. Water seals in gullies, sinks and W.C. pans must be maintained.

All external ventilation stacks must be provided with wire balloons fixed in the top of each pipe. Access to roof tops, via the outside of vertical pipes close to walls, can be avoided by fixing 20 gauge metal pipe guards to the pipe by an adjustable metal collar and projecting about 22cm. Cone guards must fit tightly against the wall, whilst square guards are best built into a brick joint and should have their edges turned down by about 5cm.

Insects and rodents thrive in warm conditions. Effective ventilation is required to keep food rooms as cool as possible. All ventilation openings, including opening windows, must be adequately proofed to avoid pests gaining access, for example, ventilation grids and air bricks should be proofed externally either with 6mm mesh, 24 gauge expanded metal or equivalent materials. It should be noted that if a pencil can pass through a gap, so can a young mouse.

Rats require a free water source and therefore denying access to water will assist control. Dripping taps, defective gutters, leaking roofs and puddles are all examples of common sources, which must be removed.

Good housekeeping

Despite all proofing precautions, pests will inevitably get into a building at some time. There is a difference, however, between the occasional invader and the establishment of a stable population. To reduce the risk of an infestation, it is important to deny the lone invader the conditions it likes and in particular to ensure that:

◆ premises are kept in a **clean** and tidy condition to reduce sources of food and harbourage. Attention must be paid to staff locker rooms, changing, dining and washroom areas. The consumption of food should be restricted to dining areas. Lift shafts must be regularly inspected to remove debris and food deposits. Adequate cleaning and dust extraction equipment is essential to avoid dust build-up, especially when handling dry powders such as flour. Fixtures and fittings should be at least 250mm above the floor to facilitate cleaning. Cooperation between cleaners and pest control contractors is essential to ensure baits are not removed, repositioned or washed away;

◆ spillages are cleared away promptly and food is not left outside;

◆ food is kept in rodent-proof containers and lids are always replaced; used ice cream tubs are ideal for use in catering operations;

◆ **stock rotation** is carried out and all stock is stored correctly;

◆ unused equipment, packaging material and similar articles are rotated and checked frequently as rodents prefer living in undisturbed areas;

◆ special attention is paid to waste disposal. Receptacles should be of adequate capacity to avoid overflowing and external containers should be provided with tight-fitting lids or covers. Waste must be removed promptly and efficiently and refuse areas should be hosed down after waste is collected. Receptacles must be cleaned after emptying to prevent deposits providing breeding sites for flies. Incinerators must not be allowed to cause problems and food premises should not be built on or adjacent to refuse tips;

◆ vegetation, old equipment, rubbish and other cover or harbourage must be removed from the immediate vicinity of the site. It may be appropriate to undertake joint action with neighbouring premises to, as far as practicable, keep adjacent areas pest free; and

◆ all raw materials, including food, packaging, equipment and laundry must be checked to ensure their freedom from infestation.

Correct storage

The correct storage of goods is essential to reduce pest incidence. The following principles must be adhered to:

◆ all areas must remain accessible for cleaning and inspection, which should be carried out at frequent and regular intervals;

◆ damage to containers must be minimised to reduce spillage;

◆ all goods must be kept clear of the walls, windows and ventilators (at least 500mm);

◆ adequate gangways must be left for inspection between stacks;

◆ all goods must be kept off the floor, for example, on pallets or low stands, taking care that enough room is left to clear spillages;

◆ all areas must be well-ventilated and lighted;

◆ storage areas must be in good repair and effectively proofed against pest entry;

♦ storage space should be cleaned and inspected before new stock arrives; and
♦ goods that are infested or susceptible to infestation must be segregated from those that are not; raw materials, packaging and finished products should be stored separately.

PEST CONTROL STRATEGIES

The risk of infestation will always remain, however effective the environmental management and the storage practice. It is therefore essential to have a pest control strategy in place. There are two options for developing such a strategy, either the use of a professional pest control contractor or the development of an in-house pest control competency.

The use of contractors

Most food businesses rely on the expertise of a pest control company, or the local authority, to ensure their freedom from infestations. The final decision on whom to choose normally depends on the type of pest and the methods required for its control. However, the destruction of pests that are observed in the premises is not sufficient; regular inspections should be carried out to ensure the complete absence of pests from the immediate surrounding area.

It should be noted that the use of contractors does not absolve managers from their responsibility of keeping premises pest free. Furthermore, their use in isolation, is not a defence, should legal proceedings be instituted for a complaint regarding food contaminated with insects or parts of rodents or their droppings. However, food authorities should consider the attitude of, and precautions taken by, companies when deciding whether or not to institute proceedings, and the court will also take these factors into account when considering a **due-diligence** defence or the level of fine.

Selecting a contractor

The following matters should be considered when selecting a contractor:
♦ the ability of the contractor to undertake a complete survey and provide a clear report of recommendations and action required. The contract should detail pests covered, frequency of visits and reports, arrangements for additional treatments, including emergency response, preventive measures and include an unambiguous quotation;
♦ the experience of the contractor of pest control in the food industry and provision of appropriate references from current clients;
♦ the adequacy of appropriate insurance cover with regard to product, public and employer's liability together with evidence of financial viability;
♦ the contractor must have sufficient resources in terms of trained/qualified staff and the necessary equipment to carry out proper pest control services. It is a legal requirement for all of the contractor's staff to be trained to a competent level;
♦ clear reporting procedures and accountability must be established;
♦ the methods and materials used for pest control treatment have to be approved under The Control of Pesticides Regulations, 1986 and it is illegal to use as a pesticide any substance not so approved. Contractors should provide the relevant Safety Data Sheets and demonstrate knowledge of COSHH. Some contractors now provide a pest **risk assessment** as part of the contract, which may assist clients taking

advantage of the **due-diligence** defence in food safety legislation;

♦ the ability of the company to provide a complete service, including preventive measures such as proofing and the installation, maintenance and cleaning of electronic flying insect killing equipment. Reports of inspections should include advice on good housekeeping, storage and any preventive work required; and

♦ the company should be a member of the British Pest Control Association (BPCA) and employ staff that hold the Association's certificate of proficiency or its equivalent.

Liaison with the contractor

The contractor should provide the client's management with details of all preparations used, supply a written report on each visit and make any necessary recommendations with regard to proofing, waste disposal, stock control, housekeeping, cleaning or access. Action points should then be agreed and follow-up visits made to ensure the remedies are carried out. Whichever firm is chosen, to ensure successful control, it will need the full cooperation of the client and the contractor should be called in immediately when evidence of a pest is discovered. Dates of visits should be recorded. Additionally:

♦ close contact and regular liaison should be made with the contractor;

♦ written notes on any unsatisfactory housekeeping should be made and immediate action taken to remedy defects;

♦ the position of bait boxes should be noted; ideally maps should be produced;

♦ regular inspections of bait boxes should take place to look for droppings and dead bodies, which should be removed immediately;

♦ if necessary, fresh bait should be laid at the end of a week, by which time weekly inspections may well suffice; and

♦ when no further evidence of infestation appears, intensive baiting can be discontinued and proofing carried out. Permanent baits should be maintained.

Development of an in-house pest control competency

An alternative to contracted pest control is to develop an in-house pest control expertise. This option is used by a number of larger food manufacturers and processors.

The perceived advantages of developing such a strategy are that:

♦ the responsibility for the pest control work remains directly within the line and functional management responsibility of the unit;

♦ management has greater control over response times and flexibility of response; and

♦ staff used are more familiar not only with the structure of the facility, but also with manufacturing processes used and the work practices employed. They will also know and be known by both managers and workers on site, increasing opportunities for cooperation between departments.

Ownership of a pest problem is very clear, for example, if pest control responsibility lies within the hygiene unit, which is also responsible for work relating to hygiene and proofing, there is no doubt about who is responsible for pest control-related problems.

It is essential, however, that all the criteria used for employing a contractor, in terms of skills, competency, reporting procedures and safety procedures, are applied equally to an in-house scheme so that standards are maintained. In-house pest control must not be seen as a cheap alternative.

THE ROLE OF MANAGEMENT IN PEST CONTROL

The role of supervisors and managers will depend on the size of the operation and the pest control strategy employed. However, responsibilities may include:

♦ ensuring the provision of proactive pest control management to assist a **due-diligence** defence, if required. This will include effective systems for checking deliveries of raw materials and laundry;

♦ arranging for the instruction of staff, especially cleaners, to recognise pests or signs of pests and the importance of staff immediately reporting signs of infestation;

♦ supervisors conducing regular audits, as well as daily inspections, to monitor that the integrated pest management system is working effectively and that waste disposal procedures are being carried out. This will include routinely inspecting vulnerable areas for pests, signs of pests and poor maintenance or proofing. Staff should be instructed to report any condition, such as damaged flyscreens, that could permit pest entry or encourage the development of an infestation such as a build-up of waste in the external refuse storage area. The importance of good housekeeping and the adherence to cleaning schedules and waste disposal procedures should also be emphasised;

♦ arranging for defects and poor housekeeping to be remedied and for the contractor to be requested to deal with any infestation;

♦ ensuring that any contaminated food is destroyed and any food-contact surfaces are cleaned and **disinfected** before use if they may have been in contact with rodents;

♦ ensuring that the contractor does not expose food to risk of contamination during treatment, for example, spraying near **open food**;

♦ walking the site with the contractor, probably after the treatment, and acting on his recommendations. The supervisor may also have the responsibility of monitoring the performance of the pest contractor, so should ensure that the procedures for routine visits, reports of visits and recording and implementation of corrective actions are adhered to. The supervisor should also be required to report to senior management non-compliances relating to the pest control contract.

♦ ensuring that any **food-contact surfaces** that may have been contaminated are cleaned and disinfected after treatment; and

♦ being aware of the position of bait boxes and traps and arranging for them to be checked regularly. Knowing how to deal with bait boxes and dead bodies. Staff should be instructed not to touch or move bait boxes.

As well as taking remedial action in the event of an infestation or issues highlighted in the routine reports of pest control visits, the supervisor may need to report to senior management structural defects, and other conditions like the failure of contractors to empty waste bins according to the waste disposal contract. The supervisor may also have a responsibility to communicate with, or seek advice from, the enforcement authority regarding pest control concerns.

RODENTS AND RODENT CONTROL

The three rodents that may infest food premises in this country are:

♦ *Rattus norvegicus* (Common Rat, Norway Rat or Brown Rat);
♦ *Rattus rattus* (Ship rat or Black rat); and
♦ *Mus domestics/musculus* (House Mouse).

The provision of food stores gives rodents the ideal conditions for rapid multiplication; food, shelter and no predators or competition. Furthermore, the transportation of food in containers has meant that rodents can easily be brought into premises, if suitable precautions are not taken during unloading and emptying.

Surveys

Certain members of staff should be specifically trained to identify evidence of rats or mice. These people should carry out regular inspections of the premises, both internally and externally, to look for signs such as:

♦ droppings, if very recent they are shiny and soft;
♦ footprints in dust;

Mouse tracks on sacks of imported peanuts.
(Courtesy of Vic George.)

Rodent damage caused by gnawing.

Rodent damage and smears.

- gnawing marks and damage, for example, holes in sacks;
- smear marks from the fur of rodents where their bodies are in regular, close contact with surfaces, for example, horizontal pipes adjacent to light-coloured walls;
- holes and nesting sites;
- rat runs in undergrowth; and
- the animals themselves, either dead or alive.

The reporting of signs should not be restricted to specific people, all staff should be aware of the problems of rodents and must observe their responsibility to notify their supervisor, if they believe them to be present.

The House Mouse

The cosmopolitan *Mus domesticus* is normally found inhabiting buildings, where it finds harbourage, warmth, food and nesting materials. Unlike the Norway Rat, the House Mouse is an inquisitive animal, investigating new objects in its environment rather than avoiding them. It does, however, rapidly pass on to other objects. For this reason the mouse tends to feed little and often, possibly feeding at some 20 points in a night. Effective control is therefore best achieved by placing many, small bait points or traps. The House Mouse is also a very good climber, spending much of its time off the ground if it can. This three dimensional activity should be reflected in the distribution of control points such as baits.

The success of the House Mouse to coexist with man can be attributed to its ability to live in a wide range of habitats, to its immense reproductive capacity and its omnivorous feeding habits (a pair of mice can, given ideal conditions, produce up to 2,000 young within a year).

House Mouse.   Norway Rat.

The Norway or Brown Rat

Rattus norvegicus is the predominant rat in the UK and is essentially an outdoor species, sometimes moving indoors to feed. It is rarely found living only indoors. When it is found indoors, it will usually be entering through, under, over or round doors, holes in walls, through the drains (the usual route when rats are found in or on a roof), or burrowing under foundations and entering through cavity walls.

Rats pose a serious public health threat as they often carry pathogens. The Norway Rat is omnivorous but has a preference for cereals. Theoretically a pair of rats can produce hundreds of offspring within a year; fortunately many fail to achieve maturity. However, once a pair of rats becomes established, failure to implement immediate eradication measures can soon result in a major infestation.

Norway Rats prefer stable environments and are neophobic, (they will avoid new objects placed in their environment, such as baits and bait boxes, until they get used to them). Rat control therefore requires patience.

The Black Rat

Rattus rattus is also omnivorous but has a preference for fruit and vegetables. It is rarely found in mainland Great Britain, although some infestations can still be found in port areas. It is an excellent climber and is often found in the upper storeys of buildings and roof spaces. The Black Rat is more difficult to control because of its food preference and its ability to climb, making access for control difficult. In many parts of the world, particularly in the tropics, it remains the dominant commensal rodent species.

Black Rat.

Barbecued mice – caused by gnawing a live electric cable.

A COMPARISON OF COMMON RODENTS

	Norway Rat	Black Rat	House Mouse
Body/weight	Thick set 100-500g	Slender 100-300g	Up to 20g
Snout	Blunt	Pointed	Slightly pointed
Ears	Small	Large	Large
Tail	Shorter than head plus body	Longer than head plus body	Much longer than head plus body
Colour	Variable: brown on back, grey belly	Variable: black or brown back, dark/white belly	Grey back, light grey belly
Feet	Large	Large	Small

Survey and monitoring

The key to all good rodent control is an effective survey, to know when an infestation is present and to identify the extent of the infestation. There are obvious signs of rodent infestation and those involved with pest control should be actively seeking out these signs on a regular basis. However, all staff, especially cleaners, should be aware of rodent signs and what to do if they see them.

Monitoring, together with the survey data, is a more planned and conscious attempt to identify activity. It uses a range of specially developed baits and traps that are used in high-risk areas particularly and are visited and inspected on a regular basis. These include:

- bait points, using both toxic and non-toxic baits;
- activity indicators on bait boxes;
- tracking dust, including fluorescent dust in some rare situations;
- break back traps; and
- live capture traps.

The information gained from effective surveying and monitoring should detect infestation as soon as it develops and will assist in monitoring the progress of the control operations.

Control and treatment

Can be divided into chemical and physical.

Chemical control

Chemical control involves the use of toxic rodenticides. Rodenticides are chemicals used for killing rodents and may be divided into three groups:

- chronic rodenticides;
- **acute rodenticides**; and
- sub-acute rodenticides.

Chronic rodenticides

These chemicals are all anticoagulants and are designed to be ingested by rodents in small doses over several days, to ensure that a lethal dose is absorbed. Even the more toxic anticoagulants work as multi-dose **(chronic) poisons** and are not usually lethal after the first feed that a rodent takes. This is mainly because the behavioural characteristics of both Norway Rats and House Mice ensure that first feeds are small. Correct and thorough use of anticoagulants can provide 100% mortality.

The anticoagulants work by preventing blood coagulation or at least by prolonging the time that coagulation takes, so that the animal haemorrhages, mostly internally, and dies. Whilst this sounds unpleasant, the symptoms are far less dramatic than the acute rodenticides and this, together with the relatively slow-acting nature of the anticoagulants, means that the rodents do not develop poison or bait shyness as they do with the acute rodenticides if sub-lethal doses are consumed.

THE ANTICOAGULANTS AVAILABLE IN THE UK CAN BE DIVIDED INTO TWO GROUPS	
First generation	**Second generation**
Warfarin (S)	Difenacoum (S)
Chlorophacinone (S)	Bromadiolone (S)
Diphacinone (S)	Brodifacoum (P)
Coumatetralyl (S)	Flocoumafen (P)

The second generation anticoagulants are the more recent anticoagulants and are usually more toxic to rodents and to non-target species than the first generation anticoagulants, although this is not always the case. Most anticoagulants should be applied using what is known as saturation or surplus baiting (S), essentially making sure that the rodents always have bait on which to feed. Two may be applied using pulsed baiting (P) because they are more toxic than the rest. This means that less bait is required and a break of a few days in feeding is not so critical to success. However, weekly visits to check on all baits are still recommended. Both the anticoagulants that are recommended for pulsed baiting (brodifacoum and flocoumafen) must, however, only be used "indoors" in the UK, thus restricting their use.

Resistance

Physiological resistance to the chronic rodenticides is a problem in some areas. This is recognised in the field by continued feeding of anticoagulant baits over many weeks, without the expected mortality. In house mice, resistance to the first generation anticoagulants is now so widespread that there is little point in using them. There is also resistance to both difenacoum and bromadiolone, but the extent and distribution is not known.

In Norway Rats, resistance to the first generation anticoagulants is mainly in central southern England, where there is also resistance to both difenacoum and bromadiolone. Similar resistance is found elsewhere but the problem is less intense. To date, resistance in Norway Rats has only been found on farms and holdings, but none in urban areas of the UK.

Acute rodenticides

There are only two acute rodenticides currently registered for use in the UK. Zinc phosphide (used for Norway Rat control) and alphachloralose (works through hypothermia and only used for House Mouse control). Both work fast and cause relatively painful symptoms. Unless a lethal dose is taken very rapidly, the animal stops feeding, eventually recovers and avoids the bait and poison if it encounters them again (bait shy).

Zinc phosphide should only be used following prolonged prebaiting, alphachloralose should be used following a thorough removal of alternative foods and then both intensively and extensively in the infested area. Neither is likely to give 100% control, an average mortality of about 70% to 80% is more likely.

Sub-acute rodenticides

Only one rodenticide belongs to this group, calciferol (vitamin D2/D3). This rodenticide causes death through hypercalcaemia and kidney failure. It is very effective against house mice, but is not effective against Norway rats, unless prebaiting is used.

Rodenticide formulations

The rodenticides may be used in a number of different formulations. By far the most frequently used are edible baits. There are a range of bait formulations, the most palatable of which are the loose cereal baits. Canary seed is particularly palatable to house mice. Pellets and wax block formulations are also available. Wax blocks usually have holes in them so that they can be tied down.

Contact rodenticides are also available. Both contact dust and contact gels are used, although the dust formulation is more commonly available. Both can be placed in the rodent's normal runs and the rodent picks them up on their fur and ingests the rodenticide whilst grooming. These contact formulations should not be used where food or food preparation surfaces may become contaminated.

A variation on this theme is the development of a "wick" formulation. Wicks are impregnated with a waxy formulation of brodifacoum, and positioned in the middle of a long tube with entrances at both ends. The mice push past the wick and get the wax on their fur, which is then ingested when grooming.

Liquid rodenticide formulations may also be used. These are placed so that the rodents are able to drink from them and thus ingest the rodenticide. They can be productive in very dry situations but great care must be taken in their use.

Physical control

There are a number of physical control techniques available for rodent control. By far the most widely used are traps.

Traps

Traps may be used if there is a particular risk of contaminating food, to remove a very small infestation or to catch a few survivors of a treatment. They are unlikely to lead to the control of larger infestations. The advantage of the trap is that it prevents rodents dying in

The use of rodenticide wicks within a tube to control House Mice. (Courtesy of Sorex)

The use of "activity indicators" incorporated into the entrance of a mouse bait box to detect mouse activity - not active. (Courtesy of Sorex)

Live capture rodent traps.

inaccessible places and causing offensive odours or blowfly problems. Traps should be placed on runs, at the entrance of harbourage or at right angles to walls, with the treadle nearest the wall. They should be examined daily so that if necessary they can be reset or dead rodents can be removed. The policies of some companies only allow the use of "live capture traps".

Rodent sticky boards

These may be used to eliminate the occasional survivor of a treatment. A piece of hardboard is coated with 3mm of a very sticky substance, which holds any rodent that comes into contact with it. Boards should be fastened down and baiting around the edge of the boards increases their effectiveness. The BPCA's Code of Practice for operational procedures concerning the humane use of boards, should be adhered to.

Safety precautions

The position of all bait points should be numbered. All bait boxes should be given a corresponding number and be dated to show when the bait was last inspected or replaced. A plan of the premises, showing the location of all bait points, should be kept by the senior person responsible. It is important to keep accurate details of visits by contractors, and a pest control book should be kept on the premises under the control of management. The following information should be recorded:

- the results of the initial survey;
- the work carried out as a result of the survey;
- the degree of infestation found and the type of pests;
- details of each treatment carried out and the rodenticide used;
- the recommendations made by the technician on each visit and the action taken;
- a record of any special or emergency visits made by the contractor; and
- all reported sightings by staff of pests on or around the premises.

Baits must not be positioned where they could expose food to risk of contamination and all boxes must be labelled "poison". Most rodenticide baits now contain bitrex, a human taste deterrent, to reduce the chances of ingestion by humans. Suitable **protective clothing** and waterproof gloves must always be worn when handling rodenticides, rodents or traps. It is essential that the label recommendations be followed when using rodenticides.

All persons involved with pest control must have regard to the Health and Safety at Work, etc. Act, 1974 and the Control of Substances Hazardous to Health (COSHH) Regulations 2002 (as amended).

INSECTS AND INSECT CONTROL

Any insect in food premises is a pest. However, apart from those insects that wander in, there are many that will cause extensive problems if they become established. Insect pests can attack and destroy large quantities of food, which become contaminated with their bodies, webbing and excreta. In addition, several insects are capable of transmitting pathogens, including food poisoning organisms. No food is safe from insect attack, although beans, cereals, flour, dried fruits and some dried meats are amongst the most susceptible to infestation.

Common insect pests of food premises include:

- flies;
- wasps;

- stored product insects, including moths;
- psocids and mites;
- silverfish;
- cockroaches; and
- ants.

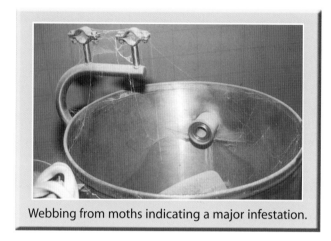

Webbing from moths indicating a major infestation.

FLIES AND FLYING INSECTS

The order Diptera contains approximately 78,000 species. Those of particular importance to the food industry are: *Musca domestica* (Common Housefly), *Fannia canicularis* (Lesser Housefly), *Calliphora spp.* (Bluebottle), *Lucilia spp.* (Greenbottle) and *Drosophila spp.* (Fruit Fly).

Flies contaminate food in four ways:

- to feed, they regurgitate enzymes and partly-digested food from the previous meal;
- they continually defecate;
- they carry **bacteria** on the hairs on their body and legs; and
- **pupal** cases, eggs and dead bodies end up in our food.

The danger to health from flies must not be underestimated. Many pathogens have been found on and in flies and their droppings. Furthermore, flies have been allegedly involved in the transmission of *E. coli* O157, *Shigella spp.* and food poisoning organisms. The close proximity of sources of pathogens, such as **faecal material** or raw meat/poultry, the number of flies landing on **high-risk food** and the temperature abuse of contaminated food will significantly increase the risk of illness.

The life cycle of flies depends on the breeding site temperature and the amount of available food. Typical breeding sites are accumulations of waste **organic** matter, such as refuse, and refuse tips. The female Housefly deposits around 600 eggs during her life span. From egg to adult is normally less than two weeks in warm weather. Maggots grow to around 9mm. Blowflies usually breed on decaying matter of animal origin, especially meat.

Fruit Flies generally occur in bakeries, fruit-canning factories and beer cellars, as **fermenting** organic materials attracts them. Food debris swept under inaccessible machinery bases and kept wet by "spray" from regular wet cleaning or condensation provides ideal conditions for **larvae**. Uncleaned pipes connecting beer or fruit juice dispenser drip trays to drains may also cause problems. Some species lay their eggs in unwashed milk bottles, when the pupal cases may be found cemented to the inside of the bottles.

Drain Flies may cause similar problems because of a failure to clean up or remove organic residues. Condensation and a failure to clean underneath uninsulated ice bins may result in a wet, slime **fungus**, which produces good conditions for larvae.

Housefly and pupae.

The presence of these flies should generally be regarded as bad management. They are more of a nuisance than a health **hazard**, control is usually achieved by removal of the breeding material and keeping potential breeding sites clean and dry. In the case of an infestation, suspect areas such as drains may be checked by using an inverted jar when closing the food premises and inspecting the jar for the presence of flies on arrival the following morning. Wet accumulations of debris should be inspected for the presence of larvae and pupae, using a magnifying glass if necessary. Glue board type **UV fly killers** may also provide an early warning of the presence of small flies.

Wasps

Wasps may contaminate food by transferring bacteria from their legs and are a nuisance during the late summer in such premises as bakeries and fruit factories. Proofing is essential. Nests should be located and destroyed, but wasps fly considerable distances. External perimeter attractants, which drown wasps, may be successful.

Flying insect control

Wherever possible, emphasis should be placed on environmental and physical control methods to reduce the risk of food contamination. The areas around food premises should be kept clean and tidy and all possible breeding sites should be removed. Drainage gullies, effluent treatment plants and waste disposal areas can all cause problems if neglected. Within kitchens, the high-risk areas tend to be the base of lift shafts, behind deep freezers, fridges and cookers. Air curtains are occasionally used to keep out flying insects.

All refuse containers should be kept clean and in good repair. Lids should always be tight fitting. If skips are used, completely enclosed, compacting types are preferable. Waste-food containers, such as syrup tins, which attract insects, should be washed thoroughly before storage outside. All refuse areas should have well-drained hard-standings, which are kept clean. Polythene sacks are recommended for internal use.

Proofing

Proofing is usually designed to prevent access by highly mobile, adult stages of the insect. Food safety legislation requires that windows that can be opened in rooms where food is prepared, treated or processed, must, where necessary, be fitted with insect-proof screens, which can be easily removed for cleaning.

Windows and other openings used to provide ventilation must, where necessary, be fitted with cleansable fly screens. Roof access at apexes and eaves should also be screened. Doors should be kept closed or provided with cleansable screens or clear, heavy-duty plastic strips. Self-closing doors and double door air locks are useful.

Electronic flying insect killers

Those insects gaining entry to food areas should be destroyed using suitably sited **electronic fly killers** (EFKs). Flies are attracted by an ultraviolet light and then electrocuted on charged grids. Performance is proportional to total light wattage of each unit. Units are most effective in subdued light, away from windows and fluorescent lights. They should not be positioned over food or food equipment or in draughts, as dead flies may be blown out. Neither should they be positioned in such a way that they might attract insects from outside, opposite doors or windows for instance.

Some units use **insecticide** and many now incorporate a system to prevent insect particles falling out, for example, the use of UV light-transmitting polymer film. Glue-board EFKs are becoming the most popular as, provided the board is changed when necessary, they reduce the risk of dead flies dropping into open food.

Catch-trays should be emptied frequently and the units regularly serviced. Tubes should be replaced every six months, at the beginning of the fly season, or as recommended by the manufacturers. Due to risk of explosions, they should not be sited where there are high concentrations of flour or sugar dust.

An important function of EFKs is that they may be used as a means of monitoring the flying insect activity in their vicinity. To do this the contents of the catch trays should be identified on a regular basis and action taken as necessary.

Sticky flypapers

These are very useful to supplement EFKs in areas to which the public are not admitted. Useful protection can be given

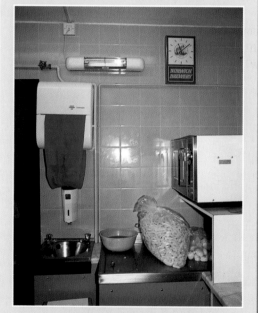

A badly sited electronic fly killer.

to storage areas, refuse areas and bakeries. They should not be positioned near heat sources and should be changed as often as necessary.

Chemical control of flying insects

Insecticides are chemical substances, that kill insects. They should only be used as a back-up to physical control methods. Only insecticides that are cleared for use in areas where food is prepared, stored or processed should be used where food may become contaminated. The insecticide labels will identify where this is possible. Before treatment, food and equipment should be removed, or protected, to prevent risk of contamination from chemicals or insects. After treatment, all food-contact surfaces should be cleaned and disinfected and dead insect bodies should be removed.

The use of residual insecticides in food rooms is not recommended because of the danger of dead insects dropping into food. However, treatment of corridors, or vestibules in non-food areas, with residual insecticides may be useful. Synthetic pyrethroids are the most common of the residual insecticides used in these areas. Where there is a severe problem of flying insects that requires immediate control, ultra low volume (ULV) application of insecticide may be used. ULV mists are designed to control flying or exposed insects, which collide with the very small droplets produced. ULV formulations do not produce significant insecticide residuality.

It is essential that COSHH assessments are undertaken prior to the use of any pesticides and that label recommendations are followed at all times.

STORED PRODUCT INSECTS (SPIs)

This is a large group of insects, that attack foodstuffs in storage, transport and manufacture. It includes beetles, weevils and moths. Cereals, flour, beans, dried products and nuts may all be attacked.

These insects have no direct health significance, although they do cause considerable economic loss. Infestations are often difficult to detect due to the small size of the insects and because the SPIs often live within the food or commodity itself. They can also remain hidden in the building structure, concealed in the crevices and inaccessible, dark corners. Signs to watch for include tiny moving adult insects, unusual debris or speckling, fine strands of webbing and tunnels in some foods. If evidence of infestation is discovered, a specialist pest control contractor must immediately be asked to carry out treatment.

Infestations may be introduced into the food premises with the raw materials or possibly arise due to breeding in materials that are poorly rotated. Inaccessible, poorly cleaned structures also provide useful breeding sites. Panelling of walls increases problems significantly. Infested pallets may be a source of infestation. It is essential that all raw materials be thoroughly inspected when unloaded at the premises. Containers or sacks showing evidence of damage or holes should be regarded with suspicion. If adequate inspection is not possible when unloading, the new materials should be segregated from existing stocks. All raw materials, which are held for considerable periods, should be inspected at least weekly. This includes paper and other stationery stocks. All spillages and residues must be removed as soon as possible.

Insect control

To successfully control SPIs it is necessary to know:

- the species involved;
- the source of the infestation; and
- the size of the infestation and its location.

To identify this information, it is essential to introduce an effective monitoring strategy. This may be based upon a range of techniques including sticky traps and live capture traps, incorporating species-specific pheromone lures. Alternatively, specially designed probe or pitfall traps may be used.

Should an infestation occur, despite environmental control, insecticides will have to be used. Trained specialists using approved insecticides should undertake the treatment. The formulation and insecticide used will depend on the site of infestation and the type of insect. Infestations of raw materials should be dealt with immediately. In some cases treatment may be successfully employed, for example, **fumigation**. However, quite often the food will need to be destroyed.

Fumigation is the application of a toxic chemical in the form of a gas, vapour or volatile liquid in a closed container or to a food stack under gas-proof sheets. The required concentration of gas must be maintained for a specific period. For some pests, such as insects in cereals, fumigation is the only satisfactory method of treatment.

Psocids or Booklice

Psocids are small (1–2mm), cream, light brown or dark brown insects, which are being reported more frequently in food premises and are resulting in increasing numbers of food complaints. They are omnivorous and commonly infest flour, grain, nuts, chocolate, fish and meat products. They also feed on **moulds** and **yeasts** and infestations are often associated with packaging materials and pallets. Their presence usually indicates conditions of high humidity. They are mainly of nuisance value but they may be responsible for disseminating **spoilage** bacteria.

Control involves high standards of hygiene, which prevent mould development. Adequate ventilation and dry conditions are particularly important. Residual insecticides may be applied to pallets, walls or other surfaces, although fumigation of product may also be necessary.

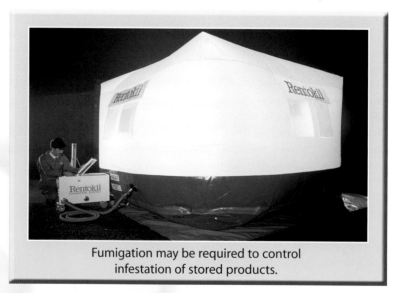

Fumigation may be required to control
infestation of stored products.

Mites

Mites are similar to insects but adults have eight legs. They appear to the naked eye as coarse dust and can only be detected by their movement and through the use of specially designed traps incorporating attractive baits. A variety of food may be infested including flour, cheese and smoked meats. They are particularly likely to be found in damp, poorly ventilated stores where they taint food. They may cause dermatitis and allergies.

Mites require high humidity in order to survive and are best controlled by drying and high temperatures, although some insecticide applications are available for treating infested food (acaricides).

Silverfish and firebrats

These essentially nocturnal insects are either bright or dull silver and are the shape of miniature carrots about 10mm long. Identification is made easier because of the two large antennae on the head and the bristles on the abdomen. They move about very quickly and, although they are frequently found in food premises, they are of little health significance. However, as with all other insects, infestations cannot be tolerated.

Stored product pests
a) *Stegobium paniceum* (Biscuit Beetle). **b)** *Sitophilus granarius* (Grain Weevil).
c) *Liposcelis bostrychophilis* (Booklice). **d)** *Ptinus tectus* (Australian Spider Beetle).

a) Larva, webbing and damage by *Ephestia elutella* (Warehouse Moth).
b) *Plodia interpunctella* (Indian Meal Moth).
c) *Tineola bisselliella* (Clothes Moth).
d) *Hofmannophila pseudospretella* (Brown House Moth).
e) *Ephestia kühniella* (Mill Moth).

Good housekeeping and denial of harbourage are essential for successful control. Crumbs and spillages must be cleared up and particular attention paid to waste disposal. Sources of moisture, including condensation, must be removed. Hundreds of Silverfish can live under defective surfaces, especially badly fixed tiles, and in cracks and crevices. Infestations thrive on tea and coffee waste trapped behind sink units.

Live insects may be killed with aerosol sprays for specific crawling insects, provided that the usual precautions are taken. Residual insecticides may need to be applied by a pest control operator where other control measures fail.

COCKROACHES

Only two species of cockroach are widely distributed in this country:
♦ the German Cockroach (*Blattella germanica*); and
♦ the Oriental Cockroach (*Blatta orientalis*).

Occasional problems are caused by the larger American Cockroach (*Periplaneta americana*), for example, in hotels, dock areas, zoos and schools, where they have escaped from laboratories. Some other cockroach species may also occur and it is essential if effective control is to be achieved, that correct identification is undertaken. Incorrect identification is likely to result in inappropriate and incorrect use of control techniques.

Cockroach habits
Cockroaches are gregarious, omnivorous, nocturnal insects and give off an unpleasant characteristic odour. During the day, they hide in cracks, pipe ducts, electric motors, behind skirtings and in stores. Their presence is normally detected by faecal pellets or their smell. The periods of maximum activity are just before dawn and just after dusk. Neither species fly, although the German cockroach may glide for short distances.

Cockroaches are capable of carrying various pathogens, which may lead to outbreaks of disease, although there is little evidence that they are a common vector for spreading infection. Over 40 pathogenic organisms have been isolated from cockroaches collected from a variety of premises, either in the faeces or contaminating their legs or antennae, including:
♦ *Staphylococcus aureus;*
♦ *Salmonella* Typhimurium; *and*
♦ *Salmonella* Typhi.

For this reason and the fact that their faecal pellets, moult debris and dead bodies contaminate food, cockroaches in food premises must be destroyed.

The German Cockroach (Steam Fly)
Probably now the most commonly encountered of all the cockroach species in the UK. The adult is 10 to 15mm long and is yellowish-brown. It is capable of climbing smooth vertical surfaces such as painted walls. German Cockroaches prefer warm, moist conditions and are commonly found in kitchens, pantries, restaurants and especially ships' galleys. Particular problems have been encountered over recent decades in blocks of flats, where the warm conditions and relatively easy access between accommodation units have led to their rapid spread and difficulties with control. At 30°C, the life span is around three to 12 months and the female produces approximately 250 to 300 eggs. The eggs hatch to produce nymphs, which are miniature versions of adult cockroaches. The nymphs pass through a series of moults,

when they shed their rigid exoskeleton, to become adults. The number and size of nymphs, egg cases, discarded exoskeletons and adults are useful to assess the size and age of the infestation.

Oriental Cockroach, with protruding ootheca.

Two German Cockroaches, one with protruding ootheca.

The Oriental Cockroach

The adults grow to about 24mm long and are shiny dark brown to black. They can climb rough vertical surfaces, such as brickwork, and often congregate around water sources. Oriental Cockroaches are frequently found in cellars, kitchens, bakeries and drains. Long-term survival and breeding externally, for example, in refuse tips and gardens, is possible. For this reason, it may be necessary to incorporate external control operations when treating a known infestation within a building or within ducting. Thorough survey and monitoring will help identify the extent of the infestation.

The eggs are laid in an **ootheca** (egg case) and take around two months to hatch at 25°C, but this period is extended in cooler conditions. It takes between six and 12 months to reach adult stage in heated buildings with good food supplies. The female can produce over 150 young in its lifetime.

Monitoring

Any effective cockroach control programme must incorporate an effective monitoring strategy. Such monitoring must identify the species involved, the size and distribution of the infestation and the progress of the control operations.

Sticky traps are the most effective method of monitoring even minor infestations. Traps may incorporate a hormone or other attractive tablet. The traps are placed throughout the areas where infestation is suspected, and beyond. It is essential that the full scope of the infested area, both vertically and horizontally, be identified. These small adhesive cockroach detectors are very effective in identifying even minor infestations and the species of cockroach involved.

Torch light surveys at night or the application of an insecticide with a flushing action, such as pyrethrum, during the day should also form a part of the survey and monitoring programme.

Cockroach control

Prevention is of prime importance when considering cockroach control in food premises. Cockroaches may be brought into the building with food containers, raw materials or laundry. It is imperative to ensure that commodities entering the food premises are not a constant source of supply of cockroaches.

Sound building structure is important as it precludes the entry of a large number of cockroaches through openings and helps eliminate harbourage. Crevices may be sealed with putty, and service pipes or conduits passing through walls should be cemented in position. Ill-fitting panels that are not removed, are often likely to harbour cockroaches. Strict hygiene should discourage infestations. Food should be stored in containers with close-fitting lids and spillage should be removed promptly.

Areas inaccessible for cleaning should be eliminated. Particular attention should be paid to drains and refuse areas.

There are number of insecticide formulations available for the control of crawling insects such as cockroaches. It is essential to select the one most suitable, both for the species involved and the circumstances of the infestation. Formulations include wettable powders, dusts, emulsion concentrates and space sprays. It is essential to use these in such a way that the life cycle is broken and that repeat applications target susceptible stages of the life cycle.

Because of problems of natural repellency to spray insecticides and the move to environmentally friendly controls, more emphasis is being placed on the use of edible baits for cockroach control, these contain insecticides such as boric acid, fipronil and hydramethylnon.

It is advisable to sketch a plan of the rooms, including details of the plant layout, to achieve effective control. Established infestations are often difficult to eliminate and reinfestation from isolated pockets commonly occurs. Sound planning and the "block control" approach will be necessary for larger scale infestations.

Cockroach traps

Several types of cockroach trap have been developed with varying degrees of success. They may be useful to monitor the extent of infestations and to determine whether any cockroaches have survived a treatment with insecticide.

ANTS

The Garden Ant (*Lasius niger*)

The black Garden Ant nests outside but often becomes a persistent pest of food premises, as it forages for food. It is mainly of nuisance value, although contaminated food must be discarded. Successful control depends on the destruction of the nest. This may be achieved using residual sprays, dusting powder or insecticidal baits.

Pharaoh's Ant (*Monomorium pharaonis*)

Pharaoh's Ants are pinkish and approximately 2mm in length. They are often found in seemingly impenetrable food containers. Infestations are usually restricted to permanently heated buildings, especially hospitals, bakeries, hotels, residential properties and kitchens. All kinds of food may be attacked, although there is a preference for sweet and high-protein food. Physical transmission of pathogens to food is possible as they may visit drains, excreta and soiled dressings.

Effective control requires the destruction of the ants' nests, rather than simply a proportion of the working ants. However, nests are very difficult to detect and destroy. Control may eventually be achieved using baits containing boric acid or hydomethylnon as an insecticide or methoprene as a growth regulator. Baits are more effective because the ants take the bait containing the active ingredient back to the nest. Residual sprays, powders and lacquer formulations are not usually effective as they only affect the ants that wander on to the treated surface.

BIRD PESTS AND THEIR CONTROL

Birds that commonly gain access to food premises are sparrows and feral pigeons, although other species, such as starlings, occasionally attain pest status. Sometimes, more unusual species, such as seagulls, may cause problems, but this is usually associated with their roosting in outside areas where they may cause fouling and contamination. Warehouses and large food factories are prime targets, although bakeries and supermarkets may also be affected.

Reasons for control:

♦ to prevent the contamination of food or equipment by droppings, feathers, regurgitated pellets and nesting materials;
♦ to prevent the transmission of food poisoning organisms such as salmonella and campylobacter;
♦ to remove sources of insect and mite infestation provided by nests, excreta and the birds themselves;
♦ to prevent blockages of gutters, which may result in flooding and expensive maintenance;
♦ to prevent defacement of buildings; bird droppings encourage the growth of microflora and **fungi**, which attack stone and brickwork;
♦ to prevent roosting on fire escapes and similar structures, which may result in a safety hazard for human occupants; and
♦ to prevent damage to food packaging.

Proofing and exclusion

Control of birds is best considered during the planning stage of new buildings. Food premises should be designed to prevent ingress of birds, as it may be extremely costly to proof against entry once the building is completed. Ledges and perches should be eliminated.

Good housekeeping

There is clear evidence that the size of any localised bird population, particularly feral pigeons, is related directly to the amount of food available. Remove the food source and the bird activity will be significantly reduced.

As with other forms of pest control, prevention is better than cure. Good housekeeping is essential. All food spillages, which attract birds, must be removed as soon as possible. Waste receptacles should be provided with tight-fitting lids and not overfilled. Waste areas must be kept in a clean condition.

Proofing

It is not always possible to solve a bird access problem with hygiene improvements alone. They usually have to be used in conjunction with proofing and exclusion techniques. All openings, whether large or small, should be proofed to prevent the entry of birds. The roof apex, open eaves, louvres and ventilation and other openings should be protected with 15mm galvanised chicken wire or preferably knotted polyethylene netting.

There are a range of techniques available for fixing these nets, but whichever technique is used, it is essential that the correct mesh sizes are used to protect against the species causing the problem.

THE FOLLOWING MESH SIZES ARE RECOMMENDED	
seagulls	100mm (4") mesh net
feral pigeons	50mm (2") mesh net
starlings	28mm (1 1/8") mesh net
house sparrows	19mm (3/4") mesh net

It is essential that the nets be installed correctly, leaving no opportunity for further bird access. Netting probably provides the best means of preventing access to areas.

Plastic strips

Doors should be self-closing and heavy-duty. Overlapping plastic strips should be fitted if factory doors are constantly left open or are used for forklift trucks.

Point systems

These involve the use of strips of plastic into which upward pointing, thin steel wires have been embedded. The strips are secured, usually by adhesive, on to the surfaces being protected. The wires interfere with the bird's ability to use the ledge or surface and they move elsewhere! It is essential that such systems be correctly installed if they are to be successful. The technique is not usually effective against smaller birds and is most effective against feral pigeons. Special point systems for use against gulls are also available.

Birdwire systems

This involves the erection of stainless steel wire, tensioned with a spring, supported on a variety of posts and brackets. Once again, the wire suspended across and over the surfaces used by the birds causes them to move elsewhere. The technique is recommended only for use against feral pigeons and gulls, if special equipment is used.

It is important when using any deterrent device, such as spike or birdwire systems, to bear in mind the degree to which the birds want to be at any particular point. Sometimes the birds are not particularly worried if they use an area or not, at other times, usually because they feed from the point or nest at a point, they have a strong urge to return. It is necessary to use the more intense and effective systems when the birds have a strong urge to return.

Repellent gel

Thick inert gels have been used, with limited success, to prevent birds perching. Birds feel insecure on contact with the gel and look for alternative sites.

Scaring

There is a range of visual and acoustic scarers on the market. These include both live predatory birds and artificial predatory birds, distress calls that copy the species-specific distress call that some birds make and simply loud scary noises!

These vary in terms of their effectiveness. It is essential when using any of them to ensure that their application procedure is both varied and reinforced, otherwise the birds rapidly acclimatise to their presence and they lose any effectiveness that they may have.

Scaring is not usually an effective method of solving serious bird activity problems.

Maintenance

All buildings should be well maintained and any holes that remain after alterations should be filled as soon as possible. Broken windows must be repaired immediately. Regular checks should be made in roof spaces, as roof linings and girders often provide ideal nesting or roosting sites; nests must be removed and a search made to locate points of entry.

Culling of birds

Clearly one way of reducing the number of birds in an area or within a building is to kill them, as we do with other hygiene pests. With birds this approach is unlikely to be effective in anything but the short term. Birds can be killed, but if the food supply remains the same, the population will rapidly return to the original size, as a result of breeding or immigration from elsewhere.

It is also essential to ensure that when culling birds, all legal constraints are both fully understood and **complied** with. In the UK all birds are protected, although "authorised" persons in certain circumstances may take some. "Authorised" in this context means that those killing the birds have the approval of the owner/occupier of the land on which the work is being undertaken.

Prevention of the spread of disease is an approved purpose for which feral pigeons, house sparrows and starlings may be taken. It is essential that anybody becoming involved with the culling or taking of birds, familiarises himself/herself with all aspects of the relevant legislation under the Wildlife and Countryside Act 1981.

Traps

Traps may be used against both house sparrows and feral pigeons. The birds are attracted into correctly positioned traps using food. This often results in birds being caught that were not part of the original problem. In addition the traps should be regularly visited, ideally twice a day. There is frequently strong adverse public reaction to this method of control.

Shooting

The use of suitable air rifles may be quite successful, especially if control is carried out at night, when birds are roosting. Foods must not be exposed to risk of metal pellet contamination during shooting. Reinvasion is likely unless proofing is carried out. The benefit of shooting over other removal techniques is that the birds actually causing the problem can be targeted. It is essential that only those who are trained and competent to use an air rifle be used on such work.

Narcotising

The use of poisons against birds is prohibited by legislation. However alphachloralose is available for use under licence from government departments in special circumstances. Alphachloralose is a stupefying substance, which may be used successfully in a bait base attractive to birds. Those that succumb may be disposed of by humane methods and protected species can be released. Chances of success are increased if all alternative sources of food, such as spillages, are removed. It is important to ensure that all baits are collected after treatment.

It is essential that correct procedures be applied. The efficiency of narcotics against birds is very low.

Mist netting

The use of mist netting is rather like fishing for birds. The nets are very fine and are not detectable by birds. They are fitted over doorways and other flight paths of birds. It is a humane technique; protected species can be released and pest birds disposed of. Once again, only licensed operators are permitted to use mist nets. Nets must be removed when the operator leaves the premises.

The control of bird problems requires a high degree of expertise and it is essential that legal constraints be recognised at all times.

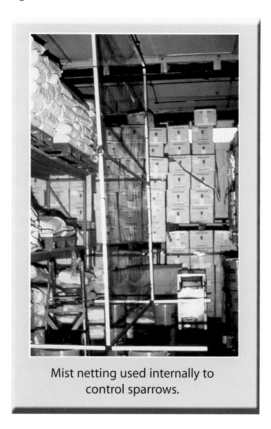

Mist netting used internally to
control sparrows.

Most of the photographs used to illustrate this chapter were provided courtesy of Anticimex and Rentokil Initial plc.

14 Control & monitoring of food standards & operations

Control and monitoring are integral parts of all food safety management systems and essential functions of management, which complete the circle of responsibility. Cost-effective operations that produce **safe food** will only be achieved if managers:

♦ set the requisite standards/objectives;

♦ provide the resources and establish systems and controls, including documentation, to achieve the standards;

♦ communicate the standards required to staff;

♦ train and motivate staff to ensure their competence to produce safe **food**, especially in relation to the control of **hazards**;

♦ provide effective supervision; and

♦ monitor, analyse, compare actual standards with those required and, if necessary, take corrective action and improve performance to facilitate achievement of objectives.

Monitoring of all food operations is essential to:

♦ confirm that expected standards/controls are achieved;

♦ ensure the production of safe, **wholesome food** of good quality and **shelf life**;

♦ ensure **compliance** with specific legislation and to facilitate the use of the due-diligence defence;

♦ identify problems, for example, **sources** of **contamination**;

♦ satisfy customers and enforcement officers and to minimise complaints;

♦ facilitate modification of procedures;

♦ encourage commitment and improve motivation of staff; and

♦ assist in the development of a food safety culture.

Commitment

Notwithstanding the legal and moral responsibilities of managers, satisfactory standards of **hygiene** will not be achieved without the commitment of all involved in the **food business**. Commitment is required from the owners, the board of directors, the managing director, the **food handlers** and all levels of management. If this commitment is not forthcoming, then inadequate resources will be made available to provide the basic framework essential to achieve the necessary standards. Resources are required to plan, design and construct food premises so that they can operate hygienically, to provide satisfactory facilities and to secure the employment and training of suitable staff. Commitment of owners will only be achieved when they believe that poor hygiene, food complaints, **food poisoning**, prosecutions and adverse publicity will threaten the profitability, or even the existence, of the business.

The commitment of management is essential to motivate and effectively supervise staff, and develop a food safety culture. Managers must always lead by example and provide staff with suitable incentives to encourage the maintenance of standards.

Staffing requirements

As part of management commitment to the provision of adequate resources, staffing requirements include adequate numbers of trained staff sufficient to effectively implement the business's food safety and quality procedures. Depending on the size and nature of the food business, it may be necessary to bring in expertise that is not available within the business. For example, there may be a requirement for outside contractors to provide pest control, cleaning and maintenance services, or consultancy in quality systems and HACCP implementation. It is essential that only reputable contractors or consultants should be employed, as part of management's exercise of due diligence. Seasonal peaks in demand may require extra staffing. It is common practice to use an agency to provide temporary staff. Care must be taken to select an agency that has thoroughly vetted personnel as to their suitability to work in a food business. As with the employment of other contractors, the contract must be carefully drawn up clearly specifying what the agency is expected to provide, for example, experienced staff with appropriate food hygiene training. Management should ensure that agency staff receive induction training prior to commencing work and close supervision during employment.

Food safety policies

A planned approach is a prerequisite of hygienic operations. The standards required and the way they can be achieved should be incorporated into a food safety policy in the same way that safety matters are included in the safety policy required by the Health and Safety at Work etc. Act, 1974. This policy document would be extremely useful to support a **due-diligence** defence. It can be used as an effective way of communicating the requisite standards to staff and for determining their training requirements. To remain effective the document must be reviewed regularly.

A responsibility flow chart showing management structure and individual responsibilities with regard to hygiene should be included. The document should be brought to the attention of all staff and written in a way that demonstrates company commitment to producing **safe food**. All aspects of hygiene should be covered by the policy, which should include:

- ◆ a commitment to produce safe food;
- ◆ a commitment to observe all relevant legal requirements, industry guides to good hygiene practice and government codes of practice;
- ◆ a commitment to implement a food safety management system based on the principles of HACCP;
- ◆ staff training and the implementation of a planned **food hygiene** training programme that results in the competency of all staff (training records should be maintained);
- ◆ procedures to ensure that all food and water suppliers are satisfactory/approved. Suppliers should provide a copy of their food safety policy and customer references. Procedures for removing unacceptable suppliers from the approved list;
- ◆ a commitment to provide the necessary premises, equipment, facilities and maintenance to achieve high standards of hygiene, including **personal hygiene**;
- ◆ satisfactory temperature control and monitoring systems for food ingredients and products during storage, preparation/processing, distribution and display. Procedures should be identified for safe alternatives if equipment is defective;
- ◆ systems to ensure satisfactory **cleaning** and, where necessary, disinfecting of the premises, equipment and facilities (cleaning schedules will be required);

♦ adequate **pest** control measures including proofing, the use of specialist contractors and maintaining records;

♦ procedures and systems for health screening and the reporting of staff illness, dealing with visitors, contractors, enforcement officers, food poisoning incidents, customer complaints, delivery of raw materials, traceability and product recall, hazard warnings and waste management;

♦ effective quality assurance/control systems, including **stock rotation**, foreign body control, **organoleptic** assessment, sampling, food labelling and in-house **audits**; and

♦ a commitment to provide the resources for and training of managers to ensure the implementation, updating and enforcement of the policy throughout the business.

EFFECTIVE COMMUNICATION IN THE FOOD BUSINESS

The importance of good communication

The aim of effective communication is to promote employees' complete understanding of food safety messages such as the need for safety and quality policies, and the procedures required to implement those policies. A business operator cannot communicate effectively with employees, customers and suppliers unless the business has defined aims. A business culture that practises good communication begins with management setting specific standards to be achieved including measurable financial goals, and safe food of a quality expected by the customer. The policies and standards will be the rule book of the business. Unless senior management is committed to, and fully understands, their policies and standards communication will be ineffective. Wordy, unclear, inaccurate, inconsiderate communications waste valuable time and can cause offence to staff and customers.

Formulation of policy and its communication down the chain of command is exclusive to senior management and business owners because they have control of resources, such as finance and staffing, and they determine the overall strategic aims of the business. However, other employees such as supervisory, quality or technical staff will make a significant contribution within businesses that value participation and commitment from employees in the development of the business. A clearly defined management structure where responsibilities and lines of communication are established and fully implemented will be essential if a culture of effective communication is to operate.

There are many obstacles that cause a breakdown in effective communication. Introduction of new procedures, for example, a HACCP-based management system may encounter resistance to change. Production or kitchen employees may not understand the reasons for changes in working practices if they are not fully explained. Production staff having a poor command of English may not understand, for example, procedures to prevent cross-contamination or when and how to wash their hands. Poorly drafted and inadequately explained work instructions are unlikely to be understood by line staff with English as a second language. Supervisors may be overwhelmed by a flood of documentation from senior management or head office, and spend too much time in reacting to everyday production problems rather than focusing on contributing to continuous improvement of quality and food safety procedures, and their implementation, in the business.

Management needs to determine why effective communication is necessary and beneficial to the organisation. Time and effort should be allocated to preparing an effective and understood message. This is essential in the day-to-day operation of the business and also when management introduces change such as the introduction of a documented food safety management system replacing informal working procedures. Implementation of changes in how the food business operates implies reorganisation posing perceived threat to the security of employees. Changes in working practice threaten the 'status quo' and challenge old ideas. Good communication of the reasons for and benefits of change is essential in effectively managing resistance to change.

Communications from management should answer the basic questions: 'who, what, where, why and when?' For example, why a food safety management system is to be introduced should be explained, and reassurances given to staff, including an explanation of advantages to employees. The message should be relevant to the reader or listener. Management communications to employees must focus on the receiver's prior knowledge, job role and command of written and spoken English. For example, technical language might be appropriate in memos regarding HACCP operations to line supervisors. However, for production staff clear simple understandable instructions about how to perform their job roles, such as taking and recording of temperatures, would be relevant. Communications should adopt the right tone, avoiding possible offence from appearing, flippant or condescending. Communication is a two-way process and opportunities for feedback from staff should be given to ascertain whether the message, such as written instructions regarding changes in working practices, has been fully understood.

Methods of communication in the food business

There are two forms of communication, written and oral. If an immediate response is required then an oral channel is a better choice. If the message contains complex information that should be filed for future reference, such as the results of an audit, then written communication will be appropriate. Written communication is important to all food businesses. Therefore managers and supervisory staff must develop effective writing skills. The fundamental principles of effective written communication require simple words, a clear message targeted at specific readers, short sentences and a lack of jargon.

Written communication methods within businesses include:

♦   bulletin boards, magazines and newsletters can be employed by management to overcome the inability of management in large companies to speak to each employee personally. These forms of written communication explain management policies, changes in organisation or development of new products. A regularly changed attractively presented updated newsletter can keep employees' attention and interest by, for example, including recognition of employee work achievements or the award of a quality accreditation to the business. The advent of desktop publishing has enabled even small food businesses to use these forms of communication;

♦   posters relating to correct food safety practices or health and safety rules can be displayed in production areas and staff facilities. Posters are useful as an on-going reinforcement of training programmes;

♦   e-mail is important in large businesses, especially those spread over a number of sites. Senior management can communicate quickly with departments. Over-use of e-mail communication will be ineffective if communications of key issues or memos are lost within a plethora of trivia and/or if messages are badly written;

♦   quality and food safety manuals and documents such as staff job descriptions are the essential paper-based systems underpinning senior management's communication of policy, standards, and responsibilities throughout the business; and

♦ audit reports whether internal or, for example, from a third party are a key tool in continuous improvement within food businesses. Well written, constructive and structured reports highlight weaknesses requiring corrective actions. Reports from line supervisors communicate quality and safety issues to senior management.

Outside the business written communications include:
♦ specifications setting out raw material or service requirements;
♦ reports from third party auditors such as those conducted by the European Food Safety Inspection service (EFSIS);
♦ letters including those from enforcement officers requiring actions to comply with notices or letters regarding customer complaints;
♦ website articles and reports, for example, The Food Standards Agency website covers a wide range of issues relating, for example, to new food safety legislation, guidance on the implementation of legislation and items of topical importance, such as food safety alerts requiring product recalls; and
♦ e-mails that may cover many of the communications set out above.

Technological changes include the increasing use of video or telephone conferencing. This reduces the need for expensive, time-consuming travel to distant conference locations.

Oral communications are an essential area for managers and supervisors to develop their skills. Management functions may include:
♦ presentations that are well structured and attractive can generate employee or customer interest and confidence in the business. Presentations also form part of employee training programmes and management's promotion of changes in the organisation;
♦ meetings that are well structured and efficiently conducted with a clear agenda are valuable. Meetings are a means of relating to employees, to explain the need for organisational or operational change, or to address problems raised by employees or customers;
♦ effective appraisals, interviewing for new employees or one-to-one employee coaching all require the development of interpersonal communication skills. These are valuable ways of improving an employee's performance; and
♦ telephone calls should be conducted as with any other form of oral communication. Calls should be planned as to their purpose, with consideration given as to the best time to call to ensure a positive reception. Good listening skills are essential in understanding, for example, a customer's complaints or enquiries. Questions should be asked in order to aid understanding.

There is a key role for employee feedback. The culture of the business should be to encourage employees to contribute, without fear of sanctions or criticism, constructive feedback on the business's quality and food safety systems. Opportunities should be available for employees to be able to express their thoughts on the effectiveness of management communication with the workforce. Employee views on the best methods of communicating management policy throughout the business should be sought without staff expecting rejection of potentially good suggestions. Where management is to introduce changes in working practice or organisation, employees should be given full explanations and information. There should be opportunities for employees to ask for information about management plans for change and make constructive suggestions on improvements in working practices. Carefully and fully explained reasons for change in working practices will assist in overcoming employee resistance and encourage cooperation with management.

Supervisors will have a key role in representing employee concerns to management. Well conducted staff meetings where the tone is conducive to honest discussions can be used to convey employee views to management. One-to-one discussions can also be effective in consulting employees. In all situations where management interact with employees good listening skills are essential. This is a neglected area of oral communication. Good listening skills are essential in dealing with employee grievances or concerns about organisational change. Listening involves empathy and interest in the speaker. The listener should concentrate on the message and be prepared for discussion. Questions may be asked to ensure understanding of the employees' point of view. Managers and supervisors should prepare for potentially difficult meetings and avoid arguments or interruptions. Taking notes is to be recommended and management should summarise employees' concerns to ensure that the right message has been received.

The role of the supervisor

The supervisor has a key role acting as the link between senior management and food-handling staff. The supervisor has responsibility for implementing the food business's hygiene policies and procedures. The supervisor implements the business's HACCP and quality systems, and contributes to their development and maintenance. The supervisor has a key role in communicating management's policies and procedures to all food handlers by carrying out the training policy's legal requirements that includes the responsibility to train, supervise and/or instruct food handlers in food hygiene matters commensurate with their job roles. Management may also require supervisors to report on the staff views, for example, regarding practical issues of implementing hygiene procedures is undertaken.

The supervisor has a key responsibility to monitor the effective operation of essential hygiene practices that include, for example, staff personal hygiene (especially handwashing, reporting of illnesses and correct protective clothing). The supervisor will implement the cleaning schedules and monitor their effective operation, as well as the safe use and storage of cleaning chemicals. Hygiene procedures will be checked to ensure that the business's legal responsibility to protect food from contamination.

The supervisor will provide management with information about the operation of the food safety and quality systems. Information will be gathered and reports produced from the supervisor's observations, audits, inspections, and monitoring records, together with feedback from staff about food safety issues such as problems with supplier performance or a poorly performing pest contractor. The supervisor may organise a programme of random micro-biological sampling to verify the effectiveness of cleaning and disinfection procedures. Results will be recorded and trends analysed and reported to management as part of the information required for planned management reviews.

For supervisors to fulfil their roles within the business, management should ensure that appropriate training is provided in food safety, for example, Level 3 Awards accredited by the awarding bodies. As supervisors may have a key role in the implementation of HACCP-based food safety management systems, appropriate HACCP training should be provided. The supervisor's role will include some or all of the following: writing audit reports for management or updating food safety and quality procedures, communicating management's policies and procedures to employees, training and supervising food handlers, conducting one-to-one employee tuition, making presentations, delegating responsibilities like monitoring, and managing staff meetings. These roles require good time management and verbal and writing skills.

Appropriate training should be provided. There will be considerable demands on the supervisor's time. Management should ensure that the supervisor has sufficient time to successfully fulfil the required roles, as well as good time management skills.

Supervisors may also have an important role regarding visitors such as environmental health officers/practitioners or third party auditors. Supervisors may be required, for example, to liaise with visitors regarding inspection and audit programmes and time allocations for visiting departments. Supervisors may accompany inspectors or auditors and arrange for key staff to be available, answer auditors' or officers' questions, ensure that all required documentation is available and provide adequate facilities, such as an office, if required.

HAZARD ANALYSIS CRITICAL CONTROL POINT (HACCP)

Food product safety is ultimately a management responsibility and is regarded as an absolute requirement by the customer. If a manager is to do more than hope that the hygiene standards he/she has set are being achieved consistently and that every item of food sold is safe, it is necessary to establish a food safety management system.

A food safety management system includes the policies, procedures, practices, controls and documentation that ensure the food sold by a food business is safe to eat and free from contaminants.

It is possible to define a safe food product by setting acceptable limits for relevant **pathogenic micro-organisms**. It is then theoretically possible to control the product safety within these limits, whatever the quality of ingredients or process, by not releasing the food for sale until it has passed microbiological and/or toxicological analysis. Control by such end-product testing, however, is not physically possible if the gap between production and consumption is short, as in conventional catering, and little information is provided as to why a product has failed to meet a standard. Consequently, a preventive approach, involving control of the ingredients, process and processing environment, is always preferable.

HACCP is a food safety management system designed to control hazards at points critical to food safety. HACCP systems prioritise controls so that resources can be concentrated at fewer points in the process. It was developed in the early 1960s by Pillsbury, NASA (National Aeronautics Space Administration) and US Army Natick Laboratories to apply a nil-defects programme for the manufacture of food for astronauts. As you will appreciate, safe food was essential - the consequences of astronauts suffering from diarrhoea and vomiting in a space suit with no gravity would be horrendous.

Prior to the introduction of HACCP, most hygienic food businesses were aware of potential food safety problems and implemented appropriate controls. However, resources were often spread very thinly over many controls. Very little attempt, especially in catering and retailing, was made to determine which controls were the most important to reduce the risk of **food poisoning**. Furthermore, it was rare to find food safety management systems which analysed food preparation to determine which controls early in the process were not essential because of controls later in the process which could be relied on to remove the problem before the food was consumed. In manufacture, control relied heavily on end-product testing. Internal and external inspections/audits were also used to determine the safety of operations.

However, many inspections concentrated on walls, floors and ceilings, and bad practices, but not necessarily on those points which were critical to food safety.

Terminology associated with HACCP

- ◆ *Acceptable level* – the presence of a hazard at a level that is unlikely to cause an unacceptable health **risk**.
- ◆ *Control measures* – actions or activities required to prevent or eliminate a food safety hazard or reduce it to an acceptable level.
- ◆ *Control point* – a step in the process where control may be applied, but a loss of control would not result in an unacceptable health risk.
- ◆ *Corrective action* – the action to be taken when results of monitoring at a CCP indicate loss of control, i.e. a critical limit is breached.
- ◆ *Criteria* – specified characteristics of a physical (for example, time or temperature), chemical (for example, **pH**) or biological (for example, sensory) nature.
- ◆ *Critical control point (CCP)* – a step in the process where control can be applied and is essential to prevent or eliminate a food safety hazard or reduce it to an acceptable level.
- ◆ *Critical limit* – a monitored criterion which separates the acceptable from the unacceptable.
- ◆ *Decision tree* – a sequence of questions applied to each process step with a potential hazard to identify those which are critical to food safety.
- ◆ *Deviation* – failure to meet a critical limit.
- ◆ *Flow diagram/chart* – a systematic representation of the sequence of steps or operations involved with a particular food item or process, usually from receipt of raw ingredients to consumer.
- ◆ *Food safety management system* – the policies, procedures, controls and documentation that ensure the food sold by a food business is safe to eat and free from contaminants.
- ◆ *HACCP (hazard analysis critical control point)* – a food safety management system which identifies, evaluates and controls hazards which are significant for food safety.
- ◆ *Hazard* – a biological, chemical or physical agent in, or condition of, food with the potential to cause harm (an adverse health effect) to the consumer. (N.B. most biological hazards are microbiological.)
- ◆ **Hazard analysis (Codex Alimentarius)** – the process of collecting and evaluating information on hazards and conditions leading to their presence to decide which are significant for food safety and should therefore be addressed in the HACCP plan.
- ◆ *Monitoring* – the planned observations and measurements of control parameters to confirm that the process is under control and that critical limits are not exceeded. "Am I in control?" Present tense.
- ◆ *Prerequisite programmes* – the good hygiene practices a business must have in place before implementing HACCP, to enable the HACCP plan to concentrate on the most significant hazards.
- ◆ *Severity* – the magnitude of the hazard or the seriousness of the possible consequence.
- ◆ *Target level* – control criterion that is more stringent than the critical limit, and which can be used to reduce the risk of a deviation.
- ◆ *Tolerance* – the specified degree of latitude for a control measure, which, if exceeded, requires immediate corrective action.

♦ *Validation* – obtaining scientific evidence that elements of the HACCP plan are effective, especially the critical control points and critical limits. "Will I achieve control?" Future tense.

♦ *Verification* – the application of methods, procedures and tests, in addition to the monitoring, checking records and auditing to confirm compliance with the HACCP plan. (Includes prerequisite programmes.) "Was I in control?" Past tense.

Advantages of HACCP

♦ proactive remedial action can be taken during processing/production, i.e. before serious problems occur;

♦ control parameters are relatively easy to monitor, for example, time, temperature, pH, texture, appearance;

♦ cost-effective because it targets resources to the control of critical points and reduces the need for end-product testing. Wastage, complaints and recalls should be reduced.

♦ the operation is controlled on the premises;

♦ reduces business risk and demonstrates management commitment;

♦ all staff can be involved with product safety;

♦ safety introduced during product development;

♦ reduced product loss and avoidance of expensive reprocessing;

♦ complementary to quality management systems, for example, ISO 9000;

♦ useful in demonstrating **due diligence**;

♦ provides greater confidence in product safety and management;

♦ compliance with legal requirements* and the requirements of third party auditors;

♦ internationally recognised (facilitates international trade);

♦ generates a food safety culture; and

♦ brand protection.

Reasons for failure of HACCP

♦ general hygiene standards (prerequisite programmes) poor;

♦ lack of management commitment;

♦ lack of knowledge/training and understanding, especially science-based knowledge;

♦ lack of resources, especially time for implementation, monitoring and verification;

♦ too complex, not understood by staff involved in implementation;

♦ too much paperwork or poor inaccurate records;

♦ not science-based;

♦ the imposition of an external "off-the-shelf" consultancy-based package when there has been little contribution from relevant staff within the organisation;

♦ the HACCP manual is left in the manager's office. HACCP should be brought into food rooms and CCPs clearly identified; and

♦ too many control points wrongly identified as critical control points.

Prerequisite programmes for HACCP

Prior to the implementation of HACCP, it is essential that the food business is operating in accordance with good hygiene practice or, in the case of factories, good manufacturing practice. Management commitment, adequate resources and suitable facilities must be provided. It is usually considered that to successfully implement HACCP and reduce the

---

*Legislation relating to HACCP is dealt with in Chapter 15.

number of critical control points to a manageable level, the following prerequisite programmes will be required:

♦ approved suppliers;
♦ premises and equipment well designed, constructed and maintained. Contingency plans in case of breakdown. Equipment calibrated. Where practicable there should be a unidirectional product flow;
♦ water and ice used in food production must be potable;
♦ staff and managers must be trained commensurate with their work activities i.e. they must be competent. They should have high standards of **personal hygiene**, especially in relation to handwashing. A health and exclusion policy should exist to screen new employees and ensure that food handlers with diarrhoea and/or vomiting do not handle food until they are symptom-free for at least 48 hours and, when they return to work, they can be relied on to thoroughly wash their hands after using the toilet;
♦ effective, planned cleaning and **disinfection** and the use of cleaning schedules for monitoring purposes;
♦ **integrated pest management**;
♦ stock rotation;
♦ thorough washing and disinfecting of all ready-to-eat fruit and salad vegetables;
♦ effective waste management; and
♦ labelling, traceability and recall procedures.

The seven HACCP principles (as defined by Codex Alimentarius)

HACCP is a food safety management system based on the following seven principles.

1. Conduct a **hazard analysis**. Prepare a flow diagram, identify the hazards and specify the control measures.
2. Determine the **critical control points (CCPs)**.
3. Establish critical limits.
4. Establish a monitoring system for each CCP.
5. Establish corrective actions to be taken when a CCP is breached.
6. Establish verification procedures to confirm that HACCP is working effectively.
7. Establish documentation and records concerning all procedures appropriate to these principles and their application.

The implementation of HACCP
1. Assemble and train the HACCP team

The HACCP team must be proportionate to the size, risk and complexity of the business. In a large business the team will be multi-disciplinary and will include people who are aware of the hazards, risks and controls associated with the products forming part of the study. Team expertise will be required for all aspects of the process including user target groups and abuse potential. Knowledge of microbiology, hazards, controls, monitoring, corrective action, the technology used in the process including the equipment, the product characteristics (a_W, pH, composition and use of preservatives), packaging, distribution and HACCP will be required. The role of each team member and the team leader should be clearly defined. In small businesses, one person may be the sole team member, although external consultants may also assist.

Team responsibilities

Team members will need to undertake research and obtain as much information as possible in relation to the products and processes. Short-term members may be invited to join the team because of their specific expertise. The team will need to communicate effectively with the rest of the food handlers and may need additional training. They will need to draw up flow diagrams relating to the processes and check they accurately reflect what happens in practice. Records relating to monitoring should be carefully considered and verification and documentation will be required.

Team members may obtain information from a number of sources, including websites, seminars, The Food Standards Agency (web-based), consultants, laboratories, food poisoning data, enforcement officers, codes of practice and industry guides. Television, radio, books, trade associations and national statistics relating to foodborne illness may also be useful.

Define the terms of reference and scope of the HACCP study

The starting point is to decide which operations or processes, which products and which hazards are to be included within the HACCP study.

It is sometimes preferable to concentrate on one type of hazard, for example, microbiological. It is also important to decide the starting point, for example, the purchase of foods from a cash and carry and the finish point, for example, the consumption of the food by the consumer.

Grouping of products

Although HACCP is usually applied to each specific product in manufacturing, this is rarely the case in catering or retailing. Because of the large numbers of varied products and frequent menu changes, products prepared in a similar way or subject to the same process may be dealt with as a group. Typical types of catering processes, which can be used as a basis for producing flow diagrams, include:

- high-risk food prepared and served cold;
- perishable raw food, cooked and served or held hot then served;
- high-risk food reheated and served or held hot and served;
- frozen high-risk food, served cold or reheated and served or held hot and served;
- low-risk food, cooked and served hot or held hot and served or cooled and served cold;
- frozen raw food, cooked and served or held hot and served or cooled and served cold; and
- perishable raw food, cooked, cooled and served cold or reheated and served or held hot and served.

2. Describe the products or processes

Products will need to be described in relation to their composition, the potential hazards and **risks** associated with them, their suitability for bacterial multiplication, methods of processing, cooking, storage and distribution. The intended shelf life of the product, packaging and labelling instructions, presence of allergens such as nuts, and legal requirements will need to be considered.

The abuse potential from customers is also important. Will food be taken home immediately? Will it be left in the car boot on a hot day? Will the food be reheated and will it be eaten immediately after cooking? Is it likely to be reheated again?

3. Identify intended use

The likely customers should be considered. They will include vulnerable (sensitive) groups such as babies, elderly people, pregnant women, ill people, those who suffer allergic reactions and those with immune deficiency such as drug abusers. Institutional feeding will need to be considered.

GENERIC FLOW DIAGRAM

PURCHASE

DELIVERY

STORE (CHILLED)

PREPARE

COOK

COOL

SERVE

4. Construct a flow diagram

A flow diagram is a systematic representation of the sequence of steps or operations involved with a particular food item or process, usually from purchase of raw ingredients to the consumer.

5. Validate the flow diagram

Most flow diagrams will be written in the office and it is important to ensure that the flow diagram accurately represents what happens in practice. Over a period of time it is possible that some steps in the process have been omitted or substituted with other procedures.

In catering in particular, different chefs may produce a dish in a variety of ways, which may be different from the flow diagram. This should not occur and the flow diagram may need to be modified. Once it has been confirmed that the flow diagram is accurate you are ready to start your **hazard analysis**.

6. Conduct a hazard analysis (Principle 1)

Hazard analysis involves:
 ♦ identifying the **hazards** that may affect the process;
 ♦ identifying the steps at which the hazards are likely to occur;
 ♦ deciding which hazards are significant i.e. their elimination or reduction to acceptable levels is essential to the production of safe food; and
 ♦ determining the measures necessary to control the hazards.

Hazards (See Chapter 5)

Food safety hazards are biological, chemical, physical or allergenic contaminants with the potential to cause harm to the person who consumes the contaminated food. The most common biological hazards are microbiological.

Biological hazards include **bacteria** or their **toxins, viruses, moulds** and **parasites** that may cause foodborne illness. They involve:
 ♦ the contamination of **ready-to-eat food** by sufficient numbers of **pathogens** to cause illness;
 ♦ the multiplication of **micro-organisms**; and
 ♦ the survival of micro-organisms, for example, as a result of undercooking.

Chemical hazards

Chemicals rarely cause **food poisoning**; however, major **outbreaks** occasionally arise. Chemical hazards may be delivered with the raw materials or may be introduced during processing. Chemical hazards include **pesticides**, herbicides, **fungicides**, fertilisers, heavy metals, **antibiotics**, hormone residues, natural toxins and industrial chemicals. Chemical hazards introduced during processing include fumes, cleaning chemicals, lubricants, refrigerants, and excessive **additives**. Chemicals may migrate from plasticisers, inks or adhesives from packaging.

Physical hazards

Physical hazards occasionally make food unsafe to consume. Problems include choking, cuts, penetration, burning and broken teeth. People may require surgery to remove the hazards. Physical hazards may be brought into the food business with the raw materials or be introduced by food handlers. Sources of physical contaminants include the building, equipment, notice boards, packaging, **pests**, maintenance operatives, visitors and cleaning activities. An example of a serious physical hazard in 2001 involved a dome-shaped jelly sweet with a hard fruit centre, which was linked to the deaths of at least 16 children, in several countries, through choking.

Allergenic hazards

Some people are allergic to specific types of food; foods that cause the most serious reaction are listed in Chapter 5. When allergen sufferers eat the food for the second time their immune system responds by producing large amounts of antibodies which result in a wide variety of symptoms. In very severe cases anaphylactic shock and even fatalities may occur.

Occasionally some people suffer from food intolerance. However, this does not involve the immune system and although unpleasant rarely results in fatalities.

A comprehensive hazard analysis for any food product should include a consideration of likely events in distribution, storage and retailing as well as the potential for consumer abuse.

Once the detailed **hazard analysis** has been completed, it may be possible to eliminate some of these **hazards** by making changes to the ingredients, process or processing environment. This is easier to do if a hazard analysis of proposals is undertaken at the planning stage of a new product. Actions such as the creation of physical barriers to prevent **cross-contamination** are extremely beneficial because alternative attempts to control the hazard will probably involve a complex set of activities which will be expensive in time and resources throughout future production.

In catering, hazard analysis is usually applied generically or to specific types of catering processes. It is rarely necessary or feasible to apply **HACCP** to each individual menu item.

Control measures

Control measures are those actions taken to prevent or eliminate hazards or reduce them to an acceptable level. In the case of **micro-organisms**, controls to prevent multiplication can be applied to temperature, time, pH (measure of acidity or alkalinity), a_W (water activity - the amount of moisture available for micro-organisms), the size, shape or weight, for example, of a joint of meat and the quantity and type of **additives** used, especially preservatives. Control measures should be scientifically validated.

Most factories will have glass and wood policies in place to reduce the risk of contamination from these substances. They may also have metal detectors fitted to remove any products that may be contaminated with pieces of metal. Chemical control measures involve storing chemicals separately from food, not storing chemicals in unmarked or food containers, not storing food in chemical containers, rinsing following chemical cleaning and following strict rules when using **pesticides** or **cleaning**.

7. Determine the critical control points (CCPs) (Principle 2)

Critical control points in the process are those steps where control measures must be used to prevent or eliminate the hazard or reduce it to an acceptable level. A failure to apply the necessary control measures will result in **food poisoning,** injury or harm. By contrast, loss of control at a control point will not result in an unacceptable health risk.

Careful consideration of each step in the process and having regard to control measures applied later in the process, will enable critical control points to be established. This determination can be assisted using the **Codex Alimentarius** decision tree, although a simplified decision tree is much more likely to be used in catering or retailing.

For example, control measures should be applied to the preparation of raw poultry to prevent contamination by, and/or multiplication of, salmonella. However, because the poultry will be cooked, and proper cooking will destroy any salmonella present, the preparation of raw poultry is a control point. By contrast, the preparation of cooked poultry is a critical control point as contamination by, and/or multiplication of, salmonella is likely to result in food poisoning. Unless the poultry is thoroughly reheated before serving, there is no further step in the process after the preparation of cooked poultry that would destroy salmonella. Good hygiene practice, high standards of **personal hygiene** and effective cleaning and **disinfection** will apply at control points and critical control points. However, the time food is at ambient temperature and the temperature of food will be strictly monitored at critical control points. Additional training and effective supervision are also important for staff involved with steps which are critical control points.

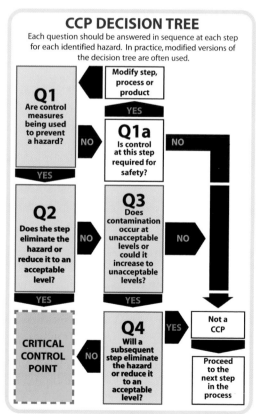

The number of critical control points should be as few as possible, so that resources can be concentrated at these points. One way of checking the selection of CCPs in manufacturing and retailing, especially for physical and chemical **hazards**, is to consider whether or not a product that had been distributed and was later discovered to have failed a critical limit at a CCP, would have been recalled. If it is decided not to recall the product then perhaps it should not have been a CCP.

8. Establish critical limits for each CCP (Principle 3)

Critical limits are the values of monitored actions at **critical control points** which separate the acceptable from the unacceptable. Critical limits must be measurable and the results obtained on site, preferably instantaneously, for example, temperature, time, **pH** and physical parameters such as weight and size of food. Bacteriological sampling may take several days to obtain the number of specific bacteria that are present and therefore this can not be used as a critical limit.

Critical limits can be determined empirically from the basis of experimentation. However, they can also be derived from theory and published information and guidelines.

Temperature limits may apply to a position within the food but may also, for practical reasons, need to apply to the air or heat transfer medium surrounding the food. In the latter case it is still the temperature of the food which is significant. Where such indirect temperature limits are used, it is essential to understand the relationship between these and the actual temperature of the food.

Target levels and tolerances

If a critical limit is breached a significant amount of food may need to be destroyed. It is preferable to set target limits which may enable a potential breach of a critical limit to be detected and remedied before the food becomes unfit. The difference between a critical limit and a target level is known as a tolerance.

For example, a critical limit for refrigerated storage of high-risk food could be 8°C for 4 hours. If this critical limit was exceeded all the food in the refrigerator would have to be destroyed. It is therefore sensible to set a target figure of 5°C. If the target limit is breached, for example, if the food is at 6°C this would allow action to be taken before the 8°C was breached and avoid the need to throw the food away. Adjustment of the thermostat may be the only action necessary to bring the process back under control.

9. Monitoring of control measures at each CCP (Principle 4)

Monitoring or checking of control measures at **critical control points** is essential to confirm that the process is under control and critical limits are not exceeded. Whichever type of observation or measurement is used for monitoring it must permit rapid detection and correction. "Am I in control?" Present tense.

Monitoring methods include the monitoring of time/temperature, **pH**, physical dimensions, **organoleptic** assessments (smell, touch and appearance), **auditing**, visual inspections and checking records and competency. Microbiological analysis is more appropriate for verification.

Monitoring systems should state: WHAT the critical limits and target levels are; HOW the monitoring should be undertaken; WHERE the monitoring should be undertaken; WHEN the monitoring should be undertaken; and WHO is responsible for monitoring. The frequency of monitoring must be cost-effective and sufficient to ensure that the **hazard** is controlled.

Monitoring can be automatic or manual and continuous or at set frequencies. Arguably, continuous automatic monitoring, for example, the use of temperature data-loggers fitted with alarms, may be more cost-effective and the records provided are likely to be more accurate than manual monitoring with a probe thermometer that is hand-recorded. Busy periods of work or forgetfulness often result in the bad practice of records being completed at the end of the day or even the end of the week. Monitoring of data-logger records by supervisors will be necessary at daily or weekly intervals.

In manufacturing it is important to be able to relate the results of monitoring to discrete batches of food. This will reduce waste and assist in recalls in the event of a failure of critical limits.

Managers are often somewhat distant from production, and the monitoring of CCPs is carried out by operatives who may be the same people responsible for the activities that are designed to limit the hazards. It is therefore essential that understanding and commitment to the system are fostered in all levels of staff within the establishment.

10. Establish corrective actions (Principle 5)

Corrective action is the action to be taken when a critical limit is breached. Corrective action usually involves two distinct actions: firstly, dealing with any affected product and secondly, bringing the critical control point and the process back under control. Procedures for corrective action should specify the action to be taken, the person responsible for taking action and who should be notified. Management usually take the decision on whether production/sales should be stopped and when they can be restarted. A clear chain of command is required to avoid delays and ensure the correct action is taken.

There are several ways in which the product outside the critical limit can be treated, for example, the product may be quarantined and subject to microbiological analysis. The process may be continued, for example, the cooking time can be extended, the product may be destroyed or the shelf life may be reduced, for example, eat within 12 hours instead of 3 days. Similar actions might be taken following testing of food held in quarantine, including using the product for a different purpose, releasing the product or destroying it.

If a product has been released and it is discovered that a critical limit has been breached, for example, cooked meat contaminated with glass or poisonous chemicals, it will need to be recalled. All products must therefore be clearly labelled and traceable.

Supervisors have a key role to play in carrying out corrective actions as part of their responsibilities concerning the implementation of HACCP procedures. Food handlers may have specific responsibilities for monitoring critical control points such as checking that cooking temperatures achieved are within critical limits. Supervisors will ensure that food handlers are fully trained, for example in the use of temperature probes and the recording of temperature checks. Food handlers will require instruction about actions to be taken, for example, in the event of critical limits being exceeded, reporting procedures relating to refrigerators or freezers failing to maintain correct temperatures, daily checks to remove out-of-date or unfit foods from display or sale, or actions to be taken if chilled and frozen foods are found to be left out of chilled or freezer display. Supervisors' responsibilities include initiating and maintaining checks that CCP control measures are being correctly implemented, carrying out corrective actions such as retraining, monitoring the correct completion of CCP monitoring records and reporting CCP non-compliances to senior management where necessary.

11. Establish verification procedures (Principle 6)

Verification involves the use of methods, procedures and tests, checking records and auditing, to confirm compliance with the **HACCP** plan. "Was I in control?" Past tense. Validation is obtaining scientific evidence that elements of the HACCP plan are effective, especially the critical control points and critical limits. "Will I achieve control?" - Future tense. For example, what evidence has been obtained to prove that 75°C is a satisfactory temperature for cooking raw meat and destroying any **pathogens** that are likely to be present? In practice, small catering and retail businesses are likely to use generic critical limits which are generally accepted by the industry, the scientific community and the enforcement agencies.

However, manufacturers must carry out detailed tests to ensure that, for example, the time and temperature of processing will be sufficient to reduce the numbers of specific pathogens that may be present to a safe level. The time and temperature may vary considerably between factories producing the same product, depending on composition, type of packaging, type of processing equipment and cooling systems employed.

Verification will usually involve **auditing** against the HACCP plan to ensure the correct implementation and ensuring that the flow diagram remains valid, **hazards** are being controlled, monitoring is satisfactory and, where necessary, appropriate corrective action has been or will be taken. The scientific data relating to hazards and **risks** may be re-examined along with monitoring records. Random bacteriological sampling, end-product testing and analysing complaints for types and trends are also verification techniques. Verification frequency should ensure confidence in the system to provide safe food and may require external expertise.

The HACCP plan should be reviewed periodically to ensure that it remains effective. New epidemiological information or the availability of new technology or scientific information may trigger reviews.

Reviews may be required if:

♦ raw ingredients are changed, for example, the use of fresh chicken instead of frozen;
♦ the recipe changes, for example, salt is removed;
♦ equipment changes, for example, a blast chiller is introduced;
♦ packaging or distribution changes, for example, refrigerated transport is utilised; and
♦ a justified complaint is received or illness occurs.

Reviews are useful to identify new products that have not been added to the HACCP plans. They should also be used to identify weaknesses in the system and to eliminate unnecessary or ineffective controls.

12. Establish documentation and record-keeping (Principle 7)

The amount and type of paperwork required to support HACCP systems varies considerably depending on the type and size of food business and the risks involved with the processes. Generally, documentation and record-

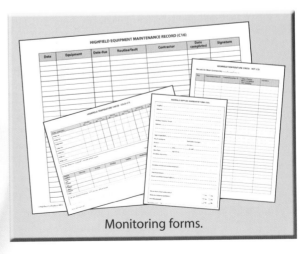

Monitoring forms.

keeping must be proportionate to the particular size and type of business. Documentation is useful to demonstrate that food safety is being managed and, provided records are completed accurately at the appropriate time, they are useful to support a **due-diligence** defence if this is required in court.

Records are very useful for investigating food complaints and alleged **food poisoning** claims. Managers use them when auditing and enforcement officers/external auditors will wish to examine them.

Documentation includes the HACCP plan and details of the prerequisite programmes.

Records include:

♦ CCP monitoring activities;
♦ deviations and corrective actions;
♦ audit reports;
♦ customer complaints;
♦ calibration of instruments; and
♦ prerequisite programme monitoring activities.

All monitoring records should be signed and dated by the food handler undertaking the monitoring and countersigned by the supervisor.

The HACCP plan

The HACCP plan is a written document that describes all of the procedures involved in implementing the seven HACCP principles. The HACCP plan may include:

♦ the details and responsibilities of the HACCP team;
♦ the scope and terms of reference;
♦ a description of the process, product and intended use;
♦ flow diagrams clearly identifying the CCPs;
♦ consumers;
♦ all information relating to the hazard analysis and CCP determination;
♦ the critical limits and the evidence used to establish these limits;
♦ the target levels, taking into account the accuracy of monitoring and processing equipment;
♦ monitoring and record-keeping procedures and determination of frequency of monitoring;
♦ the action to take when target levels are exceeded;
♦ the corrective action to take when a critical limit is exceeded, i.e. a deviation occurs. This will include testing, destruction, recall and traceability;
♦ a record of the reasons for critical decisions and modifications to the plan; and
♦ validation, verification and review procedures.

A HACCP control chart can be used to record a significant amount of the information within the HACCP plan.

HACCP CONTROL CHART

Date .... Approved by .... Page .... of ....

Process step	Hazards (Sources & causes)	Controls	CCP	Critical limit	Monitoring (Frequency & person responsible)	Corrective action (Person responsible)

Flexibility and HACCP

Guidance from the EU and the Food Standards Agency (FSA) make it clear that Article 5 does not require all food businesses to implement a Codex based HACCP system. In practice, the Codex approach has not proved successful for small catering or retail businesses. In certain food businesses it is not possible to identify critical control points and good hygiene practices may be sufficient to comply with the law, for example, a newsagency selling sweets and small business only handling low-risk foods.

In small catering and retail businesses, food safety management systems which ensure that safe food is produced may:
- avoid using HACCP jargon;
- use generic controls, e.g. cook to 75°C;
- use pre-validated procedures (e.g. by the FSA or the food industry);
- combine good hygiene practice and HACCP;
- use practical craft skills, sensory observation and supervision instead of numerical critical limits;
- use minimal documentation; and
- use exception recording, i.e. writing down important changes, e.g. to equipment or menu items or when something goes wrong, e.g. food complaint/poisoning.

The Food Standards Agency have developed the following food safety management systems, all of which use the above approach to take advantage of the flexibility allowed.

Safer food better business (SFBB)

SFBB is a food safety management system developed by the Food Standards Agency (England) for small catering organisations. It is divided into two parts. The first part provides safe methods and the second part is concerned with monitoring and verification. The safe methods relate to cross-contamination (including personal hygiene), cleaning (including handwashing), chilling and cooking. There is also a section on management which provides guidance on opening and closing checks, proving methods are safe, a safe method completion record, training and supervision, stock control and selecting suppliers and contractors.

Opening checks include: checking fridges and equipment; staff fitness; cleanliness of surfaces; and that adequate cleaning materials are provided.
Closing checks include: no food left out; out-of-date food discarded, all dirty cloths replaced; and all waste removed.

The monitoring section includes a cleaning schedule, a suppliers' list, staff training records, a diary to record daily events and a four-weekly review to support verification. The safe method sheets are based on good catering practice. They identify generic hazards and critical control points and describe how to prepare safe food. Safe method sheets must be completed by each business to ensure that the pack is customised to reflect the critical control points specific to their operation. The business must complete all safe methods relative to their operation and, if necessary, develop their own safe methods for menu items or practices not included in the pack. The manager must sign the diary every day to confirm that all safety checks were carried out and that the safe methods were followed. If something different happens or something went wrong, this should be recorded in the diary, together with the corrective action that was taken to make the food safe to eat. Verification that the system remains effective is achieved by the four-weekly audit, inspections by environmental health practitioners/officers and the validation (prove-it) part of the management section. SFBB does not require the daily use of a probe thermometer. However, the correct use of a probe thermometer, for example, to check deliveries and storage temperatures, to confirm cooking temperatures and to confirm that food on display is kept below 8°C or above 63°C, will enhance the safety of the operation. SFBB is also available in Chinese and Welsh.

The FSA (England) has introduced a version of the SFBB pack called 'SFBB for Retailers'. The pack is suitable for those small retail businesses that sell food including any foods that need to be kept chilled or frozen. Such businesses might include small convenience stores, delicatessens, confectioners, newsagents and tobacconists. However, the system is not suitable for specialist retailers including butchers, fishmongers and bakers. The pack's content is similar to that of SFBB for caterers. The Cooking and Preparation sections cover methods most likely to be used in retail premises' rotisserie cooking of chicken. In Scotland, 'Retail Safe' based on 'CookSafe' is available.

Safe Catering - your guide to HACCP (Northern Ireland model)

The Safe Catering model was developed by the Northern Ireland Southern Group Environmental Health Committee in 1999. It was given to food businesses in the Southern Group's geographical area, which adopted the model in their own operations. Following discussions with other regional environmental health teams, the approach was applied throughout the province of Northern Ireland.

Like SFBB, Safe Catering is a simplified HACCP approach where hazard analysis has already been done for a variety of catering operations. Unlike SFBB, the term HACCP has been included. Processes have been colour coded and the caterer ticks the boxes for each process that occurs in his/her business and then follows through to the corresponding control chart. Here there are lists of possible control and monitoring options and the caterer chooses the ones that match his/her operation.

The manual also contains useful forms for monitoring HACCP and prerequisite programme elements and a guidance section with additional food safety information. There is some information on allergens as a food safety issue and HACCP charts for allergen management, and the control of foreign objects and chemical contamination are included.

CookSafe (Scotland)

'CookSafe' (Scotland) has been designed as suitable for most catering businesses. Like 'Safe Catering', the system is a more traditional generic application of HACCP principles. CookSafe is divided into five sections. The first is an introduction containing guidance on HACCP terminology used in the manual. The second section provides guidance and templates for the construction of flow diagrams that can be adapted for different catering businesses. The third section consists of a series of HACCP charts that show what could go wrong at each process step and what controls the caterer will need to put in place. The fourth section covers 'House Rules' (hygiene and food safety) with guidance and templates to help the caterer to write house rules that build upon the business's day-to-day safe working practices. The final section contains guidance and templates for records that can be used in all the other sections. The manual also contains an Action Plan for the caterer to record progress made as the five sections are worked through. The system is flexible because the manual can be adapted to the caterer's additional process steps or different control measures that are already in use as part of the business's daily routine.

A science-based and validated approach to implementing HACCP in catering, developed by Dr Peter Snyder, is based on his assessment of the twelve most important controls to prevent hazards.

1. Effective handwashing (1,000,000 to 1 reduction of **pathogens**) on entering the kitchen and when the hands become contaminated.
2. Effective **cleaning** and **disinfection** of food and hand contact surfaces (100,000 to 1 reduction of pathogens).
3. Procedures for preventing physical hazards.
4. Procedures for preventing chemical hazards, including allergens.
5. Double wash of **ready-to-eat** fruit and vegetables (100 to 1 reduction of pathogens).
6. Refrigeration of all raw perishable food below 13°C.
7. Cooking to achieve a salmonella kill of 100,000 to 1 (71°C for 5 seconds)
8. Hot holding above 54°C.
9. Cooling from 54°C to 7°C within 15 hours (<1 log multiplication of *Cl. perfringens*).
10. Refrigeration of **high-risk** food based on the multiplication of listeria: 2°C 19 days; 5°C 7 days; 7°C 4 days.
11. Cold salad sandwiches precooled to <10°C (prevent the multiplication/**toxin** production of *S. aureus*).
12. Leftovers - never add fresh to old (microbiological and allergen contaminants).

Reasons for modifying HACCP applied to catering
♦ no multidisciplinary team, small numbers of employees;
♦ little technical/microbiological and scientific expertise;
♦ little knowledge of ingredient characteristics, for example, a_w and **pH**;
♦ no linear product flow and little consistency;
♦ large numbers of different suppliers;
♦ lack of **auditing** skills (required for verification and validation);
♦ major potential for **cross-contamination**;
♦ large numbers of constantly changing menu items;
♦ language, literacy problems and high staff turnover; and
♦ catering based on flair and imagination not science, laboratory testing and documentation.

The effective inspection of food premises
An inspection of a food business will only be effective if the person undertaking the inspection has a clear understanding of the reason for the inspection, and he/she has the relevant technical knowledge, skills and experience. It is essential to plan and prepare adequately and allow sufficient time to achieve the objectives of the inspection.

After the inspection, the data collected should be analysed to determine the appropriate action to be taken to rectify the defects. A comprehensive report of the inspection should always be written and problems must be followed up.

The purpose of the inspection will dictate the timing of the inspection, the time spent inspecting, whether or not to give advance warning of the inspection and the equipment needed during the inspection.

As with any type of inspection, proficiency in food safety inspections of food premises will only be achieved through the experience of inspecting a large number of similar types of

AN EXAMPLE OF A HACCP CONTROL CHART SHOWING STEPS IN THE OPERATION CRITICAL TO FOOD SAFETY

STEP	Hazards	Controls & target levels	Critical limits	Monitoring+	Corrective action*
PURCHASE	Contamination with harmful bacteria, toxic chemicals, allergens or foreign bodies.	Use only approved suppliers. Select least hazardous ingredients. Product specification. Purchase branded products.	P	Ensure supplier has effective HACCP system and good hygiene practices. Obtain HACCP documentation. Inspect supplier's premises. Utilise customer references.	Revisit/audit supplier's premises. Review product specification. Warn supplier. Change supplier.
DELIVERY AND UNLOADING	Contamination with harmful bacteria, toxic chemicals, allergens or foreign bodies.	Food covered/protected or in suitable containers. Segregation of raw and high-risk food. Segregation of allergens. Deboxing area. Use only approved suppliers. Date codes/labels. Specific delivery requirements. (NOT with toxic chemicals.)	A of C P	Observation, supervision and sensory checks. Condition of packaging/food. Condition of vehicle/driver. Supplier on the approved supplier list. Food is within date code. Food is delivered in accordance with specification.	Change supplier. Review/reissue product specification/instructions. Refuse delivery. Return stock. Inform chef or manager. Review systems/training.
	Multiplication of food poisoning bacteria.	Chilled food below 5°C. Frozen food below −18°C. Move to storage within 15 minutes of unloading.	8°C for 2 hours −15°C	Temperature of food using calibrated probe thermometer. Time to move to storage.	
CHILLED STORAGE	Contamination with harmful bacteria, toxic chemicals, allergens or foreign bodies.	Food covered/protected. Segregation of raw and high-risk food. Segregation of allergens. Use disinfected temperature probe. Food not stored in open cans. Load food correctly.	A of C P	Observation and supervision. Condition of food. Condition of packaging.	Inform chef or manager. Discard unfit, contaminated or out-of-date food. Review systems/training.
	Multiplication of food poisoning bacteria.	Chilled food below 5°C. Don't overload refrigerator. Good stock rotation procedures. Date codes/labels.	8°C for 2 hours	Air temperature. In-between pack temperature. Temperature of food. Time above 8°C. Door seals. Food is within date code.	Adjust thermostat. Reorganise refrigerator in order to allow good air circulation. Call out refrigerator engineer. Repair/replace fridge. Implement contingency plan. Discard any food >8°C for >2 hours.
FROZEN STORAGE	Multiplication of food poisoning bacteria.	Food frozen below −18°C.	−15°C (quality)	Air temperature. In-between pack temperature. Temperature of food.	Inform chef or manager. Discard unfit or out-of-date food. Review systems/training. Adjust thermostat. Call out refrigerator engineer. Replace freezer. Implement contingency plan.
DRY STORAGE	Contamination with harmful bacteria, toxic chemicals, allergens or foreign bodies.	Food covered/protected or in suitable containers. Care in handling. Segregation of allergens.	A of C P	Observation and supervision. Condition of packaging. Condition of food. Condition of canned goods. Housekeeping.	Inform chef or manager. Discard contaminated food. Review systems/training. Building maintenance to remove dampness.
	Multiplication of food poisoning bacteria.	Maintain in a cool, dry condition. Food within date code. Good stock rotation.			Store out of direct sunlight. Discard damp or spoilt food.

Personal hygiene and training, **pest control** and **cleaning** and **disinfection** are dealt with as prerequisite programmes.

P = Prerequisites **A of C** = Absence of contamination

STEP	Hazards	Controls & target levels	Critical limits	Monitoring+	Corrective action*
PREPARATION	Contamination with harmful bacteria, toxic chemicals, allergens or foreign bodies.	Separation of raw and high-risk food. Use separate equipment. Colour coding. Organisation/workflow. Disposable cloths/paper roll. Minimise handling of ready-to-eat food where practical. Thoroughly wash all ready-to-eat produce and garnishes. Don't top up sauces. Segregation of all allergens. Exclude staff with food poisoning symptoms.	A of C P	Observation and supervision. Staff sickness record and exclusions.	Inform chef or manager. Discard contaminated food. Review systems/training.
	Multiplication of food poisoning bacteria.	Maximum time at room temperature 30 minutes. Pre-cool salad sandwich ingredients. Minimise quantities prepared. Portion control.	**2 hours**	Temperature of food. Time at room temperature.	Discard high-risk food left at room temperature for >2 hours. Reduce quantities prepared.
THAWING	Multiplication of food poisoning bacteria.	High-risk food should be thawed in a refrigerator. Use thawed food within 24 hours. (Label)	**2 hours once thawed**	Temperature of food.	Inform chef or manager. Discard food which has thawed and then been left at room temperature for >2 hours.
	Contamination with harmful bacteria, toxic chemicals, allergens or foreign bodies.	High-risk and raw food should not be thawed in the same area. Raw food should not be thawed in areas used for cooling cooked food. Segregation of allergens.	A of C P	Placement of food. Observation and supervision.	Discard contaminated food. Review systems/training.
	Survival of food poisoning bacteria (during cooking).	Raw frozen food must be completely thawed, especially poultry.	**Absence of ice**	Temperature/visual and physical checks.	Continue thawing. Allow longer thawing time in future.
COOKING/REHEATING	Survival of harmful bacteria/spores and/or toxins.	Cook thoroughly to 78°C. Boil liquids. Don't reheat more than once. Contingency plans. Cook/reheat just before eating. Follow microwave procedures. Follow instruction on packaging. Stir liquids. Ensure frozen meat and poultry is completely thawed prior to cooking.	**75°C or equivalent time and temperature**	Core temperature of food. Observation and supervision.	Inform chef or manager. Extend cooking time until core temperature of 78°C is reached. Allow longer cooking time/higher oven temperature in future. Carry out cooking trials. Discard simmering high-risk liquids that have not been stirred for more than 2 hours. If less than 2 hours, stir liquid and bring to boil. Call out engineer. Implement contingency plan. Review systems/training.
	Contamination with toxic chemicals, allergens or foreign bodies.	Avoid copper and aluminium for acid food. Protect from contamination. Segregation of allergens. NB Cooking oil.	A of C P	Observation and supervision.	Repair/replace unsatisfactory equipment and pans. Discard contaminated food.

+ Frequency of checks and person responsible should be included. Monitoring records will usually be needed at most steps.

* Person responsible for corrective action should be included.   **P** = Prerequisites **A of C** = Absence of contamination

STEP	Hazards	Controls & target levels	Critical limits	Monitoring[+]	Corrective action[*]
COOLING	Contamination with harmful bacteria, toxic chemicals, allergens or foreign bodies.	Separation of raw and high-risk food. Segregation of allergens. Protect from contamination.	**A of C** **P**	Observation and supervision.	Inform chef or manager. Discard contaminated food. Review systems/training.
	Multiplication of food poisoning bacteria, formation of toxins and/or germination of spores.	Rapid cooling (blast chiller) and refrigeration. Minimise weight/thickness of joints, e.g. 2 kgs. Cool liquids in clean, shallow trays (maximum depth 25mm.) Blast chiller (90 minutes.) 63°C to 20°C in <2 hours. 20°C to 7°C in <4 hours.	**3 hours** **5 hours**	Time to cool. Temperature of food.	Discard food if not cooled and refrigerated within critical time. Call out engineer. Repair/replace blast chiller.
HOT HOLDING	Contamination with harmful bacteria, toxic chemicals, allergens or foreign bodies.	Protect from contamination. Sneeze guards etc. if hot holding for service. Use disinfected temperature probe. Segregation of allergens.	**A of C** **P**	Observation and supervision.	Inform chef or manager. Discard contaminated food. Review systems/training.
	Multiplication of food poisoning bacteria, formation of toxins and/or germination of spores.	Maintain at the correct temperature (minimum 63°C). Minimise quantities. Preheat hot-holding equipment. Contingency plans.	**63°C for** **2 hours**	Time and temperature of food.	Adjust thermostat. Discard any food that has been maintained at below 63°C for more than 2 hours. Call out engineer. Repair/replace equipment. Implement contingency plan.
COLD DISPLAY	Contamination with harmful bacteria, toxic chemicals, allergens or foreign bodies.	Food covered/protected, e.g. sneeze screens. Segregation of raw and high-risk food. Segregation of allergens. Use disinfected temperature probe. Minimise handling, use long-handled tongs/serving utensils.	**A of C** **P**	Observation and supervision.	Inform chef or manager. Discard contaminated food. Review systems/training.
	Multiplication of food poisoning bacteria.	Food stored below 5°C. Good stock rotation.	**8°C for** **2 hours**	Air temperature. In-between pack temperature. Temperature of food. Time above 8°C. Food is within date code.	Adjust thermostat. Discard any food >8°C for >2 hours. Call out engineer. Implement contingency plan.
SERVICE	Contamination with harmful bacteria, toxic chemicals, allergens or foreign bodies.	Protect from contamination. Minimise handling. Separate staff handling raw and high-risk food. Staff knowledge of allergens in products. Colour coding. Handwashing between handling soiled crockery and/or cutlery.	**A of C** **P**	Observation and supervision.	Inform chef or manager. Discard contaminated food. Review systems/training.
	Multiplication of food poisoning bacteria.	Minimise time high-risk food is at room temperature. Serve within 15 minutes of cooking, hot holding, chill storage or preparation.	**8°C for** **2 hours**	Time and temperature of food.	Discard any food >8°C for >2 hours.

N.B. Effective supervision, instruction and competency training are controls at each step. High standards of personal hygiene, integrated pest management, effective cleaning and disinfection and maintenance are prerequisites to the implementation of HACCP and are not included within the HACCP control chart. However, they are controls that apply at most steps. Chemical and physical hazards are mainly dealt with through the prerequisite programmes. Allergenic hazards will require specific controls.

premises, to enable the inspector to develop a mental picture of satisfactory premises. A comparison between this "ideal model" and the food premises being inspected enables data to be obtained, findings considered, results analysed and conclusions drawn. This will then enable recommendations to be made regarding corrective action.

Auditing versus inspection

The terms "auditing" and "inspection" are often used interchangeably, although auditing is more fashionable and perceived to be of higher status. In practice, audits are essentially concerned with comparing what is actually being done with a specific standard. They may be complex and require a considerable amount of skill; however, they are often undertaken by people with limited food safety experience using a checklist.

A food safety inspection may be considered as the systematic gathering and recording of data from observations, examinations and discussions with food handlers and managers. It also involves the analysis and interpretation of data collected and the preparation of an understandable and actionable report.

Auditing the cleaning process.
(Courtesy of Vikan Ltd).

Purpose of the inspection process

The main purpose of a food safety inspection should be to ensure the food business is capable of producing safe food, and to identify and prevent foreseeable incidences of food poisoning or injury. This will involve assessing the food safety knowledge and commitment of the manager, the effectiveness of the food safety management system, including HACCP, and the competency of the food handlers to produce safe food.

It may not be possible to achieve the objective during a single visit as the whole operation, from delivery to service, will need to be observed. It is usually appropriate, therefore, to consider the inspection as part of a process as opposed to a single visit. Several visits will be required at varying times to ensure everything is seen.

Knowledge of the inspector

If the primary focus of the inspection is the prevention of food poisoning, then the inspector must be fully aware of the causes of food poisoning. This will include the proximate causes of food poisoning, as described by Roberts, and the management failures that all too frequently result in food poisoning, as described by North (see chapter 1). It is essential to keep up to date with the latest information on sources, organisms, food **vehicles** and causes of food poisoning.

The inspector will also require knowledge of the type of operation, including relevant technology, for example, **cook-chill**, as well as an understanding of HACCP and its application to the business. A significant amount of research may sometimes be required to obtain sufficient knowledge to ensure an effective inspection can be undertaken.

Equipment required during the inspection

Equipment required may include a carrying case, protective clothing (coat, hairnet, hard hat, ear plugs and gloves), a calibrated digital thermocouple thermometer and probes, a pH meter, **disinfectant** wipes, a torch and spare batteries, a magnifying glass, a camera, a small mirror, pyrethrum spray, cockroach traps, tweezers, sterile sample bags or jars, a scraper, a screwdriver, a penknife, a clipboard, notebook or dictaphone, a mobile telephone and blue waterproof dressings. It is also useful to have the last completed report.

Skills of the inspector

The inspector should be able to recognise hazards and assess risks. He/she should have the ability to investigate, analyse and resolve problems. He/she will need to make appropriate and consistent judgement, proportionate to the risk. He/she must be competent to use all equipment and, in particular, to take accurate temperatures and other measurements. All inspectors must have good communication skills, including listening, questioning, interviewing and advising, as well as accurate recording of observations and effective report writing.

A Comark UKAS accredited laboratory, used to calibrate and certify thermometers. (Courtesy of Comark Ltd)

Planning and preparation

Planning of inspections is an important but often overlooked part of inspections. The scope of the inspection must be determined. Which hazards will be considered - physical, chemical and microbiological? Is it intended to inspect all of the business or just part of the business? Enquiries into the two major food poisoning outbreaks, John Barr and Stanley Royd Hospital, both concluded that a cursory, superficial inspection was a waste of time and could give a misleading impression.

Having decided on the type of inspection, the records of previous inspections should be examined, relevant codes of practice, industry guides and legislation should be checked and inspectors should ensure they have the knowledge and skills to undertake a competent inspection. From all this information and the experience of the inspector visiting similar premises, he/she will be able to build a picture of what standards he/she expects from the type of operation. Any shortfall between this theoretical model and the actual conditions found during the inspection will form the basis of the report and the necessary corrective action.

Modelling

Getting the specific model correct is essential. Further information to complete the specific model can be obtained at the pre-meeting with the manager, prior to the physical inspection. For example, different standards will be expected in a raw vegetable area compared with a cooked chicken area. If it is a catering unit, do they also undertake outside functions? The standards at the beginning of the production/preparation will vary from standards at the end. The facilities may be satisfactory for a small butcher's shop but what if there is a major wholesale supply element from the same operation? Several well-known outbreaks of food poisoning have arisen because the inspector failed to appreciate the full extent of the business and therefore inspected using the wrong model.

Timing of inspections

Over a period of time the inspection should cover all hours of operation including early morning starts, evenings, weekends and shift work. It is common to observe different procedures during the day, compared with an evening operation. It is important to be present at peak periods of activity to ensure there is a sufficient numbers of staff and adequate temperature control facilities, which minimises the time high-risk food is in the **danger zone**.

The frequency of inspections should be related to the risks, the level of complaints and the standard achieved on previous inspections.

Pre-meeting

Prior to undertaking the inspection it is very useful to have a pre-meeting with the manager/proprietor. The manager can be advised of the purpose of the inspection and will be able to provide full details of the business activities, including the customers supplied, for example, wholesale, the elderly, children or hospitals. The manager should be asked about the food safety management systems in place and the documentation available, for example, the HACCP plan. The inspector should assess the commitment of the manager to food safety and his/her understanding of the hazards and risks associated with the business and the controls implemented. A cursory examination of paperwork and records at this stage should suffice, as the effective assessment of food safety can only take place where food is actually being handled and prepared, not in the manager's office.

The inspection

Ideally, an inspector would like to observe the food handlers carrying out their work activities as they normally would. Unfortunately, the very presence of an inspector, who is there to assess, among other things, whether or not practices are satisfactory, will change the behaviour of those being observed. A good inspector tries to be as unobtrusive as possible, keeps out of the way and is courteous and friendly. The "royal tour" with a high profile entourage is the worst possible type of inspection, which will achieve very little.

The inspector should lead by example, always ensuring he/she wears the appropriate protective clothing, washes his/her hands properly on entering each new food room, introduces himself/herself to the manager of each area and always ensures that the best hygiene practices are followed.

The inspection should be methodical. A typical routine will be to start at a defined point

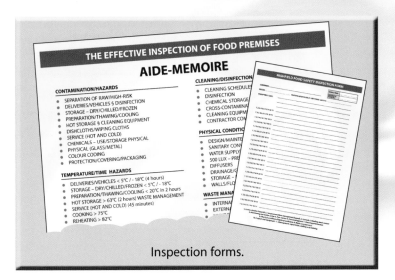

Inspection forms.

within a room, for example, the washbasin, and progressively examine all relevant items around the perimeter of the room until arriving back at the washbasin. Then follow the same ordered routine and examine all central fittings, installations and equipment.

The inspection is hard work, and must be thorough. Look under work surfaces and equipment, get steps to look at high shelves and the tops of cupboards, pull open drawers, check ducting and if you need to get on your knees or even lie on your back to view something, so be it. Remember; if you cannot see it, you cannot inspect it. It may not be enough to look at a piece of equipment; instead, it may need to be moved or even dismantled. Cupboards may need to be partially or wholly emptied and surfaces may need to be scraped or tapped to assess soundness. In this respect full use should be made of the senses: sight, smell, hearing, and touch.

An *aide-memoire* can be useful but a detailed inspection form may be detrimental, unless extremely well designed.

Observations

Observation during inspection can be direct, for example, when looking at surfaces and equipment or indirect, which is the best method for watching people. Food handlers can be watched discreetly, the inspector appearing to be doing something else.

Semi-covert observation could involve, for example, the inspector going into the premises, as a cleaner or joining the maintenance team. Covert observation would involve using CCTV. This can be an excellent training medium provided the staff, and unions, are aware of the cameras and the purpose for which they will be used. The main benefit of CCTV is that, after a short while, food handlers will behave completely normally.

The HACCP approach to inspection

One way of ensuring a thorough and orderly inspection is to use the HACCP approach. Start with deliveries and follow the passage of food through storage, preparation, cooking or processing, preparation, service or distribution. At each stage contamination, multiplication and survival hazards should be considered, together with controls, monitoring, especially at CCPs, and corrective action. Standard of suppliers, design of premises and equipment, workflow, water supply, personal hygiene, competency of food handlers and supervisors, pest control, cleaning and disinfection and waste management should all be assessed.

Documentation and records will need to be examined but should not be relied on in isolation. Many cases of inaccurate and falsified records have been reported by experienced inspectors. Discuss systems and procedures with relevant staff, ask for a demonstration, for example, how do they clean the equipment? Can they show you how they take centre temperatures of cooked food? What is the company policy if staff are suffering from symptoms of food poisoning?

Recording of data

Extensive note-taking throughout the inspection or immediately thereafter is essential. Descriptions should be quantified, for example, heavy, medium or light soiling, the depth or area, whether soiling is fresh or long standing, the colour and odour of soil, etc. Both good points and bad practices should be noted. Sketches and plans can be very useful. Areas of **cross-contamination** can be highlighted by crossover of, for example, raw food workflows drawn in red and high-risk food workflows drawn in blue. As far as practicable, data should be verified. Conclusions are more suspect if based on uncorroborated data.

Examples of key questions to answer
- ♦ Does the design and layout of the premises minimise the risk of contamination of high-risk food?
- ♦ Are the staff competent as far as food safety is concerned?
- ♦ Are the procedures and practices effective in preventing the contamination of ready-to-eat food or the multiplication of bacteria?
- ♦ Is the equipment provided capable of preventing the multiplication or destruction of food poisoning bacteria?
- ♦ Do the management have the knowledge and commitment to ensure the sale of safe food free of contaminants?

Analysis and interpretation

The simple findings during the inspection should be analysed before corrective actions are taken.

For example, if a soap dispenser is empty, the written instruction in a report three days later to "fill the soap dispenser" is almost irrelevant. It should be filled immediately and will probably have been refilled several times before the report arrives. The inspector needs to consider why the soap dispenser was empty. Has it happened before? How many soap dispensers are empty? If the soap dispensers are regularly found empty, in a high-risk area, this paints a picture of a management that have little regard for food safety and indicates that there are no effective controls and monitoring in place.

All items of a similar nature can be grouped together in an effort to determine common causation. For example, several work surfaces in different rooms were not properly cleaned. This may be because of an ineffective cleaning team or inadequate time allowed for cleaning by the food handlers themselves.

A single fault may have multiple causation, for example, a dirty slicer may be because of the **culture** of the organisation, lack of resources, lack of training, inadequate time allowed for cleaning or poor supervision. Always look for the real problem behind the symptom in an effort to achieve a permanent solution. Why were staff wearing dirty protective clothing? Was it because they didn't know the replacement procedure, or they had to launder it themselves, or because adequate replacement clothing was unavailable?

Remember things are not always what they seem. Allow for intelligent compromises and do not jump to conclusions. Do not be offended or annoyed if someone challenges your view and asks you to justify your reasons for requesting a particular course of action. If a small business has a sickness problem and two out of the four staff are unexpectedly ill, the manager may carry out a risk assessment and prioritise their work to deal with temperature control and cross-contamination. There may be a pile of dirty crockery and the floor may need to be cleaned. However, an inspector who orders the manager to clean up immediately, by removing staff from high-risk tasks, will be giving a totally inappropriate instruction.

Post-inspection discussions

Discussions with management following an inspection are essential. Summarise your preliminary findings, discuss failure to meet standards, and discuss unidentified hazards, risks and any other deficiencies in the food safety management system. Invite a response; do not assume; obtain further information. Ensure the accuracy of your records. Recommendations should be practical. Agree the corrective action required and the timescale, for example, immediate, one week, one month or three months. Keep a record of the agreement.

The report

The report is a powerful tool of communication, which is intended to achieve change. It is much more than a list of faults. Readability and clarity are essential. A summary can be helpful and jargon should be avoided. Compliment good practices and achievements. Apply rigorous science and avoid ritualistic, impractical solutions. Distinguish recommendation and requirements and prioritise the work required. Offer cost-effective solutions that work and try to assist rather than condemn. A report that makes life easier is much more likely to be favourably received. Although consistency of outcome is important, advice may change as science, experience and understanding progress.

Before sending the report, read it through again. How would you react if you received it? Will it promote change? Can it be implemented within the required timescales and, if so, what will be the outcome?

Suppliers and raw materials

The quality and safety of the final product depends, among other things, on the standard of the raw materials. Consequently, food should be obtained from reputable sources. Hygiene officers may be employed to inspect the premises of main suppliers to ensure that they are capable of providing a satisfactory product, which consistently meets the agreed specification. When it is impracticable to inspect the suppliers' premises, managers have to use alternative assessment techniques to determine acceptable suppliers. Requesting a copy of the food safety policy, the HACCP plan, the prerequisite programmes and the monitoring records would be an excellent start. References from other customers, absence of complaints and **bacteriological** sampling of results provide useful indicators. The appearance of delivery staff, their adherence to basic hygiene rules and the condition of the delivery vehicle may be considered as a likely reflection of the hygiene standards of the supplier. Carriage of cooked and raw meats in the same container, high-risk food delivered at unsafe temperatures or deliveries placed in unsuitable areas are an indication of a poor supplier.

Specifications should be set for raw materials and may include bacteriological standards, flavour, colour, temperature and permissible levels of contamination. For example, an occasional pod in a delivery of peas may be acceptable, a rat dropping would not. Certain foodstuffs carry official certificates of inspection, for example, all red meat carcases intended for human consumption must bear an official inspector's stamp. Imported food must be accompanied by documents certifying fitness.

Raw materials should be checked on arrival before unloading and regular samples should be obtained for bacteriological and chemical assessment. Dry herbs and spices are a frequent source of undesirable and pathogenic micro-organisms and must not be overlooked. The time of delivery, the weight and condition of the load and the type and condition of packaging should all be noted. The presence of decomposition, mould, unusual odours, dampness, undesirable levels/types of micro-organisms, dirt, insects, parasites, foreign bodies, pesticides, veterinary drugs, blown or leaking containers, and severely damaged packaging will usually require the rejection of the delivery (as would unacceptable temperatures of refrigerated food stuffs), unless normal, hygienic sorting and/or processing would remove or reduce the contaminants to an acceptable level.

Management action against supplier non-compliances

The identification of decomposition, mould, unusual odours, dampness, undesirable levels/types of micro-organism, dirt, insects, parasites, foreign bodies, pesticides, veterinary drugs, blown or leaking containers and severely damaged packaging will require placing the delivered consignment 'on hold', pending an investigation and a report to management. (This would also include deliveries of refrigerated or frozen foods at an unacceptable temperature). If deemed necessary, expert advice should be sought from a consultant or the local authority. Normal, hygienic sorting and/or processing may remove or reduce contaminants to an acceptable level. Where this is not possible, the consignment should be returned to the supplier, after a careful note has been made, for due diligence, about the reason for the rejection (whether a quality or food safety issue). The supplier should be informed in writing of the reasons for the rejection. The supplier should then provide information about corrective actions to be taken to prevent a recurrence of out-of-specification deliveries. If there is a documented recurring problem with a supplier, management may, as part of its review of supplier performance, instigate an audit of the supplier's food safety and quality system. The audit may be either conducted by in-house staff or by a third party. The audit results or a failure to take corrective actions may require the de-listing of the supplier, and a search for a suitable alternative.

Quality systems accreditation

Food businesses face many challenges including maintaining profitability, compliance with food safety legislation, and being able to compete successfully in local, national and international markets. A food business may achieve a nationally or internationally recognised quality standard. By doing so, the business will demonstrate to its customers, prospective customers and suppliers that it operates to a comprehensive documented quality and food safety system. A quality standard is normally achieved through objective, third party external validation and verification in the form of a rigorous audit and inspection process.

The operation of an effective accredited quality and safety food management system assists in raising business efficiency, and in demonstrating legality and due diligence through a process of continuous improvement. Achievement of quality assurance through recognised accreditation opens up market opportunities to the business. All kinds of food businesses within the food chain operate to a quality standard, for example, food manufacturers, multiple retailers and catering outlets, contract caterers and fast-food chains. A number of quality and safety standards are available to food businesses seeking accreditation:

♦ **ISO9001:2000 Series** is a generic title applied to a family of standards formulated to provide a framework within which a quality management system can be achieved. The ISO9000 is the most commonly used and recognised international standard.

♦ **ISO22000** is a Food Safety Management Standard developed by the International Organisation for standardisation. It is a derivative of ISO9000 and incorporates interactive communication, system management, prerequisite programmes and HACCP principles. ISO22000 assists food businesses in achieving a standard above that required for compliance with food safety legislation. (http://www.iso.org/iso/home.html)

♦ **British Retail Consortium [BRC]** is a trade association formed in 1992 for the UK retail industry. (www.brc.org.uk) In 1988 it produced its first Food Technical Standard and Protocol for food suppliers to improve standards and reduce the ever increasing number of duplicate food manufacturing audits by retailers. The BRC now has a suite of four technical standards, referred to as the BRC Global Standards. These specify the requirements that an organisation must achieve to ensure the production, packaging, storage and distribution of safe food and consumer products. The standards are built on principles of risk-based requirements, informative reports and auditor competence. Certification to the Global Standard is achieved through audit by a third-party Certification Body. This reduces the need for retailers and manufacturers to carry out their own audits.

♦ **The Global Food Safety Initiative [GFSI]** was launched in May 2000 following several international food safety scares and is managed by the Consumer Goods Forum (www.mygfsi.com). The GFSI Technical Committee and Foundation Board are promoting auditor competence and the convergence of food safety standards worldwide so avoiding unnecessary duplication of audits. The five main recognised food safety standards are; BRC; IFS (International Food Standard); Dutch HACCP; SQF (Safe Quality Food); and FSSC22000 (Food Safety System Certification 22000).

♦ **European Food Safety Inspection Service [EFSIS]** is a leading global inspection and certification service. EFSIS inspects against a wide range of industry quality assurance standards including ISO9001:2000 and the BRC Global Food standard.

♦ **The Guild of Q. Butchers** is open to independent butchers that are regularly audited by EFSIS to rigorous 'above the norm' quality and food safety standards.

♦ **The Safe and Local Supplier Approval scheme [SALSA]** is a new low-cost but rigorous accreditation scheme designed for small food producers and manufacturers who may not have the staffing or financial resources to achieve, for example, the BRC Global food standard. Successful certification removes many of the obstacles preventing small businesses from directly supplying local retailers and caterers. The scheme was developed jointly by the BRC, The National Union of Farmers, The Food and Drink association and The British Hospitality Association. SALSA is funded by Defra and has the support of the Food Standards Agency.

Organoleptic assessment of food

The appearance, smell, texture, taste and other physical characteristics of food are valuable for obtaining a rapid assessment of food standards (quality, taint and spoilage). However, food contaminated by pathogenic bacteria may appear in all respects fit to eat and suspect food should not be tasted. Specific indicators include:

♦ *Smell* – good food should smell fresh, pleasant and natural. Unusual, stale, musty or rancid smells should invite suspicions. Chemical smells may indicate chemical contamination. Ammonia smells in some fish are an early sign of decomposition.

♦ *Taste* – unusual bitterness, sweetness, a soapy taste or any untypical flavour may indicate unfitness.

♦ *Appearance* – food should be visibly free from signs of spoilage, **fungal** growth, slime, darkening or other change in colour, untypical wetness and mechanical damage. Absence of foreign objects and dirt in finished goods, including pests, pest debris and parasites, is important. Meat, poultry and fish should be free from signs of disease or other pathological conditions. In frozen food, excessive ice can be an **indicator** of mishandling, as can large ice crystals within the texture; loose foods such as peas should not weld together. A final judgement of frozen food can only be made after defrosting.

♦ *Sound* – many packed foods, especially canned goods, emit a characteristic sound on being tapped or shaken. Any such food or pack emitting an untypical sound is suspect.

♦ *Texture* – unusual softness, hardness, brittleness or change in texture may be indicative of unfitness. Meat, fish and certain other products such as cheese should display a springy texture. Light pressure from a finger that causes an indentation to remain can be significant.

In all situations, the key to a sound judgement is to use all the relevant senses and to make a decision on the basis of all the available evidence. In cases of doubt, advice should be obtained from local authority environmental health officers/practitioners or consultants.

Microbiological testing and food safety management

Historically the microbiological testing of end products in manufacturing along with inspections of premises (typically a "floors, walls and ceilings" type inspection) formed the basis of food safety management. With the advent of the HACCP approach some people felt there was little value in microbiological testing and in some cases it could be discontinued. Others argue that microbiological testing is of even more value today. Studies have shown that businesses with access to microbiological testing facilities produced foods with a better, i.e. lower, microbiological count, than those without access.

Sampling can be undertaken using in-house facilities or samples sent to accredited external laboratories. The advantage of external laboratories include economies of scale, the ability to use the latest often more rapid "high cost" equipment and the ability to work with pathogens at a site "removed" from production. A disadvantage is that an outside body with less knowledge of the production site may be processing anonymous samples and may have less insight into how the results need to be interpreted.

VALUE OF MICROBIOLOGICAL TESTING

Building a profile of product quality	Validation of control measures
Indication of trends in product quality	Verification of food safety programmes
Assess variation between batches	Problem-solving
Information about shelf life	Risk assessment and contribution to FSOs and POs
Demonstration of due diligence	Identification of sources of contamination
Compliance with criteria	
Evaluation of plant layout and Identification of difficult to clean areas	Outbreak investigation and linking "apparently unrelated " cases of food poisoning
Evaluation of equipment design	

DISADVANTAGES ASSOCIATED WITH MICROBIOLOGICAL SAMPLING

It is usually retrospective and cannot be used to verify product safety where there is a short time between production and consumption, for example, in conventional catering or for products with short shelf lives.

It is relatively expensive.

Considerable expertise may be needed to interpret results and relate them to product age.

The non-uniform distribution of bacteria in foods and the effect of different laboratory techniques and sampling methods significantly affect the results.

The operation is being controlled by a laboratory technician, who may be remote from the food production.

Only a limited number of samples can be taken.

Not all hazards are identified.

Only a small section of the workforce assumes responsibility for product safety.

The microbial population of a food sample will change over time starting with the micro-organisms that make up the raw materials, the hygiene of the production facility and the effects of any processing, preservatives and packaging used. After production the microbial count, depending on how the food is stored, will further change throughout the food's shelf life. The value/uses of microbiological testing (predominantly, but not exclusively bacteriological testing) can be divided into a number of areas:

Shelf life and challenge testing

Shelf life determinations are designed to answer the question – how long is it possible to keep the food until it deteriorates to a level of unacceptability or becomes unsafe? Shelf life should be considered at the product design/formulation stage. However, samples of the product produced under "routine manufacturing" conditions and treated in a manner representative of normal distribution, storage and use should be tested for organoleptic and microbiological properties. Additionally, if necessary, batches can be stored under conditions of abuse (e.g. for perishable foods, several degrees above the maximum recommended storage temperature) to provide an additional margin of error, and "standardised" allowances have been proposed to represent realistic consumer abuse. Whichever approach is used microbiological samples are taken at regular intervals (depending on the product and proposed/desired shelf life) and examined for key spoilage, indicator or marker organisms as well as pathogens. Where safe to do so these results are considered in relation to the food's organoleptic properties. One or two days may be deducted from the product's actual shelf life in anticipation of consumer retention and use beyond the stated date. The whole process needs to be replicated several times to generate sufficiently reliable data for decision making. In accelerated shelf-life testing, often used for canned or bottled foods, a portion of the batch is incubated at a much higher temperature, e.g. up to 55°C for thermophiles in canned foods. The product is examined visually, e.g. for gas production, and microbiologically for signs of spoilage. In this instance the growth of the spoilage organism has been "accelerated" by using more favourable growth conditions.

Microbial challenge testing is mostly used for assessing food safety but can also be used for specific spoilage organisms to answer the question – is the food capable of allowing (or preventing) the growth of a specific pathogen (e.g. identified by the HACCP plan) or spoilage organism to an unacceptable level over the course of its shelf life? This is performed by deliberately adding the organism under test at varying concentrations to samples of the food, followed by monitoring its growth and comparing to controls of uninoculated product. The organisms used to challenge the food may be ones that could gain access to the product via raw materials or through processing, e.g. listeria species in samples of chilled ready-to-eat foods.

Surface and air testing

Cleaning and disinfection of food-contact and non-food-contact surfaces are important parts of food safety and should ideally, certainly in larger businesses, be validated, monitored and verified. This can be achieved in a variety of ways including visual, rapid chemical residue detection, e.g. Adenosine triphosphate (ATP), and microbiological. Microbiological testing is particularly useful in validation but is of less use in monitoring due to the length of time taken for the results to be obtained. Surfaces can be tested for general counts, indicator organisms or for pathogens to help prevent cross-contamination. It has been shown that the microbial populations of food-contact surfaces, and in some cases equipment used for cleaning, contribute directly to the microbial population of the foods being produced. Studies have also shown that the microbial population of a food business can be relatively persistent over time inhabiting the plants for many years in some cases. Routine surface testing is particularly important for some pathogens, e.g. listeria. What is of great importance is that the results of microbiological surface monitoring are communicated to the correct people (not just filed in a cabinet) acted upon and subjected to trend analysis, i.e. patterns of results over time are studied.

Microbiological air testing can also be undertaken especially in certain types of food plants, e.g. bakeries, cheese or meat-cutting plants. The microbiological quality of the air will vary with conditions (temperature, UV light, RH etc.). Settle plates (petri dishes with their lids off) can be left on surfaces and the colonies they subsequently grow examined. In general this is a much less effective way of air sampling than the use of slit or other types of "activated" air sampling where the air is sucked into a device containing an agar plate. This allows greater quantities of air and the particles in it to be sampled.

Outbreak investigation

Microbiological testing of both foods and premises can be an important part of investigating an outbreak. This can be undertaken using traditional and newer genetic methods. The latter have revolutionised the epidemiological study of foodborne disease and allow investigators to identify the source of an outbreak, track exactly how contamination of the product may have occurred, and link apparently "unrelated" cases to the same source.

Product testing: raw material and in-process testing

Microbiological testing of raw materials can be used to check that the raw materials conform to purchasing specifications (important in relation to any later processing) and can provide an indication of what micro-organisms are being imported into the food production plant. It can also be used to compare raw materials from different suppliers and even countries. In one study suppliers were buying strawberries at different times of the year from different countries. The strawberries were used for making fruit-topped custard desserts but the supplies from one country differed markedly in their microbiological properties from those of the other. This was of particular concern as the strawberries were unprocessed and being added to a potentially high-risk product with a shelf life of four days. This meant that the microbiological quality of the end product differed considerably at different times of the year depending upon country of strawberry origin and this could have influenced the shelf life and/or safety of the product.

Microbiological results from raw materials should also be monitored as part of trend analysis and feedback given to suppliers along with requests for information on the cause of any variations or spikes in microbial counts.

An often previously neglected use of microbiological testing is the testing of the food being produced at various stages of its production. End-product testing tells you something has gone wrong (indicated by high counts/presence of particular organisms). In-process testing provides the producer with information that things may be going to go wrong and where that is occurring or has occurred. Increasingly, risk assessment is being used by larger manufacturers and retailers to set food safety objectives (FSO) - aspects of microbial quality in the finished product, e.g. the level of *Listeria monocytogenes* in the end product must not exceed 10^2 cfu/g at the time of consumption. Linked to this is the setting of performance objectives (PO) - microbial quality at a point in production or other point in the food chain. By following the microbial counts during production and transport up to the point of consumption, in-process microbiological testing allows the producer to see if the final product is likely to be microbiologically satisfactory. This can empower the producer in a way that end-product testing alone cannot. Additionally, in-process testing can be used to validate control measures at specific points in the production process.

Product testing: end-product testing

End-product testing has a number of disadvantages and alone cannot guarantee food safety or quality. It is retrospective, i.e. detects things after the event. Nor, due to the distribution of micro-organisms in food, plus problems of detecting and isolating organisms from food, can it guarantee that a food that may test negative is acceptable and free of a particular pathogen. This does not mean it is of little value. Microbiological end-product testing can be of considerable value including informing the food producer of the efficacy of his food safety management system, i.e. verification of HACCP plans. Again the greatest value from end-product testing is gained with the use of trend analysis: recording and then analysing the results over time, looking for consistency and identifying trends and patterns in microbial quality. This can, where necessary, then be linked to problem-investigating techniques such as root cause analysis.

Product testing: sampling and analysis

Prior to any microbiological testing is the collection of a sample. Samples may need to be randomly taken but as part of a routine sampling programme and not a "grab" sample, i.e. where the nearest product to hand is taken just so an analysis can be performed. Alternatively, samples may be specifically taken from part of the batch, e.g. the outside, if it is suspected that it has experienced temperature abuse, or the inside of a sample at the coldest point if validating a control measure. The sample must be correctly taken aseptically using sterile equipment/utensils. A number of potential prosecutions have been rejected due to inappropriate sampling protocols. After collection, the sample must be transported to the laboratory using an appropriate validated and monitored method.

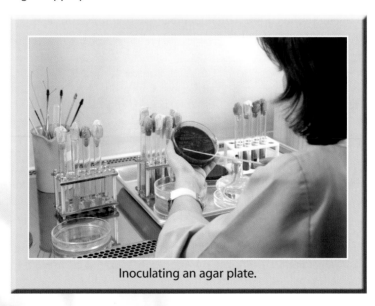

Inoculating an agar plate.

Once in the laboratory the sample can be analysed using traditional or rapid methods: quantitatively, i.e. how many general or specific organisms are there, or qualitatively, i.e. what types of organisms are there or are any pathogens present? Depending upon the food, a general bacterial count, the most common type being an aerobic colony count (ACC described in terms of colony forming units or cfu/g), or a mould/yeast count can be used as a general measure of shelf life but may tell you little about its safety or hygienic status. An ACC in excess of 10^6 (except for products like yogurt) indicates that spoilage is imminent. To assess safety, foods can be examined directly for the presence of specific pathogens. These may be ones that should be absent completely (e.g. *Salmonella spp*) or ones that can be present but below certain levels (e.g. *Clostridium perfringens* below 20 cfu/g). However, the probability of detecting/finding pathogens such as salmonella can be low and frequently foods are sampled for indicator organisms. Commonly used ones include Enterobacteriaceae (widely used in Europe), coliforms (Enterobacteriaceae that ferment lactose and more commonly used in the USA) and faecal streptococci sometimes used for frozen foods as they survive drying better than coliforms and are slightly more resistant. Faecal coliforms include *E. coli* and are more indicative of faecal pollution or poor hygiene and are capable of growth at 44-45°C. Indicator organisms are ones normally associated with the presence of specific pathogens and tell you something about the hygienic handling of the food. They are normally found in higher numbers than the pathogen and are easier to detect. Their presence in high numbers indicates either poor plant hygiene possibly due to post-processing contamination or that processing has not been as effective as it should have been.

CHARACTERISTICS OF A GOOD SAFETY INDICATOR ORGANISM

Definable group/single species
Similar growth/survival and death rates to important pathogen
Present in higher numbers than the related pathogen
Non-pathogenic itself
Easily/cheaply detected
Correlates with presence of particular pathogen

Microbiological criteria

A microbiological criterion (singular criterion – plural criteria) defines the acceptability of a product, or food lot, based upon the presence or absence of a number of micro-organisms and/or their toxins or metabolites per unit(s) mass, volume or area. There are three main types of microbiological criteria: specifications, guidelines and standards. Specifications are agreed between suppliers and purchasers and most large producers and retailers make use of these. Guidelines are used to indicate the microbiological condition of food and deviation from them requires investigation. Environmental health practitioners/officers may make use of these in assessing food samples. Microbiological standards are criteria contained in laws or regulations and failure to meet these may be an offence with foods being classified as unfit for consumption. The EU Microbiological Criteria Regulations are divided into Food Safety Criteria, if these are breached the relevant authorities must be notified and food withdrawn, and Process Hygiene Criteria which if exceeded require appropriate internal corrective action to be taken.

RAPID METHODS FOR MICROBIOLOGICAL TESTING*

The term "rapid method" in **microbiology** has numerous connotations. To microbiologists, a rapid test is one that has a significant time-saving over more traditional methods. However, a rapid test for one manager (producing a long shelf life product) may be unacceptable to another. The selection of a particular rapid method therefore depends upon the individual circumstances of a particular company/product.

Rapid versus traditional methodology

Assessment of the microbiological quality of food has traditionally been determined by the use of standard **plate counts**. This has often incorporated the use of specialist media to isolate a particular organism, for example, salmonella or listeria, followed by a confirmatory test. These methods involve a growth stage and hence can take several days between analysis of the sample and obtaining the result.

Rapid methods are usually based on a few technologies such as those of DNA detection, immunoassay and biochemical determination, although other novel methods do exist. However, for the vast majority, enrichment (broth) culture is required to allow organisms to be detected, which can take up to 24-48 hours. It should, of course, be stressed that for routine purposes, culture is still the most sensitive method with the lowest limit of detection being one **colony** forming unit (CFU). One has to realise that detection of an organism at a high level of sensitivity is significantly different from the traditional numbers game where microbiological specifications are designed to reflect the number of permissible viable organisms within a food. This leads to the main problem with rapid methods – drawing inappropriate conclusions from the results obtained.

Even with significant advances in technology, however, a truly rapid method (taking only a few hours), requiring minimal resources and with the ability to detect low levels of specific pathogens, does not really exist at the time of writing this book.

Advantages and disadvantages of rapid methods

Rapid methods:

♦ provide real time results, leading to rapid clearance of raw materials and products. This provides savings in warehouse/cold storage space due to shorter release time;

♦ are in some cases very easy to use, for example, adenosine triphosphate (ATP) - photometry can be carried out by non-specialist staff after a short training session. However, it should be stressed that in the usual way of using ATP-photometry, the test is non-specific and will not discriminate between pathogens and other microbial flora;

♦ will not solve hygiene/spoilage problems; they will only allow them to be detected over a shorter time span – they will **not** make the problem easier to find;

♦ have to be commissioned and this may be relatively slow as protocols will have to be designed and optimised to fit in with the production process. This will ensure that the information obtained is relevant to the process being monitored; and

♦ require the education of line managers, and supervisors since a test result will probably not be expressed as CFU/ml or gram and there is often confusion in relating metabolic measurements to the real life situation.

*Originally written by Dr Paul Beers (University of Humberside) and edited by Dr Adrian Eley (University of Sheffield)

Rapid methods available

Impedance method

This method refers to the measurement of impedance (the degree of resistance to an electric current) within a culture medium. Micro-organisms will metabolise substrates as they grow, decreasing the impedance of the medium. It is possible to directly relate the changes in impedance to cell numbers. The bactometer is a commercial instrument that uses this technique. Numerous specific methods have been developed for the detection of coliforms, including the detection in meat samples. Individual organisations can develop their own protocols in consultation with the companies producing the instrumentation.

DNA methods

Different DNA methods include the use of a DNA-probe, designed to detect a single organism or a group of organisms. The future of rapid methods lies in the DNA-based methods, as they can be used to detect and amplify bacteria, for example, the polymerase chain reaction (PCR). Although PCR is a rapid technique, insufficient sensitivity for detection of pathogens in foods has necessitated enrichment culture for up to 24 hours. Additional problems have been difficulties over specificity of the target, which may also be found in non-pathogenic organisms. Improved sensitivity may be achieved by TaqMan (Tm), which is a newer real-time PCR method, giving results in only a few hours. This technology combines DNA amplification and detection of the products in a single tube, which reduces the contamination risk (false-positives). It is also less time-consuming than gel-based analysis and can supply a quantitative and qualitative result.

Adenosine triphosphate bioluminescence (ATP)

All organic matter, including bacteria (small amounts), and food (large amounts) contain ATP, the main energy store for living organisms. This biochemical test uses the enzyme luciferase, that emits light if ATP is present and this light can be measured with a luminometer. In 20 seconds, the test will indicate whether or not a surface is clean. However, it cannot distinguish between food residues and micro-organisms. The test is very sensitive with less than 1ppm food residues being detected.

Protein and sugar tests

Like ATP, these tests are used to monitor the cleanliness of surfaces not specifically to detect the presence of micro-organisms. Although not as sensitive as ATP tests, these biochemical tests produce rapid colour change if protein/amino acids or sugars are present. Reaction time varies between one and ten minutes. Although micro-organisms are not identified, they are likely to be present on any surface where food residues have been detected.

Culture media

The addition of identifiable substrates (i.e.

Swabbing a knife blade for ATP testing
(Courtesy of Biotrace.)

substrate that is used by a particular group of micro-organisms leading to an observable change within the media) to existing culture media is another expanding area. These methods may shorten the time to make a positive identification and have the advantage, for food industry personnel, of expressing the results in the same format as traditional methods. One such method is the addition of 4-methylumbelliferyl-D-glucuronide (MUG) to culture media. Most *Escherichia coli* convert this non-fluorescent substrate into a fluorescent product, causing the media to fluoresce under a simple UV lamp. More recently, there has been a growing interest in the use of chromogenic media, for example, 5-bromo-4 chloro-3 indoxyl-B-D-glucuronide (BCIG) to detect *E. coli* O157. They can, however, seem rather costly although they may save time and expense in confirming suspect colonies.

Immuno methods

There are many types of immunological assay available, which can be divided into those based on **enzyme** linked immunosorbant assay (ELISA) with or without immunomagnetic separation, and latex agglutination methods. The ELISA method involves the use of antibodies to detect a particular organism or group of organisms that are linked to an enzyme system, which changes colour if the organism is present. A wide variety of organisms can be detected using ELISA, although the method can take 24-48 hours for a result, is not particularly sensitive and is labour-intensive. Immunomagnetic separation increases sensitivity as the **antigen** is concentrated, using paramagnetic beads coated with an **antibody** to the target organism or toxin and then applying a powerful magnet. In latex agglutination, the antibody is attached to an inert **carrier** particle, such as latex, which enhances visible clumping of the antigen. This is a rapid method of identifying the target organism but because the inherent sensitivity is poor, an enrichment procedure is often required. Alternatively, this method known as reversed passive latex agglutination (RPLA), can be used to detect toxins such as *Bacillus cereus* diarrhoeal enterotoxin.

Biochemical methods

Another common way of rapidly identifying isolated organisms is by the use of biochemical profiles, achieved through addition of the test organism to a range of different substrates, often in a kit form. The biochemical profile of an organism will denote the "best fit" identification. Several automated systems are available, allowing for testing of a large number of organisms.

Selection of a rapid method

Further information can be obtained from food microbiology textbooks, reviews of current methodology and more importantly from trade literature. If managers intend to introduce rapid microbiological testing, the following points should be considered.

Firstly, identify if current methods are adequate for the company's needs. If they are, then a change is probably unnecessary. If existing methods are inadequate then:

♦ review the current information available on rapid techniques and identify any that may be of benefit;

♦ collect as much information as possible on reliability, ease of use and sensitivity (including false positive and negative rate). However, one needs care in interpreting data. Information provided depends on the gold-standard or reference method, which can only be reliably compared if all data was generated in the same trial;

♦ contact the manufacturers and ask for a demonstration;

♦   set up a trial of the method to run in parallel with existing tests; and

♦   ascertain if the results of the trials lead to an improvement in the information obtained.

If this is the case the test may be adopted, otherwise continue to use existing methods or select an alternative rapid method.

Food MicroModel

This is not a rapid method in itself but is a computer-based system for predicting the growth, death and survival of foodborne pathogens. It can be used to help determine the microbiological safety of food and reduce the number of **challenge tests** when developing new products.

Bacteriological food sampling by enforcement officers

The Food Safety Act, 1990 formalised the administrative procedures for the taking and examination of food samples. Food liaison groups, involving environmental health practitioners/officers from adjacent authorities, Public Health Laboratory food examiners, trading standards officers, and sometimes, public analysts and have introduced coordinated sampling programmes within their areas. These groups also cooperate with the Food Standards Agency and the Local Authorities Coordinators of Regulatory Services (LACORS) to obtain food samples to comply with the requirements of the EU with regard to national sampling programmes.

EU legislation is increasing the emphasis on bacteriological standards as a way of improving food safety. Standards exist for many foods including egg products, milk and milk products and shellfish. However, EU policy dictates that inspection and sampling are primarily undertaken at the production premises in the country of origin and not at frontiers between member states (EU Directives 89/397 and 89/662).

Samples of food may be taken for bacteriological examination to determine the acceptability or safety of a batch of food intended for human consumption, for example, a consignment of imported food or a quantity of food suspected of being contaminated by pathogens. As bacteria are unevenly distributed throughout food, a statistical sampling plan should be used to ensure that an adequate number of random samples are taken, on which to base a decision regarding the whole consignment.

However, most routine bacteriological sampling by enforcement officers is carried out at food shops, factories and restaurants, etc., to support observations regarding the standard of hygiene within the premises. When sampling from retail outlets, it is preferable to take samples of several different high-risk foods from one or two premises, as opposed to taking samples of the same type of high-risk food from many premises.

Unacceptable numbers of bacteria in the sample usually reflect poor handling techniques, under-processing, post-process contamination or incorrect storage. Due to the uneven distribution of bacteria, unsatisfactory results should not usually be used to support an opinion about any food remaining on the premises. However, the presence of pathogens or a suspicion of under-processing would require the detention and further sampling of any of the original food that had not been used or sold.

If only one or two samples out of many taken from a premises are unacceptable, this may be due to an unsatisfactory delivery of the specific food. If several samples from a single premises are unsatisfactory, for example, because of the presence of *Escherichia coli,* and all of the food originated from different suppliers, this would indicate that it was more likely a handling or storage problem at the retail outlet or restaurant.

The routine use of statistical sampling plans requiring many samples of the same food to be taken from one premises is not practicable or necessary to determine whether a particular food sample has been handled hygienically. However, a sampling programme should be designed to ensure the appropriate frequency of sampling of specific foods from particular premises. The programme may be based on the risk of food hygiene associated with particular foods, the history of premises with regard to food poisoning and food complaints and the nature of the food industry within a particular area.

When procuring a food sample, the officer obtains as much information as possible concerning its handling. This would include method of distribution, date of delivery, date of production, temperature of storage, type and condition of packaging, and any significant information regarding hygiene associated with the product, for example, risks of cross-contamination, handling techniques, personal hygiene of operatives and hygiene of premises and equipment.

The food is usually placed in an insulated container, to avoid the multiplication of bacteria prior to testing, and taken to the public health laboratory. The bacteriologist examines the food to establish the total number of bacteria present per gram of food and whether any indicator or pathogenic organisms are present. On completion of incubation, typically 48 hours at 37°C, the number of bacteria are counted and a report forwarded to the environmental health department. As none of the methods used by laboratories can be guaranteed completely accurate, tolerances must be allowed. Furthermore, if comparisons are to be made or standards established, it is important that the same methods and procedures are used by all laboratories involved in analysis, as well as by all enforcement officers.

Interpretation of results
Bacteriological counts

The total number of living bacteria in a food sample is usually expressed as the **total viable count** (TVC) and is used as a microbiological indicator of food quality. The temperature of incubation used varies depending on the type of bacteria likely to be present if the food has been mishandled. A temperature of 37°C is usually employed by the PHLS, as they are interested in the presence of mesophilic bacteria and the opportunity for pathogen growth. A TVC in excess of 10^4g in most high-risk foods indicates either gross contamination or old product, together with storage at incorrect temperatures. High counts at 20°C on chilled foods indicate inadequate, or lack of, refrigeration.

Indicator organisms

Indicator organisms are organisms that are usually present in very large numbers in environments inhabited by pathogens. The usual indicator organisms used by food microbiologists belong to the Enterobacteriaceae family, many of which live in the intestine of man and animals, and include coliform organisms, faecal coliforms and *Escherichia coli*.

Faecal streptococci

Faecal streptococci include *Streptococcus faecalis, Streptococcus faecium, Streptococcus bovis and Streptococcus equinus* – this group is serologically defined as Lancefield group D. They are normally present in mammalian faeces but are more resistant to drying, high temperatures and disinfectants than Enterobacteriaceae. Their presence usually indicates poor plant hygiene or a failure of a specific heat process to destroy them; post-process contamination may or may not have occurred.

THE ENTEROBACTERIACEAE FAMILY

Lactose fermenting coliforms (also some species of Salmonella and Shigella).

Coliforms/Enterobacteriaceae

Coliforms are those members of the Enterobacteriaceae that **ferment** lactose and produce gas. They are sensitive to heat and their presence in food usually indicates post-process contamination or poor hygiene. The presence of coliforms in water, or food, may be a result of recent faecal contamination but as some coliforms exist in soil and on plants, this is not always the case. However, the presence of E. coli does indicate recent human or animal faecal contamination and also the likelihood of pathogenic contamination. Faecal coliforms are those coliforms that can be successfully incubated at the higher temperature of 44 to 45.5°C and include E. coli.

Pathogenic contamination

Pathogens should not be present in hygienically handled and effectively processed high-risk food, even though some microbiologists believe that levels of 10^3 *Staphylococcus aureus*, *Clostridium perfringens* or *Bacillus cereus* per gram are insignificant. However, notwithstanding the fact that such low numbers are extremely unlikely to cause food poisoning, such food is potentially hazardous and has not been handled hygienically.

In high-risk food presence of:

♦ *Staphylococcus aureus* usually indicates a breakdown in personal hygiene or the handling of food;

♦ *Clostridium perfringens* usually indicates prolonged warm storage after cooking; and

♦ *Salmonella* indicates cross-contamination, under-cooking/inadequate thawing or faecal contamination from a carrier.

Microbiological guidelines

The Health Protection Agency has published microbiological guidelines for **ready-to-eat foods** sampled at point of sale. The microbiological quality of the food is based on the **aerobic colony count (ACC)**, indicator organisms and common foodborne pathogens, and ranges from satisfactory to potentially hazardous. Foods are divided into five categories; however, the guidelines relating to pathogens are the same for categories one to five. Category one foods have stricter guidelines for aerobic plate counts than category two foods, which have stricter guidelines than category three etc. Although the guidelines are not a legal requirement, they may be referred to in the event of enforcement action.

GUIDELINES FOR THE MICROBIOLOGICAL QUALITY OF CATEGORY 1 READY-T0-EAT FOODS

Beefburgers/kebabs, sausage rolls, pickled fish, scotch eggs, bhajis, pasties, meat pies, pork pies, mayonnaise, mousse

Criterion	Microbiological quality (CFU per gram unless stated)			
	Satisfactory	Acceptable	Unsatisfactory	Unacceptable/ Potentially hazardous*
Aerobic colony count† 30ºC:48h ∓2h	$<10^3$	$10^3 - <10^4$	$\geq 10^4$	N/A
Indicator organisms‡				
Enterobacteriaceae§	<100	$100 - <10^4$	$\geq 10^4$	N/A
E. coli (total)	<20	$20 - <100$	≥ 100	N/A
Listeria spp. (total)	<20	$20 - <100$	≥ 100	N/A
Pathogens				
Salmonella spp.	absent in 25g			present in 25g
Campylobacter spp.	absent in 25g			present in 25g
E. coli O157 & other VTEC	absent in 25g			present in 25g
V. cholerae	absent in 25g			present in 25g
V. parahaemolyticus¶	<20	$20 - <100$	$100 - <10^3$	$\geq 10^3$
L. monocytogenes	$<20**$	$20 - <100$	N/A	≥ 100
S. aureus	<20	$20 - <100$	$100 - <10^4$	$\geq 10^4$
C. perfringens	<20	$20 - <100$	$100 - <10^4$	$\geq 10^4$
B. cereus and other pathogenic Bacillus spp.#	$<10^3$	$10^3 - <10^4$	$10^4 - <10^5$	$\geq 10^5$

[*] Prosecution based solely on high colony counts and/or indicator organisms in the absence of other criteria of unacceptability is unlikely to be successful.

[†] Guidelines for aerobic colony counts may not apply to certain fermented foods – for example, salami, soft cheese, and unpasteurised yogurt. These foods fall into category 5. Acceptability is based on appearance, smell, texture, and the levels or absence of indicator organisms or pathogens.

[‡] On occasions some strains may be pathogenic.

[§] Not applicable to fresh fruit, vegetables and salad vegetables.

[¶] Relevant to seafood only.

[#] If the Bacillus counts exceed 10^4 CFU/g, the organism should be identified.

[**] Not detected in 25g for certain long shelf life products under refrigeration.

[N/A] Not applicable.

Enterobacteriaceae tests have replaced coliform tests and will include non-lactose fermenting organisms such as salmonellas. However, the criteria listed for Enterobacteriaceae do not apply to fresh fruits, vegetables or sandwiches containing salad vegetables, as they often carry high levels of the organisms as part of their normal flora.

GRADES OF MICROBIOLOGICAL QUALITY

The terms used to express the microbiological quality of ready-to-eat foods are:
- satisfactory ~ test results indicating good microbiological quality;
- acceptable ~ an index reflecting a borderline limit of microbiological quality;
- unsatisfactory ~ test results indicating that further sampling may be necessary and that authorised officers may wish to undertake a further inspection of the premises concerned, to determine whether or not hygiene practices for food production or handling are adequate;
- unacceptable/potentially hazardous ~ test results indicating that urgent attention is needed to locate the source of the problem; a detailed risk assessment is recommended. Such results may also form a basis for prosecution by environmental health departments, especially if they occur in more than one sample. Food examiners will wish to draw on their own experience and expertise in determining the advice and comments they wish to give and they will be required to do this if invited to give an expert opinion during legal proceedings.

If the food fails to achieve a reasonable bacteriological quality, then an investigation is usually carried out to ascertain the reasons for this and advice will be given on how to prevent further unsatisfactory results by ensuring that:
- the product is acceptable when delivered to the premises;
- stock rotation is effective;
- handling techniques are hygienic;
- cleaning and disinfection is satisfactory;
- proper temperature control is exercised at all stages of manufacture, distribution and sale;
- packaging is satisfactory; and
- staff training is effectively carried out.

Repeat samples should be taken until a sequence of satisfactory results is obtained.

Official control of food premises

In the UK, central government has given the responsibility for protecting public health and ensuring food businesses comply with food hygiene legislation to local authorities. Authorised officers with a wide range of qualifications, experience and expertise are necessary to enable authorities to carry out the significant range of food hygiene and food safety controls that now exist. The most common local authority officer involved in food hygiene control is an environmental health practitioner/officer. Authorities may also appoint technical officers with specialist food qualifications.

The functions of authorised officers in the field of food hygiene and food safety include:
- ensuring product safety and fitness for consumption;
- reducing possible sources of contamination entering the food environment;

- monitoring conditions and hygienic operations within the food environment;
- ensuring compliance with relevant legislation;
- establishing the competency and attitude of management and effectiveness of control procedures; and
- offering professional guidance, particularly when legislation is changing.

Authorised officers undertake the above functions:
- during routine visits to and inspections of food premises;
- whilst investigating food poisoning outbreaks and incidents;
- whilst investigating food complaints;
- by lecturing on hygiene courses and seminars and giving related talks;
- by using the media, for example, press releases, committee reports and hazard warnings;
- whilst dealing with planning and licence applications;
- by developing partnerships with businesses' decision-making bases in the local authority's area (often referred to as the "Home Authority Principle"); and
- by developing local business forums for the exchange of information and the provision of advice.

Hygiene inspections of food premises by authorised officers

Inspections should be carried out at all stages of production, processing and distribution to ensure compliance with food law. The main purpose of a hygiene inspection is to ensure food is being handled and produced hygienically and to identify forseeable incidences of food poisoning or injury resulting from consumption of the food.

The main objectives of primary food hygiene inspections are the:
- determination of the scope of business activities and the relevant food safety legislation, which applies to the operations taking place at the premises;
- thorough and systematic gathering and recording of information, from observations of practices, procedures and processes, including procedures based on HACCP principles, and discussion with food handlers, contractors, food business operators and managers;
- identification of potential hazards and associated risks to public health;
- assessment of the effectiveness of process controls to achieve safe food;
- assessment of the HACCP based food safety management system operated by the business;
- identification of actual or potential breaches of food law and, if appropriate, the gathering and preserving of evidence;
- consideration of appropriate enforcement action, (proportionate to risk), to secure compliance with food safety legal requirements;
- provision of advice and information to food business proprietors and food handlers, in accordance with industry guides and codes of practice; and
- determination of the need to collect samples of food or materials and articles in contact with food for analysis and/or examination.

Secondary inspections may involve visits: for sampling; to investigate food complaints, to discuss food safety management systems; for training; and to check work carried out (revisits).

LACORS has issued advice on food hygiene inspections, which reflects the main purposes of an inspection. LACORS guidance emphasises the need for local authorities to have an appropriate management system, to ensure enforcement officers undertake inspections in a consistent manner. The various stages of a food hygiene inspection are specifically addressed, including planning for the inspection, preliminary interviews, the inspection of premises, the post-inspection interview and post-inspection administration.

Before carrying out a food hygiene inspection, authorised officers will take account of a number of issues. These will include:

♦ reviewing the premises' previous history, including information on its operations and systems, previous complaints and responses to previous inspection outcomes;
♦ timing of inspection – generally unannounced, although advance notice may occasionally be appropriate to ensure relevant persons are present;
♦ equipment availability, for example, calibrated temperature recording equipment;
♦ appropriate protective clothing; and
♦ assessing the need for additional expertise, for example, food examiners.

Before commencing an inspection, the officer will explain the purpose of the inspection and what it will entail to the manager. Inspections will include:

♦ a preliminary assessment of the food hazards associated with the business; and
♦ determining whether the business has a satisfactory system for assessing food hazards and controlling risks at those points that are critical to food safety.

The approach to inspection will depend significantly on whether such a system exists. LACORS guidance on food hygiene inspections therefore emphasises the central role of a preliminary interview. Discussion at an early stage of the inspection about the hazards associated with the business, and any system in place for assessing those hazards and controlling the risks, allows an officer to properly plan the subsequent detailed inspection of the business operations and premises. The officer should examine any food safety policy, the HACCP plan and other relevant documentation.

Businesses may have various types of hazard analysis systems in place. Only a minority will have a formal documented HACCP system; most are more likely to have implemented some less formal system. Different approaches to auditing such systems are necessary. LACORS guidance on risk assessment provides detailed advice on assessing different types of systems. It emphasises the flexibility officers must have in recognising that food businesses may use a variety of methods to identify and assess relevant food hazards and control risks. It also recognises that, with this new requirement, many businesses will need advice on how to develop systems. Officers are seen as central to enabling proprietors to develop relevant systems.

In addition to considering any systems in place, an inspection will include a visual and physical examination of the premises and its operations. Officers will have particular regard to the food hazards and the control and monitoring procedures in place at the critical points. LACORS guidance on risk assessment includes advice on the broad stages of a risk-based inspection and the judgements officers must take. The guidance emphasises going beyond simply identifying hazards. It recognises that action taken to control hazards, without any consideration of the risk, can result in unnecessary controls being imposed on food businesses.

Food hygiene inspections should include:
- a review of the information held on record by the food authority in relation to the food business;
- a preliminary discussion with the duty manager/proprietor, which should include:
    - an explanation by the officer of the purpose of the inspection;
    - identification of all the food-related activities undertaken by the business, for example, the areas of the premises used for the preparation/production/storage of foodstuffs, the processes used, and the staff involved;
    - identification of the customer base of the business;
    - identification of any food safety management systems that may be in use;
    - an assessment by the officer of the hazards posed by the business's activities;
    - an assessment of the manager's/proprietor's understanding of the hazards posed by the business and the application of appropriate controls;
    - an examination of any documented food safety management system/hazard analysis;
    - an assessment of the provision of supervision and instruction and/or training of staff;
- a discussion with any staff responsible for monitoring and corrective action at CCPs to confirm that control is effective;
- a physical examination of the premises to assess if all the critical controls have been identified, whether those controls are in place and to assess compliance with the relevant legislation; and
- an assessment whether to take microbiological or chemical samples.

The physical examination of the premises will usually consider the following areas:
- temperature controls during storage, cooking, processing, cooling, reheating, thawing, preparation and distribution. Physical checks will be made and records examined, including action taken in the event of breakdown, for example, the failure of refrigeration;
- the absence of cross-contamination and the use of good handling techniques. Work flows will be examined to ensure separation of high-risk food from raw food and waste. The use of staff and equipment will be considered and particular attention paid to thawing and cooling. The protection/covering and packaging of food will be included;
- cleansing and disinfection. The physical and bacteriological cleanliness of premises and equipment, evidence of a planned cleaning programme/cleaning schedules;
- personal hygiene and training. The hygiene awareness of managers and staff, the standard of supervision, procedures for appointments, medicals and exclusions. Procedures for replenishment of soap, towels and replacement of soiled protective clothing. The availability of training records;
- the delivery and handling of raw materials, including the use of specifications, checking food on arrival, dealing with non-food items such as packaging, to avoid food contamination and reject procedures;
- pest control including absence of pests, proofing and control. Records of visits, treatment and recommendations will be required;

- ◆ complaints. An examination of records and action taken on receipt of complaints.
- ◆ recall systems and product traceability will be checked. Foreign body detection equipment such as metal detectors, and systems will be examined;
- ◆ waste and refuse. Procedures for handling and removal of waste and for dealing with detained or unfit food;
- ◆ visitors. Procedures for dealing with visitors, including enforcement officers, engineers and contractors;
- ◆ food storage and stock rotation. Systems and documentation, including staff awareness;
- ◆ finished product. Handling, wrapping, storage and distribution;
- ◆ management control systems, including the hygiene policy and the application of hazard analysis and control. Monitoring of procedures at critical points will be examined. Contracts, for example, pest control, cleaning, equipment maintenance, waste disposal and catering. Quality assurance/quality control systems including microbiological monitoring, records and action taken in event of adverse results. Hygiene audit records should be available; and
- ◆ structure, equipment and facilities including design, lighting, ventilation, drainage, water supply, staffrooms, first aid, storage areas, facilities for washing hands, equipment and food, and external buildings and yards.

It will be clear from the above that comprehensive inspections of food premises by authorised officers may take several hours or even days, depending on the size of premises, the type of operation and the standards of hygiene. Furthermore, inspections may take place at any time of the day or night depending on the hours of operation.

Some form of post-inspection interview should occur at a closing meeting, to enable the officer to discuss any significant findings including any contraventions of food hygiene laws with the manager/proprietor. At all times, officers should clearly distinguish those matters that are contraventions from recommendations of good practice. The closing meeting should include:

- ◆ a discussion regarding any hazards that have been identified by the officer and have not been covered by the business's systems;
- ◆ a discussion regarding failures to implement or monitor any critical controls that have been identified by the business;
- ◆ a discussion regarding any contravention of the relevant legislation;
- ◆ any recommendations of best practice the business may wish to consider; and
- ◆ a discussion regarding the timescale for any remedial work needed and any follow-up action the officer intends to take.

Authorised officers should report back in writing after every relevant inspection. The reports should include the following information:

- ◆ name and address of premises;
- ◆ person seen/interviewed;
- ◆ type of premises;
- ◆ date and time of inspection;
- ◆ specific legislation under which inspection was conducted;
- ◆ areas inspected (whole or part of premises (specify areas));
- ◆ records/documents examined (and outcome);

- details of any samples procured including description and batch number;
- summary of matters discussed at closing meeting; and
- summary of action to be taken by the authority, for example, standards satisfactory, a letter or improvement notice.

It is quite common for such reports to be provided at the end of the inspection, in handwritten form. The summary of action should confirm whether any further measures will follow, for example, an advisory letter or service of a notice.

Action taken as a result of an inspection

During an inspection, an officer may identify contraventions of food hygiene legislation and/or poor or unsafe **food handling** practices. Several options exist to remedy the contravention and detailed guidance is found in the Food Law Code of Practice as to the most appropriate action. In addition, LACORS has published guidance on food enforcement policies. The guidance stresses the range of options available to local authorities and provides detailed criteria that may be applicable to them. The options available and potential outcomes for all food hygiene inspections include:

- verbal advice/warnings or informal written advice/warnings where the officer is confident the work will be carried out;
- a hygiene improvement notice, for contraventions of food hygiene legislation; allowing not less than 14 days to comply;
- the detention or seizure of unsafe food, where food does not comply with the food safety requirements;
- a hygiene emergency prohibition notice, where there is an imminent risk of injury to health, requiring closure of the premises or prohibition of processes or use of equipment;
- a formal caution where an offence exists but it is not considered in the public interest to prosecute through the courts; and
- prosecution, where it is considered in the public interest.

Frequency of inspections

Effective inspection programmes recognise that the frequency of inspection will vary according to the type of food business, the nature of the food, the degree of handling and the size of the business. Essentially, those premises posing potentially a higher risk should be inspected more frequently than those premises with a lower risk. The Food Law Code of Practice details an inspection rating scheme for assessing premises for this purpose.

Premises are rated in the following areas:

- potential hazards and significance of risk associated with the premises:
  - type of food and method of handling, including risks from *E. coli* O157, other VTEC, *Clostridium botulinum*, salmonella or *Bacillus cereus*;
  - method of processing, including cook-chill, small-scale production of cooked meat or milk and dairy products, purification of shellfish, thermal processing and aseptic packaging of **low-acid foods**, vacuum packing including sous vide but excluding raw and unprocessed meat and dried foods; and
  - consumers at risk;
- level of current compliance with regard to:
  - food hygiene/safety, including practices, procedures and temperature controls; and

     ♦   structure, including cleanliness, layout, lighting, ventilation and facilities;
♦ confidence in management/control systems including:
     ♦   previous history;
     ♦   management attitude;
     ♦   the technical knowledge available on hygiene and food safety matters, including HACCP; and
     ♦   documented procedures and HACCP-based food safety management systems.

The officer determines the score for each of the categories, in line with the code's detailed guidance. The total score is used to determine the minimum frequency of inspection and the date of the next inspection. Businesses processing high-risk food, are at risk from *E. coli* O157, other VTEC or *Clostridium botulinum*, or supplying vulnerable consumers, are likely to be inspected at least every six months. Establishments scoring less than 31 points are deemed to be low-risk and may be subject to an alternative enforcement strategy instead of routine inspections, for example, hygiene questionnaires. However, inspections must be carried out in the event of consumer complaints, application for registration and significant changes in activities. It would be beneficial if the scoring system was simplified to improve consistency.

Provided premises comply with hygiene legislation, it should be noted that the interval between inspection will be greater if the officer has confidence in the management and the control systems. This enables local authorities to target their resources at those businesses that fail to make efforts to comply and in which the authorities have little or no confidence.

Managing visits from Enforcement Officers

Food businesses receive visits from different enforcement agents including Environmental Health Officers/Practitioners, Trading Standards Officers, Health and Safety Executive Officers and Fire Officers. Most visits will be routine inspections or advisory visits. On occasion, the officer may serve an enforcement notice. Under Section 32 of the Food Safety Act, an Environmental Health Officer (Practitioner) has the right of entry into food premises at any reasonable time of the day. Visits may be by appointment but the officer has the right to make unannounced visits. It is the responsibility of the food business operator and employees to cooperate with the enforcement officer in the exercise of his/her legal duties.

The food business operator (manager or owner) must allow access to all parts of the business as requested. Management must respond to all the officer's enquiries, including requests for relevant documentation such as the food safety management system. Where applicable, management must ensure that personnel are available for interview and permit the officer to ask questions of the employees.

Management should request written confirmation of the visit and information about any actions required. As the officer may have provided advice, management should take notice of any reasonable recommendations to ensure compliance with the hygiene legislation. The management should confirm receipt of the officer's letter and give details about how the business will comply with the officer's requirements. If an enforcement notice is served then, where applicable, the food business owner, line manager or directors should be immediately informed. Management must ensure compliance with the requirements of enforcement notices, recording all corrective actions that are required and implemented.

Employees such as supervisors should immediately inform their manager or the owner in the event of an enforcement officer's visit. All employees in the business have a responsibility to cooperate with the enforcement officer.

The investigation of food complaints

Food safety legislation contains a number of offences that may be relevant to food complaints. There is a general offence regarding selling foods that do not comply with food safety requirements, which includes food that is either injurious to health, unfit for human consumption or so contaminated (whether by extraneous matter or otherwise) that it would not be reasonable to expect it to be used for human consumption. The act also contains an offence of selling food not of the nature, substance or quality demanded by the purchaser. These offences cover a whole range of food complaints, including food that would be harmful if it were consumed, food contaminated by foreign bodies, contamination by mould and food in dirty containers (a particular problem with reusable bottles).

Local authorities investigate food complaints as part of the general enforcement service to the public. The purpose of investigating complaints includes:

♦ resolving problems that pose a risk to public health;
♦ the provision of information to the food industry in order to raise and maintain standards;
♦ the prevention of future complaints; and
♦ fulfilling the duty of enforcement contained in the act.

To ensure a consistent approach to the investigation of food complaints, LACORS has published specific guidance on dealing with and investigating those made to local authority environmental health departments. A structured and systematic approach is necessary in investigations because what may appear to be a simple isolated problem could have significant, possibly national or international, implications.

The first stage of any investigation will be receipt of the complaint, when information will be obtained from the complainant. Various details are necessary to assist the future investigation. At this early stage, a decision must be made confirming that it is the responsibility of the authority that has received the complaint to investigate.

The relevant local authority officer, usually an environmental health practitioner/officer, will then inspect the food in question and arrange, if necessary, to further interview the complainant. The complainant will usually be asked to provide a written statement, detailing various matters including information on when, where and by whom the food was purchased, what happened to the food after purchase and when, where and by whom the problem with the food was discovered. Details of the vendor and, if relevant, the manufacturer and importer will be noted. Some form of proof of purchase is desirable to supplement the statement of the complainant, for example, a till receipt or distinctive packaging.

At this early stage, the officer will consider whether the complaint may relate to national/widespread problems or malicious contamination. The Food Law Code of Practice provides guidance on further action to be taken in the event of a food incident or hazard. The officer will also assess whether the complaint is associated with illness and, therefore, whether it is necessary to initiate a food poisoning investigation.

The retailer, caterer or manufacturer where the food was purchased or produced will then be visited. Where the retailer is within the officer's local authority area but the manufacturer is outside that authority's area then, after visiting the local retailer, the officer will make contact with the local authority environmental health department responsible for the manufacturer (often referred to as the home or originating authority) to obtain further information. Food legislation empowers **authorised officers** such as environmental health practitioners/officer to enter business premises outside their area to identify evidence of contraventions, which may encompass, amongst other things, the investigation of food complaints. However, authorities generally rely on the reports from home or originating authorities for detailed information on such premises as this is seen as a more cost-effective option.

At this stage, further information obtained may suggest that a national or widespread problem exists. In most cases, however, the officer will proceed with a detailed investigation and inspection of all relevant premises. The investigation will seek to confirm if an offence has been committed, the alleged person(s)/enterprise responsible and the precautions taken to prevent such a complaint.

Food complaint investigations will, on occasions, necessitate formal interviews having regard to all the relevant law on criminal evidence and, in particular, the Police and Criminal Evidence Act, 1984 and its associated codes of practice. This will occur when the officer considers that an offence exists and the outcome of the investigation is likely to result in a recommendation to prosecute. In addition to interviews with persons, officers may formally request confirmation, in writing, of details from manufacturers and other relevant enterprises relating to the complaint and, in particular, precautions taken to prevent such complaints.

The usual outcome of food complaint investigations is that advisory or warning letters are sent to the business responsible. However, if an officer believes a prosecution may be appropriate, the following factors should be considered:

- ◆ the sufficiency of the evidence including:
    - ◆ the reliability and credibility of witnesses and their willingness to cooperate;
    - ◆ the alleged persons(s) have been identified;
    - ◆ any explanation offered by the suspect;
    - ◆ the likely success of a defence, especially a due-diligence defence; and
    - ◆ that it is in the public interest.
- ◆ the seriousness of the offence;
- ◆ the likelihood of a nominal penalty;
- ◆ the offence was committed as a result of a genuine mistake or misunderstanding (balance against seriousness); and
- ◆ whether other action such as issuing a formal caution or service of a hygiene improvement notice would be more appropriate.

The reference in the Food Hygiene (England) (Scotland) (Wales) (NI) Regulations 2006 and the Food Safety Act, 1990 to the defence of "**due diligence**" with regard to food-related offences is worthy of specific note. The legislation creates a number of offences known as "strict liability". In such a case, it does not matter that the person accused did not intend to break the law. The mere fact that there is clear evidence that the statute has been contravened is sufficient for a conviction. This regime of strict liability was perceived as causing injustice if a person was held to have committed an offence for which he/she had no responsibility at all, or because of an accident or some cause completely beyond his/her control. In order to create a balance of fairness, a defence was included which has become known as the "due-diligence defence".

The legislation specifically states that it is a defence to prove that all reasonable precautions were taken and all due diligence exercised to avoid the offence. Through legal precedent, various principles have been confirmed as necessary if a defence is to succeed. Some positive steps will always be required. Taking reasonable precautions involves the setting up of a system of control, having regard to the nature of the risks involved. Due diligence involves securing the proper operation of that system. Where there is a reasonable precaution then it should be taken. Nevertheless, what is reasonable will depend on particular circumstances including the size of the business. All relevant aspects of the operations of the business must be included in any control system and the operation of the system must be kept under review and amended as necessary.

Food complaint investigations may, therefore, involve considerable time and effort on the part of the investigating authority. In addition to determining whether there is admissible evidence to provide a realistic prospect of conviction for any food complaint offence, authorised officers will also consider whether it is in the public interest to prosecute. It is likely that only those food businesses that have failed to fulfil their legal and moral responsibilities will find themselves in court for food complaint offences.

Occasionally, criminally-minded members of the public attempt to extort money from food companies by making fraudulent claims. In 2005, Anna Ayala and her husband were jailed for nine and twelve years respectively for trying to extort $205 million from Wendys (USA). Ayala claimed she had bitten into a finger served in a bowl of chilli. The fast-food chain lost $2.5 million because of bad publicity and had to lay off dozens of workers. Ayala's husband obtained the finger from a friend who had lost it in an accident.

Management of complaints

It is essential that management has a policy and procedures in place relating to customer food safety complaints. A serious complaint may lead to a product withdrawal or a full product recall. An unsafe food product, for example, glass splinters in a jar of jam, has the potential for enforcement or civil action, adverse publicity and high costs of mounting a product recall. Management must immediately initiate an investigation to ascertain the origin and nature of the contaminant prior to implementing corrective actions.

The company's documented traceability system may point to the glass contamination as originating in the factory. The investigation must determine whether the entire batch from which the contaminated jar originated is unsafe. If it is, then the recall procedure will need to be instigated as soon as possible. If an investigation reveals that the glass contamination could not have occurred from within the factory, then an independent laboratory analysis should be carried out to determine the possible source. It might be that the contamination was a deliberate act on the part of individuals outside the business. In this case, the matter should be referred to the police.

The BRC Guidelines give details on how management can establish a complaints handling system. There should be a procedure for logging in complaints with a range of information including a detailed description of the nature of the complaint, traceability coding and date of the complaint. It is recommended that there should be separate files for complaints such as from enforcement authorities and retailers. Once the complaint has been logged, management should write to the complainant stating that the complaint is under investigation with an appropriate date of completion. Complaints should be investigated as soon as possible in order to prevent further complaints and reassure the customer that the business takes the complaint seriously.

Management should investigate thoroughly, focusing on the appropriate records. For example, a complaint relating to metal contamination would include analysis of documentation such as metal detection records for the appropriate production period, metal detector maintenance, operator training and finished product physical tests.

It is necessary to analyse trends in complaints to assist in identifying production problems and the appropriate corrective actions. The collection of complaints information is valuable as a management tool and may be used to inform employees about their performance and act as a motivation to improve quality and safety.

Once the investigation has been completed and corrective actions have been carried out to prevent a recurrence of the incident, the complainant should be informed in writing.

Accurate and completed relevant documentation is required to contribute to due diligence should the business be subject to an investigation following a customer complaint. Examples of necessary documentation include:

♦ HACCP plans for individual products;
♦ customer correspondence;
♦ customer complaints logs;
♦ complaint trends analysis; and
♦ production records.

Reviewing food safety procedures

The investigation of a customer complaint should be followed by a review of the food safety and quality management system. Examples of the kind of complaints that would necessitate an immediate review include:

Labelling mistakes: Mistakes regarding labelling could expose consumers to harm. For example, failure to include allergenic ingredients, such as peanuts, on food labels risks causing an allergic reaction in susceptible consumers, with possibly fatal consequences. Wrong 'use by' dates on high-risk foods might also result in enforcement action because the manufacturer supplied food potentially injurious to health.

Microbiological and chemical analyses by customers, enforcement authorities or as part of the manufacturer's routine analysis of food samples: The presence of pathogens in food such as *Listeria monocytogenes* or *Salmonella spp.* renders the food injurious to consumer health. Natural substances present at above normal levels such as histamine in fish may also compromise consumer health. Chemical residues such as veterinary medicines present in food pose the risk of both immediate and long-term harm to the consumer.

Foreign body contamination: The presence of metallic or glass contamination and foreign bodies from pest infestations, for example, rodent droppings in cereals, are a frequent cause of customer complaint.

Third Party Audits: Food safety non-compliances regarding documented food safety and quality systems may be identified during Third Party audits. Failure to review the business's food safety and quality system may result in the loss, for example, of accreditation to the British Retail Global Food Standard. As a result, customers may be lost to the business.

Enforcement action: If, for example, a Hygiene Improvement Notice or a Hygiene Emergency Prohibition Notice is served on the food business operator, then the issues raised by the Notice will require a review of the food safety management system as part of the corrective actions required to comply with the Notice.

Traceability

The legal definition of traceability in EU law is: "The traceability of food, feed, food-producing animals and any other substance intended to be, or expected to be incorporated into a food or feed at all stages of production, processing and distribution" [EC Regulation 178/2002 Article 18 (1)]

The Regulation applies to any food business at all stages in the food chain. However, records need only be kept from business to business transactions, not to the final consumer.

Food retailers like supermarkets do not have to keep records of sales to the final consumer because consumers are not food businesses. Other food business operators such as manufacturers and wholesalers supplying to other food businesses, for example, caterers must have a traceability system extending back to their suppliers and forward to their customers. Caterers will keep records of purchases from suppliers but are not required to keep records of sales to the final consumer like restaurant customers.

Why are traceability systems necessary?

A traceability system does not guarantee food safety. It forms part of the controls operating within an effective food safety management system based on HACCP principles.

Apart from the business's legal requirement, a traceability system fulfils the following roles within a food safety management system:

♦ to protect public health by assisting the targeted and accurate withdrawal or recall of unsafe food products from the market;

♦ to provide information about the withdrawal or recall for the competent authorities; and

♦ to contribute to providing informed consumer choice through accurate information. An effective traceability system has the potential to verify label information on product or ingredient history.

Although there is no legal requirement for an internal traceability system, food business operators such as manufacturers put internal traceability systems in place from raw material intake to dispatch. This assists in the rapid identification of failure at a particular stage in the production process in the event of a customer complaint, such as metal or glass contamination.

Food business operators working towards or maintaining a quality management system such as ISO 9000: 2001 or the BRC Global Food Standard will be required to demonstrate effective internal traceability.

How may businesses comply with the Regulation?

Traceability systems may be paper-based or computer-based. Businesses should record, as a minimum, the address of the supplier or customer, what was supplied, the quantity, and the dates of the transaction and delivery. Where applicable, the item's batch number or shelf life should also be recorded. Information may be included in a bar code system. Businesses, such as caterers, do not necessarily have to maintain a formal traceability system. It is the requirement to provide information, not the format, which is important. For example, caterers will indicate on their menus items when potential allergens like nuts are present. Food businesses are required to provide traceability information, when required, to the competent authorities such as their local enforcement authority and the Food Standards agency.

Traceability systems do not need to be complex. An effective and practicable system will be one that is integrated into the normal working practices of the business. It is essential that the information should be kept and organised by the business in such a way that it can be immediately available to the competent authorities in the event of a withdrawal or recall being required.

Managing the operation of the traceability system

Management should establish a traceability policy and communicate the written policy and procedures through, for example, training and staff briefings. Traceability procedures appropriate to the size and nature of the business will be established. Management should regularly test the traceability system at least every 12 months, preferably in conjunction with tests of the product recall procedure. Planned internal management food safety and quality audits will include traceability procedures. Non-conformity with the procedures trigger documented corrective actions.

A fully documented system whereby the business can trace all the raw material inputs that make up the final product for the consumer is fundamental to demonstrating 'due diligence'. If there is a problem with a food product, being able to demonstrate that the system works efficiently will have a number of benefits, including the protection of the company's reputation and brand, because management can quickly identify and put right quality and food safety problems. Testing traceability also gives consumers confidence that the business has effective food safety and quality controls in place. Quality assurance systems like ISO 9001:2001, ISO 22000 and the BRC Global Food Standard require documented traceability systems. It is not enough to establish a documented system - the business must be able to demonstrate that it works. For example, there is a fundamental requirement within the BRC Global Food Standard for management to regularly test the system 'to ensure that traceability can be determined from raw material to finished product, and vice versa'.

The role of the consultant environmental health practitioner (EHP) - formerly EHO

Some of the largest food manufacturers, retailers and caterers employ EHPs or hygiene technologists to help them formulate and manage their own hygiene policies.

However, many companies use the services of hygiene consultants. There are a number of experienced and self-employed EHPs providing consultancy services and some companies offer a national service.

Consultants provide an independent and objective assessment of a food operation and can help companies formulate policies to improve the management of their hygiene standards. Consultants often fulfil a troubleshooting role but increasingly their advice is sought on a proactive basis, as the food industry recognises the benefits that accrue from a proper investment in hygiene. They may be utilised to assist with the implementation of ISO 9000 and HACCP and to approve potential suppliers. The considerable demand for hygiene training created by food safety legislation has resulted in many consultants specialising in this area of work.

The introduction of compulsory competitive tendering has resulted in some local authorities using consultants in areas not subjected to competition, including food hygiene inspections, and this trend may increase.

The role of the expert witness *by Dr Slim Dinsdale*

Evidence given by expert witnesses on the technical issues of a case, in both criminal and civil litigation, can play an important role in assisting the court to arrive at a fair decision regarding guilt or liability.

The expert's role begins with instructions to produce a report from a solicitor on behalf of the defence or the prosecution. A bundle of documents is provided, consisting of the charges against the food business, witness statements, and various exhibits such as microbiological results from food samples, public analyst's reports, inspection reports, etc. These must be critically examined and any errors, unsubstantiated assumptions, and lack of continuity noted. Nothing should be taken for granted and every avenue explored to identify the strengths and weaknesses of the case. Unused material held by the prosecution should always be requested, as it may contain information that could assist the defendant's case, and a thorough examination of all the material will show where further information and/or experimental work is needed. For example, assumptions may have been made that food that has been cooked may have been cooled too slowly. Simple experiments using recording thermometers, used with the food produced and stored as stated, can provide convincing information. Genetic profiling of bacteria isolated from suspect food, and stool samples of patients, can also help to establish whether or not a link exists between the food and the food poisoning.

The skills of expert witnesses can only be fully used when they are part of a team, dedicated to maximising the chances of success. From a defence viewpoint, the inter-relationships of lawyer, the food company, and the expert witness are crucial and are outlined in the illustration below.

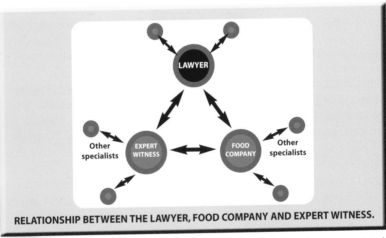

RELATIONSHIP BETWEEN THE LAWYER, FOOD COMPANY AND EXPERT WITNESS.

With the lawyer occupying the key position, it is essential that only appropriately qualified lawyers are instructed to deal with the case, and this is amply illustrated in the Oakwood Deli case (R-v-Kashioulis, 2000) where the specialist food law firm was Birmingham-based Margetts and Ritchie.

The Oakwood Deli case

The Crown alleged that chopped liver sold by the Oakwood Deli, in North London, was at the centre of an outbreak of *Salmonella* Enteritidis phage type 4 (SET4) food poisoning involving more than 150 people. The Crown's case was based upon microbiological and epidemiological evidence, both of which had been "tainted" to such an extent as to make them unreliable sources of evidence. In particular, the sampling protocol for food adopted by the local authority bringing the charges used a spoon, which was disinfected with sanitising wipes instead of being sterilised. This was a clear breach of Code of Practice No. 7, "Sampling for Microbiological Analysis and Examination", and any results from such foods should have automatically been regarded as unreliable. In an attempt to recover the situation and demonstrate that the sampling method was adequate, the prosecution commissioned the PHLS to carry out an experiment to determine the validity of the disinfection protocol.

A minced meat sample was spiked with SET4 and sampled with the original spoon; subsequent examination of the mince showed that SET4 was detected. The spoon was then wiped with sanitising wipes and used to sample liver pâté known to be free from salmonella. The subsequent examination of the pâté did not identify any SET4. The conclusion was that the sanitising wipes had removed any SET4 that was on the spoon and therefore the method was acceptable for taking formal food samples.

There was a fundamental flaw in this experiment, in that it was assumed that the spoon was contaminated with SET4 after sampling the 'spiked' mince, but this was not demonstrated since the spoon itself was not sampled. Further, the SET4 in the spiked minced meat sample was diluted greater that 100,000:1 with the indigenous bacterial flora. This would have further reduced the chances of any SET4 getting on to the spoon during the sampling of the spiked minced meat. This mistake was one of a number that fatally weakened the prosecution's case, and ended with an acquittal on all the charges.

Giving oral evidence

Oral evidence enables complex issues, such as those involving micro-organisms and microbiological results from food, to be explained to the court in an understandable way. Therefore these issues can be seen in the light of the whole food process, enabling a clear picture to be painted in support of any argument for or against the allegations. Oral evidence given under oath may carry as much weight in the court as written statements or records.

Conclusion

In conclusion, there are three pieces of advice that the expert witness should heed. First, be wary of accepting instructions from lawyers who appear to know little about the issues involved, and who seem reluctant to spend the time necessary to construct a good case. Second, carry out a thorough investigation, assume nothing, and adopt some lateral thinking when approaching brick walls. Third, and most importantly, be independent, produce a fair report and do not hesitate to state that there could be difficulties supporting a particular aspect of the case. Doing this will make the expert a much more credible witness and greater weight will be given to the evidence when the time comes for the court to make a decision.

Organisations involved in food control

The food control service operated by EHPs relies from time to time on advice and assistance from other organisations including LACORS (Local Authorities Coordinators of Regulatory Services), the Health Protection Agency, the public analyst, the Food Standards Agency, the Health Protection Agency Centre for Infections, research establishments, and, with regard to animals, veterinary investigation centres. In addition, a considerable amount of work on the microbiology of food is undertaken by the Food Hygiene Laboratory at the Central Public Health Laboratory at Colindale.

LACORS and the coordination of local authorities

LACORS (www.lacors.gov.uk) is a local government central body charged with the task of coordinating local authority trading standards and food enforcement activity. Its terms of reference were extended in 1992 to encompass local authority food hygiene and food safety functions. This reflected the need for local authorities to ensure delivery of an effective enforcement service that was both coordinated and consistent.

LACORS is funded by local government monies and is answerable to a group of local authority elected members, appointed through the local authority associations, which make up the LACORS Management Committee. It has a small administrative and professional secretariat but is reliant on the hard work, experience and expertise of a large group of local authority advisers, who volunteer, through the associations, their time and efforts to assist LACORS in its work. Advisers include directors, chief officers, experienced managers and practitioners, who are organised into various technical panels and working groups to address specific enforcement issues requiring coordination.

LACORS has identified three key coordinating strategies, which have been applied to food hygiene and food safety. Firstly, through LACORS advisers, it emphasises the need for common-sense, pragmatic interpretations and application of food hygiene laws and a consistent approach to inspections, investigations and outcomes. LACORS identifies and promotes existing good enforcement practice, encouraging local authorities to ensure enforcement policies are based on protecting the public.

The second strategy involves encouraging the development of local authority food liaison groups. These groupings of local authorities enable EHPs to raise enforcement difficulties and potential inconsistencies and resolve them through peer group discussion.

The third strategy is known as the Home Authority Principle. This involves local authorities taking particular responsibility for those food businesses whose decision-making bases are located in their areas (usually the head office). The role of a home authority is to assess a food business's own system for ensuring that food hygiene and food safety issues, including legal compliance, are properly addressed. It acts as a focal point for liaison with other authorities, who inspect the business's decentralised branches or units situated in their area. However, the final decision to pursue legal action in the event of a contravention always remains with the authority where the offence occurred.

In April 2009, a new scheme came into effect: primary authority (PA). This statutory scheme is administered by the Local Better Regulation Office (www.lbro.gov.uk). Businesses operating in more than two authorities can, with the agreement of the authority, select an authority to become its PA. Costs incurred by the PA can be recovered from the business. If the business follows the advice of the PA it should not face action by other authorities. Furthermore, if another local authority wishes to take action against the business it must liaise with the PA.

The public analyst

Food authorities appoint a public analyst to provide, among other things, a service of chemical analysis and advice. Work is also undertaken for private companies. However, public analysts must not engage in any food business that is carried on in the area to which their appointments apply. Food and water are analysed using extremely sensitive and sophisticated equipment to confirm the presence, or absence, of specific contaminants, pesticides, additives, trace metals or taints. Tests can be carried out to ascertain whether an item has undergone a particular process - for example, the phosphatase test is used to determine whether an insect has been subjected to heat treatment or cooking. The composition of food and the amount of water present can also be ascertained.

15 Food safety legislation

The law is a complex subject. Most acts and regulations affecting the **food** industry are difficult to interpret. However, ignorance of the law is no defence in the event of a prosecution. All managers must make a special effort to become conversant with legislation that affects their business.

This chapter is intended only as a general outline of the most important legislation relating to **food** and **food hygiene**. There are differences in the way that food law has been implemented in England, Wales, Scotland and Northern Ireland. However, since this law originates from the same European regulations and directives, such differences are minor in nature.

It is not intended to provide a concise legal document. As legislation is constantly changing, regard must always be had to any new legislation that may have been introduced since this book was written. Should information or advice be required regarding the interpretation of a particular section or the current legislation applicable, the local environmental health practitioner/officer or a solicitor should be consulted. UK legislation consists of:

Acts of Parliament

These are statutes passed by Parliament that can only be modified by parliamentary procedure. Acts are normally concerned with principles of legislation and must pass through the House of Commons and the House of Lords before receiving royal assent.

Regulations and orders

Regulations and orders are delegated legislation made by the appropriate Minister, who is empowered to do so under a specific act. For example, The Food Labelling Regulations, 1996 were made under the Food Safety Act, 1990. Regulations normally deal with specific premises or commodities in much greater detail than acts.

Local acts or bylaws

These are made or adopted by local authorities and are legally binding only within the area of the particular authority. Bylaws must be formally approved by a specified minister before they can take effect.

The European Union (EU)

When the UK joined the European Union, most food safety legislation originated from directives which required member states to provide regulations to achieve the objectives of the specific directive. It now appears that the EU prefers to issue regulations which are binding on all member countries without the need for each country to introduce their own legislation.

Copies of legislation can be purchased from Her Majesty's Stationery Office. Regulations are known as statutory instruments (SI) and are numbered to enable rapid identification when ordering.

Acts and regulations applicable to the food industry are concerned with:
♦ preventing the production or sale of injurious, unsafe or unfit food;
♦ preventing the **contamination** of food and food equipment;
♦ the **hygiene** of food premises, equipment and personnel (including training);

- temperature control and the prevention of contamination;
- the implementation of food safety management systems based on the principles of HACCP;
- the provision of sanitary accommodation, water supplies and washing facilities;
- the control of **food poisoning**;
- the importation of food;
- the composition and labelling of food; and
- the registration and licensing of food premises and vehicles.

LEGAL TERMS

Court of Appeal (Criminal Division)

This division deals with appeals from the crown court against conviction or sentence. Usually three or five judges sit to hear an appeal.

Crown court

This court is responsible for serious criminal trials of indictable offences and also hears appeals from magistrates' courts.

County court

The county court is responsible for dealing with civil offences, for example, claims for damages from persons who have suffered food poisoning.

Indictable offences

Serious crimes usually tried by a judge and jury in the crown court. The accused is given a full written statement setting out each alleged offence. This document is known as an indictment and each offence is called a count.

Information

A statement of the alleged contravention(s), which is sent to the justices' clerk by the prosecuting authority. On receipt of the information the clerk issues the summons. This is the usual method of instituting criminal proceedings before a justice of the peace.

Judge

An officer of the Crown, appointed on the advice of the Lord Chancellor, who sits in court to administer justice according to the law. Most judges are barristers and will have had several years of experience before appointment; however, some are solicitors.

Justices of the peace (JP)

Persons from all walks of life, appointed by the Crown to preside over magistrates' courts in a particular area. They act judicially in the case of summary offences and initiate proceedings and commit the accused for trial in the case of indictable offences. They receive expenses only and must attend training courses prior to appointment.

Magistrates' court

A court that deals with summary offences in a particular geographic area. Usually presided over by three justices of the peace or a single stipendiary magistrate. Each bench of magistrates is assisted by a legally qualified justices' clerk.

At the court hearing the accused has to plead guilty or not guilty. If he pleads guilty the magistrates will then sentence him, taking into account previous convictions. If he pleads not guilty the prosecutor will call witnesses to prove his guilt. The solicitor acting for the accused will cross-examine the prosecution witnesses, the accused will give his own evidence and may produce his own witnesses to prove his innocence.

The prosecution has to prove the guilt of the accused beyond all reasonable doubt. After the closing speech by the defence solicitor, the magistrates will state whether or not they find the case proved. If the accused is found guilty, he will then be sentenced.

Statutory instrument

Subordinate legislation, such as regulations and orders, which the appropriate minister is empowered to lay before Parliament.

Stipendiary magistrate

A salaried magistrate who is a legally qualified barrister or solicitor with at least seven years' experience.

Summons

A document signed by a magistrate and issued by the justices' clerk on receipt of the information, requiring the attendance of the accused in court on a particular date.

THE LAW GOVERNING THE SALE OF FOOD

Regulation (EC) No 178/2002 general principles of food law and procedures in matters of food safety

Definitions

"Food" includes drink, chewing gum and any substance, including water, intentionally incorporated into the food during its manufacture, preparation or treatment.

"Food business" means any undertaking, whether for profit or not and whether public or private, carrying out any of the activities related to any stage of production, processing and distribution of food.

"Food business operator" means the natural or legal persons responsible for ensuring that the requirements of food law are met within the food business under their control.

"Retail" means the handling and/or processing of food and its storage at the point of sale or delivery to the final consumer, and includes distribution terminals, catering operations, factory canteens, institutional catering, restaurants and other similar food service operations, shops, supermarket distribution centres and wholesale outlets.

"Primary production" means the production, rearing or growing of primary products including harvesting, milking and farmed animal production prior to slaughter. It also includes hunting and fishing and the harvesting of wild products.

"Final consumer" means the ultimate consumer of a foodstuff who will not use the food as part of any food business operation or activity.

"Placing on the market" means the holding of food for the purpose of sale, including offering for sale or any other form of transfer, whether free of charge or not, and the sale, distribution and other forms of transfer themselves.

The general food law relates to all stages of the production, processing and distribution of food. Food law must achieve a high level of protection of human health and life and should be based on risk analysis (risk assessment, risk management and risk communication).

Article 7 (the precautionary principle)

In cases where the possibility of harmful effects on health have been identified but scientific uncertainty persists, proportionate risk management measures may be adopted, to protect health, pending further scientific information for a more comprehensive risk assessment (a scientifically based process consisting of hazard identification, hazard characterisation, exposure assessment and risk characterisation).

Food law should involve open and transparent public consultation.

Article 14

This Article prohibits food being placed on the market if it is unsafe. Food is considered to be unsafe if it is injurious to health or unfit for human consumption. The Article applies to all food business operators including, for example, those who supply foods to charitable and similar events. Only food produced for domestic consumption is excluded.

To determine whether a food is unsafe or injurious to health, the following considerations are to be taken into account:

♦ how the food is used. For example, chicken would be considered unsafe if it was inadequately cooked to eliminate salmonella;

♦ for whom the food is intended. For example, if a product containing nuts is sold as nut-free to those with a nut allergy the food would be considered injurious. However, the Article would not prevent the sale of foods containing, for example, peanuts as long as the food was correctly labelled as such, simply on the grounds that some consumers are allergic to nuts; and

♦ not only the likely immediate or short-term effects of the food on the consumer, but also the long-term and cumulative toxic effects.

Once a food business identifies hazards that might render the food injurious to health, the associated risk should be evaluated. There are two key issues having regard for the above considerations:

1. *What harm might be caused?*
2. *How likely is it?*

To determine the risk, the food business may need to seek expert advice, for example, from food research associations or enforcement authorities.

The key issue in determining whether a food is unfit is 'unacceptability'. Food may be deemed unacceptable by virtue of its contamination with extraneous matter such as glass, or is obviously noxious, decayed or subject to putrefaction.

If part of a batch or consignment is found to be unsafe, then it should be presumed that all the food in the batch or consignment is also unsafe. However, a full risk assessment may find that there is no evidence that the rest of the batch or consignment is unsafe.

Article 15

Feed is not to be placed on the market or fed to any food-producing animal if it unsafe. Feed is considered to be unsafe if it adversely affects human or animal health, and if the food derived from food-producing animals is unsafe for human consumption.

Article 16

Labelling, advertising and presentation of food must not mislead consumers.

Article 18

Operators of food businesses must establish traceability systems for food, animal feed, food-producing animals and any other substances to be used in food or feed. The traceability system must apply to all stages of production, processing and distribution. The food business operator must establish systems and procedures that enable traceability information to be available to the **competent authority**.

Article 19

If a food business operator has reason to believe that a food is unsafe then the food business operator must immediately withdraw the food from the market. If the food product has already reached the consumer, the food business operator must immediately inform the consumer of the reason for its withdrawal. At the same time, the competent authority must be informed of the reasons for the withdrawal and the steps taken by the food business operator to prevent risks to the consumer. The food business operator must also cooperate with the competent authority to avoid or prevent risk to the consumer.

This Regulation established the European Food Safety Authority including its mission, tasks and organisation. It also established a rapid alert system to facilitate crisis management and for dealing with emergencies throughout the EU.

The General Food Regulations 2004 (No.3279)

These Regulations align the Food Safety Act, 1990, with the general principles and requirements of Regulation (EC) No. 178/2002.

They confirm the competent authorities as the Food Standards Agency, the Port Health Authority or the Food Authority. The competent authorities are provided with new enforcement powers in respect of Articles 14, 16, 18 and 19 of Regulation (EC) No. 178/2002. Penalties for contraventions are also confirmed.

Regulation 4a. It is an offence to place food on the market if it is unsafe (injurious to health or unfit for human consumption) i.e. in contravention of Article 14 of Regulation (EC) No. 178/2002.

Regulation (EC) No 852/2004 on the hygiene of foodstuffs

Article 1

This Regulation repeals Directive 93/43/EEC which was enforced by the Food Safety (General Food Hygiene) Regulations 1995. It applies directly to all members states and lays down general hygiene rules for food business operators based on the following principles:

- (a) primary responsibility for food safety rests with the food business operator;
- (b) food safety must be ensured throughout the food chain, starting with primary production;
- (c) the cold chain must be maintained for food that cannot be stored safely at ambient temperatures;
- (d) procedures should be based on good hygiene practices and HACCP principles;
- (e) guides to good practice are invaluable to aid compliance with hygiene rules and the application of HACCP principles;
- (f) microbiological criteria and temperature control based on a scientific risk assessment;
- (g) imported food must be of the same hygiene standard as Community food.

The regulation does not apply to:

(a)   primary production for private domestic use;

(b)   domestic preparation, handling or storage for domestic consumption;

(c)   the direct supply, by the producer, of small quantities of primary products to the final consumer or to local retail establishments supplying the final consumer.

N.B. Recital 9 of Regulation 852/2004 states that community rules should only apply to undertakings, the concept of which implies a certain continuity of activities and a certain degree of organisation.   The scope, therefore, excludes activities such as the occasional preparation of food by individuals or groups for gatherings or for sale at charitable events or where, for example, hairdressers offer refreshments to their customers.

Article 2

Definitions

"Food hygiene" means the measures and conditions necessary to control hazards and to ensure fitness for human consumption of a foodstuff taking into account its final use.

"Establishment" means any unit of a food business.

"**Contamination**" means the presence or introduction of a hazard.

"Wrapping" means the placing of a foodstuff in a wrapper or container in direct contact with the foodstuff concerned, and the wrapper or container itself.

"Packaging" means the placing of one or more wrapped foodstuffs in a second container, and the latter container itself.

"Processing" means any action that substantially alters the initial product, including heating, smoking, curing, maturing, drying, marinating, extraction, extrusion or a combination of those processes. (Excludes mincing, chilling and freezing).

Article 3 (General obligation) Food business operators shall ensure that all stages of production, processing and distribution of food under their control satisfy the relevant hygiene requirements.

Article 5 (HACCP) Food business operators must implement a food safety management system based on the following HACCP principles:

(a)   identifying hazards;

(b)   identifying the **critical control points** (CCPs) at the steps at which control is essential to prevent or eliminate a hazard or to reduce it to acceptable levels;

(c)   establishing critical limits at CCPs which separate acceptability from unacceptability;

(d)   implementing effective monitoring procedures at CCPs;

(e)   establishing corrective actions when a CCP is out of control;

(f)   establishing verification procedures;

(g)   establishing documents and records commensurate with the nature and size of the food business. (Documents must be kept up-to-date and retained for an appropriate period.); and

(h)   the system must be reviewed if the product, process or any step is modified.

This article does not relate to primary production and transport related to primary production.

Article 6 Food business operators must register with the **competent authority** (usually the local authority).

Significant changes in activities must be reported to the competent authority.

Articles 7 & 8 of Regulation 852/2004 on the hygiene of foodstuffs makes provision for the development of national guides to Industry Good Hygiene Practice and for the application of HACCP principles required under Article 5. New guides are being developed, and two were published in 2007. The Regulation encourages the use of national guides as an effective way of complying with food hygiene legislation. The general principles for the development of national guides are set out in Article 8. Guides are to be developed for specific sectors like catering or retail in consultation with representatives of interested parties such as trade associations and consumer groups. The contents of the sector guides are to be of practical application for the sectors to which they refer and should have regard to Codex Alimentarius codes of practice.

The Food Standards Agency has published Guidelines for the development of national voluntary guides to good hygiene practice and the application of HACCP principles in accordance with EC food hygiene regulations. Use of recognised guides by food business operators is voluntary and compliance with the regulations may be achieved in other ways. However, if a food business follows the guidance in a recognised guide, the enforcement authority must take this into account when assessing compliance with food hygiene legislation. Article 8 of Regulation 852/2004 permits Industry Guides to Good Hygiene Practice, drawn up in accordance with the obsolete Directive 93/43/EEC, to remain in use. These older guides may continue to be used by food business operators in so far as they are compatible with the new hygiene regulations.

Article 9 of Regulation (EC) 852/2004 makes provision for the development of community guides approved at EU level. These guides will have EU-wide status. The Commission has published guidelines describing how community guides will be developed and assessed. Details of any community guides developed will be included in the FSA's list of guides. Information about progress in the publication of the national and community guides can be accessed from the FSA's website at www.food.gov.uk/foodindustry/

Annex II (General hygiene requirements)
Chapter I (General requirements for food premises)
(1) Food premises are to be kept clean and maintained in good repair and condition.
(2) The design, layout, construction, siting and size of food premises are to:
  (a) permit adequate maintenance cleaning and/or disinfection, minimise airborne **contamination**, and provide adequate working space to allow for the hygienic performance of all operations;
  (b) be such as to protect against the accumulation of dirt, contact with toxic materials, the shedding of particles into food and the formation of condensation or undesirable mould on surfaces;
  (c) permit good food hygiene practices, including protection against contamination and, in particular, pest control; and
  (d) where necessary provide suitable temperature controlled handling and storage conditions of sufficient capacity for maintaining foodstuffs at appropriate temperatures to be monitored and, where necessary, recorded.
(3) An adequate number of flush lavatories are to be available. Lavatories are not to open directly into rooms in which food is handled.

(4)　An adequate number of washbasins are to be available, suitably located and designated for cleaning hands. Washbasins are to be provided with hot and cold running water, materials for cleaning hands and for hygienic drying. Where necessary, the facilities for washing food are to be separate from the handwashing facility.

(5)　There is to be suitable and sufficient means of natural or mechanical ventilation. Mechanical air flow from a contaminated area to a clean area is to be avoided. Ventilation systems are to be so constructed as to enable filters and other parts requiring cleaning or replacement to be readily accessible.

(6)　Sanitary conveniences are to have adequate natural or mechanical ventilation.

(7)　Food premises are to have adequate natural and/or artificial lighting.

(8)　Drainage facilities are to be adequate for the purpose intended. They are to be designed and constructed to avoid the risk of **contamination**.

(9)　Where necessary, adequate changing facilities for personnel are to be provided.

(10)　Cleaning agents and disinfectants are not to be stored in areas where food is handled.

Chapter II (Specific requirements in rooms where foodstuffs are prepared, treated or processed)

(1)　The design and layout of the rooms are to permit good food hygiene practices, including protection against contamination between and during operations. In particular:

(a)　floor surfaces are to be maintained in a sound condition and be easy to clean and, where necessary, to disinfect. This will require the use of impervious, washable and non-toxic materials, unless the food business operators can satisfy the competent authority that other materials used are appropriate. Where appropriate, floors are to allow adequate surface drainage;

(b)　wall surfaces are to be maintained in a sound condition and be easy to clean and, where necessary, to disinfect. This will require the use of impervious, washable and non-toxic materials and require a smooth surface up to a height appropriate for the operations, unless food business operators can satisfy the competent authority that other materials used are appropriate;

(c)　ceilings and overhead fixtures are to be designed, constructed and finished so as to prevent the accumulation of dirt and to reduce condensation, the growth of undesirable moulds and the shedding of particles;

(d)　windows and other openings are to be constructed to prevent the accumulation of dirt. Those which can be opened to the outside environment are, where necessary, to be fitted with insect-proof screens which can be easily removed for cleaning. Where open windows would result in contamination, windows are to remain closed and fixed during production;

(e)　doors are to be easy to clean and, where necessary, to disinfect. This will require the use of smooth and non-absorbent surfaces, unless the food business operators can satisfy the competent authority that other materials used are appropriate; and

(f)　surfaces (including surfaces of equipment) in areas where foods are handled and in particular those in contact with food are to be maintained in sound condition and be easy to clean and, where necessary, to disinfect. This will require the use of smooth, washable, corrosion-resistant and non-toxic materials, unless food business operators can satisfy the competent authority that other materials used are appropriate.

(2) Adequate facilities are to be provided, where necessary, for the cleaning, disinfecting and storage of working utensils and equipment. These facilities are to be constructed of corrosion-resistant materials, be easy to clean and have an adequate supply of hot and cold water.

(3) Adequate provision is to be made, where necessary, for washing food. Every sink or other such facility provided for the washing of food is to have an adequate supply of hot and/or cold potable water, and be kept clean, and where necessary, disinfected.

Chapter III (Requirements for market stalls or mobile sales vehicles, premises used primarily as a private dwelling house, premises used occasionally for catering purposes and vending machines)

Premises and vending machines are, so far as is reasonably practicable, to be sited, designed, constructed, kept clean and maintained in good repair and condition as to avoid the risk of **contamination**, in particular by animals and pests.

Surfaces in contact with food are to be in a sound condition and be easy to clean and, where necessary, to disinfect.

Where necessary, there are to be facilities to maintain adequate personal hygiene and for the cleaning and, where necessary, disinfecting of working utensils and equipment.

Adequate facilities and/or arrangements for maintaining and monitoring suitable food temperature conditions are to be available.

Foodstuffs are to be placed so as to avoid the risk of contamination.

Chapter IV (Transport)

Conveyances and/or containers used for transporting foodstuffs are to be kept clean and maintained in good repair and condition to protect foodstuffs from contamination, and are, where necessary, to be designed and constructed to permit adequate cleaning and/or disinfection.

Chapter V (Equipment requirements)

All articles, fittings and equipment with which food comes into contact are to:

(a) be effectively cleaned and, where necessary, disinfected. Cleaning and disinfection are to take place at a frequency sufficient to avoid any risk of contamination;

(b & c) be so constructed, be of such materials and be kept in such good order, repair and condition as to minimise any risk of contamination and to enable them to be kept clean and, where necessary, to be disinfected; and

(d) be installed in such a manner as to allow adequate cleaning of the equipment and the surrounding area. Where necessary, equipment is to be fitted with any appropriate control device to guarantee fulfilment of this regulation's objective.

Chapter VI (Food waste)

Food waste, non-edible by-products and other refuse are to be removed from food rooms as quickly as possible, so as to avoid their accumulation.

Waste is to be deposited in closable containers (unless the competent authority agree otherwise). Containers are to be of an appropriate construction, kept in sound condition, be easy to clean and, where necessary, to disinfect.

Adequate provision is to be made for the storage of waste. Refuse stores are to be kept clean and free of animals and pests.

All waste is to be eliminated in a hygienic and environmentally friendly way and is not to constitute a direct or indirect source of contamination.

Chapter VII (Water supply)

An adequate supply of potable water must be provided and used to ensure foodstuffs are not contaminated. Ice is to be made from potable water, if it could contaminate the food. It is to be made, handled and stored to protect it from **contamination**.

Where heat treatment is applied to foodstuffs in hermetically sealed containers it is to be ensured that water used to cool the containers after heat treatment is not a source of contamination for the foodstuff.

Chapter VIII (Personal hygiene)

Persons working in food handling areas are to maintain a high degree of personal cleanliness and wear suitable, clean and, where necessary, protective clothing.

No person suffering from, or being a carrier of, a foodborne disease or afflicted with infected wounds, skin infections, sores or diarrhoea is to be permitted to handle food or enter any food handling area in any capacity if there is a likelihood of direct or indirect contamination. Any person so affected and employed in a food business who is likely to come into contact with food is to report immediately the illness or symptoms, and if possible their causes, to the food business operator.

Chapter IX (Provisions applicable to foodstuffs)

Contaminated or decomposed raw materials must be rejected unless normal sorting and hygienic preparation will ensure their fitness for human consumption.

All food must be protected against contamination during handling, storage, packaging, display and distribution.

Effective pest control procedures must be implemented.

Food likely to support the reproduction of pathogenic micro-organisms or the formation of toxins is not to be kept at temperatures that might result in a risk to health. Food businesses manufacturing, handling and wrapping processed foodstuffs are to have suitable rooms, large enough to separate the storage of raw materials from processed material, and sufficient separate refrigerated storage.

Where foodstuffs are to be held or served at chilled temperatures they are to be cooled as quickly as possible following the heat-processing stage, or final preparation stage if no heat process is applied, to a temperature which does not result in a risk to health.

The thawing of foodstuffs is to be undertaken in such a way as to minimise the risk of growth of pathogenic micro-organisms or the formation of toxins in the foods.

Hazardous and/or inedible substances, including animal feed, are to be adequately labelled and stored in separate and secure containers.

Chapter X (Provisions applicable to the wrapping and packaging of foodstuffs)

Materials used for wrapping are not to be a source of contamination. They must be stored in such a manner that they are not exposed to a risk of contamination.

Wrapping and packaging operations are to avoid contamination of the products. The integrity and cleanliness of cans and glass jars are to be assured.

Reusable wrapping and packaging materials are to be easy to clean and, where necessary, to disinfect.

Chapter XI (Heat treatment)

Heat treatment of food in hermetically sealed containers should conform to an internationally recognised standard (for example, pasteurisation, ultra high temperature or sterilisation). Every part of the product should achieve a given temperature for a given period of time.

Chapter XII (Training)

Food business operators are to ensure:
(1) that food handlers are supervised and instructed and/or trained in food hygiene matters commensurate with their work activity;
(2) that those responsible for the development and maintenance of the HACCP system or for the operation of relevant guides have received adequate training in the application of the HACCP principles; and
(3) compliance with any requirements of national law concerning training programmes for persons working in certain food sectors.

The Food Hygiene (England) (Scotland) (Wales) (NI) Regulations 2006
Part 1   Preliminary
Reg 1.   Each country has its own specific regulations. However, they are almost identical and are all intended to achieve the same objective.

Reg 2.   "Authorised officer" means any person authorised in writing by an enforcement authority to act in matters arising under the Hygiene Regulations (examples include environmental health practitioner/officer, technical officer etc.)
"Enforcement authority" means either the Food Standards Agency or the food authority in whose area the food business operator carries out his operations.
"Hygiene Regulations" means these Regulations and Regulation (EC) 852/2004 on the hygiene of foodstuffs, Regulation (EC) 853/2004 for food of animal origin and Regulation (EC) 854/2004 for controls on products of animal origin intended for human consumption as amended by Regulation EC 882/2004 and as read with Directive 2004/41.
"Premises" includes any establishment, any place, vehicle, stall or moveable structure and any ship or aircraft.

Reg 3.   Food commonly used for human consumption found on food premises shall be presumed, until the contrary is proved, to be intended for human consumption.

Reg 5.   The Food Standards Agency shall enforce the Hygiene Regulations in relation to primary production, slaughterhouses, game handling establishments, fresh meat, cutting plants, egg operations and matters relating to raw cows' milk. The Food Authority shall enforce the Hygiene Regulations in all other food premises.

Part 2   Main provisions
Reg 6.   An authorised officer can serve a **hygiene improvement notice** on the food business operator of a food business, for failing to comply with Hygiene Regulations. The **notice** must state the grounds for non-compliance, specify the contraventions and measures necessary to secure compliance, and the time (not less than 14 days) allowed. Failure to comply is an offence.

Reg 7.   If a food business operator is convicted of an offence under the above regulations **and** the court is satisfied that the business, any process/treatment, the construction or condition of any premises or the use or condition of any equipment involves a risk of injury to health, they **shall** impose a **hygiene prohibition order**. A **hygiene**

prohibition order can apply to the use of a process/treatment, the premises (or part thereof) or any equipment. A copy of the **hygiene prohibition order** must be conspicuously fixed on the premises and contravention of the **order** is an offence. The hygiene prohibition order ceases to have effect when the enforcement authority issues a certificate, which states that there is no longer a health risk. On application by the food business operator, the enforcement authority must determine within 14 days whether the health risk has been removed and if so satisfied, issue the certificate within three days.

The court may also impose a prohibition on the proprietor or manager participating in the management of any food business. (Only a court can lift a **hygiene prohibition order** on a food business operator.) This prohibition applies for at least six months.

Reg 8.   If an authorised officer of an enforcement authority is satisfied that there is an imminent risk of injury to health, he/she may issue a **hygiene emergency prohibition notice** requiring the immediate closure of the premises. An application for a **hygiene emergency prohibition order** must then be made to the court within three days of serving the notice, and at least one day before the date of application, the food business operator must be advised of this intention. (Saturdays, Sundays and Bank Holidays are excluded.)

The **hygiene emergency prohibition notice** and **hygiene emergency prohibition order** must be served on the food business operator and conspicuously displayed on the premises. Any contravention is an offence. A hygiene emergency prohibition notice ceases to have effect if no application for an order is made to the court. A **hygiene emergency prohibition notice/order** ceases to have effect when the enforcement authority issues a certificate, stating that there is no longer a health risk. Compensation is payable by the enforcement authority in respect of loss suffered in complying with the **notice**, unless an application is made for a **hygiene emergency prohibition order** within three days (five days in Scotland) **and** the court is satisfied that the health risk condition was fulfilled.

The Food Law Code of Practice provides guidance on the use of hygiene improvement notices and prohibition procedures.

Reg 9.   If an authorised officer of an enforcement authority is satisfied that the Hygiene Regulations are being breached in respect of an establishment subject to approval under Regulation 853/2004 (mainly slaughterhouses and cutting premises), he may serve a remedial action notice. This notice may prohibit the use of any equipment or part of the establishment, impose conditions on or prohibit a process or require the rate of operation to be reduced or stopped.

An authorised officer may also serve a detention notice requiring the detention of any animal or food for the purposes of examination or sampling.

Failure to comply with either of the above notices is an offence.

Reg 10. Enables proceedings to be taken against another person when the offence was due to his/her act or default.

Reg 11. It is a defence for the accused to prove that he took all reasonable precautions and exercised all **due diligence** to avoid commission of the offence by himself or by a person under his control.

If the defence relates to the offence being due to another person, at least seven clear days before the hearing or within one month of his first court appearance the accused must notify the prosecutor in writing identifying that other person.

Part 3 Administration and enforcement

Reg 12. Empowers an authorised officer to purchase or take samples of food, food sources, & 13. contact materials or any article or substance required as evidence. Such samples should, if considered necessary, be submitted for analysis by a public analyst or examination by a food examiner, who shall provide a certificate specifying the result of the analysis or examination.

Reg 14. Empowers an authorised officer, on production of an authenticated document showing his/her authority, to enter any premises within his/her area at all reasonable hours to carry out his/her duties under the hygiene regulations. In the case of a private dwelling house, entry cannot be demanded unless 24 hours' notice has been given to the occupier. An authorised officer is also empowered to enter any business premises outside his/her area for the purpose of ascertaining whether or not there are any contraventions of the hygiene regulations or regulations/orders made thereunder. Warrants may be issued by a justice of the peace authorising entry, by force if necessary, when entry is refused.

Authorised officers can inspect, seize and detain records, including computer records, required as evidence. Improper disclosure of information so obtained is an offence.

Reg 15. It is an offence to obstruct persons executing the provisions of the hygiene regulations, including the failure to assist or provide information (unless it incriminates them) or the furnishing of false information.

Reg 16. Prosecutions must commence before the expiry of three years from the commission of the offence or one year from its discovery by the prosecutor, whichever is the earlier.

Reg 17. A person guilty of an offence under these Regulations shall be liable on:
(a) summary conviction to a fine not exceeding the statutory maximum (level 5*); or
(b) conviction on indictment to imprisonment for up to two years and/or an unlimited fine.

The penalty for obstruction on summary conviction shall be a fine not exceeding Level 5* and/or up to three months' imprisonment.

Reg 18. Where an offence by a body corporate has been committed with the consent or connivance or due to the neglect on the part of any director, manager, secretary or similar officer, he shall also be liable to prosecution.

Reg 20. Enable aggrieved persons to appeal to the magistrates' court or the crown court. & 21.

Reg 22. Allows for appeals against hygiene improvement notices and remedial action notices.

Reg 23. Section 9 of the Food Safety Act 1990 (inspection and seizure of suspected food) applies to these regulations as regards an authorised officer of an enforcement authority.

Part 4 Miscellaneous and supplementary provisions

Reg 24. Empowers the Secretary of State to issue codes of recommended practice for the guidance of food authorities as regards the execution and enforcement of the Hygiene Regulations. The Food Standards Agency may issue a food authority a direction requiring their compliance with any code. Food authorities must have regard to any such code.

*The Criminal Justice Act, 1991 provided fines for summary offences in magistrates' courts to be placed on a scale of levels 1 to 5, unless otherwise stipulated in a particular act.
Level 1 – £200   Level 2 – £500   Level 3 – £1,000   Level 4 – £2,500   Level 5 – £5,000

Reg 25. Officers of enforcement authorities are not personally liable for acts involved with the execution of the Hygiene Regulations provided they honestly believed such action was necessary.

Reg 27. When an authorised officer certifies that food has not been produced, processed or distributed in accordance with the Hygiene Regulations, it shall be treated as failing to comply with food safety requirements in accord with Section 9 of the Food Safety Act. All food within a batch shall be treated as certified until it is proved that the rest of the food was dealt with in compliance with the Hygiene Regulations.

Reg 28. Relates to the service of documents.

Schedule 4 Temperature control requirements

(1) Schedule does not apply to slaughterhouses and cutting premises or any food business operations on ships or aircraft.

Chill holding requirements

(2) No person shall keep any food likely to support the growth of pathogenic micro-organisms or the formation of toxins in a food premises at a temperature above 8°C. (Excludes mail order to an ultimate consumer as long as there is no risk to health).

General exemptions from the chill holding requirements

(3) Paragraph 2 shall not apply to:
   (a) food which:
   - ♦ has been cooked or reheated;
   - ♦ is for service or on display for sale; and
   - ♦ needs to be kept at or above 63°C in order to control the growth of pathogenic micro-organisms or the formation of toxins;
   (b) food that, for the duration of its **shelf life**, may be kept at **ambient temperatures** with no risk to health;
   (c) food that is being or has been subjected to a process such as **dehydration** or canning, intended to prevent the growth of pathogenic micro-organisms at ambient temperatures, but this paragraph shall not apply in circumstances where:
   - ♦ after or by virtue of that process, the food was contained in a hermetically sealed container; and
   - ♦ that container has been opened;
   (d) food that must be ripened or matured at ambient temperatures, but this paragraph shall cease to apply once the process of ripening or maturation is completed; and
   (e) raw food intended for further processing (which includes cooking) before human consumption, but only if that processing, if undertaken correctly, will render that food fit for human consumption.

(4) If food is kept above 8°C, it is a defence for the person charged to prove that:
   (a) a food business responsible for manufacturing, preparing or processing the food has recommended that it is kept:
   - ♦ at or below a specified temperature above 8°C; and
   - ♦ for a period not exceeding a specified shelf life;
   (b) the specified temperature is on a label on the packaging or is a written instruction;
   (c) the food was not kept above the specified temperature; and

(d) the specified shelf life had not been exceeded.

A food business shall not recommend food is kept above 8°C for a specified shelf life, unless there has been a well-founded scientific assessment.

Chill holding tolerance periods

(5) It is a defence for a person charged under paragraph 2 to prove that the food:
(a) was for service or on display for sale;
(b) had not previously been kept for service or on display for sale at a temperature above 8°C; and
(c) had been kept for service or on display for sale for less than four hours.

It is also a defence to prove that the food:
(a) was being transferred to or from a food business vehicle to premises at which the food was going to be kept at or below 8°C;
(b) was kept above 8°C for an unavoidable reason such as:
♦ to accommodate the practicalities of handling during and after processing or preparation;
♦ the defrosting of equipment; or
♦ the temporary breakdown of equipment
and was kept at a temperature above 8°C for a limited period consistent with food safety.

Hot holding requirements

(6) No person shall in the course of a food business keep any food that:
(a) has been cooked or reheated;
(b) is for service or on display for sale; and
(c) needs to be kept at or above 63°C in order to control the growth of pathogenic micro-organisms or the formation of toxins at or in food premises at a temperature below 63°C.

Hot holding defences

(7) It is a defence for any person charged under paragraph 6 to prove that:
(a) a well-founded scientific assessment indicates there is no risk to health if food held for service or on display is kept at a specified temperature below 63°C for a period not exceeding a specified period of time and this time/temperature had been adhered to.

It is also a defence to prove that the food:
(a) had been kept for service or display for less than two hours; and
(b) had not previously been kept for service or on display by that person.

Schedule 6 Restrictions on the sale of raw milk intended for direct human consumption.

Raw milk can only be sold direct to the final consumer by the occupier of a premises at which milk producing cows are kept or a distributor. The raw milk must meet the following standards:

♦ Plate count at 30°C (cfu* per ml)   <20,000
♦ Coliforms (cfu per ml)   <100

* cfu - colony forming units

The Food Hygiene (Scotland) Regulations 2006
Schedule 4 Temperature Control Requirements
Chill and hot holding offences
Food should be kept in a refrigerator, a cool ventilated place or above 63°C unless:
- ♦ it is undergoing preparation for sale;
- ♦ it is exposed for sale or has been sold;
- ♦ it is being cooled under hygienic conditions as quickly as possible to a safe temperature, immediately following cooking or the final processing stage;
- ♦ it is reasonable to store it at a different temperature so as to be conveniently available for sale on the premises to consumers; or
- ♦ for the duration of its shelf life, it may be kept at ambient temperatures with no risk to health.

Reheating of food
   Food which has been heated and is thereafter reheated before being served for immediate consumption or exposed for sale, shall be raised to a temperature of not less than 82°C. (It is a defence to prove that reheated food could not be raised to 82°C without a deterioration of its qualities.)

Schedule 6 Restrictions on the placing on the market of raw milk or raw cream
   It is an offence for any person to place on the market raw milk or raw cream intended for direct human consumption.
   It is a defence to prove that the raw milk or raw cream was intended for export, for example, to England, Wales, Northern Ireland or other member state or third country as long as it complies with Regulation 253/2004 and any relevant national rules.

Offences and penalties
Any person guilty of an offence against these regulations shall be liable:
- ♦ on summary conviction, to a fine not exceeding the statutory maximum; or
- ♦ on conviction on indictment, to a fine or imprisonment for a term not exceeding two years, or both.

Regulation (EC) No 2073/2005 on Microbiological Criteria for Foodstuffs
   Food must not be placed on the market if it is unsafe (EC 178/2002). To comply with this requirement, all food business operators involved in the production and handling of food shall ensure that foodstuffs comply with set microbiological criteria. This is also a requirement in Articles 1 and 4 of EC852/2004. Microbiological criteria define a limit above which a food should be considered unacceptably contaminated with the micro-organisms for which the criteria are established. The latter are set out in Annex 1 of the Regulation and require a sampling and testing programme appropriate to the size and nature of the food business.

   Microbiological criterion means a criterion defining the acceptability of a product, a batch of foodstuffs or a process, based on the absence, presence or number of micro-organisms, and/or the quantity of their metabolites per unit(s) of mass, volume, area or batch.

   Food safety criterion means a criterion defining the acceptability of a product or batch of foodstuff applicable to products placed on the market.

Process hygiene criterion indicates the acceptable functioning of the production process. Such a criterion is not applicable to products placed on the market. It sets an indicative contamination value above which corrective actions are required in order to maintain the hygiene of the process in compliance with food law.

Batch means a group or set of identifiable products obtained from a given process under practically identical circumstances and produced in a given place within one defined production period.

Microbiological testing cannot, by itself, guarantee the safety of food because of the limitations of sampling and the uneven distribution of micro-organisms throughout the food. However, testing against microbiological criteria is one of the ways of validating controls in place within a food safety management system based on HACCP principles. Small food businesses such as caterers may be able to demonstrate compliance with the Regulation in other ways by implementing food safety management systems such as 'Safer Food Better Business' or 'CookSafe', without having to operate a sampling and testing programme. However, enforcement officers may decide to carry out testing to support evidence of compliance or non-compliance with food safety regulations if they identify a food safety problem or if they are carrying out food hygiene surveys.

Food Safety Act, 1990

As a result of EU Regulations, especially Regulation EC No 852/2004 and the food hygiene regulations 2006, many of the food safety provisions included within the Food Safety Act, 1990 are no longer applicable to the majority of food businesses. This Act is now primarily concerned with food standards.

The Act consists of four parts and five schedules.

Part I Preliminary

Section 1. Extends the definition of "food" to include water that is bottled for sale or used as an ingredient (water supplied to the premises is excluded).

Section 2. Extends the meaning of sale to include food that is offered as a prize or reward or given away in connection with any entertainment for the public.

Section 3. Food, or ingredients, commonly used for human consumption are presumed, until the contrary is proved, to be intended for sale for human consumption.

Section 5. "Food authorities" include the council of London and metropolitan boroughs, districts and counties.

"**Authorised officer**" means any person authorised in writing by a food authority to act in matters arising under the Food Safety Act, 1990.

Section 6. Requires every food authority to enforce within their area those parts of the act for which they are responsible.*

---

*The Food Safety (Enforcement Authority) (England and Wales) Order, 1990 (SI 1990 No. 2462) sets out the division of responsibility for enforcing the act.

Part II Main provisions

Section 7. It is an offence to treat food so as to render it injurious to health, with the intent that the food will be sold in that state. Regard shall be had to the cumulative effect of foods consumed over a long period.

Section 9. An authorised officer of a food authority may seize or detain food (for up to 21 days), which fails to comply with **food safety requirements** or that is likely to cause **food poisoning** or a **foodborne disease**. Food that is seized has to be dealt with by a justice of the peace. Any person liable to be prosecuted in respect of such food is entitled to make representations to the justice of the peace. If the food is not condemned, or detained food is cleared, compensation can be claimed. Any expenses incurred in the destruction of condemned food must be paid by the owner of the food.

If such food is part of a batch, then the whole batch shall, until the contrary is proved, be presumed to fail to meet the **food safety requirements**.

The Food Law Code of Practice provides guidance on the seizure and detention of food.

Section 13. Empowers the minister to issue an **emergency control order**, prohibiting the carrying out of commercial operations in respect of food, food sources or contact materials that involve an imminent risk of injury to health. Failure to comply is an offence and expenses for "work in default" can be recovered.

Section 14. It is an offence to sell, to the prejudice of the purchaser, any food that is not of the **nature** (different kind or variety) or **substance** (not containing proper ingredients) or **quality** (inferior, for example, stale bread) demanded by the purchaser.

Section 15. It is an offence to sell, display or have in possession for the purpose of sale, food that is falsely described or labelled, which is misleading as to the nature or substance or quality.

Sections 16, 18 & 26. Empower the ministers to make regulations, including those relating to composition, fitness, processing, hygiene, labelling and for securing food safety and the training of **food handlers** (Schedule 1).

Section 17. Empowers the ministers to make regulations to secure compliance with Community obligations.

Section 19. Empowers the Ministers to make regulations requiring the registration of food premises, and for the licensing of premises to secure compliance with food safety requirements or in the interest of public health or protecting the interests of consumers.

Section 20. Enables proceedings to be taken against another person when the offence was due to his/her act or default.

Section 21. It is a defence for a person to prove that he/she took all reasonable precautions and exercised all **due diligence** to avoid the commission of the offence, by himself/herself or by a person under his/her control.

In the case of persons not involved with the preparation or importation, for example, a retailer, charged with an offence under Sections 8, 14 or 15 it is a defence to prove:

- the offence was due to another person;
- that he/she carried out all reasonable checks or it was reasonable to rely on checks carried out by his/her supplier; and
- he/she did not know or suspect his/her act or omission would amount to an offence.

Section 23. Enables a food authority to provide training courses on food hygiene within or outside their area.

Section 25. Empowers ministers to make orders to facilitate the exercise of functions, i.e. to provide for the detailed enforcement of the act. The section also specifies the circumstances when it will not be an offence for a person to disclose information obtained by means of an order.

Part III Administration and enforcement

Section 27. Requires food authorities to appoint a public analyst.

Sections 29 & 30. Empowers an authorised officer to purchase or take samples of food, food sources, contact materials or any article or substance required as evidence. Such samples should, if considered necessary, be submitted for analysis by a public analyst or examination by a food examiner, who shall provide a certificate specifying the result of the analysis or examination.

Section 31. Empowers ministers to make regulations relating to sampling and analysis. (The Food Safety (Sampling and Qualifications) Regulations, 1990 (SI. No. 2463) lay down procedures for enforcement officers when taking samples for analysis or **microbiological** examination.)

Section 32. Empowers an authorised officer, on production of an authenticated document showing his/her authority, to enter any premises within his/her area at all reasonable hours to carry out his/her duties under the act. In the case of a private dwelling house, entry cannot be demanded unless 24 hours' notice has been given to the occupier. An enforcement officer is also empowered to enter any business premises outside his/her area for the purpose of ascertaining whether or not there are any contraventions of the act or regulations/orders made thereunder. Warrants may be issued by a justice of the peace authorising entry, by force if necessary, when entry is refused.

Authorised officers can inspect, seize and detain records, including computer records, required as evidence. Improper disclosure of information so obtained is an offence.

Section 33. It is an offence to obstruct persons executing the provisions of the act, including the failure to assist or provide information (unless it incriminates them) or the furnishing of false information.

Section 34. Prosecutions must commence before the expiry of three years from the commission of the offence or one year from its discovery by the prosecutor, whichever is the earlier.

Section 35. The penalty for obstruction on summary conviction shall be a fine not exceeding level 5* and/or up to three months' imprisonment.

The penalty for the remaining offences is:
♦ on conviction on indictment to an unlimited fine and/or up to two years' imprisonment; or
♦ on summary conviction to a fine not exceeding the relevant amount and/or imprisonment for up to six months. (In the case of Sections 7, 8 or 14 the relevant amount is £20,000; the amount for the other sections is level 5.)

Part IV Miscellaneous and supplemental
Section 40. Empowers the ministers to issue codes of recommended practice for the guidance of food authorities, as regards the execution and enforcement of the act and regulations/orders made thereunder.

Section 41. Requires food authorities to provide reports, returns and information to the minister.

Section 42. Enables the minister to empower another food authority, or one of his/her officers, to discharge the duty of a food authority that has failed to discharge that duty and the failure affects the general interests of consumers of food. The authority in default will be responsible for the payment of reasonable expenses.

Section 49. Relates to the form and authentication of documents.

Section 50. Relates to the service of documents.

Section 54. Deals with the application of the act to the Crown, i.e. the removal of Crown immunity.

Statutory codes of practice
Section 40 of the Food Safety Act 1990 and Regulation 24 of the Food Hygiene (England) (Scotland) (Wales) (NI) Regulations 2006 permit ministers to issue codes of practice for enforcing authorities regarding the execution and enforcement of food law.

Currently there is one Food Law Code of Practice to which enforcement authorities must have regard when discharging their duties. There is also additional advice provided in a Food Law Practice Guidance to which enforcement officers may wish to adhere.

The Food Safety (Sampling and Qualifications) Regulations 1990 (SI 1990 No. 2463)
These Regulations set out the procedures to be followed by enforcement officers, when taking samples for analysis or microbiological examination and also set out qualification requirements for public analysts and food examiners.

Regulation (EC) No. 853/2004 laying down specific hygiene rules for food of animal origin (Effective from 1 January 2006)
The Regulation repeals many of the vertical directives and regulations made thereunder relating to food of animal origin. It applies to both processed and unprocessed products of animal origin.

The requirements do not usually apply to food containing both products of plant origin and processed products of animal origin.

"Processed products" means foodstuffs resulting from the processing of unprocessed products. These products may contain ingredients that are necessary for their manufacture or to give them specific characteristics.

"Unprocessed products" means foodstuffs that have not undergone processing, and includes products that have been divided, parted, severed, sliced, boned, minced, skinned, ground, cut, cleaned, trimmed, husked, milled, chilled, frozen, deep-frozen or thawed.

"Mechanically separated meat" means the product obtained by removing meat from flesh-bearing bones after boning or from poultry carcases, using mechanical means resulting in the loss or modification of the muscle fibre structure.

The Regulation supplements Regulation (EC) No. 852/2004 and applies to slaughterhouses, for both red meat and poultry, cutting plants, game handling establishments, premises producing minced meat, meat preparations or mechanically separated meat, despatch centres for live bivalve molluscs, vessels used to harvest fishery products, establishments handling fishery products, milk production holdings, establishments for the manufacture of eggs and egg products.

The Regulation is concerned with:

♦ the hygiene of the above premises;
♦ the transport of live animals to the slaughterhouse (including domestic ungulates (domestic cattle and bison, pigs, sheep, goats and horses/mules), poultry and lagomorphs (rabbits and hares);
♦ the hygiene requirements for the production and harvesting of live bivalve molluscs, and fishery products including heat treatment, relaying of molluscs, health standards, wrapping and packaging, labelling, storage and transport;
♦ the health requirements for raw milk production;
♦ hygiene during milking, collection and transport;
♦ the microbiological criteria for raw milk;
♦ the hygiene of dairy products, including temperature requirements, wrapping and packaging and labelling;
♦ the hygiene requirements for the manufacture of egg products, including analytical specifications and labelling;
♦ the hygiene of businesses preparing frogs legs or snails;
♦ the hygiene requirements for the preparation of rendered animal fat and greaves;
♦ the hygiene requirements for businesses treating stomachs, bladders and intestines;
♦ the hygiene requirements for the manufacture of gelatin and collagen;
♦ slaughter hygiene, including cutting and boning;
♦ emergency slaughter outside the slaughterhouse and slaughter on the farm; the hygiene requirements during storage and transport;
♦ the hygiene requirements for cutting premises;
♦ the hygiene requirements for hunting and handling wild game; and
♦ the hygiene requirements of businesses producing minced meat, meat preparations, mechanically separated meat and meat products.

Milk and dairy processing

Milk and dairy processing operators must ensure that milk is quickly cooled to not more than 6°C upon acceptance, and maintained at that temperature until processed. Milk may be held at a higher temperature if processing begins immediately after milking or within four hours of acceptance at the processing establishment. Where milk or dairy products are subject to a heat treatment, food business operators must ensure that this conforms to the requirements in Annex II Chapter XI (EC852/2004). If raw milk is to be subject to a heat treatment such as pasteurisation, the food business operator must have regard for the procedures developed in accordance with HACCP principles to comply with the requirements in EC854/2004 and Article V in 852/2004. Food businesses manufacturing dairy products must ensure that immediately before processing raw cows' milk, used to prepare dairy products, has a plate count of less than 300,000 per ml at 30°C. If dairy products are to be produced from processed cows' milk, the plate count at 30°C must not exceed 100,000 per ml. The sealing of packages for the consumer must be carried out hygienically, immediately after filling in the establishment where the last heat treatment of liquid dairy products takes place, so as to prevent contamination.

The Regulation does not usually apply to retail businesses. However, it may apply to operations supplying food of animal origin to another establishment (excluding businesses only involved in storage or transport). In this latter case, specific temperature requirements outlined in Annex III will apply, for example offal<3°C and other meat<7°C.

The Regulation does not apply to retail premises supplying other retailers if the supply is marginal, localised or restricted.

Primary production for private domestic use and the direct supply of small quantities of product to the final consumer are also excluded. National rules are required to ensure the hygiene and welfare of such operations.

Food business operators shall:

◆ be registered with or approved by the competent authority;
◆ health mark products of animal origin placed on the market;
◆ ensure certificates or other documents accompany consignments of products of animal origin.

Regulation (EC) No. 854/2004 laying down rules for official controls on products of animal origin

This Regulation applies to the activities and persons within the scope of Regulation 853/2004. It includes requirements for:

◆ the approval of establishments (must comply with Regulations 852/2004 and 853/2004);
◆ the auditing and inspection of businesses to ensure compliance with the regulations;
◆ the inspection of red meat animals and poultry (ante-mortem and post-mortem) including animal welfare. Inspection includes microbiological criteria;
◆ live bivalve molluscs;
◆ fishery products;
◆ raw milk and dairy products;
◆ action to be taken in the event of non-compliance;
◆ tasks of the official veterinarian and official auxiliaries;
◆ lagomorphs (rabbits and hares); and
◆ farmed and wild game.

Regulation (EC) No. 882/2004 on official controls to ensure compliance with food law and animal health

The Regulation lays down general rules for the performance of official controls which should be carried out regularly, on a risk basis and with appropriate frequency.

Official controls, for example, audits, inspections, surveillance, verification, sampling and analysis should take account of:

♦ identified risks associated with food or food business;
♦ the food business operator's past record of compliance;
♦ the reliability of any own checks carried out; and
♦ any information that might indicate non-compliance

Official controls, except audits, should be without prior warning

The competent authorities shall ensure that:

♦ official controls on food are effective;
♦ staff have no conflict of interest;
♦ they have sufficient qualified and experienced staff;
♦ they have access to an adequate laboratory;
♦ they have appropriate facilities and equipment;
♦ they have the legal powers to carry out official controls;
♦ they have contingency plans in the event of an emergency;
♦ food business operators assist staff to accomplish their tasks;
♦ official controls are impartial, consistent and transparent; and
♦ staff receiving appropriate training.

Requirements are also included for:

♦ inspection methods and techniques;
♦ sampling and analysis;
♦ third country imports;
♦ fees or charges;
♦ registration/approval of food business establishments;
♦ community and national reference laboratories;
♦ multi-annual national control plans and reports;
♦ community controls, including audits of member states; and
♦ enforcement measures for non-compliance.

Animal By-Products Regulations 2005

Animal by-products waste is defined as entire bodies or parts of animals or products of animals or products of animal origin not intended for human consumption. Animal by-products waste originates, for example, from slaughterhouses and butchers, manufacturing businesses such as bakeries, catering establishments, and retail stores. The Regulations classify animal by-products into three categories according to risk to human health:

♦ Category 1 is the highest risk, covering animals suspected or confirmed as being infected with, for example, Bovine Spongiform Encephalopathy (BSE), specified risk material such as spinal cords.
♦ Category 2 covers high risk waste including, for example, condemned meat or fallen livestock (dying on the farm). These types of waste must not be disposed of to landfill but must be collected by licensed contractors, and be subject to processes such as

incineration, or rendering prior to incineration in plants approved under either the Animal By Products Regulations or under the EC Waste Incineration Directive.

♦ Category 3 is the lowest risk, covering 'former foodstuffs' that were previously fit for human consumption, including catering waste such as fully cooked foods, fruit and vegetables or foods past their 'use by date'. Catering waste cannot be fed to livestock and may be sent to landfill, for example, fully cooked meat and fish products. However, there are preferred alternative means of disposal that will be increasingly used, such as incineration, composting or biogas production. Fruit, vegetables, bread and confectionery products like cakes may be fed to livestock only if these foods have been strictly segregated from products of animal origin during production, storage and transport.

The Official Feed and Food Controls (England) Regulations 2007

These Regulations revoke The Official Feed and Food Controls (England) Regulations 2006. The Regulations implement the food and feed elements in the EC Regulation 882/2004 on official controls. Official controls are any form of check carried out by the competent authorities to establish whether or not feed/food business operators are complying with the Regulations. These checks include inspections, audits, sampling and analysis. The Regulations, in particular, cover enforcement of controls, to protect public health, over imports of feed and food of non-animal origin imported from outside the European Community. There is a prohibition on the import of food and feed that does not comply with food safety requirements as set out under Articles 14 and 15 of Regulation (EC) 178/2002. The 2007 Regulations designate the competent authorities responsible for the national official control arrangements required under the Regulations. These are The Food Standards Agency, local food authorities, port authorities and Her Majesty's Revenue and Customs.

The Quick-frozen Foodstuffs (England) Regulations, 2007

These regulations replace The Quick-frozen Foodstuffs Regulations 1990 (as amended) and apply only to England.

These Regulations apply to "quick-frozen foodstuff", i.e. food that has undergone "quick-freezing", whereby the zone of maximum crystallisation is crossed as rapidly as possible and is labelled for the purpose of sale to indicate it has been subjected to quick-freezing.

Quick-frozen foodstuff intended for supply to the ultimate consumer, must be suitably pre-packaged so as to protect it from microbial and other contamination and dehydration and must remain so packaged until sale. Such food shall, if intended for supply without further processing, be labelled with:

♦ an indication of the date of minimum durability;
♦ an indication of maximum advisable storage time;
♦ an indication of the temperature and the equipment in which, it is advisable to store it;
♦ a batch reference; and
♦ a clear message not to refreeze after defrosting.

Quick-frozen food must, subject to permitted exceptions, be maintained at or below −18°C. (Exceptions relate to local distribution and storage in retail display cabinets consistent with good storage practice.) Air temperature monitoring or recording instrumentation must be fitted by businesses involved with the storage, distribution and sale of quick-frozen foodstuffs. Records must be retained for at least one year.

All new temperature monitoring instruments must comply with specific European standards from 1st January 2006. Instruments installed prior to 1st January 2006 can be used until 31st December 2009. All temperature monitoring instruments must meet European standards from 1st January 2010. Food business operators must keep all relevant documentation showing that their temperature monitoring instruments meet the relevant European standards.

The Diseases of Animals (Waste Food) Order, 1973 (SI No. 1936)

All waste food, including meat or animal products, must be processed before being used for feeding to animals. It is an offence for any caterer to allow the removal of waste food unless the person holds a current licence issued by the Department of the Environment, Food and Rural Affairs (Defra). Conditions regarding the type and cleaning of vehicles used to convey waste are laid down. The order also applies to Scotland.

Office of Fair Trading

The Director General of Fair Trading is empowered, under Part III of the Fair Trading Act, 1973, to seek written assurances from a person carrying on a business, which has persistently operated to the detriment of the interests of consumers. Assurances are usually sought from persons who ignore repeated complaints, warnings and prosecutions.

Where a person refuses to give, or breaks, an assurance, the Director General can apply to a county court for a court order requiring the person to operate within the law, for example, by giving the court an undertaking to protect food from risk of contamination. If the person fails to observe the order, the court can impose very heavy penalties for contempt of court.

The Police and Criminal Evidence Act, 1984 (PACE)

Section 67 of this act requires persons charged with a duty of investigating offences to have regard to codes of practice made under Sections 60 and 66. The act, therefore, applies to environmental health practitioners/officers investigating contraventions of food legislation. The first code of practice came into force on 1 January 1986 and has superseded the judges' rules in relation to questioning of suspects.

Persons suspected of an offence must be cautioned prior to asking questions intended to obtain evidence for use in court. The Criminal Justice and Public Order Act, 1994 requires the caution to be in the following terms: "You do not have to say anything. But it may harm your defence if you do not mention, when questioned, something which you later rely on in court. Anything you do say may be given in evidence." (Minor deviations are allowed.) Persons must also be advised that they are not under arrest and may leave the premises but if they stay they may wish to seek legal advice.

In most cases involving food/hygiene offences, persons suspected of the offence will be invited to attend an interview at the council's offices and advised to discuss the matter with their solicitor, who may wish to be present at the interview. A signed record of the time and content of the caution, together with relevant information regarding the interview including all those present, must be retained. Tape-recorded interviews are commonly held.

Code B of PACE requires enforcement officers to go through a set procedure for obtaining warrants and conducting searches (and seizures), when there are grounds for suspicion that an offence has been committed. Provisions are available for enforcement officers to issue "Search with Consent" notices, which advise the person whose premises are being searched of his/her rights. However, these are only required to be issued in circumstances where the enforcement officer is acting outside of his/her statutory powers. Particular procedures are laid down for dealing with juveniles, the mentally ill or handicapped and persons requiring an interpreter, and obtaining written statements.

SPECIFIC LEGISLATION RELATING TO FOOD POISONING AND FOODBORNE ILLNESS

Public Health (Control of Disease) Act, 1984

Section 11. Medical practitioners must notify cases, or suspect cases, of food poisoning to the proper officer of the local authority immediately. This requirement also applies to medical practitioners in hospitals. Telephoned or faxed notifications are preferred.

Section 18. The occupier of any premises in which there is, or has been, someone suffering from food poisoning, must provide any information within his/her knowledge that may be required to enable the proper officer to prevent the spread, or trace the source, of food poisoning.

Section 20. The proper officer can require any person to discontinue work to prevent the spread of typhoid and paratyphoid, dysentery, scarlet fever, acute inflammation of the throat, **gastroenteritis** and undulant fever. The local authority must compensate persons suffering any loss by discontinuing their work.

The Health Protection (Notification) Regulations 2010 (SI 2010/659)

These Regulations, applying only to England, build on the concept of the Health and Social Care Act 2008, which introduced an "all hazards" approach to health protection. Doctors must notify the Proper Officer if they suspect a patient has a notifiable disease, as listed in the Schedule to the Regulations, an infection or is contaminated in a way which could present significant harm to human health. (This could include emerging pathogens, chemicals or radiation) Notification must be in writing within 3 days or less if it is urgent, in which case it can be oral. The Proper Officer must notify the Health Protection Agency. The Operator of a laboratory has a duty to notify causative agents isolated from human samples to the Health Protection Agency in writing within 7 days.

National Health Service (Amendment) Act, 1986

This act removed Crown immunity from health authority premises.

Section 1 removes Crown immunity from health authorities in England and Wales and health boards in Scotland for the purposes of the Food Safety Act, 1990 and any regulation made thereunder.

Section 2 removes Crown immunity from health authorities and health boards for the purposes of the Health and Safety at Work, etc. Act, 1974 and regulations, orders and other instruments made thereunder. The act also removes any protection afforded to members and officers of health authorities and health boards by Section 125 of the National Health Service Act, 1977 or *Section 101* of the National Health Service (Scotland) Act, 1978. In effect this means that, where appropriate, legal action can be taken against individuals for contraventions of food or health and safety legislation.

The National Health Service (Food Premises) Regulations, 1987 (SI No. 18)

These Regulations provide that health authorities in England and Wales shall be treated as both owners and occupiers for the purposes of food legislation.

The Health Protection Agency (HPA)

The HPA is a national organisation for England and Wales, created on 1 April 2003 to protect people's health by minimising risks from infectious diseases, poisons, chemicals, biological and radiation hazards. The HPA incorporates several organisations, including the Public Health Laboratory Service (PHLS), the Health Protection Agency Centre for Infections, the Central Public Health Laboratory and NHS public health staff responsible for infectious disease control. The HPA is responsible for: advising the government on public health matters;

delivering services to protect public health; providing impartial advice and information to professionals and the public; providing a rapid response to health protection emergencies; and improving knowledge of health protection through research, development, education and training.

THE LAW RELATING TO FOOD STANDARDS

Food standards requirements are those that relate to the labelling, composition, quality and fair trading of foods. Food standards legislation is usually enforced by trading standards officers except in London and in metropolitan and unitary authorities where environmental health practitioners/officers have this responsibility.

The food labelling law

The advertising, describing and presenting of foods is regulated by many pieces of legislation and the primary purpose of the law is to protect consumers.

Consumers need to be able to make informed choices about the food they buy. The law covers, amongst other things, claims for diet and health, labelling accuracy and cost. Regulations are subject to change as scientific evidence becomes available and while manufacturers are guided on how claims and information should be presented, much of what we see on food labels is down to the manufacturer.

The Food Standards Agency (FSA) ensures that mislabelling and misdescription does not take place. In some circumstances contraventions can be described as fraud.

The Food Labelling Regulations 1996

These Regulations require food packaging to be marked or labelled with certain information including:
- the name of the food;
- a list of ingredients (in order of quantity);
- the amount of an ingredient which is named or associated with the food (for example 80% beef in a pie);
- an appropriate durability indication (this may be use-by or best-before depending on the type of product);
- any special storage conditions – such as keep refrigerated or frozen;
- the name of the business and manufacturer and in certain cases information to enable quick traceability of the product;
- the place of origin, this information can also be used for ease of traceability;
- the process used in manufacture, for example, roasted or baked; and
- instructions for use to include the way the food should be cooked.

Expected shelf life	Date marking allowable
Highly perishable and likely to constitute an immediate danger to health.	Use-by 1st April 2011 (year can be omitted).
3 months or less.	Best-before 1st April 2011 (year can be omitted).
3 to 18 months.	Best-before 1st December 2012 or Best-before end of December 2012.
More than 18 months.	Best-before December 2012 or Best-before end of 2012.

Food Compositional Legislation requires that minimum quantities of ingredients are used in a food. The European Marketing Standards define how a food may be marketed including:

♦ fresh fruits and vegetables;
♦ canned sardines and tuna;
♦ olive oil;
♦ alcoholic spirit drinks: whisky, gin, and so on;
♦ eggs in shell;
♦ organic food; and
♦ foods of designated geographic indication or origin, such as Parma ham and West Country Cheddar.

A European-wide review of the general labelling of food including nutritional claims began in 2004. The outcome of this work will allow a single Regulation to be used for all member states of the European Union.

Nutritional labelling of food

The Food Standards Agency has agreed a system to be used for a consistent approach to front of pack labelling that will provide 'at a glance' information on labels about the nutritional content of foods.

Signposting aims to make it easier for people to choose a healthy diet. The 'traffic light' information will help consumers easily see how much fat, saturated fat, sugar and salt is in a product.

Much of the Food Standards Agency's work on the nutritional labelling of food allows manufacturers, retailers and caterers to use the information produced voluntarily. This work and consumer demands have, over recent years, driven standards on the clarity of information available on packaging and menus. An example of promotional work carried out after commissioned research findings is the salt reduction target. The FSA have now published revised salt reduction targets for 2012, and maintain their advice that everyone should aim to reduce their salt intake to less than 6g a day.

Health claims on food

Any manufacturer of food who wishes to make a health claim on their products must substantiate the claim with validated research. There are restrictions regarding the types of health claim which can be considered by the FSA and these include:

♦ nutrients which help growth, development and functions in the body; and
♦ nutrients which aid slimming, weight control and reductions in the sense of hunger.

The Plastic Materials and Articles in Contact with Food Regulations, 2009

These Regulations cover the manufacturing, conversion, use, importing or selling to commercial customers or consumers any food packaging materials and articles made from plastic for use in contact with food.

Any material which a food comes into contact with must not contaminate that food. The Regulations cover everything from small self-adhesive stickers on fruit and vegetables to containers which may be reused for another purpose other than the original design. Recent concerns over the substance bispenol-A in plastics have instigated further research into whether this chemical can affect the endocrine system in humans.

The Genetically Modified and Novel Foods (Labelling)(England) Regulations, 2000 (SI No. 768)

These Regulations require businesses to provide advice to consumers regarding the presence of genetically modified (GM) ingredients. In restaurants, cafes and the like, this advice may be provided verbally by trained staff, as long as a notice is displayed on the premises that informs customers how to obtain such information.

European Regulations 49/2000 and 50/2000 brought in additional requirements for the labelling of GM ingredients by manufacturers. The Regulations introduce a threshold of 1% adventitious contamination of ingredients by GM food, below which there is no requirement to declare the presence of the GM food. This can only be done where the manufacturer has taken positive steps to prevent such adventitious contamination from occurring.

The Food (Lot Marking) Regulations, 1996 (SI No. 1502)

These Regulations require that a unique identification or "lot" number be applied to prepacked foods. The purpose of this number, is to facilitate easy product recall in the event of a defect occurring in the food. The lot mark does not have to be understood by the consumer but if not obvious, should be prefixed with the letter "L". It is acceptable for the durability date to also act as a lot number.

Food additives are substances that are not usually consumed as a food on their own and are not normally used as an essential ingredient of a food. However, they are intentionally added to give the food certain desirable properties. Examples include colours, sweeteners and preservatives and their use in food is controlled by:

♦ the Sweeteners in Food Regulations, 1995 (as amended)(SI No. 3123)
♦ the Colours in Food Regulations, 1995 (as amended)(SI No. 3124)
♦ the Miscellaneous Food Additives Regulations, 1995 (as amended)(SI No. 3187)

Regulation (EC) No. 1935/2004 on Materials and Articles Intended to come into Contact with Foodstuffs

These Regulations set out the general requirement that all food contact materials and articles should not transfer their constituents to food in quantities which could endanger human health, or make the food otherwise unacceptable to consumers.

Regulation (EU) No. 1169/2011 on the Provision of Food Information to Consumers

These Regulations establish the general principles, requirements and responsibilities governing food. They apply throughout the food chain to all foods where information to consumers is provided.

THE LAW AFFECTING HEALTH AND SAFETY

The Health and Safety at Work, etc. Act, 1974

A major piece of legislation that incorporated a completely new approach to health, safety and welfare. It applies not only to employees but also to members of the general public and the self-employed. The Act created the health and safety executive, working under the direction of the Health and Safety Commission and also applies to Scotland. The objectives of the Act include:

♦ to secure the health, safety and welfare of persons at work;

♦ to protect non-employees and members of the public against risks to health and safety, arising from the activities of persons at work; and

♦ to control the keeping and use of dangerous substances.

The Act attempts to create an awareness of the need for high standards and encourages management to promote health and safety. Supervision and training must be given to all staff.

A further requirement is the duty placed upon employers to prepare and revise a written safety policy and to bring this document to the attention of their staff. Businesses with less than five employees are exempt. Safety policies should consist of three parts, the first part being a general statement of policy, the second the organisation and thirdly the arrangements for implementing the policy and bringing it to the attention of all employees. Unions may appoint safety representatives and, at the request of the representatives, an employer must set up a safety committee.

The Control of Substances Hazardous to Health (COSHH) Regulations, 2002 (as amended)

These Regulations introduce a legal framework for the control of substances hazardous to health in all types of businesses, including factories, farms, retail and catering premises, stalls and delivery vehicles. The Regulations set out essential measures that employers (and employees) have to take to ensure people are protected from the hazardous substances they may encounter.

Substances **hazardous to health** include substances labelled as dangerous (i.e. toxic, harmful, irritant or corrosive) pathogens and substantial quantities of dust.

Employers must carry out an assessment of all work that is liable to expose any employee to hazardous solids, liquids, dusts, fumes, vapours, gases or micro-organisms. The assessment involves evaluating the risks to health and then deciding on the action necessary to remove or reduce those risks. Equipment must be properly maintained and procedures observed. Employees should be informed, instructed and trained about the risks and the precautions to be taken. In some circumstances it may be necessary to monitor the exposure of employees and to carry out an appropriate form of surveillance of their health.

The Reporting of Injuries, Diseases and Dangerous Occurrences Regulations 2013 (RIDDOR 2013)

These regulations require employers to notify enforcing authorities of any death or specified injury in the workplace immediately, a telephone service is available for these reports only, telephone reports must be followed up with a written report within 10 days. Injuries which cause an employer to be off work or unable to carry out their normal duties for over 7 days also require a written report in this case within 15 days. Certain occupational diseases when notified to the employer by a medical practitioner require reporting within 10 days of diagnosis. Dangerous occurrences require reporting immediately. 2 online forms are available for reporting a F2508 for Injuries and Dangerous Occurrences and a F2508A for Occupational Diseases.

The Electricity at Work Regulations, 1989 (SI No. 635)

Employers must ensure electrical equipment and systems are in good condition and have been correctly installed. Fixed wiring systems and portable equipment must be checked and records of inspection and maintenance retained. Electricians employed must be competent.

The Management of Health and Safety at Work Regulations, 1999 (SI No. 3242)

These Regulations set out broad duties for employers, which include a requirement that the health and safety of employees is assessed, so that any necessary preventive and protective measures can be identified. Emergency procedures must be set up and employees must be given appropriate health and safety information and training.

The Workplace (Health, Safety and Welfare) Regulations, 1992 (SI No. 3004)

Aspects covered include maintenance of workplaces and equipment, ventilation, temperatures, lighting, cleaning, room dimensions, workstations, seating and sanitary accommodation.

The Health and Safety (Display Screen Equipment) Regulations, 1992 (SI No. 2792)

Covers the use of computers including the assessment of the workstation, eyesight tests, training and the provision of information.

The Provision and Use of Work Equipment Regulations, 1998 (SI No. 2306)

General duties are placed on employers to ensure that equipment is suitable for its use, in good repair and, where necessary, guarded. Employees must be given adequate information, instruction and training to use equipment.

The Manual Handling Operations Regulations, 1992 (SI No. 2793)

Include provisions relating to the avoidance of manual handling, assessment of risk, the reduction of risk of injury, training and information as to loads.

The Personal Protective Equipment at Work Regulations, 1992 (SI No. 2966)

These Regulations require employers to provide and maintain suitable protective equipment, following risk assessment. Equipment must be replaced when necessary and employees must be provided with appropriate information, instruction and training.

THE ENFORCEMENT OF FOOD LAW IN ENGLAND AND WALES

The Food Standards Agency (FSA) (www.food.gov.uk) was brought into being on 1st April 2000 by the Food Standards Act, 1999 and has the overall responsibility for the enforcement of food law. The FSA is accountable to Parliament but acts as an independent watchdog, with the intention of putting consumers first and being accessible.

The FSA's primary aim is to protect the health of the public in relation to food by:

- reducing foodborne illness;
- helping people eat more healthily;
- promoting honest and informative labelling to help consumers;
- promoting best practice within the food industry;
- improving the enforcement of food law; and
- earning people's trust by what they do and how they do it.

Food hygiene legislation is enforced by authorised officers (environmental health practitioners/officers) employed by local authorities or port health authorities, and food standards legislation is enforced by trading standards officers and technical officers.

Some legislation is enforced by both local authorities and by officers employed by central government. In the case of meat legislation, the Meat Hygiene Service (MHS), a division of the Food Standards Agency, regulates conditions in slaughterhouses, cutting plants and cold stores licensed under fresh meat legislation. The Dairy Hygiene Inspectorate (DHI), a division of Defra, is responsible for the inspection of dairy farms.

Food incidents and hazards

A food incident occurs when a food authority or the FSA becomes aware that food or its labelling fails to meet food law requirements. If the incident has the potential to cause harm to the customer it becomes a food hazard. Localised food hazards which are not considered serious are dealt with by the food authority. Serious localised food hazards, for example, involving *E. coli* O157, *C. botulinum* or *Salmonella* Typhi or affecting vulnerable groups, or likely to involve large numbers or deaths, and non-localised hazards when food is distributed beyond the boundaries of the food authority, should be notified to the FSA and other relevant agencies at the earliest opportunity by the quickest available means.

Food alerts and recalls

A 'food alert' is a communication from the FSA to a food authority concerning a food hazard. The authority may or may not be required to take action. The FSA also issues information on product recalls. The largest recall made to date involved the illegal carcinogenic dye Sudan 1 which was found in hundreds of food products in the UK in 2005.

The Food Law Code of Practice provides food authorities with guidance for responding to food alerts and recalls.

Product withdrawal

If a food business operator considers, or has reason to believe, that a food does not comply with food safety requirements, the food must be removed from the market. This includes foods that have left the immediate control of the initial food business up to and including the retail stage. If the food is regarded as unsafe, that is, 'injurious to health' (as defined in Article 14 EC178/2002), the food business operator must immediately inform the Food Standards Agency and the local food authority. Examples of non-conforming products that would be subject to withdrawal and/or recall include:

- failure to include ingredients on food labels that could cause an allergic reaction in susceptible consumers;
- chemical residues, such as veterinary medicines, present in food;
- natural substances present at above normal levels, such as histamine in fish;
- pest infestations, such as rodent droppings in cereals;
- wrong 'use by' dates on high-risk foods;
- presence of metallic or glass contamination; and
- presence of pathogens in food such as *Listeria monocytogenes* or *Salmonella*.

Failure to remove an unsafe product from the market can have serious consequences for public health in terms of illness and even fatalities. Adverse publicity may seriously damage a food business's reputation and result in heavy financial penalties resulting from criminal prosecution and civil claims, as well as the costs of recall. The risk of harm to the consumer increases the longer the product remains on the market. It is therefore essential that the unsafe food product is removed from the market as quickly as possible.

It is essential to establish a Procedure to ensure that a recall is carried out as quickly and effectively as possible. Management must have a written Recall Policy in place, and be fully committed to implementing and regularly testing an effective Recall Plan. The effective written Recall Plan consists of the following elements:

♦ a realistic up-to-date assessment of the significant hazards particular to the business, that could give rise to a serious product safety incident;

♦ a constituted Product Recall Team consisting of management representatives and other appropriate staff;

♦ a nominated coordinator or team leader with the responsibility for convening the team in the event of a serious risk to health being identified from a product through internal testing or as a result of a customer complaint;

♦ arrangements in place to ensure that all members of the Recall Team and all affected members of staff, have received appropriate training. Training will encompass what constitutes an incident that may require a withdrawal and/or recall of product, the overall purpose of the Plan, and individual responsibilities;

♦ arrangements made for the coordinator to immediately inform the Food Standards Agency and the Food Authority of the recall, as well as other business operators within the supply chain that might be affected by the recall, such as distributors and wholesalers;

♦ completion by the Recall team of all required incident reporting forms, for example, those required by the Food Standards Agency;

♦ action of recommendations for handling the incident from the Food Standards Agency and the local Food Authority;

♦ an arrangement to inform the affected customers as soon as possible of the need for a recall, the reasons for the recall and the procedure for the quarantine of affected product, collection from consumers, and return or destruction of affected product;

♦ arrangements made to inform the public through, for example, newspaper advertisements, internet, radio and television reports of details concerning the affected product, the reasons for the recall, and what action should be taken;

♦ arrangements in place for a regular testing of the product recall procedure, for example, every six months; and

♦ corrective actions after the incident to prevent a recurrence of the incident. This will include a review of food safety controls within the business including such issues as effective traceability of product.

The British Retail Consortium Guidelines - 'Product Recall Testing' states that a product recall simulation has an important role within the product recall plan.

The simulation should be carried out regularly, for example, every six months as appropriate. The exercise will give an insight into the effectiveness of the Recall Plan in the event of a serious incident. The purpose of the simulation is to identify areas of weakness in the Recall Plan and its operation, as well as training needs. Possible additional resources may be required such as a public relations agency or recall insurance. The effective recall simulation has the following elements:

♦ the scenario chosen for simulation should be as realistic as possible, and should involve an incident relevant to the business such as the presence of a specific contaminant in the product;

♦ only a few staff (possibly excluding the Recall Team) should know the date and time of the simulation;

♦ the simulation should be carried out at times when it can be tested effectively. Many incidents occur out of hours when the business is especially vulnerable;

◆ an independent observer of the exercise, such as a supplier is recommended; and

◆ after the exercise, the simulation should be critically assessed and corrective actions put in place.

SCOTTISH LEGISLATION

Scotland has a different legal system to England, being founded on principles originating from Roman law. In the event of any legal query, it is always best to consult someone conversant with the specifics of both the legal system and the subject matter in question.

Scottish legal terms

Licensing board

The statutory body made up of appointed councillors, which meets every three months to grant licences to premises serving alcohol.

Licensing committee

Part of a council's committee structure, which meets every committee cycle to grant licences to premises under the Civic Government (Scotland) Act. A major part of their time is taken in processing applications for licences not connected with the food trade, for example, taxi drivers.

Procurator fiscal (sometimes abbreviated to either procurator or fiscal)

A full-time head of a department servicing each sheriff court. Officers of this department are responsible for the independent assessment of the validity of all cases that would be taken to a sheriff court or above. Members of this department are responsible for the presentation of prosecution evidence to the court. The staff who present evidence to a sheriff court are solicitors.

Sheriff court

This court is the equivalent of the English stipendiary magistrates' court. It is the usual location for all food cases to be heard.

Sheriff

A full-time paid official presiding alone over a sheriff court. They are usually QCs with considerable experience. The sheriff principal is the senior sheriff for a Scottish region.

High Court

If a sheriff feels that a case merits a greater sentence than he/she is empowered to impose, he/she can refer it to this court for sentence. The court moves around the country on circuit. It is presided over by a single Scottish Law Lord and has 15 jurors.

Court of Session

The highest Scottish Court – presided over by three Scottish Law Lords.

The Public Health etc. (Scotland) Act 2008

The Act places a duty on Scottish Ministers, health boards and local authorities to protect public health.

Part II of the Act is concerned with notifiable diseases. A list of notifiable diseases, including food poisoning, and foodborne diseases is provided in Schedule 1. Medical practitioners must notify the relevant health board, in writing, within 3 days if they suspect that a patient is suffering from a notifiable disease. In urgent cases oral notification must be made as soon as reasonably practicable.

Part III of the Act is concerned with public health investigations and **Part IV** the health functions of health boards.

Section 33 enables a health board to apply to a sheriff for a person to be medically examined when they know or suspect a person has an infectious disease and there may be a significant risk to public health.

Section 37 empowers a health board to exclude from any place, a person who has an infectious disease (or has been exposed to the organism) and there is a significant risk to public health.

A health board may compensate a person subject to an exclusion order who incurs any loss in complying with the order.

Licensing (Scotland) Act 2005

This Act makes provision for regulating the sale of alcohol, and for regulating licensed premises and other premises on which alcohol is sold.

Section 50 of the Act requires that a premises licence application must be accompanied by a food hygiene certificate, if food is to be supplied on the premises.

The food hygiene certificate is issued by the Food Authority (environmental health department) confirming that the premises complies with the relevant food safety regulations relating to construction, layout, drainage, ventilation, lighting, water supply, sanitary and washing facilities.

Civic Government (Scotland) Act, 1982

This Act requires the licensing of street traders, market stalls, places of public entertainment and late night caterers. These licences are issued by the licensing committee of the relevant unitary authority.

The Food Hygiene (Scotland) Amendment Regulations 2012 (2012 No.75)

These Regulations:
  (a) extend the use of remedial action notices (RANs) to all food businesses in Scotland (not just "approved premises");
  (b) provide for compensation to be payable to a food business operator for loss suffered by complying with a remedial action notice, which is subsequently cancelled by a court on appeal; and
  (c) add a new Schedule 6A which specifies the requirements for the special health mark.

16 Managing food safety:
being a manager edited by Euan MacAuslan

Background

Any successful food business is likely to have a quality management system. Quality, applied to food, can be considered to be all aspects of it including taste, nutrition, safety, etc. A component of any quality management system is likely to be its food safety management system and in many countries some or all of this will need to be documented. For example, EU Regulation 852/2004 Article 5 (1) states that:

"All food businesses, other than primary producers, put in place, implement and maintain a permanent procedure or procedures based on HACCP principles, including documentation and records".

However there is considerable flexibility in the requirement for documentation and record keeping which should be "commensurate to the size and nature (level of risk) of the business". A small catering business will not require as much as a very large manufacturer or a large supermarket chain. The latter may have thousands of branches and will need to try to ensure that all of them use the same procedures and this will require written instructions.

Food safety management can be defined as "the coordinated activities to direct or control food safety" or "the attainment of food safety goals in an effective and efficient way through planning, staffing, organising, directing and controlling its resources". Documented systems will be required to achieve these aims and to comply with any relevant legislation. However, many companies, for marketing or other purposes, are choosing to exceed legislative requirements and have their systems externally audited and accredited against international third party standards (see quality systems accreditation and the role of the Global Food Safety Initiative (GFSI)). Having a documented system in addition to any legislative or other requirements demonstrates planning and control, helps to ensure consistency and repeatability as well as helping to ensure "due diligence".

Having such a system should set out how food safety in the business is to be achieved. However, having such a system in place does NOT in itself guarantee that it will be followed and management systems are intimately linked to the food safety culture within the business. It is a combination of these two factors which will deliver the appropriate "operational food safety performance" (OFSP), i.e. those hygiene behaviours which are necessary to produce safe food, comply with legislation and **are routinely used and practised**. Once a food safety management system is devised it will need to be fully implemented, maintained and reviewed.

Management systems

Depending on their size and complexity businesses can design their food safety management system using a range of different approaches. One thing that is critical is that there is a "Documented food safety management system" and NOT a "System of food safety documents". This sounds like a play on words but it contains an important message. The documents must be part of a "living and breathing" system which is practical and used by people (food safety is "everyone's" responsibility and not just a select few) and not simply a collection of documents (in some cases plagiarised from another company) placed on a shelf and pulled down when an auditor arrives.

One approach is to classify them as "manufacture control systems" (PRPs, HACCP, etc.) with others being "Corporate control systems" (e.g. product traceability and recall, document control). The former is more product specific the latter company wide. Another approach is to simply divide them into HACCP and PRPs and both these terms are widely used. In an ISO 22000 based system an additional category "Operational prerequisite programmes" (OPRPs) are also used. However, in larger businesses these two or three methods used to group control measures should be supported by microbiological testing programmes and increasingly by a documented risk assessment. One type of hierarchy of management systems:

*These are indicative examples only of possible prerequisite programmes and are not a complete list.

The numbers and types of systems in use will relate to the size and risk of the company and its products. In many catering operations HACCP and PRPs may be combined in a single system, e.g. Safer Food Better Business with no microbiological monitoring. Whereas in a large manufacturing operation all of the above may be used and required.

At the end of the day it is important to remember what the objective of the documented system is:

"A measure of a good safety management system is not how complicated you can make it but how simple it can be to ensure food safety" (Owen - Griffiths)

Each area identified as needing management is likely to have documentation at a number of levels. Policies are aspirational statements of intent, form the basis for actions and decisions, guide staff and are signed by executive management, e.g. Food Safety Policy or Cleaning Policy. They set out in writing what the business wants to achieve with respect to that specific element of food safety, e.g. cleaning. These should not be copied from other companies or taken lightly as they will form the basis of a company's food safety culture and are likely to be audited. The Level 2 documents describe the processes used to achieve the policy objectives, who is responsible, contain manuals of what is to be undertaken, the procedures used and

FOOD SAFETY MANAGEMENT SYSTEMS
– LEVELS OF DOCUMENTATION

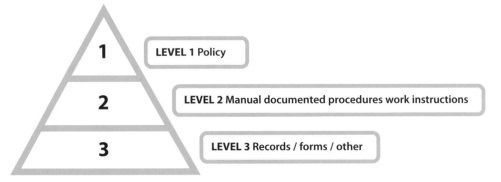

1 LEVEL 1 Policy

2 LEVEL 2 Manual documented procedures work instructions

3 LEVEL 3 Records / forms / other

how they will be implemented, e.g. cleaning procedures and schedules containing standard operating procedures (SOPs), work instructions, specifications and standards etc. Level 3 documents relate to the record keeping, receiving checklists, ongoing monitoring results, e.g. from cleaning and process control charts. These should be completed correctly (not made up or filled in dishonestly "before or after" the event) signed, dated and stored appropriately e.g. critical control point monitoring records, time/temperature records, corrective action reports. All the documents in the system require scrupulous control e.g. to make sure the ones in use are current, widely circulated and out of date documents are withdrawn.

Whilst food safety is everyone's responsibility, in anything other than the smallest business, it needs to be managed and this is likely to be a team approach. Members of this team should act as a role model for others, be trained in food safety, committed to ensuring the company's policy objectives are achieved, empowered with responsibility and take a lead in ensuring compliance with legislation. Meetings of the food safety management team should be documented, transparent and auditable.

SOME AREAS LIKELY TO BE DOCUMENTED/REQUIRE DOCUMENTATION

- Food safety policy
- Organisational structure and responsibilities
- HACCP plans
- Internal audit
- Purchasing
- Supplier approval
- Documentation control
- Training
- Corrective and preventative action
- Traceability
- Product withdrawal and recall

- Complaints procedure
- Maintenance programmes
- Food safety management meetings
- Microbiological testing
- Cleaning
- Waste management
- Pest control
- Product control
- Control of non-conforming product
- Process control
- Personal hygiene
- Risk assessment

"It is noble to be good, and it is nobler to teach others to be good – and less trouble!"

Mark Twain

Being a manager

In 2001 the Food Standards Agency identified that 87% of all food businesses in the UK employ less than ten employees. However, no matter what the size of the business, staff management is an essential part of food safety management. It is surprising how many managers can communicate well with their customers but who have difficulty in communicating with their employees. Poor communication is the main reason for staff dissatisfaction or non-conformance with expected standards.

What is management? Perhaps it could be described as "the art of getting four food handlers to do the work of four food handlers." It is unfortunately more than being based on a simple definition. One possible definition of a managerial role is "any role in an organisation where the occupant is authorised to get part of his/her work done through employed subordinates for whose work s/he remains wholly accountable." Every manager is a supervisor and every supervisor is a manager.

Essential management skills

"Give a man a fish and you feed him for a day. Give him a fishing rod and teach him how to use it and you feed him for life." (Chinese proverb). An effective manager is someone who can get people to do something correctly on the first time of asking, and in future, without continuous supervision. To do this he/she needs essential management skills.

Essential management skills required include:

♦ leadership;
♦ motivation;
♦ training/coaching;
♦ team building;
♦ communication;
♦ cultural awareness;
♦ influencing; and
♦ monitoring and evaluation.

With these skills, plus suitable and sufficient food safety training, a manager of a food business will be able to identify and implement food safety training needs. He/she will also be able to:

♦ observe employee performance;
♦ question or survey employees to identify areas of weakness;
♦ review past food safety inspection reports for violations related to employee performance; and
♦ test employees' food safety knowledge.

An IPM consultative document, *"Managing People - The Changing Frontiers",* published in Personnel Management in November 1993 stated that *"There is an increasing awareness that all managers will need a better understanding of how to manage and lead people…However…the implications in terms of training and development required are not fully appreciated."* Unfortunately, the quotation is equally relevant today, particularly in small and medium-sized food businesses.

Consider one of the essential management skills listed above. "Influencing" – what does it mean? Below are some words which will help the manager influence people at work. The questions posed are deliberately provocative. They may raise further questions about a manager's level of training and ability to put into practice what has been taught.

Watching: If you want to learn how staff work just watch them. Consider how many times they wash their hands in a food room, or how they use disposable gloves. There is no need to talk to them. Behavioural patterns will be picked up and identified. How do the staff interact? Is the sous-chef setting an example to the kitchen porter? Do the staff shut the back door after delivery?

Listening: Does the Head Chef motivate or shout at staff? Do employees comment on how senior managers never set an example when in a food room? Maybe if someone identifies food safety issues, such as incorrect temperatures or mouldy stock then he/she needs to talk to someone. How is the message conveyed and acted upon? Does the manager acknowledge the contribution made to food safety by the staff member who raised the issues in the first place?

Understanding: Employees have now been watched and listened to. Build up some kind of picture of the food handlers that matter. Are they managing to succeed or succeeding to fail in their post because, for instance, no-one in the business has helped them apply the knowledge gained on a course in a supervised practical way? Perhaps the observer may like to reminisce about the practical application difficulties he/she ran into as a trainee.

Be part of the picture: How do the staff see the observer? Never sets an example? Leads by example or by "Do as I say but not do as I do"?

Influencing: Establish how much influence you may have. How is it applied and received? Has the influencing succeeded or failed? Maybe there was a better or alternative way that the situation could have been handled.

Changing: Food safety practices will not be changed overnight. It is better to lead and motivate employees. Begin with something small and use that as a building block. For instance it could be handwashing, changing the uniform or encouraging team hygiene discussions.

An essential management skill is *communication*. Just how well qualified is a manager to understand cultural and religious issues which may affect the work of a food handler without involving the individual concerned? How much training has the manager received to effectively assess the English capabilities of a food handler who does not speak, read or write English as a first language – especially when that manager may have been born outside the UK? What about assessing special educational needs of food handlers such as dyslexia, dyspraxia, colour blindness? How many food handlers have suffered attending food safety courses because their manager did not enquire about language support, special considerations or opportunities for any reasonable adjustment? How many managers have assumed an individual can read the joining instructions for a course or follow the documented food safety management system without taking into account these issues? Britain has perhaps the worst record in the European Union of failing to have an adequate workforce who can speak two or more languages. An inability to communicate leads to lost opportunities, isolation and suspicion. Figures from the ONS (September 2010) identified that 75% of food handlers in London did not speak English as a first language. Failure to communicate represents a major food safety issue. A good small business manager should not shy away from acting as a mentor.

Currently, there is no legal requirement for managers of food businesses to show that they are competent or qualified in any of the essential management skills. If there was, then managers would have to become more involved in the practical implementation of food safety matters by themselves and their employees. An issue encountered in the UK's food businesses is the high turnover of employees – especially first tier workers. Men and women with poor literacy are least likely to be in full-time employment at the age of thirty. 63% of men and 75% of women with very low literacy skills have never received a promotion. (Literacy: State of the Nation, March 2010, National Literacy Trust). But even these days with a highly mobile workforce, managers and supervisors from a range of countries come and go. Whilst learning English and broadening their experience as managers they must not neglect their responsibilities in managing food hygiene.

Perhaps the worst employees within a food business to train are managers. One of the main, but not only, reasons is because they feel they have more to consider in running the business than just food safety. However, changing management attitudes and food hygiene practices are equally as important as changing attitudes and practices of other employees within the business. An effective manager will:

♦ set the required food safety standards;
♦ provide the resources to achieve standards;
♦ implement and devise systems to achieve standards (HACCP for example);
♦ inform and discuss standards with employees;
♦ motivate and train employees;
♦ provide effective supervision and instruction; and
♦ monitor, review and improve performance.

Take a look at the next two sections and compare the diagrams. Consider what sort of management attitudes count. Decide if you are a good or bad manager. Without an open mind this is something difficult to do. After reading the whole of this book go back to the diagrams and decide what you do well and what you could do better if you had the support. Contact your local college, Business Link, Institute for Leadership and Management, or go on-line for management advice and training.

What sort of management attitudes count?

A good manager will think about and demonstrate some of the following characteristics (which include good management techniques) and thereby work towards high standards of food safety:

A bad manager will adopt unacceptable food safety practices and neglect needs of staff. This leads to a lack of or breakdown in a food safety culture within a business, and the consequences that go with it.

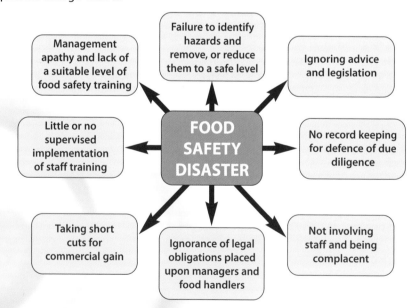

For the Defence of Due Diligence to succeed a manager must demonstrate how "all reasonable precautions" have been taken. In respect of training it is simply not enough to send employees on a classroom-based course without identifying the training needs of individuals and giving them the post-course practical supervision and guidance that is essential. Unless employees are in jobs which require knowledge of multi-skilling, the traditional one-day classroom-based courses may be totally inappropriate as a stand-alone solution. The manager should also consider training records. Sound systems that can be demonstrated have two key advantages: a reduced risk of prosecution, and a higher standard of food safety. These in turn lead to increased staff motivation and customer confidence.

Are food business operators and managers food handlers?

The legal definition of a food handler is "any person in the food business who handles food, whether open or packaged (food includes drink and ice)". Compare this with the definition given in the Institute of Food Science and Technology's "Food Hygiene Training: A guide to its responsible management" (1992). The definition reads:

"A food handler means any person involved in a food business who, by his actions, or management, or decision, or advice, can influence the hygiene or quality of any food handled by that business at any stage."

Therefore using this definition "any person" could be extended to the General Manager, Purchasing Manager, Supervisors and others involved in the operation of a food business - not just chefs, catering staff and kitchen porters. Managers of food businesses need to demonstrate an awareness of current legal requirements for food safety and standards. In addition, they must demonstrate that they have taken appropriate steps to inform, train, keep up to date and supervise their employees. The manager of a food business may also be the food business operator. A 'food business operator' means the natural or legal person responsible for ensuring that the requirements of food law are met within the food business under his/her control. This relates to managers or employees in charge at the time of the local authority's food safety inspection. Food safety knowledge is not enough on its own to meet food safety law requirements. Only when combined with effective management skills will a properly functioning food safety culture prevail in the organisation or business concerned.

Consider the following:

A kitchen porter attends a one-day Level 2 Award in Food Safety in Catering course, and a waiter attends a Level 1 Award in Food Safety in Catering course. The premises manager who sent them has not received any training higher than Level 2, and this was four years ago. A chef in the 100-seated restaurant with a brigade of 12 staff only has the equivalent of Level 2 training. In both cases neither manager has up-to-date or a level of training that could be described as "commensurate with their work activities". Neither of the managers may be able to help the newly trained staff put the theory into practice, and both may have slipped back into old and bad food hygiene practices. The result of which could mean that the staff become de-motivated and there is no visible room for improvement.

What are the best solutions in addressing the problems faced above?
♦ The general manager or food business operator needs to develop a training strategy and seek advice about effective training methods.

- If the subordinates are to attend courses they should be relevant to their work activities and their managers should explain what help is to be given on their return to implement practical application of theory taught. They could put together a "commitment to action" plan. This will enable managers and subordinates to work together to practically improve standards.
- Consideration needs to be given to determine if the course booked was suitable for a job-specific employee or a multi-skilled employee.
- Managers need to enquire about the subject content. For instance, if they run a vegetarian restaurant why, for example, are the candidates being tested on their knowledge of defrosting chickens?
- Both the manager and chef would benefit from the equivalent of Level 3 or 4 food safety training that is more suited to their roles as managers.

Many organisations and businesses will have a key link between the staff and management which should not be overlooked if a business is to be well managed and the burden of responsibility can be diluted to allow other management functions to take place but not at the expense of food safety. That link is in the form of a supervisor. Supervisors may be considered as members of the junior management team. They act as the link to enable food safety policies, practices, controls, and training to be implemented.

Failures of management

Ineffective management is brought about by a number of pressures which include lack of higher and lower management support, insufficient or inadequate training, and disagreements with those above and below their position, work overload, undefined work role, and changes in technology which are not accounted for.

As part of Richard North's thesis (A management perspective on the causation of food poisoning, 1991, referred to in Chapter 1) he proposed ten "rules" for managers and supervisors. These do not just call upon food safety knowledge and its application, but they also call upon effective people management skills:

1. Carry out risk assessments before making changes to any ingredients, processes or recipes, and implement any food safety requirements identified.
2. Be prepared for breakdowns, crises or unexpected changes - plan alternative arrangements for production, storage and/or delivery of high-risk foods.
3. Check whether your management systems or structures penalise staff for maintaining good hygiene - do your staff lose out if they stick to the rules?
4. Make sure bad practice and hazards can be notified to people who have the authority to deal with these problems, and pass back information on hazards down the chain.
5. Ensure that systems and processes are regularly reviewed by persons who are fully competent to recognise hazards and report on them.
6. Rapidly and fully investigate any food safety incidents (including food poisoning), evaluate the findings and ensure that any changes needed are fully implemented.
7. Identify and eliminate conflicts between "best practice" and actual working practices, whether arising from unit design or management/commercial requirements.
8. Establish safe procedures for all high-risk operations and check to see that they are carried out consistently.

9. Prevent the misuse of equipment and do not allow (or require) production levels over and above the safe capacity of the operation.
10. Make sure your staff (and your under-managers/supervisors) have the means, knowledge and resources to carry out your instructions on good practice.

It should be emphasised that this model does not replace food handlers' rules. It is intended to provide a specific focus for those in management positions in food businesses. However, the formulation of such rules, based on the identification of management perspective causal factors, in food poisoning incidents, offers exciting possibilities for improved prediction and control of food poisoning risks in commercial premises. The model above will only be effective if managers have received proper food safety and management skills training. An example of failings in both areas resulted in 19 patients dying and 455 falling ill from salmonella at the Stanley Royd Hospital, Wakefield in 1984. Over a hot summer's weekend there was a lack of communication between senior management and the kitchen staff.

Thinking tactics

Reuven Feuerstein is generally acknowledged as the founding father in the field of determining skills and strategies necessary to make a person a free and independent thinker. The trainer and manager can use Feuerstein's Top Ten Thinking Tactics to help with problem solving in a business. These are:

1. Pinpointing the problem.
2. Systematic search.
3. Planning – rehearsing a way forward before attempting a solution.
4. Check and change – constantly checking on the way something is done and accepting the need for change.
5. Correct communication – making instructions and wishes clear.
6. Comparison and contrasting – seeing fine points of difference between apparently similar material and events.
7. Getting to the point – through the initial fog of confusing information, by comparing and contrasting, trying to detect a common theme.
8. Using several sources – being able to think about more than one piece of information at a time, combining the pieces to make sense of the whole task.
9. Self Awareness – becoming aware of an individual's learning style.
10. Setting your own targets – understanding what your purpose is and having ideas about what you want to achieve.

Managers need to know about the concepts, skills and strategies involved in human problem solving. Food handlers will be motivated, develop self-esteem, and be better learners if they have a better understanding about when they are doing a task and why they are doing it.

Suggested management responsibilities

Managers who work in food businesses have a number of food safety responsibilities which need to be combined with management skills. Examples of these are below:

♦ Be aware of their own and their employees legal requirements in respect of instruction, supervision and training to ensure that these are commensurate with their work activities.

- Understand the legal requirements for minimum standards of food safety. Managers should strive for higher standards.
- Set a good example to subordinates. For example handwashing on entering a food room.
- Involve staff in the food safety management decisions and discuss food safety issues at team meetings. Give employees the opportunity to make suggestions at meetings, face to face, in a suggestions book, or to participate in completing food safety management procedure documentation. These methods are often disregarded as a training method. But they can be put down to a learning experience for both employees and line managers.
- Managers need to keep up to date. Attend refresher or higher levels of training, go to hospitality and food safety exhibitions, attend conferences or local food clubs, and make use of the internet.
- Learn how to carry out food safety audits or inspections and observe individuals performing food handling tasks. Ask questions to assess the need for further appropriate training interventions.
- Learn basic training techniques suitable for both training room style and one-to-one coaching or for in situ workplace training.
- Help individuals who may not speak English as a first language, or those with special educational needs and learning difficulties. Do not assume that the person in front of you has the ability to attend a course that you have chosen for him/her without first making an informed decision.
- Use a food safety management procedure based on the principles of HACCP as a management tool. This will help to highlight training, instruction and supervision needs.
- If interviewing new food handlers test them on their food safety knowledge rather than taking any food safety certificate they may possess on face value.

Management skills required for food business managers

Occupation	Examples of skills required
Managers of medium and large food businesses	Leadership skills Company strategy Quality standards Service commitments Change management Effective enhanced communication skills Management and leadership skills Level 3 or 4 qualification in food safety
Owners and Managers of small and medium food businesses	Multi-skilled Customer liaison Cost management Team management Management and leadership skills Customer services management Change management Equal opportunities training Basic training skills Levels 3 or 4 in food safety Developing food safety cultures

Getting the best out of your food handlers

Many organisations encourage managers to use tried and tested techniques to get the best out of their employees. Examples of these are as follows:

♦ Provide job variety to prevent fatigue and to improve employee inspiration.
♦ Promote a team spirit.
♦ Be firm but supportive in supervision.
♦ Gain staff loyalty by providing relentless support to your food handlers.
♦ Observe and learn from overseas trained individuals.
♦ Be aware of religious and social backgrounds by removing barriers.
♦ Know about your food handlers and help them to overcome learning and language difficulties.
♦ Develop a mentor/mentee food safety scheme.
♦ Create a training regime and keep your employees informed about why, where and when it may involve them.

Where next?

Mike Jacobs in his Safe food handling: a training guide for managers of food service establishments (Geneva, WHO, 1989) recommends that managers should organise training of their food handlers, and themselves by taking responsibility to supervise operational procedures. In summary, as part of an effective hygiene management system managers will also need to:

♦ be adequately trained in food safety and people management skills;
♦ know how to supervise staff in food safety matters;
♦ be responsive to suggestions and comments which may contribute to improved standards;
♦ develop a food safety culture;
♦ review systems and change practices or processes as necessary;
♦ help staff to turn the theory of food safety into meaningful practice; and
♦ keep up to date with good food safety and people management skills.

If you cannot manage people do not expect to see effective changes in your operation's food safety management systems. As Goethe put it: "Knowing is not enough; we must apply. Willing is not enough; we must do."

17 *Food safety culture* edited by Professor Chris Griffith

Background

A good food safety management system meets all necessary legal requirements and should ensure safe food is produced. However, failure to comply with quality and food safety management system requirements can be both widespread and problematic. Inspections within the public sector and audit reports from the private sector have identified in businesses varying and often frequent degrees of non-compliance with food safety requirements. Repeated research studies have indicated that food safety is not just a microbiological problem but that it also has a major behavioural component. It has been suggested that 97% of food poisoning outbreaks traced to non-manufacturing food businesses involve a food handler error/malpractice. A number of food poisoning outbreak investigations in food manufacturing have identified an inappropriate food safety culture as a contributory factor.

Why food handlers choose not to implement known hygiene practices has been studied and approaches to predicting behaviour examined. Such studies indicate that whilst some aspects of behaviour relate to the individual over 40% of non compliance may be related to the prevailing food safety organisational culture. Culture is to do with groups of people (not individuals alone) within a business, how they interact, how they behave and what an organisation is about. Food handlers are only as hygienic as the business requires, allows and encourages them to be and this is influenced by the facilities provided as well as the management systems and culture in place.

ORGANISATIONAL AND FOOD SAFETY CULTURE

The concept of workplace culture affecting employee behaviour, whilst largely ignored in the food industry, has been studied in a number of other industries, including aviation and nuclear for over 30 years. Interest in food safety culture only started about 5-6 years ago but is rapidly increasing. Calls have been made for more specific research on food safety culture although results from the limited research to date indicate the concept and its importance is poorly understood by all levels in industry including middle and top management.

There are many definitions of culture, although there is no universally agreed definition of organisational food safety culture or indeed the interaction between this and organisational food safety climate. However, one possibly over-simple practical interpretation can be "the way we do things round here" (as opposed to systems which specify what should be done) although in practice it is recognised to be more complex and deep rooted. In turn culture is a reflection of the attitudes, beliefs and behavioural norms of food handlers, supervisors and managers.

ALL food business possess a "food safety culture". This may be known and understood by management or, as is more likely, will be unknown. Of importance is that culture does not happen by accident but is created by management. In a positive food safety culture hygiene requirements are considered to be of a high priority to the business, this is understood by the work force, they are actively achieved and there is a high level of compliance with documented requirements. There is a willingness to learn from mistakes/errors with strategies in place to prevent problems recurring. A negative food safety culture is where food safety has a low priority and is not perceived to be of prime importance, resulting in frequent non-compliance with good hygiene practices or documented requirements. A negative culture may be passively acquired as the result of ignorance of its importance or lack of management interest in food safety which is then transmitted to individual food handlers. However, a negative food safety culture can also be actively acquired by food handlers as a result of inappropriate management decisions/directives e.g. management considers that, other business aspects such as the need to save money, cut corners in order to maximise profit or meet demand at any price, are more important than food safety.

Any business's food safety culture is likely to lie on a continuum from very positive to very negative. Towards the centre of this continuum lies a neutral point and this is often a characteristic of the culture found in some larger businesses especially those with multiple outlets or sites (linked to the strength of the culture). Such companies have become complacent about their systems believing them to be foolproof and all that is required to produce safe food. This complacency has possibly in part been fostered by the drive in previous years towards improving management systems to get external accreditation and the belief that a set of papers/documents is all that is needed to produce safe food.

A strong food safety culture is consistent throughout the organisation, centered around "core" values with the beliefs about their importance strongly held across all levels within the business. A weak food safety culture may be fragmented across different levels, composed of smaller subcultures where food safety is perceived to be of greater or less importance.

It is possible to assess and map a company's food safety culture using strength and positivity and in turn use these as the basis for formulating an improvement strategy.

What is food safety culture?

There is no universally accepted definition of food safety culture although one of the most widely used is:

"the aggregation of the prevailing relatively constant, learned, shared attitudes, values and beliefs contributing to the hygiene behaviours used in a particular food handling environment". (Griffith)

This definition tries to encompass in a simple way a range of complex issues. Points to note are that:

♦ food safety culture represents the collective attitudes, values and beliefs, i.e. those held across a range of food handlers and not those specifically held by individuals. Beliefs and attitudes in turn feed into behaviour, i.e. food safety practices used;

♦ a business's food safety culture is learnt by new employees when they first start and can override any individual food safety beliefs they may have about what the correct hygiene behaviour is or should be in that particular business. New employees perceive the culture as the "correct way to think and behave"; and

♦ food safety culture is relatively constant and does not vary widely over time.

Research into organisational culture has identified a wide range of contributing factors. These have been considered in many different combinations and using different approaches although they all generally (the vocabulary used may differ) cover the following topics. Each one of these major categories can itself be composed of a wide range of sub-factors:

- ◆ leadership and standards;
- ◆ communication;
- ◆ commitment;
- ◆ resources;
- ◆ assessment and monitoring; and
- ◆ consequences.

Creation of a food safety culture is a management responsibility. Within a business this culture or cultures (a business can be composed of many different subcultures) may vary between units, depending on local managers and can vary between different levels within an organisation. Research undertaken within one multinational food company indicated there was a significant difference in the perception of the prevailing food safety culture between different levels within the same organisation giving rise to a plurality of cultures with top management having an "optimistic" perception of reality. The food handlers themselves had a very different perception of what hygiene practices they should be practically implementing. The role of top management involves a number of key elements, including culture, strategy development and measuring cultural performance, although these are often unfortunately neglected and poorly understood within businesses.

Having an appropriate positive food safety organisational culture is essential to maintaining a successful brand and top management needs to be aware of their own role and responsibilities and to equip their managers with the skills to create and maintain a positive food safety culture at unit level.

DEVELOPING A POSITIVE FOOD SAFETY CULTURE

Leadership

There is often much talk about food safety management but relatively little said about food safety leadership, yet leadership is an essential component of food safety culture. Leadership in food safety starts at the top and then permeates down through the different management/supervisory levels. Food safety leadership is NOT the same as food safety management although the two do overlap.

"Managers do things right, leaders do the right things" (Bennis)

The above quote is one simple attempt to distinguish between them, although in reality it is far more complex. Some implied key differences are that leadership is more about setting direction, selecting strategies, communicating with and motivating. One definition of food safety leadership is:

"The extent to which business leaders are able to engage staff in behaving hygienically and comply with the business's food safety goals /visions/standards and requirements" (Griffith)

To succeed, food businesses need both strong food safety management and strong food safety leadership – neither is inferior to the other.

The word leadership is derived from the Anglo Saxon word " lead " meaning path or road and leadership implies a sense of direction. A leader must have a strong commitment to food safety, perceiving it to be of prime importance to the business with vision of the type of food safety behaviours they wish implemented within their business. However, what is important is that leaders do not just say that food safety is a key business priority but they must be able to prove it. Unfortunately a strong commitment to food safety may be overridden by a competing desire to maximise profit and save money at any cost or achieve other business targets. Leaders must then formulate goals and objectives in order to achieve their vision. Goals should lead to the production of safe food, be realistic and achievable by staff. Setting unattainable goals which cannot be achieved only encourages a culture of non compliance.

Standards

Leaders need to set high standards (which in turn can be used to set high expectations). This is reminiscent of the head chef who like a general, used to line staff up before every shift and inspect their personal hygiene standards. Food handlers need to know the standards that are expected of them and take pride in their achievement. This is of particular importance when hiring and inducting new staff so that they can be exposed to the food safety standards that will be required of them. Leaders must themselves display the highest standards of food safety – if hand hygiene or protective clothing is required for entry into a food area they themselves must follow the requirements i.e. lead by example and ensure there are no exceptions. One very important function a new leader must assume is, where necessary, to change an existing inappropriate food safety culture.

Communication

A leader's requirements/standards in turn need to be communicated to individual food handlers. They will not be hygienic if they do not know how to behave and what is expected of them. Training is obviously a crucial element in this but in many businesses tends to be "a one off" whereas in reality it is ongoing. Communication about food safety and its importance should be continuous and can take many different forms (see Chapter 14). More obvious forms are reminders such as posters. However, these may have an initial impact but soon become part of the "wallpaper" and such reminders need to be simple, specific and changed regularly. More recently novel communication strategies including food safety "info sheets" available to all staff, have had some success. These vary in content but can include discussions of recent food poisoning outbreaks, or interviews and pictures of victims. However, food handlers often pick up on the more subliminal communication messages sent by managers who refuse to invest in necessary food safety requirements citing their "perceived high cost" and the "need" to save money as reasons. Staff will soon pick up on the fact that food safety is of secondary importance. These may not just be limited to equipment but also to staffing. One of the main reasons given by food handlers for non compliance with food safety requirements is lack of time – often linked to low staffing. One department in a delicatessen normally had 4 staff working – yet they all went for lunch between 12 and 2 pm, sometimes with only 2 on duty, leaving the counter short staffed at its busiest time for serving customers. A particular problem in food service might be that staff are forced to decide whether to implement known food safety practices or not comply with hygiene requirements in order to serve a possibly growing queue of impatient customers. Another example of miscommunication occurred when a business awarded staff a bonus for reducing food wastage. In itself this may be a good ambition but in at least one instance it led to staff re-coding out-of-date food to give it a longer shelf life (hence compromising food safety) in order to achieve lower wastage targets – with staff believing this was the company priority not food safety. Communication of food safety issues should be planned (should have a strategy) and make use of a range of different mechanisms and methods relevant to that business. Methods should be selected to both increase awareness as well as others designed to lead where necessary to behavioural change. Of crucial importance is that information flow is in all directions – not just top down. Staff must be prepared to report problems they have to their superiors

Commitment

Making sure that each member of staff has a high standard of food safety commitment and is provided with all the necessary resources (time, equipment, consumables, etc.) will lead to strong positive food safety culture and high standards of compliance. Food safety commitment can be defined as:

"a measure of the extent (qualitative and quantitative) to which a person considers their own values and beliefs over food safety correspond or align to those stated by the organization and the extent to which they want to follow company requirements" (Griffith)

As stated earlier food safety commitment starts at the top and permeates down through all levels and this is especially important in larger organisations or ones with multiple outlets. It has been shown hygiene practices, based on the same set of documents, can vary widely between different units depending on the manager in charge. Managers and supervisors must remove any barriers to compliance and motivate staff to be hygienic (see consequences) and the staff themselves should take pride in achieving or exceeding the hygiene expectations of their managers. Good hygiene should be the "norm" and staff should feel free to make suggestions on how hygiene (and compliance) can be improved. They should feel free to bring inappropriate behaviour to the attention of their colleagues or supervisors without fear of reprisals or sanctions. Staff should be encouraged to report poor practices and a clearly understood line should be drawn amongst staff about what is acceptable and what is not. This should give rise to an open and transparent culture with "peer pressure" to act in a hygienic manner.

Resources

Staff can only be as hygienic as the environment and available resources allow them to be. Failure to provide adequate resources can be a major barrier to the practice of good hygiene. All food handlers need to practise good hand hygiene yet one auditor found that out of 7 wash hand hygiene stations 5 had empty paper towel dispensers. At least 2 had been like this for several days. When asked whose responsibility it was to ensure they were checked and refilled an adequate reply was not forthcoming. This illustrates the need to manage the provision of hygiene resources and this should be part of a company's documented management system. A poor working environment and premises design can make it very difficult for staff to be hygienic and in particular make the prevention of cross-contamination very difficult. Adequate provision of resources not only ensures that everything necessary to be hygienic is available but also sends out a message to staff and demonstrates the commitment that management have to ensuring food safety is practised

Assessment and monitoring

A crucial factor is knowing whether the communicated food safety goals are being implemented. Internal audits can to an extent measure compliance, although there is always the concern that what is seen during the audit may not be representative of the normal way of doing things. It is known that some staff may falsify or make up records or behave differently during an audit/inspection – ironically demonstrating they know what they should be doing but choosing not to do this all the time. Auditing can therefore usually only assess food safety climate – the outer more visible level of food safety culture – not the deeper layers of food safety beliefs and values. A good food safety leader knows "how" their staff feel and think as well as behave both during and between audits and inspections. A variety of ways can be used to assess food safety performance other than direct observation including, for example, frequency of handwashing by monitoring soap/paper towel usage. Nevertheless assessing what is routinely undertaken by observation is crucial to creating a positive food safety culture providing it is linked to feedback and consequences relating to an individual's food safety behaviour.

Consequences

High standards of food safety behaviour should be rewarded and poor standards of behaviour sanctioned. When rewarding people for being hygienic most minds immediately turn to financial rewards. Whilst these can be important – awarding bonuses for achieving food safety targets, other factors can be equally or even more important. It has been said that financial rewards can help to stop people becoming dissatisfied but may not in themselves make them "more" satisfied. Other aspects such as perceived status and value at work, job satisfaction, responsibility and recognition can be more powerful motivators than money. Businesses can develop a range of strategies to ensure that good hygiene is rewarded in a non- financial sense. This can range from simple regular praise and positive feedback when good behaviour is observed to the use of badges and prizes with a high workplace profile. Different food handlers will respond in different ways and a good supervisor or leader will know how to motivate specific individuals. Poor food hygiene behaviour needs to be sanctioned but prior to any sanctions, which could ultimately lead to warnings and dismissal, a good leader will investigate why an individual is not complying. In many cases there may be good reasons, which need to be corrected, for them not being as hygienic as they should. Any barriers to staff practising good hygiene need to be removed.

Continuous improvement

Food pathogens and the foods causing food poisoning are changing and evolving, this means food safety practices need to be constantly reviewed and updated. Food safety culture can change over time with new staff and managers in place and companies must always assess and modify culture and continually improve. It is important to remember that the type of food safety culture created in, and possessed by, a business is a matter of choice. The top manager/person in charge must make that choice!

Appendix I Food processing

These days, there is not only a greater consumer demand for quality foods but also for foods that are convenient to prepare and serve. Many consumers are particularly concerned that the **food** is as "natural" as possible and free from food **additives** and **contaminants**. This is not always easy to achieve. Virtually all foods that we consume are subjected to some form of **preservation**, even if it is only chilling, packaging in a modified gas atmosphere or freezing. There is a demand for "fresh food" but usually to present such food to the consumer, who might be miles away from the production point, requires the application of very sophisticated food technology. This may range from plant breeding to give the desired properties, for example, seedless grapes or potato varieties suitable for crisp making, to packaging in containers that will control the ripening rates of fruits.

The technology of food processing draws upon the principles of chemistry, physics and biology, along with those of engineering, to ensure **safe food** manufacture.

The general techniques of preservation used in food processing have been dealt with in Chapter 7. This section is primarily concerned with specific processing techniques and foods.

HEAT PRESERVED FOODS

These foods are made **commercially sterile**, principally by the application of a predetermined amount of lethal heat. Various types of hermetically sealed containers are used such as cans, retortable plastic trays and pouches, to prevent post-process **contamination**. The use of the term "canning" tends to be generic to all these types of packs. Unlike most other forms of preservation, the food inside the can remains an ideal medium for **bacterial** growth. It is therefore imperative that:

♦ the heat process is adequate to destroy all **pathogenic** and **spoilage** organisms, which are capable of growth within the **anaerobic** conditions of the can;

♦ the closure of the can precludes the entry of **micro-organisms**; and

♦ the post-process handling of the can prevents damage and subsequent contamination.

The most heat-resistant pathogenic organism is *Clostridium botulinum*. This bacterium will not grow below a **pH** of 4.5 (or an a_w of 0.94). Consequently, when determining the heat process, regard must be had for the pH of the can contents. Foods with a pH of less than 4.5 are known as acid foods and those with a pH of more than 4.5 are termed **low-acid foods**.

Fruits have a pH of less than 4.5 and consequently only receive a relatively low **pasteurising** heat process. Vegetables and meats have pH's much higher than 4.5 and are given a process known as a "botulinum cook" to render them commercially **sterile**.

Before canned food is heat processed, it is normally prepared in some way. The actual preparation will vary depending on the food type but the following flow chart shows the usual processes involved.

Exhausting

Exhausting is only carried out for cold fill ingredients. The exhausting process is usually done by blowing steam into the headspace (space above can contents at top of can). This has the effect of producing concave ends on the can after processing and cooling, due to the

A SCHEMATIC DIAGRAM OF CANNING OPERATIONS

Canning plant

Cans | **Raw materials**

Delivery ▶ **Storage** ◀ **Delivery**

Cans
inverted and washed

or air rinsed using de-ionised air

Raw materials

Preparation

*Fruit & vegetables - washing, peeling, grading and blanching
Meats - cleaning, boning, cutting and curing
fish - washing, degutting and brining
Milk products - filtering, standardising and homogenising*

Filling
(normally hot)

Inspection
(including metal detection and magnets)

Sealing
to create vacuum and coding

Double seam to hermetically seal the can

Processing:
The "BOTULINUM COOK"

This is normally done in retorts, hydrostatic pressure vessels or horizontal cookers

Cooling

Chlorinated water

Shrink wrapping ◀ **Labelling** ◀ **Drying**

Storage ▶ **Distribution**

SHOP

©Highfield.co.uk Ltd 2014

formation of a vacuum when the steam condenses. The removal of oxygen from the can also reduces the **risk** of oxidative corrosion of the inner can surface and helps to maintain the nutritive quality of the food.

Coding and sealing
After filling, the cans are coded, usually by video jet, and then sealed before being sent for retorting.

Container seams and seals
The construction and size of the container seams are very important to ensure integrity and safety of the food. The diagram below shows the construction of a can seam.

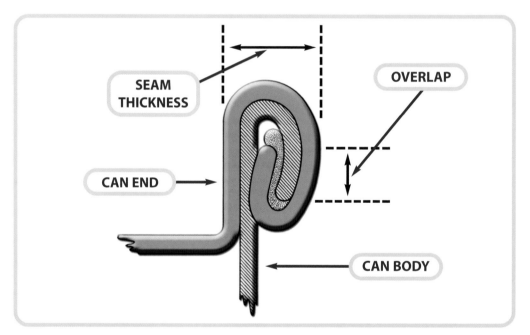

Processing
The actual process time and temperature must be determined for each can size of low-acid food and will depend on such things as weight, composition, headspace, viscosity, presence of preservatives and intended storage conditions. Scheduled processes for all low-acid products have been established by the Campden and Chorleywood Food Research Association.

The minimum safe thermal process for a low-acid canned food, is one which would reduce the chance of survival of one **spore** of *Clostridium botulinum* to less than one in 10^{12} (considered to be the equivalent of 121°C for three minutes, i.e. an F_0 value of 3.0).

F_0
F_0 is the measure of the lethal effect of processing. It is the sum of the lethal effects of a heat process equated to minutes at 121°C. An F_0 of 6.0 is therefore equivalent to heating at 121°C for six minutes. The higher the temperature, the shorter the time of heat processing necessary to achieve the same degree of microbial destruction.

The can contents are heated by either convection or conduction. The headspace is critical if the pack heats by convection, for example, mixed packs of solid and liquid, such as potatoes in brine, as there will be dimensional increases and movement of contents.

For solid fill packs, such as corned beef, heat by conduction and headspace is not an issue.

To destroy the more heat-resistant food spoilage organisms, such as *Bacillus stearothermophilus*, a process in excess of an F_0 of 3.0 must be given.

SOME TYPICAL EXAMPLES OF F_0 VALUES*

Product	F_0
Canned salmon	7.0
Canned strawberries	1.0 (high-acid product)
Beans in tomato sauce	5.0
Whole chicken in broth	4.0
Sterilised milk	5.0
Dog food	14.0

Various types of retorts depend on different heating media including steam, hot water, steam-air mixtures, and "raining" hot water systems using recycled water. The use of microwaves has now been reported in Europe, but so far not in the UK. The validation and control of these heating systems are essential to the assured achievement of sterility.

Cooling

After the heating process, the containers must be quickly cooled with chlorinated water. It is essential that cooling water is brominated or chlorinated before use to ensure its freedom from bacteria. A **contact time** of 20 minutes must be allowed to ensure complete **disinfection**. The level of chlorine in the water should be kept as low as possible (two to five parts per million) to avoid the corrosion of cans. A residual level of 0.5 ppm is normally the target. Pasivation (prevention of electrolysis) and rust inhibitors may be added to the water. Regular samples, both chemical and bacteriological, should be taken from the cooling water. To avoid post-process contamination, handling of the hot cans must be prohibited. Cans should be cooled to between 32°C and 43°C to prevent "stack burn".

After processing, the cans dry naturally, are labelled and then shrink wrapped. The cooled and labelled cans must be completely dry before storage so as to prevent any rusting. Cans that are made of sheet steel with only a thin layer of tin on each side, may suffer damage which results in rusting of the iron.

Underprocessing

Underprocessing may result in the production of gas, due to the action of the surviving micro-organisms, which causes the can to swell. The contents may also undergo some other undesirable changes without gas production. In the latter case, spoilage is only detected after opening, these cans are known as flat sours.

* Source: Introduction to Food Technology, Open Learning Module, Humberside University, 1989. ISBN 0 903057 06 9.

Sources of contamination in canneries

Contamination may be either bacteriological, chemical or physical (see chapter 5).

Bacteriological contamination

Contamination or spoilage of food in cans may occur because of:

♦ defects in the can such as unsatisfactory welding, pinholes in the plate or a damaged flange;
♦ a change in raw materials with an increased loading of **thermophilic** organisms;
♦ poor hygiene prior to filling, which may result in a build-up of thermophiles in the blancher;
♦ underprocessing or uneven processing;
♦ post-process contamination, for example, because of a defective end-seam or infected cooling water;
♦ storage temperatures above 45°C, allowing the multiplication of thermophiles; or
♦ damage to the can in distribution, storage or retail.

If the examination of blown cans reveals the presence of one or two heat resistant thermophiles, then underprocessing is the likely cause. If a general flora of **mesophiles** is isolated, this usually indicates leaker spoilage. Apart from the **moulds** *Byssochlamys fulva* and *B. nivea*, which are occasionally responsible for the spoilage of canned fruit, **yeasts** and moulds are relatively easy to destroy by heat. They are usually present because of post-process contamination. Similar faults may also occur with plastic containers.

Post-process contamination

The greatest care must be taken after heat treatment, especially whilst the can is still warm and wet, and before the sealing compound has hardened. Bacteria are capable of being sucked into visually satisfactory cans through microscopic holes in the seams. If these bacteria are spoilage or pathogenic organisms, problems will occur.

Post-process contamination may arise because of:

♦ contaminated or unchlorinated cooling water;
♦ contaminated runways;
♦ operatives handling warm and wet cans; or
♦ damage to cans, especially while still warm.

It is recommended that cooling water contains less than 100 organisms per ml and that post-process conveying systems have less than 100 organisms per 500 square millimetres.

Blown cans

Cans may be blown, for example, because of carbon dioxide produced by micro-organisms or because of hydrogen production. The vacuum created during processing normally ensures that the can ends are concave, but the production of gas eventually destroys the vacuum and the can becomes blown. The first stage of this positive pressure is known as a flipper. This is a can with a slightly distended end, which can be pressed back to the normal position with very light pressure. When the end is banged it flips out. The next stage is known as a springer. This is a can with one end distended, which when pushed back to the normal position, causes the other end to spring out. A hard swell is the final stage of blowing when both ends of the can are permanently distended.

COMMON THERMOPHILIC SPOILAGE BACTERIA OF CANNED FOODS

BACTERIUM	Foods commonly spoiled	REMARKS
Aerobic spore formers *Bacillus stearothermophilus* *Bacillus coagulans*	Low-acid foods, such as vegetables. Low and medium acid foods, especially foods such as tomato juice.	Can referred to as a flat sour. Acid produced but no gas production and no swelling of the can.
Anaerobic spore formers *Clostridium thermosaccharolyticum*	Meat, fish and vegetables.	Carbon dioxide and hydrogen produced, contents often have a cheesy odour.
Desulfotomaculum nigrificans	Meat, fish and vegetables.	Hydrogen sulphide gas produced but is soluble and may be absorbed, so preventing swelling. Rotten egg smell. Contents may go black as the hydrogen sulphide reacts with the iron of the container.
Clostridium sporogenes	Fish and meat.	Gas production, contents foul smelling.

Hydrogen swells

This condition results from the action of the contents on the internal surface of the can. It is a problem with acid foods such as canned tomatoes and fruits. Not only is there a build-up of hydrogen causing the can to pass through the flipper, springer and hard swell stages, but also lacquer stripping and a metallic **taint** of the contents occur, along with a high tin content of the food (maximum limit is 200mg/kg). Hydrogen swells are indistinguishable from a can damaged by microbial action and the cans must be discarded.

Certain cans containing foods rich in sulphur, for example, corned beef, sardines and legumes may show a dark staining of the inner surface of the can. This is due to the formation of hydrogen sulphide during processing, which reacts with the tin lining to give tin sulphide. Whilst looking unpleasant, it will normally present no danger to the consumer unless the can has become perforated.

Overfilling

Due to the expansion of the contents during heating, the can becomes strained and distorted. These cans must be regarded with suspicion and can only be confirmed by physical or bacteriological checks of the contents.

Damage

Damage is caused by a variety of reasons including perforation by nails, sharp crates, dockers' hooks, knives used to open cardboard cartons in shops, and denting due to mishandling cases. Considerable bacteriological significance should be placed on damaged cans: leakage introduces an infection from the atmosphere and possibly subsequent bacterial spoilage and/or mould growth. Cans with badly damaged seams should be rejected. External wetting, for example, in flooding or fire-fighting, may re-introduce the risk of post-process contamination through seams, especially on handling.

Incorrect storage

Apart from thermophilic spoilage, high temperature storage may result in internal corrosion. Furthermore, if conditions are too humid, external rusting and eventual pinholing of the can may occur.

Pasteurised canned foods

As discussed earlier, most low-acid canned foods are processed to a minimum standard of the "botulinum cook". However, some foods if fully processed, would be inedible. One example of this is canned cured ham. This product only receives a pasteurisation process (a centre temperature of about 70°C). This means that other precautions are necessary to ensure that it does not become a source of *Clostridium botulinum* **food poisoning**. It is the presence of curing salts (sodium or potassium nitrite and sodium chloride), which help to inhibit the growth of botulinum organisms and make canned cured ham a safe food. The combined inhibitory effect of curing salts and sodium chloride on spore germination is referred to as the perigo effect. A sufficient combination of heat process temperature and curing salt level may render the product ambient stable. Lesser treatments may necessitate the use of subsequent chilled storage. It is essential to first evaluate the stability of new products, in order to establish if chilled storage is needed.

Retortable pouches

The development of thermally processed foods in flexible packaging was led by the United States during the 1970's. The aim was to serve the Apollo astronauts with high quality, nutritious food, which did not require a "toothpaste tube" style system. The commercial development of the pouches and much of the filling/sealing equipment has been led by Chinese and Japanese manufacturers. It is only in the last few years that UK processors have exploited the potential of flexible packaging.

The pouch itself is a tri-layer polymeric construction with the most common laminate layers being:

Outer layer:	Polyester (affords tensile strength to the pouch).
Middle layer:	Aluminium foil (acts as an effective oxygen, light and water barrier).
Inner Layer:	Polypropylene/polyolefin (acts as an inert barrier in contact with the food).

In common with traditional metal cans, flexible pouches are double-sealed. However, this sealing is achieved by applying heat and pressure to the pouch in two stages. The first stage creates a seal 3mm in width, whilst the second stage creates two additional seals, 5mm either side of the first one. The filling of these pouches can have a direct influence on the integrity of these seals. Splashing of the product needs to be avoided during the process.

Once filled, the pouch is processed in a horizontal orientation that offers the highest surface area to volume ratio, typically the pouch presenting a profile only 19mm thick. This thickness, provides the processor with the opportunity to use a shorter **sterilisation** time than with the same product weight in a traditional can, resulting in greater retention of nutrients, flavour and taste whilst still achieving a suitable F_0. However, the shorter time/temperature regime can present a problem if the pack is poorly loaded into the formers or is otherwise distended. An increase in pack thickness of just 2mm can reduce the F_0 value from 3.0 to an unsafe 1.6, leading to the possibility of *Clostridium botulinum* spore survival. Furthermore the fill weight must be tightly controlled to prevent over-filling, which would alter the surface area/volume ratio and also reduce the F_0 value of the product.

Aseptic production technology

This differs from canning as the sterilisation of the product is carried out as a separate operation from package sterilisation, prior to filling aseptically. Various types of heat exchangers are used for these continuous flow processes. Ohmic heating may be used, whereby heating is induced by passing a high-voltage electric current directly through the food material. It is then packed under aseptic conditions into sterilised packaging containers, for example, multi-layered plastic film bags. The finished product has an extended **shelf life** and is stable at **ambient temperatures**. Ohmic heating may be combined with other forms of heating, such as plate heat exchange systems.

DAIRY PRODUCTS

The processing and testing of milk

In 1887, Anthony Hailwood produced sterilised milk and by 1920 pasteurised milk had been developed. From this time, there has been a gradual improvement in the quality of milk and **hygienic** methods of production. The most important factor in securing improvements, has been the introduction of refrigeration on the farm and the use of insulated tankers to transport milk to the dairy. Moreover, better use of refrigeration and reducing contamination during packaging and bottling have extended the shelf life of milk even more.

Most milk sold in this country is heat-treated by one of three methods:

◆ pasteurisation;
◆ sterilisation; or
◆ ultra heat-treated (U.H.T.).

Pasteurisation ensures the destruction of pathogens and most **vegetative organisms**. However, heat-resistant organisms and spores survive, which accounts for milk souring after a few days. Sterilisation and UHT treatment destroy all organisms and this ensures a prolonged shelf life, even without refrigeration. It is essential that the pathogenic contamination of heat-treated milk is prevented, as the milk, devoid of its natural flora, is more likely to support the rapid multiplication of the pathogens.

The production of pasteurised milk

The heating process for producing pasteurised milk in the UK was based on the destruction of two potential pathogens, namely, *Mycobacterium tuberculosis/bovis* and *Brucella abortus*. Whilst destroying these organisms and many other pathogens and spoilage organisms, pasteurisation is a relatively mild heat treatment and has a minimal effect on the flavour and nutritional value of milk. However, even with pasteurisation, up to 10% of many vitamins will be lost.

Pasteurised milk is usually produced by a heat treatment involving a high temperature for a short time (HTST process, which involves heating to at least 71.7°C for 15 seconds), or a process using different time/temperature combinations to obtain an equivalent effect (e.g. the Holder Process involves 63°C for 30 minutes).

Pasteurised milk must:

♦ show a negative reaction to the phosphatase test and a positive reaction to the peroxidase test (high temperature pasteurisation produces a negative reaction to both tests); and

♦ meet certain microbiological standards in random sampling checks carried out at the treatment establishment, including the absence of pathogens in 25g and only one out of five samples with a coliform (per ml) count of less than 5.

Milk arriving at the dairy is weighed and checked for its quality, for example, added water, the presence of any blood and its microbiological load. It is then placed in holding tanks where it will be mixed with milk from many other farms, so ensuring a consistent product. It is then filtered to remove gross contamination and pumped to a balance tank, which maintains an even flow rate through the next part of the HTST plant where the heat exchange takes place.

The cold milk entering the plant is preheated by the hot milk leaving the processing plant. It is finally heated to the required temperature of 72°C by using hot water at around 75°C. At no time do the water and milk come into direct contact. The heat exchange takes place through thin stainless steel plates. Regular checks of the unit, particularly the seals, must be made to ensure its integrity. The heated milk flows through a holding tube for 15 seconds, before passing a flow diversion valve. If the milk is below 71.7°C, a bell rings, the milk is diverted back to the balance tank and goes through the whole process again. If the temperature is at or above 71.7°C, the milk passes out of the heat exchange, heating up incoming milk.

To preserve the cream line and reduce caramelisation, dairies operate as close as possible to 72°C for 15 seconds. After heat treatment, the milk is cooled rapidly to below 10°C. This prevents the multiplication of heat-resistant organisms, maintains the cream line and improves the keeping quality. As a temperature of 72°C stimulates the germination of any *Bacillus cereus* spores that may be present, cold storage is particularly important to prevent the multiplication of the vegetative bacteria produced. After cooling, the milk is bottled or filled into cartons and stored under refrigeration. Strict **stock rotation** is essential to avoid complaints of souring, especially during the warm summer months. Regular testing ensures that the milk has a reasonable shelf life and has been given a satisfactory heat treatment.

The methylene blue test

This dye reduction test is a chemical method of assessing the microbiological quality of the milk. Methylene blue is added to the milk which is incubated at 37°C for 30 minutes. If the milk/methylene blue is decolourised in this time, it indicates that the level of micro-organisms present is unacceptably high and the milk is rejected. The test does not differentiate the type of organism causing the contamination.

The phosphatase test

This test is used to determine whether or not the milk has been pasteurised satisfactorily and to ensure that raw milk has not been added after processing. Such contamination is likely to occur if the seals on the heat exchange units are defective. The test relies on the fact that the enzyme phosphatase, which is present in raw milk, is destroyed by effective pasteurisation.

The chemical di-sodium para nitrophenyl, which turns yellow if phosphatase is present, is added to the milk and the depth of colour is examined against a standard sample using a comparator. A figure of more than 10g represents a failure of the test.

The production of sterilised milk

The prolonged life of sterilised milk is obtained at the expense of flavour changes. This is due to the caramelisation of lactose, and results in a loss of nutritional value (approximately 50% of vitamins are destroyed). Sterilised milk can be produced by heating milk at around 110°C for 30 minutes in a hermetically sealed container, the seal of which must remain intact during such heat treatment, or by use of the continuous flow process.

The turbidity test

This test is to measure the degree of protein **denaturation** that has taken place. When heated to a sterilisation level the proteins, albumen and globulin, are denatured. If ammonium sulphate is added, the protein casein is precipitated and can be filtered out. The filtrate will be clear and if this is further heated to boiling point, it will turn cloudy (turbid) if any protein has not been already precipitated. Thus, a turbid solution indicates that the original milk had not been adequately sterilised.

Ultra heat treated milk

UHT milk is produced by a continuous flow process with the application of a very high temperature for a short time (not less than 135°C for not less than a second). This is so all residual spoilage micro-organisms and their spores are destroyed, but the chemical, physical and organoleptic changes to the milk are minimal. Immediately after heat treatment, the milk is filled into opaque containers, or containers made opaque by the packaging. It will store for several months without refrigeration.

If the heat treatment involves direct contact with steam, it must be from **potable** water, must not adversely affect the milk, for example, by leaving foreign matter, and must not change the water content of the treated milk.

Sterilised (and UHT) milk must:

♦ not contain any unacceptable levels of any pharmacologically active substance;
♦ not contain any added water; and
♦ after 15 days in a closed container at 30°C (or seven days at 55°C) be **organoleptically** normal, not show any sign of deterioration and have a plate count at 30°C≤ 100 per ml.

Since 1997, problems of spoilage have resulted from spores of *Bacillus sporothermodurans* which have survived UHT processing.

Thermised milk

Thermised milk is obtained by heating raw milk for at least 15 seconds, between 57°C and 68°C, so as to show a positive reaction to the phosphatase test.

Raw milk tests at the dairy

Raw milk must come from healthy animals on a registered production holding. Such animals must not show any disease symptoms, udder wounds or have recently been treated with dangerous substances. Herds must be tuberculosis and brucellosis free.

Raw milk must not contain added water or unacceptable **antibiotic**, hormonal, **pesticide** or detergent residues or other harmful substances. Raw cow's milk must have a plate count at 30°C of ≤100,000 per ml and a somatic cell count of ≤400,000 per ml.

If raw milk is not heat treated at the dairy within four hours of acceptance, it must be cooled to 6°C. If not treated within 36 hours and the plate count at 30°C exceeds 300,000 per ml, it must not be used for the production of heat-treated milk.

Milk is examined for the presence of taint, dirt, blood and antibiotics and several tests are carried out before processing. Unsatisfactory milk can then be rejected.

Brucella abortus ring test

An **antigen** is added to milk at 37°C and if the milk is positive for the organism, a blue ring rises to the top with the cream.

Freezing point test

This test is carried out to ascertain the addition of water to milk. The milk is frozen and if this occurs at between 0.53°C and 0.565°C it has not been adulterated. Freezing at higher temperatures indicates the addition of water.

The Gerber test (fat content)

The Gerber test is used to determine the fat content of milk. It is an electronic method, which involves using a milkotester. The result is obtained in 15 minutes.

The hydrometer test

The hydrometer test is used to check the density (total solids) of milk. If the fat content is known, the solids-not-fat can then be calculated by subtracting the fat per cent from the total solids per cent (approximately 87% of milk is water).

The resazurin test

Resazurin is a violet dye, which is decolourised by souring organisms. The resazurin is added to the milk and then left in a water bath at 37°C for ten minutes. The milk will first go pink and eventually colourless, depending on the number of organisms present. After ten minutes the colour is checked using a Lovibond comparator. A reading of 3.5 or less indicates the milk is unsatisfactory.

Problems encountered with milk

Milkstone

When milk is heated, phosphate and albumen are deposited as milkstone. This normally occurs above 72°C and is not a great problem in pasteurisation. Milkstone harbours bacteria and causes **cleaning** problems. When it does occur, the plant should be given an **acid clean**, for example, with phosphoric acid.

Milk taint

Either odour or taste taint may be caused by:
- ♦ treatment of cows with particular medicines;
- ♦ certain types of animal feed such as turnips or kale;
- ♦ certain illnesses such as **mastitis**, which may produce bitterness;
- ♦ storage of uncovered milk near paint, manure or strong-smelling substances;

- ♦ cows near the end of lactation producing a rancid taste;
- ♦ sunlight or contact with copper, which may produce an oily taint; or
- ♦ phenol from cleaning chemicals at the farm, a rare but serious problem.

Taints of bacteriological origin increase with age; those due to feeding are strong, fresh from the udder. Taints may be retained by milk products.

Blood
May be introduced into milk because of animals suffering from clinical mastitis or from sore udders. Herds infected with mastitis produce a reduced yield and the compositional quality of the milk falls. The milk is tested for the presence of blood at the dairy.

Ropey milk
The milk is slimy, which is caused by *Bacillus aerogenes*. It may be associated with faulty cleaning or disinfection. This is now rare due to improved cooling and cold storage.

Leucocytes
Occasionally, complaints are received about rusty droplets in bottles of homogenised milk. These deposits consist of milk fat, casein and large numbers of leucocytes, commonly referred to as milk slime. Leucocytes are a type of cell found in the udder. The number present in milk increases if cows are suffering from mastitis. The presence of leucocytes in heat-treated milk is purely an aesthetic problem.

Souring of milk
Lactic acid bacteria break down lactose to produce lactic acid. Bacteria involved include *Staphylococcus* and *Streptococcus lactis*. *Bacillus proteus* forms whey.

Cream
The butterfat in milk is present as small globules, which gradually rise to the surface, as they are less dense than milk. This cream line can be seen in bottles of pasteurised milk that have not been homogenised. To speed up the process, a mechanical separator that acts like a centrifuge is used. The stainless steel separator consists of an outer casing, which encloses a stack of conical plates. Pre-warmed milk is fed into the separator, which rotates at around 6,000 revolutions per minute. The lighter cream collects in the centre of the unit and is drawn off, heat treated and cooled. The heavier skimmed milk passes through the plates and is also drawn off, flash heated to around 80°C and then cooled to around 5°C. A valve may be used to control the fat content of the cream.
The cream may contain the same pathogens as milk. It is normally pasteurised in an HTST plant at not less than 72°C (or the equivalent), for not less than 15 seconds and then cooled to less than 5°C. It is normally aged before filling into suitable cartons. Homogenisation is sometimes used to thicken the cream.

Sterilised cream
Homogenised cream is canned or bottled and then sterilised, at a temperature of not less than 108°C, for not less than 45 minutes (or the equivalent) and then cooled. Sterilised cream will keep for prolonged periods but obviously has a different flavour from pasteurised. The

legislation relating to milk applies to cream. In addition, specific regulations lay down the appropriate compositional standards for particular types of cream; double cream must contain at least 48% milk fat; single cream must contain at least 18% milk fat.

Imitation or non-dairy cream
   This is a substance, which is produced by **emulsifying** edible oils or fats with water. Imitation cream is mainly used by bakeries for filling, in place of dairy cream. It is often prepared from palm kernel oils with egg yolk, water, sugar and milk powder.

Yogurt
   To manufacture yogurt, skimmed milk, sugar and water are mixed together and heated to approximately 95°C, for around 30 minutes. The mix is then cooled to around 43°C, filled into incubation tanks, and a starter culture, for example, *Lactobacillus bulgaricus* or *Streptococcus thermophilus*, is added. These bacteria produce lactic acid, the **fermentation** process is allowed to continue until a pH of approximately 4.0 is achieved and the yogurt has thickened considerably. The mix is then cooled to below 5°C. Unless plain yogurt is required, fruit is added and the mix is then filled into cartons and placed in cold storage.

Yogurt spoilage
   Bacterial spoilage is inhibited by the acidity of the yogurt and low storage temperatures. However, unless the mix is heat treated after fermentation, the starter culture will continue to produce acid and after approximately ten days, the yogurt becomes unpalatable. Yeast and moulds are more likely to cause problems. Fermentation of sugar by yeast causes the production of carbon dioxide, which results in a strained convex cap. Mould may be observed as a white or green clump on the surface.

Butter
   Cream is held at 5°C in large, insulated, stainless steel tanks until required. It may be necessary to add lactic acid-producing bacteria (starters) and warm the cream to ensure the correct acidity. The temperature and pH are dictated by the flavour required. The cream is then pumped into a large, stainless steel churn which operates half full and at a temperature of around 7°C. The churn revolves for 40 minutes which allows the fat globules to coalesce. The fat granules formed are the size of a grain of wheat.
   The buttermilk is then drawn off and the butter sprayed with chilled water to remove any traces of buttermilk. Excess water is drained off and salt may be added, depending on the flavour required. The churn is rotated slowly to disperse moisture and salt and to ensure a smooth finished product. This stage is known as "working the butter". When the butter is removed, the moisture content must, by law, not exceed 16%. After packing, the butter should be stored away from chemicals or other food with strong odours. Modern manufacture is by continuous buttermakers, which operate on the same principle but produce five tonnes per hour.
   Defects in butter may be due to poor quality cream, production errors or post pasteurisation contamination. The butter may be sour, rancid or cheesy, normally because of bacterial action. It is essential, therefore, to maintain high standards of factory hygiene and develop suitable quality control checks, including bacteriological examination of raw materials and finished product.
   Growth of bacteria, yeast and moulds may occur rapidly if butter, especially unsalted, is

stored above 16°C. The keeping quality depends on the bacterial load, type of organisms and storage temperature. Chilled or refrigerated storage is advisable. Growth of salmonellae has been recorded in butter kept at room temperatures (25°C).

Margarine
Margarine is produced from a blend of fat-free milk and vegetable, animal and marine oils or fats.

Cheese
Cheese may be made from:
♦   whole milk, for example, Cheddar;
♦   skimmed milk, for example, Dutch; or
♦   milk to which cream has been added, for example, Stilton.

There are three main types of cheese:
♦   *Hard cheeses*
These have relatively low-moisture content and possess excellent keeping qualities. Examples include Cheddar, Lancashire and Cheshire.

♦   *Soft cheeses*
Those which are allowed to drain naturally as the curd is not pressed, such as, Camembert, Limburger and Cambridge.

♦   *Blue-veined varieties*
These cheeses have a high-moisture content and soft curd. They are ripened by normal organisms and by the growth of specific moulds.

Cheese manufacture
Pasteurised milk is run into long stall troughs, and milk cultures of *Streptococcus lactis* are added to ensure the correct acidity. Rennet is then added and the milk-clots form a curd and a liquid whey, which is drained off. The curd is cut into small cubes and then heated to expel moisture and assist in whey drainage. Higher temperatures are used to produce the drier, hard cheeses.

The cubes coalesce and the resultant mass is cut into slabs, which are piled up to increase whey drainage. The dry, firm curd is then passed through a milling machine, which tears it into small pieces, and salt is added. After salting, the cheese is filled into moulds or vacuum packs, pressed and then ripened at 10°C and 80 to 90% relative humidity. Ripening can take from three months to a year. Most types of cheese, once cut, should be stored in a refrigerator, provided that they are well-wrapped.

CHEESE FAULTS
Defects in cheese may occur because of:
♦   the use of unsatisfactory milk;
♦   the presence of foreign substances;
♦   the growth of abnormal bacteria; or
♦   production errors.

Bacterial faults include sliminess, bitterness, rancidity and pigmentation. Scrupulous attention must be paid to the quality of raw materials and to hygiene during production. Food poisoning incidents, including salmonella and staphylococcal, have been traced back to contaminated cheese. In 1984, imported Camembert and Brie from France resulted in several cases of *E. coli* food poisoning. Listeriosis has often resulted from the consumption of contaminated soft cheeses. Food poisoning and **foodborne disease** incidents are more commonly associated with cheese made from unpasteurised milk.

Mycotoxin-producing moulds have been isolated from a number of cheeses including Cheddar.

Condensed milk

There are two types of condensed milk:
♦ sweetened condensed milk; and
♦ unsweetened evaporated milk.

Sweetened condensed milk

The milk is preheated, filtered and separated (separation is not carried out if full-cream condensed milk is to be produced). Further heating is carried out to destroy bacteria, moulds and **enzymes**. Sugar is added at a concentration that ensures preservation, by producing a high osmotic pressure. The sweetened milk is pumped into an evaporator, where approximately 60% of the water is boiled off under vacuum at around 55°C. The milk is cooled carefully, to prevent the formation of large lactose (milk sugar) crystals, and canned.

Thickening of condensed milk may be caused by micrococci and contamination by gas-producing yeast may cause the can to blow.

Unsweetened evaporated milk

The production of this milk is very similar to sweetened condensed milk, apart from the fact that no sugar is added. After evaporation, the milk is homogenised to prevent the separation of fat and then cooled and filled into cans. The filled cans are heated to 115°C for 20 minutes to ensure their safety and shelf life.

Underprocessing of evaporated milk may allow the survival of *Bacillus subtilis, Bacillus coagulans* or *Bacillus cereus*, which give the can contents a coagulated appearance.

Dried milk

The standardised raw milk is preheated and filtered before the removal of water. There are several methods available for the production of dried milk.

Roller drying

The milk is spread, as a very thin film, on an internally-heated, revolving, horizontal steel cylinder. The resultant dried milk is automatically scraped off.

Spray drying

After an initial boiling under vacuum, the concentrated milk is pumped into the top of a hot-air tower as a very fine spray. The resulting dried milk powder collects at the base of the tower and is cooled. The burnt particles are removed and it is then packed in air-tight containers.

Accelerated freeze drying

To improve reconstitution, this method may be used. The milk is frozen and then heated under vacuum, so that the water is removed by **sublimation**. Salmonellae have been isolated from dried milk powder made from unpasteurised milk. There is also a possible risk if *Staphylococcus aureus* is present and allowed to multiply prior to drying, as heat-resistant **toxins** may be produced.

Ice cream

Ice cream may be made with milk fat, sugar, eggs and cornflour, or vegetable fat, separated milk powder, sugar, gelatin, emulsifiers and water. Manufacture consists of mixing, pasteurising, homogenising, freezing and packaging. Alternatively, the mix may be sterilised and frozen, or **dehydrated** and sold as a complete cold mix, which is reconstituted by the addition of water.

Pasteurised ice cream

Pasteurisation may be carried out by heating to not less than:
 ♦   65.6°C for at least 30 minutes; or
 ♦   71.1°C for at least ten minutes; or
 ♦   79.4°C for at least 15 seconds.

After heating, the mixture is homogenised and cooled to below 7.2°C, within one and a half hours and then frozen and packaged. The HTST plant must be provided with a flow diversion valve to redirect ice cream, which has not been heated to the correct temperature. Indicating and recording thermometers should be provided and records kept for at least one month.

Sterilised ice cream

If the mixture is sterilised, it must be heated to not less than 148.9°C for at least two seconds and then cooled to below 7.2°C within one and a half hours, or alternatively canned under sterile conditions. If the can is opened, the ice cream must be cooled to below 7.2°C and kept at this temperature until frozen.

Soft ice cream

Soft ice cream is freshly frozen ice cream, which is normally sold to the public direct from the freezer. When using a complete cold mix, it is essential that after reconstitution, the mix is frozen in the soft ice cream machine within one hour. (For cleaning a soft ice cream machine, see chapter 12.)

Ice cream spoilage

Ice cream may become either sour or rancid. Sour ice cream is caused by prolonged storage before freezing or the use of sour milk. Rancid ice cream is caused by the use of rancid fat.

The methylene blue test

This test is used to determine the bacteriological standard of ice cream. The ice cream is mixed with methylene blue and Ringer solution and then incubated in a water-bath at 20°C for 17 hours. It is then incubated at 37°C and inverted every 30 minutes until decolourised.

INTERPRETATION OF RESULTS	
Grade	Time to decolourise (hrs)
1	4.5
2	2.5 to 4
3	0.5 to 2
4	0

Most samples should be grade 1 or 2 and, although not legally binding, consistent grade 3 or 4 samples indicate poor hygiene at some stage of production or handling.

Liquid egg

The objective in pasteurising liquid egg is to destroy pathogenic organisms, especially salmonellae, without affecting the physical and functional properties of the raw egg. Thus, the time and temperature used are critical to achieve this state of affairs. Liquid whole egg can be pasteurised at 60°C for three and a half minutes, or a temperature of not less than 64.4°C for at least two and a half minutes, or another time and temperature that has the same lethal effect on vegetative, pathogenic organisms. Following the pasteurisation process, the treated egg must satisfy the alpha-amylase test. This is another enzyme test (similar to the phosphatase test for pasteurised milk). Absence of the enzyme signifies that the liquid egg has been adequately pasteurised.

Pasteurised shell egg

Eggs can now be pasteurised, in the shell, by using warm water or humidity-controlled air. Eggs pass through a warm water bath of aerated air at a temperature and time which results in a 5 log reduction (100,000 to 1) of any salmonella that may be present. For example, 57°C for 30 minutes. At this temperature, the albumen is not denatured. The eggs are then chilled in a cool water bath. They can be sealed with a food grade wax to prevent future contamination and then stored at 7°C.

Shellfish *by Vic George*

Shellfish may often be contaminated with food poisoning organisms, especially bivalves such as cockles, mussels, oysters and clams, as they obtain their nutrients by filter feeding in coastal waters that may contain sewage effluent. A stringent heat processing routine for commercially cooked shellfish, mainly cockles, should eliminate the risk. However, those shellfish that are eaten raw (oysters), or lightly cooked mussels, need to contain minimal amounts of contamination, if illness is not to result.

Significant numbers of shellfish (mainly oyster) associated incidents of viral **gastroenteritis** still occur, however, bacterial food poisoning is less common and usually results from post-process contamination.

Bivalve molluscs are controlled from the growing areas through to sale under the provisions of Regulation (EC) No 853/2004, Regulation (EC) No 854/2004, Regulation 852/2004 and the Food Hygiene (England) (Scotland) (Wales) (NI) Regulations 2006. The Food Law Code of Practice gives guidance to enforcement authorities on how these regulations should be enforced.

The Regulations place a duty on local authorities to take regular (usually monthly) microbiological samples from bivalve harvesting areas, the results of the samples enable the Food Standards Agency to classify areas, depending on the *E. coli* content of the shellfish.

CLASSIFICATION OF SHELLFISH AREAS BASED ON *E. COLI*

CAT A*	<230 *E. coli*/100g Nil Salmonella/25g	May go for direct consumption
CAT B+	<4,600 *E. coli*/100g	Must be depurated
CAT C+	<46,000 *E. coli*/100g	Relay (2 months) to meet A or B category
Unclassified	>46,000 *E. coli*/100g	Prohibited

*Draft EU Regulations for Microbiological Criteria for Foodstuffs 2005
+Annex III Section VII, Chapter V of the Regulation (EC) 853/2004

The most common form of **depuration**, usually referred to as "purification", involves immersing the shellfish in a tank of seawater under strictly controlled conditions. The shellfish should resume their normal filter feeding within the depuration tank and thereby expel pathogens into the water, which will then be destroyed as the water is passed by ultra violet light. The UK operate a standard purification time of 42 hours, although this varies in other countries, from 24 to 48 hours.

The requirement to healthmark each batch of molluscs from a purification plant with the premises approval number and date of dispatch provides traceability of product. Separate monitoring is undertaken for algal toxins. Diarrhetic, paralytic and amnesic shellfish poisoning toxins are becoming more widespread and are causing increasing concern to the enforcement agencies and the shellfish trade.

A food authority may make a temporary prohibition order, prohibiting the collection of any live shellfish from a specified area, if it is satisfied that the consumption of those shellfish would be a risk to public health. Although used in cases of chemical contamination (oil spillages) and sewage contamination, local authorities are increasingly having to use these powers in respect of algal toxins. Many algal toxins are heat stable and the normal cooking process will not inactivate them. The temporary prohibition orders last for up to 28 days after which, if the problem still exists, they must be renewed.

Appendix II

EMPLOYEE MEDICAL QUESTIONNAIRE

NAME.. OCCUPATION ....

ADDRESS... DEPARTMENT..

....

....

....

(1) Have you ever had or been a **carrier** of:

A **foodborne disease**	**YES/NO**
Typhoid or paratyphoid	**YES/NO**
Tuberculosis	**YES/NO**
Parasitic infections	**YES/NO**

(2) Has any close family contact suffered from any of the above?   **YES/NO**

(3) Have you suffered from any of the following:

Serious diarrhoea or vomiting	**YES/NO**
Skin trouble	**YES/NO**
Boils, styes or septic fingers	**YES/NO**
Discharge from the ears, eyes, gums/mouth	**YES/NO**

(4) Please give details of any other medical problems that may affect your employment as a **food handler**, for example, recurring **gastrointestinal** disorder.

....

....

(5) Have you been abroad within the last two years?   **YES/NO**

WHERE? ....

(6) Should it be necessary, will you agree to provide such specimens that may be required by the company, to ensure that you are not a carrier of any organism that may infect food?   **YES/NO**

I declare that all the foregoing statements are true and complete to the best of my knowledge and belief.

Signed ....

Appendix III Food safety qualifications

Food business operators must ensure that food handlers are supervised and instructed and/or trained in food hygiene matters commensurate with their work activity. This means that staff must have the necessary competencies to produce safe food. The flexibility of EU legislation enables staff to achieve competencies in a variety of ways, including accredited training, in-house training, on-the-job training or e-learning.

However, many food handlers attend food safety courses to obtain a nationally recognised accredited qualification provided by one of the following awarding bodies:

Organisations providing food safety courses for food handlers

- Highfield Awarding Body for Compliance (HABC)
  Highfield House, Heavens Walk, Lakeside, Doncaster DN4 5HZ
  Tel: 0845 2260350 www.highfieldabc.com
- Royal Society for Public Health (RSPH)
  John Snow House, 59 Mansell Street, London E1 8AN
  Tel: +44 (0)20 7265 7300 www.rsph.org.uk
- Chartered Institute of Environmental Health (CIEH)
  Chadwick Court, 15 Hatfields, London SE1 8DJ Tel: 020 7928 6006 www.cieh.org
- The Royal Environmental Health Institute of Scotland (REHIS)
  19 Torphichen Street, Edinburgh EH3 8HX Scotland. Tel: 0131 229 2968
  www.rehis.com

A list of trainers and courses can be found on www.foodsafetytrainers.co.uk.

Choosing an awarding body

All of the above awarding bodies have the same status and offer a similar package of Ofqual accredited and non-accredited food safety qualifications. The following information is provided to assist in choosing an awarding body that best meets your requirements:

- **Customer service** – Are the staff friendly, helpful, accurate and knowledgeable? If necessary, can you speak to a manager with the ability to make immediate decisions? Do you feel that there are unnecessary, bureaucratic barriers in place? Are results and certificates dispatched quickly or do you have to wait several weeks?
- **Quality control** – Have you confidence that the systems and procedures in place ensure the security, integrity and quality of qualifications to meet awarding body and regulatory requirements?
- **Value for money** – Are the qualifications, and ancillary costs including, postage, replacement certificates, replacement out-of-date examination papers, etc. competitively priced?
- **Technical expertise** – Are you able to speak to a subject matter expert who can provide technical information regarding the syllabus and the examination questions?
- **Examination papers** – Do the examination papers accurately reflect the assessment criteria agreed by the Sector Skills Councils? Are questions fair and practically based? Are questions unambiguous, easy to understand with only one clear answer?
- **Proactive and flexible** – Is the awarding body receptive to your requirements? Do you feel they are working with you?

In 2006, National Occupational Standards (NOS) in Food Safety were produced for Catering, Retailing and Manufacturing, by their respective Sector Skills Councils. The Awarding bodies use the NOS to develop food safety qualifications specific to the three food sectors. The qualifications appear on the Qualification and Credit Framework (www.accreditedqualifications.org.uk/qualifications-and-credit-framework-qcf.htm) once the qualifications have been accredited by the Office of the Qualifications and Examinations Regulator (www.ofqual.gov.uk). In Scotland the equivalents are the SCQF and the Scottish Qualification Authority; in Wales they are DCELLS; and in Northern Ireland they are CCEA.

The following levels apply:

♦ **Level 1 (up to 3 hours)** - Will probably be part of the induction programme. Aimed at those food handlers who are new or have relatively low-risk jobs.

♦ **Level 2 (6 to 9 hours)** - Intended for high-risk food handlers and replaced the Foundation qualifications.

♦ **Level 3 (21 to 25 hours)** - Intended for supervisors, especially in high-risk food businesses. This replaced the Intermediate qualifications.

♦ **Level 4 (around 40 hours)** - Intended for managers and those food handlers who have significant responsibilities for food safety, for example, HACCP team members, QA staff in factories, trainers or auditors. This replaced the Advanced qualifications.

The syllabuses for the qualifications remain very similar to those of the replaced qualifications, although there is increased emphasis on allergens, hazards, controls, monitoring and recording (HACCP) and items of food safety of practical relevance to the particular sector (catering/manufacturing/retail). The level 3 and level 4 syllabuses have a greater emphasis on supervisory and management responsibilities together with a requirement for a greater knowledge of HACCP principles.

The relevant Sector Skills Councils for food safety are:
♦ **People 1st** - Catering www.people1st.co.uk
♦ **Improve** - Manufacturing www.improveltd.co.uk
♦ **Skillsmart** - Retail www.skillsmartretail.com

Qualifications offered by **Highfield Awarding Body for Compliance (HABC)**

Level 1 Award in Food Safety in Catering / Manufacturing / Retail
Level 1 Award in Health and Safety for Catering
Level 2 Award in Food Safety in Catering / Manufacturing / Retail
Level 2 Award in HACCP for Catering / Manufacturing
Level 3 Award in Supervising Food Safety in Catering / Manufacturing / Retail
Level 3 Award in Supervising HACCP for Catering / Manufacturing
Level 3 Award in Effective Auditing and Inspection Skills
Level 4 Award in Managing Food Safety in Catering / Manufacturing
Level 4 Award in HACCP Management for Food Manufacturing

Qualifications offered by the **Royal Society for Public Health (RSPH)**

Certificate in Food Hygiene Awareness – **Level 1**
Fundamentals of Food Safety – **Level 2**
Fundamentals of Food Safety for the Food Industry – **Level 2**
Level 2 Award in Food Safety in Catering / Manufacturing / Retail
Level 3 Award in Supervising Food Safety in Catering / Manufacturing / Retail
Level 4 Award in Managing Food Safety in Catering / Manufacturing
Foundation Certificate in HACCP – **Level 2**
Fundamentals of HACCP – **Level 2**
Level 3 Award in HACCP for Food Manufacturing
Level 4 Award in HACCP Management for Food Manufacturing

Qualifications offered by the **Chartered Institute of Environmental Health (CIEH)**

Level 1 Award in Food Safety Awareness in Catering / for Retail
Level 1 Award in Induction into Food Safety for Manufacturing
Level 1 Award in Induction into Safety in Food Premises
Level 2 Award in Food Safety in Catering / for Manufacturing / for Retail
Level 2 Award in Food Safety in Catering / for Manufacturing / for Retail Refresher
Level 2 Award in Cleaning in Food Premises
Level 3 Award in Supervising Food Safety in Catering
Level 3 Award in Food Safety Supervision for Manufacturing / for Retail
Level 3 Award in HACCP for Catering
Level 3 Award in HACCP for Food Manufacturing
Level 4 Award in Food Safety in Catering / for Manufacturing

Qualifications offered by the **Royal Environmental Health Institute of Scotland (REHIS)**

The Royal Environmental Health Institute is Scotland's Awarding Body for qualifications in food safety. Scotland has its own national qualification and accreditation system which is not regulated by Ofqual. All the Institute's food safety qualifications have been developed using the national occupational standards produced by the Sector Skills Councils and are suitable for staff employed in all sectors of the food industry and also for teachers and members of the public. REHIS qualifications are equivalent to Level 1 to 4 Awards in England, Wales and Northern Ireland.

Introduction to Food Hygiene - **Level 1**
Elementary Food Hygiene - **Level 2**
Intermediate Food Hygiene - **Level 3**
Advanced Food Hygiene - **Level 4**
Elementary Food and Health - **Level 2**
Introduction to HACCP and Hazard Analysis - **Level 2**
HACCP for Caterers - **Level 2**
Intermediate HACCP Practices - **Level 3**

Glossary

Acid	A chemical, with a pH of less than 7, which forms hydrogen ions in solution, the hydrogen being replaceable by a metal to form a salt. Used for removing hard water scale. Generally corrosive and turns litmus paper red.
Acute disease	A disease that develops rapidly and produces symptoms quickly after infection. Patients soon recover, or die. Does not imply severity: an acute disease may be mild.
Acute poison	A poison, that takes effect rapidly. In the case of rodenticides, it usually involves a single dose.
Additives	Preservatives, antioxidants, colourings, emulsifiers, stabilisers, artificial sweeteners and flavourings added to food to improve quality, taste, shelf life, function or appearance.
Aerobic	Using oxygen.
Aerobic colony count	The count of viable aerobic bacteria per gram of product (based on the number of colonies grown on nutrient agar plate).
Aerosol	Airborne contamination.
Agar	A seaweed extract used to form a gel as the basis for culture plates, on which bacteria can be grown.
Air-off temperature	The temperature of the cold air, leaving the evaporator coil, where it enters the multi-deck refrigerated cabinet.
Air-on temperature	The temperature of the warmer air measured at the return air vent in the multi-deck refrigerated cabinet.
Algae	Simple plants capable of photosynthesis, most commonly found in aquatic environments or damp soil, for example, seaweed and spirogyra (forms bright green slimy masses in ponds).
Alkali	A chemical, with a pH greater than 7, which reacts with an acid to form a salt and water only.
Allergy	An identifiable immunological response to food or food additives, which may involve the respiratory system, the gastrointestinal tract, the skin or the central nervous system. In severe cases this may result in anaphylactic shock.
Ambient temperature	The temperature of the surroundings. Usually refers to the room temperature.
Anaerobic	Using little or no oxygen.
Anorexia	Loss of appetite.
Antibiotic	A chemical used to destroy, or inhibit the growth of, pathogenic bacteria within human or animal bodies. Often extracted and refined from moulds.
Antibody	A protein produced by white blood cells to destroy antigens and protect the body against disease. Antibodies are produced when we are vaccinated and provide immunity from specific infections.
Antigen	A foreign protein that can trigger an immune response resulting in the production of an antibody, as part of the body's defence against infection. Antigens include viruses, bacteria and their toxins.
Antiseptic	A substance that prevents the growth of bacteria and moulds, specifically on or in the human body.
Antiserum	Blood serum containing specific antibodies. Used for typing species of bacteria and the treatment of some diseases.
Aseptic	Free from micro-organisms.
Aspic	A clear savoury meat jelly used as a decorative glaze on prepared foods. An ideal growth medium for bacteria.
Asymptomatic	Without symptoms.

Audit	A systematic and independent examination to determine whether activities and related results comply with planned arrangements and whether these arrangements are implemented effectively and are suitable to achieve objectives (Regulation (EC) No 854/2004).
Authorised officer	Any person who is authorised by a food authority, in writing, to act in matters arising under the Food Safety, Act 1990.
Autolysis	The self-destruction of cells, including bacteria, as a result of the action of their own enzymes.
A$_W$ (water activity)	A measure of the water in food available to micro-organisms. Most bacteria prefer values of 0.995 to 0.980. $$A_W = \frac{\text{Water vapour pressure of food}}{\text{Water vapour pressure of pure water}}$$
Bacteraemia	The presence of bacteria in the blood, usually without multiplication.
Bacteria (singular bacterium)	Single-celled micro-organisms with rigid cell walls that multiply by dividing into two. Some bacteria cause illness and others cause spoilage.
Bactericide	A substance that destroys bacteria.
Bacteriostat	A substance that inhibits the growth and multiplication of bacteria.
Bacteriology	The study of bacteria, especially those that cause disease.
Bacteriophage	A parasitic virus of bacteria.
Binary fission	Asexual method of reproduction by the division of the nucleus into two daughter nuclei, followed by similar division of the cell body. The method of reproduction used by bacteria.
Biodegradable	Chemicals and materials that can be broken down by bacteria or other biological means (usually during sewage treatment).
Biosecurity (of poultry and farm animals)	Taking all necessary measures to prevent the contamination of feed and water and the infection of animals from all sources and vehicles of pathogens, including pests, birds, animals, dust, soil, feed, people, waste, the environment, premises and equipment. It may also include the exclusion of toxic chemicals.
Blanching	The immersion of, for example, vegetables in hot water for up to a minute to destroy enzymes and reduce spoilage, during the storage of frozen food. It also helps to preserve colour and flavour.
Botulinum cook	The thermal process applied to low-acid canned food, which reduces the chance of survival of one spore of *Clostridium botulinum* to less than one in 10^{12}. (Equivalent to 121°C for three minutes)
Carcinogen	A substance capable of causing cancer. Carcinogens may be chemical, physical or biological.
Carrier	A person who harbours, and may transmit, pathogenic organisms without showing signs of illness.
Case	See clinical case.
Case control study	An epidemiological study, in which the characteristics of cases of disease (for example, food histories) are compared with a matched control group of people without the disease, for example, to determine a food vehicle.
Challenge testing (microbiological)	The inoculation of a product with specific pathogens to determine, for example, the critical limits for cooking, by subjecting the product to various time/temperature combinations.
Causal factors (food poisoning)	How the food vehicle became contaminated and the stage of food preparation that allowed bacterial multiplication or survival.
Causative agent	The organism, toxin or poison associated with the illness, which is recovered from sufferers and/or food and/or the environment under investigation, for example, salmonella, scombrotoxin or mercury.
Chronic disease	A disease, that usually develops slowly, and symptoms last for a prolonged period.

Chronic poison	A substance, that is used at low concentration and relies on repeated intake by the target pest to ensure elimination.
Cleaning	The process of removing soil, food residues, dirt, grease and other objectionable matter.
Clean surface	A surface that is free from residual film or soil, has no objectionable odour, is not greasy to touch and will not discolour a white paper tissue that is wiped over it.
Clinical case	A person with symptoms who has become ill.
Cohort study	An epidemiological study of a population to compare the incidence of disease in persons exposed and not exposed to possible causal factors. For example, comparing the attack rates of persons with food poisoning, based on those who ate a specific food and those that did not.
Colony	A cluster of bacteria grown on a culture plate in sufficient numbers as to be visible to the naked eye.
Commensal	A usually harmless micro-organism, but one that may cause illness in immunocompromised persons.
Commercially sterile food	Food that has been subjected to treatment, that has destroyed all pathogens and organisms capable of causing problems, such as spoilage, under normal storage conditions, for example, low-acid canned food.
Competent authority	The central authority of a member state competent to ensure compliance with relevant regulations, or any other authority to which that central authority has delegated that competence.
Compliance	Measures that satisfy a legal requirement.
Compressor (refrigerator)	A mechanical pump which moves up and down in a cylinder containing the refrigerant gas and pumps it round the system, starting with the condenser.
Condenser (refrigerator)	A unit that looks like a car radiator with a fan in front of it. The fan draws air from the room across the surface of the condenser, which cools the gaseous refrigerant, delivered from the compressor, and returns it to a liquid state.
Contact time	The period of time required by a disinfectant to achieve disinfection, for example, of a surface.
Contamination	The presence or introduction of a hazard. (EC Regulation No. 852/2004)
Cook-chill	A system of food preparation in which food is cooked in advance and rapidly cooled for chilled storage to be reheated several days later. Strict control of chilled storage temperature is required to ensure the safety of the food.
Core temperature	The temperature found at the centre of the thickest part of a piece of food.
Coved	Rounded finish to the junctions between walls and floors, or between two walls, to make cleaning easier.
Critical control point (CCP)	A step in the process where control can be applied and is essential to prevent or eliminate a food safety hazard or reduce it to an acceptable level.
Cross-contamination	The transfer of bacteria from contaminated foods (usually raw) to ready-to-eat foods by direct contact, drip or indirect contact using a vehicle such as hands or a cloth.
Cryogenics	A system of refrigeration using injection of liquefied gas into the storage chamber.
Cuisine sous vide	A system of cooking (pasteurising) raw or par-cooked food in a sealed pouch under vacuum. After pasteurisation, the pouch is cooled and stored below 3°C. Products have a shelf life of up to 21 days (eight in the UK) and are regenerated using heat, immediately before consumption.
Culture	A liquid or solid medium used to grow a population of a particular type of micro-organism as a result of the inoculation and incubation of the medium.

Danger zone of bacterial growth	The temperature range within which the multiplication of some pathogenic, mesophilic bacteria is possible, i.e. from 5°C to 63°C. Most rapid growth occurs between 20°C and 50°C.
Dehydration (of food)	The reduction of the available water in food to prevent the growth of micro-organisms.
Dehydration (of people)	The loss of water and salt from the body, for example, as a result of serious diarrhoea. 60% of a man's body weight and 50% of a woman's body weight is water. This percentage is necessary for the healthy functioning of cells.
Denaturation	Disruption.
Deoxyribonucleic acid (DNA)	The genetic material found in all cells of every organism.
Depuration	The process of purifying shellfish, by re-laying them in clean water for around 42 hours .
Detergent	A chemical or mixture of chemicals made of soap or synthetic substitutes; it facilitates the removal of grease and food particles from dishes and utensils and promotes cleanliness, so that all surfaces are readily accessible to the action of disinfectants.
Disinfectant	A chemical used for disinfection.
Disinfection	The reduction of micro-organisms to a level that will not lead to harmful contamination or spoilage of food. Chemical agents and/or physical methods, which are used, should not adversely affect the food. The term disinfection normally refers to the treatment of premises, surfaces and equipment, but may also be applied to the treatment of skin.
Dormant	The description of bacteria that are not growing or multiplying, but are waiting to multiply when favourable conditions return.
D value	The time, in minutes, required at a given temperature, to reduce the number of viable cells or spores of a given micro-organism by 90%.
Due diligence	The legal defence in the Food Safety Act, 1990, and the Food Hygiene (England) (Scotland) (Wales) (NI) Regulations 2006 that a person charged with an offence had taken all reasonable precautions and exercised all due diligence to avoid the commission of the offence by himself or a person under his control.
Electronic or UV fly killers	Equipment to control flying insects consisting of a UV light, that attracts the insect, which is then destroyed on a high voltage grid or captured on a sticky board.
Emulsification	The production of a mixture of two immiscible liquids, one being dispersed in the other in the form of fine droplets.
Encephalitis	Inflammation of the brain.
Endemic	A disease, that is prevalent in a particular area.
Endocarditis	Inflammation of the internal lining of the heart, especially the valves.
Endotoxin	Toxins present in the outer membrane of the cell of many gram-negative bacteria. They are released on the death of the bacteria.
Enteritis	Inflammation of the intestine.
Enterotoxigenic	Able to produce a toxin adversely affecting the intestines.
Enterotoxins	Exotoxins that affect the gastrointestinal tract.
Environmental control/management	The denial of access to pests, by design maintenance and proofing of buildings and the denial of food and harbourage by good housekeeping.
Enzyme	A protein that regulates the rate of chemical reaction in the body.
Epidemic	A sudden spread of a large number of cases of disease within a community, when there are usually much smaller numbers present.
Epidemiological surveillance	The study of the distribution and trends in incidence of disease in a population through the systematic collection, consolidation and evaluation of morbidity and mortality reports and other relevant data, including incidence, sources, causes, mode of spread, distribution and control. Surveillance includes the

	dissemination of information to all those who need to know, so that appropriate action can be taken.
Evaporator (refrigerator)	Consists of a long tube bent many times and passed through hundreds of aluminium fins. Air from the cabinet is drawn over the evaporator and heat is transferred to the liquid refrigerant, delivered from the condenser, which boils and reverts to a gas.
Evisceration	Removal of the internal organs and intestines.
Exotoxin	Highly toxic proteins, usually produced during the multiplication or sporulation of some gram-positive bacteria. They are often produced in food.
Extraneous matter	Any contaminant of raw material or food. Usually referred to as "foreign bodies", in the finished product.
Extrinsic contaminants	Contaminants that are not part of the food.
Faecal material	Excreta. Stools. The indigestible residues voided from the alimentary canal after digestion and absorption of food and water. One third of the dry weight of human faeces is bacteria, mainly *Escherichia coli* and *Streptococcus faecalis*.
Fermentation	The process involving the growth of beneficial micro-organism and the production of acid in food such as yogurt, cheese, salami and sauerkraut.
First aid materials	Suitable and sufficient bandages and dressings, including waterproof dressings and antiseptic. (All dressings to be individually wrapped.)
Fomites (singular fomes)	Inanimate objects such as clothes, books and bedding that can harbour pathogens and act as vehicles of infection.
Food	Food includes drink, ice and chewing gum but excludes live animals or birds, fodder or animal feeding stuffs, or controlled drugs.
Foodborne disease	Illness resulting from the consumption of food or water contaminated by pathogenic micro-organisms and/or their toxins. Characterised by having a low infective dose and no requirement for the multiplication of the organism within the food to cause illness.
Food business	Means any undertaking, whether for profit or not, and whether public or private, carrying out of any of the activities related to any stage of production, processing and sale of food.
Food-contact surface	A surface that comes into contact with food, for example, a cutting board or a knife.
Food handler	Any person in a food business who handles food, whether open or packaged (food includes drink and ice).
Food handling	Any operation in the production, preparation, processing, packaging, storage, transport, distribution and sale of food.
Food hygiene	The measures and conditions necessary to control hazards and to ensure fitness for human consumption of a foodstuff taking into account its intended use. (EC Regulation No. 852/2004)
Food poisoning	An acute illness of sudden onset caused by the recent consumption of contaminated or poisonous food.
Food vehicle	The food eaten, that contained the pathogen (causative agent), which gave rise to, for example, food poisoning.
Freezer burn	The loss of moisture from the surface of unwrapped frozen food. Results in a parchment-like appearance or spongy pale brown or yellow patches.
Fumigation	The application of a toxic chemical in the form of a gas, vapour or volatile liquid in a closed container or to a food stack under gas-proof sheets.
Fungi	Plants unable to synthesise their own food and are usually parasitic or saprophytic. Includes single-celled microscopic yeasts, moulds, mildews and toadstools. Yeasts are used to produce alcohol, moulds cause food spoilage and ringworm is a fungal disease of animals.

Fungicide	A substance that kills fungi and mould.
Galvanised metal	Iron or steel, that has been coated with zinc for protection against corrosion.
Gastroenteritis	An inflammation of the stomach and intestinal tract, which normally results in diarrhoea.
Germicide	An agent used for killing micro-organisms.
Germination	The process resulting in the formation of a new mature vegetative bacterium from a spore, following heat activation and slow cooling.
Grease trap	A device fitted into a drainage system to prevent fat and grease entering the sewer.
HACCP (hazard analysis critical control point)	A food safety management system which identifies, evaluates and controls hazards which are significant for food safety. *Please see full HACCP Glossary on page 271.*
Hazard	A biological, chemical or physical agent in, or condition of, food with the potential to cause harm (an adverse health effect) to the consumer. (NB most biological hazards are microbiological).
Hazard analysis (codex alimentarius)	The process of collecting and evaluating information on hazards and conditions leading to their presence to decide which are significant for food safety and therefore should be addressed in the HACCP plan.
Haemoglobin	The oxygen-carrying pigment of red blood cells. The oxygen and haemoglobin join together to form oxyhaemoglobin.
Halophilic organisms	Organisms that can grow in high concentrations of salt.
Haloduric organisms	Organisms that can survive in high levels of salt but do not grow.
Hand-contact surface	A surface touched by the hand, for example, door handle, drawer handle, tap, nail brush, soap dispenser lever, toilet seat and knife handle.
Heat labile	Unstable at high temperatures.
Hermetically sealed	A package for a foodstuff with an airtight seal, to protect it from contamination, for example, cans, plastic pouches and cartons. Food may be pasteurised or sterilised after sealing in the pack, or beforehand and then packed in a sterile environment.
Health declaration	A medical questionnaire completed, for example, when applying for a job or on return to work after an illness, to determine fitness for food handling duties.
High-risk foods	Ready-to-eat foods, which, under favourable conditions, support the multiplication of pathogenic bacteria and are intended for consumption without treatment, which would destroy such organisms.
Host	An organism providing food and shelter for a parasite that lives in or on the host.
Hygiene	The science of preserving health and involves all measures necessary to ensure the safety and wholesomeness of food.
Immune system	The cells and proteins that fight invading pathogens and protect the body from infection.
Immunity	The ability to resist an invading organism so that the body does not develop the disease.
Immuno-compromised	An individual who is unable to produce a normal immune response to an infection.
Incubation period	The period between infection and the first signs of illness.
Indicator organism	Generally a non-pathogenic organism, not usually present in the food, the presence of which suggests poor hygiene and that the food may be contaminated with pathogenic organisms.
Infective dose	The number of a particular micro-organism required under normal circumstances to produce clinical signs of a disease.

Infestation	The presence of rats, mice, insects or mites in numbers or under conditions that involve an immediate or potential risk of contamination, loss or damage to food. The term usually implies the existence of a breeding population but may be used to denote the presence of individuals.
Inorganic	Substances that do not contain carbon, such as salt or metal.
Insecticides	Chemical substances used to kill insects.
Inspection	The systematic gathering and recording of data from observations, examinations, and discussions with food handlers and managers, the analysis and interpretation of data collected and the preparation of an understandable and actionable report.
Integrated pest management	The cost-effective implementation of prevention and eradication strategies based on the biology of pests, intended to ensure a pest free operation.
Intrinsic contaminants	Already present in the food, for example, stalks and leaves in vegetables or bones in fish.
Isolate	A single species of a micro-organism, originating from a particular sample or environment, growing in a pure culture.
Lag phase	The first phase of bacterial growth when there is no multiplication and the bacteria acclimatise to their new environment.
Larva (plural larvae)	The immature stage of an insect that undergoes complete metamorphosis (Egg > larva > pupa > adult).
Lassitude	A feeling of weakness or tiredness.
Load lines	Lines marked on refrigerated units above, or in front of, which product will be out of refrigeration or obstruct airflow, resulting in a failure to keep food at the correct temperature.
Low-acid foods	Food with a pH above 4.5.
Low-dose pathogen	A pathogen capable of causing illness with very few organisms, for example, less than ten. Foodborne diseases are usually caused by low-dose pathogens.
Low-risk foods	Ambient stable foods that do not normally support the multiplication of pathogens. However, they may occasionally be responsible for foodborne illness if they are ready-to-eat foods contaminated with low-dose pathogens, for example, lettuce.
Lux	A measure of light levels.
Malaise	A vague feeling of being ill.
Mastitis	Inflammation of the mammary gland.
Median	Situated towards the middle. The middle number or average of the two middle numbers in an ordered sequence of numbers, for example, 8 is the median of 2, 8, 32 and 1, 6, 10, 14.
Mesophiles	Organisms that have a growth range of 10°C to 56°C, with an optimum of 20°C to 46°C.
Metabolism	A term used to describe all of the chemical processes that occur in the body.
Microaerophilic organisms	Organisms that prefer to grow in an environment of approximately 5% oxygen, for example, campylobacter.
Microbiology	The science of studying micro-organisms.
Micro-organisms	Any minute living organisms including bacteria, viruses, yeasts, moulds, protozoa and prions.
Modified atmosphere packaging	The replacement of air in a package by one or more gases followed by sealing to prevent re-entry of air.
Mildew	A type of fungus similar to mould.
Morphology	The study of the structure and form of micro-organisms.
Moulds	Microscopic plants (fungi) that may appear as woolly patches on food.
Mycotoxins	Poisonous chemicals (toxins) produced by some moulds, for example, *Aspergillus flavus*.

Neonate	A newborn child up to four weeks old.
Neurotoxin	A poison/toxin produced by pathogens, for example, *Cl. botulinum*, which affects the nervous system.
Onset period	The period between consumption of the food and the first signs of illness. (Where incubation of micro-organisms within the body does not take place.)
Ootheca	The egg case of a cockroach.
Open food	Unwrapped food that may be exposed to contamination.
Optimum	Best.
Organic	Relating to or derived from plants or animals and having a carbon basis.
Organoleptic	Involves the use of the five senses: sight, smell, hear, taste and touch.
Osmophiles	Organisms that can grow in high concentrations of sugar.
Osmoduric	Organisms that can survive in high concentrations of sugar without multiplying.
Outbreak	An incident in which two or more people, thought to have a common exposure, experience a similar illness or proven infection (at least one of them having been ill).
Outbreak location	The place where the food vehicle was prepared or served.
Parasite	An organism that lives and feeds in or on another living creature, known as the host, in a way that benefits the parasite and disadvantages the host. In some cases, the host eventually dies.
Pasteurisation	A heat treatment of food at a relatively low temperature that destroys vegetative pathogens and most spoilage organisms, so prolonging the shelf life. Toxins and spores generally survive and rapid cooling and refrigerated storage is usually essential.
Pathogen	Disease-producing organism.
Personal hygiene	Measures taken by food handlers to protect food from contamination from themselves.
Pests (food)	Animals which live in or on our food. They contaminate food and are destructive noxious or troublesome.
Pesticide	A chemical used to kill pests.
pH	An index used as a measure of acidity or alkalinity.
Phage type	A variety of bacteria within a particular species, distinguished on the basis of their susceptibilities to a range of bacteriophages.
Plate count	The number of colonies of bacteria growing on an agar plate.
Potable	Safe to drink and acceptable for use in food preparation.
Preservation of food	The treatment of food to prevent or delay spoilage and inhibit growth of pathogenic organisms, which would render the food unfit.
Primary production	Those stages in the food chain up to and including, for example, harvesting, slaughtering, milking and fishing.
Prions	Proteinaceous infectious particles.
Probe	The part of the thermometer that is inserted into food or between packs to obtain temperature readings.
Product code	The date marking on product packaging to show its safe shelf life within which time it should be consumed.
Protective clothing	The clothing worn by food handlers to prevent contamination of food, including hairnets, hats, coats, apron, gloves and boots.
Proteolytic	Having the ability to break down proteins.
Protozoa (singular protozoan)	Single-celled organisms, which form the basis of the food chain. Live in moist habitats such as oceans, rivers, soil and decaying matter. Some are pathogenic, for example, *Entamoeba histolytica*.
Psychrophiles	Organisms that have a growth range of –8°C to 25°C with an optimum below 20°C.

Psychrotrophs	Organisms that have a growth range of –5°C to 40°C with an optimum above 20°C.
Pulmonary	Pertaining to the lungs.
Pupa (plural pupae)	The third stage of development of an insect that undergoes complete metamorphosis.
Quats	A popular name for quaternary ammonium compounds (disinfectant).
Radicidation	The use of irradiation to destroy non-spore-forming pathogens, pests and parasites.
Radurisation	The use of irradiation to destroy spoilage organisms, prolong shelf life and reduce micro-organisms to a safe level.
Ready-to-eat foods	Foods that are intended for consumption without any treatment that is intended to destroy any pathogens that may be present. They include all high-risk foods and such foods as fruit, salad, vegetables and bread.
Rehydration	The addition of liquid, usually water or milk, to dry foods.
Residual insecticide	A long-lasting insecticide applied in such a way that it remains active for a considerable period of time.
Respiration	The loss of water by evaporation, for example, from fruit.
Risk	The likelihood of a hazard occurring in food.
Risk assessment	The process of identifying hazards, assessing risks and severity and evaluating their significance.
Route	The path along which bacteria are transferred from a source to ready-to-eat foods.
Safe food	Food that is nutritious, compositionally sound, free from contaminants at levels that could cause harm or illness and is labelled with the correct safety instructions for use and storage.
Sanitiser	A chemical agent used for cleansing and disinfecting surfaces and equipment.
Saprophyte	An organism that lives on dead organic matter.
Septicaemia	Blood poisoning. Rapid multiplication of bacteria and toxin production within the blood.
Serotyping	A test used to distinguish between different sub-types of the same species of bacteria, for example, *Salmonella* Typhi and *Salmonella* Enteritidis.
Shelf life	The period within which food is safe and of the best quality.
Shelf-stable	Foods that do not normally suffer microbiological spoilage at room temperature.
Sneeze guards	Screens fitted to food display units, intended to protect food from customers sneezing or coughing.
Source (of pathogens)	A source may be considered as the origin of the pathogen (causative agent), for example, the cow on the farm or the vehicle that brought the pathogen into the premises, for example, the milk.
Spoilage	Food deterioration resulting in off-flavours, odours and change in appearance, indicating the products are unsuitable for sale or consumption.
Sporadic case	A single case of disease apparently unrelated to other cases or carriers.
Spore (bacterial)	A resistant resting-phase of bacteria, which protects them against adverse conditions.
Spore (fungal)	The reproductive body of a fungus.
Sporulation	The production of spores, for example, in adverse conditions.
Sterile	Free from all living organisms.
Sterilisation	A process that destroys all living organisms.
Stock rotation	The practice of ensuring the oldest stock is used first and that all stock is used within its shelf life.
Sublimation	The process of ice, under vacuum, changing directly into water vapour without going through a liquid phase.
Surveillance	See epidemiological surveillance.

Symptomatic	With symptoms.
Synergism	A phenomenon whereby two chemicals in combination have a greater effect than the sum of their individual efforts.
Systemic disease	A disease affecting the whole of the body, as opposed to being localised.
Taint	Contamination of food from undesirable flavours or odours, for example, butter absorbs paint fumes, and chocolate stored next to detergent washing powders will taste soapy.
Tap proportioner	A device fitted to a tap, which delivers the right amount of detergent or sanitiser to the water.
Taxonomy	The naming of organisms (nomenclature), the grouping of organisms (classification) and the identification of organisms.
Terrazzo flooring	Coloured marble chips set in portland cement in a mosaic fashion. (May be attacked by acids and alkalis.)
Thermophilic organisms	Organisms that prefer to multiply above 45°C.
Thermoduric organisms	Organisms that can survive but do not multiply at temperatures above 45°C.
Total viable count	The total number of living cells detectable in a sample. The number of cells is assessed from the number of colonies, which develop on incubation of a suitable medium, that has been inoculated with the sample of bacteria.
Toxins (bacterial)	Poisons produced by pathogens, either in the food or in the body after consumption of contaminated food.
Typing (bacteria)	Any method used to distinguish between closely related strains of micro-organisms, for example, members of the same species.
Use-by date	The date mark required on high-risk perishable prepacked food, which must be stored under refrigeration. The food should be consumed on or before the use-by date. It is an offence to sell food after its use-by date.
Vegetative bacteria	Viable bacteria capable of multiplication.
Vehicles (for pathogens)	Things used by bacteria to transfer them from sources to ready-to-eat foods, including hands, cloths and equipment, hand-contact surfaces and food-contact surfaces.
Virology	The study of viruses.
Virulence	The ability of a pathogen to cause disease, for example, the number of deaths, the proportion of people exposed to infection who became ill and how rapidly the infection spreads through the body.
Viruses	Microscopic pathogens that multiply in the living cells of their host.
Water activity a_W	A measure of the available water in a food.
Water hardness	Water containing dissolved calcium and magnesium salts. Temporary hardness results from the presence of bicarbonates and these form a scale when water is heated. Permanent hardness involves sulphates and is unaffected by heat. Soft water usually has up to 60ppm of salts, whereas hard water is over 120ppm. Hardness interferes with the action of soap causing a scum.
Water softener	A unit to remove water hardness salts to prevent a scale build-up in water heating equipment.
Wholesome food	Sound food, fit for human consumption.
Xerophilic organisms	Organisms capable of growth under dry conditions at lower levels of air.
Yeast	A unicellular fungus, which reproduces by budding and grows rapidly on certain foodstuffs, especially those containing sugar. Yeasts are the chief agents of fermentation. (Sugar converted to alcohol and carbon dioxide.)
Zoonoses	Diseases, that can be transmitted naturally from animal to man and vice versa.
Z value	The change in temperature in degrees celsius required for a ten-fold change in D value.

Abbreviations

Commonly used abbreviations in Hygiene for Management

ACC	Aerobic colony count
ATP	Adenosine triphosphate
A$_W$	Water activity
BMI	Body mass index
BMR	Basal metabolic rate
BPCA	British Pest Control Association
BSE	Bovine spongiform encephalopathy
CAP	Controlled atmosphere packaging
CCDC	Consultant in communicable disease control
CCP	Critical control point
CCTV	Closed circuit television
CDSC	Communicable Disease Surveillance Centre
CFU	Colony forming unit
CHIPS	Chemicals, hazards, information and packaging for supply
CIEH	Chartered Institute of Environmental Health
CIP	Clean-in-place
CJD	Creutzfeldt-Jacob disease
COSHH	Control of substances hazardous to health
CPU	Central production unit
DEFRA	Department of the Environment, Food and Rural Affairs
DH	Department of Health
DNA	Deoxyribo nucleic acid
EDTA	Ethylene diamine teracetic acid
EFKs	Electronic fly killers
EHO	Environmental health officer
EHP	Environmental health practitioner
ELISA	Enzyme linked immunosorbant assay
EU	European Union
FSA	Food Standards Agency
FSA (Ireland)	Food Safety Authority of Ireland
GMP	Good manufacturing practice
HABC	Highfield Awarding Body for Compliance
HACCP	Hazard analysis critical control point
HDL	High density lipoprotein
HOCI	Hypochlorous acid
HPA	Health Protection Agency

HTST	High temperature short time
HUS	Haemolytic uraemic syndrome
IPM	Integrated pest management
LACORS	Local Authorities Coordinators of Regulatory Services
LDL	Low density lipoprotein
MAP	Modified atmosphere packaging
MEL	Maximum exposure limits
NAMAS	National measurement accreditation service
NVQs	National vocational qualifications
PCR	Polymerase chain reaction
PPE	Personal protective equipment
PVC	Polyvinyl chloride
QA	Quality assurance
QACs	Quaternary ammonium compounds
QC	Quality control
REHIS	Royal Environmental Health Institute of Scotland
RNA	Ribonucleic acid
RSPH	Royal Society for Public Health
SI	Statutory instrument
SOFHT	Society of Food Hygiene and Technology
SPI	Stored product insect
TVC	Total viable count
UHT	Ultra heat treatment
UK	United Kingdom
USA	United States of America
UV	Ultraviolet
ULV	Ultra low volume
VCJD	Variant Creutzfeldt-Jacob disease
VTEC	Vero cytotoxin-producing *E. coli*
WHO	World Health Organisation

Useful websites for further information & guidance

Ask Cedric - Safety and Quality Information	www.askcedric.org.uk/business-index.php
Awarding Bodies	See Appendix III
Centers for Disease Control (USA)	www.cdc.gov
Codex Alimentarius Commission	www.codexalimentarius.net
Dept of Environment, Food & Rural Affairs	www.defra.gov.uk
Department of Health (DH)	www.doh.gov.uk
European Law	http://eur-lex.europa.eu/en/index.htm
European Food Information Council (EUFIC)	www.eufic.org
European Food Safety Authority	www.efsa.eu.int
Food & Drink Federation	www.fdf.org.uk
Foodlaw - Reading	www.foodlaw.rdg.ac.uk
Foodlink	www.foodlink.org.uk
Food Safety Authority of Ireland	www.fsai.ie
Food Safety Information (USA)	www.foodsafety.gov
Food Safety Trainers	www.foodsafetytrainers.co.uk
Foodservice (USA)	www.foodservice.com
Food Standards Agency	www.food.gov.uk
Hospitality Institute of Technology & Management (USA)	www.hi-tm.com
Health Protection Agency	www.hpa.org.uk
Health Protection Scotland	www.hps.scot.nhs.uk
Institute of Food Science & Technology	www.ifst.org
LACORS	www.lacors.com
Office of Public Sector Information	www.opsi.gov.uk
United States Dept of Agriculture (USDA)	www.usda.gov
World Health Organisation	www.who.int

Bibliography

Eley R. (Ed.) (1996). Microbial Food Poisoning.
London: Chapman & Hall.

Food Standards Agency. (2008). Management of Outbreaks of Foodborne Illness in England and Wales. FSA/1250/0508.

Health Protection Agency. (2009). Guidelines for Assessing the Microbiological Safety of Ready-to-Eat Foods. (Draft).

Jay James M. (2005). Modern Food Microbiology.
New York: Springer.

MacAuslan E. M.R. (2004). Effective Food Hygiene Training.
Doncaster: Highfield.co.uk ltd.

Mclauchlin J. and Little C. (2007).
Hobbs' Food Poisoning and Food Hygiene. London: Hodder Education.

North R. (1999). Some Observations on Food Hygiene Inspections.
London: Chadwick House Group Ltd.

Sheard M. and Church I. (1992). Sous-Vide Cook-Chill.
Leeds: Leeds Metropolitan University.

Sprenger R.A. (2011). Supervising Food Safety (Level 3).
Doncaster: Highfield.co.uk ltd.

Wallace C. (2012). Intermediate HACCP.
Doncaster: Highfield.co.uk ltd.

Yiannas F. (2009). Food Safety Culture.
New York: Springer.

Index